Wisden Cricketers of the Year

Wisden Cricketers of the Year

A Celebration of Cricket's Greatest Players

Simon Wilde

With a Foreword by David Gower

JOHN WISDEN

First published in Great Britain 2013

John Wisden and Co
An imprint of Bloomsbury Publishing Plc
50 Bedford Square
London WC1B 3DP

www.wisden.com
www.bloomsbury.com

Bloomsbury Publishing, London, New York, Berlin and Sydney

A CIP catalogue record for this book is available from the British Library

ISBN 97814081 40840

10 9 8 7 6 5 4 3 2 1

Designed by Marcus Duck
Printed and bound in Italy by L.E.G.O. S.p.A.

Contents

Foreword

IT IS AN HONOUR THAT COMES YOUR WAY BUT once and once alone – and, for any cricketer, to be named as one of *Wisden*'s Five Cricketers of the Year is an illustrious accolade.

For me it came early, after just one reasonably glorious year of Test cricket, and I suspect that I was too young, too naïve, too keen to just get on and play the game, to fully appreciate the honour. Don't get me wrong, it was a mighty proud moment and I was suitably chuffed, but there was still so much to learn and a lot of cricket still to be played. I would definitely have had summers later on that merited the recognition more, but that is the nature of the beast; once the great God, *Wisden*, has identified you as one of the chosen ones, that is it. You are there for ever.

Others have waited a lot longer; Jack Simmons was 44 when he was named in 1985, proving that a little stamina – and a few fish-and-chip suppers! – never go amiss. The satisfaction is no less for the wait; indeed the honour is probably greater.

As I look through this stupendous collection of all those recognised since the award was first conceived for the 1889 *Wisden*, it takes no effort to realise that this is in effect a potted history of the game, defined by those who left the most vivid of marks upon all those summers since. Each and every man is affectionately recognised for his skill, his artistry, his dedication; whatever attribute it was that marked him out as special from the previous English summer. I chanced at random on the pages for 1901, when four Yorkshiremen made the list, including one John Tunnicliffe, who *Wisden* noted was a non-drinker and a lay preacher. He was also tagged "one of the best professionals never to play for England". I wonder how many more in these pages suffered the same fate.

This is a glorious volume, fascinating and easy to dip into at any point. After turning to see what was said about me in 1979 I'm going to pick a year, any year, and take it from there...

David Gower, April 2013

Introduction

WISDEN'S CRICKETERS OF THE YEAR IS THE oldest individual award in cricket. Dating back to 1889, it is almost as old as the competition for the Ashes – indeed at its inauguration Australia had yet to win back the urn presented to Ivo Bligh, the captain of the English team, in Melbourne during the 1882-83 tour – and first appeared a year before the official constitution of the county championship. Future stars of both England-Australia Test matches and the championship would feature prominently in what became the nearest thing the sport has had to a "Hall of Fame". The International Cricket Council introduced its own "Hall of Fame" in 2009 but, given its long history, *Wisden*'s award certainly holds more cachet. It is the only "Hall of Fame" judged contemporaneously.

Taken as a whole, *Wisden*'s Cricketers of the Year represent a gallery of almost every cricketer of note since the game acquired a global dimension – provided at some stage they played in England and did something of note there.

In the early days, it seems, selection as a Cricketer of the Year escaped the notice of some players. Harry Calder, chosen as one of five schoolboy cricketers of the year in 1917, when first-class cricket was in abeyance because of war, only found out a year before his death aged 94 that he had once been picked. But for many people it was a cherished acknowledgement of their abilities as cricketers, and such was the significance of the award that a succession of editors has felt the annual weight of responsibility surrounding his choice of a "Five".

Even Sydney Pardon, who did more than anyone to establish the reputation of the feature during his long editorship from 1891 to 1925, sometimes prevaricated over his choice. In the Preface to the 1911 edition, he admitted he had changed his mind: having originally intended to pick five young batsmen he felt obliged to include "Razor" Smith, the Surrey bowler who had such a remarkable season in 1910. A year later, he expressed regret at not picking Johnny Douglas, who as Pardon penned his Preface to the 1912 *Wisden* was starring as England's stand-in captain in Australia. Almost every editor at some stage bemoaned the difficulty of his task. Matthew Engel in 1995 described picking five Cricketers of the Year as a "perk" but also as "frightening".

Today, players are chosen by *Wisden* primarily for their influence on the previous English season, but the original concept was less specific and it took several years for the feature to settle into its recognised form. There is plenty of evidence in the pre-1940 era in particular to suggest that editors were influenced by the selection of English players for major winter tours overseas and even by how they had performed in the early weeks of those tours. But it was rare indeed for anyone to be chosen who had not featured fairly prominently in the most recent English season.

The "rules" governing selection are stated in the most recent editions of *Wisden* as:

"The Five Cricketers of the Year are chosen by the editor of *Wisden* … Excellence in and/or influence on the previous English summer are the major criteria for inclusion as a Cricketer of the Year. No one can be chosen more than once."

These "rules" were only made clear in relatively modern times, and it was not immediately understood that any player could only be chosen once. In 1897 *The Times* criticised *Wisden* for not including J. T. Hearne among its Five – "his bowling was better than that of anyone else during the season" – seemingly unaware that Sydney Pardon would not be choosing Hearne again as he had already picked him in the 1892 edition. However, Pardon had made it clear that that no player would be chosen more than once in the short introductory explanation to the "Five" which was a standard feature until 1898. In 1895 for example he complained that it was becoming "less and less easy to find a suitable picture for *Wisden*, the portraits of so many of the best players having [already] been given."

Alongside his annual "Notes", the task of naming a new "Five" each year might be regarded as an editor's chief duty. The former constituted his verdict on the state of the game – a sermon, a state-of-the-nation address; the latter was his judgment on which players deserved the papal blessing. If those chosen as Cricketers of the Year were mainly cricket's star performers, there was often room to pay tribute to its stalwarts. The award's merit came from *Wisden*'s reputation for even-handedness, and a willingness to look beyond the logic of who had scored most runs and taken most wickets to an individual's greater worth. "I cannot recall in any of the biographies which he wrote – a marked feature of *Wisden* – an unkind word about any cricketer," Pelham Warner – a Cricketer of the Year himself in 1904 – stated on Sydney Pardon's death. "Criticism was sometimes imperative but the charitable touch was never wanting."

The principle that no player could be chosen more than once was to prove central to the feature's charm and success. Some critics have maintained that *Wisden* erred in not simply picking its five best players of the previous season, even if they had appeared before, but this would have denied many fine cricketers the recognition they deserved as well as leading to many tedious selections. How many times would Don Bradman or Garry Sobers have appeared among the Five? What would there have been left to say about them?

When the Cricketers of the Year first appeared, *Wisden* had been in publication for 26 years. Originally, the idea was an attempt to revive interest in an annual that hit hard times following the death of W. H. Knight, its first long-serving editor, in 1879. In 1884, John Wisden himself, a former Sussex and All England bowler of great repute and the almanack's publisher, had also died. So bad had things become that the 1886 edition only appeared the following year, when Harry Luff, who had purchased the Wisden sports outfitting business as well as the almanack, brought in Charles Pardon as editor. Pardon, who had co-founded the Cricket Reporting Agency in 1880, was charged with not only ensuring *Wisden* appeared on time but injecting it with vim and vigour. He proved an inspired choice, not least because he brought along as associates his brothers Sydney and Edgar, and C. Stewart Caine. This quartet would edit *Wisden* for the next 47 years and secure its position in British sporting and cultural life.

It was in Charles Pardon's third year as editor that he alighted on the notion of picking out for special treatment some of the star players of the day. There were sound cricketing reasons for the innovation: in a wet summer, the England-Australia Tests of 1888 had seen outstanding bowling performances, particularly from three Australians about whom English audiences knew little. "It has been thought appropriate, in consequence of the exceptional quality and effectiveness of last season's bowling, to publish some medallion portraits of prominent men," the editor explained. The idea bore immediate fruit too, the 1889 edition being the first to run to a second edition. By 1892, the almanack had expanded to a healthy 448 pages without increase in the one shilling price.

The idea was not so much to provide written profiles as to display "medallion portraits". At this time published photographs were a great novelty. *The Daily Graphic*, the first national newspaper to use a significant number of illustrations, did not start publication until 1890, the year after *Wisden* first began its feature, and even then the *Graphic* concentrated on line-drawings rather than photographs. Within three years, Sydney Pardon was sufficiently confident in the feature's success to predict, on taking over as editor, that no future edition would appear without a portrait (in fact, there would be a few war-time issues in which no photographs appeared).

The concept was not entirely Charles Pardon's own: like all good journalists, he took an idea from someone else and made it better. In 1882, a new competitor had entered the cricket publications market – *Cricket: A Weekly Record of the Game*, edited by Charles Alcock, the secretary of Surrey and a prime mover behind the creation of both Test cricket in England and the FA Cup. Alcock also edited the other main cricket annual of the day, *James Lillywhite's Cricketers' Annual*, which had appeared since 1872. In both *Cricket* and the *Lillywhite Annual*, Alcock had shown a sharp eye for giving the public insights into the game's leading performers. *Cricket* routinely ran a lengthy front-page profile of a star player accompanied by a line-drawing, while the *Lillywhite Annual* ran a special feature on either a notable player or, more usually, a team. In 1876 it featured Alfred Shaw, and in 1877 W. G. Grace. Then, in

1888 – just 12 months before Pardon introduced his "medallion portraits" – it saluted Arthur Shrewsbury's great season the previous year.

Alcock's mistake was that he did not persist with this idea, or expand it. He did not feature another player until 1897, by which time *Wisden*'s five "special portraits" was firmly established. The *Lillywhite Annual* ceased publication in 1900, and *Wisden*'s improvement under the Pardons certainly contributed to its demise. Reviewers of *Wisden* in 1890s routinely paid tribute to the player portraits situated near the front of the book.

The extent to which the photographs rather than the words were important was evident from the first year's entries. Only 80 words were devoted to Robert Peel's entry and not many more to George Lohmann's. C. T. B. Turner, Australia's star bowler, received the lengthiest tribute at just over 300 words (*Wisden* explained that less description was required of the Englishmen "as they are all familiarly known to the cricket public").

And it was no doubt precisely because once a player's photograph had appeared in *Wisden* there was not much point publishing it again that the practice was immediately adopted of no cricketer being chosen more than once. The notion of a "Hall of Fame" had well and truly taken hold by the time *Wisden* in 1914 included for the first time a full list of those selected for portraits – exactly 25 years after the first photographs had appeared.

The emphasis on portraiture survived a surprisingly long time, even if the accompanying written profiles grew longer and more ambitious in scope. The single page containing five medallion photographs remained the only photographic presence in the almanack until a general overhaul of lay-out took place under Wilfrid H. Brookes in the 1938 edition, when team photographs were introduced and the five players, appearing in alphabetical order, were given small headshots alongside their entries.

Between 1889 and 1937, extra kudos was accorded the player whose medallion portrait was situated in the centre of the page. Sydney Pardon wrote in the 1901 edition that he would like to have included Lord Hawke, the Yorkshire captain, among his "Five" but would have had to give him centre spot among the photographs (presumably on grounds of social standing); and that place clearly had to go to R. E. Foster, the Worcestershire amateur who had enjoyed a sensational season. Fourteen years later, Pardon alluded to Johnny Douglas's "paramount claims to be in the centre". A review of the 1924 *Wisden* in *The Times* commented that Maurice Tate had earned his place "in the middle of the portrait page". (In this book, the players who were accorded the central portrait are listed first).

It was noticeable that when first-class cricket was in abeyance during the First World War and two sets of public schools cricketers were chosen for the 1918 and 1919 issues, the portraits were retained but not the written profiles – even though the editor had some difficulty getting hold of the necessary photographs (brief descriptions of the players were incorporated into the Schools Review). When *Wisden* occasionally abandoned its selection of a "Five" and opted instead for a special tribute of one player, the main attraction was that this one player was accorded a full-page photograph.

Even if there was plenty of agonising in the early years over precisely what format it should take, the feature was an immediate success and by the fifth year the almanack was flagging up the identities of the chosen players on the title page. However, it was not until 1928 that the label was expanded from "Special Portraits" to "Special Portraits of Five Cricketers of the Year". Nor was it until 1939 that *Wisden*'s full list of those who had been chosen appeared under the heading, "Five Cricketers of the Year", rather than "Portraits in *Wisden*". Previously this list had been prefaced with the introductory comment, "In the issue for 1889 the idea of having photographs of prominent cricketers in *Wisden* was first adopted." At the same time, Wilfrid H. Brookes, the editor, spelt out for the first time that those chosen were cricketers "who, in the opinion of the editor, most deserved the honour by reason of their accomplishments during the previous season". This was changed in the 1954 edition, to "especially during the previous season", and in the 1977 edition, to "not necessarily, during the previous season" – the latter probably to accommodate the inclusion of long-serving Derbyshire wicketkeeper Bob Taylor. The full list was dropped in 1979 (when chosen players were instead identified under their entries in Births and Deaths of Cricketers) only to be restored in 1994, though no longer with any explanatory note.

Matthew Engel outlined the criteria in the preface to the 1995 *Wisden* before modifying them in his 1997 preface. From 2004, there was an explanatory note introducing the Cricketers of the Year, and since 2010 a "*Wisden* Honours" page immediately before the Editor's Notes states the Cricketers of the Year "rules".

At the outset, the photographs were taken by E. Hawkins and Co, who had run a studio in Brighton since the early 1860s and had specialised in photographs of individual cricketers and cricket teams since 1884 (the studio had actually passed out of the hands of the Hawkins family in 1887 and was run by George Thatcher). *Wisden* was clearly pleased with the association, stating in its 1889 edition that the reputation of Hawkins and Co "will certainly not suffer by the present specimen of their ability". With Hawkins and Co pretty much cornering the market, *Wisden* continued to exclusively use them until the First World War. Thereafter, photographs were drawn from a variety of sources.

The only early exception to the standard "head-and-shoulders" portrait came with W. G.

Grace's solo appearance in 1896 when a full-page portrait showed him at the crease, in readiness to receive a ball, a clearly stage-managed shot. The first action pictures of Cricketers of the Year appeared with the first post-Second World War selection in the 1947 edition.

As soon as he became editor, Sydney Pardon made one important change to the "Special Portraits" feature introduced by his brother: he reduced the number of players commemorated to five, a number he stuck to – save for the special features on Grace in 1896, John Wisden in 1913 and Pelham Warner in 1921 – for the rest of his editorship. It set a pattern which subsequent editors adhered to, with just two notable exceptions.

The first came in 1926, in the first *Wisden* edited by C. Stewart Caine, who took over the editorship following the death of Pardon in November 1925 and opted for a special tribute to Jack Hobbs for passing Grace's career tally of 126 centuries the previous season. Hobbs had already been a Cricketer of the Year in 1909. The second occurred in 2011 when Scyld Berry chose only four players because one of his original choices – presumed to be Mohammad Amir – was among three Pakistan cricketers suspended by the International Cricket Council over allegations of spot-fixing during the last Test match of the 2010 season. The three players were subsequently jailed. The previous year, Berry had chosen the first – and so far only – woman to be a Cricketer of the Year, Claire Taylor.

Another departure from tradition came in 2000 when Matthew Engel based the award on the players' impact on cricket worldwide rather than the preceding English season. In 1997 he chose Sanath Jayasuriya even though he had not played in England the previous year, but he justified this on the basis that Jayasuriya's performances at the 1996 World Cup (which was held in Asia) had a significant influence on the English season that followed. However, the 2000 change was shortlived: in 2004 the decision was reversed and a separate award for "Leading Cricketer in the World" was introduced (see page 370).

It might be argued that in some years editors found it difficult to arrive at five worthy choices; certainly some of them bemoaned the paucity of available options. Perhaps four Cricketers of the Year might have been a better idea. But once the international schedule expanded, and overseas stars flooded into county cricket in the late 1960s, the reverse seemed to be the case, and many fine players found themselves unable to gain entry to the Hall of Fame. Inzamam-ul-Haq was not chosen despite playing 120 Tests and scoring more than 8,800 Test runs. Nor was Chaminda Vaas, who took 355 Test wickets, or Wasim Bari, who executed more than 220 Test dismissals. Of England's 79 Test captains, 22 were never recognised by *Wisden*, although only three of these date from the last 60 years – Tony Lewis, Chris Cowdrey and Mark Butcher. Lewis's eight Tests as captain were all overseas while Cowdrey and Butcher, though they led England at home, did so only once.

In 2008, *Wisden* named the five best players since 1889 not chosen as Cricketers of the Year: they were Inzamam and four bowlers who took 892 Test wickets between them, Wes Hall, Bishan Bedi, Jeff Thomson and Abdul Qadir.

By the time *Wisden* celebrated its 150th edition in 2013, its Hall of Fame had acquired 570 members.

Notes for the Reader

- The following symbols appear throughout this book:

   batsman
   bowler
  / ● allrounder
  Ⓜ wicketkeeper

- The year in which a Cricketer of the Year is selected in all cases reflects the edition in which he/she is named, even though his/her selection is based on performances in the previous year.

- A year in square brackets after a cricketer's name indicates the year in which that player was a Cricketer of the Year.

- All ages relating to selection are as at April 1st of the year in which the player is chosen.

- Statistical tables at the end of each year's summary are not comprehensive in every case and include only the categories of matches that the author judged were material to the players' selection.

- 'List A' matches refer to all limited-overs games of 40 overs per side or more, as officially sanctioned by the relevant governing bodies.

- All current statistics in the book are accurate to May 1 2013.

Part One: 1889 to 1917

When Wisden introduced its new feature in 1889, English cricket was essentially confined to a group of eight first-class counties, and Test matches between two countries, England and Australia. Although South Africa are now deemed to have played their first Test in March 1889, their early matches were only later accorded Test status, and their early tours of England were low-key affairs. Had it stayed like this, *Wisden* might have struggled to find enough good new players worthy of commendation.

Fortunately, things changed. Over the next 15 years the number of first-class counties doubled from eight to 16, while by the late 1890s England and Australia were reciprocating series of five matches rather than three. South Africa's cricket also developed sufficiently that by 1907 they were playing Tests in England, and two of their new-fangled googly bowlers featured among *Wisden*'s five Cricketers of the Year (although South Africa's first Cricketer of the Year, wicketkeeper Ernest Halliwell, had appeared following their non-Test tour of 1904).

Naturally, *Wisden*'s selections were largely based on which players had done well during the previous season's County Championship and – if there were any – Test matches, although the annual Gentlemen v Players encounters were also significant measures of a player's standing. Selection for a major tour also seemed to count, although clearly no one was going to be chosen for a tour on the back of a bad English season. Between the 1895 and 1914 editions, Sydney Pardon chose 21 Cricketers of the Year who had been picked for a Test tour of Australia or South

Africa in the winter following the English season covered by the Almanack, and of these 14 had yet to play a Test. Pardon's thinking may simply have been that he saw these players as rising stars whose faces might be of interest to the public by the time the Almanack came out (during this period *Wisden* was usually published before the end of January, before most winter tours were complete).

With the medallion portraits the main attraction, it took a few years for the accompanying biographies to acquire an authoritative feel. In most instances a formulaic style was followed, each entry beginning with the player's name (prefaced by "Mr" in the case of amateurs) and the first or second sentence containing his place and date of birth. Notable exceptions were W. G. Grace in 1896 and Pelham Warner in 1904. Perhaps Grace was considered too well known for it to be necessary to provide such basic information, but with Warner there may have been some reluctance to highlight the Caribbean origins of England's new captain.

Few biographies shed much light on the subject's life outside cricket. They stuck to steadfastly recounting a player's progress for his county or, in the case of amateurs, at school. If an amateur had not gone to a public school of note, *Wisden* usually mentioned neither the school nor where his early cricket had been played. In this regard, the entry for Frank Foster in 1912 was typical: "Nothing was known of him outside local cricket till the season of 1908 when in five matches for Warwickshire he took 23 wickets…" Seemingly, little attempt was made to dig deep for information not readily available in the sporting press or previous editions of the Almanack. Players certainly weren't interviewed. The first evidence of *Wisden* contacting a player for assistance with a biography came in 1910, when Sydney Pardon wrote to Douglas Carr, sensationally plucked from the obscurity of club cricket to play for Kent and England the previous summer. Pardon quoted Carr's reply at some length.

Controversy was also avoided. While *Wisden* was not afraid to select professionals who had been in dispute with their county clubs over pay (a not uncommon occurrence), it shrank from airing the details. This is what it said in 1909 about Walter Brearley's turbulent relationship with Lancashire: "Into the question of the foolish quarrel – happily made up last spring – which threatened to terminate his connection with Lancashire there is no need in this place to enter." A year later it said just as little about Sydney Barnes's troubles with the same county: "The disagreement that caused him to drop out of the XI was an even greater misfortune to Lancashire than to the player himself. There is no need at this distance of time to go into the merits of the quarrel."

Most disappointing, though, was the treatment in 1904 of Walter Mead, who had fallen out with Essex over a request for more pay. "It is a thousand pities that after the close of the past season he should have become estranged from his county over a question of money," said *Wisden*. "Into the merits of the dispute this is not the place to enter, but one cannot help expressing the opinion that Mead was very ill-advised to press for an increase of winter pay at a time when the finances of the county club were in such a bad state." What it did not say was that Mead had asked for more money because his wife and child had died, and he needed help supporting his other children.

Reading these early biographical essays, it would be possible to surmise that there was no such thing as womankind, players' wives not even meriting a mention even when, as in the cases of Mead and Bill Lockwood (1899), they had recently died. The first (passing) reference to a woman came in Walter Brearley's 1909 entry, when readers were informed that Brearley's friends – presumably male – had recently had the pleasure of congratulating him on his marriage. More than 100 Cricketers of the Year had been profiled at this point.

Just as the "old" counties who played before 1889 continued to dominate the Championship up to 1914, so they dominated *Wisden*'s Cricketers of the Year (see table). But *Wisden* was not slow to recognise newcomers. When Somerset finished third in their second year in the Championship in 1892, two of their players were chosen. Dick Lilley was similarly acknowledged after two seasons with Warwickshire, who had joined the Championship in 1895, while George Thompson was selected after starring in Northamptonshire's maiden Championship season of 1905. When Warwickshire became, in 1911, the first of the new counties to win the Championship, *Wisden* chose both Frank Foster, their captain, and Sep Kinneir.

Championship winners usually had at least one representative among the Five. The only years when this did not happen – apart from the exceptional cases of 1896 and 1913 when a Five was not chosen – were 1897 (when Yorkshire had been the champions the previous year), 1900 (Surrey), 1903 (Yorkshire) and 1914 (Kent). Six of Surrey's regulars in 1900 had already been chosen. Yorkshire had four representatives in 1901, to mark their extraordinary title win of the previous year when they went unbeaten in 28 games. Surrey provided three of the Five in 1907, even though they had only finished third the previous year; Kent, the champions, contributed two.

Australian touring teams had three

representatives following the 1888, 1899 and 1902 visits, but none after the 1905 trip. Three Australians were chosen while playing for counties – Albert Trott, Frank Tarrant and Alan Marshal – as was the South African Charles Llewellyn, and the West Indian Sydney Smith. K. S. Ranjitsinhji, an Indian, was chosen after becoming the first non-white to play for England.

As far as English cricketers from this period were concerned, 13 were chosen following seasons in which they had appeared in home Tests for England (including Ranjitsinhji). Three such players were picked following the 1888 and 1896 seasons, and none following 1902 and 1907. Of course, many of those who represented England had already been chosen in earlier years: in 1902, the England XI that took the field in the First Test against Australia at Edgbaston – a famously powerful side – had all been Cricketers of the Year, Johnny Tyldesley and Len Braund having been selected earlier that summer.

With fewer opportunities available to them, several notable cricketers from overseas missed out on selection. Perhaps the most striking Australian omission of the era was the fast bowler Ernie Jones, who might have been picked after the 1896 or 1899 tours. Doubts over Jones's action may have played a part, *Wisden* being a vocal critic of throwing (although this did not get in the way of Arthur Mold's selection in 1892). But perhaps the finest cricketer of all from this period who missed out was Aubrey Faulkner, the South African all-rounder, who averaged 40.8 with the bat and 26.6 with the ball in Tests. He would probably have been chosen following South Africa's 1912 tour, but *Wisden* did not pick a Five the following year, preferring instead to commemorate the life of John Wisden as a way of marking the publication of the 50th Almanack.

The England player who appeared in most Tests during this period without being a Cricketer of the Year was Frederick Fane, who won 14 caps, three as captain. Ted Arnold

of Worcestershire, who played eight Tests against Australia and gathered more than 15,000 runs and 1,000 wickets in his career, was never chosen. Nor were George Dennett, the Gloucestershire slow left-armer who took 2,151 wickets between 1903 and 1926, or the Leicestershire pair of J. H. King and C. J. B. Wood, who scored 25,122 and 23,879 runs respectively in careers running from the mid-1890s to the mid-1920s. The Lancashire all-rounder Jack Sharp was another notable omission: he helped win the Championship in 1904, scored more than 22,000 runs in his career, and hit England's only hundred of the 1909 Ashes series. He remains one of only two people to score a home century for England v Australia since the award was introduced in 1889 not to be picked – the other being Mark Butcher, maker of a famous match-winning hundred at Headingley in 2001. Kent's Fred Huish, who became the first wicketkeeper to complete 100 dismissals in a season (something he did twice) was also never chosen.

Of the 107 English players chosen, 43 held amateur status, or 40%, which roughly equated to the proportion of amateurs representing England in Tests during this period – suggesting commendable class impartiality on *Wisden*'s part. Of these, one was a wicketkeeper, two were spinners, three fast bowlers, eight all-rounders, and 29 batsmen. During the first four years of the award, only one English amateur (Gregor MacGregor) was chosen, but after that the only Five lacking an English amateur presence was 1908 (though Reggie Schwarz was in effect an English-born amateur who had switched to South Africa's camp). Five English amateurs were chosen in 1893, and four in 1898.

The youngest players to be chosen during this period were Jack Crawford and Donald Knight, both 20 when *Wisden* selected them; John Ferris, Sammy Woods, Wilfred Rhodes and J. W. "Young Jack" Hearne were all 21. Although amateurs tended to be younger – many peaked in their early twenties before moving into business – they also provided the three oldest picks, in Lord Hawke (aged 48), W. G. Grace (47) and Levi Wright (43).

Six died during military service in the First World War – Major Booth, Kenneth Hutchings, Colin Blythe and Alfred Hartley were killed in action, while Schwarz and Alan Marshal died of illness. John Ferris died during the second Boer War. Four took their own lives – Arthur Shrewsbury, Drewy Stoddart, Albert Trott and Albert Relf. Dick Pilling died shortly after the *Wisden* in which he was named among Five Great Wicketkeepers was published, having not played for 18 months.

CRICKETERS OF THE YEAR 1889–1915

(Teams they represented in the English season prior to selection)

Team	Years	Awards	Batsmen	Bowlers	Allrounders	WK
Surrey	1889–1915	23	11	7	3	2
Yorkshire	1889–1914	15	7	3	5	0
Lancashire	1889–1911	12†	6	4	1	1†
Nottinghamshire	1890–1914	11	6	3	1	1
Kent	1892–1915	11	4	4	3	0
Middlesex	1892–1912	8	3	2	3	0
Essex	1898–1915	5	1	2	2	0
Sussex	1895–1914	4	3	0	1	0
Warwickshire	1897–1912	4	1	0	2	1
Hampshire	1900–1914	4	3	0	1	0
Gloucestershire	1896–1899	3	1	0	2	0
Somerset	1893–1902	3	2	0	1	0
Derbyshire	1899–1906	2	1	0	0	1
Worcestershire	1900–1911	2	2	0	0	0
Northamptonshire	1905–1915	2	0	0	2	0
Leicestershire	1904	1	1	0	0	0
Staffordshire	1910	1	0	1	0	0
Cambridge University	1889-1901	6	2	1	2	1
Oxford University	1893-1915	4	4	0	0	0
Australians	1889-1910	16	6	4	4	2
England	1889-1912	13	3	6	2	2
South Africans	1905-1908	3	0	2	0	1
TOTAL		**153***	**67**	**39**	**35**	**12**

*In total, there were 131 Cricketers of the Year between 1889 and 1915. However, the figure of 153 awards shown in the table reflects the fact that twenty players appeared for two teams during the season in question (11 for a county plus Tests for England; 1 for a university plus England; 1 for a university plus Australia; 7 for a university and county). One player, Stanley Jackson, appeared for three teams (university, county and country).

†Dick Pilling of Lancashire did not appear during the previous season because of illness.

1889

Six Great Bowlers of the Year

John Ferris (Australians) ●

Charles Turner (Australians) ●

Johnny Briggs (Lancashire and England) ●

George Lohmann (Surrey and England) ●

Bobby Peel (Yorkshire and England) ●

Sammy Woods (Cambridge University and Australians) ●

HEADLINE EVENTS FROM 1888

- Unofficial county champions – Surrey

- England win the Test series with Australia 2-1

THE STELLAR PERFORMANCES OF THE ENGLAND and Australia bowlers in the three Tests of 1888 gave Charles Pardon a natural group to choose as his first selection. Charles Turner in particular made a big impression for the Australians, shaking the confidence of batsmen up and down the country with his knack of making the ball lift, and earning himself the nickname of "The Terror". Although England won the series 2–1, Australia's victory in the first match at Lord's – where the home side were dismissed for 53 and 62 – signalled a revival in Australian cricket following a string of Test defeats.

Pardon chose the three bowlers on either side who did almost all the bowling. Turner, John Ferris and Sammy Woods – aged respectively 25, 21 and 21 and new to English audiences – took all 37 wickets claimed by Australia, while Bobby Peel, Johnny Briggs and George Lohmann accounted for 47 of the 55 taken by England. This was not quite as crude a decision as it may sound; history would show that Pardon had chosen well. Turner, Lohmann and Briggs were magnetic personalities, while Peel joined them among the first five bowlers in history

to take 100 Test wickets. Lohmann, who took 150 wickets or more in seven successive English seasons from 1886 to 1892, was also one of the great slip catchers.

In what was admittedly a bowler's summer, what these two triumvirates showed was how sophisticated bowling had become thanks to regular international contests between the countries since 1877.

In fact, in the case of the Australians, Turner and Ferris were essentially seen as a great partnership with Woods in support: that a photograph of Turner and Ferris together took pride of place on the page of medallion portraits accurately reflected their status. Pardon admitted that Woods only narrowly gained selection ahead of several unnamed bowlers from Kent and Nottinghamshire.

Woods, a powerful man who also played international rugby union, was an out-and-out quick bowler. Briggs, who stood only 5ft 5in and was first chosen for England as a batsman, operated in a style that would be recognisable to modern slow left-arm spinners, coming in off a short run and using variations of spin and flight

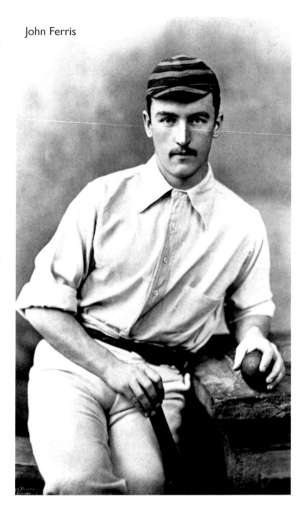
John Ferris

to deceive batsmen. The others were essentially medium-pacers (Turner the briskest) who altered their speeds and could cut or spin the ball in or out. Like Briggs, Ferris and Peel were left-armers.

Pardon wrote in Briggs's entry: "It is curious, as showing how fashions and methods of attack change in cricket, that not more than one of these six bowlers can be called slow, and only one of them, Woods, can be properly described as fast. The rest vary between slow, medium, and fast, and their ability is shown in nothing else so much as in the way they mix up the pace. This is a change indeed from the condition of things ten years ago before Australian influence was felt."

Pardon devoted most words to Turner, who had produced some great performances against English teams in Australia and now took 21 Test wickets at 12.42 apiece (outstanding figures that Peel nevertheless beat with 24 at 7.54). He described Turner's style of bowling as "above medium pace, with a beautifully easy delivery, his hand not being very high at the moment the ball quits it. He has a fine break from the off, and bowls a wonderful yorker, but the great thing about him is that he makes the ball rise from the

Sammy Woods

Sammy Woods:
"He bowls very fast right-hand, now and then sending in a good yorker"

CRICKETERS OF THE YEAR 1889 – Performances in the English season 1888

Name	Age*		Matches	Runs	Bat ave	Wickets	Bowl ave	Catches (/st)
J Briggs	26	First-class	26	872	21.26	160	10.49	11
		Tests	3	39	13.00	12	7.83	0
JJ Ferris	21	First-class	37	489	11.92	199	14.74	16
		Tests	3	66	22.00	11	15.18	1
GA Lohmann	23	First-class	29	628	16.10	209	10.90	45
		Tests	3	64	21.33	11	13.09	8
R Peel	32	First-class	31	669	13.38	171	12.22	9
		Tests	3	48	12.00	24	7.54	0
CTB Turner	26	First-class	36	789	14.61	283	11.68	17
		Tests	3	59	9.83	21	12.42	0
SMJ Woods	21	First-class	18	459	17.00	87	16.82	16
		Tests	3	32	5.33	5	24.20	1

* as at 1/4/1889

The England team that beat Australia in the 2nd Test match at The Oval in August 1888. Back row (l-r): Frank Sugg [1890], Billy Barnes [1890], Henry Wood [1891]. Seated: John Shuter, **George Lohmann**, W. G. Grace [1896] (captain), George Ulyett, Walter Read [1893]. On ground: Bobby Abel [1890], **Johnny Briggs**, **Bobby Peel**

George Lohmann:
"One of the best bowlers and most accomplished all-round cricketers ever seen"

pitch faster perhaps than any bowler we have seen." Turner got this lift despite being by modern standards short for a fast bowler at 5ft 9in. Archie MacLaren [named as a Cricketer of the Year in 1895] later claimed that Turner grew his nails long so he could gouge the seam of the ball.

They may have been among the greatest bowlers of their era, but the future was not kind to the three English professionals, nor to Ferris. Shortly after playing alongside Peel and Briggs together in Tests for the last time in Australia in 1891-92, Lohmann developed tuberculosis; he moved to South Africa, and died there in 1901 aged 36. Peel was peremptorily sacked by Yorkshire in 1897 after taking the field drunk. Briggs suffered an epileptic attack during a Test against Australia at Leeds in 1899, was admitted to

an asylum, and died there in 1902 in his 40th year.

Turner and Ferris toured England in 1890, but Woods never played for Australia again. He had come to England for his schooling, and was only co-opted onto the 1888 tour after doing well for Cambridge University. He remained in England, enjoying a gilded career as amateur cricketer, rugby player and footballer, representing England at cricket and rugby, and serving in the First World War with the Somerset Light Infantry. Ferris also settled in England: he played for Gloucestershire, and once for his adopted country against South Africa in what is now regarded as a Test match, before dying of enteric fever in 1900 during the Boer War. He was only 33. Turner outlasted them all, living until 1944.

Charles Turner

Nine Great Batsmen of the Year

Arthur Shrewsbury (Nottinghamshire) *i*

Bobby Abel (Surrey) *i*

Billy Barnes (Nottinghamshire) *i*

William Gunn (Nottinghamshire) *i*

Louis Hall (Yorkshire) *i*

Robert Henderson (Surrey) *i*

Maurice Read (Surrey) *i*

Frank Sugg (Lancashire) *i*

Albert Ward (Lancashire) *i*

HEADLINE EVENTS FROM 1889

- A team led by C. Aubrey Smith tours South Africa and plays what subsequently are declared to be the first Test matches between England and South Africa; England win both games

- Unofficial county champions – Surrey, Lancashire and Nottinghamshire

HAVING PICKED BOWLERS IN HIS FIRST SELECTION, Charles Pardon turned to batsmen in his second, although he was at pains to point out that the decision was the proprietor's and not his own.… Why nine is unclear, but with no Test cricket in 1889 eight came from the three counties who shared the last unofficial championship title: Surrey, Nottinghamshire and Lancashire.

All nine were professionals, which with the exception of one man was a fair reflection of the state of amateur batting in England. The exception was Grace [1896], who scored the most first-class runs (1,396) in the season at an average (32.5) bettered by only four. It was a curious decision, as some of those chosen were no more than journeymen pros, but as would become clear *Wisden* regarded Grace as a special case who would be dealt with in due course.

The Nottinghamshire players must have been among the easier picks. Although Pardon hailed him as the "greatest professional batsman of the day", Arthur Shrewsbury had in fact been a more reliable batsman than Grace for most of the 1880s, during which he took defensive play to new levels, hanging on the back foot and playing the ball as late as possible. In 1887 Shrewsbury averaged 78.71 in first-class cricket, surpassing Grace's 78.25 in 1871, both amazing figures for their day, and although he missed the 1888 season (staying behind in Australia after a cricket tour to manage what is now recognised as the first British Lions rugby tour) he had performed strongly on his return. No one would score more Test runs before 1900 than his 1,277.

Billy Gunn, a late-developing protégé of Shrewsbury's who stood 6ft 2in tall, topped the national averages and was described by Pardon as "emphatically the most successful batsman of 1889". Billy Barnes, while not as versatile a batsman as either, had been for years a central

The strong Surrey team of the 1880s. Back row (l-r): **Bobby Abel**, Charles Horner, Monty Bowden, Edwin Diver, Walter Read [1893]. Front: Edward Barratt, Kingsmill Key, **Robert Henderson**, John Shuter (captain), **Maurice Read**, William Roller

figure for Nottinghamshire and England, as all-rounder and carouser-in-chief – two years earlier at Sydney he had injured himself throwing a punch at Australia's captain Percy McDonnell.

Maurice Read and Bobby Abel of Surrey were also seasoned campaigners, into their thirties and experienced in touring overseas. They had already successfully played Test cricket, although ten of

Bobby Abel:

"His present high position among professional cricketers may be described as a triumph of perseverance"

Read's Tests had taken place abroad; he had not been chosen at home since the infamous defeat to Australia in 1882 that created the Ashes legend (he returned in 1890 to great effect). His 1889 season would have been better but for injuries. Abel, 5ft 5in and a former hop porter, had been the star batsman in the bowler's summer of 1888. He would become one of the most prolific run-scorers in England, topping 2,000 runs in eight successive years from 1895 and not playing his last Test until 1902. He was also a regular captain of the Players against the Gentlemen.

Frank Sugg and Albert Ward topped Lancashire's averages. Ward, at 23 the youngest of the nine, was an exciting prospect, Pardon rightly predicting great things for him: "Standing 6ft in height, and having great power and reach, Albert Ward possesses every qualification for a first-class batsman, and it seems reasonable to expect a brilliant career for him." Ward would be England's leading run-scorer during the Ashes-winning tour of 1894-95. By contrast, Sugg – an attacking batsman who had previously played for Yorkshire and Derbyshire – would not add to his two Test caps of 1888.

Frank Sugg

Billy Barnes

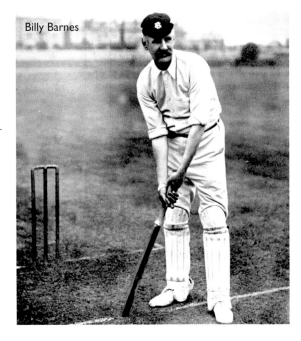

Albert Ward

William Gunn

Arthur Shrewsbury

Wisden alerted readers to Hall's forthcoming benefit, a crucial event in the life of every professional. Some of this group did well out of their benefits (Ward the best with £1,700), and spent the money wisely. Others did not. Barnes became a publican and was dead within five years. Shrewsbury and Gunn, who did not play in a Test in 1896 after demanding (along with Abel) a pay rise for the professionals, were among the leading cricket entrepreneurs of their day, organising tours and developing sports-equipment businesses. Gunn, the first professional elected to a county committee, eventually left £57,000 in his will. In tragic contrast, Shrewsbury, unable to face life without playing, committed suicide at 47.

Abel, who fathered 11 children, set up a cricket manufacturing business that folded after eight years; he later went blind. Sugg, a grammar-school boy who opted for professional cricket and football rather than a legal career, published a cricket annual and established a successful sports-goods firm with his brother, before gambling away much of his wealth. Read took up a job on the Tichborne estate in Hampshire, made huge scores in club cricket, and lived until he was 70. Henderson, who enjoyed a better benefit than Hall, Gunn, Shrewsbury or Abel, spent his last 56 years as chorister and churchwarden in Beddington, Surrey.

The most surprising inclusions were Louis Hall and Robert Henderson, neither of whom scored a century in 1889 or ever came close to playing for England. Henderson, born in Wales, played arguably the innings of the year, an unbeaten 59 that carried Surrey to victory over Yorkshire in near-darkness – a game remembered as the "Gaslight Match" because the street lights around The Oval were burning bright by the end. Hall was a stonewalling opener whose defence was so solid that he carried his bat 15 times, and whose nature was quiescent enough (he was a Nonconformist lay preacher and teetotaller) that he was often entrusted with captaining Yorkshire when Lord Hawke [1909] was absent.

Arthur Shrewsbury:
"His batting during the last few years... has been some of the most remarkable in the history of the game"

CRICKETERS OF THE YEAR 1890 – Performances in the English season 1889

Name	Age*		Matches	Runs	Bat ave	Wickets	Bowl ave	Catches (/st)
R Abel	32	First-class	25	1095	28.81	2	44.50	29
W Barnes	37	First-class	27	1249	34.69	15	22.40	20
W Gunn	31	First-class	26	1319	37.68	0		13
L Hall	37	First-class	21	975	26.35	0		16
R Henderson	25	First-class	18	550	22.91	4	19.50	10
JM Read	31	First-class	17	847	33.88			15
A Shrewsbury	33	First-class	12	522	37.28			12
FH Sugg	28	First-class	20	747	26.67			12
A Ward	24	First-class	21	822	30.44	0		7

*as at 1/4/1890

Louis Hall

1891

Five Great Wicketkeepers

Jack Blackham (Australians) Ⓜ
Gregor MacGregor (Cambridge University and England) Ⓜ
Dick Pilling (Lancashire) Ⓜ
Mordecai Sherwin (Nottinghamshire) Ⓜ
Harry Wood (Surrey) Ⓜ

HEADLINE EVENTS FROM 1890

• County champions – Surrey

• England win the series against Australia 2-0, the Manchester Test being abandoned without a ball bowled

FOLLOWING THE UNTIMELY DEATH OF HIS brother Charles at the age of 40, Sydney Pardon took over the editorship of *Wisden* for 1891, and immediately picked out for commendation a cricketer – Dick Pilling of Lancashire – whose ill-health had prevented him taking the field the previous summer (hence the title Five Great Wicketkeepers rather than Five Great Wicketkeepers of the Year). Even though Pilling had not played, Pardon felt it would have been "an obvious mistake" to omit him from such a Five. Pilling was the only person chosen for the award before 1996 who did not play cricket during the previous English season.

When the profiles were written, Sydney Pardon knew only that Pilling had been seriously ill, but within three months of *Wisden*'s publication he had died – on March 28, 1891, aged 35. Having just returned from what had been intended as a recuperative trip to Australia paid for by his county club, Pilling possibly never even knew of his selection. At least his wife Emma and daughter Mary had the proceeds of his 1889 benefit, worth a then-record £1,600, on which to live.

Pilling, who also worked as a stonemason, was recognised from the outset as a natural wicketkeeper and was, in the opinion of many, the finest in England during the 1880s, a period when rough-and-ready pitches and flimsy gauntlets made the craft a hazardous one. Nor was his health ever very sturdy. His fortunes took a decisive turn for the worse during the winter of 1889-90, when he fell ill after playing football.

Wisden was unequivocal in its praise. "Much might be said about Pilling's special excellence as a wicketkeeper, but we will content ourselves by expressing a very strong opinion that during the last 12 years he has had no superior but [Jack] Blackham. His style may be described as the perfection of neatness and rapidity, without the least unnecessary show." Pilling might have played more often for England but for the practice (not abandoned until 1899) of the counties staging Tests being responsible for the selection of the XI, and often favouring local players. Pilling played only three Tests in England – all on his home ground of Old Trafford.

Without Pilling, the various selection committees agreed that the previously untried Gregor MacGregor was indisputably England's best gloveman. He retained the

Mordecai Sherwin

Jack Blackham

in England on his home ground at The Oval in 1888. He might not have had the best hands behind the stumps, but he demonstrated his capabilities in front of them by scoring 134 not out against South Africa at Cape Town in 1892 in what would subsequently be regarded as a Test match: Wood thus became the first wicketkeeper to record a Test hundred.

There was no chance of Sherwin doing such a thing. Although quite agile for his size, he weighed around 17st and his highest score in a first-class career spanning 20 years was 37. He did not lack for competitiveness, though, as *Wisden* discreetly hinted: "Though the applause and laughter of the spectators may occasionally cause him to go a little too far, he has certainly never done anything to really lay him open to censure." Until Grace [1896] was chosen, Sherwin was at 40 the oldest to be recognised by *Wisden*.

position throughout the home series against Australia in 1890, and again in 1893. Born in Edinburgh, educated at Uppingham, and the first British-born amateur to be picked by *Wisden*, MacGregor was in his third year at Cambridge in 1890, where he had made his name keeping to Woods [1889]. He was also a capable batsman in an era when keepers were not expected to score heavily. His career first-class batting average of 18.02 was the best of the Five, ahead of Harry Wood (16.94), Jack Blackham (16.78), Pilling (9.85) and Mordecai Sherwin (7.59). He captained Middlesex to the Championship in 1903.

Wood, who left his native Kent for Surrey and stood only 5ft 3½in, had played his one Test

Jack Blackham:

"He is the greatest wicketkeeper the world has yet seen"

Harry Wood

While England chopped and changed, Australia were rarely in doubt about their best keeper: Blackham was given the gloves in 32 of their 39 Tests up to 1894. At 10st 6lb, he weighed rather less than Sherwin, and was fearless standing up to the stumps. He was the first keeper regularly to dispense with a long-stop to fast bowling. A fierce, anxious competitor, he was staunch with the bat, good enough to play three Tests purely as a batsman. The 1890 tour of England saw him at the age of 36 playing somewhere near his best despite Australia being a weak team. *Wisden*'s verdict on this pioneer was that he was "the greatest wicketkeeper the world has yet seen".

MacGregor, who became Middlesex's treasurer, and Blackham, a sometime bank clerk, both patrolled money as they once had the stumps, but Sherwin – who also kept goal for Notts County in his younger days – was less fortunate. He was awarded a benefit match against Cambridge University which drew a poor gate… and no proceeds.

Pardon said that had he named seven wicketkeepers he would have included Hylton "Punch" Philipson (Oxford University) and Yorkshire's David Hunter. Neither was ever chosen, though Hunter completed more than 1,250 dismissals.

Gregor MacGregor

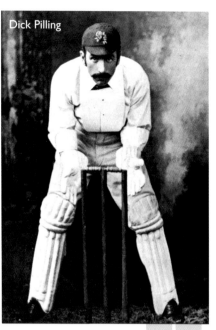

Dick Pilling:
"No professional cricketer is held in higher regard than the Lancashire wicketkeeper"

CRICKETERS OF THE YEAR 1891 – Performances in the English season 1890

Name	Age*		Matches	Runs	Bat ave	Wickets	Bowl ave	Catches (/st)
JM Blackham	36	First-class	28	655	15.59	0		38/27
		Tests	2	17	4.25			1/2
G MacGregor	21	First-class	19	628	20.25			25/12
		Tests	2	3	1.50			3/2
M Sherwin	40	First-class	26	139	5.79			59/10
R Pilling	Would have been 35; did not play in 1890 and died March 28,1891							
H Wood	37	First-class	16	308	17.11			31/8

* as at 1/4/1891

1892

Five Great Bowlers

William Attewell (Nottinghamshire) ●
Jack Hearne (Middlesex) ●
Fred Martin (Kent) ●
Arthur Mold (Lancashire) ●
John Sharpe (Surrey) ●

HEADLINE EVENTS FROM 1891

- County champions – Surrey

- Somerset admitted to the county championship

ARTHUR MOLD PROVED TO BE WISDEN'S FIRST controversial pick. A fast bowler from Northamptonshire (not then a first-class county) who joined Lancashire, he was one of the quickest in the country, and among the most successful, but opponents constantly grumbled about the legitimacy of his action. As Sydney Pardon wrote in his obituary of Mold, who died in 1921, those doubts dated from his Northamptonshire days: "He was extremely lucky to bowl for so many seasons before being no-balled. To pretend that a perfectly fair bowler could have been condemned as he was is absurd… He did wonders for Lancashire but personally I always thought he was in a false position." But it did not stop Pardon picking Mold among his Five at a time when throwing had yet to become the hot topic it later became.

Perhaps Pardon felt that in the absence of any umpire calling him for throwing – something that did not happen until 1900, when he was in the twilight of his career – he must recognise Mold's considerable efforts. In his debut season, he had finished third in the national averages with 102 wickets at 11.9 apiece, and in 1891 he took 138 at 12.5, an average bettered only by J. T.

"Jack" Hearne among the Five. *Wisden*'s tribute highlighted the dangers he posed: "Mold's bowling is so formidable as to make him worth his place in any XI. Bowling with a high action, he has tremendous speed, and, considering his pace, the amount of work he can get on the ball is astonishing. On anything like a rough or bumpy wicket he is, beyond all question, the most difficult and dangerous bowler of the day, the ball getting up from the pitch so high and so fast as to intimidate all but the very pluckiest." When Mold played his only Tests in 1893, the Australians also regarded him as suspect.

There was nothing dubious about Jack Hearne, a medium-pacer who could cut the ball in and swing it away. He had a beautifully economical action that served him well during a career spanning 35 years in which he claimed 3,061 first-class wickets, a haul only ever bettered by three people (all spinners). He was 24 years old in 1891 and relatively inexperienced, having played half a season for Middlesex the previous year, but in the next few years he performed great feats, taking 257 wickets in 1896, ten of them against Australia at The Oval, and a hat-trick against them at Headingley in

1899, the first for England on home soil. Like Mold, he was born in a non-first-class county, Buckinghamshire, where he was spotted by the Middlesex captain A. J. Webbe.

Dick Attewell was even harder to score from than Hearne. His favoured method was to bowl outside off stump to a packed off-side field. He was also credited in some quarters with developing an early googly. He played ten Tests against Australia, and his economy-rate of 21.96 runs per 100 balls remains the best among Test bowlers who have delivered 2,000 or more. A butcher by trade, Attewell was also a handy batsman – by far the best of this Five – and a fine cover point. He played for Nottinghamshire until his 49th year.

John Sharpe and Fred "Nutty" Martin proved less durable. Sharpe, who had lost his right eye as a youth and moved to Surrey after being unwanted by his native Nottinghamshire, was a 5ft 7in fast-medium bowler who broke the ball back into the right-hander, and was an early exponent of the yorker and surprise faster ball. Alongside George Lohmann [1889], he helped Surrey win the 1890 and 1891 titles, two seasons in which he took 247 wickets. But the 1891-92 tour of Australia contributed to his rapid burnout. By the age of 27 in 1894 he had played the last of his 82 first-class matches, and went back to work as a framework knitter.

Martin, a late-developing slow-medium left-armer, had three outstanding years between 1889 and 1891, but after that lost his powers of spin and managed only one more good season, though he played on until 1899. With Peel and Briggs for competition, he played only two Tests for England, in the first of which, at The Oval in 1890, he took 12 Australian wickets.

While Mold was cast out of the game after a vote of the (amateur) county captains in 1901

William Attewell:
"Since Alfred Shaw there has probably been no bowler with such a uniformly accurate pitch and... no one from whom it is so hard to get runs"

The England team that toured Australia in 1891-92. Back row (l-r): Bob Carpenter (umpire), **William Attewell**, George Lohmann [1889], Maurice Read [1890], George Bean, **John Sharpe**, Bob Thoms (umpire). Seated: Johnny Briggs [1889], Gregor MacGregor [1891], W. G. Grace [1896] (captain), Bobby Peel [1889], Drewy Stoddart [1893], Bobby Abel [1890]

Arthur Mold

went against him 11–1, Hearne moved easily among his social superiors, spending several winters coaching for the Maharajah of Patiala, gaining election to the Middlesex committee in 1920, and later coaching at Oxford University alongside Tom Hayward [1895]. Mold at least had the proceeds of a healthy benefit worth £2,050 to live off.

Although three of them moved away from home to play their county cricket, Hearne, Martin, Mold and Sharpe all died in the places in which they were born.

Fred Martin

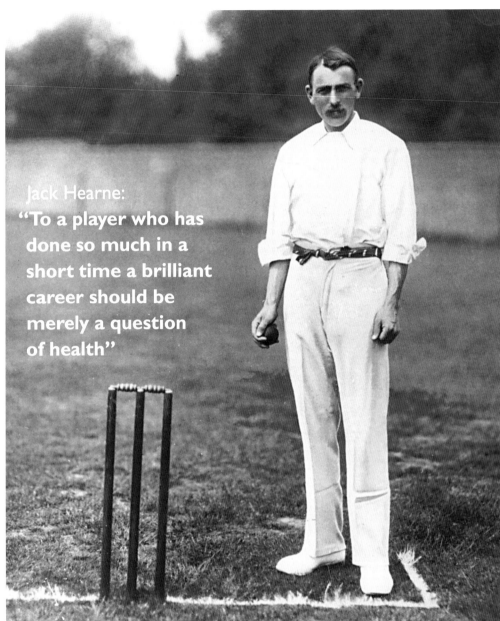

Jack Hearne: "To a player who has done so much in a short time a brilliant career should be merely a question of health"

CRICKETERS OF THE YEAR 1892 – Performances in the English season 1891

Name	Age*		Matches	Runs	Bat ave	Wickets	Bowl ave	Catches (/st)
W Attewell	30	First-class	28	532	16.12	153	13.93	26
JT Hearne	24	First-class	18	142	6.76	129	11.23	16
F Martin	30	First-class	22	188	8.95	140	13.37	8
AW Mold	28	First-class	19	130	8.66	138	12.49	9
JW Sharpe	25	First-class	21	183	8.71	108	13.84	14

as at 1/4/1892

1893

Five Batsmen of the Year

Walter Read (Surrey) *i*
Herbie Hewett (Somerset) *i*
Lionel Palairet (Oxford University and Somerset) *i*
Stanley Scott (Middlesex) *i*
Drewy Stoddart (Middlesex) *i*

HEADLINE EVENTS FROM 1892

• County champions – Surrey

• English teams tour both Australia and South Africa in 1891-92, playing Tests in both countries: England win the only Test in South Africa, but lose the Ashes to a revitalised Australia

WHEN WISDEN HAD FIRST RECOGNISED SOME of the country's leading batsmen, after the 1889 season, they had all been professionals. This time, in choosing five amateurs, it was acknowledging that amateur cricket had emerged from the doldrums. If Walter Read and Stanley Scott both belonged to an earlier generation, and Drewy Stoddart had developed his game in London club matches, Herbie Hewett and Lionel Palairet ushered in an era of brilliant cricketers to come out of public schools.

It was surprising that Grace [1896] was again ignored. Although his record in 1892 was unexceptional, his average of 31.02 was only fractionally inferior to Stoddart's or Hewett's, and his total of 1,055 runs was more than Scott managed. Grace's claims were noted by Sydney Pardon in his introduction: "Inasmuch as Mr Grace, fresh from his successes with Lord Sheffield's team in Australia [in 1891-92], made over 1,000 runs in first-class matches, it would have been quite appropriate to have included him in the group, but if the portrait of our greatest cricketer should ever be presented to the readers… it will, we fancy, appear by itself."

Hewett went to Harrow and Oxford, and Palairet, six years his junior at 22, to Repton and Oxford, but both ended up opening the batting for Somerset, who had only achieved first-class status the previous year. Their fame was cemented by a partnership of 346 against Yorkshire – then a first-wicket record and the county's best for any wicket until 2012 – but they were consistent throughout that season (which for Palairet began at Oxford) and helped Somerset finish third in the Championship. They scored 2,750 first-class runs between them.

Their attacking approach caused real excitement. *Wisden* described Hewett as "beyond a doubt the finest left-handed batsman in England", before adding: "Like most left-handers, he plays his own game, with no very strict regard for orthodox rules, and it is a long time since we have had so fearless and daring a hitter. Bad and good wickets seemed to come pretty well alike… he demoralised the bowlers. Had it been necessary last August to put a representative England XI into the field, Hewett would undoubtedly have been given a place."

In fact, Hewett never played Test cricket. Short of fuse, he quit the Somerset captaincy and regular county cricket in 1893 after public criticism of the way he handled a rain-delayed match against the Australians. A similar incident in a festival match two years later led him to walk out after the first session.

Palairet, who came from Huguenot stock, played only two Tests (in 1902), but he gained an enduring reputation as a stylist. The Repton coaches weren't solely responsible; Palairet's father recruited William Attewell and Fred Martin [both 1892] to teach him at home. "He has almost every good quality as a batsman, combining strong defence with fine hitting, and playing always in beautiful style," *Wisden* stated. "Among the young cricketers of the day there is no one better worth looking at."

Stoddart, in historical terms the most substantial of the Five, played in the same spirit. A gifted rugby player who had played on the inaugural British Lions tour of Australasia that Arthur Shrewsbury [1890] organised, his serious cricket career took time to flourish. He did not play for Middlesex until he was 23, but batted with power and adventure, and was reckoned one of the finest counter-attackers of fast bowling there had been. He had already been on two cricket tours of Australia, scoring 134 in one of the Tests in 1891-92, but it was for organising and captaining two subsequent trips there in 1894-95 and 1897-98 – the first of them won 3–2 in a series that gripped England from afar – that

Stanley Scott

Lionel Palairet:
"He has almost every good quality as a batsman, combining strong defence with fine hitting, and playing always in beautiful style"

Walter Read

CRICKETERS OF THE YEAR 1893 – Performances in the English season 1892

Name	Age*		Matches	Runs	Bat ave	Wickets	Bowl ave	Catches (/st)
HT Hewett	28	First-class	24	1407	35.17			14
LCH Palairet	22	First-class	26	1343	31.97	30	24.13	21/3
WW Read	37	First-class	23	1088	34.00	6	35.16	14
SW Scott	39	First-class	17	1015	39.03	0		12
AE Stoddart	30	First-class	26	1403	31.17	9	53.33	17

as at 1/4/1893

Andrew Stoddart

Lionel Palairet (left) and **Herbie Hewett** pose with W. G. Grace

Andrew Stoddart:
"His position among the great players of the day has been unassailable"

he would be chiefly remembered. In 1893, he became the second (and as it transpired last) man to captain England at cricket and rugby, after A. N. Hornby. Tragically, declining health and failing finances drove him to suicide in 1915.

For most amateurs, the means of funding their cricket was a concern. Walter Read, hailed by *Wisden* as Surrey's finest batsman to date and credited with developing the pull shot, was unable to play regularly for many years because he needed to teach in Reigate. In the end Surrey, realising his value, paid Read to act as assistant secretary, a job that conveniently never stopped him playing. (It was this kind of "shamateurism" that so incensed professionals.) Read, a hero of England's original Ashes-winning campaign of 1882-83, and the scorer of a hard-hit century against Australia from No.

10 in 1884, recaptured some of his best form in 1892 at the age of 37 to help Surrey win a third successive title.

Money was less of a problem for Scott, who had gone straight from school to the London Stock Exchange. It was only several years later, in 1878, that he started playing for Middlesex. Neither before nor after did he touch the heights he managed in 1892 when, at the age of 39, he led the national averages for much of the summer. His 224 against Gloucestershire was the season's highest individual score, and he also made runs in Gentlemen–Players matches. He did not do much else than bat, though – *Wisden* said "it would be flattery to describe him as a first-rate field" – and after one more season he gave the Stock Exchange his full attention once again.

1894

Five All-round Cricketers

Stanley Jackson (Cambridge University, Yorkshire and England) / ●
George Giffen (Australians) / ●
Alec Hearne (Kent) / ●
Harry Trott (Australians) / ●
Ted Wainwright (Yorkshire and England) / ●

- County champions – Yorkshire

- England win back the Ashes, taking the three-match series 1-0

As WISDEN SEARCHED FOR WAYS TO KEEP ITS feature fresh, all-rounders presented a natural group. As pitches improved and scoring levels rose, fielding sides needed more time and more bowlers to dismiss the opposition. The days of two men bowling unchanged through an innings were dying out. When England scored their highest total in a home Test of 483 at The Oval in 1893 – the young Stanley Jackson scoring a brilliant century in his second match – George Giffen and Harry Trott were among seven bowlers used by Australia.

The world's most celebrated cricketer, Grace [1896], had done the match double of 100 runs and 10 wickets an incredible 17 times, although the last instance had been in 1886. By now, he was a batsman and captain who only occasionally bowled. Giffen, a tireless but relatively expensive bowler, had achieved the match double seven times (and would do so twice more), but his record was less impressive in England, where conditions were less suited to his aggressive batting.

In 1893, Giffen made few runs against the stronger sides. "It would be flattery to pretend… that his play came up to anticipation," *Wisden* observed, before adding: "Whatever his shortcomings in England in 1893, his record during the last ten years in Australia is sufficient to stamp him one of the world's greatest all-round players." That said, Giffen – one of the first to make extensive use of a slower ball – took 16 wickets in the Tests, whereas Trott, Jackson and Ted Wainwright claimed none. Nor was Giffen finished. When England toured Australia in 1894-95, his return in five Tests was a staggering 475 runs and 34 wickets.

The great strength of Jackson and Trott was their big-match temperament. Few have announced themselves in Tests with quite the élan of Jackson, who had preceded his century at The Oval with an enterprising 91 at Lord's on debut. He was only 23, but *Wisden* rated him as strong an attacking leg-side player as anyone in the game. Jackson declined to play in the Third Test as he preferred to turn out for Yorkshire, even though the counties had agreed to make players available for England and Yorkshire had already won the Championship. Trott, who had started out as chiefly a leg-break bowler, showed immense character in leading Australia's bid to escape with a draw in the Second Test, scoring 92 after his side followed on 392 behind.

Alec Hearne

Jackson and Trott were born leaders, who would later captain their countries to the Ashes – Trott in 1897-98 and Jackson in 1905, when he topped the batting and bowling averages and won all five tosses. Their styles of leadership and their backgrounds, though, could hardly have been much more different. Jackson had been educated at Harrow and Cambridge, and was the son of Lord Allerton, who had served in the Cabinet for seven of the previous eight years. Trott had no such advantages, but was more popular with his men. "By sheer force of character," *Wisden* stated in its obituary of Trott, "he overcame the disadvantages involved in lack of education, and won the warm regard of men with whom, apart from the comradeship of the cricket field, he had nothing in common." Jackson's reputation as a martinet would be largely forgotten amid his glamorous

George Giffen

Harry Trott

George Giffen:
"For some time past [he has] been regarded as the greatest all-round cricketer yet produced by the Australian Colonies"

Hon. F. S. Jackson

Hon. F. S. Jackson:
"Mr Jackson has great confidence and splendid hitting power"

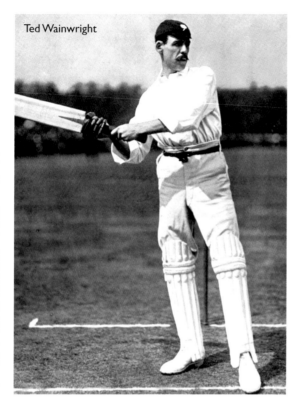

Ted Wainwright

In retirement he worked as a postman; Jackson died with an estate worth £85,620.

Wainwright never cracked Test cricket. He was an immense player for Yorkshire, whom he would help to win five Championships, and had a great record as an off-spin bowler on rain-affected pitches, but when he toured Australia in 1897-98 his bowling was ineffective. "The contrast was bewildering," said *Wisden*. In 1893, he played in the First Test, was dropped for the Second, and like Jackson played for Yorkshire instead during the Third. Unlike Jackson, Wainwright was never chosen for a home Test again.

Alec Hearne – the youngest and the best of three cricketing brothers, and a cousin of Jack Hearne [1892] – had an excellent season, scoring 266 runs and taking 17 wickets in five matches against the Australians without appearing in the Tests. A versatile cricketer who switched from bowling leg-breaks to off-spin in the 1880s, and liked to uppercut fast bowlers over the slips, he was described by *Wisden* after his death in 1952 as "one of the best cricketers who never played for England". In fact, in 1891-92 he played in a match at Cape Town now regarded as a Test, with one brother alongside him in the England team and another, who had emigrated to South Africa, in the opposition.

achievements on and off the field. While Jackson rationed the time he spent playing cricket (he never toured Australia) in order to pursue business, soldiering and politics, Trott acutely felt the burden of leadership, and suffered bouts of depression, rarely playing again after 1898.

CRICKETERS OF THE YEAR 1894 – Performances in the English season 1893

Name	Age*		Matches	Runs	Bat ave	Wickets	Bowl ave	Catches (/st)
G Giffen	35	First-class	29	1133	23.12	118	19.04	27
		Tests	3	91	18.20	16	21.37	4
A Hearne	30	First-class	24	906	22.65	86	17.95	23
FS Jackson	23	First-class	21	1328	41.50	57	20.56	13
		Tests	2	199	66.33	0		2
GHS Trott	27	First-class	31	1269	24.40	38	23.86	15
		Tests	3	146	29.20	0		1
E Wainwright	28	First-class	26	696	18.31	125	14.66	25
		Tests	1	27	13.50	0		0

* as at 1/4/1894

1895

Five Young Batsmen of the Season

Bill Brockwell (Surrey) *

Jack Brown (Yorkshire) *

C. B. Fry (Oxford University and Sussex) *

Tom Hayward (Surrey) *

Archie MacLaren (Lancashire) *

HEADLINE EVENTS FROM 1894

• County champions – Surrey

HAVING CONSIDERED BUT REJECTED CHOOSING five county captains on the grounds that it would have been invidious, Sydney Pardon went for five young batsmen – and picked well. Bill Brockwell's inclusion could be questioned – although statistically the batsman of the season with 1,491 runs and five centuries (having never made one before), he was hardly "young" at 29 – but the others were all under 25 and went on to great things.

Jack Brown and Archie MacLaren, in fact, did so within weeks of the 1895 Almanack appearing, scoring centuries in the deciding Test of the winter's epic Ashes series in Australia. MacLaren scored 120 in the first innings and Brown a rapid 140 in the second to lead England to a famous six-wicket win. Neither had played in Tests before that tour. Later that year, MacLaren scored a world-record 424 for Lancashire at Taunton, and by 1898 Brown (twice) and Tom Hayward had also achieved triple-centuries in the Championship. Grace [1896] was the only other batsman who had managed this by that point.

Charles Fry, the youngest of the Five at 22 in 1894, took longer to break through. A fine academic, he appeared destined for a lofty career in the civil service but, amid personal problems, he took only a fourth-class degree from Oxford in 1895. It was only then that he threw himself into sport. By 1898 he was one of the most effective batsmen in the country.

Fry had been at Repton alongside Lionel Palairet [1893], but lacked the style and self-belief of many former public-schoolboy contemporaries, of whom MacLaren – like Hewett [1893] and Jackson [1894] a product of Harrow – was a prime example. While MacLaren was a polished player by the time he made a century in his first match for Lancashire at the age of 18, Fry took years to develop from an ungainly leg-side player into a fully rounded batsman. This was curious given his varied sporting gifts; he had already won Blues at football and athletics, and in 1893 claimed a share of the world long-jump record (losing it again in 1894). "We would not put Mr Fry as a batsman in the same class with such a player as Mr MacLaren," *Wisden* said, "but he has any amount of pluck and resolution."

But in the long run Fry's first-class record dwarfed MacLaren's and almost everyone else's:

Bill Brockwell

C. B. Fry

Archie MacLaren

C. B. Fry:

"We would not put Mr Fry as a batsman in the same class with such a player as Mr MacLaren, but he has any amount of pluck and resolution"

at the end of his career in 1922 his batting average of 50.22 stood second only to that of his close friend Ranjitsinhji [1897], while his 94 first-class centuries was topped only by Grace's 126 and Hayward's 104. While at the height of his cricketing fame, he played once for England at football and also appeared in an FA Cup final for Southampton.

The measure of MacLaren, Hayward and Fry was that they became so central to England's fortunes that usually one of them (and sometimes two) would open the batting in Ashes Tests until 1905. Indeed, England had never had such a dependable first-wicket pair as MacLaren and Hayward, who gave them some great starts in Australia in 1901-02. Hayward, who came from an extended Cambridge family of professional cricketers, finished with marginally the best Test record of the three. Pardon had little doubt about Hayward's potential: "His method of play is so admirable that no distinction of the cricket field should be beyond his reach."

One thing, of course, was beyond reach: as a professional, Hayward was not going to captain England. For MacLaren and Fry, though, leadership was a social right, and by 1894 MacLaren was already Lancashire captain while Fry had led Oxford. MacLaren would succeed Grace as England captain in 1899, and he led them in five of their next seven Ashes series. All five were lost, although this was not all his fault, and Stanley Jackson [1894] thought him an able lieutenant in 1905. MacLaren could be arrogant and wrong but he was also tough, and some of his hunches, such as the selection of Sydney Barnes [1910], were inspired. Fry captained England in 1912 and, benefiting from Barnes's presence, won four out of six Tests in the ill-fated Triangular Tournament. Neither Fry nor MacLaren was always flush for money; Fry taught and wrote, as did MacLaren, to help make ends meet.

MacLaren died at 72, leaving £6,535, and Fry at 84, leaving £9,197.

Held in high regard as a model professional, Hayward did enjoy the rare honour for a pro of sometimes leading Surrey during his final season in 1914, and he later assisted in the development of a future England captain in Douglas Jardine [1928], whom he coached at Oxford. Hayward was also a capable medium-pace off-break bowler who took 481 first-class wickets.

As with MacLaren, Brown's northern upbringing taught him to bat on any kind of wicket. Had there not been such stiff competition, Brown might have played more for England; as it was, he appeared in only three more Tests. Lord Hawke [1908] said Brown's head was turned by his success in Australia, but he recovered strongly from a poor season in 1895. Short and stocky, Brown remained among the most effective openers in county cricket. A drinker and smoker, he developed asthma and heart trouble and was forced to give up playing in 1904; later that year he died, aged 35.

Brockwell, who played seven Tests – five in Australia in 1894-95 – without making much impact, also met a sad end. A stylish player who was always smartly turned out, he later took up coaching, writing and photography, but died in poverty aged 70.

Jack Brown

Tom Hayward

Tom Hayward:
"His method of play is so admirable that no distinction of the cricket field should be beyond his reach"

CRICKETERS OF THE YEAR 1895 – Performances in the English season 1894

Name	Age*		Matches	Runs	Bat ave	Wickets	Bowl ave	Catches (/st)
W Brockwell	30	First-class	32	1491	38.23	19	23.84	26
JT Brown	25	First-class	31	1399	30.41	1	109.00	16
CB Fry	22	First-class	16	713	26.40	25	28.40	13
TW Hayward	24	First-class	26	884	26.78	11	18.72	9
AC MacLaren	23	First-class	27	1105	25.69			15

* as at 1/4/1895

1896 Cricketer of the Year

W. G. Grace (Gloucestershire) ❋

WG AT LAST – AND, AS SYDNEY PARDON HAD predicted in 1893, his portrait appeared by itself.

Grace had a sensational summer in 1895, scoring 1,000 runs in the first month of the season and the 100th first-class century of his career, both unprecedented feats. He simply was *the* man of the season, and Pardon's decision to let his photograph stand alone was recognition both of this unarguable fact and his special place in the game. So brilliant was Grace in a season in which he turned 47 years of age that the editor's decision to opt not for five Cricketers of the Year but one seemed entirely appropriate.

"It had for some time been intended to publish in *Wisden*'s Almanack a portrait of W. G. Grace," Pardon explained, "and it was felt before the season of 1895 had been many weeks in progress that the most suitable time had arrived… Mr Grace last summer played with all the brilliancy and success of his youth." Pardon wrote a brief tribute, and commissioned lengthier appreciations from two people who had played cricket with Grace and, like him, captained England – Lord Harris and A. G. Steel.

As Steel pointed out, Grace's "Champion" status rested on his batting. He had been very successful with his slow flighted bowling, off which he was a terrific fielder, but it was his amazing feats with the bat that had set him apart in the 1860s and '70s. According to Steel, his strengths included opening up the leg side as a scoring area, dominating fast bowlers whose short balls he square-cut, and displaying immense patience. In essence, he showed the world how to build a long innings.

For Harris, Grace's dedication was the key. "This super-excellence was not the result of eminent physical fitness only, it depended a good deal also on the careful life the old man led," he wrote. "He did not play brilliantly despite how he lived, as some, whose all too brief careers I can remember, did, but he regulated his habits of life with such care and moderation that his physical capacity was always at its best."

When Grace began playing, individual scores of 100 were rare, but for him they became commonplace and, by the start of 1895, most contemporary sources reckoned he had made 98 of them at first-class level, with Arthur Shrewsbury [1889] a distant second on 41. His hundredth hundred came for Gloucestershire at Ashley Down, Bristol, only a few miles from his birthplace at Downend. He reached three figures off the bowling of Sammy Woods [1889] and with his godson Charles Townsend [1899] at the non-striker's end. "This was the one and only time I ever saw him flustered," said Townsend. Recovering his poise, Grace went on to score 288.

Grace had always been a popular figure (Harris called him "the kindest and most sympathetic cricketer I have ever played with") and, thanks to the beard he had worn since his early twenties, an instantly recognisable one, but his latest achievements created a fresh mania. Three testimonial funds raised a staggering £9,073.

Grace's capacity for making money despite playing as an "amateur" had already caused disquiet. He had toured Australia in 1891-92 for a fee of £3,000 that was ten times the amount paid to the professionals; partly as a result, Arthur Shrewsbury and Billy Gunn [1890] declined to go. Grace's testimonial riches may have encouraged five professionals – with Gunn again to the fore – to threaten not to play in the Oval Test of 1896 unless their fees were raised from £10 to £20. Grace, it emerged, was receiving as much as them to cover his expenses. Writing in the 1897 *Wisden*, Pardon defended Grace, arguing that as cricket's great populariser he was entitled to such special treatment: "Nice customs curtsey to great kings."

Grace, a qualified but hardly overworked medical practitioner, gave up playing Test cricket in 1899 aged 50, played his last first-class match at 59, and was still playing club cricket a year before his death in 1915 aged 67. In all recorded matches he scored more than 80,000 runs and took over 7,000 wickets.

His extraordinary year helped cement the idea that *Wisden*'s feature should recognise those who had enjoyed an outstanding season; distinguished past service, or the promise of future greatness, alone was not enough.

Had five Cricketers of the Year been chosen in 1896, the ill-fated George Davidson of Derbyshire, the only player to do the double in 1895, who died of pneumonia in 1899 aged 32, would surely have been chosen. Harry Baldwin took 114 wickets in his first full season aged 34, as Hampshire returned to first-class status.

W. G. Grace: **"The greatest cricketer the world has ever seen"**

Middlesex's Timothy O'Brien, who would captain Ireland and England at cricket, scored 1,079 runs, and Warwickshire's captain Herbert Bainbridge 1,162.

CRICKETER OF THE YEAR 1896 – Performances in the English season 1895

Name	Age*		Matches	Runs	Bat ave	Wickets	Bowl ave	Catches (/st)
WG Grace	47	First-class	29	2346	51.00	16	32.93	31

* as at 1/4/1896

1897 Five Cricketers of the Season

K. S. Ranjitsinhji (Sussex and England)

Syd Gregory (Australians)

Dick Lilley (Warwickshire and England)

Tom Richardson (Surrey and England)

Hugh Trumble (Australians)

THIS PROVED THE MOST ILLUSTRIOUS SELECTION yet, just shading 1889 and 1895. All five shone in the Ashes series of 1896, and all five enjoyed glittering careers: had *Wisden* chosen a World XI from the pre-1914 era, each would have been a strong contender for inclusion.

Aided by quick feet and a good batting technique, the diminutive Syd Gregory – whose family provided Australia with four international cricketers – played Tests for 22 years, and his 58 caps remained a record until 1930. He was the first man to score a Test double-century in Australia (in defeat at Sydney in 1894-95), his average of 31.82 in 1896 was the highest achieved on a tour of England so far, and he was, at cover point, the finest fieldsman Test cricket had yet seen. He played for so long in part because business ventures fared poorly, ending on a low note in 1912 (his eighth Ashes tour) as captain of a weakened and ill-disciplined Australian team in England.

Gregory's team-mate Hugh Trumble – who stood 6ft 5in to Gregory's 5ft 4in – got through more bowling than anyone in Tests up to 1914, by which time his 141 wickets had been bettered only by Sydney Barnes [1910].

Trumble's selection for the 1896 tour was queried in advance, but it proved a turning point in his career; he got the ball to lift off an immaculate length and spin either way just enough to beat the stroke. At The Oval, he showed how good he could be on a rain-affected surface. "He convinced Englishmen he was entitled to rank among the great bowlers of Australia," *Wisden* said. Trumble quit Tests after taking a second hat-trick against England in 1903-04. Having worked in banking during his playing days, he later became a long-serving secretary of the Melbourne Cricket Club.

Dick Lilley, with 70 catches and 22 stumpings, stood as the most successful Test keeper until 1933. The first player chosen from among 1895's new first-class counties, he was a natural gloveman whose hands remained undamaged by his craft, but his batting took time to develop, and benefited from the coaching of Arthur Shrewsbury [1890]. *Wisden* frowned on his method of standing back to the pacemen, but maybe the reality was that bowlers were becoming quicker. He remained England's first-choice keeper until 1909, and Warwickshire's until 1911 when he fell out with Frank Foster [1912].

Sydney Pardon wrote that "as a matter of absolute justice" Bill Storer [1899] ought to have been chosen, but Lilley's selection for all three Tests gained him preference.

If Kumar Shri Ranjitsinhji and Tom Richardson proved less durable – Richardson played his last Test at 27, Ranji at 29 – they were nevertheless absolute champions and hugely popular. When Richardson died in France at 41, *Wisden* hailed him as "perhaps the greatest of all fast bowlers", while Ranji became the first batsman to score runs all round the wicket, his invention of the leg-glance being only one part of this radical process.

After ironing out early flaws in his action, Richardson, the son of a groom, was stupendous at his peak, his haul of 1,005 wickets in four seasons from 1894 to 1897 – 246 of them in 1896 – never being bettered by a bowler of genuine pace. Tall and strong, he could break the ball back into the batsman from outside off stump at speed. But he was overbowled and he drank too much, and consequently his fitness and form deteriorated. "Too much was exacted from him but he ought not to have gone off as soon as he did," *Wisden* said in its obituary. "He began to lose efficiency before he was 28... A great

Dick Lilley

Tom Richardson

Tom Richardson:
"No professional cricketer in England enjoys greater popularity with the general public and among his brother players"

CRICKETERS OF THE YEAR 1897 – Performances in the English season 1896

Name	Age*		Matches	Runs	Bat ave	Wickets	Bowl ave	Catches (/st)
SE Gregory	26	First-class	31	1464	31.82			11
		Tests	3	182	30.33			0
AFA Lilley	30	First-class	26	979	24.47	12	18.83	58/10
		Tests	3	92	23.00	1	23.00	9
KS Ranjitsinhji	24	First-class	29	2780	57.91	10	42.90	23
		Tests	2	235	78.33			2
T Richardson	26	First-class	34	270	7.71	246	16.32	19
		Tests	3	20	6.66	24	18.29	2
H Trumble	29	First-class	30	628	19.62	148	15.81	39
		Tests	3	55	13.75	18	18.83	5

* as at 1/4/1897

increase in weight rather than hard work was responsible for his comparatively early decline." He played only four Tests at home, three of them in 1896 – taking 11 wickets at Lord's and 13 at Old Trafford, where in a three-hour spell he nearly bowled his country to victory.

Ranji, who came to England from rural India to attend Cambridge University, where as captain Stanley Jackson [1894] was slow to recognise his unusual talent, was the first non-white to make a mark on cricket – there would not be another until Charles Llewellyn [1911]. Once established with Sussex, Ranji rose fast; 1896 was only his second full season, and yet he broke the record for most runs in a season held by W. G. Grace [1896] since 1871. There was confusion in 1896 as to whether he should be deemed eligible for England, but Lancashire settled that argument by picking him for the Second Test at Old Trafford, where Ranji

K. S. Ranjitsinhji

sensationally scored 62 and 154 not out on debut.

He soon twice improved on his 1896 tally of 2,780 runs with 3,159 in 1899 and 3,065 in 1900, which gave him the three highest seasonal aggregates on record at the time. *Wisden* suggested that Ranji's methods, relying on a good eye and flexible wrists, could not be imitated: "For any ordinary player to attempt to turn good length balls off the middle stump as he does, would be futile and disastrous… if the somewhat too-freely-used word genius can with any propriety be employed in connection with cricket, it surely applies to the young Indian's batting."

Ranji's serious career ended early because of his political ambitions, and in 1907 he was chosen by the British Government as Jam Sahib of Nawanagar, where he ruled until his death in 1933. Having started with nothing, he left an estate worth almost £130,000.

Syd Gregory

K. S. Ranjitsinhji:
"If the somewhat too-freely-used word genius can with any propriety be employed in connection with cricket, it surely applies to the young Indian's batting"

Hugh Trumble

1898

Five Cricketers of the Year

Gilbert Jessop (Cambridge University and Gloucestershire) ● ●
Frederick Bull (Essex) ●
Willis Cuttell (Lancashire) ●
Frank Druce (Cambridge University and Surrey) ●
Jack Mason (Kent) ● ●

HEADLINE EVENTS FROM 1897

- County champions – Lancashire

GILBERT JESSOP'S BATTING CAUSED ALMOST AS much of a sensation in the 1897 season as that of Ranjitsinhji and Grace in the previous two years. Jessop, who turned 23 in May, had previously concentrated on bowling fast, but a change in method produced startling results. Only 5ft 7in, he crouched more in his stance in preparation to step out and attack the ball, and dropped his hands lower on the bat handle. The game's most ferocious hitter before the modern era was born.

Jessop had an incredible July, scoring 42 in 17 minutes for Cambridge in the Varsity Match, 67 in 35 minutes in his first Gentlemen–Players encounter at Lord's – meting out brutal punishment to Richardson [1897] – and 101 in 40 minutes for Gloucestershire against Yorkshire on a small ground at Harrogate. This stood as the fastest century in first-class cricket until 1920.

"The public dearly love a fearless hitter," enthused *Wisden*. "We have never before produced a batsman of quite the same stamp. We have had harder hitters, but perhaps never one who could, in 20 minutes or half an hour, so entirely change the fortunes of a game… To hit fast bowling as he hits it is scarcely given to half a dozen batsmen in a generation." Jessop took risks as only an amateur could.

Jessop did the 1,000-run/100-wicket double, and ought to have gone on the 1897-98 tour of Australia, but his heroics came late – the team was finalised by the first week in August – and he missed out. Despite his gifts – he was also the finest outfielder England had so far produced – he would rarely be a Test regular, but this did not curb his fearlessness: at The Oval in 1902 he scored perhaps the greatest match-winning century in Test history, 104 in 75 minutes to turn around a desperate position.

Two young amateurs who did go to Australia as a result of their performances in 1897 (combined with the unavailability of several big-name batsmen) were Frank Druce, Jessop's captain at Cambridge, and Jack Mason of Kent. Druce, a talented strokemaker, topped the national batting averages, though most of his runs came for his university rather than Surrey. His finest innings came against the Gentlemen of Philadelphia, whose attack included Bart King, who had mastered swing better than any English bowler.

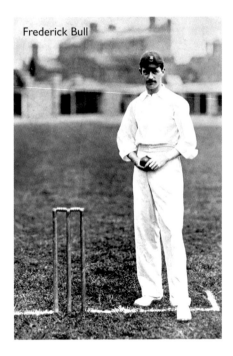

Frederick Bull

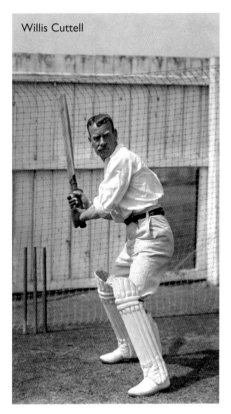

Willis Cuttell

Wisden hinted that the inclusion of Mason – "whose portrait ought to have been seen before this" – had been bolstered by his appointment as Kent captain for 1898 and an innings of 128 not out against Victoria early in the Australia tour. He was a tall front-foot player, and struggled badly in the Tests, starting the series as opener but finishing it at No. 8. Druce did slightly better, always getting a start but making only one fifty. Out of the shared misfortune of a disastrous tour (England were beaten 4–1), Mason and Druce – products of Winchester and Marlborough respectively – became firm friends, Mason carrying with him for the rest of his life a photograph of himself and Druce reclining on the MCG outfield. Neither would play for England again.

The stories of Jessop, Druce and Mason – as well as Frederick Bull – illustrate how difficult it was to play regular cricket as an amateur in what had grown into a full-on season lasting five months. Jessop, who had got into Cambridge on a clergy scholarship but left without a degree, kept afloat working as a journalist and in the City, latterly as chairman of the sports-equipment business of Frank Sugg [1890], although Gloucestershire looked after him too. Mason – whose career batting and bowling statistics rivalled Jessop's – cut back on his commitments from 1903 to work as a solicitor, while Druce – who became a successful distiller – barely played again after Australia.

Bull, 22, took 120 wickets in the second of what proved to be only four full seasons with Essex. He could make the ball break both ways. "It is indeed no flattery to say that on a good lively pitch Mr Bull can get more spin on the ball than any other English-born slow bowler now before the public," *Wisden* said. Essex helped him financially by making him assistant secretary, but after he lost form he moved north for work, only to turn professional in 1905 to play in the leagues. He drowned in the sea off St Annes in 1910, only a month after playing his last match for Rishton.

Willis Cuttell, the only professional among the Five, was a different fish, having come to county cricket at 32 from the leagues, where he had played for Accrington, then Nelson. Barely known outside Lancashire, he had great success in 1897 as a medium-pace bowler armed with a well disguised leg-break. He helped Lancashire win their first official title, and in 1898 did the double before touring South Africa, where he played what are now regarded as two Tests. He later ran a tobacconist's and coached at Rugby School, where he helped Jack Bryan [1922].

CRICKETERS OF THE YEAR 1898 – Performances in the English season 1897

Name	Age*		Matches	Runs	Bat ave	Wickets	Bowl ave	Catches (/st)
FG Bull	22	First-class	18	311	16.36	120	21.95	14
WR Cuttell	34	First-class	29	428	12.96	120	16.45	25
NF Druce	23	First-class	14	928	51.55	2	15.00	19
GL Jessop	23	First-class	26	1219	29.73	116	17.85	30
JR Mason	24	First-class	22	1377	35.30	51	22.86	24

* as at 1/4/1898

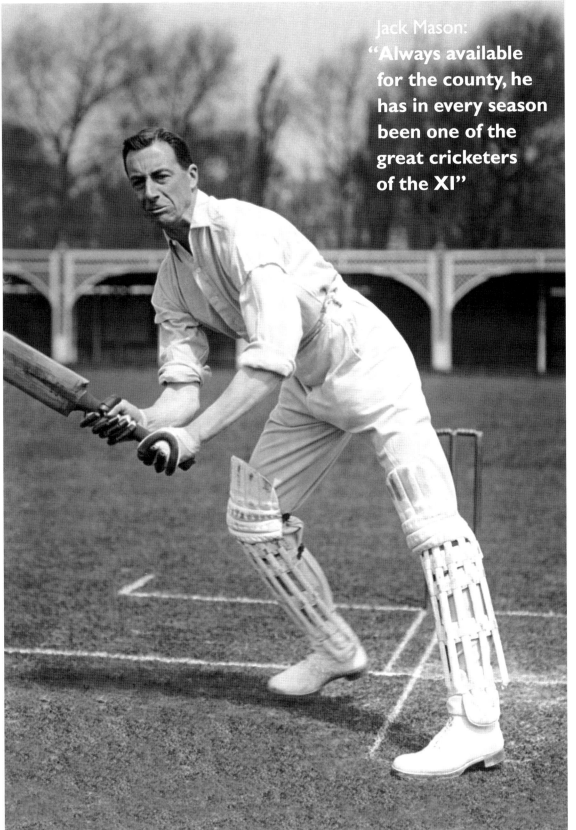

Jack Mason:
"Always available for the county, he has in every season been one of the great cricketers of the XI"

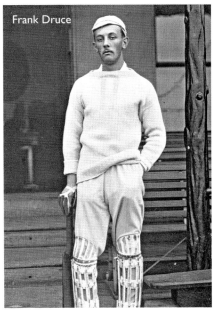

Frank Druce

Gilbert Jessop

Gilbert Jessop:
"It is perfectly safe to say that there are few more popular figures on the cricket field"

1899

Five Great Players of the Season

Charles Townsend (Gloucestershire) / ●
Bill Lockwood (Surrey) / ●
Wilfred Rhodes (Yorkshire) ●
Bill Storer (Derbyshire) ⫿
Albert Trott (Middlesex) ●

WILFRED RHODES BECAME THE YOUNGEST Cricketer of the Year so far. Only 20, he had taken 154 first-class wickets in 1898, a haul that has never been beaten by a bowler in his debut season. Rhodes may have lacked experience, but he had such a naturally good action and such an ability to spin the ball on a rain-affected pitch – of which there were plenty this year – that there were few more dangerous bowlers in the country.

The weather, though, was not always going to play into his hands, so Rhodes turned himself into the most resourceful of cricketers. Having taken 1,058 wickets in his first five seasons, he embarked on a remarkable rise as a batsman that saw him share in Test stands of 130 for the tenth wicket and 323 for the first in the space of nine years. He took more than half his 127 Test wickets between 1899 and 1904, and scored more than half his 2,325 Test runs between 1909 and 1914, but he was an all-round force in county cricket for years, achieving the last of his record 16 doubles in 1926, the season in which he was recalled at 48 to help England regain the Ashes.

When he retired in 1930, he had played more matches (1,107) and taken more wickets (4,187) in first-class cricket than anyone else ever

had (or still has). Rhodes's determination to maximise his abilities may have stemmed from the circumstances behind his early selection as Yorkshire's left-arm spinner: he was brought in after Bobby Peel [1889] had forfeited his place through misconduct. Rhodes gave no one the chance to drop him.

The stories of *Wisden*'s other four picks – all gifted all-round cricketers – confirmed how transient success could be.

Even more than Rhodes, Charles Townsend was a boy wonder. Son of Frank, once a Gloucestershire regular, and godson to W. G. Grace [1896], he had been given his chance by the county in 1893, when he was 16 and still at Clifton College, and caused a sensation by taking 130 wickets with his leg-breaks. Physical frailty hindered his progress, but in 1898 he was one of only three players to perform the double, then in 1899 became the second after Grace to manage 2,000 runs and 100 wickets in a season.

Wisden was excited about Townsend's potential, but 1900 proved to be his last full season, as he chose at 24 to concentrate on working as a solicitor. Thus the two Tests he played in 1899, chiefly as the team's sole left-

HEADLINE EVENTS FROM 1898

• County champions – Yorkshire

• Australia regain the Ashes, winning 4-1 at home in 1897-98

Charles Townsend (right) with his godfather W. G. Grace [1896]

Wisden did not mention this domestic tragedy, but praised Lockwood for returning to first-rate physical condition. He nearly did the double in 1898, did manage it in 1899 and 1900, and was still going strong in 1902, when he starred in England's win at The Oval.

Albert Trott, another talented youngster and the brother of Harry Trott [1894], had shone with bat and ball in three Tests for Australia in 1894-95, but was inexplicably omitted from the 1896 tour of England even though Harry was captain. Severing his ties with Australia, Albert moved to England and

Bill Lockwood

handed batsman, were all his England career amounted to. One of his sons also played for England.

Bill Lockwood's selection was as much a celebration of a career saved as a tribute to a mercurial talent. Some who faced both reckoned Lockwood could be even more dangerous than his regular partner Tom Richardson [1897] – Lockwood had the better strike-rate in Tests – but he lost his way after the death of his wife and child, and spent most of 1897 out of the team.

Charles Townsend:
"Except Mr Grace himself, and Ranjitsinhji, there is no more interesting figure in the cricket field at the present time"

Bill Storer

qualified for Middlesex, and in the 1898 season – his first with the county – took 130 wickets with a rich variety of deliveries (like the American Bart King, he had played baseball and swung the ball better than Englishmen).

Trott had a pair of mighty hands, and if his main strength was with the ball, he was also a danger with the bat. In 1899 and 1900 he scored 1,000 runs and took 200 wickets, a double no one had done before, and in the first of these years he hit a ball from Monty Noble [1900], preferred to him as Australia's all-rounder, over the Lord's pavilion (still a unique feat). But after his career as player and umpire petered out, Trott fell on hard times and, with only £4 and one piece of furniture to his name, shot himself in 1914.

A near miss in 1897, Bill Storer was one of the finest wicketkeeper-batsmen of the era. *Wisden* cryptically remarked that he might have kept wicket in the 1896 Tests but for "some little unpleasantnesses – for which he was not free from blame", before he performed creditably in Australia in 1897-98. He kept wicket in only half his games in 1898 (often bowling in the rest) to rest his hands, but scored more runs (1,548) than any other wicketkeeper in the year preceding their *Wisden* selection until Les Ames [1929]. He started the 1899 Ashes as keeper but made a costly error in the First Test. Dick Lilley [1897] was recalled, and Storer never played for England again.

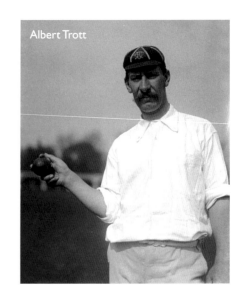

Albert Trott

Wilfred Rhodes

Wilfred Rhodes:
"His qualities as a slow bowler struck everyone as being exceptional... on some days he was irresistible"

CRICKETERS OF THE YEAR 1899 – Performances in the English season 1898

Name	Age*		Matches	Runs	Bat ave	Wickets	Bowl ave	Catches (/st)
WH Lockwood	31	First-class	26	878	30.27	134	16.62	8
W Rhodes	21	First-class	33	557	17.40	154	14.60	18
W Storer	32	First-class	24	1548	41.83	32	34.40	41/2
CL Townsend	22	First-class	25	1270	34.32	145	20.64	23
AE Trott	26	First-class	19	482	20.08	130	17.94	24

as at 1/4/1899

1900

Five Cricketers of the Season

Robert Poore (Hampshire) *i*

Joe Darling (Australians) *i*

Clem Hill (Australians) *i*

Arthur Jones (Nottinghamshire and England) *i*

Monty Noble (Australians) *i* •

THE CHOICE OF THREE AUSTRALIANS REFLECTED the achievement of Joe Darling's team in becoming the first visitors to win a series of more than one Test in England. They took a close-fought five-match series only 1–0, but were the more stable and unified side. In Darling they had the master tactician, in Clem Hill the leading batsman, and in Monty Noble the best all-rounder.

Sydney Pardon wrote that no apology was needed for giving three places to Australians; in fact, he might have picked a fourth in Ernie Jones, the star fast bowler, who took ten wickets in the decisive win at Lord's, but he was curiously overlooked. The legitimacy of his action had once been questioned, but not now.

Instead, the last two places went to an English Jones – Arthur, of Nottinghamshire, who made his debut in the final Test – and Robert Poore, a soldier who had come late to county cricket and scored prolifically for Hampshire before leaving for Africa in the autumn to fight in the Boer War, an event that would dominate British life. Poore's military status probably secured him the central photograph.

Darling, Noble and Hill were central figures in what became a great era for their side. Between them they captained Australia from 1899 to 1911-12, during which five out of eight Ashes series were won, before Hill, along with several others, fell out with the Australian board and missed the tour of England in 1912.

As a youngster, Darling nearly turned to farming, but insisted to his father that he should give cricket a go (he returned to agriculture later). He had the strength of a farmer, driving and defending with muscular resolve, and had already taken three hundreds off England in 1897-98. They would be his only Test centuries, but he played some important innings during the 1899 series, including a match-saving 71 at The Oval. His total of 1,941 first-class runs on the tour was the best by a visiting batsman to this point.

Noble was arguably the best Test all-rounder of the pre-1914 era: unlike Wilfred Rhodes, he was a force with bat and ball at the same time. Australia certainly would not have held on to their lead without his tenacious batting. At Old Trafford, where a draw ensured the retention of the Ashes, Noble batted 510 minutes for 60 not out and 89, an exceptional period for a three-day

HEADLINE EVENTS FROM 1899

- County champions – Surrey

- Joe Darling's Australians retain the Ashes, winning the first five-match series in England 1-0

- England win both Tests in South Africa in 1898-99

Wisden Cricketers of the Year 1900 | 37

The powerful Australian touring side of 1899. Back row (l-r): Ben Wardill (manager), Alfred Johns, Jim Kelly [1903], Frank Iredale, Frank Laver. Middle: Bill Howell, **Joe Darling** (captain), Ernie Jones. Front: Jack Worrall, **Clem Hill**, Syd Gregory [1897], Charles McLeod, Victor Trumper [1903], **Monty Noble**

Test. "No Australian batsman has ever shown better cricket during his first visit to England," *Wisden* judged. He also caused England problems with the late swerve of his bowling.

As shrewd and capable as Darling, Noble led his country to home-and-away Ashes wins in 1907-08 and 1909, and later became one of the best of the early radio commentators. He was also a banker and a dentist, though not at the same time.

Being a less orthodox left-hander than Darling, his fellow South Australian, Hill gave

opponents nightmares about how to bowl to him. He was another of the new breed who scored strongly through the leg side off straight balls. Still only 22, he had already played a major match-winning innings of 188 during the 1897-98 series, and now played another of 135 at Lord's. He contributed 301 runs before illness ruled him out of the last two Tests.

Hill was the first great Test No. 3, scoring 2,514 of his 3,412 runs in that position in an era in which only a handful had an aptitude for the role. *Wisden* rated him in its profile second only

Joe Darling:
"No left-handed batsman in our time has possessed quite such a defence"

Robert Poore

to Ranjitsinhji [1897], and from 1902 until 1924 he stood as Test cricket's highest run-scorer.

Jones – who turned 27 on the final day of his first Test – was a late developer, but justified his England selection with his all-round form and positive approach. Although he started creditably, he never quite established himself in Test cricket, which made it surprising that he was invited to captain England in Australia in 1907-08, even though he had just led Nottinghamshire to the title. Illness and anxiety ruined his tour, and declining health led to his early death from tuberculosis in 1914.

Jones's greatest contribution to the game was the quality of his close-to-the-wicket catching. He set new standards, and is credited with creating the gully position.

Poore, who was born in Dublin, developed his cricket while on army service in India and South Africa, where he played in what are now regarded as three Tests against England in 1895-96. Sometimes garrisoned in Hampshire, he played two half-seasons for the county in 1898 and 1899, averaging an unprecedented 91.23 in 12 matches in the second one, despite failing in two Gentlemen–Players matches. His seven centuries included scores of 104, 119 not out and 304 against Somerset.

Poore stood 6ft 4in, an advantage when it came to front-foot drives, if not fielding. "At times [he] finds some difficulty in getting down to the ball," *Wisden* said. Little more was seen of him on the cricket field, and he died a Brigadier-General in 1938.

Arthur Jones

CRICKETERS OF THE YEAR 1900 – Performances in the English season 1899

Name	Age*		Matches	Runs	Bat ave	Wickets	Bowl ave	Catches (/st)
J Darling	29	First-class	35	1941	41.29	0		32
		Tests	5	232	25.77			3
C Hill	23	First-class	16	879	39.95	1	16.00	11
		Tests	3	301	60.20			1
AO Jones	27	First-class	23	1609	44.69	36	35.50	18
		Tests	1	31	31.00	3	38.66	2
MA Noble	27	First-class	33	1608	37.39	82	22.90	23
		Tests	5	367	52.42	13	31.23	2
RM Poore	34	First-class	12	1551	91.23			5

as at 1/4/1900

1901

Mr R. E. Foster and Four Yorkshiremen

Reginald "Tip" Foster (Oxford University and Worcestershire) ⟋

Schofield Haigh (Yorkshire) ◑

George Hirst (Yorkshire) ⟋ ●

Tom Taylor (Cambridge University and Yorkshire) ⟋

John Tunnicliffe (Yorkshire) ⟋

HEADLINE EVENTS FROM 1900

• County champions – Yorkshire

YORKSHIRE BECAME THE FIRST TEAM TO HAVE four players chosen in the same year, an achievement not matched, let alone beaten, until five England players were selected in 1938 and five Australians in 1949.

Yorkshire won the Championship decisively, going unbeaten in 28 matches. Tom Taylor – like Tip Foster – was only 22 in 1900 and an amateur who would play only rarely after 1902, but George Hirst, Schofield Haigh and John Tunnicliffe were seasoned professionals who devoted their lives to the game. After long playing careers, each went into coaching, Hirst helping to develop several future Cricketers of the Year at Yorkshire.

Pardon stated in his Preface that he would have liked to include Yorkshire's captain Lord Hawke [1909], "but I could only have put him in the centre of the picture and Mr Foster's claims to the place of honour were paramount".

Hirst was born in the same village of Kirkheaton near Huddersfield as Wilfred Rhodes [1899], was brought up above a pub, and left school at ten. He was, in *Wisden*'s opinion, "a small Hercules… who would never fail for want of strength or stamina." By 1900, when he scored 1,960 runs and took 62 wickets, his left-arm fast-medium bowling was not fully developed. In 1901, though, he mastered the art of late swing which the Australians had pioneered. That year he took 183 wickets to add to his 1,950 runs. From 1903 to 1913 he completed 11 successive doubles, including in 1906 the unique union of 2,000 runs and 200 wickets.

He was a considerable batsman who hit hard and relished a crisis; among genuine all-rounders only Grace [1896] had bettered his 60 centuries by the time he retired. Hirst had his moments in Tests, but was rarely effective with the ball in Australia, and his overall record in 24 matches was unexceptional. Of a sunnier disposition than Rhodes, he was a popular figure, and his benefit realised £3,703, a record for this period. Haigh (£2,071) and Tunnicliffe (£1,750) would also do well.

Haigh, also born in a village near Huddersfield, was another immense county performer. In 1900 his bowling took a big step forward when he modified his action and began unleashing devastating off-cutters; he finished with 163 wickets at 14.82. He was off-colour in 1901, but after that he topped the national

Tom Taylor

George Hirst:

"A better man in a county team than Hirst is at the present time not easy to find"

bowling averages five times in eight years. He was near-unplayable on rain-affected pitches, but less dangerous on hard ones. Of the 22 wickets he took in 11 appearances for England, 12 came in two matches against South Africa only retrospectively granted Test status.

Wisden reckoned Tunnicliffe one of the best professionals never to play for England. As a non-drinker, lay preacher and opening bat, he was Yorkshire's natural successor to Louis Hall [1890]. Tunnicliffe and Jack Brown [1895] may have been chalk and cheese as people, but they were the most dependable opening pair in county cricket: in 1898 they shared a partnership of 554 against Derbyshire, a world record that was not bettered until 1932. At 6ft 2in, Tunnicliffe was tall for a batsman, hence the nickname Long John o'Pudsey. Although Sydney Pardon decried the general standard of fielding in 1900, Hirst was outstanding at mid-off and Foster and Tunnicliffe were brilliant slips; among non-keepers, Tunnicliffe was the leading catcher in eight seasons out of 11 from 1894.

A Yorkshire trio: **George Hirst** (left) and **Schofield Haigh** flank Wilfred Rhodes [1899]

R. E. Foster

R. E. Foster:

"As a batsman he has almost every good quality – a strong defence, self-restraint when it is needed, a free, attractive style, and truly magnificent hitting powers all round the wicket"

Taylor had shone at Uppingham as a wicketkeeper-batsman, but Yorkshire could not accommodate him as keeper, only as a versatile batsman. His maiden century came against the 1899 Australians, and his two hundreds the following year were both off Surrey. He captained Cambridge in 1900 – in opposition to Foster at Oxford – and was seen as a future Yorkshire leader. But after being England's 12th man at Lord's in 1902, Taylor opted to stay in Japan the following year on the way home from a non-Test tour of Australasia, and when he returned he devoted himself to engineering. He was Yorkshire's president for 12 years up to his death in 1960.

Foster, on the other hand, secured a lasting reputation through some brilliant performances during his short career. Along with two elder brothers H. K. [1911] and W. L. – there were seven Foster brothers in all, each of whom learned the game at Malvern where their father taught – he helped Worcestershire gain entry to the Championship in 1899. In 1900 he set new standards for university batsmen by scoring 930 runs at an average of 77.5, before making centuries in both innings of a Gentlemen–Players match, something never done before. The lateness and wristiness of his strokes won comparison with Ranjitsinhji [1897].

By 1903 Foster, who worked as a stockbroker, was rarely turning out in first-class cricket, but he still joined the 1903-04 tour of Australia and scored 287 in the First Test at Sydney, which stood as the biggest innings in Tests until 1930, and remains the highest on debut. In 1907, he came out of semi-retirement to captain England in three Tests against South Africa (thus making him the first and still only man to captain England at cricket and football, at which he won five caps). He died of diabetes aged 36, while his six brothers lived to an average age of 76.

Foster's career contributed to the idea that amateurs could turn up and play well for England with little preparation. It worked for him but few others.

John Tunnicliffe

CRICKETERS OF THE YEAR 1901 – Performances in the English season 1900

Name	Age*		Matches	Runs	Bat ave	Wickets	Bowl ave	Catches (/st)
RE Foster	22	First-class	23	1807	51.62	13	31.84	31
S Haigh	30	First-class	33	760	18.53	163	14.82	19
GH Hirst	29	First-class	36	1960	40.83	62	26.90	31
TL Taylor	22	First-class	26	1461	39.48			22/1
J Tunnicliffe	34	First-class	32	1551	33.00	1	12.00	49

* as at 1/4/1901

1902 Five Cricketers of the Year

Johnny Tyldesley (Lancashire) *

Len Braund (Somerset) * *

Charlie McGahey (Essex) *

Frank Mitchell (Yorkshire) *

Willie Quaife (Warwickshire) *

HEADLINE EVENTS FROM 1901

• County champions – Yorkshire

FOUR OF THE FIVE WERE MEMBERS OF THE England team that toured Australia in the winter of 1901-02, a badly planned mission that ended in heavy defeat. Many leading amateurs were unavailable, and Yorkshire refused to release key players, which created opportunities for the likes of Charlie McGahey and Willie Quaife. *Wisden* went to press before the fate of the Ashes was known, but Sydney Pardon may have feared the worst. He referred to his Five as "not I hope an unhappy choice". In fact, McGahey and Quaife never played for England again after that tour.

Len Braund and Johnny Tyldesley proved more significant figures at international level. Tyldesley, a teetotaller, was a class act, a small man who put bat to ball in a way to match the best amateurs. He scored 3,041 runs in 1901, the most by someone in the season prior to his *Wisden* selection until M. J. K. Smith [1960], and among his nine centuries were innings of 140 for Players v Gentlemen and 221 to save Lancashire from defeat at Trent Bridge. Although he managed only two fifties in the Tests in Australia, Tyldesley soon established himself as a dependable No. 3, and played a decisive role in the retention of the Ashes in

1905. He was among the three best England professional bats of the pre-1914 era, along with Tom Hayward [1895] and Jack Hobbs [1909].

Braund was a wrist-spinner – "one of the very best of the new leg-break bowlers," in *Wisden*'s words – but also a batsman of substance. Having been inexplicably released by Surrey in 1898, he rebuilt his career with Somerset, and in 1901 achieved the double for the first time. For the next four years he ranked as one of the game's best all-rounders, his big-turning leg-breaks embarrassing even the biggest names. With 256 runs and 21 wickets in the Tests – including a half-century and a five-for in England's only win – he could not be blamed for the defeat in Australia, and enjoyed another productive tour there in 1903-04. He later lost ground to the emerging googly bowlers.

At 5ft 5in, Quaife was even shorter than Tyldesley, something *Wisden* thought a serious disadvantage. Pardon reproached him for keeping his average "a little too much before his mind… [he] is apt to play a slow game when caution is the last thing needed by his side". Quaife was not in future to better his season's average of 56.66 in 1901, but proved remarkably durable, playing

Willie Quaife

regular county cricket until the age of 55 and scoring a century in 28 of out 29 seasons. Having overcome doubts about his action, he was – like McGahey – also an effective leg-break bowler. Both Quaife and McGahey did the match double of 100 runs and 10 wickets in 1901.

McGahey played for Essex as an amateur, but his background was modest – his father was a railway clerk – and he often struggled for money. The club had recently helped out, appointing him assistant secretary on a salary of £200, making him as well-paid as the professionals. *Wisden* expressed only qualified approval of his game, attributing much of his success – he scored 1,838 runs, average 48.36 – to Leyton's friendly pitches. "McGahey is not quite so straight and fine a player as Perrin… falling a little short of the front rank of batsmen," it said. Percy Perrin [1905] was the other main pillar of Essex's batting, and onlookers had difficulty telling the "Essex twins" apart.

McGahey captained Essex from 1907 to 1910, and after serving as a private in the 1914–18 war helped the club for three more seasons as player and five as coach. Braund, who also umpired, coached at Cambridge University while Tyldesley coached Lancashire as well as investing a healthy benefit (£3,111, the second-best of the pre-1914 era) into a sports-outfitting business. Quaife's long career earned him, uniquely for the time, two benefits; he went into bat manufacturing.

Johnny Tyldesley

Johnny Tyldesley:
"Whether at third man or long-off he is magnificent, covering a lot of ground"

CRICKETERS OF THE YEAR 1902 – Performances in the English season 1901

Name	Age*		Matches	Runs	Bat ave	Wickets	Bowl ave	Catches (/st)
LC Braund	26	First-class	26	1587	36.06	120	30.62	27
CP McGahey	31	First-class	24	1838	48.36	52	28.50	11
F Mitchell	29	First-class	31	1807	44.07			14
WG Quaife	30	First-class	23	1360	56.66	44	23.15	23
JT Tyldesley	28	First-class	35	3041	55.29			20

as at 1/4/1902

Frank Mitchell led a very different life. Like Gilbert Jessop [1898], he left a minor public school and taught for two years before going up to Cambridge. But unlike Jessop he played only two full county seasons – scoring 1,748 runs in 1899 and 1,807 in 1901, when he topped Yorkshire's averages. Between these two years he volunteered for the Boer War in South Africa – he had toured there in 1898-99, playing what are now regarded as two Tests – and by the time of *Wisden*'s tribute it was clear he would not be returning to Yorkshire in 1902.

He settled in Johannesburg, and worked for businessman and politician Abe Bailey, who was to be a prime mover in the administration and financing of South African cricket. Through

Bailey, Mitchell captained South Africa on a non-Test tour of England in 1904 and in three Tests at the Triangular Tournament of 1912. He had also won six England rugby caps in 1895-96.

Len Braund

Frank Mitchell

Charlie McGahey

Len Braund:

"A fine bat on all sorts of wickets, a beautiful field in the slips, and one of the very best of the new leg-break bowlers"

1903

Five Cricketers of the Year

Victor Trumper (Australians) *

Warwick Armstrong (Australians) * •

Cuthbert Burnup (Kent) *

James Iremonger (Nottinghamshire) *

Jim Kelly (Australians) Ⅲ

HEADLINE EVENTS FROM 1902

• County champions – Yorkshire

• Joe Darling's Australians beat England 2-1 in England, having beaten them 4-1 in Australia a few months earlier

---

THE 1902 ASHES SERIES WAS ONE OF THE MOST dramatic of all time: Australia, who took the series 2–1, won one match by three runs, England another by one wicket. But 14 of the 16 who appeared for England had already been recognised by *Wisden*, including the entire XI who played in the First Test. Nor did *Wisden*'s Five contain anyone from Yorkshire, who won a third title in a row. Seven of their regulars had already been picked.

If this made Sydney Pardon's job tricky, he still had the victorious Australians to choose from (five of whom had been selected before) and, as he wrote in his Preface, "No apology is needed for including three members of the Australian team."

One of them picked himself. Victor Trumper was the undoubted man of the season, batting with such daring and brilliance in a wet summer that Pardon acclaimed him as "by general consent, the best batsman in the world… he put into the shade everything that had ever before been done in England by Australian batsmen."

Trumper had shone at 21 on the 1899 tour, when he had scored a fine hundred in the Lord's Test and a triple-century against Sussex, but he now moved onto a different plane. His play was all the more sensational after his poor form at home to England in 1901-02, when an office job between matches had taken its toll. Now, in a season in which only two others topped 2,000, he scored 2,570 runs.

Trumper survived in difficult conditions because of his lightning footwork; he was rarely caught out of position. He scored a hundred before lunch during four of his 11 centuries, including in the first session of the Old Trafford Test, which Australia won. For such an attacking batsman, he was rarely stumped – in 2.7% of all innings, compared to 7.6% for Jessop [1898].

A gentle and unassuming hero, Trumper drove a generation of writers to lyricism, and his early death at 37 from Bright's Disease only cemented the legend. Despite ill-health, Trumper scored more Test centuries (eight) than anyone else in the pre-1914 era, and more runs (3,163) than all bar Clem Hill [1900].

The choice of team-mates Warwick Armstrong and Jim Kelly was less clear-cut. Armstrong, a capable Aussie Rules player and trimmer now than he would later become, was a young man of potential – but although his overall tour figures were good he did little in the Tests, usually batting low in the order and playing only a small part with his accurate, gently-turning leg-breaks. But Pardon noted his efforts the previous winter, when as last man he shared a stand of 120 that killed England off in the Second Test, and Armstrong was also to star in three Tests in South Africa on the way home, carrying his bat for 159 in the second one.

Armstrong, who stood 6ft 3in, became a figure of great influence, rounding off his Test career by leading Australia to crushing back-to-back Ashes wins in 1920-21 and 1921, making "Armstrong's Australians" a phrase that echoed down the years. Off the field, he forcefully championed the cause of players against querulous administrators. A whisky merchant, he died a wealthy man.

Kelly mustered only 46 runs and six dismissals in the Tests, and two fifties on the entire tour. He had moved to New South Wales from Victoria, where Jack Blackham [1891]

Jim Iremonger

Warwick Armstrong: **"Few players coming to England for the first time with an Australian team have done better work"**

held sway. Kelly's fortunes had been mixed on two previous tours of England, when he had problems keeping to the tearaway Ernie Jones, but *Wisden* now rated him "better than ever". He pulled off a crucial stumping during the Old Trafford win. He toured again in 1905, when a blow over the heart expedited his retirement.

He died on the same day in 1938 as his team-mate Hugh Trumble [1897].

Amateur and professional, Cuthbert Burnup and Jim Iremonger had in common an unusual "double" – both played for England at football but not cricket, though they were unlucky not to do so. A product of Malvern and Cambridge, Burnup batted with the doggedness of a professional. He had scored steadily for Kent for several years and was the first batsman to make a double-century for them, but 1902 was easily his best season so far, bringing him 2,048 runs at 39 – though he improved his average in Kent's first title-winning season of 1906, when he led the national lists with 1,207 runs at 67.05.

Iremonger won the last of his three international football caps shortly before the 1902 cricket season. A powerful figure who played for Nottingham Forest for 15 years, he was signed by Nottinghamshire as a bowler, but made his name as opening partner to A. O. Jones [1900]. When his batting declined, Iremonger transformed himself into a frontline medium-pacer who took 565 wickets in six years and won a place on the 1911-12 Ashes tour. He became a highly successful coach, playing a major part in the development of Harold Larwood [1927], Bill Voce [1933] and Joe Hardstaff [1938].

Cuthbert Burnup

Victor Trumper

Victor Trumper:
"At the present time, by general consent, the best batsman in the world"

Jim Kelly

CRICKETERS OF THE YEAR 1903 – Performances in the English season 1902

Name	Age*		Matches	Runs	Bat ave	Wickets	Bowl ave	Catches (Ist)
WW Armstrong	23	First-class	35	1075	27.56	72	18.90	30
		Tests	5	97	13.85	2	61.50	7
CJ Burnup	27	First-class	33	2048	39.38	26	24.19	21
J Iremonger	27	First-class	24	1358	39.94	2	39.50	13
JJ Kelly	35	First-class	24	326	14.17			22/13
		Tests	5	46	11.50			3/3
VT Trumper	25	First-class	36	2570	48.49	20	20.75	25
		Tests	5	247	30.87	2	50.50	2

*as at 1/4/1903

1904

Five Cricketers of the Year

Pelham Warner (Middlesex) /
Colin Blythe (Kent) •
John Gunn (Nottinghamshire) / •
Albert Knight (Leicestershire) /
Walter Mead (Essex) •

**HEADLINE EVENTS
FROM 1903**

• County champions – Middlesex

PELHAM WARNER WAS THE MAN OF THE MOMENT. As vice-captain he had helped Middlesex to their first official Championship and was chosen, rather surprisingly, to lead the first English side to tour Australia under MCC's banner in 1903-04.

Born in Trinidad to a colonial officer, and educated at Rugby and Oxford, where he studied law, "Plum" Warner was perhaps the first man to captain England in a major series whose leadership qualities counted for more than his playing abilities. He had already made five minor tours to three continents, two of them as captain. His appointment was a triumph: England took the series 3–2, although he himself contributed only 249 runs.

He had scored only 1,141 runs in 1903: not since Archie MacLaren [1895] had a specialist English batsman been chosen by *Wisden* on the back of fewer runs. It was a wet summer, though, and Warner had been a dependable scorer since 1900, when he had helped out the first West Indian side to visit England, led by his brother Aucher.

Although he made occasional Test appearances up to 1912 and played for Middlesex until he led them to another title in 1920 (prompting a special portrait in the 1921 *Wisden*), Warner soon developed parallel careers in administration and journalism. Such conflicts of interest aroused some press criticism, but he was knighted for services to the game in 1937. "Cricket is the very breath of his nostrils," said *Wisden*.

With Wilfred Rhodes [1899] available, neither John Gunn nor Colin Blythe – also slow left-armers – went to Australia. *Wisden* rated Gunn as second only to Hirst [1901] as an all-rounder for the season. In May he scored 294 in 270 minutes against Leicestershire, sharing a third-wicket stand of 369 with his uncle William Gunn [1890], and during six days in August took 28 wickets in two matches in which he bowled unchanged. Gunn, who had toured Australia in 1901-02 with mixed success, was to do the double in the next three seasons as well, and finished with 20,000 runs and 1,000 wickets for Nottinghamshire alone.

Good judges rated Colin "Charlie" Blythe a more skilful bowler than Rhodes, but he was a weak batsman – Rhodes was often preferred by England even though Blythe was more consistently excellent. During the 1900–14

Colin Blythe

Colin Blythe:
"He is a slow bowler of varied gifts"

period, Blythe took 100 wickets at an average below 20 in 13 seasons, on the first occasion at the age of 21. He was a key factor in Kent winning four titles.

By the time England first paired them together, in 1907-08, Blythe was clearly superior, and in five Tests in tandem he took 31 wickets to Rhodes's six. But Blythe, an epileptic, found Test cricket a strain, and largely opted out from 1909 onwards. He was killed in action at Passchendaele in 1917, aged 38; the other members of this Five lived to ages between 73 and 89.

Walter Mead narrowly beat Blythe at the top of the national bowling averages with 131 victims at 13.67. A successful and versatile operator, Mead spun the ball sharply both ways at pace, his stock delivery an accurate off-break with the leg-break for variation. The downside was that he plainly changed grip, so sharp-eyed batsmen knew what was coming.

He also needed help from the pitch, plenty of which he got in 1903. His one Test, in 1899, was played on a true surface and he claimed only one wicket. His record against many of the better sides was only modest. Like Blythe, he was no batsman.

Shortly after the 1903 season Mead got into a dispute with Essex which resulted in his missing much of the next two seasons. His wife and infant daughter had died and he asked for a small pay rise, but the club pleaded poverty – genuinely so, although that had not stopped their generosity towards the amateur Charlie McGahey [1902]. *Wisden* sided with the club, saying Mead had been "very ill advised" and had "alienated a good many of his friends". He eventually backed down, and returned to top 100 wickets in 1906 and 1907, after which his form tailed away. Further tragedy was in store: Mead's son Harold, who had played with him, died of wounds sustained in the 1914–18 war.

Albert Knight, a batsman with a cast-iron defence whose five centuries included a faultless 139 for Players v Gentlemen, was the first Leicestershire player chosen by *Wisden*. His reward for scoring 1,834 runs was selection for Warner's team to Australia, where he played three Tests and scored a painstaking 70 in the win that gave England the series. A Methodist lay preacher, Knight would offer a prayer before facing his first ball.

In 1906, he wrote a controversial book in which he criticised MCC for supporting a system which saw "many an 'amateur', so termed… more heavily remunerated than an accredited professional". He, like Mead, never played cricket for England again.

CRICKETERS OF THE YEAR 1904 – Performances in the English season 1903

Name	Age*		Matches	Runs	Bat ave	Wickets	Bowl ave	Catches (/st)
C Blythe	24	First-class	22	254	12.70	142	13.75	14
JR Gunn	27	First-class	27	1665	42.69	118	19.34	15
AE Knight	31	First-class	27	1834	45.85	1	3.00	13
W Mead	36	First-class	23	195	7.80	131	13.67	9
PF Warner	30	First-class	21	1141	39.34			10

* as at 1/4/1904

On top Down Under: the England team that won the Ashes in 1903-04. From left: **Albert Knight**, George Hirst [1901], Tom Hayward [1895], John Tyldesley [1902], Wilfred Rhodes [1899], Bernard Bosanquet [1905], Ted Arnold, Len Braund [1902], Dick Lilley [1897], **Pelham Warner** (captain), and "Tip" Foster [1901]

Walter Mead

Pelham Warner:
"A more enthusiastic player it would be impossible to find anywhere"

John Gunn

1905

Five Cricketers of the Year

Bernard Bosanquet (Middlesex) / ●
Ernest Halliwell (South Africans) �
James Hallows (Lancashire) / ●
Percy Perrin (Essex) /
Reggie Spooner (Lancashire) /

HEADLINE EVENTS FROM 1904

- County champions – Lancashire

- P. F. Warner leads the first MCC touring team to a 3-2 series victory in Australia in 1903-04 to regain the Ashes for England

- For the third time, a South African team tours England but does not play any Tests

BERNARD BOSANQUET'S SUCCESS IN 1904 MARKED a watershed in the game. Bowlers had apparently experimented with the googly before, but none had deployed it with such prominent success as he did this year. Having bowled England to victory at Sydney to clinch the Ashes in March, he returned home to claim 132 wickets at 21.62, cementing a reputation as the most dangerous slow bowler in the world, and triggering a race among others to master the new weapon.

Bosanquet, of Huguenot descent, emerged at Eton and Middlesex as a batsman who bowled useful medium-pace, but in 1901 switched to leg-breaks. He also worked on developing a ball which spun the other way without any apparent change in delivery, but experienced little joy until 1903, when he took 63 wickets. "This was," as Wisden noted, "something almost entirely new… how he manages [this] one cannot pretend to say."

Wisden hoped that Bosanquet would figure prominently at home to Australia in 1905, and he duly won the First Test with eight second-innings wickets. But his command of the googly faltered, and from 1906 on he took only 22 more wickets at first-class level, even though

he continued playing (chiefly as a batsman) until 1919.

His new trick – dubbed the "Bosie" – was soon being deployed to even better effect by South Africans and Australians. Indeed Reggie Schwarz [1908] had used it on behalf of the South Africans in England in 1904 (when no Tests were played). With the Boer War over, South Africa started to exchange regular tours with England: in 1905-06 they fielded Schwarz and three other googly bowlers, and won by four Tests to one.

Ernest "Barberton" Halliwell, who kept wicket to Schwarz, became the first member of a South African touring team to be chosen by Wisden. Several English cricketers had rated him the world's best keeper on South Africa's previous visit in 1901. He was also a handy batsman and wise counsel, having played for his country since 1891; he turned 40 on the last day of the tour. He had once championed the selection of Krom Hendricks, a coloured fast bowler, but could find no seconder. Few keepers any longer stood up to fast bowlers, but Halliwell sometimes still did, perhaps partly because he was reckoned to have devised the

Bernard Bosanquet:
"How he manages to bowl his off-break with apparently a leg-break action one cannot pretend to say"

Percy Perrin

Ernest Halliwell

ploy of putting steaks in his gloves to protect his hands, a ruse many would imitate.

Reggie Spooner, a star batsman at Marlborough who scored 44 and 83 on his Championship debut at 18 in 1899, had served two years in the Boer War (he was later wounded in the First World War). He returned to play rugby for England and score heavily for Lancashire, whom he helped to win the Championship without losing a game in 1904. Business commitments restricted his involvement in county cricket, but he topped 1,500 runs in five of his six full seasons. He scored fifties in his first two Tests against Australia, in 1905, and took a hundred off South Africa in 1912. Spooner would have captained the 1920-21 tour of Australia, but was ruled out through injury. He was rated among the most stylish batsmen of his era, and was also a brilliant cover point.

For the first time, Lancashire had two representatives among *Wisden*'s Five (they had had two in 1890, when nine players were chosen), something that would not happen again until 1971. James Hallows, a left-handed bat and left-arm fast-medium bowler, was even more central to their title win than Spooner, achieving the double in Championship matches alone. A talented player, his career was blighted by epilepsy, and 1904 – when for once he enjoyed

good health – turned out to be easily his best season. He played his last game in 1907, and died aged 36 in 1910.

Like Spooner, Percy Perrin was an amateur famed for his drives, but unlike Spooner had no need to work, having inherited a fortune from his father's chain of public houses. In a career spanning 32 years, he appeared in more Championship matches (496) than any other amateur. In 1904, he played an extraordinary innings of 343 not out, peppering the Chesterfield boundary for 68 fours (a record till Brian Lara broke it 90 years later during his 501 not out), but still finished on the losing side. This was one of Perrin's best seasons, but he had a habit of performing well in non-Test match summers, and this, allied to a reputation as a poor fielder, prevented him ever appearing for England. "He seems to lack entirely the born fieldsman's power of anticipating the direction of a hit," observed *Wisden*. (He also never played for Gentlemen v Players, perhaps because he wasn't regarded as enough of a gentleman.) Not that this prevented Perrin from assisting England in other ways. His experience and sound judgement made him one of the best Test selectors – he sat on the panel in 1926 which astutely recalled the 48-year-old Wilfred Rhodes [1899] for the decisive final Ashes Test at The Oval, and again from 1931 to 1939.

Reggie Spooner

Reggie Spooner:
"Among the public-school batsmen of the last ten years there has assuredly been no one to compare with R. H. Spooner"

James Hallows

CRICKETERS OF THE YEAR 1905 – Performances in the English season 1904

Name	Age*		Matches	Runs	Bat ave	Wickets	Bowl ave	Catches (/st)
BJT Bosanquet	27	First-class	27	1405	36.02	132	21.62	17
EA Halliwell	40	First-class	21	475	20.65	0		35/13
J Hallows	31	First-class	25	1071	39.66	108	19.37	13
PA Perrin	28	First-class	19	1486	53.07	0		18
RH Spooner	24	First-class	31	1889	43.93	4	79.00	18

* as at 1/4/1905

1906

Five Cricketers of the Year

David Denton (Yorkshire and England) /
Walter Lees (Surrey) ●
George Thompson (Northamptonshire) / ●
Joe Vine (Sussex) /
Levi Wright (Derbyshire) /

WISDEN VENTURED INTO LITTLE-CHARTED territory by picking its first player from Northamptonshire – new arrivals to the Championship in 1905 – its second from Derbyshire, and its third from Sussex. When the 1906 Almanack appeared in early January, the ages of the Five ranged from George Thompson's 28 years to Levi Wright's 43, which made him the second-oldest pick so far behind W. G. Grace [1896].

In his Preface, Sydney Pardon wrote that he would have liked to include Walter Brearley, the Lancashire fast bowler who had an outstanding season, "but a difficulty arose over which I had no control". Could this have been a problem over a suitable photograph? Brearley was eventually chosen in 1910.

For the first time, no member of an Australian touring team was recognised, while England, who dominated the 1905 Ashes, had just one representative in David Denton, who played one Test as stand-in and failed in both innings. Many of those involved in the Ashes had already been selected – 15 Englishmen and seven Australians.

Denton, one of the more attacking professional batsmen, was nicknamed "Lucky"

because of the frequent let-offs he enjoyed in the field, but he was actually unfortunate not to play more often for England. Despite scoring a thousand runs in 21 of his 22 seasons and being a fine fielder in the deep, he was never chosen for another home Test, and made two difficult tours of South Africa against the new googly bowling. His only success was a rapid century at Johannesburg in 1909-10. Plum Warner [1904] described him as "the hardest hitter of his size and weight I have ever seen, and no one timed the ball better".

Denton had a wonderful year in 1905, scoring 2,405 runs with eight centuries, and fully deserved to go to South Africa the following winter. The same was true of Walter Lees, an accurate fast-medium bowler who did not make his mark with Surrey until 1903, when he was 26. Best suited to hard pitches from which he could extract bounce, Lees was the leading wicket-taker in 1905 with 193 wickets. But on matting pitches in South Africa he was still effective, and took 26 wickets in five Tests, though an under-strength England side lost 4–1.

Lees had another big year in 1906, taking 168 wickets, but in the build-up to England's next Test series in 1907 he was injured and lost out to two amateur team-mates from Surrey in Jack Crawford and Neville Knox [both 1907]. He had two more good seasons, but in 1911 lost his Surrey place. A move to Lancashire League cricket fizzled out, and he died of pneumonia in 1924 at 47, not much beyond the age at which the other four played their last first-class matches. *Wisden* described Lees as a bowler as "very good without being great".

Joe Vine

Walter Lees

Joe Vine:

"He plays the game with an evident sense of enjoyment... no day is too long for him"

Thompson, a burly all-rounder whose size helped him get lift out of his fast-medium bowling and distance with his shots, was a central figure in Northamptonshire's elevation to first-class status. Educated at Wellingborough School he, like Frederick Bull [1898], provided a rare case of an amateur turning professional – in Thompson's case in 1897 aged 19. His achievements in the Minor Counties championship earned him invitations to tour with MCC and appear for Players v Gentlemen, and he had no trouble adjusting to the County Championship. In 1905 he scored 652 runs and took 127 wickets, and in ten full seasons up to 1914 topped 10,000 runs and 1,000 wickets. He was instrumental in Northamptonshire managing top-four finishes in 1912 and 1913.

David Denton

George Thompson

George Thompson:
**"One could
imagine him
being unplayable
on the crumbling
wickets with which
bowlers of the last
generation were
often favoured"**

Thompson played one Test against Australia in 1909, and five the following winter in South Africa, where he was England's star all-rounder with 267 runs and 23 wickets. He fared better with the bat than all but Jack Hobbs [1909].

Joe Vine was also a versatile all-rounder, who established himself with Sussex as a youngster but did not blossom until 1904. Vine was an effective opening partner for C. B. Fry [1895], although expected to play second fiddle. He topped 1,500 runs in eight seasons, but never bettered his aggregate of 1,871 in 1905. A revival in form as a useful if expensive leg-break bowler saw him tour Australia in 1911-12 and play two Tests. He made 399 consecutive Championship appearances from 1899 to 1914.

Wright, the only amateur among the Five and the only one not to play Tests, was, like Thompson, a pioneer for his county. Born in Oxford, he moved to Derby to teach, and there developed as a cricketer with Derbyshire and footballer for Derby County and Notts County. He had first played for Derbyshire in 1883, and except for a couple of early years had stayed involved ever since, despite the club returning to second-class status between 1888 and 1894. *Wisden* reckoned Wright was as good a player as he had ever been in 1905, when he scored 1,855 runs at 42.15 and remained a brave silly point. Made captain for 1906, he declined in form during two difficult seasons at the helm.

Thompson, who was injured during the First World War, and Vine became school coaches, while Denton had a spell as Yorkshire's scorer before becoming an umpire.

Levi Wright

CRICKETERS OF THE YEAR 1906 – Performances in the English season 1905

Name	Age*		Matches	Runs	Bat ave	Wickets	Bowl ave	Catches (/st)
D Denton	31	First-class	37	2405	42.19	1	49.00	40/1
		Tests	1	12	6.00			0
WS Lees	30	First-class	34	771	16.40	193	18.01	16
GJ Thompson	28	First-class	22	652	18.62	126	17.57	14
J Vine	30	First-class	34	1871	34.01	29	35.62	11
LG Wright	44	First-class	23	1855	42.15			18

as at 1/4/1906

1907

Five Cricketers of the Year

Kenneth Hutchings (Kent) /

Jack Crawford (Surrey) / ●

Arthur Fielder (Kent) ●

Ernie Hayes (Surrey) /

Neville Knox (Surrey) ●

HEADLINE EVENTS FROM 1906

- County champions – Kent

- P. F. Warner's England side are crushed 4-1 in South Africa in 1905-06

THE LEADING PUBLIC SCHOOLS PRODUCED plenty of fine cricketers, but most were attacking batsmen. Jack Crawford – though he could bat with ferocity – and Neville Knox were young bowlers, one fast-medium and the other outright fast, who provided eye-catching exceptions to the rule.

Crawford, who played in glasses, enjoyed an extraordinary year in 1906. Aged 19, he began it by touring South Africa, where he contributed 281 runs and nine wickets in five Tests, before returning home to perform the double, averaging 30.10 with bat and 20.28 with ball. England would not field another teenager until Ian Peebles [1931] in 1927-28; nor would anyone younger achieve the double until Brian Close [1964] in 1949. At 20, he was the youngest so far to be chosen by *Wisden*.

Crawford, who came from a large cricketing family, must rank as one of the finest English schoolboy cricketers of all. Two years at St Winifred's in Henley-upon-Thames brought him 2,093 runs and 366 wickets; four subsequent seasons at Repton produced 2,098 runs and 244 wickets. Surrey picked him at 17, and in his sixth match he took ten Gloucestershire wickets.

Knox, a product of Dulwich College – where his team-mates included P. G. Wodehouse – also made his Surrey debut in 1904, aged 19. Like Crawford, he brought the ball back in to right-handers from outside off stump, but Knox was much quicker. He took 129 wickets in 1905 and 144 in 1906, which included 12 wickets for the Gentlemen at Lord's, where his pace rattled several professionals.

The emergence of this pair caused great excitement, but neither lasted on the big stage. Crawford did the double again in 1907 and toured Australia the following winter, where his ability to make the ball deviate off flat pitches brought him 30 wickets in five Tests. But his protests at Surrey's treatment of professionals, including the suspension of Alan Marshal [1909], led to a split with the club; he emigrated to Adelaide, where he taught and coached, and played for South Australia.

Knox, who played two Tests against South Africa in 1907, was already struggling with sore shins, too often playing rather than resting, and by 1910 his career was over at 25. He took to acting, understudying Basil Foster – brother of R. E. [1901] and H. K. Foster [1911] – in the

Arthur Fielder

Players against the Gentlemen at Lord's in the game in which Knox caused such a stir (Fielder still finished on the losing side). He claimed 13 other hauls of six or more wickets for Kent, for whom he took 172 wickets.

Fielder had toured Australia in 1903-04 after one full season of county cricket. Returning there in 1907-08, his method of bowling outside off stump, and varying break-backs with the occasional outswinger, brought him 25 wickets in four Tests. He was also an improbable batting hero at Melbourne, where his unbeaten 18 helped England to a one-wicket win.

With his ultra-attacking batting, Hutchings – the youngest of four cricketing brothers – fitted the conventional image of the ex-public-schoolboy cricketer. Having been an outstanding performer at Tonbridge, he was playing his first full county season in 1906, and by scoring 1,454 runs at great speed for Kent was, according to *Wisden*, the batting sensation of the year. He looked to score off many more balls than most. "He suggests to a far greater extent than Trumper muscular power, his forearms being immensely strong," said *Wisden*. Hutchings's high-risk game was never as consistently successful again, although dazzlingly he scored 126 in just over two hours during the Test at Melbourne in 1907-08 in which Fielder also starred. He gave up regular cricket in 1912, and worked as a paper manufacturer.

West End. Jack Hobbs [1909] described him as "the best fast bowler I ever saw".

Ernie Hayes, another Surrey player, was one of the best and most enterprising of professional batsmen, who, by scoring 2,309 runs in 1906, improved his best aggregate for the eighth season in nine. He scored a hundred before lunch during three of his seven centuries, and coped well with Knox at Lord's. He was also a useful leg-break bowler, and a first-rate slip whose 54 catches was the most by any non-keeper in the year of his *Wisden* selection until Stuart Surridge [1953]. He had played three Tests in South Africa in 1905-06 despite illness, and appeared in two more at The Oval in 1909 and 1912.

Alongside Kenneth Hutchings, Arthur Fielder – the son of a farmer's bailiff – played a leading role in Kent's title win, but his season was best remembered for his 14 wickets, including all ten in the first innings, for the

In picking five players from south-east counties, Sydney Pardon said "For once there were no new northern players with any strong claim to be included." George Dennett, the Gloucestershire slow left-armer, was unlucky to miss out, having taken all ten against Essex and finished seventh in the national averages with 175 wickets.

Hutchings was killed in action in September 1916. Hayes, as a commissioned officer, was wounded and decorated, while Knox served as a lieutenant, later rising to major.

Kenneth Hutchings

Kenneth Hutchings: **"Batting so remarkable and individual as his, has not been seen since Ranjitsinhji and Trumper first delighted the cricket world"**

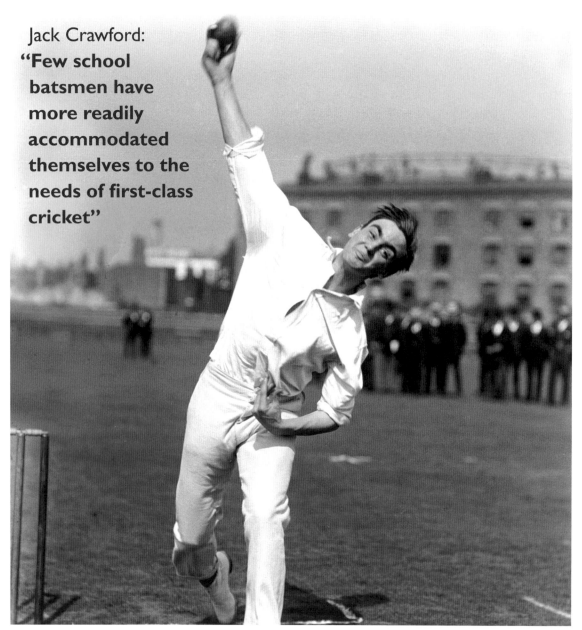

Jack Crawford:
"Few school batsmen have more readily accommodated themselves to the needs of first-class cricket"

Ernie Hayes

Neville Knox

CRICKETERS OF THE YEAR 1907 – Performances in the English season 1906

Name	Age*		Matches	Runs	Bat ave	Wickets	Bowl ave	Catches (Ist)
JN Crawford	20	First-class	30	1174	30.10	118	20.28	16
A Fielder	29	First-class	25	188	11.75	186	20.19	11
EG Hayes	30	First-class	35	2309	45.27	43	25.37	54
KL Hutchings	24	First-class	21	1597	53.23	16	27.75	14
NA Knox	22	First-class	24	258	9.92	144	19.63	9

* as at 1/4/1907

1908

Five Cricketers of the Year

Frank Tarrant (Middlesex) / ●
Albert Hallam (Nottinghamshire) ●
Reggie Schwarz (South Africans) ●
Ernie Vogler (South Africans) ●
Tom Wass (Nottinghamshire) ●

HEADLINE EVENTS FROM 1907

• County champions –
Nottinghamshire

• England, under R. E. Foster,
win a three-Test series against
South Africa 1-0

THE 1907 SUMMER WAS ONE OF THE WETTEST and coldest on record, which played into the hands of bowlers, and *Wisden* chose five players who all took 100 wickets at less than 16 runs apiece. A diverse bunch, they all faced difficult decisions about who to play for, and three of them switched continents. None of them played for England.

Reggie Schwarz, whose 137 wickets cost him only 11.79 apiece, and Ernie Vogler played a big part in South Africa making a successful first Test tour, winning 21 matches and losing only four. One defeat came in the only Test with England that was decided, but by just 53 runs.

Schwarz, born in England to a merchant of Silesian Jewish stock, showed more talent at St Paul's and Cambridge for rugby than cricket, playing three times at half-back for England between 1899 and 1901. He appeared occasionally for Middlesex while working on the London Stock Exchange, but his cricket career only really took off after he left for South Africa in 1902, colour-blindness having dashed his hopes of joining the navy. Like Frank Mitchell [1902], he worked for Abe Bailey. Touring England with South Africa in 1904, he

learned the googly from watching his former Middlesex team-mate Bernard Bosanquet [1905], and enjoyed immediate success. He turned the googly prodigious distances, and used it as a stock ball, taking 18 Test wickets at home to England in 1905-06 on matting pitches, and 25 more on the hard surfaces of Australia in 1910-11.

Schwarz fought in German South-West Africa, then as a major in France, being twice wounded and awarded the Military Cross, before dying of Spanish flu in 1918 aged 43.

Vogler was one of several South Africans shown the googly by Schwarz, but he disguised it better than anyone and used it as a sparing variation to his fast leg-breaks. It took him until 1906-07 to perfect, but when he did the results were startling: in one innings for Eastern Province he took all ten for 26, the best figures in first-class cricket until 1929. In 1907, he took 15 wickets in three Tests, and was hailed by England's captain R. E. Foster [1901], writing in *Wisden*, as the world's most dangerous bowler. "This new kind of bowling is a very great invention," he added. Vogler lived up to the label with 36 England wickets in five Tests in 1909-10, but a year later was hit out of

Tom Wass

The 1907 South African team, which narrowly lost their inaugural Test series in England. Back row (l-r): Aubrey Faulkner, Dave Nourse, Jimmy Sinclair, George Allsop (manager), Stanley Snooke, **Ernie Vogler**, Gordon White. Seated: Maitland Hathorn, **Reggie Schwarz**, Percy Sherwell (captain), Johannes Kotze, William Shalders, Louis Tancred. On ground: Tip Snooke, Harold Smith

Reggie Schwartz:
"He fairly puzzled Ranjitsinhji"

the attack by the Australians. By offering his financial support, Abe Bailey had once deterred Vogler from pursuing a career with Middlesex, but Bailey now cut him off, accusing him of excessive drinking. Vogler, also a useful lower-order hitter, moved to England in 1912 and played club cricket into the 1920s.

Middlesex's use of foreigners was a contentious issue. In 1903, Frank Tarrant had followed Albert Trott [1900] in swapping

CRICKETERS OF THE YEAR 1908 – Performances in the English season 1907

Name	Age*		Matches	Runs	Bat ave	Wickets	Bowl ave	Catches (/st)
AW Hallam	38	First-class	24	155	9.68	168	12.69	15
RO Schwarz	32	First-class	26	644	20.77	137	11.79	16
		Tests	3	7	7.00	9	21.33	4
FA Tarrant	27	First-class	32	1552	32.33	183	15.70	26
AEE Vogler	31	First-class	25	723	21.26	119	15.62	20
		Tests	3	47	9.40	15	19.66	0
TG Wass	34	First-class	22	89	5.23	163	14.28	8

as at 1/4/1908

Melbourne for Marylebone, where he embarked on one of the most successful careers by a player never to feature in Tests. Tarrant – given the central photograph – achieved the first of eight successive doubles in 1907, when he claimed 1,552 runs and 183 wickets, and became recognised as second only to George Hirst [1901] as an all-rounder in English cricket. Unlike Hirst, Tarrant often opened the batting.

During one period in 1907, Tarrant, a slow-medium left-arm spinner, took ten wickets in five successive matches; later, within eight days, he claimed nine for 59 against Nottinghamshire and nine for 41 against Gloucestershire (including four wickets in four balls). In the winter, he returned to Victoria but, despite scoring heavily, was not picked by Australia, and did not play there again until 1924-25. After the outbreak of war, Tarrant developed a career in India, where he coached and played, and became wealthy trading racehorses. He umpired England's first two Tests there, and managed the first visit by an Australian side in 1935-36.

That Nottinghamshire won the title without being beaten was largely due to Tom Wass and Albert Hallam. In 19 matches, Wass took 145 wickets and Hallam 153, with no one else claiming more than 25. With the tall Wass bowling fast-medium leg-breaks, and Hallam operating at an accurate slow-medium, they helped dismiss opponents for less than 100 on 13 occasions. Wass was included in England's squad for the First Test of the summer; Hallam was invited to take part in the Third, only to withdraw with a bruised hand.

Wass, a miner, started out in the leagues, and turned down a contract with Lancashire. He convinced his native county of his qualities after bowling Arthur Shrewsbury [1890] in the nets, and developed into one of the most tireless wicket-takers in England, finishing at the age of 46 in 1920 with a record 1,653 for Nottinghamshire.

Frank Tarrant

Frank Tarrant:
"The best all-round cricketer of 1907"

Hallam started with Leicestershire, then spent six years at Lancashire before moving back to the county of his birth in 1901. In most seasons, Hallam – the senior partner by four years – was outperformed by Wass, but this year he took more wickets at a lower average. Needing more help from pitch conditions, he claimed 100 wickets in only two other seasons, compared to Wass's nine. Neither was much of a batsman.

Albert Hallam

1909

Lord Hawke and Four Cricketers of the Year

Lord Hawke (Yorkshire) *

Walter Brearley (Lancashire) ●

Jack Hobbs (Surrey) *

Alan Marshal (Surrey) *

John Newstead (Yorkshire) * ●

JACK HOBBS MIGHT HAVE BEEN CHOSEN A YEAR before this after scoring 2,135 runs in a bowler's summer, but the case was now overwhelming. In 1908, he finished second in England's averages in his maiden Test series in Australia, before falling only slightly short of 2,000 again in the English season. "There is perhaps no better professional batsman in England, except Hayward and Tyldesley," wrote Sydney Pardon.

Hobbs showed in the next three years that he was better than any batsman alive, scoring 539 Test runs in South Africa, where he tamed the googly bowlers, and 662 in Australia. He may have depended on cricket for his livelihood but he played with real dash, scoring a century before lunch on the first day of a match on an unprecedented 13 occasions, nine of them by 1914.

Born and bred in modest circumstances in Cambridge, Hobbs was encouraged by Tom Hayward [1895] to qualify for Surrey, and made up for a late start by scoring 88 and 155 in his first two matches in 1905, when he was 22. By maintaining exceptional fitness and technical expertise into his fifties, Hobbs left a statistical legacy still revered today: 61,237 runs and 197

centuries in first-class cricket, both records, and 5,410 runs and 15 centuries in Tests, neither of which had been bettered when he retired in 1930. He was knighted in 1953.

If Hobbs's selection was cast-iron, Lord Hawke's was less clear-cut. As a player, he had done nothing exceptional, but Martin Hawke was finally giving up regular cricket aged 48 and had just led Yorkshire to an eighth title in 16 seasons. *Wisden*'s tribute was therefore essentially valedictory. Pardon confined himself to a short sketch, skipping over the usual biographical details, and no reference was made to Hawke's playing abilities – in more than 25 years he had scored only 13 first-class hundreds. Instead Pardon focused on his merits as leader and spiritual guide.

These were beyond dispute. Apart from the Championship wins, the Eton- and Cambridge-educated Hawke had done much for the lot of professionals, introducing winter pay and the practice of two-thirds of a player's benefit money being invested safely on his behalf. "I am only regarding him as the good genius of Yorkshire cricket," explained Pardon.

In future, Hawke would concentrate on cricket administration and chairing the Oxo

HEADLINE EVENTS FROM 1908

- County champions – Yorkshire

- Monty Noble's Australia side regain the Ashes, winning 4-1 in 1907-08

Walter Brearley

had two big seasons. The first was 1905, when he dismissed Victor Trumper [1903] six times, and played in two of the Tests. The second was 1908, when he claimed 21 five-fors and took 25 wickets in two Roses matches. His "inexhaustible vitality… is half the secret of his success," said *Wisden*. He should have played more for England, but his untameable nature led to frequent clashes with Lancashire, whom he left after 1911. The last of his four Tests came in 1912, when he was playing for Cheshire. He later became a significant coach.

Alan Marshal also fell out with his county. Standing 6ft 3in, he was the first cricketer of note from Queensland (not yet a Sheffield Shield side). He came to England in 1905, and qualified for Surrey after topping 4,000 runs in all matches in 1906, blossoming excitingly in 1908. "Marshal has not Jessop's ability to score in all directions from bowling of all kinds of length, but with his immense advantages of height and reach… he can certainly send the ball further," *Wisden* stated. He also had success as fast-medium bowler, taking 12 for 73 against Derbyshire.

He never touched such heights again. In 1909 he was suspended after not co-operating with police after Surrey players were caught in trivial nocturnal high jinks; his contract was terminated the next year. Marshal returned to Queensland, but opportunities were limited. He died of enteric fever while serving in the war, aged 32.

Jack Hobbs

Jack Hobbs:
"Very keen on the game and ambitious to reach the highest rank"

Company. His personal wealth enabled him to tour widely; he captained in what are now regarded as five Tests in South Africa in 1895-96 and 1898-99. He was also instrumental in creating, in 1899, a selection panel for home Tests, and sat on it for many years. He was the first Championship-winning captain to be chosen as a Cricketer of the Year.

Walter Brearley, an energetic fast bowler and spirited amateur who was nearly picked by *Wisden* in 1906, was not always available because of business commitments (he never toured). Coming late to county cricket, he

Alan Marshal

CRICKETERS OF THE YEAR 1909 – Performances in the English season 1908

Name	Age*		Matches	Runs	Bat ave	Wickets	Bowl ave	Catches (/st)
W Brearley	33	First-class	20	193	7.14	163	16.17	6
Lord Hawke	48	First-class	24	317	15.85			7
JB Hobbs	26	First-class	36	1904	37.33	6	22.00	13
A Marshal	25	First-class	33	1931	40.22	56	18.83	26
JT Newstead	31	First-class	36	927	25.05	140	16.50	26

* as at 1/4/1909

The emergence of John Newstead, a star of Yorkshire's season, was a surprise. Aged 30, he had been tried five years earlier, after which Lord Hawke arranged for him to join the Lord's groundstaff; he had also coached in South Africa. Recalled as a stand-in in 1907, he took 11 for 70 against Worcestershire, and in 1908 scored 927 runs and took 140 wickets as a probing fast-medium bowler. These amounted to nearly half

Lord Hawke:

"The good genius of Yorkshire cricket"

his career haul; after a moderate year in 1909, he drifted back into the leagues. He was the only Cricketer of the Year known to have died and not obituarised contemporaneously in the Almanack; a notice eventually appeared in 1994, 41 years late.

John Barton King, a "swerve" bowler on his third tour with the Gentlemen of Philadelphia, topped the 1908 first-class averages with 87 wickets at 11.01 apiece, but was overlooked.

The Yorkshire cricket team, circa 1908. Back row (l-r): **John Newstead**, James Rothery, Mr Hoyland, David Denton [1906], William Wilkinson, William Bates. Seated: David Hunter, George Hirst [1901], **Lord Hawke** (captain), Schofield Haigh [1901], Wilfred Rhodes [1899]. On ground: Hubert Myers, Charles Grimshaw

1910

Five Cricketers of the Year

Sydney Barnes (Staffordshire and England) ●
Warren Bardsley (Australians) *i*
Douglas Carr (Kent and England) ●
Arthur Day (Kent) *i*
Vernon Ransford (Australians) *i*

HEADLINE EVENTS FROM 1909

• County champions – Kent

• Australia retain the Ashes in England, winning the series 2-1

SYDNEY BARNES HAD BEEN ARGUABLY THE best bowler in England since 1901, but through selectorial myopia and his own preference for league and Minor Counties cricket – it paid better than county cricket and spared him dealing with high-handed officialdom at Lancashire, where he had played two seasons – he had rarely featured in big matches.

Ironically, England's strategic planning was a shambles during the 1909 Ashes, but Barnes was chosen for three matches despite having appeared in only one home Test before. Although he took 17 wickets, the series was still lost 2–1. The Australians were amazed England did not pick him more often at home, because he had already toured their country twice and taken 43 wickets in eight Tests.

Monty Noble [1900] rated him during the 1907-08 tour as the world's best bowler, and this Barnes probably remained until 1914, when he played the last of 27 Tests, in which he claimed 189 wickets, a record that stood until 1935. Barnes played league cricket with phenomenal success until well into his sixties, and dismissed eight of the South African touring team for 41 while playing for Minor Counties in 1929. He was then 56.

Barnes, who stood 6ft 1in and bowled with a high action, operated only at a brisk medium-pace, but was relentlessly accurate and had all the tricks. He generally bowled from wide of the crease and broke the ball from leg, but could bring it back from the off, and was a master of flight. He is rated by some good judges as the greatest bowler there has ever been, but he did not help himself by being so cussed.

Warren Bardsley and Vernon Ransford were central to Australia's Ashes victory, and Sydney Pardon said he was bound to include them among his Five. These two left-handers, who had enjoyed prolific home seasons before they arrived in England, were the leading run-scorers in the Tests. Ransford contributed an unbeaten 143 at Lord's, and 45 and 24 in a low-scoring game at Leeds – both of which Australia won – while Bardsley, in becoming the first batsman to score centuries in each innings of a Test, blocked England's path at The Oval. Ransford, a fine baseballer, also shone in the field. "No safer catch or more untiring worker in the deep field has ever been seen," *Wisden* said.

Sydney Barnes

Sydney Barnes:
"Few bowlers have sprung into fame more suddenly"

Warren Bardsley

Bardsley had taken longer to come through than Ransford, who was playing for Victoria at 18 and Australia at 22, but of the seven men Australia tried as openers during the Tests it was Bardsley, the new boy, who proved most effective. He was to open almost 50 times in Tests up to 1926, second only to Trumper [1903] among Australians to that point – and Bardsley had the superior average, at 41.78 to Trumper's 33.00. His appetite for the game was insatiable, and through long hours of practice he developed great style and a wide range of scoring options. He topped 2,000 runs on the 1909 tour, a feat he repeated in 1912 and 1921. He was left partially deaf by a blow to the head from Ted McDonald [1922].

Ransford, more of a dasher, failed to live up to his promise. In two subsequent Test series he failed to score another century, and missed the 1912 tour of England because of an administrative dispute. Although he battled ill-health to play for ten years after the First World War, he was not the cricketer of old.

Douglas Carr, who opened the bowling with Barnes in the Fifth Test, experienced an extraordinary season – one which *Wisden* claimed was unique in cricket history.

A 37-year-old schoolteacher "inclined to stoutness", Carr breathed life into a routine club career by turning himself, after three years of trying, into a capable googly bowler. Available to Kent outside term-time, he took seven wickets on debut against Oxford University and 15 in two appearances for Gentlemen v Players, getting the better of several big names. Desperate both for a win and for a successor to Bernard Bosanquet [1905], England named Carr in the squad for the Fourth Test before he had even played a match in the Championship, and then stuck him in the XI for The Oval, where he started well but was overbowled, finishing with seven for 282 from 69 overs.

Carr would never appear in another Test, but with 51 wickets in eight matches he played a big part in Kent winning the title. He took at least 50 wickets in the second half of each of the next four summers, in two of which Kent were also champions.

Vernon Ransford

The Kent side which won the County Championship in 1909. Back row (l-r): Arthur Fielder [1907], Fred Huish, Frank Woolley [1911], Walter Hearne (scorer), Edward Humphreys, Colin Blythe [1904]. Seated: Sam Day, Kenneth Hutchings [1907], Jack Mason [1898] (captain), **Arthur Day**, **Douglas Carr**. On ground: Bill Fairservice, James Seymour

Arthur Day, the youngest of three brothers who learnt the game at Malvern and played for Kent, was also a key figure in the Championship win, contributing 905 runs at 45.25 and topping the national averages in all matches. Here was fulfilment for someone who had struggled to hold down a regular place since scoring 1,149 runs in his debut season in 1905 at the age of 20. He remained an erratic performer, but sparkled briefly again by averaging 111.00 in four Championship matches in 1921.

Douglas Carr:
"There is no other instance of a man playing for England in a Test match in his first year in good-class cricket"

CRICKETERS OF THE YEAR 1910 – Performances in the English season 1909

Name	Age*		Matches	Runs	Bat ave	Wickets	Bowl ave	Catches (/st)
W Bardsley	27	First-class	33	2072	46.04	0		11
		Tests	5	396	39.60			1
SF Barnes	36	First-class	6	34	5.66	34	15.79	2
		Tests	3	2	0.50	17	20.00	1
DW Carr	38	First-class	16	94	6.71	95	18.27	6
		Tests	1	0	0.00	7	40.28	0
AP Day	24	First-class	20	1014	44.08	0		13
VS Ransford	25	First-class	32	1736	43.40	1	27.00	16
		Tests	5	353	58.83			1

* as at 1/4/1910

1911

Five Cricketers of the Year

William Smith (Surrey) ●
Henry Foster (Worcestershire) ◢
Alfred Hartley (Lancashire) ◢
Charles Llewellyn (Hampshire) ◢ ●
Frank Woolley (Kent) ◢ ●

BORN IN PIETERMARITZBURG TO A WELSH father and Indian mother, who was herself born on St Helena in the south Atlantic, Charles "Buck" Llewellyn was the second non-white chosen by *Wisden* after Ranjitsinhji [1897]. Having been picked for Natal without his colour being an issue (as it later would be), he had first appeared for South Africa in what is now regarded as a Test in 1895-96, aged 19. He was his country's first outstanding slow left-armer, mixing orthodox spin with occasional wrist-spin, and was a capable if inconsistent batsman.

Llewellyn was first employed as a clerk by the father of Herby Taylor [1925] but, with the help of Robert Poore [1900], moved to England to play professionally for Hampshire. He did the double in his first full season in 1901, and nearly repeated the feat in 1902. *Wisden* recognised him after his third double in 1910.

Initially, South Africa continued calling on Llewellyn. He helped out on non-Test tours of England in 1901 and 1904, and appeared in three home Tests against Australia in 1902-03 (taking 25 wickets), but by then England had included him in a Test squad at Edgbaston in 1902 without fielding him. His professional status was deemed unacceptable by some in South Africa, and he stopped playing there.

By the time of his *Wisden* selection, Llewellyn had been controversially recalled for a tour of Australia in 1910-11, but his return to the side proved brief. In 1911 he started a long career in the English leagues, first joining Accrington, who paid better than Hampshire, although he still appeared for South Africa in the 1912 Triangular Tournament in England. He died in Surrey in 1964.

Like Llewellyn, Frank Woolley was an all-rounder who batted left-handed and bowled slow left-arm. He was still in the formative stages of an immense career that would span 29 seasons and yield 58,969 runs, 2,068 wickets and 1,018 catches (a record for a non-wicketkeeper).

Aged 23 in 1910, Woolley, who had started out on the Tonbridge groundstaff, achieved the first of eight doubles (in a record four of which he topped 2,000 runs), but his batting only really blossomed on the 1911-12 tour of Australia, with a rapid triple-century and a maiden Test hundred. "He often starts badly and there is something wanting in his defence," *Wisden* stated. "It ought to be a harder matter than it is to bowl him out."

HEADLINE EVENTS FROM 1910

• County champions – Kent

• England are beaten in South Africa 3-2 in 1909-10

Henry Foster

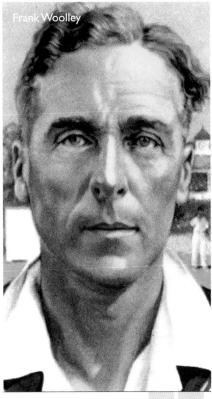
Frank Woolley

Woolley was a constant presence in the England side between 1909 and 1926, but it was not until after the 1914–18 war that he spent more time in the top half of the batting order than the bottom. Serenely stylish for a tall batsman, Woolley in full flow was an enchanting sight, but in Tests he didn't convert enough fifties into hundreds.

The three other members of *Wisden*'s Five never played Tests, although Henry Foster was sometimes involved with England as a selector, starting in 1907 when his younger brother R. E. Foster [1901] captained the side. Henry devoted more time to cricket than any of his six brothers, playing three years at Oxford and captaining Worcestershire for 12 seasons. Although he topped 1,000 runs in 1910, this was not one of his best years, and *Wisden*'s decision owed something to his status as leader: "There is a certain appropriateness in giving his portrait in *Wisden* now, though it should have appeared long ago, as he captained the Gentlemen last season both at The Oval and Lord's."

Frank Woolley:
"As a small boy he was always to be found on the Tonbridge Cricket Ground"

But Woolley was a free-scoring player, one of the fastest of his generation.

Originally chosen by Kent as a stand-in for Colin Blythe [1904], Woolley remained a significant bowler into the 1920s. In 1910, he finished ahead of Blythe in the averages, and took five-fors against Surrey, Middlesex and Lancashire (twice), all sides that pushed Kent for their third title in five seasons. In 1912, he took ten for 49 in a Test against Australia.

Alfred Hartley

In his Preface, Sydney Pardon said that he had originally intended to pick five young batsmen, but had changed his mind. One of the reasons, he implied, was that he was "obliged" to have William Smith, nicknamed "Razor" because of his slight frame, who had an extraordinary season and was given pride of place with the central photograph.

Smith, an off-spinner who claimed many victims with a ball that swerved from leg, took 247 wickets, 72 more than anyone else. *Wisden* rated him the best slow right-armer in the country. Hampered by ill-health, he had taken a long time to command a regular place with Surrey, but in four seasons from 1909 to 1912 he took 614 wickets.

Alfred Hartley – the fifth of nine children to a Southport cotton merchant and a mother from New Orleans, where he was born – had scored 1,000 runs in the two previous seasons for Lancashire as an obdurate top-order batsman, sometimes appearing alongside his elder brother Charles. In 1910, Alfred managed 1,585 runs thanks to some big innings against weaker counties, although he also performed well in a low-scoring game for Gentlemen v Players. "Hartley is not a batsman to draw the crowd," *Wisden* said bluntly.

His form declined in 1911, but following his father's death he and Charles had to attend to family business. Alfred was killed in action four weeks before the Armistice, aged 39.

William Smith

Charles Llewellyn

Charles Llewellyn:

"As a batsman he is one of the most punishing left-handers now before the public"

CRICKETERS OF THE YEAR 1911 – Performances in the English season 1910

Name	Age*		Matches	Runs	Bat ave	Wickets	Bowl ave	Catches (/st)
HK Foster	37	First-class	16	1032	36.85			6
A Hartley	31	First-class	31	1585	36.86	1	39.00	6
CB Llewellyn	34	First-class	26	1232	29.33	152	19.27	19
WC Smith	33	First-class	36	476	9.71	247	13.05	29
FE Woolley	23	First-class	31	1101	24.46	136	14.50	33

*as at 1/4/1911

1912

Five Members of the MCC's Team in Australia

Frank Foster (Warwickshire)
Jack Hearne (Middlesex)
Septimus Kinneir (Warwickshire)
Phil Mead (Hampshire)
Herbert Strudwick (Surrey)

HEADLINE EVENTS FROM 1911

- County champions – Warwickshire

SYDNEY PARDON CHOSE FIVE MEMBERS OF WHAT proved to be a triumphant Ashes-winning England side in Australia, although he picked them before the tour was far advanced, meaning selection must have rested on how they performed in the 1911 season. Indeed, he expressed regret about his choice in his Preface, written after two of the five Tests had been played. "I wish now that I had included Mr J. W. H. T. Douglas," he wrote. Douglas [1915] had taken over the captaincy early in the tour after Pelham Warner [1904] fell ill.

Warwickshire in 1911 became the first of the "new" counties to win the Championship. Much was due to the inspiration of Frank Foster, who at 22 remains the youngest captain to win the title and the only one to do so while performing the double. Pardon gave Foster's photograph pride of place, and said: "In any picture he would have had a place." Sep Kinneir, who turned 40 during the season, was Warwickshire's leading run-scorer.

Foster and Kinneir, like "Young Jack" Hearne and Phil Mead, made their Test debuts during the series in Australia. Bert Strudwick, 31, had already toured Australia once before, and appeared in five Tests in South Africa.

Although Hearne, himself only 20, started the Ashes series with scores of 74, 43 and 114, Foster proved the real star, claiming 32 wickets with his left-arm swing bowling as he and Barnes [1910] swept England to a 4–1 triumph. Foster also scored three half-centuries.

During the previous sweltering summer, Foster's supercharged confidence helped him to hit a whirlwind 200 in three hours against Surrey, plunder 284 runs and 18 wickets from two games with Yorkshire, and snap up the last three wickets as Warwickshire clinched the title with victory over Northamptonshire in their final fixture.

Foster, who came from a wealthy family unrelated to the Worcestershire clan of Fosters, was a free-spirited amateur who had previously achieved little with his gung-ho batting. "Everything is possible at three and twenty," *Wisden* said. "Cricket at its brightest is a young man's game, and Foster is the very personification of youthful energy."

But tragedy lurked. Foster did the double again in 1914, but a motorcycle accident the following year meant his playing days were over at 26. He fell into debt, was dismissed from the family business, and became a suspect in the

The England team which won in Australia in 1911-12, providing all five Cricketers of the Year in 1912. Insets (top): **Sep Kinneir**, Jim Iremonger [1903]. Back row (l-r): **Bert Strudwick**, Tiger Smith, Bill Hitch [1914], Joe Vine [1906], George Gunn [1914], **Philip Mead**. Seated: Sydney Barnes [1910], Johnny Douglas [1915], Pelham Warner [1904] (captain), Jack Hobbs [1909], Wilfred Rhodes [1899]. Insets (bottom): **Frank Foster**, Frank Woolley [1911], **Jack Hearne**

1914

Five Cricketers of the Year

Lionel Tennyson (Hampshire) /

Major Booth (Yorkshire) / ●

George Gunn (Nottinghamshire) /

Bill Hitch (Surrey) ●

Albert Relf (Sussex) / ●

HEADLINE EVENTS FROM 1913

• County champions – Kent

SYDNEY PARDON WROTE THAT HE HAD ARRIVED at his choice only "after some deliberation" – suggesting he was not totally convinced by his picks – but George Gunn, aged 34 and already a star on two Test tours of Australia, was overdue his recognition. He finished third in the national averages in 1913, and scored centuries of contrasting moods against Championship runners-up Yorkshire at Trent Bridge – the first occupying 360 minutes, the second 85. In the return fixture at Dewsbury he carried his bat, as he did against Middlesex at Lord's.

Gunn, a nephew of William [1890] and younger brother of John [1904], had a fine defence, though he did not always show it, preferring to skip down the pitch to bowlers of all types. This maverick streak played its part in Gunn being often overlooked in selection for England and the Players. He appeared in only one home Test, in 1909.

Gunn was troubled by ill-health, and was convalescing in Australia when he was called up as replacement during the 1907-08 Ashes tour. He scored 119 and 74 in his first Test and added a second century in the final match of the series. A full member of the 1911-12 side, he was a key figure in England's victory, making six scores between 43 and 75 at No. 3. Three months later, when the Triangular Tournament began, he was dropped for Reggie Spooner [1905], who in his place scored 1, 1, 1 and 0 against Australia. "The absence of his name from the England team… caused astonishment in Sydney and Melbourne," *Wisden* said.

Gunn appeared in one more Test series in the West Indies in 1929-30, when he was 50, and did not stop playing for Nottinghamshire until he was 53, finishing as the leading run-scorer in their history.

Albert Relf, a more prosaic talent who turned 39 in June 1913, had also been a strong performer for some time. He had topped 1,000 runs in his maiden season in 1900, made Test tours of Australia and South Africa, and now performed the double for the eighth time, a record bettered at the time only by George Hirst [1901]. He was rewarded with a place on the winter tour of South Africa, where he played his part in England's 4–1 win.

Lionel Tennyson – playing his first season of first-class cricket at 23 – could not have been chosen any sooner by *Wisden*. A grandson of the poet Alfred, Lord Tennyson, he had made little

George Gunn

> George Gunn:
> **"He showed such powers of defence that his ultimate success was almost taken for granted"**

Albert Relf

impression as a player at Eton, where he was picked as a fast bowler, or Cambridge, before joining the Coldstream Guards. But in 1913, when he was available for the second half of the summer, he scored a century on debut for MCC v Oxford University before adding hundreds away at Essex and Nottinghamshire in his second and third Championship matches. He then scored 96 at Yorkshire. "It is scarcely too much to say that Tennyson's success as a batsman was the most surprising feature of last season's cricket," said *Wisden*. "Rarely indeed has a player quite new to first-class matches done so much."

Tennyson played all five Tests in South Africa, and although he appeared infrequently in 1914 he was to prove among the more durable and capable of amateur captains during the post-war period. He led Hampshire for 15 seasons – the last five after succeeding to the family title – and briefly took over the England captaincy in crisis in 1921, leading a fightback with pugnacity.

Bill Hitch, another taken to The Oval from Cambridgeshire by Tom Hayward [1895], was the country's fastest bowler in 1913. A Surrey regular since 1908 and a support bowler during the 1911-12 Ashes, he now combined pace, control and fitness. His haul included ten-fors in seven matches, as well as innings figures of seven for 59 for Players v Gentlemen at Scarborough, where he also scored 53 and 68. *Wisden* also hailed him as "the best short leg in the world". He played two Tests after the war, one under Tennyson in 1921.

CRICKETERS OF THE YEAR 1914 – Performances in the English season 1913

Name	Age*		Matches	Runs	Bat ave	Wickets	Bowl ave	Catches (/st)
MW Booth	27	First-class	35	1228	27.28	181	18.46	26
G Gunn	34	First-class	22	1697	49.91			24
JW Hitch	27	First-class	30	597	15.30	174	18.55	18
AE Relf	39	First-class	34	1846	31.82	141	18.09	41
Lord Tennyson	24	First-class	10	832	46.22	0		5

* as at 1/4/1914

Major Booth

Lionel Tennyson

Bill Hitch

Like Relf, the unusually named Major Booth, a product of the Pudsey St Lawrence club, did the double, finishing as the country's leading wicket-taker. A rare right-armer in the Yorkshire attack, he could break the ball back from the off or swing it away late. He took 17 five-fors and bowled 1,156.5 overs, a big workload for a tall man not rated as especially strong.

Booth played two Tests during the winter in South Africa, where he was injured in a car crash, and had another excellent season with the ball in 1914. Tragically, he was to die as a second lieutenant on the first day of the Somme Offensive in 1916, aged 29. Roy Kilner [1924] named his son Major after him. Gunn also served in the war before being invalided out, as did Hitch and Tennyson, who was wounded three times.

Relf, who had turned to coaching, committed suicide in 1937, mistakenly believing his wife was terminally ill. She inherited £20,880, a greater estate than those of the other four players combined.

Lionel Tennyson:
"He may or may not have the qualities that make for permanent success"

1915

Five Cricketers of the Year

John Douglas (Essex) *I* ●
Percy Fender (Surrey) *I* ●
Wally Hardinge (Kent) *I*
Donald Knight (Oxford University and Surrey) *I*
Sydney Smith (Northamptonshire) *I* ●

No previous Cricketers of the Year selection could have felt as irrelevant as that for the 1915 Almanack. Britain had entered the European War in August 1914, and while it was the job of *Wisden* to record the cricketing events of the previous year, the world at large had other priorities, as did the cricketers themselves.

The four Englishmen among the Five – Sydney Smith was by birth and upbringing a West Indian, the first such to be chosen – were all to see active service, Johnny Douglas and Donald Knight as soldiers, Percy Fender as an air pilot and Wally Hardinge as a seaman. All survived to take part in England's next home Test series in 1921.

Sydney Pardon in his Preface wrote that Douglas "has paramount claims to be in the centre of the picture", because in the previous 12 months he had been captain of the successful team in South Africa and his bowling had won the Gentlemen-Players match at Lord's.

Douglas had also captained England to victory in Australia in 1911-12 as stand-in skipper, and this excellent record of leadership counted in his favour when a captain was required to take a team to Australia after the war (when England lost 5–0). Some reckoned Douglas lacked imagination as captain, but he was a supremely fit and resourceful cricketer.

Having first played for Essex in 1901, the year he left Felsted, Douglas took five seasons to establish himself and another five after that to be made captain. In 1914 he achieved the double for the first time and took 13 wickets for Gentlemen v Players with his fast-medium swing bowling, which regularly caused trouble to Jack Hobbs [1909], whom he dismissed more times than any other bowler.

The elder son of a wealthy timber merchant and influential sports administrator, Douglas was well placed to follow his father's passion for cricket and boxing (as well as football, at which he won an England amateur cap). A muscular middleweight, Douglas took gold at the London Olympics of 1908. Purportedly, it was through his father, who held the mortgage on the Leyton ground, that Douglas became Essex captain; once removed in 1928, he refused to play again. Douglas died with his father at sea off Denmark during a timber trip in 1930.

Fender and Knight were two young members of a Surrey side that won their first title since

Johnny Douglas

Johnny Douglas:
"**The position Mr Douglas now holds in the cricket world has been won by sheer hard work and perseverance**"

Sydney Smith

1899 – though because the programme was cut short by war they were not confirmed as champions until November. Fender was thought to be of Jewish origin, something that may have played a part in his never captaining England. He turned 22 in August, and Knight turned 20 in May. Only Jack Crawford [1907] had been chosen by *Wisden* at as young an age as Knight.

Fender had already played two full seasons for Sussex, but a switch to his native Surrey for 1914 saw a dramatic improvement. He took a hat-trick in his second game and scored 140 in two hours in his fifth. "He is not a cricketer whose value can in any way be gauged from the figures or averages," *Wisden* stated. "As a match-winning factor he is a far greater force on a side than his records would suggest."

Knight started county cricket even earlier than Douglas or Fender, playing occasionally for Surrey during each of his last three years at Malvern. In 1914, he rejoined them after finishing his first year at Oxford; always stylish, he scored Championship centuries against Kent and Gloucestershire.

After the war, Fender remained one of the best all-rounders and slip catchers in the country, and an innovative captain for Surrey for 12 seasons, as well as an engaging wine merchant. He should have appeared more than 13 times for England, but fell out with authority and played only one Test after 1924. Knight played only

one more full season – with great success in 1919 – before teaching limited his availability. His subsequent championing of pad-play aroused the ire of Sydney Pardon.

Smith, a left-handed batsman and slow left-arm spinner, played six years for Trinidad before settling in England after touring with a West Indian side in 1906 (not a Test tour). After qualifying for Northamptonshire, he was a key figure, along with George Thompson [1906], in the county finishing second in 1912. Smith took over as captain in 1913, did the double and led them to fourth place. He achieved the double again in 1914, and scored two half-centuries for the Gentlemen at Lord's. He emigrated for a second time in 1915, to New Zealand, where he performed strongly for Auckland into his mid-forties.

Hardinge was a gifted dual sportsman who played for Kent from the age of 16 to 47 – developing into one of the country's most reliable opening batsmen – and an inside-forward for Newcastle, Sheffield United and Arsenal. He represented England once at football in 1910 and once at cricket in 1921, when he opened the innings with his county team-mate Frank Woolley [1911]. He scored only four centuries in 1914, but fell five times in the eighties. He bowled with his left arm but threw with his right. He worked as a sales rep for John Wisden and Co towards the end of his playing days.

Percy Fender

Percy Fender:
"As a match-winning factor he is a far greater force on a side than his records would suggest"

CRICKETERS OF THE YEAR 1915 – Performances in the English season 1914

Name	Age*		Matches	Runs	Bat ave	Wickets	Bowl ave	Catches (/st)
JWHT Douglas	32	First-class	25	1288	35.77	138	19.10	15
PGH Fender	22	First-class	25	820	22.77	83	23.09	29
HTW Hardinge	29	First-class	29	1768	37.61	5	26.20	21
DJ Knight	20	First-class	20	1204	41.51			9
SG Smith	34	First-class	21	1373	42.90	105	16.25	16

as at 1/4/1915

Wally Hardinge

1916 1917

No award

WITH FIRST-CLASS CRICKET IN ABEYANCE because of the war, *Wisden* suspended its Cricketers of the Year feature. As the conflict dragged on, cricket at lower levels gradually picked up, notably in some northern leagues where some high-profile cricketers were involved. Services charity matches featuring prominent players also became popular, encouraging Sydney Pardon to propose in the 1917 Almanack that in line with some other sports county cricket should resume. But logistically this was impractical.

Donald Knight

Part Two: 1918 to 1946

The period between the First and Second World Wars witnessed the internationalisation of the *Wisden* award. The proportion of Cricketers of the Year provided by overseas touring teams rose from 15% in 1889–1915 to 24.5% between 1922 and 1940. This increase reflected the rapid growth in Test tours: intermittent until 1927, they were thereafter annual events, with West Indies (1928), New Zealand (1931) and India (1932) all joining the rota of Test visitors to England.

England Test players were themselves more heavily represented. Whereas only 12.2% of English players chosen as Cricketers of the Year in 1889–1915 had appeared in Tests during the previous season, that figure now rose to 33 out of 73, or 45.2%. All five cricketers chosen for the 1938 Almanack had played Tests for England the summer before, the first time this had happened. In addition to the 33, another 15 English players were chosen for major winter tours. In 1929, all of *Wisden*'s Five had been chosen for what proved to be a triumphant tour of Australia under Percy Chapman during the 1928-29 winter (the Almanack went to press before the outcome of the series was known).

Despite the shift in emphasis, only three Test XIs during this period consisted solely of former Cricketers of the Year – the England sides that took the field against Australia at Sydney in December 1924, and at Lord's and Leeds in 1930. (Various England XIs on the 1924-25 and 1928-29 Ashes tours came close to providing full complements, but for one or two players named in the 1925 and 1929 Almanacks respectively).

However, those Cricketers of the Year drawn from domestic teams were more than ever representative of home-grown English talent, the only exceptions being two young Indians, K. S. Duleepsinhji and the Nawab of Pataudi senior, who had refined their batting skills at Cambridge and Oxford Universities. Both opted to play first for England, though Pataudi later captained India. No overseas players were chosen while playing for counties (although Ted McDonald spent several seasons at Lancashire after being picked as a member of the 1921 Australian touring team).

This period also saw a strong growth in the award's popularity and reputation. By 1923, *The Times* was describing the "honour of the photograph" as the highest in the power of the editor to bestow. The identity of the Five had begun to generate lively debate in cricketing circles during the winter months, and made the publication of *Wisden* an event in itself. *The Times* greeted the 1932 Almanack with an article containing the cross-heading "The Chosen Five", and the words "They are at last known". The players themselves were starting to regard selection as a privilege. "That it is an honour greatly appreciated no one talking with first-class cricketers can possibly doubt," wrote A. S. Dixon in an article on the Cricketers of the Year published in the 1945 *Wisden*.

The editorship changed several times between the wars, leading to changes in presentation. Following Sydney Pardon's death in 1925, the editor was successively C. Stewart Caine (1926–33), Sydney J. Southerton

(1934–35), Wilfrid H. Brookes (1936–39) and Haddon Whitaker (editor from 1940–43, but the selector of only one Five before war led to a suspension in play). Under Caine the length of the biographical entries almost doubled from 1927 to 1930 – from a total of four pages to almost seven. Even though Caine remained editor for another three years, the writing of the biographies then passed to Southerton, who filled nearly ten pages in 1931 and 12 in 1935, which was the second and last year of his own editorship. Brookes, who oversaw a general rationalisation of the Almanack's contents, cut the entries back to seven or eight pages but also moved them to the front of the book, making the Cricketers of the Year the first feature readers came to. He also abandoned the practice of five medallion portraits appearing on one page; instead each player was given a small headshot alongside their respective entries, which were arranged alphabetically. Some critics felt this layout looked less dignified – and it would not in fact last long.

Of the 73 English cricketers chosen by *Wisden* (including Duleepsinhji and Pataudi), only 21 were amateurs, or 28.8%, compared to 40% in 1889–1915. In the seven years from 1932 to 1938, only four English amateurs were selected – Pataudi, Freddie Brown, Cyril Walters and Errol Holmes. And perhaps the most striking single omission by *Wisden* during the period was that of Gubby Allen, whose appearances for Middlesex were severely limited by business commitments but who nevertheless clocked up 22 Tests between 1930 and 1937 (plus three more in 1947-48), and captained England on an Ashes tour of Australia. Allen himself long maintained that he should have been chosen by *Wisden*.

If the lengths varied, the style of entries remained much the same – factual and pretty strait-laced, but even-handed in judgement and not sparing in criticism if shortcomings were evident. The practice of beginning each entry with the player's full name, and place and date of birth, continued – and sometimes sprang a surprise, as in the case of Jim Smith in 1935. Smith had always been referred to in *Wisden's* scorecards as "Smith, J." (professionals always had their initials placed after their name), and would continue to be so, but the start of his Cricketer of the Year entry revealed that he possessed a much longer name: "Cedric Ivan James Smith, more generally known as Smith, J., of Middlesex…"

Caine appears to have begun the practice of contracting out the writing of some of the biographical essays (although there is nothing to suggest he did not pick the Five). In 1928, for the first time, an author other than the editor was credited with writing a profile: J. A. H. Catton, a former long-serving editor of the Manchester-based *Athletic News* who closely followed Lancashire cricket, contributed the entry on Charles Hallows. The following year, it appears that all five profiles – which were relatively short in length – were written by F. B. Wilson, whose name appeared after the final entry. Caine then handed over the writing of all biographies to Southerton in 1931, 1932 and 1933. As editors, Southerton and Brookes apparently wrote them themselves, but Whitaker – primarily a publisher who acted as caretaker editor – almost certainly commissioned someone else to write the profiles for the 1940 edition, as he did the Notes.

The award was spread more evenly among the counties than had been the case in 1889–1915. Five counties won the Championship (Yorkshire 12 times, Lancashire five, Middlesex two, Derbyshire one, Nottinghamshire one) but they claimed only 33 Cricketers of the Year compared to the 39 secured by the 12 counties that didn't. Sussex, Surrey and Gloucestershire, who all finished runners-up at various times but were never champions, produced 18 Cricketers of the Year between them. In no year did any county have more than two representatives. Somerset (in 1925), Leicestershire (1927) and Worcestershire (1934) all had their first picks for 23 years. Derbyshire in 1934 had their first for 28 years – then added three more in as many years.

Apart from Gubby Allen, other significant performers who played predominantly during this period, and might have been chosen but weren't, included Jack O'Connor of Essex, who scored 28,764 first-class runs in his career; Alf Dipper, of Gloucestershire, who scored 28,075; and the Lancashire trio of Harry Makepeace, Frank Watson and Jack Iddon, all of whom topped 22,000 runs. Dave Nourse scored 1,924 runs in 45 Tests for South Africa between 1902 and 1924 but was never picked (though his son Dudley was chosen in 1948). Hampshire's Jack Newman, who scored more than 15,000 runs,

CRICKETERS OF THE YEAR 1918–40
(Teams they represented in the English season prior to selection)

Team	Years	Awards	Batsmen	Bowlers	Allrounders	WK
Yorkshire	1920-40	10	5	4	0	1
Nottinghamshire	1923-40	7	4	3	0	0
Sussex	1924-39	7	2	2	3	0
Surrey	1920-37	6	4	1	1	0
Lancashire	1920-38	6	3	2	0	1
Middlesex	1920-40	6	3	2	1	0
Gloucestershire	1923-38	5	3	2	0	0
Kent	1922-40	4	1	2	0	1
Essex	1922-39	4	2	1	1	0
Derbyshire	1934-37	4	2	1	1	0
Somerset	1925-36	3	1	1	1	0
Glamorgan	1927-31	2	1	1	0	0
Leicestershire	1927-33	2	0	0	2	0
Northamptonshire	1928-34	2	1	0	1	0
Warwickshire	1930-35	2	1	1	0	0
Hampshire	1933	1	0	0	1	0
Worcestershire	1934	1	1	0	0	0
Cambridge University	1922	2	2	0	0	0
Oxford University	1931-32	2	1	1	0	0
England	1925-40	33	15	10	6	2
Australians	1922-39	11	6	3	1	1
South Africans	1925-36	5	4	0	0	1
New Zealanders	1928-32	2	1	0	1	0
Indians	1933-37	2	1	0	1	0
West Indians	1934-40	2	1	0	1	0
Public Schools	1918-19	10	2	6	1	1
TOTAL		**141***	**67**	**43**	**23**	**8**

*In total, there were 105 Cricketers of the Year between 1918 and 1940. However, the figure of 141 awards shown in the table reflects the fact that thirty-four players appeared for two teams during the season in question (32 for a county plus Tests for England; 2 for a university and county). One player, Ian Peebles, appeared for three teams (university, county and England)

took more than 2,000 wickets and did the double five times, missed out, as did Reg Perks of Worcestershire, who retired in 1955 with 2,233 wickets to his name.

Arthur Mailey, who took 260 first-class wickets with his leg-breaks and googlies on Australia's 1921 and 1926 tours combined, including 26 in eight Tests, was not chosen. Nor was another Australian, Chuck Fleetwood-Smith, a left-arm wrist-spinner who captured 194 wickets on the 1934 and 1938 tours.

Aside from the schoolboys chosen in 1918 and 1919, the youngest Cricketers of the Year during this period were three batsmen – Denis Compton (aged 20), and Len Hutton and Tuppy Owen-Smith (both 21). The oldest were two bowlers picked in 1933, Ewart Astill (45) and Alex Kennedy (42). Arthur Wood, a wicketkeeper, was picked at 40, as was another bowler in Charlie Parker, a member in 1923 of the oldest-ever quintet (average age 34).

War or misfortune scarred many of these lives. George Geary, Jack Mercer, Andrew Sandham and Roy Kilner were all wounded during the First World War; Bert Oldfield survived being buried alive at Ypres in 1917. Dodger Whysall died of septicaemia aged 43, Ted McDonald in a car accident aged 46, and Lionel Hedges of influenza at 32. Fred Bakewell's career was ended by a car crash, and Vallance Jupp was sentenced to nine months in jail after killing a motorcyclist while at the wheel of his car. Andy Ducat died while batting at Lord's, and the Nawab of Pataudi senior while playing polo in Delhi. Enteric fever killed Kilner at 37 and Jock Cameron at 30; Cameron is the only person to be posthumously named a Cricketer of the Year (Dick Pilling died in 1891 three months *after* being chosen). George Macaulay, Hedley Verity, Maurice Turnbull and Kenneth Farnes all died on service during the Second World War.

1918

School Bowlers of the Year

Clement Gibson (Eton) ●
Harry Calder (Cranleigh) ●
John Firth (Winchester) ●
Gerard Rotherham (Rugby) ●
Greville Stevens (University College School) ●

AFTER A SUSPENSION OF TWO YEARS, WISDEN restored its Cricketers of the Year. The carnage continued on the Western Front – this issue of the Almanack alone recorded the deaths of more than 400 cricketers – and the first-class game remained in abeyance, but Sydney Pardon decided to select five players from the leading public schools which were still fulfilling fixtures.

It was a poignant act, designed to lift spirits among the wider public and at the public schools, where former pupils were suffering particularly high losses in battle. "So much interest was taken in the matches that I thought portraits of some of the leading players [from the public schools] would lend attraction to a necessarily rather gloomy *Wisden*," Pardon explained in his Preface.

In theory, there would have been nothing to stop *Wisden* choosing players from the leagues that were active. However, since May 1916 all men aged between 18 and 41 had been under mandatory conscription, so selecting adults would have drawn attention to those exempted from service, and might have been contentious.

While the Five schoolboys (all picked for their bowling) no doubt performed creditably in 1917, the name of only one – Greville Stevens, who played ten Tests for England, one as captain – would resonate with later generations.

Of the others, only Clem Gibson and Gerard Rotherham managed even one full season of county cricket. John Firth appeared in two matches for Nottinghamshire, while Harry Calder – uniquely for a Cricketer of the Year – never played at first-class level. In fact Gibson, Rotherham and Calder all moved overseas in 1921.

Stevens, who averaged 58.18 with the bat and 8.65 with his leg-breaks and googlies for UCS, was to rise fast. In 1919, his final year at school, he scored 466 in a house match, returned match figures of ten for 136 on debut for Middlesex, and was chosen for the Gentlemen at Lord's. The following year, outside term at Oxford, he helped Middlesex win the Championship with 44 wickets and 440 runs in 11 matches.

Overall, though, Stevens's Test career was a disappointment. He did little on two tours of South Africa, deputising unsuccessfully as captain in the final Test of 1927-28; needing only a draw to take the series, England lost heavily. His one notable performance came

SCHOOL BOWLERS OF THE YEAR

G.T.S. STEVENS
University College
School.

J.E.D'E. FIRTH
Winchester.

C.H. GIBSON
Eton.

G.A. ROTHERHAM
Rugby.

H.L. CALDER
Cranleigh.
School.

in the Caribbean in 1930, when he took ten wickets in Barbados.

Gibson was rated the standout bowler. He might have been a significant swing bowler but soon lost pace, and after leaving Cambridge returned to his native Argentina. By taking six for 64 to help a makeshift England XI inflict the only defeat on the 1921 Australians, he won the lasting support of his captain Archie MacLaren [1895], who was the prime mover behind a controversial invitation to Gibson to join the Ashes tour of 1924-25 even though he had not been involved in county cricket. Gibson sensibly declined.

Along with Stevens, Rotherham – who with bat and ball averaged 47.42 and 11.75 – was rated the best all-rounder. After leaving Rugby he won Blues at Cambridge in 1919 and 1920 before taking 88 wickets with his fast-medium bowling for Warwickshire the following season. He then emigrated to New Zealand, where he played a few games for Wellington.

Firth, who bowled brisk leg-breaks, took eight for 48 against Harrow and all ten for 41 against Eton; *Wisden* said that what he lacked in an ungainly action he made up for in brains

and determination. His main handicap was severe short-sightedness; he wore pebble-stone glasses which tended to steam up the more he bowled, and he was never going to play regular serious cricket. He became a schoolmaster and chaplain at Winchester College, and later Master of the Temple and Canon Emeritus at Winchester Cathedral.

Calder, whose father played for Hampshire in the 1880s, was born in South Africa but moved to England for his schooling. With his off-spin he finished top of Cranleigh's bowling averages for the third year in a row. Not turning 17 until January 1918, and being a few days younger than Stevens, he was – and remains – the youngest person chosen as a Cricketer of the Year. He appeared for Surrey's Second XI in 1920 while working for Barclays Bank, but gave up the game after being transferred to Johannesburg. Calder was unaware he had been chosen by *Wisden* until tracked down in Cape Town a year before his death, in 1995, aged 94.

Had they been born two years earlier, this Five might all have died in the war. As it was, they lived to an average age of 76.

G.T.S. Stevens

CRICKETERS OF THE YEAR 1918 – Performances in the English season 1917

Name	Age*		Matches	Runs	Bat ave	Wickets	Bowl ave	Catches (Ist)
HL Calder	17	School		163	20.37	36	10.08	
JED'E Firth	18	School		2	2.00	29	6.55	
CH Gibson	17	School		92	18.40	43	9.97	
GA Rotherham	18	School		332	47.42	36	11.75	
GTS Stevens	17	School		640	58.18	66	8.65	

as at 1/4/1918

1919

Five Public School Cricketers of the Year

Norman Partridge (Malvern) 🖊 ●
Percy Adams (Cheltenham) 🏏
Percy Chapman (Uppingham) 🖊
Adrian Gore (Eton) ●
Lionel Hedges (Tonbridge) 🖊

WITH THE WAR CONTINUING, THOUGH NEAR AN end, *Wisden* again chose five public-school cricketers – this time two batsmen, an all-rounder, a bowler and a wicketkeeper. Again, only one of the Five would make a lasting name for himself – Percy Chapman, who captained England in two successful Ashes series – although *Wisden* might have considered several other schools cricketers who went on to enjoy significant careers.

These included two future Cricketers of the Year in Beverley Lyon [1931] and Douglas Jardine [1928]. Lyon was described by *Wisden* as "a brilliant player" at Rugby in 1918, but Jardine, in his third year at Winchester, was reckoned to have "hardly improved as much as expected".

Chapman was a key figure in the revival of English cricket in the 1920s. Standing 6ft 3in, he was a left-handed batsman of effortless power, and a breathtaking catcher, who played with rare enthusiasm and self-confidence. These were necessary qualities if England were to turn the tide against Australia's might.

Even so, it came as a surprise when the untested Chapman was summoned as captain for a must-win Test in 1926, but he had the belief to get the job done and later led a happy team to a 4–1 victory in Australia in 1928-29. He won his first nine Tests as captain, and overall lost only two out of 17.

The son of a schoolteacher, Chapman was a dominant batsman at Uppingham, and rose so easily through the ranks that he appeared in six Tests before qualifying for Kent. He scored a century on debut for Cambridge in 1920 and two years later cemented his star status with centuries at Lord's in the Varsity Match and for Gentlemen v Players. Sydney Pardon once wrote that Chapman had "the genius of the game in him".

Chapman married the sister of Tom Lowry, a Cambridge contemporary and New Zealand's first Test captain, and became a prominent celebrity, funding his lifestyle through work for a Kent brewery, something which may not have helped his cricket. His defence was too loose for consistent performances at Test level. A swashbuckling 121 at Lord's in 1930 was his only century, and he was replaced as captain after averaging 10.71 during a 1–0 defeat in South Africa the following winter.

FIVE PUBLIC SCHOOL CRICKETERS OF THE YEAR

A.C. GORE
Eton

A.P.F. CHAPMAN
Uppingham.

N.E. PARTRIDGE.
Malvern

P.W. ADAMS.
Cheltenham

L.P. HEDGES.
Tonbridge

Chapman spent the next six years leading Kent but, deprived of the limelight, his game deteriorated, and in retirement he sank into alcoholism and depression.

Norman Partridge, another product of Malvern, was the star all-rounder of 1918 with 514 runs at 102.80 and 32 wickets at 11.56. In some matches he was irresistible with both bat and ball – 229 not out and 11 wickets against Repton, and centuries and five-fors in two matches against Cheltenham. *Wisden* described him as "quite the hero of the school season… very few in any year have approached him".

In 1919 Partridge was invited to represent the Gentlemen at The Oval, but Malvern refused him leave. He subsequently spent one year at Cambridge – where he played alongside Chapman – before embarking on a long career with Warwickshire, appearing frequently at first but later seldom for more than a few matches a season. His main value was as a bowler, although *Wisden*'s obituary highlighted doubts about his methods: "Bowling fast-medium in-swingers, he had… a rather ugly action which, though he was never no-balled, was regarded by some as slightly suspect."

Lionel Hedges was, like Chapman, a gifted batsman and fine fielder. In 1919, in his last year at Tonbridge, he scored 1,038 runs as captain and first played for Kent; in 1920, he won his Blue at Oxford as a freshman and scored a match-winning Championship century against Yorkshire. He had another solid year in 1921. However, after leaving university he took up teaching in Cheltenham and was restricted to occasional appearances for Gloucestershire. Praised for his exceptional personality, he was an accomplished amateur stage actor, and appeared in the 1931 film *Tell England*. He died two years later of influenza, aged just 32.

Adrian Gore had striking success with his fast-medium inswing bowling for Eton, demolishing a string of opposition line-ups and finishing the season with 40 wickets at 7.95 apiece. Embarking on a career in the army with the Rifle Brigade in 1919, he never played county cricket, but did make occasional first-class appearances for the Army between 1921 and 1932. He rose to the rank of Brigadier, and was awarded the DSO.

Not many Cricketers of the Year laid more tenuous claim than Percy Adams, the Cheltenham wicketkeeper. *Wisden* was impressed by his neatness behind the stumps, but pointed out a rather unfortunate failing in a gloveman, that "he gets his hands damaged rather easily". As a batsman he was nothing out of the ordinary, averaging 15.57 in 1918 with a top score of 35. Adams made one appearance for Sussex, against Cambridge University in 1922, when the county's first-choice keeper George Street played as a batsman.

A. P. F. Chapman

CRICKETERS OF THE YEAR 1919 – Performances in the English season 1918

Name	Age*		Matches	Runs	Bat ave	Wickets	Bowl ave	Catches (/st)
PW Adams	18	School		109	15.57			
APF Chapman	18	School		472	52.44	15	17.73	
AC Gore	18	School		32	4.00	40	7.95	
LP Hedges	18	School		632	63.20			
NE Partridge	18	School		514	102.80	32	11.56	

* as at 1/4/1919

1920 Five Cricketers of the Year

Patsy Hendren (Middlesex) *

Andy Ducat (Surrey) *

Percy Holmes (Yorkshire) *

Herbert Sutcliffe (Yorkshire) *

Ernest Tyldesley (Lancashire) *

HEADLINE EVENTS FROM 1919

- County champions – Yorkshire. Matches are played over two days for the only time

WITH THE RETURN OF COUNTY CRICKET IN 1919, *Wisden* picked five professional batsmen. It chose well. The five would score 540 first-class centuries in their careers – their tally was 43 at this point – and Patsy Hendren, Herbert Sutcliffe and Ernest Tyldesley would each finish as the leading all-time run-scorers for their counties (which they remain). Hendren and Sutcliffe were as tough and dependable cricketers as England have ever had.

In his Preface, Sydney described the selections of Hendren, Sutcliffe and Percy Holmes as "inevitable", saying that Hendren "rose to the rank of an England player" – he alone was picked for the 1920-21 Ashes tour – while as Yorkshire openers Holmes and Sutcliffe "made themselves the talk of the season".

Sutcliffe, by a distance the youngest of the Five at 25, had not played at first-class level before, but he had played plenty of league cricket during the war despite earning a regimental commission, and this helped his strong start. No one has ever bettered his 1,839 runs in a debut season.

Hendren, Tyldesley and Holmes, who all saw little or no military action, had similarly kept their cricket going (Tyldesley was stationed solely in the UK, because his commanding officer was keen on cricket), so it was unsurprising they managed strikingly better seasons than before the war.

They were all soon promoted to international level. While Hendren, who finished second in the national averages in 1920, was England's third-best Test run-scorer in Australia, Tyldesley, Holmes and Andy Ducat all made their England debuts at home in 1921. Sutcliffe had to wait until 1924, but then showed the ideal temperament for Test cricket. Nothing fazed him, as perhaps it wouldn't someone orphaned at the age of ten.

Wisden rightly predicted great things for him, but its assessment that his defence was not as strong as that of Holmes, his Yorkshire team-mate, sounds odd to modern ears. Few England batsmen have shown a better defence – and none has bettered Sutcliffe's Test average of 60.73 – but in these early days there were flaws to iron out; in 1920 and 1921 he averaged in the low thirties, before topping 2,000 runs for the next 14 seasons.

Sutcliffe formed two great opening partnerships: with Holmes for Yorkshire – who won the title on 12 occasions during Sutcliffe's time – and Jack Hobbs [1909] for England. It was not until his ninth match that Sutcliffe was promoted to open with Holmes, but in the rest of the season they shared five hundred partnerships. They shared 69 first-wicket century stands in their career, the highest a then-world record of 555; it still stands as the best for any wicket for an English side.

Hobbs and Sutcliffe blocked Holmes's path to a substantial England career, but he ought to have gone to Australia in 1920-21 to open with Hobbs after enjoying another fruitful season in 1920. He was chosen for the First Test of 1921 at home, but despite top-scoring in the first innings was promptly dropped. He did not return until 1927-28 when, in the absence of Hobbs, he partnered Sutcliffe in South Africa.

Like Holmes, Hendren – also a skilful footballer for several clubs – blossomed in post-war cricket into an attacking batsman willing to take on the fastest bowlers. The fourth of six children to Irish immigrants, Hendren was a popular figure, in his pomp in the early 1920s when he topped the national averages three times in four seasons, but durable enough to score a Test century in 1934 and the last of his 170 first-class hundreds in 1937, when he was 48.

Tyldesley – who shared a birthday with Hendren, a unique coincidence for two chosen in the same year – benefited from the coaching of J. T. Tyldesley [1902], his elder brother by 15 years, who played alongside him regularly for the last time in 1919 (finishing only slightly behind him in the averages). Ernest started the season slowly, before a golden run saw him amass 746 runs in six Championship matches, which in a one-off experiment were limited to two days.

Ernest subsequently took over Johnny's No. 3 spot for Lancashire, but despite a patient, dependable style he rarely got the chance to emulate his brother's success in that position for England, losing out to Frank Woolley [1911]. In his 14 Tests, he scored three centuries and averaged 55.00.

Ducat was a significant all-round sportsman who, in this same year as he was chosen by *Wisden*, captained Aston Villa to victory in the FA Cup final, and played three times for England at football (he won six caps in all). *Wisden* praised his stamina, saying: "Hard work seems to agree with him… he always looks a model of physical fitness."

Ducat scored four centuries in the space of eight matches for Surrey in 1919, including an unbeaten 306 against Oxford University. He was chosen for his sole Test at Leeds in 1921, but his fate – caught at slip as his bat disintegrated against the pace of Ted McDonald [1922] – symbolised England's inadequacy against Australian post-war might.

After retiring in 1931, Ducat went into coaching, working at Eton at the same time as Hendren was head pro at Harrow.

Andrew Ducat

Andrew Ducat:
"He always looks a model of physical fitness"

CRICKETERS OF THE YEAR 1920 – Performances in the English season 1919

Name	Age*		Matches	Runs	Bat ave	Wickets	Bowl ave	Catches (/st)
A Ducat	34	First-class	23	1695	52.96	2	44.00	20
EH Hendren	31	First-class	23	1655	61.29	17	42.29	20
P Holmes	33	First-class	32	1886	43.86			36
H Sutcliffe	25	First-class	31	1839	44.85			22
GE Tyldesley	31	First-class	24	1635	44.18	0		8

* as at 1/4/1920

Ernest Tyldesley

Herbert Sutcliffe:
"His record for a first-season man in big cricket must be almost without parallel"

Herbert Sutcliffe (on the left) and **Percy Holmes** in 1932

Patsy Hendren

1921 No award

A REMARKABLE CLIMAX TO THE 1920 COUNTY Championship, which saw Middlesex win their last nine matches to take the title, prompted Sydney Pardon to abandon the Five Cricketers of the Year in favour of a special photograph of Pelham Warner [1904] who, at the age of 46 and playing his last season, masterminded Middlesex's triumph. Warner left the field after the final game in a blaze of glory after Surrey were beaten with ten minutes to spare. "It was suggested that though he had already found a place in the *Wisden* portrait gallery there could be no more appropriate picture for this year's issue… than a special photograph of him at the end of his career," explained Pardon, who claimed that "no cricketer has ever had a more dramatic finish to a brilliant career".

There being no Test tour of England in 1920, interest focused on the Championship and on discussion of which players might be taken to Australia in the winter for the resumption of the Ashes. Several players who were never chosen as Cricketers of the Year did well. Harry Makepeace, an opening batsman with Lancashire, performed steadily enough to go to Australia, where he scored a century in the Fourth Test. Harry Lee, who during the war had been shot in the leg, declared dead, and taken prisoner, played some vital innings for Middlesex, including a century in the decider against Surrey. Laurence Cook, a medium-pacer with Lancashire, took 156 wickets at 14.88 each, while Abe Waddington won a tour place with 141 wickets at 16.72 for Yorkshire. Freddy Calthorpe, a future England captain, did the double in his first season as Warwickshire leader.

He died of heart failure while batting at Lord's during a Home Guard match in 1942. Holmes was released by Yorkshire in 1933 over concerns about his problems with lumbago, a decision that inspired members to force a vote of no confidence which the committee survived. Holmes later worked in mills around Huddersfield and coached at Scarborough College.

Tyldesley turned amateur in 1936 in a failed attempt to become Lancashire captain, while Sutcliffe grew wealthy through a sports-outfitting business and a managerial post in the paper trade.

HEADLINE EVENTS FROM 1920

• County champions – Middlesex

1922 Five Cricketers of the Year

Charlie Macartney (Australians) *
Hubert Ashton (Cambridge University and Essex) *
Jack Bryan (Cambridge University and Kent) *
Jack Gregory (Australians) * ●
Ted McDonald (Australians) ●

HEADLINE EVENTS FROM 1921

- County champions – Middlesex

- Glamorgan, the seventeenth county, take part in the championship for the first time

- Australia under Warwick Armstrong win the Test series 3-0, having months earlier beaten England 5-0 at home

JACK GREGORY AND TED MCDONALD WERE a fitting selection as the first pair of Test fast bowlers chosen in the same year. They terrorised England in 1921, throwing them into disarray from the first session of the series. Their combined hauls were 16 wickets at Trent Bridge, 13 at Lord's and 10 at Leeds, to deliver Australia three decisive victories. Precisely half their 46 victims were bowled.

They complemented each other well. The 6ft 4in Gregory, a farmer and natural athlete, bounded in before delivering the ball with a giant leap; it was never quite certain where he would make it land. McDonald, also tall but leaner, glided in on a sinuous run, posing less of a threat to the batsman's ribs but moving the ball around dangerously off a good length.

Gregory, a cousin of Syd Gregory [1897], had burst on to the scene during an Australian Imperial Forces tour in 1919. For two years he touched heights rarely matched by any all-rounder. A hard-hitting left-hand batsman, he meted out brutal punishment in the middle order and pulled off stupendous slip catches, but it was ferocious bowling that secured his reputation.

In the Ashes series in Australia that directly preceded the one in England, Gregory's return was 442 runs, 23 wickets and 15 catches (a record for any Test series), and in South Africa en route home from England he struck a century in 70 minutes, still the fastest Test hundred in terms of time. He would help Australia retain the Ashes in 1924-25, but was never so phenomenal again.

McDonald, the first Cricketer of the Year born in Tasmania, did not make his mark in state cricket until he was 24. He had done little in the series in Australia but was in his element in English conditions, and finished the tour as the leading wicket-taker. *Wisden* described him as the best of his type since Bill Lockwood [1899].

McDonald returned to England in 1922 after accepting an offer to play league cricket, and by 1924 had embarked on a brilliant career with Lancashire that brought 1,053 wickets in eight seasons and four Championship titles. His health was only moderate – he was a heavy smoker – but England's cooler climes suited him. He was killed in a car crash near Bolton aged 46.

If Gregory and McDonald demoralised England's batsmen, Charlie Macartney did the

The strong Australian team of 1921. Back row (l-r): Tommy Andrews, Bert Oldfield [1927], Jack Ryder, **Jack Gregory**, Edgar Mayne, Stork Hendry, **Ted Macdonald**, Clarence "Nip" Pellew. Seated: Warren Bardsley [1910], **Charlie Macartney**, Warwick Armstrong [1903] (captain), Herbie Collins, Arthur Mailey. On ground: Johnny Taylor, Hanson Carter

Charlie Macartney:

"Owing little or nothing to coaching he made himself a batsman by watching the big matches in Australia, and by persistent practice"

CRICKETERS OF THE YEAR 1922 – Performances in the English season 1921

Name	Age*		Matches	Runs	Bat ave	Wickets	Bowl ave	Catches (/st)
H Ashton	24	First-class	21	1294	39.21			24
JL Bryan	25	First-class	24	1858	50.21	9	41.77	11
JM Gregory	26	First-class	27	1135	36.61	116	16.58	37
		Tests	5	126	21.00	19	29.05	8
CG Macartney	35	First-class	31	2317	59.41	8	30.00	5
		Tests	5	300	42.85	0		1
EA McDonald	31	First-class	26	257	12.23	138	16.55	10
		Tests	5	92	46.00	27	24.74	1

as at 1/4/1922

same to their bowlers. Macartney, now in his mid-thirties, was transformed from the self-taught cricketer who had first appeared for Australia as an all-rounder; an audacious and quick-footed No. 3, he attacked any bowling, thinking nothing of late-cutting fast bowlers off his stumps. "A law unto himself – a triumph to individualism – he is not a model to be copied," *Wisden* said.

Macartney scored Australia's only century of the series, at Leeds, but his tour was chiefly remembered for an innings a week earlier in which he plundered 345 in four hours against Nottinghamshire. He returned to England in 1926 to score hundreds in three successive Tests, in one of which he emulated Victor Trumper [1903] by reaching a century before lunch on the first day.

Australia might have merited a fourth Cricketer of the Year. Wrist-spinner Arthur Mailey, who had captured 36 wickets in the Ashes series in Australia, followed up with 134 first-class wickets in England.

Sydney Pardon preferred to salve battered English pride. Hubert Ashton was one of the few English batsmen to have much success against the Australians, scoring 107 not out for Cambridge University, 90 for Essex, and a dashing 75 for an England XI that inflicted their only defeat of the tour.

Such accomplishment against good bowling was to be rare; Ashton's career record for Cambridge (2,259 runs, average 64.54) would owe much to the plundering of weak amateur attacks. A front-foot player, he did little in Championship cricket or for the Gentlemen, although he played little after leaving university and joining the Burmah Oil company.

Ashton – one of three brothers who captained Winchester and Cambridge, while a fourth appeared for Essex – had won the Military Cross during the war. He later married the sister of Hugh Gaitskell, the future Labour

leader, but served 14 years as a Conservative MP. He received a knighthood and had a term as MCC president.

Like Ashton, left-hander Jack Bryan went up to Cambridge late after the war; in 1921 he turned 25 (Ashton was 24) and finally broke into the side. In the space of eight matches for Cambridge and Kent he scored 1,030 runs, taking 231 off Surrey and 106 off Lancashire, and carrying his bat against Yorkshire.

This was his only full season. After taking up teaching at St Andrew's, Eastbourne, he played for Kent in the holidays, although he took leave to join the 1924-25 Ashes tour as reserve opener. Like Ashton, Bryan had brothers who played county cricket, and he captained two of them at Dover in 1925.

Jack Gregory:
"He was certainly faster than anyone else"

Hubert Ashton

Jack Bryan

1923

Five Cricketers of the Year

Jack Russell (Essex)
Arthur Carr (Nottinghamshire)
Tich Freeman (Kent)
Charlie Parker (Gloucestershire)
Andy Sandham (Surrey)

HEADLINE EVENTS FROM 1922

• County champions – Yorkshire

ALL THESE FIVE HAD SIGNIFICANT CAREERS. Arthur Carr captained England against Australia. Tich Freeman took 3,776 first-class wickets and Charlie Parker 3,278, placing them second and third on the all-time list. Andy Sandham scored 107 centuries and Jack Russell 71. Yet all experienced disappointment at the highest level, none enjoying an extended run with England.

With an average age of 34 at selection, they were the oldest Five ever chosen. Hampshire's Alex Kennedy [1933] was unlucky to miss out, after gathering 1,129 runs and 205 wickets in the season.

Freeman and Russell, as cousins, were the first relatives to be chosen in the same year. Cricket ran deep in the family: Freeman's uncle and Russell's father had played together for Essex in the 1890s, and Freeman's elder brother John was now Russell's opening partner at Essex, where Freeman himself started on the groundstaff before moving to Kent. Freeman's uncle also assisted in the development of Carr as the pro at Sherborne School.

The son of a stockbroker, Carr had assumed the Nottinghamshire captaincy after the war and retained it until his sacking in 1934 amid the fallout from Bodyline, a strategy he helped develop but later renounced. He played with the same gusto as Percy Chapman [1919], whose thirst for alcohol and the good life – if not matinee-idol looks – he shared, winning the loyalty of his players, who delivered him the Championship in 1929.

Carr had a good season for Nottinghamshire in 1922, but it was a hard-hitting innings of 88 for the Gentlemen at Lord's that won *Wisden*'s approval. By 1926, he was captaining England, but was replaced by Chapman for the deciding match of the series after a string of errors at Leeds (including leaving out Parker) and falling ill (some suspected of drink) at Manchester. He made a short-lived return as England captain in 1929.

Carr's Test debut came in South Africa in 1922-23, where Russell and Sandham opened the batting for a below-strength England side. These two might have opened in more Tests in another era, Russell especially. He had recently scored three hundreds against Australia, was the leading run-scorer of the 1922 season, and heroically battled illness to score twin centuries in the deciding, timeless Test in South Africa. "Judged

Tich Freeman lives up to his name, between two other Kent greats, Percy Chapman [1919] and Frank Woolley [1911]

Tich Freeman:

"It was an inglorious scramble. Freeman paralysed the batsmen"

Charlie Parker

Jack Russell

by results since the war he is an exceptional player and yet his batting lacks the quality that fascinates," said *Wisden*. "A master of on-side play, he is rather too utilitarian to rank among the great ones." In fact, he never played for England again.

Sandham had served in the Sportsman's Battalion of the Royal Fusiliers during the war, before being invalided home following an appendix operation. A largely self-taught player, he was expert in English conditions, forming a great opening partnership with Jack Hobbs [1909] for Surrey, but his England opportunities mainly came overseas in the absence of first-choice players. He made

only one Test fifty in South Africa, but his England career finished on an improbable high in Jamaica in 1929-30 when, nearly 40, he scored Test cricket's first triple-century, using a borrowed bat and ill-fitting boots.

Despite 400 wickets between them, neither Freeman nor Parker went to South Africa, where the Tests were played on matting. Alfred "Tich" Freeman (he stood only 5ft 2in) bowled straight and flat with heavy use of a top-spinner; many batsmen found him hard to score off and about half his wickets were taken bowled, lbw or caught and bowled. But the really good players were untroubled, and his record against strong

Arthur Carr

Arthur Carr:
"His straight-driving could almost have been described as the restoration of a lost art"

sides was unexceptional. He failed in the Ashes Tests of 1924-25.

But no bowler so regularly cut a swathe through ordinary county line-ups. In one Sussex innings in 1922 he took nine for 11 (17 for 67 in the match) and over the years he won Kent numerous matches, averaging 8.5 wickets in victories and routinely helping them finish in the Championship's top five (though never first). He was given a huge amount of bowling; inevitably, his rewards were plentiful. Of the top 11 hauls in an English season, Freeman owns six, including the all-time best of 304 in 1928.

Parker's brisk left-arm spin was also difficult to get away, and he too became the mainstay of his county's attack, although Gloucestershire weren't a force until the late 1920s. This may be one reason why he played only one Test (in 1921) and never joined a major tour, although he was neither athletic nor conciliatory. "He must at times have bewailed his luck in playing for a county so weak in batting," *Wisden* said. "No matter how cheaply he got the other sides out he could seldom hope to be rewarded by victory."

Parker was not a real force until his late thirties; he still took 200 wickets in a season five times (lastly at the age of 48), and remained successful into his fifties. In 1922, aged 39, he took nine for 36 against Yorkshire in his benefit match (hitting the stumps with five successive balls, one of which was a no-ball) and nine for 87 (eight bowled) against Derbyshire.

Freeman ran sports shops. Russell, Sandham and Parker went into coaching, umpiring or scoring in retirement, Russell dying in some poverty. Carr died aged 69 after collapsing while shovelling snow outside his home.

Andy Sandham (right) with his most famous opening partner, Jack Hobbs [1909]

CRICKETERS OF THE YEAR 1923 – Performances in the English season 1922

Name	Age*		Matches	Runs	Bat ave	Wickets	Bowl ave	Catches (/st)
AW Carr	29	First-class	33	1749	39.75	1	48.00	27/1
AP Freeman	34	First-class	28	237	13.16	194	14.63	12
CWL Parker	40	First-class	31	524	12.47	206	13.16	4
CAG Russell	35	First-class	32	2575	54.78	28	32.46	22
A Sandham	32	First-class	28	1875	46.87			3

* as at 1/4/1923

1924 Five Cricketers of the Year

Maurice Tate (Sussex) •
Arthur Gilligan (Sussex) •
Roy Kilner (Yorkshire) •
George Macaulay (Yorkshire) •
Cec Parkin (Lancashire) •

- County champions – Yorkshire

- England beat South Africa 2-1 in South Africa in 1922-23

- For the third time, a West Indies team tours England without playing Tests

TWO HEAVY POST-WAR DEFEATS TO AUSTRALIA had plunged English cricket into depression, but there were signs in 1923 of a bowling revival. Maurice Tate, it was clear, was a champion in the making, while Arthur Gilligan, Tate's captain and new-ball partner at Sussex, also inspired optimism, *Wisden* praising his energy, temperament and "varied gifts".

Wisden's selection looked sound. When England next took the field, at Edgbaston in June 1924, Gilligan was captain: he and Tate routed South Africa for 30, equalling the lowest Test score at the time. Tate took four for 12, including a wicket with his first ball for his country, and Gilligan six for seven. Roy Kilner and Cec Parkin were also in the XI. George Macaulay played in the Third Test of the series.

But this was an ill-fated group. Parkin, a lively and free-spirited character who had already written an autobiography, was unimpressed at being underbowled by his captain at Edgbaston, and promptly criticised Gilligan in a newspaper column, an act that cost him his place. He was never chosen again, and was denounced as a Bolshevik after calling for Jack Hobbs [1909], a professional, to captain England.

Not long after the Parkin incident, Macaulay, once described as "antagonism personified", blotted his copybook during an ill-tempered county match against Middlesex, and he – like Parkin – was a notable absentee from the winter tour of Australia led by Gilligan. Although he was one of the most successful bowlers in the country, Macaulay played only three more Tests.

Gilligan, meanwhile, was struck over the heart while batting in a Gentlemen–Players match and, unwittingly, did himself greater damage by continuing to score 112. He could act only as support bowler in Australia, and never again touched the heights of 1923, when he performed his only double, and 1924.

All this left Tate shouldering an immense burden in Australia, one he handled manfully to finish with 38 wickets in five Tests, but England went down 4–1.

Roy Kilner, a left-arm spinner and left-handed batsman whose right wrist was damaged during the war, was England's second-best bowler in Australia, but was tragically to die of enteric fever three years later, aged 37, with several more seasons in him. Kilner was a popular character, whose funeral drew a vast crowd in Barnsley. Macaulay died of illness while serving as an RAF pilot in 1940, aged 43.

Gilligan lived to 81, and remained long involved in the game as writer, commentator and administrator. One of his key contributions was encouraging the development of cricket in India while captaining MCC there in 1926-27. After his death his reputation was harmed by a controversy concerning his membership of the British Fascists in 1930.

Only Tate really fulfilled his promise, becoming the second England player after Wilfred Rhodes [1899] to do the double in Tests. Tate was not reckoned as quick through the air as Gilligan in 1923, but he made the ball nip off the pitch and either break back or go away. A spell of five wickets for no runs for England v The Rest marked him out as something special, and he finished the season with more than 1,000 runs and 200 wickets, a rare double he repeated in 1924 and 1925.

Tate beat Parkin to 200 wickets for the season by just two hours. While Tate's virtue was consistency, Parkin never stopped experimenting, mixing off-breaks with leg-breaks, top-spinners and moon-balls. "There is something fascinating in his ceaseless experiments," *Wisden* said.

Parkin learnt his craft in the northern leagues, and toured Australia in 1920-21, where he was England's best bowler, before taking up regular county cricket. When in 1926 Lancashire followed England by dispensing with his services, he went back to the leagues.

Kilner and Macaulay were key figures in Yorkshire winning the title with 25 wins and one loss. The county were short of bowlers after the war, and both came to their aid. Kilner was chiefly an aggressive batsman, but by 1922 he was topping 100 wickets a season, while the slightly built Macaulay, who could swing the new ball and spin the old, was recruited after turning in a job as a bank clerk in Kent.

Arthur Gilligan (right) tosses the coin in his first Test as England captain, in 1924, watched by South Africa's Herby Taylor [1925]

Macaulay took 101 wickets in 1921, and by 1922-23 was touring South Africa, where he vied for the new ball with Gilligan: like Tate he took a wicket with his first ball in Tests (he also hit the winning runs in a tight finish). Macaulay seemed happiest playing for his county, though life was rarely smooth. "His fault is that he is apt to become depressed and upset when things go wrong," *Wisden* stated. "His friends wish that he had a little more of Roy Kilner's cheerful philosophy."

All this Five belonged to cricketing families. Gilligan was the middle of three brothers who played together at Dulwich, the youngest of whom also captained England. Kilner's brother Norman had a long career with Yorkshire and Warwickshire. Tate's father had played one Test in 1902, and Parkin's son followed him into the Lancashire side. Macaulay's father played in the leagues.

George Macaulay

Roy Kilner

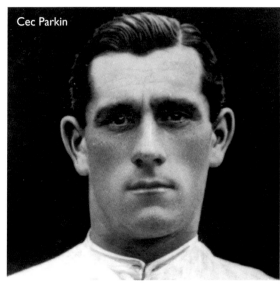
Cec Parkin

Arthur Gilligan:
"[He] has taken his place among the leading amateur cricketers of the day"

Maurice Tate

Maurice Tate:
"Nothing in last season's cricket was more striking or of better omen for the future than Tate's jump into fame as the best bowler of the year"

CRICKETERS OF THE YEAR 1924 – Performances in the English season 1923

Name	Age*		Matches	Runs	Bat ave	Wickets	Bowl ave	Catches (/st)
AER Gilligan	29	First-class	36	1183	21.12	163	17.50	17
R Kilner	33	First-class	36	1401	34.17	158	12.90	26
GG Macaulay	26	First-class	35	463	18.52	166	13.84	31
CH Parkin	38	First-class	35	581	14.17	209	16.95	18
MW Tate	28	First-class	36	1168	22.03	219	13.97	9

* as at 1/4/1924

1925

Five Cricketers of the Year

Jack MacBryan (Somerset and England) *

Bob Catterall (South Africans) *

Herby Taylor (South Africans) *

Dick Tyldesley (Lancashire and England) ●

Dodger Whysall (Nottinghamshire) *

- County champions – Yorkshire

- England, led by Arthur Gilligan, beat South Africa 3-0

HERBY TAYLOR WAS THE FIRST GREAT SOUTH African-born batsman. As captain of a moderate side, he had scored more than 500 runs against England in both the 1913-14 and 1922-23 series, in the first of which he countered Sydney Barnes [1910] at his best, as well as fashioning a win for Natal over MCC with scores of 91 and 100. Driven to distraction by Taylor's broad bat, Barnes at one point threw the ball to the ground and cried: "It's Taylor, Taylor, Taylor, all the time!"

No one played better on South Africa's matting pitches, but Taylor was less effective in Tests on English turf. In 1924, he had one good match against England, scoring two fifties at Leeds, but thanks to four centuries against weak teams he topped the overall tour averages. His selection therefore owed something to past achievements, which included winning the Military Cross during the Great War.

"It is no injustice to him to say that in this country last summer he fell far below the expectations of his friends," *Wisden* stated. "He made plenty of runs and played many a fine innings but the responsibility of captaining a losing side proved rather too much for him." This had not affected him before.

Taylor returned in 1929, aged 40, to score his only Test century in England, in the process becoming South Africa's leading Test run-scorer, a position he held until 1947.

Unlike Taylor, Bob Catterall, an enterprising young batsman and his side's leading fielder, kept his best for the Tests, scoring 120 at Edgbaston, 120 at Lord's and 95 at The Oval. A good all-round athlete, he like Taylor had learned the game from English coaches at school, in his case in Port Elizabeth before moving to the Transvaal. At home to England in 1927-28, he scored a match-winning 119 at Durban to clinch a 2–2 draw, and in the 1929 Tests had some success as a stodgy opener.

Dick Tyldesley, a rotund leg-spinner, took the England place vacated by fellow Lancastrian Cec Parkin [1924]. Tyldesley played four Tests and then toured Australia, where he struggled on the bone-hard surfaces and played only one Test .

Tyldesley won only two more caps, but he remained a successful bowler for Lancashire, helping them to four titles in five seasons. Statistically, 1924 was his best year in terms of wickets taken (184) and average (13.98), and he had some remarkable days, claiming 12 wickets in the match against the South Africans, seven for six against Northamptonshire, and five for none against Leicestershire.

A former colliery worker, Tyldesley was the youngest of four cricketing brothers from Westhoughton who were unrelated to Johnny and Ernest Tyldesley [1902 and 1920]; one brother died in the war, another in 1923. After falling out with Lancashire, Dick played in the leagues before running a pub, dying aged 46.

Jack MacBryan, who narrowly missed out on the Australian tour, was more technically accomplished than many amateurs, and regularly topped Somerset's averages. Short and strongly built, he played fast bowling well, and his success in dealing with Maurice Tate [1924], against whose Sussex side he scored two match-winning centuries, set him apart. When England experimented against South Africa after going 3–0 up, MacBryan deserved his debut, but the match was ruined by rain and he did not bat. He was not chosen again, and gave up regular county cricket in 1926.

MacBryan's life was colourful, if not always happy. Like Tyldesley, he had a

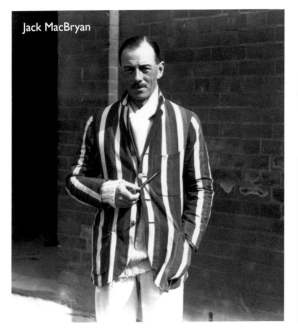

Jack MacBryan

Herby Taylor: "Taylor's style is so good and his back play so exceptionally strong that one never has the least doubt as to his class"

brother killed in action. He himself spent most of the war as a prisoner. In 1920, he won a cricket Blue at Cambridge, and took a hockey team gold medal at the Antwerp Olympics. Marriage to a Gaiety Girl proved short-lived, and a career on the Stock Exchange only left financial hardship through to his death aged 90.

William "Dodger" Whysall, who scored four centuries in ten days in June, was only one of many capable county opening batsmen, but as a part-time wicketkeeper he earned a place to Australia as reserve gloveman. In fact, after England went 2–0 down, he played three Tests purely as a batsman, and contributed 76 to the victory at Melbourne.

His reliability grew, and he topped 2,000 runs each season from 1926 to 1930, when he was recalled aged 42 against Australia for a timeless Test England needed to win (he scored 13 and 10). However, three months later he slipped on a dance floor, injured his elbow, and died within two weeks of septicaemia.

Whysall was the first of five Cricketers of the Year to attend Kirkby Woodhouse School in Nottingham, the others being Harold Larwood [1927], Sam Staples [1929], Bill Voce [1933] and Joe Hardstaff [1938].

Bob Catterall

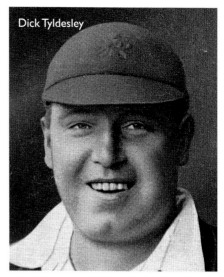
Dick Tyldesley

Dodger Whysall

CRICKETERS OF THE YEAR 1925 – Performances in the English season 1924

Name	Age*		Matches	Runs	Bat ave	Wickets	Bowl ave	Catches (/st)
RH Catterall	24	First-class	33	1329	28.27	6	44.16	11
		Tests	5	471	67.28	0		1
JCW MacBryan	32	First-class	26	1608	41.23			19
		Tests	1	0				0
HW Taylor	35	First-class	34	1898	42.17	3	28.66	13
		Tests	5	197	32.83			4
RK Tyldesley	28	First-class	36	618	18.72	184	13.98	36
		Tests	4	30	30.00	12	20.75	1
WW Whysall	37	First-class	28	1852	46.30	1	24.00	25/2

as at 1/4/1925

Dodger Whysall:
"In his style of play Whysall is a product of the new school"

1926 No award

For the third and last time, *Wisden* chose to celebrate one active cricketer, not five. As was the case with Pelham Warner in 1921, Jack Hobbs – now aged 42 – had already been a Cricketer of the Year, but it was felt that his remarkable achievements during the 1925 season demanded special treatment. A photograph bearing Hobbs's signature accompanied a two-page tribute to a season in which he scored a then-record 16 centuries, in the process overtaking the previously unrivalled career tally of 126 hundreds by Grace [1896]. It is likely that the decision to salute Hobbs was taken by Sydney Pardon before his death on November 20, 1925; his successor, C. Stewart Caine, who ensured the 1926 Almanack still came out on time, offered no clues, writing simply in his Preface: "Hobbs playing such wonderful cricket and enjoying the distinction of heading W. G. Grace's list of centuries, the customary picture of 'Five Cricketers of the Year' gives place to a full-page portrait of the great Surrey batsman."

There were no Tests in the 1925 season. Many of the leading performers were players who had been Cricketers of the Year in the past and a few who would be in the future. Those who were never chosen included Alf Dipper, a veteran with Gloucestershire aged 39, who scored 1,976 runs, and Frank Watson, 26, one of Lancashire's most valuable players, who made 1,730. Fred Root of Worcestershire took 219 wickets with his fast-medium bowling, and Glamorgan's slow left-armer Frank Ryan 139. Tiger Smith, who had been unlucky to miss out in 1913, had another good season for Warwickshire aged 39, allying 55 dismissals to his best year with the bat, scoring 1,477 runs with three hundreds. Smith, Watson and Root all went to the West Indies with MCC (a non-Test tour) in 1925-26.

HEADLINE EVENTS FROM 1925

- County champions – Yorkshire

- England lose the Test series in Australia 4-1 in 1924-25

1927

Five Cricketers of the Year

Harold Larwood (Nottinghamshire and England) ●

George Geary (Leicestershire and England) ● /

Jack Mercer (Glamorgan) ●

Bert Oldfield (Australians) �🏏

Bill Woodfull (Australians) /

ENGLAND REGAINED THE ASHES WITH AN EPIC victory at The Oval in 1926, and *Wisden* selected two heroes from that game in Harold Larwood, a young fast bowler of immense pace and promise, and George Geary, a resourceful cricketer who took three brilliant catches and the final wicket of the match. Earlier in the series, Geary's batting had saved the Leeds Test.

Both would go on to help England retain the Ashes in Australia in 1928-29 – Larwood was the match-winner in the First Test, while Geary topped the bowling averages and hit the runs that secured the series – but Larwood touched even greater heights four years later when, with rare speed and accuracy, he captured 33 wickets as England won 4–1 again, a victory forever compromised by their Bodyline tactics.

As it happened, the two Australians among this Five – both immense performers in their own right – were centre-stage when the Bodyline drama reached its peak in January 1933 at Adelaide, where Bill Woodfull was struck over the heart and Bert Oldfield, their fleet-footed wicketkeeper, hit on the head. Noble men, neither held it against Larwood.

Larwood was born in a Nottinghamshire colliery village, and his early work as a miner put strength into his 5ft 7½in frame. His rise was swift. His first match for Nottinghamshire was in 1924; two years later he had sealed his elevation to the England team by twice bowling Jack Hobbs [1909] in a county match. Sadly, Larwood's England career was over before he turned 30 when – entirely reasonably – he refused to apologise to MCC for his part in Bodyline. He later emigrated to Australia, where Oldfield and Woodfull counted among his friends.

"He gets great pace off the ground, probably because he has a perfect run up to the wicket, and at times makes the ball come back so much that he is almost unplayable," was *Wisden*'s assessment.

Armed with great guts and a straight bat, Woodfull played several courageous innings against Larwood both before and during the Bodyline series. It was after scoring his fourth century of the 1926 tour against Nottinghamshire that Woodfull was promoted to open in the Tests: he responded with 141 at Leeds and 117 at Manchester. *Wisden* named him as the most difficult Australian to bowl out.

HEADLINE EVENTS FROM 1926

- County champions – Lancashire

- England regain the Ashes, beating Australia by 289 runs at the Oval after four draws

Bert Oldfield

Bert Oldfield:

"Probably the best wicketkeeper in the world at the present day"

Bill Woodfull

Woodfull returned to England as captain in 1930 and 1934, and on both occasions regained the Ashes with a victory at The Oval completed on his birthday. After retiring with a first-class batting average of 64.99, he rose to headmaster at Melbourne High School.

Oldfield, who marked himself out as a great keeper during the 1924-25 Ashes, was said not to have made a mistake on the 1926 tour. "Neat, quiet and skilful, Oldfield showed himself as well-equipped a wicketkeeper as any side could desire," said *Wisden*. He kept with skill to fast bowlers and spinners, and remained Australia's No. 1 until 1937. His total of 54 Test caps was not bettered by any keeper until Godfrey Evans [1952] in 1954; his 52 stumpings remains a Test best.

Oldfield might not have played for Australia at all. Serving as a corporal, he was injured and buried alive for several hours at Polygon Wood during the third battle of Ypres in 1917. Stationed later in England, he was called up for an Australian Imperial Forces cricket tour there in 1919, and first showed his talent behind the stumps.

Geary, one of 16 children of a shoemaker, also escaped death during the war, when he was struck on his left shoulder and thigh by a propeller in 1914. He didn't return to his best as

CRICKETERS OF THE YEAR 1927 – Performances in the English season 1926

Name	Age*		Matches	Runs	Bat ave	Wickets	Bowl ave	Catches (/st)
G Geary	33	First-class	28	715	20.42	124	19.02	35
		Tests	2	45	22.50	3	62.66	4
H Larwood	22	First-class	31	451	12.88	137	18.31	11
		Tests	2	5	2.50	9	28.00	1
J Mercer	33	First-class	29	506	14.88	136	16.46	13
WAS Oldfield	32	First-class	21	303	18.93			21/19
		Tests	5	112	28.00			5/2
WM Woodfull	29	First-class	27	1672	57.65			17
		Tests	5	306	51.00			0

as at 1/4/1927

a player until 1922, but became one of the most tireless and versatile bowlers around, capable of moving the ball both ways through swing, seam or cut. He took 51 wickets inside three weeks in 1926, including 14 for 98 against champions-to-be Lancashire.

Geary took 12 for 130 in a Test at Johannesburg in 1927-28 before breaking down with an elbow problem that required career-saving surgery. He came back to tour Australia, and then take ten for 18 against Glamorgan in 1929, the best first-class figures in history at the time. He later coached Peter May [1952] at Charterhouse.

Jack Mercer

George Geary

Jack Mercer, also wounded badly enough in the war to be invalided out, was the first Glamorgan player to be named a Cricketer of the Year, six years after they were granted first-class status. Having previously finished at or near the foot of the table, Glamorgan were eighth in 1926, thanks to the bowling of Mercer and Frank Ryan.

Having given up on a faltering career with his native Sussex in 1922, Mercer developed into an accomplished swing bowler at his second home, becoming the first Glamorgan player to 1,000 wickets, and also taking all ten against Worcestershire in 1936. Mercer never played Test cricket but, along with Geary, he was taken on MCC's tour of India and Ceylon in 1926-27. He later became coach at Northamptonshire (for whom he made one emergency appearance aged 54) and a member of the Magic Circle.

Despite their wartime scrapes, Oldfield lived to 81, Geary to 87 and Mercer 94. Woodfull died aged 67 and Larwood at 90.

Harold Larwood

Harold Larwood:
"Few fast bowlers have jumped to the top of the tree more quickly"

1928

Five Cricketers of the Year

Walter Hammond (Gloucestershire) *

Roger Blunt (New Zealanders) * ●

Charles Hallows (Lancashire) *

Douglas Jardine (Surrey) *

Vallance Jupp (Northamptonshire) * ●

HEADLINE EVENTS FROM 1927

• County champions – Lancashire

• New Zealand tour England without playing Tests

FOUR OF THESE FIVE PICKED THEMSELVES. Wally Hammond's tally of 2,969 runs was the fourth-highest in a season since 1906, and included 1,000 before the end of May. Douglas Jardine's average of 91.09 had only once been bettered in an English summer, by Robert Poore [1900]. Charlie Hallows was, by 500 runs, the leading run-scorer for champions Lancashire, and Vallance Jupp – soon to be the first Cricketer of the Year to be imprisoned – performed the double with superior figures to Maurice Tate [1924].

Roger Blunt was something of a left-field pick, chosen for his all-round efforts for the New Zealanders on their first tour of Britain, their leading run-scorer and second-highest wicket-taker. Blunt's selection was partly recognition of his team losing only five out of 38 matches, a record that helped seal their promotion to Test cricket in 1930.

Hammond and Jardine were still making their way in the game – Hammond's first Test came on the 1927-28 tour of South Africa and Jardine's in the opening match against West Indies in 1928, when Hallows and Jupp were both briefly recalled by England after a gap of several years – but *Wisden* was in little doubt that both were destined for big things.

Quite how big, though, few could have imagined. They were to be central figures in the Ashes being won on the next two tours of Australia – Hammond with a record-breaking 905 Test runs in 1928-29, Jardine with his iron-willed execution of Bodyline in 1932-33.

As batsmen, their styles were very different. Hammond, who received his first coaching from John Tunnicliffe [1901] only after joining Gloucestershire, was attacking by instinct and armed with glorious cover-drives; Jardine, who was arguably over-coached at Winchester and Oxford, built his game on a watertight defence. As partners in England's middle order, they proved an ideal combination.

Hammond, the son of a soldier who died in the war, was educated at grammar schools in Portsmouth and Cirencester. He would establish himself as one of England's all-time greats, but before 1927 his record was unremarkable. He had not played in 1926 because of an unspecified illness (now thought to be venereal disease), and his career average was only 30.

Charles Hallows

At a time of overly cautious batting of the type favoured by Jardine and Hallows, Hammond's enterprise was admired. "Beautifully built and loose-limbed with strong and pliant wrists, Hammond is essentially a stylist in method, and moreover, a firm believer in making the bat hit the ball," enthused *Wisden*. In scoring 99 and 187 not out at Old Trafford – having struck an unbeaten 250 there in 1925 – he meted out rare punishment to Ted McDonald [1922].

Hammond, who became England captain after turning amateur in 1938, left an immense record as batsman (he held the Test run-aggregate record from 1937 until 1970), useful swing bowler and prehensile slip catcher, but inevitably suffered in comparison to Don Bradman [1931].

Jardine's own attempts to conquer Bradman with Bodyline were briefly successful, but ultimately cost him his career, the Establishment having no use for him when England and Australia next met. A fearless

Wally Hammond

Wally Hammond:
"Here we have in all likelihood one of the best professional batsmen of the future"

The first New Zealand team to play a Test in England, in 1931. Back row (l-r): Ian Cromb, Jack Kerr, Ken James, Ron Talbot, Lindsay Weir, Bill Merritt, Mal Matheson. Seated: Jack Mills, Curly Page, Tom Lowry (captain), Cyril Allcott, Stewie Dempster [1932]. On ground: **Roger Blunt**, Giff Vivian

player of fast bowling himself, Jardine did not devise leg-theory bowling but, armed with the bowlers to do so, was the person who applied it most rigorously.

Having recently qualified as a solicitor, Jardine could turn out only occasionally in 1927, but was a bolder player for it, scoring 1,002 runs in 11 matches. His five centuries included a masterly 123 for Gentlemen v Players.

Short, strong and tough, Jupp, who in 1922 left Sussex because Northamptonshire offered to employ him as secretary, had by 1933 accomplished the double ten times, a rock in a weak side. But the following year he was at the wheel of a car that struck and killed a young factory worker on a motorbike. Convicted of manslaughter, he was sentenced to nine months in jail. He resumed playing in 1936, but was a spent force.

Hallows, a prolific left-handed opener, was a key figure in Lancashire's Championship win, just as his uncle James Hallows [1905] had been when he was chosen. *Wisden* praised Charlie's style, but said he had "schooled himself to severe repression and inexhaustible patience". Hallows touched greater heights still in 1928, when he also reached 1,000 runs before the end of May, but that was his last big year; by 1932 his Lancashire career was over. He coached for 40 years up to his death.

Blunt, who was born in Durham, emigrated with his parents when he was six months old, his

Vallance Jupp (right) goes out to bat at the Scarborough Festival with Johnny Douglas [1915]

father being a university professor. He was still at school when he first played for Canterbury, originally as a leg-spinner but later as an all-rounder. He played in New Zealand's first nine Tests, and struck the first triple-century in New Zealand first-class cricket in 1931-32.

In retirement, Blunt spent much time in England as a successful businessman, in advertising and confectionery. Hammond, who struggled financially in later life, emigrated to South Africa with his second wife and spent his last 14 years there. Jardine died of cancer in Switzerland in 1958.

Douglas Jardine

Douglas Jardine:
"Above everything else stands out his splendid defence: the manner in which he watches the ball right on to the bat, stamps him at once as an accomplished player"

CRICKETERS OF THE YEAR 1928 – Performances in the English season 1927

Name	Age*		Matches	Runs	Bat ave	Wickets	Bowl ave	Catches (/st)
RC Blunt	27	First-class	25	1540	44.00	77	25.29	14
C Hallows	32	First-class	33	2343	75.58			14
WR Hammond	24	First-class	34	2969	69.04	20	44.20	46
DR Jardine	27	First-class	11	1002	91.09	3	36.00	7
VWC Jupp	37	First-class	27	1537	39.41	121	20.42	12

* as at 1/4/1928

1929

Five Cricketers of the Year

Jack White (Somerset and England) ●

Leslie Ames (Kent) ▥

George Duckworth (Lancashire and England) ▥

Maurice Leyland (Yorkshire and England) ❘

Sam Staples (Nottinghamshire) ●

HEADLINE EVENTS FROM 1928

- County champions – Lancashire

- West Indies play their first Tests in England, losing all three

- England draw 2-2 in South Africa in 1927-28

By the time Wisden went to press early in 1929, England had already retained the Ashes by winning the first three Tests in Australia. High on glory – "not for 17 years has the reputation of English cricket stood as high as at the present moment" – the editor C. Stewart Caine picked as his Five the only members of the tour party not chosen before as Cricketers of the Year.

The logic was pretty crude. Sam Staples developed rheumatic trouble on the outward voyage and was sent home without playing a match. Les Ames was the reserve keeper, and did not play a Test. Too late for Wisden to take into account, Jack White took 13 wickets (more than half his series tally) in the Fourth Test at Adelaide, while Maurice Leyland scored 137 and 53 not out in the Fifth on his only appearance.

There were other candidates. The 1928 English season provided a bumper harvest for numerous batsmen, including Frank Watson and Alf Dipper, both of whom might have been picked in 1926; their returns of 2,583 and 2,365 runs respectively were the largest seasonal aggregates to this point by players never chosen as Cricketers of the Year. Jack Newman completed his fifth double for Hampshire, and Learie Constantine [1940] did the double for the first West Indian touring team to play Tests in England.

That said, each of the Five had good seasons; had they not done so, they would hardly have toured. Ames was a standout player at the age of 23: he became the first to perform the wicketkeeper's double, scoring 1,919 runs and executing 122 dismissals (in itself then a record). He would repeat the feat in 1929 (with 128) and 1932. Many of his catches and stumpings came off Tich Freeman [1923], to whom he crouched very low.

Wisden rightly suggested that Ames might become the best wicketkeeper-batsman England had ever had; in fact when he finished, his batting average in Tests in which he kept wicket (43.40) was 13.19 clear of any other regular keeper from any country. His record of eight Test centuries as keeper was not bettered until Andy Flower [2002] went past him in 2000. Ames remains the only specialist wicketkeeper to score 100 first-class centuries.

Duckworth held off Ames's challenge to the position of England's No. 1 until 1931. His best

All *Wisden's* Five for 1929 came from the England team which won the Ashes the previous winter. Back row (l-r): **George Duckworth**, **Les Ames**, Philip Mead [1912], Maurice Tate [1924], Patsy Hendren [1920]. Middle: **Maurice Leyland**, **Sam Staples**, Wally Hammond [1928], Francis Toone (manager), Herbert Sutcliffe [1920], Harold Larwood [1927], Tich Freeman [1923]. Front: Ernest Tyldesley [1920], **Jack White**, Percy Chapman [1919] (captain), Douglas Jardine [1928], Jack Hobbs [1909]

first-class score in 504 matches was 75, but he was good in a crisis, a key figure in Lancashire's three titles from 1926 to 1928, and *Wisden* rated him the best keeper in the country to all bowling in 1928, when he also topped 100 dismissals. Although small, he was skilled at standing back to express fast bowlers. He had trialled at Warwickshire before getting his chance at Old Trafford in 1923, but within a year was playing his first Test. England have had few noisier men behind the stumps.

Leyland, the son of a former league professional, was playing Lancashire League cricket at 14, but was a late developer for Yorkshire, not scoring a century until he was 24. His figures were modest by the run-drenched standards of 1928, but he got a game when England rang the changes for the final Test. He was out for nought, but went to Australia anyway, and his century at Melbourne confirmed his big-match temperament. Seven of his nine Test centuries came against Australia, including three in 1934 when, as the principal left-hander, he was superb against the varied leg-spin of Clarrie Grimmett [1931] and Bill O'Reilly [1935]. Armed with courage and a dry wit, Leyland was the first in a noble line of gritty England middle-order lefties.

One of only three amateurs on the Australia tour, White, who came from Somerset farming stock, had been a prolific wicket-taker since 1919 – he remains his county's leading wicket-taker –

Les Ames:

"He may become the best wicketkeeper-batsman that England has ever had"

but had previously played only two Tests. His experience was invaluable, few bowlers being better at setting a challenge on any type of pitch. He finally found rich rewards in the furnace-like conditions of Adelaide, where his second-innings eight for 126 clinched victory by 12 runs. "I used a few shirts and whiskey-and-sodas," he said.

White led England in the final Test, and in three more matches against South Africa in 1929. He remained England's first-choice left-arm spinner until the emergence of Hedley Verity [1932].

Like White, Staples – the elder of two long-serving brothers at Nottinghamshire – was adept at keeping things tight with his medium-pace cutters. He was an ideal foil at his county for Harold Larwood [1927], whose colliery-town upbringing he shared. Staples played three Tests in South Africa in 1927-28, but he was not as effective on matting as had been hoped. In all first-class cricket he took more than 1,300 wickets. He retired after the 1933 season to coach Nottinghamshire, and after the war briefly fulfilled a similar role at Hampshire, where he recruited Derek Shackleton [1959].

This group lived and breathed the game. Duckworth became a baggage man to various Test touring parties. Ames acted as England selector and tour manager, and as Kent's

Jack White

secretary-manager from 1960 to 1974. Leyland was Yorkshire's head coach from 1951 to 1963, during which time the county produced eight Cricketers of the Year.

> Maurice Leyland:
> **"He has a beautiful drive past extra cover and can hit the too far pitched-up ball straight back over the bowler's head"**

CRICKETERS OF THE YEAR 1929 – Performances in the English season 1928

Name	Age*		Matches	Runs	Bat ave	Wickets	Bowl ave	Catches (/st)
LEG Ames	23	First-class	37	1919	35.53			70/52
G Duckworth	27	First-class	35	280	17.50			76/31
		Tests	1	7				2
M Leyland	28	First-class	33	1783	54.03	35	34.20	16
		Tests	1	0	0.00	1	6.00	0
SJ Staples	36	First-class	29	512	25.60	110	21.76	32
JC White	38	First-class	26	745	21.28	138	19.71	21
		Tests	1	21		3	17.66	1

as at 1/4/1929

1930 Five Cricketers of the Year

Bob Wyatt (Warwickshire and England)

Ted Bowley (Sussex and England)

K. S. Duleepsinhji (Sussex and England)

Tuppy Owen-Smith (South Africans)

Walter Robins (Middlesex and England)

HEADLINE EVENTS FROM 1929

- County champions – Nottinghamshire

- England beat South Africa 2-0

- England under Percy Chapman retain the Ashes 4-1 in Australia in 1928-29

ENGLISH AMATEUR BATTING HAD BEEN THROUGH a lean time in the 1920s, but *Wisden* could now salute Bob Wyatt and K. S. Duleepsinhji, both of whom scored more than 2,500 runs in 1929, and all-rounder Walter Robins, who did the double in his first full season of county cricket having, like "Duleep", left Cambridge the previous year. Wyatt scored 113 against South Africa at Old Trafford, the first Test century by an English amateur since the war.

Probably the most exhilarating hundred of the season was made by a young South African, Harold "Tuppy" Owen-Smith, an audacious batsman and brilliant fielder, playing what turned out to be his only series. Going into the final day at Leeds, a swift England victory looked certain, but 20-year-old Owen-Smith plundered 129, mainly in partnership with the tail. England still won, thanks in part to Ted Bowley's 46, but it was a close thing.

The Times regretted that *Wisden* did not find room for two more South Africans in "Nummy" Deane, the captain, and all-rounder Denys Morkel.

With several regulars unavailable, England gave debuts to eight players, including Duleep,

Robins and Bowley, who was 39. Wyatt, who had played three Tests in South Africa in 1927-28, was recalled.

But Duleep was given only the First Test. His uncle Ranjitsinhji [1897], who funded his upbringing, had been a contentious selection for England, and so now was Duleep, especially for a series against South Africa, where colour prejudice was entrenched. Despite six centuries for Sussex in 36 days he was chosen neither for England nor Gentlemen v Players. *Wisden* described the decisions as "unwise" and as a "surprise". "Scandalous" might have put it better.

Duleep was chosen, along with Bowley, for a winter tour of New Zealand (they scored Test centuries together at Auckland), but not for the trip to South Africa in 1930-31, even though he had confirmed his talent by scoring 173 in his first Test against Australia in 1930. In his 12 Tests he averaged 58.52 but, laid low by pulmonary tuberculosis in 1932, he played his last first-class match aged 27. Having scored 50 first-class hundreds in eight years, he was still rated by many as the best amateur batsman in England between the wars.

Ted Bowley

Wyatt, the scion of the architectural Wyatt dynasty and cousin to Woodrow Wyatt (later an MP and journalist), was described by *Wisden* as "rather retiring" in nature, but he captained England 16 times, first in the final Test of 1930 as a controversial replacement for Percy Chapman [1919]. He later succeeded Douglas Jardine [1928], to whom he had deputised during Bodyline. More available than many amateurs, he undertook six major tours.

Though painstakingly thorough as leader and batsman, Wyatt lost three big series as captain, but was unlucky with injuries. One of the greatest fighting cricketers England ever had, at various times he fractured his jaw, toes, ribs, thumb, fingers and wrist. He scored only two hundreds in 40 Tests, but in a first-class career that lasted until 1951 he totalled 39,405 runs and 901 wickets as a change bowler.

Robins was as enthusiastic and joyous as Wyatt was dour, but despite 612 runs and 64 wickets in 19 Tests was rarely a regular. Despite expensively dropping Don Bradman [1931] during the 1936-37 Ashes series (prompting

Bob Wyatt

Walter Robins

Bob Wyatt:
"Wyatt, as he has often shown, is essentially the cricketer for a big occasion"

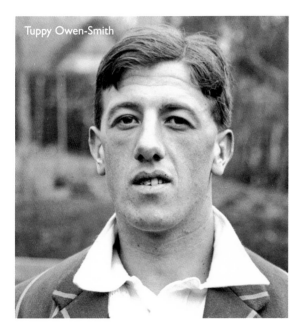
Tuppy Owen-Smith

K. S. Duleepsinhji

three seasons under Robins at Middlesex while at St Mary's Hospital. He developed into a useful bowler, but rugby became his primary sport: he represented England ten times as an outstanding attacking full-back, captaining them during the 1937 home championship.

Bowley had been a steady scorer for Sussex since rejoining them in 1920 out of the army. He topped 1,500 runs in every season bar one, and in 1929 passed 2,000 for the third successive year as well as taking 79 wickets. His best game came against Gloucestershire at Hove, where he scored 78 and 280 not out before claiming six for 31 with his leg-breaks to win the match with minutes to spare. He shared a first-wicket stand of 490 with John Langridge [1950] against Middlesex in 1933, then the third-highest partnership in first-class cricket.

Bowley went into coaching, while Wyatt and Robins became influential in selection, tour managership and administration, although Robins's track record was as chequered as it had been as a player. Wyatt died aged 93. Duleep and Owen-Smith had little more to do with cricket: Duleep joined the Indian Foreign Service and became High Commissioner in Australia; Owen-Smith returned to Cape Town to work as a GP.

the put-down from his captain Gubby Allen, "Don't give it another thought… you've just cost us the Ashes"), he was appointed England's stopgap captain in 1937. He led Middlesex to the Championship in 1947.

Owen-Smith had little further involvement in South African cricket. He returned to England in 1930 to study medicine at Oxford, where he represented the university at cricket, rugby, boxing and athletics, and later played

K. S. Duleepsinhji: "[He] has already accomplished enough in cricket to be regarded as one of the great batsmen of the younger generation"

CRICKETERS OF THE YEAR 1930 – Performances in the English season 1929

Name	Age*		Matches	Runs	Bat ave	Wickets	Bowl ave	Catches (/st)
EH Bowley	39	First-class	33	2360	43.70	79	23.62	21
		Tests	2	90	30.00	0		1
KS Duleepsinhji	24	First-class	29	2545	53.02	1	78.00	47
		Tests	1	13	6.50	0		0
HGO Owen-Smith	21	First-class	22	1168	35.39	30	25.80	13
		Tests	5	252	42.00	0		4
RWV Robins	23	First-class	34	1134	26.37	162	21.53	20
		Tests	1	4	2.00	5	15.80	0
RES Wyatt	28	First-class	34	2630	53.67	62	30.98	20
		Tests	2	119	59.50	2	37.50	0

as at 1/4/1930

1931

Five Cricketers of the Year

Don Bradman (Australians) *

Clarrie Grimmett (Australians) ●

Beverley Lyon (Gloucestershire) *

Ian Peebles (Oxford University, Middlesex and England) ●

Maurice Turnbull (Glamorgan) *

HEADLINE EVENTS FROM 1930

- County champions – Lancashire

- Australia regain the Ashes, beating England 2-1

- Two England sides undertake four-Test series abroad in 1929-30: one draws 1-1 in West Indies, the other beats New Zealand 1-0

FOR THE FIRST TIME, EACH OF THE FIVE HAILED from different countries. Don Bradman was born in Australia, Clarrie Grimmett in New Zealand, Bev Lyon in England, Ian Peebles in Scotland and Maurice Turnbull in Wales. No Cricketer of the Year had previously been born in New Zealand, and only one each in Scotland and Wales.

Bradman and Grimmett were the chief reasons why Australia regained the Ashes. Bradman, stupendous and only 21 years old, scored a record 974 runs in the five Tests, while Grimmett, a well-travelled and wily 38-year-old, took 29 wickets, the most in an Ashes series in England so far.

While Bradman's feats dominated the headlines – with 334 at Leeds he took dual possession of Test and first-class record scores, having earlier in the year scored 452 not out in a state match – it was Grimmett, with his immaculate length, well-disguised googly and deadly top-spinner, who did most to keep Wally Hammond [1928] quiet, and ensure Australia took all 20 wickets in three of the Tests.

Grimmett, who took all ten for 37 against Yorkshire, was called upon for an immense amount of work, and during the early stages of the summer was the bowler the Australians most relied on. *Wisden* thought it remarkable he did not break down under the strain, and said that without him "it is fairly certain the Australians would have gone back without the Ashes". As it was, a bruised finger limited him to 24 wickets in his last eight matches.

While Grimmett, who generally bowled in a cap to hide his baldness, had to wait until his thirties for significant success (though this did not stop him becoming the first to 200 Test wickets), Bradman struck a century in his first first-class match aged 19, and by the end of the England tour had scored 24 centuries in 56 first-class matches (a ratio he would later improve).

Although it judged (pretty accurately) that "there would seem to be no limit to his possibilities", *Wisden* expressed reservations about Bradman's technique, saying that when the ball was turning there were limitations to his skill. It judged that he still had something to learn about playing a correct offensive or defensive stroke.

Grimmett's Test career ended after he was controversially left out of Australia's 1938 tour of England, a decision for which Bradman was widely blamed and which Grimmett never forgave. He played his last big match in 1941, and later coached in schools and worked as an insurance salesman.

Peebles, a young leg-break and googly bowler, caused Bradman problems in the Old Trafford Test; Bradman admitted that he could not pick his googly. Unfortunately Peebles struggled to retain command of his leg-break, although as it happened one of the few he bowled in the Tests accounted for Bradman.

Taking more than 120 wickets in a season for the second time, Peebles appeared to be fulfilling the great hopes invested in him. Spotted in Inverness as a young teenager by George Geary [1927], he moved to London, where Plum Warner [1904] secured him a tour place to South Africa in 1927-28 even though he had not played county cricket.

Many judges felt his abilities were overestimated. Peebles did better on his second tour of South Africa, in 1930-31, and took 139 wickets in 1931, but his form then declined and he surrendered his England place to Walter Robins [1930]. He lost an eye during a wartime air raid, and later became a witty and erudite cricket writer.

Both Lyon and Turnbull led their counties enterprisingly in 1930. While Turnbull had displayed precocious batting talent at Downside School and Cambridge, Lyon's abilities were slow to ripen through school at Rugby, where he was coached by Willis Cuttell [1898], and Oxford. Lyon wore glasses, but still fielded close in order to see what his own bowlers were doing and how opposing batsmen were playing them.

Lyon's positive approach contributed to Gloucestershire winning more matches than any other county in 1929 and again in 1930, when he was their leading Championship scorer with 1,355 runs.

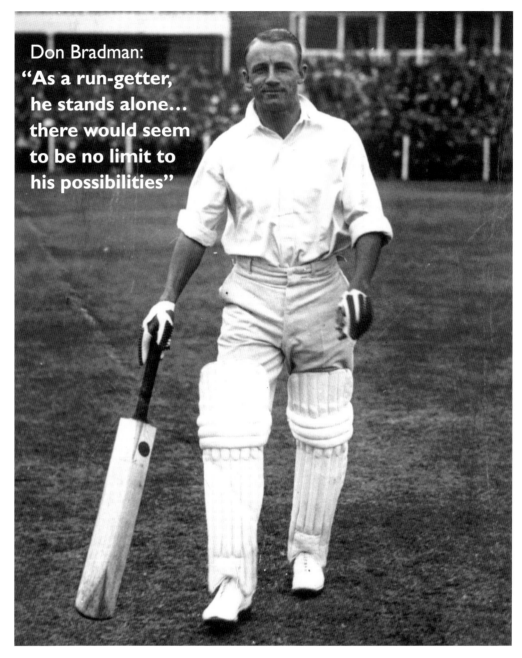

Don Bradman:
"As a run-getter, he stands alone... there would seem to be no limit to his possibilities"

Although Lyon was spoken of as a possible England captain, his unorthodoxy counted against him, and he never did play a Test. In 1931 he declared an innings after one ball to expedite a result (a tactic copied by Turnbull); he also advocated one-day cricket and Sunday play (he himself was Jewish). By 1934 he had resigned to focus on business; he co-founded Rediffusion,

Bev Lyon

Clarrie Grimmett

Maurice Turnbull

Turnbull, who played hockey and rugby for Wales, was killed in action in 1944, four years before Glamorgan won their first Championship. Bradman, accepted as the greatest batsman the game has seen, and knighted for services to cricket in 1949, lived until 2001.

Ian Peebles (right) arrives home after England's 1930-31 tour of South Africa, with (from left) Jack White [1929], George Duckworth [1929], Percy Chapman [1919], Bob Wyatt [1930] and Maurice Leyland [1929]

which distributed wireless signals and produced radio and TV sets.

Turnbull, who belonged to a prominent ship-building family from Penarth, became Glamorgan's first Test cricketer in New Zealand in 1929-30, but his energies and charm were devoted to his struggling county. He fostered a Welsh identity to the side and was heavily involved in the club's management, using business contacts to raise funds. The difference in the form of the side was immediately apparent.

CRICKETERS OF THE YEAR 1931 – Performances in the English season 1930

Name	Age*		Matches	Runs	Bat ave	Wickets	Bowl ave	Catches (/st)
DG Bradman	22	First-class	27	2960	98.66	12	25.08	12
		Tests	5	974	139.14	0		2
CV Grimmett	39	First-class	26	237	11.85	144	16.84	12
		Tests	5	80	16.00	29	31.89	2
BH Lyon	29	First-class	26	1576	38.43	5	61.40	27
IAR Peebles	23	First-class	22	279	11.16	133	18.44	13
		Tests	2	9	9.00	9	39.33	0
MJL Turnbull	25	First-class	32	1739	32.81	0		25

* as at 1/4/1931

Maurice Turnbull:
"He now stands forth as a fine off-side batsman, with a capital style, ranking high among his contemporaries"

1932

Five Cricketers of the Year

James Langridge (Sussex) / ●
Bill Bowes (Yorkshire) ●
Stewart Dempster (New Zealanders) /
Nawab of Pataudi senior (Oxford University) /
Hedley Verity (Yorkshire and England) ●

**HEADLINE EVENTS
FROM 1931**

• County champions – Yorkshire

• England lose 1-0 in South
Africa in 1930-31

• New Zealand play Tests in
England for the first time,
losing a three-match series 1-0

BILL BOWES AND HEDLEY VERITY WERE TWO
key figures in Yorkshire's first Championship
title since 1925. In what was a bowler's
summer, Verity took 138 wickets at 12.34 in the
competition and Bowes 109 at 15.29. It was
Verity's second county season and Bowes's third.

This was a youthful quintet, the first all to
be under 30 years of age on April 1 of the year of
their selection. The Nawab of Pataudi, chosen
exclusively for his performances in his final
season at Oxford, had just turned 22, Bowes was
23, James Langridge (though with eight county
seasons behind him) only 25, Verity 26, and the
New Zealander Stewie Dempster 28.

It was, then, a selection based on promise.
Verity, the only one who played for England
in 1931, would be their first-choice spinner
for the rest of the decade, but Bowes played
only 15 Tests for England and Langridge eight,
while Pataudi's career flittered mysteriously
and unsatisfactorily between England and his
native India.

It was a surprise *Wisden* did not pick
Gubby Allen, given that he scored 122 in the
First Test and took five for 14 in the Second,
but his availability was limited, and he would

have been the third Middlesex amateur chosen
in as many years.

Verity, who left school at 14 to work for
his father's coal business, and started in league
cricket with Middleton, only took up left-
arm spin in 1929 in an attempt to break into
the Yorkshire side, and almost immediately
convinced insiders that he was a worthy
successor to Wilfred Rhodes [1899]. He
topped the national averages in 1930, and in
his second Championship game of 1931 took
all ten Warwickshire wickets for 36. In July
1932 he returned what still stand as the best
innings figures in history, ten for ten against
Nottinghamshire at Headingley.

Verity ranks among the finest of slow left-
armers, phenomenally accurate and deadly on
rain-affected pitches, but *Wisden* in 1932 did
not yet rate him the equal of his predecessor:
"Verity does not yet suggest the ability to flight
the ball which was such a marked characteristic
of Rhodes's bowling," it said. "It is greatly in his
favour that, unspoilt by success, he realises that he
still has a good deal to learn." And learn he did.

Bowes first came to prominence on the
groundstaff at Lord's, where Walter Brearley

[1909] cut his run-up to ten yards. It was easy to underestimate Bowes; although 6ft 4in, he was gangly and bespectacled, and looked like a professor, an impression his batting and fielding did nothing to contradict; his bowling was fast-medium rather than fast.

By 1931, though, there was no doubting his stature. "At the end of the season [he] came to be looked upon as only second to Larwood in his particular class," *Wisden* said. "With a high action he makes the ball swerve, but he owes most of his success to the manner in which he is able to get pace off the ground, together with a decided 'lift'."

Langridge, a genuine all-rounder who like Verity bowled left-arm spin, ought in *Wisden*'s view to have already been recognised by England's selectors. Sussex knew his worth, and in 1950 made him their first modern professional captain; he led them to second place in the Championship two years later. He was the last of six players to top 30,000 runs and 1,500 wickets in a career.

In 1943, when Langridge was on duty with the national fire service, Verity died from wounds aged 38 in an Italian PoW camp. When cricket resumed, Langridge was briefly England's first-choice slow left-armer, but lost his place through injury. Bowes also spent three years as a prisoner in Italy, but lived until 1987, working

Stewie Dempster (left) with his New Zealand team-mate Lindsay Weir

for 40 years as a noted cricket writer and becoming in 1952 the first former recipient to contribute a Cricketer of the Year article himself. He wrote nine signed profiles of Yorkshire cricketers between 1952 and 1969.

Having previously shown mixed form, Pataudi scored six centuries in seven matches for Oxford in 1931, culminating in an innings of 238 not out against Cambridge at Lord's, which remained a record for the Varsity Match until 2005. He also slaughtered the bowling of Tich Freeman [1923] for the Gentlemen at Lord's.

Stewie Dempster:
"The best batsman that country [New Zealand] had ever produced"

James Langridge

CRICKETERS OF THE YEAR 1932 – Performances in the English season 1931

Name	Age*		Matches	Runs	Bat ave	Wickets	Bowl ave	Catches (/st)
WE Bowes	23	First-class	32	53	6.62	136	15.66	9
CS Dempster	28	First-class	23	1778	59.26	0		8/1
		Tests	2	173	86.50			0
J Langridge	25	First-class	31	1007	28.77	102	18.60	13
Nawab of Pataudi	22	First-class	14	1454	69.23	1	19.00	8
H Verity	26	First-class	36	234	12.31	188	13.52	17
		Tests	2	0		4	21.25	0

* as at 1/4/1932

Hedley Verity:

"Verity is the first to acknowledge the debt he owes to Wilfred Rhodes for much valuable advice"

Nawab of Pataudi senior

The Yorkshire and England pair of **Bill Bowes** (left) and **Hedley Verity**

During the winter Pataudi captained trial matches ahead of India's first Test tour of England in 1932, but in the end he played for Worcestershire and went with England to Australia in 1932-33, where he scored 102 on debut while disagreeing with Bodyline. Ill-health in 1934 ended his regular involvement with English cricket, but he captained India's tour of England in 1946, playing against Bowes and Langridge. He died of heart failure in 1952, aged 41, while playing polo in Delhi.

Dempster, who had received no formal coaching before touring England in 1927, convinced *Wisden* that he was now the best batsman New Zealand had produced. He had scored their first Test century against England in 1929-30, and now struck 53 and 120 to help draw the First Test at Lord's. Versatile and quick-footed, he coped better than most in difficult conditions.

Dempster's Test career was brilliant but short-lived. In 1933 he emigrated to England, where he worked as furniture-store manager for Sir Julien Cahn while captaining Leicestershire for three years.

Both Langridge and Pataudi had relatives who were later Cricketers of the Year: Langridge's brother John in 1950, and Pataudi's son in 1968.

1933 Five Cricketers of the Year

C. K. Nayudu (Indians) / ●
Ewart Astill (Leicestershire) / ●
Freddie Brown (Surrey and England) / ●
Alex Kennedy (Hampshire) / ●
Bill Voce (Nottinghamshire and England) ●

HEADLINE EVENTS FROM 1932

- County champions – Yorkshire

- India lose their inaugural Test in England

THE 1933 WISDEN WENT TO PRESS AS THE Bodyline series was at its incendiary height, too soon for the editor to mark England's recapturing of the Ashes by including five members of the victorious tour party as he had in 1929. He chose Bill Voce and Freddie Brown, two young players on the tour, but surprisingly not Eddie Paynter [1938], nor Tommy Mitchell, nor Gubby Allen.

Instead C. Stewart Caine honoured two players – Ewart Astill and Alex Kennedy – at unfashionable counties who had never played Ashes Tests and had been first-class cricketers for 25 years. Both were now in their forties. "[They] have surely earned recognition," wrote Caine.

In historical terms, the most significant pick was C. K. Nayudu, the fourth Indian-born cricketer to be chosen but the first to arouse popular support across India. Nayudu was born and raised in Nagpur to a Cambridge-educated father, and his prowess earned him the patronage of the Maharajah of Holkar, who employed him on a sinecure in his army. A superb athlete, Nayudu played like a free-spirited English amateur, and established himself as a national hero with a blistering 153, laden with sixes, against MCC in 1926-27.

Nayudu, who prepared for India's inaugural Test tour in 1932 by playing London club cricket the previous summer, proved the principal star. Playing all 26 first-class matches, he finished as leading run-scorer and third-highest wicket-taker, though he was little more than a change bowler. Possessing supple and powerful wrists and a good eye, he hit the ball tremendously hard, striking an unrivalled 32 sixes.

In the absence of a suitable prince to captain them, Nayudu led India in the only Test at Lord's, in which they performed creditably in defeat, and retained the captaincy when England toured in 1933-34. He played regular first-class cricket into his sixties.

Wisden might have picked India's two fastest bowlers, both of whom made a big impact: Mohammad Nissar, who took six wickets in the Test, and Amar Singh, who captured 111 first-class wickets on the tour as well as striking two centuries.

Brown, who performed the double in his first full season of county cricket, having already played for England in 1931 after leaving

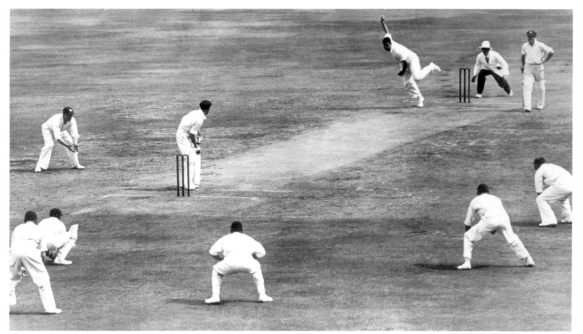

Bill Voce bowls during the 1932-33 Bodyline series

Bill Voce:

"**Voce can maintain his pace for a long period and, at his best, is undoubtedly a difficult player to face**"

Cambridge, cut a similar dash: like Nayudu, he wore a neckerchief and hit the ball hard. He scored 212 and 135 against Middlesex and 168 against Kent, but his leg-break and googly bowling was raw.

Born in Peru, where his father was in business, Brown played sporadically for Surrey during the 1930s but revived his career after the war, much of which he spent as a PoW with Bill Bowes [1932]. First with Northamptonshire, who employed him as assistant secretary, and then England, whose third choice he was to lead in Australia in 1950-51, he brought dividends with his spirited refusal to give up, though his overbearing manner intimidated some youngsters.

Voce, another product of Nottinghamshire's mining community, only turned 23 in 1932 but by then had taken 45 wickets in 11 Tests as a left-arm fast bowler, a style he only settled on in the West Indies in 1929-30 when he made his Test debut (he had started out bowling spin). For Nottinghamshire during the 1931 and 1932 seasons, he and Harold Larwood [1927] focused on the leg-theory that would shape the series in Australia, Voce – a taller, bouncier bowler – taking 259 wickets to Larwood's 291.

Although Voce was also not chosen for the 1934 Ashes, he returned to Australia in 1936-37, taking 17 wickets in two Tests won by England before back trouble hampered him. He made a third Ashes tour in 1946-47, aged 37, but had so little success that he soon retired.

Neither Kennedy nor Astill had vintage seasons, though Kennedy topped 100 wickets for the 15th and (as it proved) last time. Both had at times been considered genuine all-rounders – between 1921 and 1930 Kennedy performed five doubles and Astill nine – but bowling was their stronger suit. Kennedy's accurate inswing was reckoned not quick enough for the highest level, but that did not stop him taking all ten for Players v Gentlemen in 1927. His career haul of 2,874 wickets puts him seventh on the all-time list. Astill, a medium-pace spinner of off-breaks and leg-breaks, makes the top 15 with 2,431.

They only experienced Tests overseas –

Alex Kennedy

C. K. Nayudu

Freddie Brown

C. K. Nayudu:

"He seemed rather more comfortable on English wickets than most of his colleagues"

After winning a billiards competition for county players, **Ewart Astill** (right) receives the trophy from Douglas Jardine [1928], accompanied by the beaten finalist Alf Gover [1939].

Kennedy in South Africa in 1922-23 (where his 31 wickets in five Tests were crucial to England's series win), and Astill in South Africa in 1927-28 and West Indies in 1929-30.

As to why Kennedy never played against Australia, *Wisden* explained: "Some years ago when he was at the height of his powers there were rumours that his action was not above suspicion… Very naturally he resented in most strenuous fashion the accusation but… there remained in the minds of the successive selection committees the germ of the suspicion."

Wisden rated Astill day in and day out Leicestershire's best all-round player since the war, even though George Geary [1927] was in the side. Astill retired in 1938 to coach Leicestershire, and after serving in the army during the war coached at Tonbridge School in 1946, where Colin Cowdrey [1957] was among his charges.

CRICKETERS OF THE YEAR 1933 – Performances in the English season 1932

Name	Age*		Matches	Runs	Bat ave	Wickets	Bowl ave	Catches (/st)
WE Astill	45	First-class	31	987	21.45	78	26.53	15
FR Brown	22	First-class	31	1135	32.42	120	20.46	18
		Tests	1	30	15.00	3	34.00	0
AS Kennedy	42	First-class	32	787	17.88	144	18.79	31
CK Nayudu	37	First-class	26	1618	40.45	65	25.53	20
		Tests	1	50	25.00	2	30.50	1
W Voce	23	First-class	32	445	18.54	136	16.87	22
		Tests	1	4		5	10.20	0

* as at 1/4/1933

1934 Five Cricketers of the Year

George Headley (West Indians) *

Fred Bakewell (Northamptonshire and England) *

Stan Nichols (Essex and England) * ●

Leslie Townsend (Derbyshire) * ●

Cyril Walters (Worcestershire and England) *

HEADLINE EVENTS FROM 1933

- County champions – Yorkshire

- England beat West Indies 2-0

- Douglas Jardine's England side regain the Ashes in Australia in 1932-33 in a series scarred by the Bodyline controversy

GEORGE HEADLEY PROVIDED SYDNEY Southerton with the easiest of picks in his first year as editor. Headley, the first black player ever chosen, was an established star, having made four hundreds in four Tests against England in 1929-30 and two in five in Australia in 1930-31, as well as a string of big scores for Jamaica against English touring sides, but the West Indian tour of 1933 was itself a triumph.

"From what we had been told by English players who had been to the West Indies, we were fully prepared for Headley's success, but even so, he astonished most of us," wrote Southerton, who described him as "beyond all question the best batsman the West Indies have ever produced".

Headley's watchful style helped him adjust easily to English pitches, and although it was a batsman's summer he scored runs even when conditions favoured the bowlers. Despite missing games through injury and illness, he scored almost twice as many as any team-mate. An unbeaten 169 ensured West Indies drew the Second Test.

Born to West Indian parents in Panama, where his Bajan father worked on construction of the canal, Headley did not live in the Caribbean until he was ten, and spent the next ten years lodging with a relative. But once introduced to cricket at school he rose fast, scoring 211 in his second first-class match aged 18, and narrowly missing out on the 1928 tour of England.

Headley's success in 1933 earned him a lucrative contract to play for Haslingden, and he played English league cricket regularly before and after the 1939–45 war. Although his appearances were relatively few, only Bradman [1931] has bettered his average both in Tests (60.83) and in first-class cricket (69.86).

He carried not only a weak West Indies batting line-up but the hopes of the black English-speaking people of the Caribbean. He was the first black West Indies Test captain (though for one match only). A son and grandson also played Test cricket; another son sprinted for Jamaica at the 1964 Olympics.

Southerton might also have picked Manny Martindale, a short but powerful new-ball bowler who took 103 wickets on the tour. Instead he chose four cricketers from unfashionable counties who had been called up for England's 1933-34 tour of India.

With England on the lookout for openers, Cyril Walters and Fred Bakewell were among the leading candidates. Walters made his debut against West Indies, scoring 51 and 46 in his first two innings, while Bakewell, first tried in 1931, hit 107 on his recall in the final Test.

Walters, who had switched from Glamorgan to Worcestershire, where he was appointed assistant secretary and captain, had overhauled his technique with dramatic results, scoring nine hundreds in 1933. "Playing so well [for England]… it was at once felt a satisfactory successor to either Hobbs or Sutcliffe had been discovered," *Wisden* stated. "When he and Hammond were in together… the batting of the two men, for sheer grace of style and beauty of execution, could not have been bettered."

Bakewell, also an expert short-leg fielder, was less orthodox but even better to watch, a quick-footed shot-maker who in 1933 twice broke the Northamptonshire record with successive

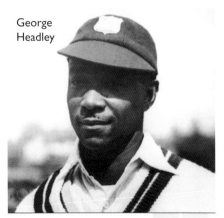

George Headley

Les Townsend

George Headley:
"[He] is beyond all question the best batsman the West Indies have ever produced"

The Players team which took on the Gentlemen at Lord's in 1934. Back row (l-r): Les Ames [1929], Hedley Verity [1932], Jack O'Connor, Jim Smith [1935], Arthur Mitchell, **Maurice Nichols**. Seated (l-r): Wally Hammond [1928], Herbert Sutcliffe [1920], Patsy Hendren [1920] (captain), Maurice Leyland [1929], Tommy Mitchell

innings of 246 and 257 against Nottinghamshire and Glamorgan. "To lovers of the orthodox Bakewell's position at the wicket is looked upon probably with disfavour," said *Wisden*. "He adopts a pronounced two-eyed stance, with his right shoulder brought round until he is facing the bowler almost full front… by reason of his watchfulness he is usually a difficult man to bowl out."

However, neither man lasted. Walters scored a century in India and 401 runs in the 1934 Ashes (captaining England in the first match), but was affected by health problems and, marrying into money, drifted out of the game. Bakewell's style proved vulnerable to leg-spin in India and he was not risked against Australia, though he did play two more Tests in 1935. His career was ended by a car crash in 1936 in which a team-mate, R. P. Northway, was killed.

After slow starts to their careers, Leslie Townsend and Morris Nichols now ranked among the leading all-rounders in the country, helping their counties to one of their best seasons. Townsend was the better batsman with a role higher in the order, Nichols much the faster and better bowler, which was the main reason why he played 14 Tests to Townsend's four. Neither had appeared for England since 1930, but Nichols was brought back for the Third Test in 1933 (scoring 49 and taking three wickets) while Townsend played three Tests to Nichols's one in India.

Nichols's finest season came in 1935, when he took six for 35 for England v South Africa and 11 for 54 for Essex v Yorkshire (as well as scoring 146). The outbreak of war deprived him of another scheduled tour of India in 1939-40, and brought an end to his first-class career. He later played as a professional in the Birmingham League.

Townsend in 1933 became the first cricketer for ten years to perform the 2,000-run/100-wicket double, but topped this as a key figure in Derbyshire's title-winning season of 1936. He was praised by *Wisden* as a model professional: his first-class career also ended with the war, but afterwards he emigrated to

Fred Bakewell

New Zealand, where he became a successful coach.

Cyril Walters

Cyril Walters:
"Essentially a stylist, Walters drives with great power and correct placing of the ball"

CRICKETERS OF THE YEAR 1934 – Performances in the English season 1933

Name	Age*		Matches	Runs	Bat ave	Wickets	Bowl ave	Catches (/st)
AH Bakewell	25	First-class	27	2149	46.71	0		31
		Tests	1	107	107.00			2
GA Headley	24	First-class	23	2320	66.28	21	34.33	17
		Tests	3	277	55.40	0		4
MS Nichols	33	First-class	34	1460	30.41	145	20.97	25
		Tests	1	49	49.00	3	29.00	0
LF Townsend	30	First-class	33	2268	44.47	100	18.71	19
CF Walters	28	First-class	30	2404	50.08	4	48.50	12
		Tests	3	99	33.00			0

* as at 1/4/1934

1935 Five Cricketers of the Year

Bill O'Reilly (Australians) ●
Stan McCabe (Australians) ●
George Paine (Warwickshire) ●
Bill Ponsford (Australians) ●
Jim Smith (Middlesex) ●

HEADLINE EVENTS FROM 1934

- County champions – Lancashire

- Australia regain the Ashes, winning 2-1

- England under Douglas Jardine win 2-0 in the first Test series played in India in 1933-34

THE SELECTION OF THREE AUSTRALIANS instrumental in their side regaining the Ashes was inevitable. Each was already of proven class but now cemented his status. Bill Ponsford scored 569 runs in the five Tests, and Stan McCabe 483. Bill O'Reilly, an aggressive bowler of fast-medium leg-breaks, googlies and top-spinners, was the leading wicket-taker in the series with 28, inflicting early psychological damage with 11 for 129 in an opening win at Trent Bridge.

When O'Reilly died in 1992, he was described by *Wisden* as "probably the greatest spin bowler the game has ever produced". Don Bradman [1931] hailed him as the greatest bowler he faced or saw. Both McCabe and O'Reilly would reaffirm their greatness on Australia's next visit in 1938, but Ponsford announced his retirement shortly after returning home. He thus provides a rare instance of *Wisden* choosing someone who had already departed the game.

O'Reilly, who like McCabe escaped much coaching by growing up in rural New South Wales, might have made the 1930 tour alongside the other two, but his career was hampered by his job as a teacher. He rarely had a bad match

and always had a good series, averaging 25 wickets in each of his five full ones. Few bowlers were collared less often, his economy-rate of 1.94 runs per over standing second only to Verity [1932] during the inter-war period. He later became a combative journalist.

McCabe, first picked by Australia at 19, was a pocket battleship of a batsman, fearless and adventurous against pace, as he had shown during the Bodyline series. With a tighter method than in 1930, he finished with most runs and centuries on the tour (just shading Bradman in both), as well as acting as a useful new-ball bowler. "He blossomed forth as an almost completely equipped batsman of the forcing type and was probably the best exponent – Bradman himself scarcely excluded – of the art of hitting the ball tremendously hard and safely," *Wisden* said.

Ponsford, who also represented Victoria at baseball, developed a batting method with the St Kilda club in Melbourne that *Wisden* described as "never graceful or elegant". In the 1920s he had set the standards for run-scoring in state cricket which Bradman overhauled – Ponsford with 429 and 437 twice improved on the world-record

Stan McCabe:
"He almost bore comparison with Bradman"

Bill Ponsford (left) and Stan McCabe go out to bat for Australia

George Paine

score which Bradman took from him early in 1930 – but a flawed technique against short-pitched bowling meant a chequered Test career.

In 1934, though, he partnered Bradman in two influential stands worth 388 at Leeds and 451 at The Oval, his shares being 181 and 266. "Opinions probably will always differ as to his ability to deal properly with fast bowling," wrote Sydney Southerton. "There have been occasions, and the writer has seen them himself, when his batting against Larwood in particular was absurdly ineffective… one would incline to the idea that he does not care for the fast rising ball on the leg stump. Far too often last season he turned his back to it and got hit."

An English player whose own Achilles' heel was fast bowling, Jack O'Connor of Essex, had his best season in 1934, scoring 2,350

runs, average 55.95, but was overlooked by *Wisden*, as was Ken Farnes [1939], who took ten wickets in the First Test and 11 in Essex's victory over Yorkshire.

Neither George Paine nor Jim Smith played in the Tests, though both must have featured in the England selectors' thoughts. Paine topped the national averages, but as a left-arm spinner was not going to displace Verity; there was speculation that England might field both in the same XI, but it did not happen. Smith, playing his first full season of first-class cricket, was a tireless and powerful 6ft 4in fast bowler who got the ball to lift off a wicket-to-wicket line. He arguably deserved a summons; playing for Middlesex against the Australians in May, he dismissed both Ponsford and Bill Woodfull [1927] for ducks.

Wisden described his omission as "something of a mystery".

Paine and Smith had been on the Lord's groundstaff together in 1926, Paine following in the footsteps of his father and grandfather, Smith having arrived from his native Wiltshire. During a few appearances for Middlesex, Paine came to the attention of Warwickshire and embarked on a career with them in 1929; Smith stayed put, but waited eight years for a Championship debut.

They were reunited in an under-strength England side that toured the West Indies in 1934-35 (too late to much influence their selection by *Wisden*), where both played all four Tests and led the attack in terms of overs and wickets. Paine was troubled by rheumatism: his form declined and he was released by Warwickshire after 1938. Smith, who played one further Test in 1937, remained a strong performer up to the war, by which time he had taken 676 wickets in six seasons and acquired fame as a prodigious hitter. He did not resume playing afterwards.

In retirement, Ponsford led a quiet life working for the Melbourne Cricket Club, and has a stand at the MCG named after him. McCabe ran a sports store in Sydney, where he hired cricket colleagues as salesmen, including O'Reilly and Ray Lindwall [1949].

Jim Smith

Bill O'Reilly

Bill O'Reilly:
"Old judges say that of his type he was the best to play for their country since George Giffen and Hugh Trumble"

CRICKETERS OF THE YEAR 1935 – Performances in the English season 1934

Name	Age*		Matches	Runs	Bat ave	Wickets	Bowl ave	Catches (/st)
SJ McCabe	24	First-class	26	2078	69.26	21	37.80	19
		Tests	5	483	60.37	4	54.75	6
WJ O'Reilly	29	First-class	19	237	26.33	109	17.04	7
		Tests	5	100	25.00	28	24.92	2
GAE Paine	26	First-class	26	613	19.77	156	17.07	16
WH Ponsford	34	First-class	22	1784	77.56			10
		Tests	4	569	94.83			5
CIJ Smith	28	First-class	34	617	13.41	172	18.88	23

* as at 1/4/1935

1936 Five Cricketers of the Year

Errol Holmes (Surrey and England)
Jock Cameron (South Africans)
Bruce Mitchell (South Africans)
Denis Smith (Derbyshire and England)
Arthur Wellard (Somerset)

HEADLINE EVENTS FROM 1935

- County champions – Yorkshire

- South Africa win their first series in England 1-0

- England lose 2-1 in West Indies in 1934-35

HORACE "JOCK" CAMERON, WHO AS wicketkeeper-batsman had just helped South Africa become the first visitors other than Australia to win a series in England, remains the only person to be posthumously named a Cricketer of the Year. He died of enteric fever on November 2, 1935, shortly after returning home, aged only 30.

Free of the captaincy he had held for two years, Cameron flourished. He turned around the Lord's Test, which South Africa won, with a hard-hit 90, of which 58 came out of 60 in half an hour; in the corresponding fixture in 1929 he had been knocked unconscious by Harold Larwood [1927]. He took 30 off an over from Hedley Verity [1932] in the defeat of Yorkshire, and in the final tour match struck 160 in 140 minutes at Scarborough.

"For all his fearless hitting, [he] will be chiefly remembered for his high place among wicketkeepers not only of South Africa but in his generation," wrote *Wisden*'s new editor Wilfrid H. Brookes. "His stumping of a batsman has been likened to the 'nonchalant gesture of a smoker flicking the ash from a cigarette'… [he] was a very fine personality, one who enriched the game and whose manliness and popularity extended far beyond the cricket field. The passing of this charming fellow was a cruel loss."

No one did more towards South Africa's triumph than Bruce Mitchell, who for 20 years was the unassuming bedrock of his country's batting. Chosen at 20 for his first tour of England in 1929, when he finished as leading run-scorer, Mitchell was arguably the most effective opening batsman in the world. An unbeaten 164 on a difficult pitch teed up the victory at Lord's; an innings of 128 at The Oval ensured the series was safe.

Mitchell was a striking batsman for his style and his quiet, calm deliberation. He made the most of his 5ft 10in, getting well over the ball, and his footwork was superb. He was also a useful leg-break bowler and brilliant slip fielder who benefited from the coaching of Ernest Halliwell [1905]. No one bettered his 3,471 Test runs for South Africa until 1999, four years after his death.

Three defeats in as many series confirmed England were in a lean period and during this series the selectors got through 25 players in five Tests.

The South African tourists of 1935. Back row (l-r): Robert Williams, Ken Viljoen, Eric Rowan [1952], Denis Tomlinson, Bob Crisp, Arthur Langton, Dudley Nourse [1948], Xen Balaskas. Seated: Jack Siedle, Cyril Vincent, **Jock Cameron**, Sibley Snooke (manager), Herby Wade (captain), **Bruce Mitchell**, Sandy Bell, Eric Dalton

Errol Holmes, who finished tenth in the national batting averages and played in the defeat at Lord's without success, was a cricketer of charm and hope, but he would not appear for England again. Born in Calcutta, he shone as an all-rounder at Malvern and Oxford before dropping out of the game to work in the City, briefly relocating to New York.

Lured back by an invitation to captain Surrey in 1934, he energised the side and spectators with his enterprise. He toured the West Indies as vice-captain in 1934-35, when his gung-ho batting came off only once; even so, after leading a goodwill tour of Australia in 1935-36 designed to smooth relations following Bodyline, he was lined up as vice-captain for the Ashes in 1936-37. He declined for personal reasons, and gave up the Surrey captaincy in 1938 after his engagement to the niece of club president H. D. G. Leveson Gower.

Jock Cameron:
"Cameron, for all his fearless hitting, will be chiefly remembered for his high place among wicketkeepers not only of South Africa but in his generation"

Denis Smith, a tall, expansive left-hander from Derbyshire who topped 2,000 runs in a season for the first (and only) time, was brought in to solve England's problems at the top of the order, where there had not been a settled pairing since 1930. Smith was due to play the First Test, but a cracked rib delayed his entry until the third match.

He did reasonably well, scoring 36 and 57 at Leeds and 35 and 0 at Manchester, but lost his place for The Oval. He was not a natural opener, and in his early days seemed uncertain facing the new ball. "It remains a problem whether No. 1 or No. 4 is the more suitable place for him to go in," said *Wisden*. Smith performed well under Holmes in Australia in 1935-36, and remained a solid scorer for his county – setting records for runs and centuries not beaten until the 1990s – but he too never played another Test.

Denis Smith

Arthur Wellard

Errol Holmes

Arthur Wellard, who came close to making his debut in the final Test, would win only two caps, but there were few more popular county cricketers. An untutored fast-bowling all-rounder who was salvaged from obscurity in his native Kent by a chance encounter that took him to Somerset, Wellard hit more than 500 sixes in his career, including what was then a season's record of 72 in 1935. He had developed a sound defence, but preferred the long handle to the long game. A capable and versatile bowler, he stands as Somerset's second-greatest wicket-taker. He made occasional, colourful appearances for Harold Pinter's Gaieties CC into his seventies.

Brookes in his Preface regretted not finding room for Yorkshire wicketkeeper Arthur Wood [1939].

Errol Holmes:
"A marked characteristic about the batting of Holmes is the ease and certainty of his strokes"

CRICKETERS OF THE YEAR 1936 – Performances in the English season 1935

Name	Age*		Matches	Runs	Bat ave	Wickets	Bowl ave	Catches (/st)
HB Cameron	30	First-class	27	1458	41.65			28/19
		Tests	5	306	38.25			7/3
ERT Holmes	30	First-class	31	1925	41.84	55	31.90	25
		Tests	1	18	9.00	0		1
B Mitchell	27	First-class	22	1451	45.34	35	19.02	22
		Tests	5	488	69.71	2	77.00	6
D Smith	29	First-class	31	2175	39.54	2	52.50	24
		Tests	2	128	32.00			1
AW Wellard	33	First-class	27	1347	31.32	114	20.68	18

* as at 1/4/1936

1937

Five Cricketers of the Year

Vijay Merchant (Indians) *

Charles Barnett (Gloucestershire and England) *

Bill Copson (Derbyshire) •

Alf Gover (Surrey and England) •

Stan Worthington (Derbyshire and England) *

**HEADLINE EVENTS
FROM 1936**

• County champions –
Derbyshire

• England beat India 2-0

BILL COPSON, A FIERY AND SKILFUL NEW-BALL bowler who only discovered cricket by chance during the General Strike, and Stan Worthington, who turned himself into an effective opening bat after sustaining a broken jaw the previous August, helped Derbyshire win their first and only Championship in 1936. Two other key members of the side had already been chosen – Leslie Townsend in 1934 and Denis Smith in 1936 – but there was again no place for wrist-spinner Tommy Mitchell, who took 100 wickets for the eighth season in a row.

Worthington also shone in his first Tests on home soil, making 87 against India at Old Trafford and 128 at The Oval, during which he shared stands of 127 and 266 with Wally Hammond [1928]. He and Copson were rewarded with places on the winter tour of Australia, but Worthington did little in three Tests and Copson, though he topped the tour averages, did not appear in the series.

Worthington never played for England again, but Copson made an impressive debut against West Indies at Lord's in 1939, only for the war to thwart his future prospects.

Both men got into cricket through colliery teams, although unlike Copson and many others Worthington, a grammar-school boy, worked as electrician rather than miner. He began his career with Derbyshire in 1924 and for many years played as an all-rounder, but his accurate fast-medium bowling was tailing off by 1935.

Copson first picked up a cricket ball in anger aged 18 when fellow miners persuaded him to join in local matches while they were absent from work during the 1926 General Strike. Naturally fast and accurate, he made his debut for Derbyshire in 1932 and dismissed Andy Sandham [1923] with his first ball. His progress was hindered by fitness issues, but he reached the heights in Derbyshire's Championship year, when he played in all but two of their 28 matches and took 140 wickets at 12.8 apiece.

Charlie Barnett, the only opening batsman to score 2,000 runs in 1936, had previously appeared in four Tests, but was recalled for the final one against India, for what proved to be a two-year run during which he scored centuries against Australia at Adelaide and Nottingham. One of the most attacking openers England have possessed, Barnett in the second of those games only narrowly failed to become the first to score a century in the opening session of a Test for England, reaching his hundred off the first ball after the interval.

Barnett's freewheeling style was well suited to Australian conditions, and he finished as leading run-scorer on the 1936-37 tour. Educated at Wycliffe College, he turned professional at 21, and ran his own meat and poultry business after giving up cricket, before returning to Wycliffe to coach.

Vijay Merchant was the undisputed star of India's tour of England. A small, quick-footed batsman who could cut and hook strongly, he was pressed into service as an opener and fared

Bill Copson

Vijay Merchant

Stan Worthington

Vijay Merchant:
"Merchant does not allow his comparatively small physique to handicap him"

so well that he scored 1,745 runs – 643 more than any team-mate. The highlights came in the north-west in late July, when he carried his bat through both innings against Lancashire at Liverpool (paving the way for one of only two wins over first-class counties), then helped salvage a draw in the Manchester Test with a second-innings century.

Born in Bombay to a family that ran textile mills, Merchant was a leader on and off the field, supporting cricketers from poor backgrounds and working on behalf of India's poor. He captained the Hindus in inter-communal matches and scored massively in Indian domestic cricket, his first-class career average of 71.22 placing him second only to Bradman [1931], but it was his success in challenging conditions in England in 1936 and 1946 that confirmed the thoroughness of his technique.

Alf Gover, like Copson, ranked among the best fast bowlers in the country, but unlike Copson took long hours of practice to hone his method. Standing 6ft 2½in, Gover generated good bounce and could swing the ball away and break it back, and by taking more than 200 wickets in 1936 (a feat he repeated in 1937) he achieved something no fast bowler had managed since Tom Richardson [1897]. Called up for the Test at Manchester, he went wicketless on the easiest batting pitch of the series and missed out on a winter tour place, though he would play more Tests at home in 1937 and 1946.

Gover was for many years the proprietor of an indoor school in Wandsworth through which many future Cricketers of the Year passed; he only retired in 1989, aged 81. In his Preface, Wilfrid Brookes indicated that Gover was the last of the Five to be included. "In deciding to include Gover, I had reluctantly to omit Fishlock, another Surrey player," he wrote. Laurie Fishlock was eventually picked in 1947.

Charles Barnett

Charles Barnett:
"Probably he will always be a player of the type prepared to run risks, and qualities of an aggressive kind form the strength of his batting"

Alf Gover

CRICKETERS OF THE YEAR 1937 – Performances in the English season 1936

Name	Age*		Matches	Runs	Bat ave	Wickets	Bowl ave	Catches (1st)
CJ Barnett	26	First-class	34	2098	38.14	43	22.16	11
		Tests	1	75	75.00			0
WH Copson	28	First-class	31	135	7.10	160	13.34	17
AR Gover	29	First-class	34	308	11.40	200	17.73	10
		Tests	1	0		0		0
VM Merchant	25	First-class	23	1745	51.32	18	34.33	15
		Tests	3	282	47.00	0		2
TS Worthington	31	First-class	30	1734	41.28	23	31.60	22
		Tests	2	215	107.50	1	52.00	3

as at 1/4/1937

1938 Five Cricketers of the Year

Tom Goddard (Gloucestershire and England) ●
Joe Hardstaff junior (Nottinghamshire and England) /
Leonard Hutton (Yorkshire and England) /
Jim Parks senior (Sussex and England) / ●
Eddie Paynter (Lancashire and England) /

HEADLINE EVENTS FROM 1937

- County champions – Yorkshire

- England beat New Zealand 1-0 in a three-match series

- England under Gubby Allen are beaten 3-2 in Australia in 1936-37 after leading 2-0

FOR THE FIRST TIME, ALL FIVE CRICKETERS OF the Year were picked after playing Tests for England the previous summer. They were an illustrious group, but at contrasting stages of their careers: Joe Hardstaff and Len Hutton were young batsmen with their best years ahead of them; Jim Parks, Eddie Paynter and Tom Goddard had all been playing regular cricket since the early 1920s. No more than four played at once in the same side in the 1937 series against New Zealand.

There could be no disputing their right to be chosen. All had mighty seasons in 1937 – Parks achieved a unique double of 3,000 runs and 100 wickets; Paynter, Hutton and Hardstaff all topped 2,500 runs; and Goddard took 248 wickets, claiming all ten in an innings against Worcestershire and ten-wicket hauls in 12 other matches.

Parks would not add to the one cap he earned in the First Test against New Zealand as opening bat (he was sacrificed to strengthen the bowling), but the others soon enjoyed rare success for their country.

Goddard, who had previously been restricted to one Test because off-spin was out of fashion with the selectors, bowled England to victory in the Second Test with six for 29. Recalled again in South Africa in 1938-39, he performed the hat-trick at Johannesburg.

Hardstaff scored centuries in the First and Third Tests against New Zealand, and Hutton one in the Second (having been dismissed for 0 and 1 on debut in the First). Greater things were to come. In the final match against Australia in 1938, Hutton broke the Test record with an innings of 364 spanning 13 hours 17 minutes, during which he put on 215 with Hardstaff, who finished unbeaten on 169.

Earlier in that series, the left-handed Paynter – already a national hero for rising from his sick bed to score 83 at Brisbane during the Bodyline tour – cemented his reputation with 216 not out at Trent Bridge. A few months later in South Africa, he scored twin centuries at Johannesburg and 243 at Durban.

Jack Cowie, an accurate and menacing opening bowler who twice despatched Hutton and Parks cheaply at Lord's, enjoyed an outstanding tour for New Zealand, but for the first time in nine years no touring cricketer was included among *Wisden*'s Five.

Tom Goddard

Hutton, the son of a builder, was brought up in a Moravian community near Pudsey, and was recommended to Yorkshire by Herbert Sutcliffe [1920]. His class was immediately apparent but, after his debut at 17, it took time for him to achieve big scores – until, shortly before his England call-up, he scored 271 not out against Derbyshire, something for him to aim at the following year at The Oval.

Wisden was not wrong when it predicted, "He [Hutton] should furnish England with one of the opening batsmen so badly needed since the breaking of the Hobbs–Sutcliffe partnership." By the time of his last Test in 1955, worn down by the cares of being England's first modern professional captain, he had to his name two Ashes wins as leader and more runs as opener than any Test batsman to that point. He was knighted the following year.

Hardstaff emerged through colliery cricket around Nottingham and, like Hutton, made his county debut as a teenager. But, unlike Hutton, he liked to cut a dash, and against Kent in August 1937 reached a hundred in 51 minutes. "Hardstaff stands as erect as a sentinel at the crease… a batsman of beautiful style," said *Wisden*.

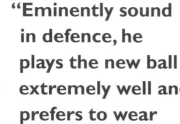

Len Hutton

Len Hutton:
"Eminently sound in defence, he plays the new ball extremely well and prefers to wear down the bowling rather than take risks"

CRICKETERS OF THE YEAR 1938 – Performances in the English season 1937

Name	Age*		Matches	Runs	Bat ave	Wickets	Bowl ave	Catches (1st)
TWJ Goddard	37	First-class	33	421	12.02	248	16.76	21
		Tests	2	5		8	17.87	0
J Hardstaff	26	First-class	28	2540	57.72	0		9
		Tests	3	350	70.00			0
L Hutton	21	First-class	35	2888	56.62	28	36.60	28
		Tests	3	127	25.40	1	15.00	2
JH Parks	34	First-class	35	3003	50.89	101	25.83	23
		Tests	1	29	14.50	3	12.00	0
E Paynter	36	First-class	34	2904	53.77	0		20
		Tests	2	114	38.00			1

* as at 1/4/1938

Paynter, Parks and Goddard all took longer to develop. Paynter, who left school at 12 to work in a cotton mill, where he lost the tops of two fingers in an accident, did not score a Championship century until he was 29, a month before making his England debut. Small, pugnacious and brave, he enjoyed great success as opener for Lancashire in 1937 – scoring 322 against Sussex – but generally batted in the middle order for England.

Parks, whose first century for Sussex came when he was 25, developed into an organised and resourceful batsman and reliable slow-medium inswing bowler; his remarkable peak in 1937 was partly testimony to his durability during a long season (he batted 63 times). "He was essentially a county player, immensely dependable, but lacking the touch of genius which marks the top class," *Wisden*'s obituary stated in 1980.

Goddard, armed with height and big hands, left Gloucestershire in 1928 after struggling as a fast bowler; joining the Lord's groundstaff, he turned to off-spin and was spotted by Bev Lyon [1931], who took him back to Bristol. Bowling round the wicket to an array of leg-side catchers, he reeled in 184 wickets in his first season and was still cutting swathes through county line-ups after the Second World War, almost propelling Gloucestershire to the title in 1947. In 1939 he took 30 Championship wickets in the space of six days at Bristol.

Hardstaff, Hutton and Parks were all members of strong cricketing dynasties; Hardstaff's father also played for England, as did a son each of Hutton and Parks. "Young Jim" Parks was a Cricketer of the Year in 1968.

Joe Hardstaff junior

Eddie Paynter

Eddie Paynter:

"Paynter came under the expert coaching of J. T. Tyldesley, to whom he says he owes practically everything for his advance in the game"

Jim Parks

1939

Five Cricketers of the Year

Hugh Bartlett (Sussex) *
Bill Brown (Australians) *
Denis Compton (Middlesex and England) *
Kenneth Farnes (Essex and England) ●
Arthur Wood (Yorkshire and England) ▥

HEADLINE EVENTS FROM 1938

- County champions – Yorkshire

- Australia retain the Ashes after the series in England is drawn 1-1

ALTHOUGH AUSTRALIA RETAINED THE ASHES with a 1–1 draw, only opening batsman Bill Brown was chosen. Three influential members of the team had been picked before. Many of the 17 players called on by England had previously appeared, leaving editor Wilfrid Brookes bemoaning his choice.

But he could now include Arthur Wood, whom he had wanted to find room for in 1936; Hugh Bartlett and Ken Farnes, who took 17 wickets in the Tests, made compelling cases with their performances in the Gentlemen–Players match; and Denis Compton was a prodigy who would have demanded attention in any year. At 21, Compton was as young as anyone so far chosen outside the schoolboy years of 1918–19.

Brown, who had scored a century in the Lord's Test of 1934, only just scraped a place on the 1938 tour, but totally vindicated his inclusion. An innings of 133 in the follow-on saved the First Test, and by carrying his bat for 206 in the Second – again at Lord's, in the first Test match to be televised – he did much to keep Australia in the game. He followed up with a career-best 265 against Derbyshire and 101

at Warwickshire. He trained with sprinters to improve his running.

The son of a Queensland dairy farmer, Brown grew up in the shadow of the Depression; his family moved to Sydney, where his cricket career developed, but he returned to his native state where he was a pioneering if self-effacing figure as player and administrator. He toured England again in 1948, but was confined to a minor middle-order role. *Wisden* described him as someone who batted with "charming skill, coolness, thoughtfulness and certainty".

Compton was the son of a decorator-turned-lorry driver from Hendon, but his talent for sport was so evident that he was encouraged to join the Lord's groundstaff straight from school; in the same year, 1936, he joined Arsenal (his elder brother Leslie also played for Middlesex and Arsenal). Denis scored 1,004 runs in his first season and 1,980 in his second, when England gave him a debut against New Zealand at 19. He made 65, and kept his place against Australia in 1938, scoring 102 in the First Test and a match-saving 76 not out in the Second.

Compton fully lived up to the expectations he aroused, winning the hearts of the nation

Bill Brown (right) goes out to bat with Don Bradman [1931] at Trent Bridge in 1938

Hugh Bartlett

after the war with his audacious and brave batting against Australia and his record-breaking feats of 1947, when he scored 3,816 runs and 18 centuries. He was among the first British sportsmen to make a healthy living out of advertisements and endorsements, his personality and his game all the more attractive for their flaws (he was a poor timekeeper and a shocking judge of a run).

"An adaptable player with a touch of genius, Compton possesses a sound defence, a wonderful eye and the right stroke for every ball," *Wisden* stated. "Among the young batsmen of the day, there is no one better worth watching."

Wood was called up for his Test debut as a late stand-in wicketkeeper for the timeless Oval Test a few days short of his 40th birthday. Asked for £7 15s by his driver for the journey

from Leeds, he said he only wanted to pay the fare, not buy the taxi. With England batting in painstaking fashion for a record 903 for seven, *Wisden* praised Wood – who contributed a brisk 53 – as "the only batsman on his side who attempted a forcing game".

Wood, who in 1939 played three more home Tests, had been a county regular since 1928, averaging 700 runs and 68 dismissals per year; in 1935 he became the first Yorkshire keeper to top 1,000 runs in a season.

By including Farnes and Bartlett, *Wisden* picked two amateurs for the first time since 1931. Farnes, who stood 6ft 5in and bowled fast off a short run-up, shone in his final year at Cambridge in 1933, when he also played for Essex and finished with 113 wickets at 18.38. The following year he took ten wickets on Test debut against Australia, but injuries and teaching commitments were to limit his appearances. Even so, he made three Test tours. In 1938, his 11 wickets helped the Gentlemen to only their second win over the Players at Lord's since 1914.

Bartlett's success as a tall attacking left-handed bat was more fleeting. A healthy run-scorer at Dulwich and Cambridge, where he arrived the year after Farnes left, he played briefly for Surrey before qualifying for Sussex: 1938 was his first full Championship season, and it remained his best. Promised his county cap if he scored fifty away to Yorkshire, he rattled up 94 in 75 minutes. He scored an unbeaten 175 for the Gentlemen, and struck a century in 57 minutes against the Australians. He toured South Africa in 1938-39, and was named for the cancelled 1939-40 trip to India, but never played a Test.

In the Second World War, Bartlett served with distinction in the army, and afterwards captained Sussex for three seasons before resigning. He was later president of the club, and died while watching a match at Hove in 1988. Farnes was killed in 1941 when he crashed his plane on his first unsupervised night flight. Brown, who also served in the air force, outlived him by 67 years.

Arthur Wood keeps wicket for England in 1939.

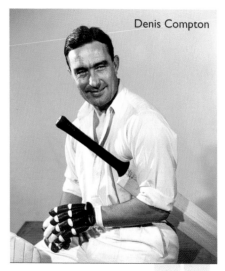

Ken Farnes

Denis Compton

Denis Compton:
"An adaptable player with a touch of genius, Compton possesses a sound defence, a wonderful eye and the right stroke for every ball"

CRICKETERS OF THE YEAR 1939 – Performances in the English season 1938

Name	Age*		Matches	Runs	Bat ave	Wickets	Bowl ave	Catches (/st)
HT Bartlett	24	First-class	21	1548	57.33	0		4
WA Brown	26	First-class	25	1854	57.93	0		14
		Tests	4	512	73.14			3
DCS Compton	20	First-class	30	1868	45.56	16	31.50	35
		Tests	4	214	42.80			4
K Farnes	27	First-class	19	136	9.71	107	18.84	14
		Tests	4	14	7.00	17	34.17	0
A Wood	40	First-class	32	661	20.65			35/22
		Tests	1	53	53.00			3

* as at 1/4/1939

1940 Five Cricketers of the Year

Learie Constantine (West Indians) ✦ ●
Bill Edrich (Middlesex) ✦
Walter Keeton (Nottinghamshire and England) ✦
Brian Sellers (Yorkshire) ✦
Doug Wright (Kent and England) ●

HEADLINE EVENTS FROM 1939

• County champions – Yorkshire. The season is cut short by war

• England beat West Indies 1-0

• England win 1-0 in South Africa in 1938-39

LEARIE CONSTANTINE, A TRINIDADIAN all-rounder, was chosen 16 years after his first tour. In 1923 he was hailed as the world's finest fielder. In 1928 he performed the double. *Wisden* did not pass up another opportunity when he topped the bowling averages in 1939. "It would have been hard if we had had to wait much longer for a photograph of the elastic and versatile Constantine," wrote a reviewer in *The Times*.

Constantine's family was steeped in cricket; his parents – the descendants of slaves – both played, and his father Lebrun twice toured England. Learie himself found sport opened doors closed to him as an ordinary individual. After the 1928 tour he resolved to improve his cricket in order to gain a professional contract in the Lancashire leagues that would enable him to pursue a legal career in England. He continued to represent West Indies, and was central to the series defeat of England in 1934-35.

In later life, he made an immense contribution to racial tolerance, especially in the UK, where he was instrumental in the passing of the Race Relations Act and became the first black peer, but his gift to the West Indies was

establishing its distinctive style of cricket.

"Who will deny that he has been all the more intriguing because of his emphatic rejection of the ordinary?" *Wisden* stated. "[He is] a cricketer who will never be forgotten, who took great heed that all nature's gifts should be, as it were, expanded by usage, a deep thinker and an athlete whose every movement was a joy to behold."

Bill Edrich's career was still in its infancy. One of four sons of a Norfolk farmer who all played first-class cricket, Edrich had marked his first full season for Middlesex in 1937, aged 21, by scoring 2,000 runs. The next year, he reached 1,000 before the end of May and again topped 2,000, but failed repeatedly for England against Australia and South Africa until, at the last gasp, he produced a fighting double-century in the Timeless Test at Durban.

That did not save his place against West Indies at home in 1939, but after a slow start he scored 2,000 runs for a third time. A powerful and aggressive player of fast bowling, Edrich was a courageous and combative batsman, useful fast change bowler and fine fielder. After surviving the war as a daytime bomber pilot, for which he received the DFC, he returned to

Learie Constantine

The Yorkshire side which won seven Championships in the 1930s. Back row (l-r): Bright Heyhirst (masseur), Len Hutton [1938], Frank Smailes, Bill Bowes [1932], Ellis Robinson, Cyril Turner, Horace Fisher, Bill Ringrose (scorer). Seated: Hedley Verity [1932], Arthur Mitchell, Maurice Leyland [1929], **Brian Sellers** (captain), Herbert Sutcliffe [1920], Arthur Wood [1939], Wilf Barber

Learie Constantine:

"A deep thinker and an athlete whose every movement was a joy to behold"

cricket as an amateur, resumed his formidable middle-order partnership with Denis Compton [1938] for county and country, and got through five marriages.

Brian Sellers was a modestly gifted middle-order batsman, but an exceptional leader who captained Yorkshire to their third title in succession and their sixth in eight years since

CRICKETERS OF THE YEAR 1940 – Performances in the English season 1939

Name	Age*		Matches	Runs	Bat ave	Wickets	Bowl ave	Catches (/st)
LN Constantine	38	First-class	22	614	21.17	103	17.77	17
		Tests	3	110	27.50	11	29.81	1
WJ Edrich	24	First-class	29	2186	49.68	15	50.80	30
WW Keeton	34	First-class	25	1765	51.91	0		4
		Tests	1	20	10.00			0
AB Sellers	33	First-class	33	708	20.22	0		19
DVP Wright	25	First-class	26	490	18.84	141	16.81	14
		Tests	3	7	7.00	6	35.33	2

as at 1/4/1940

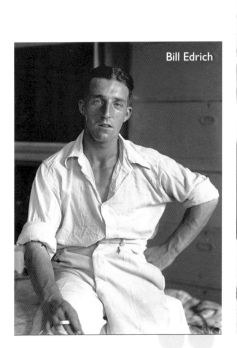

Bill Edrich

Walter Keeton (left) takes the field at Trent Bridge with Nottinghamshire wicketkeeper Arthur Wheat

Bill Edrich:

"No other cricketer has ever been so persevered with in the face of continued non-success as a run-getter"

taking regular charge in 1933 (they won another Championship under him in 1946). He was capable of playing courageous innings and was a fearless fielder, but it was his ability to keep Yorkshire functioning despite the absences of England players that marked him out.

Sellers's father Arthur, who played for the county in the 1890s, chaired the selection committee when his son started. By 1939, Brian himself was an England selector, and after retiring in 1948 began a long run as Yorkshire chairman, his autocratic style contributing to the departures of Ray Illingworth [1960] and Brian Close [1964] which triggered the club's infighting of the 1970s.

Doug Wright was a young leg-spin and googly bowler of rich promise. He was spotted by Aubrey Faulkner, who gave him a job at his Walham Green cricket school, and later mentored at Kent by Tich Freeman [1923]. After not picking him following his fine season in 1938, when he played three Tests against Australia, the editor predicted Wright was "almost sure to enjoy the honour in a future year".

Wright made sure he did not wait long by finishing as the leading wicket-taker on the 1938-39 tour of South Africa and seventh in the national averages in 1939, when he warmed up for the First Test with 16 wickets at Bath. By this time he had already performed five hat-tricks (adding two more later). He was inconsistent but dangerous, and England kept faith until 1950-51; with 108 wickets at 39.11 in 34 Tests, he is statistically the best leg-spinner they have had.

Walter Keeton, who had played one Test as a stand-in in 1934, was the third England opening partner of the summer for Len Hutton [1938] – due reward for a fine season with Nottinghamshire, for whom he scored 1,644 Championship runs, including what remains a county-record 312 not out against Middlesex.

Keeton was out for 0 and 20 at The Oval; the next day his season was ended when Ken Farnes [1939] broke his hand, although the outbreak of war in early September soon brought an end to all cricket. Keeton's career was marred by several injuries, the worst coming in 1935 when he was knocked down by a lorry. He returned after the war, and did not lose his Nottinghamshire place until he was 46.

1941 to 1946

No award

WISDEN SUSPENDED ITS CRICKETERS OF THE YEAR feature during the years of the Second World War. In his preface to the 1940 edition, Haddon Whitaker, the editor, stated that it would not reappear until after the war, thereby ruling out a repeat of Sydney Pardon's wartime selection of five public-school cricketers in 1918 and 1919 – or something similar. Whitaker wrote: "For the war years another type of choice will be made." In fact, this did not happen. With the conflict ending in May 1945, some cricket was played in England that summer – including a series of five "Victory Tests" against Australia – but *Wisden* contented itself in its 1946 edition with a full-page photograph and appreciation of Eddie Paynter, who had announced his retirement.

Doug Wright

Part Three: 1947 to 1968

THE PRESENTATION OF THE CRICKETERS OF the Year was greatly enhanced after the Second World War. Each player was accorded a full-page action photograph, and the written profiles – typically half as long again as those from earlier – provided more thorough and rounded portraits, blending technical analysis with colourful biographical details about personal lives. The modern blueprint was born.

The new approach was set with the first post-war group of 1947, when Hubert Preston, who had assumed the editorship three years earlier, commissioned his son Norman – who would succeed him in 1952 and remain editor until 1980 – to write profiles of four England players chosen for the 1946-47 tour of Australia. Norman Preston was covering the tour as an agency reporter and, leaving home with the team aboard the *Stirling Castle* on August 31 (well before the English season had finished), personally interviewed the players on the outward voyage.

During his time as editor, Hubert Preston employed at least eight different writers to produce the profiles, and most were well versed in popular journalism (Hubert Preston himself never wrote a profile as editor). The one used most often was Reg Hayter, a long-standing contributor to *Wisden*, whose close relationship with players led to him becoming one of the earliest agents to stars such as Denis Compton.

For his part, Norman Preston broke new ground in his first year by commissioning Bill Bowes, a Cricketer of the Year himself in 1932, to write the profile of Bob Appleyard, whom

Bowes had coached at Yorkshire. Bowes also wrote profiles of at least eight more Yorkshire cricketers between 1954 and 1969. He may also have been the author of an unsigned profile of Fred Trueman in 1953.

Norman Preston called on other notable cricketers to write profiles during this period. Robin Marlar wrote about his Sussex colleague Ted Dexter for the 1961 edition, and Jack Fingleton, who had toured England in 1938, contributed an assessment of Norman O'Neill, a fellow New South Welshman, in 1962. That same year, uniquely, Richie Benaud – as Australia's Ashes-winning captain – was not only chosen as a Cricketer of the Year but contributed the profile of one of the others, all-rounder Alan Davidson. Benaud later wrote six more profiles of Australian tourists, four in 1973 and two in 1976. As writers were given freer rein in what they said, so the practice of giving the player's full name and birth details in the opening paragraph was gradually abandoned. These details were provided lower down the piece.

Foreign representation continued to grow, with 46 out of 110 Cricketers of the Year in this period belonging to touring teams, a rise from 24.5% in 1918–40 to 41.8%. With only two exceptions – following the summers of 1952 and 1959, when India were the visitors – every touring team had at least one player selected, even after split tours were introduced in 1965. The famous Australian side of 1948 uniquely swept the board by claiming all five Cricketers of the Year in 1949, and four Australian tourists were picked following the 1961 Ashes series. West

Indies had four men picked after both their 1950 and 1963 tours, early markers on what proved a golden run for Caribbean cricket through to the 1990s. Fazal Mahmood became the first Pakistan player chosen following their inaugural tour of 1954, and three Asians were selected in the same year for the first time in 1968.

An additional five foreign players were picked while playing for domestic English sides: Martin Donnelly, a New Zealander, was chosen after a prolific season at Oxford University in 1947; Bruce Dooland and George Tribe, two Australians, were picked in 1955 after starring for Nottinghamshire and Northamptonshire respectively; Roy Marshall, who had toured with West Indies in 1950, was picked in 1959 when a Hampshire player; and Bill Alley, who scored 3,000 runs for Somerset in 1961, gave Australia a fifth representative in 1962.

Alley, at 43, was the oldest player chosen during this period, while Mushtaq Mohammad of Pakistan, picked the following year at 19, was the youngest: indeed he was the youngest ever, outside the schoolboy selections of 1918 and 1919.

The proportion of home-grown cricketers who had played Tests for England in the previous summer also rose, from 45.2% in 1918–40 to 69.5% (41 out of 59), reflecting the growth of international cricket. The only years no England Test player of the previous summer was chosen were 1949 and 1962, when Australians swept the board. Four were chosen in 1947, 1960 and 1967 (although one of the four in 1967 included Basil D'Oliveira, who had qualified for England by residence after emigrating from his native South Africa). All 11 England players who took the field in the Second and Fourth Tests against Australia in 1958-59 had previously been Cricketers of the Year.

This suggested that the Prestons were not much interested in left-field selections, although as we shall see in the next section Norman Preston was obliged to change tack during the 1970s. But in this era, only four of the 110 chosen players never appeared in Test cricket – John Langridge (1950), Stuart Surridge (1953), Vic Wilson (1961) and Alley (1962). Surridge (Surrey) and Wilson (Yorkshire) were both chosen as Championship-winning captains, as was Tom Dollery of Warwickshire in 1952.

The domination of Surrey and Yorkshire, who won 14 of the 20 Championship titles settled outright, was reflected in their being awarded 21 Cricketers of the Year between them (Surrey 11, Yorkshire 10). Surrey, who won seven successive Championships, actually had ten players chosen in 14 years from 1947 to 1960, and several times during 1958 fielded seven players who had been Cricketers of the Year.

Northamptonshire, Lancashire and Worcestershire were the next best, with five awards each: Northamptonshire never won the Championship, while Lancashire only shared the title in 1950. Glamorgan (in 1948) and Hampshire (1961) won their first Championships without *Wisden* recognising any of their players: both were stymied by those Australian clean sweeps. Bob Barber, who helped Warwickshire lift the Gillette Cup in 1966, was the first to be named a Cricketer of the Year after his county won a one-day competition, although his selection owed as much to a brilliant Test century in Australia the previous winter.

About 30% of the English cricketers held amateur status before the distinction between "Gentlemen" and "Players" was finally abolished in November 1962. The last amateurs to be chosen were Ted Dexter and Raman Subba Row in 1961.

With competition stiff among Australian, West Indian and South African touring players, some notable performers inevitably missed out. Sid Barnes scored prolifically for the Australians in 1948. Wes Hall, whose new-ball partner Charlie Griffith was chosen in 1964, took 34 Test wickets for West Indies on two tours. John Waite made three tours of England as wicketkeeper, scoring 684 Test runs for South Africa, whose all-rounder Trevor Goddard scored 455 runs and took 42 wickets in Tests on two tours of England. None was chosen.

With India badly beaten in 1952 and 1959, they did not have a Cricketer of the Year between 1947 and 1968. Vijay Hazare averaged 41.45 in seven Tests in England in 1946 and 1952 but missed out, as did Polly Umrigar and Vijay Manjrekar – both of whom scored more than 3,000 Test runs but did little in Tests in England.

Dick Howorth of Worcestershire, the first all-rounder to the double in 1946 and 1947, topped 10,000 runs and 1,000 wickets in his career

CRICKETERS OF THE YEAR 1947–68

(Teams they represented in the English season prior to selection)

Team	Years	Awards	Batsmen	Bowlers	Allrounders	WK
Surrey	1947-66	11	5	5	0	1
Yorkshire	1948-65	10	5	3	2	0
Lancashire	1947-68	5	2	3	0	0
Worcestershire	1950-67	5	2	1	2	0
Northamptonshire	1955-67	5	3	1	1	0
Middlesex	1948-67	4	2	0	1	1
Sussex	1949-68	4	3	0	0	1
Warwickshire	1952-67	4	2	1	1	0
Essex	1947-56	3	1	0	2	0
Nottinghamshire	1950-55	2	1	0	1	0
Kent	1951-56	2	1	0	0	1
Gloucestershire	1953-59	2	2	0	0	0
Somerset	1953-62	2	1	0	1	0
Derbyshire	1959-60	2	1	1	0	0
Hampshire	1959	2	1	1	0	0
Glamorgan	–	0	0	0	0	0
Leicestershire	–	0	0	0	0	0
Cambridge University	1952-53	2	2	0	0	0
Oxford University	1948	1	1	0	0	0
England	1947-68	41	24	10	5	2
Australians	1949-65	16	8	3	3	2
West Indians	1951-67	11	7	3	1	0
South Africans	1948-66	10	7	3	0	0
Pakistanis	1955-68	4	2	1	1	0
New Zealanders	1950-66	3	1	1	1	0
Indians	1947-68	2	1	0	1	0
TOTAL		**153***	**85**	**37**	**23**	**8**

*In total, there were 110 Cricketers of the Year between 1947 and 1968. However, the figure of 153 awards shown in the table reflects the fact that thirty-nine players appeared for two teams during the season in question (all for counties plus Tests for England). Two players, Peter May and David Sheppard, appeared for three teams (university, county and England)

without being chosen, as did Tom Cartwright and John Mortimore. Sam Cook, a predecessor of Mortimore's at Gloucestershire, took 100 wickets in a season nine times without being picked. Another Gloucestershire player, David Allen, appeared in 39 Tests between 1959-60 and 1966 without being chosen. Ken Suttle, of Sussex, ended his career in 1971 with 30,225 runs to his name, precisely the same tally as Les Berry, of Leicestershire, who had stopped in 1951. Neither was chosen, and no one has scored more runs and not been picked by *Wisden*.

1947

Five Cricketers of the Year

Alec Bedser (Surrey and England) ●

Laurie Fishlock (Surrey and England) /

Vinoo Mankad (Indians) / ●

Peter Smith (Essex and England) / ●

Cyril Washbrook (Lancashire and England) /

CHAMPIONSHIP AND TEST CRICKET RESUMED in England in 1946 after a seven-year break, and the challenge for every team was to blend new faces with old. The new faces were not necessarily young: Alec Bedser, who started his Test career in sensational fashion with 22 wickets in two matches against India, turned 28 during the season. *Wisden*'s Five had an average age of 34, making them the third-oldest quintet to date (it was soon pushed into fourth place by the 1948 selection).

The four Englishmen were all chosen for the 1946-47 tour of Australia, a party that left on August 31, before the home season ended. The profiles were based on interviews conducted during the outward voyage by Norman Preston, son of the editor Hubert Preston, who was covering the tour for the Cricket Reporting Agency. The style is less staid than before, more akin to the popular journalism of the day, and the words were, for the first time, accompanied by action photographs. All four had served in the war in various capacities.

Knighted in 1996 for services to the game, Bedser ranks among the greatest English bowlers. He caused Don Bradman [1931] as much trouble as anyone – dismissing him six times during the 1946-47 and 1948 series – and was a key figure in England's Ashes win in 1953, their first for 19 years. No more than fast-medium, but 6ft 3in tall and armed with two great weapons, a late inswinger and a sharp leg-cutter, Bedser was the mainstay of England's attack for eight years, during which he rose to become the world's leading Test wicket-taker at the time.

Bedser, who had played only a dozen first-class matches at the time of his Test debut, joined the Surrey staff in 1938 along with his twin brother Eric, who himself became a stalwart of the county side.

If Alec Bedser helped revive England after the war with ball, Cyril Washbrook did so with bat, by forming the most courageous and defiant of opening partnerships with Len Hutton [1938]. Washbrook had been a solid run-scorer for Lancashire since 1935 – and won his first Test cap in 1937 – but he took his game to a new level in 1946, finishing second in the national averages. He maintained exceptional form for county and country until 1950-51, when the runs dried up on a tour of Australia and he lost his Test place.

As a member of the selection panel,

Laurie Fishlock

Cyril Washbrook

Washbrook was persuaded into an emergency return to the side at Headingley in 1956, aged 41, and scored a vital 98 that helped turn the series England's way.

Laurie Fishlock, a left-handed bat, had also been a county regular since the mid-1930s and received an early taste of Test cricket. He played twice against India in 1936 and was taken to Australia the following winter, but his tour was ruined by a hand injury. This pattern repeated itself ten years later: he was recalled to face India in 1946 – having become the first batsman to

Cyril Washbrook:
"To see this young Lancastrian on the cricket field, one would imagine that he treats cricket solely as a serious business because he never allows his stern face to relax – the crowd calls him 'Smiler'"

CRICKETERS OF THE YEAR 1947 – Performances in the English season 1946

Name	Age*		Matches	Runs	Bat ave	Wickets	Bowl ave	Catches (Ist)
AV Bedser	28	First-class	26	494	17.03	128	20.13	10
		Tests	3	38	19.00	24	12.41	3
LB Fishlock	40	First-class	27	2221	50.47	0		8
		Tests	1	8	8.00			0
MH Mankad	29	First-class	28	1120	28.00	129	20.76	21
		Tests	3	124	24.80	11	26.54	3
TPB Smith	38	First-class	21	834	25.27	120	19.49	9
		Tests	1	0		1	58.00	0
C Washbrook	32	First-class	28	2400	68.57	0		12
		Tests	3	146	36.50			1

* as at 1/4/1947

1,000 runs in the season – before travelling to Australia, where he sustained a broken finger. He enjoyed no great days with England, but at 45 helped Surrey win the first of seven successive Championships in 1952.

Fishlock was 39 when the 1946 season began and Peter Smith 38. An occasional film actor and radio broadcaster, as well as the victim of a hoax telegram calling him to play a Test at The Oval in 1933, Smith had been an Essex regular since 1930, bowling leg-breaks and googlies and making useful lower-order runs. He had big seasons with the ball in 1937 and 1938, but his wickets never came cheaper than in 1946, when he finally made his England debut at The Oval for real. He played two Tests in Australia in 1946-47, but took only two expensive wickets.

Smith got through more than 1,600 overs in 1947 for 172 wickets, but his most eye-catching feat came with the bat, when he scored 163 – the highest ever by a No. 11 – in a last-wicket stand of 218 with Frank Vigar at Chesterfield.

Vinoo Mankad, whom Lionel Tennyson [1914] had described in 1937-38 as worthy of

Alec Bedser

Peter Smith

Alec Bedser:

"He takes a comparatively short run of eight paces and imparts all his energy at the moment of delivery. Immensely strong, he can keep bowling for long spells … he rarely sends down a loose ball"

Vinoo Mankad bats for India, with Len Hutton [1938] at slip

inclusion in a World XI, was a tireless and versatile member of India's party, and the first touring cricketer to achieve the double since 1928. He got through prodigious work with the ball, bowling 1,160 overs, 380 more than any of his colleagues. Unlike some of his countrymen, Mankad had no difficulty adapting to alien conditions; he scored two Test centuries in Australia, and at Lord's in 1952 took on England virtually single-handed, with innings of 72 and 184 as well as sending down 97 overs of left-arm spin in the match (he took five for 196 in the first innings). India still lost.

Mankad, who batted in all 11 positions for India and was used in various roles on this tour, was one of the first Test cricketers to top 2,000 runs and 150 wickets. A few months after his selection by *Wisden*, he caused a furore by running out Bill Brown [1939] at the non-striker's end at Sydney, a type of dismissal still known as "Mankading".

1948

Five Cricketers of the Year

Martin Donnelly (Oxford University) *i*
Alan Melville (South Africans) *i*
Dudley Nourse (South Africans) *i*
Jack Robertson (Middlesex and England) *i*
Norman Yardley (Yorkshire and England) *i*

HEADLINE EVENTS FROM 1947

- County champions – Middlesex

- England beat South Africa 3-0

- Denis Compton and Bill Edrich rewrite the batting record books, Compton scoring 18 centuries and 3,816 runs in the season, both still records

- Australia retain the Ashes at home in 1946-47, winning 3-0

THE CRICKET SEASON OF 1947 RANKS AMONG THE greatest: glorious weather, big crowds relishing a game denied them during the war, and batsmen in the ascendant. Denis Compton [1939] and Bill Edrich [1940], the biggest stars, had already been chosen, but *Wisden* had no difficulty finding five more batsmen to celebrate, including the England and South Africa captains.

Norman Yardley had succeeded Wally Hammond [1928] after acting as his deputy in Australia in 1946-47, where he took charge for the final Test. On a difficult tour, Yardley showed courage with bat and ball, scoring 252 runs and topping the bowling averages with ten wickets. In the First Test against South Africa he scored a defiant 99 after England followed on 325 in arrears; a stand of 237 with Compton went far towards saving the game.

Yardley was regarded as a decent, kindly leader, but was restricted by his work as a wine merchant from regular touring. He subsequently led England only at home, against Australia in 1948 (when he faced criticism for his tactics at Leeds) and – in the first three Tests – West Indies in 1950. He also led Yorkshire from 1948

to 1955, but with limited success for such a big club (just one shared title).

A talented sportsman at St Peter's, York and Cambridge, Yardley was described in his *Wisden* obituary as Yorkshire's finest amateur since Stanley Jackson [1894]. He served in the Green Howards during the war alongside Hedley Verity [1932], and was wounded.

Jack Robertson, whose opening partnership with Syd Brown at Middlesex paved the way for Compton and Edrich, had a stunning season; his tally of 12 centuries was bettered only by Compton's 18, and in the Championship – which Middlesex inevitably won – he and Compton stood equal first with 11 hundreds. He deputised for the injured Edrich in the final Test in the unfamiliar position of No. 3; as opener his Test opportunities came only when others were unavailable, though he topped the averages in the West Indies in 1947-48, and scored 121 at Lord's in 1949.

Robertson was abstemious and self-effacing, but his aggression came out against new-ball bowling. His jaw was broken by Ray Lindwall [1949], but three times he scored a century in the first session of a match, and at Worcester in 1949

Dudley Nourse

he reached 331 by stumps on the opening day. It remains Middlesex's record score.

Alan Melville, who as a schoolboy was almost taken on South Africa's 1929 tour of England, was a cricketer of immense integrity and courage who repeatedly battled illness and injury. For much of the 1930s he played for, and captained, Oxford and Sussex with success, before taking a job on the Johannesburg Stock Exchange. In 1938-39 he led South Africa against England, scoring 78 and 103 in the Timeless Test at Durban. During the war he wore a steel jacket for 11 months to overcome a back injury.

He retained the captaincy for the 1947 tour, and despite breaking a finger early on, and then straining a thigh in the match itself, he scored 189 and 104 not out in the First Test, and followed up with 117 in the Second. But the tour took a toll on his fragile health, and his form did not last. On returning home he announced his retirement, but reversed the decision in order to play one further Test.

Melville's vice-captain Dudley Nourse fully sustained his form, topping 50 in seven of his nine Test innings and finishing the series with 621 runs. By scoring 149 in a third-wicket stand of 319 with his captain, Nourse helped

Alan Melville

Alan Melville:
"A shrewd, undemonstrative captain, he inspired the affection of his own and the respect of his opponents"

CRICKETERS OF THE YEAR 1948 – Performances in the English season 1947

Name	Age*		Matches	Runs	Bat ave	Wickets	Bowl ave	Catches (/st)
MP Donnelly	30	First-class	17	1488	62.00	5	29.20	9
A Melville	37	First-class	26	1547	40.71			27
		Tests	5	569	63.22			5
AD Nourse	37	First-class	23	1453	42.73			26
		Tests	5	621	69.00			4
JDB Robertson	31	First-class	32	2760	52.07	7	38.71	31
		Tests	1	34	17.00			0
NWD Yardley	33	First-class	30	1906	44.32	11	40.45	30/1
		Tests	5	273	39.00	0		7

as at 1/4/1948

Norman Yardley

Norman Yardley:
"[He] has now reached full stature as a cricketer, his quality as an international player proven both in technique and temperament"

Jack Robertson

put South Africa in control of the First Test, but he scored an even better hundred at Old Trafford on a pitch taking spin. Taking over the captaincy, he topped his team's batting at home to England in 1948-49 and Australia in 1949-50, and finished second in England in 1951, when he scored a double-century in the opening Test with a damaged thumb.

The son of Dave Nourse, a left-handed batsman who played 45 Tests, Dudley scored his maiden first-class century against a Western Province team containing his 52-year-old father. Four years later in 1935-36, he played his finest innings, a double-century against Australia at Johannesburg.

Martin Donnelly was rated among the most attractive of all batsmen, with some acclaiming him at the time as the world's best left-hander. A gifted athlete whose twin brother died in infancy, Donnelly had toured England in 1937 as a teenager, scoring 1,414 runs.

After rising to major in the army during the war, he settled in England, returning to public attention with a dazzling century for a Dominions team at Lord's in 1945. He went up to Oxford in his late twenties, scored six centuries for the university in 1946, and added three more in 1947, by which time he had also acquired a rugby Blue and an England cap as centre against Ireland at Lansdowne Road. His finest innings of 1947 was an unbeaten 162 for Gentlemen v Players.

Donnelly's cricket career proved fleeting. Taking up a job with Courtaulds which took him to Australia in 1950, he played only occasionally for Warwickshire, and in one more Test series for New Zealand in 1949 – although it proved a tremendous farewell with three half-centuries and a sumptuous double at Lord's.

Martin Donnelly

1949

Five Cricketers of the Year

Lindsay Hassett (Australians) *

Bill Johnston (Australians) ●

Ray Lindwall (Australians) ●

Arthur Morris (Australians) *

Don Tallon (Australians) ▥

FOR THE ONLY TIME, ALL FIVE CRICKETERS OF the Year were chosen from one touring team. Under Don Bradman [1931], the 1948 Australians (since known as "the Invincibles") went unbeaten in 31 first-class matches – of which 23 were won, including four of the five Tests.

A brief introduction to the feature explained that *Wisden* had taken the decision both as a tribute to the team and in recognition that Australian cricketers had "limited opportunities… to appear in this gallery". Regrets were expressed that three more Australians had been omitted "as a reluctant necessity". They were Keith Miller and Neil Harvey, who were picked in 1954, and Sid Barnes, who never was.

There was also no room for a representative of Glamorgan, whose cricketers for the first time won the Championship: captain Wilf Wooller, leading batsman Emrys Davies and top wicket-taker Len Muncer would all have been contenders. In fact, no Glamorgan player was picked by *Wisden* between 1931 and 1969.

Lindsay Hassett, Bradman's vice-captain, was a more defensive batsman after the war, but had an established popularity among English audiences through his involvement in the 1938 tour and as leader of an Australian Services side that played Victory Tests in 1945. A small man of agile wit and feet, he assembled a formidable record, averaging 46.56 in 43 Tests and 58.24 in all first-class cricket, a figure surpassed by only four frontline batsmen at the time he retired after leading Australia in England in 1953.

Centuries from Bradman and Hassett shaped the opening Test of the 1948 series, just as they had in 1946-47. It was Hassett's only significant score in the Tests, but his support of Bradman was crucial, and in first-class matches outside the Tests he topped 1,250 runs. He started the 1953 series with centuries at Trent Bridge and Lord's, but lacked the support to prevent a 1–0 defeat.

Ray Lindwall, a bowler of rare pace, accuracy and variation who in 1956 became the first fast bowler to take 200 Test wickets, was the means of many victories. With the help of Miller and a new ball every 55 overs, Lindwall tested the nerves of many batsmen. A lot were found wanting. Of his 86 tour wickets, half were bowled.

Lindwall had been a star of the 1946-47 Ashes, when he topped the bowling averages

The "Invincible" Australians at Lord's in 1948, with the Humber cars provided for their use: (l-r) **Don Tallon** (in hat), Sam Loxton, Keith Miller [1954], Ernie Toshack, Neil Harvey [1954], Ian Johnson, **Ray Lindwall**, **Arthur Morris**, Bill Brown [1939], Sid Barnes (behind car), **Lindsay Hassett**, Don Bradman [1931], Ron Saggers, Doug Ring, Ron Hamence, Colin McCool, **Bill Johnston**

CRICKETERS OF THE YEAR 1949 – Performances in the English season 1948

Name	Age*		Matches	Runs	Bat ave	Wickets	Bowl ave	Catches (/st)
AL Hassett	35	First-class	22	1563	74.42	0		23
		Tests	5	310	44.28			6
WA Johnston	27	First-class	21	188	18.80	102	16.42	9
		Tests	5	62	20.66	27	23.33	2
RR Lindwall	27	First-class	22	411	24.17	86	15.68	14
		Tests	5	191	31.83	27	19.62	3
AR Morris	27	First-class	21	1922	71.18	2	45.50	10
		Tests	5	696	87.00	0		4
D Tallon	33	First-class	14	283	25.72			29/14
		Tests	4	112	28.00			12

*as at 1/4/1949

with 18 wickets and scored a quick hundred at Melbourne, but he was even more destructive now, topping the averages with 27 wickets, equalling the best haul to date by a visiting fast bowler in England, set by Ted McDonald [1922].

With the exception of Leeds (where he scored 77 to keep Australia in the game), Lindwall struck early in every innings he bowled. No one bowled better at Lord's, where he took eight wickets, or at The Oval, where his six for 20 routed England for 52.

Bill Johnston, whose brother was killed in the war, was not as menacing as Lindwall or Miller, but as a tall left-arm fast-medium bowler with a useful bouncer he was as effective. He matched Lindwall with 27 wickets in the Tests and, working hard on the tour as a whole, was the only bowler to top 100 wickets. With Miller not bowling much in the Second and Third Tests, Johnston shared the new ball with Lindwall and gave nothing away.

He remained a central part of Australia's attack into the mid-1950s, and topped 20 wickets in each of the next four series. His bowling dipped in England in 1953, when he succumbed to knee trouble, but he acquired a curious batting record by scoring 102 runs in 17 innings on the tour for only once out, giving him an average of 102.00. He also possessed a prodigious throwing arm.

English gratitude that Bradman was retiring was tempered by the success of Arthur Morris, who followed up three centuries in the series in Australia with three more in England, including 182 as a record 404 was chased down at Leeds. In all matches, Morris – who like Lindwall had played for the St George club in Sydney under the guidance of Bill O'Reilly [1935] – scored more runs than anyone except Bradman.

Morris's left-handedness seemed a problem to England; left-handed openers were as rare as left-arm quicks like Johnston, and his tendency to shuffle across his stumps to defend worked

well. But he later came badly unstuck against Alec Bedser [1947], who dismissed him ten times in as many matches (having done so eight times before) to keep Morris's average below 40.

Don Tallon took only 12 catches in the series – he missed the game at Leeds – and averaged less than three dismissals per game in his 21 Tests, but his reputation as a keeper brooked no argument. His contemporaries regarded him as one of the greats, and a master of slick glovework whether dealing with speed or spin. After surprisingly being omitted from the 1938 tour of England, he was kept waiting until he was 30 for his Test debut. A capable batsman, he scored nine first-class centuries, but was rarely required to make runs in Tests, though his best score of 92 hurt England at Melbourne in 1946-47.

The highlight of Tallon's 1948 tour came at The Oval, when he caught Len Hutton [1938] left-handed down the leg side at full stretch off an authentic leg-glance. He toured again in 1953, but was past his best and appeared in only the First Test.

Don Tallon

1950 Five Cricketers of the Year

Trevor Bailey (Essex and England) / ●
Roly Jenkins (Worcestershire) / ●
John Langridge (Sussex) /
Reg Simpson (Nottinghamshire and England) /
Bert Sutcliffe (New Zealanders) /

HEADLINE EVENTS FROM 1949

- County champions – Middlesex and Yorkshire share title

- England and New Zealand draw all four Tests

- England win 2-0 in South Africa in 1948-49

THE 1949 SEASON WAS LADEN WITH RUNS. Nineteen batsmen scored 2,000, and New Zealand comfortably drew all four three-day Tests, prompting a permanent move to five-day matches the following year.

Bert Sutcliffe, New Zealand's left-handed opener, scored more runs on tour than any previous visiting batsman bar Don Bradman [1931] in 1930; Reg Simpson and John Langridge both exceeded 2,500 at averages in excess of 60; and Trevor Bailey and Roly Jenkins both did the double for the first time.

There was no place, though, for Yorkshire's Brian Close [1964], who at the age of 18 also did the double, in his first season. In fact, editor Hubert Preston indicated that Warwickshire's Eric Hollies [1955], who took 166 wickets, was next in line, Jenkins being preferred only "after much discussion".

John Langridge, the younger brother of James [1932], first played for Sussex in 1928 and was now in his 40th year. Helped by four straight hundreds, he was first to 1,000 runs on June 2 and the first to 2,000 on July 11, and ended only one good innings shy of 3,000 (he had a quiet last game for Over Thirty v Under Thirty at

Hastings). His 2,441 runs and 12 hundreds for his county alone remain annual bests for Sussex.

He made a first appearance for Players v Gentlemen, but was usually ignored for representative matches, even though he was a first-rate slip and scored 2,000 in six seasons in the 1930s when England were looking for openers. He was picked for a tour of India in 1939-40, but it was cancelled because of the outbreak of war. No one has scored more centuries (76) and not played Test cricket. He later stood in seven Tests during a long umpiring career.

Simpson, who worked for the Gunn & Moore equipment company and played as an amateur, took a huge stride forward in 1949. The previous season he had averaged 29.18 and, although he toured South Africa in 1948-49, he failed in his one Test. He now produced a string of big scores on Trent Bridge's sublime surfaces, as well as an unbeaten 238 at Old Trafford. Being a fine sprinter, he also excelled at cover.

Recalled by England for the Third Test, also at Old Trafford, he not only scored a century but showed how attacking he could be, moving from 50 to 100 in 27 minutes. His next Test hundred would be even more momentous, an unbeaten 156 at Melbourne in 1950-51 which secured a first win over Australia in 15 post-war Tests. Simpson played 27 Tests in all, scoring two other hundreds, both on his home ground at Nottingham, and proved an able leader of the county.

Bailey, who combined teaching with Essex's assistant secretaryship and had declined to tour the West Indies in 1947-48, embarked on an even more significant Test career. For ten years he was England's premier all-rounder, amassing more than 2,000 runs and 100 wickets from 61 Tests. He influenced many games, most famously the Lord's Test of 1953, which he saved in a long rearguard with Willie Watson [1954]; the following year, inspired bowling brought a series-levelling win in Jamaica. He is one of only three post-war players with 20,000 runs and 2,000 wickets in first-class cricket, the others being Ray Illingworth [1960] and Fred Titmus [1963].

A product of Dulwich and Cambridge,

Bailey was most prized in 1949 for his lively and varied fast bowling. Famed later for his forward-defensive, his batting was quite aggressive at this time; in addition to taking 16 wickets against New Zealand, he scored 219 runs. A week after the final Test, he claimed all ten Lancashire wickets at Clacton.

Jenkins, one of ten children and a colourful character who, with a fidgety run-up and flail of arms, delivered sharp leg-breaks and googlies, toured South Africa in 1948-49 as a late substitute for Hollies. He postponed his wedding to go, and exceeded expectations by topping England's Test averages with 16 wickets at 30.93 apiece and outbowling Doug Wright [1940]. He fielded well and sold his wicket dearly.

Wisden said he returned home "a 50% better bowler", which he demonstrated by finishing as leading wicket-taker in the country in 1949 as Worcestershire finished third in the table. In the final Championship match, against Surrey, he took two hat-tricks. Jenkins performed the

Reg Simpson

Reg Simpson:
"When at his best Simpson is the type of batsman everyone admires"

John Langridge (right) goes out to umpire a match at Arundel in 1956 with Maurice Tate [1924]

Roly Jenkins

Bert Sutcliffe (left) with his New Zealand team-mate Jack Cowie

Trevor Bailey

double only once more, and appeared in just four more Tests, but finished with 10,000 runs and 1,000 wickets at first-class level.

Sutcliffe's rise was meteoric. After a few first-class appearances during war-time, he averaged nearly 100 across three seasons in New Zealand, three times scoring twin centuries, including once against MCC. He struggled to adjust to English conditions in 1949 at first, reaching fifty only three times in 14 innings leading up to the Tests, but once he found his feet there was no stopping him. He scored 101

in the Manchester Test. *Wisden* described him as a "well-built, good-looking, golden-haired batsman… possessing classic style, [a] master of all the strokes".

Sutcliffe later twice topped 350 in New Zealand provincial games, but his Test career suffered from playing in a weak side. He scored his only home Test century against England in 1950-51; his three other hundreds all came in India. He scored few Test runs in England in 1958 and 1965, and never finished on the winning side in 42 Tests, an unwanted record.

Trevor Bailey:
"Bailey is always experimenting. He has already changed his action five times and is ready to do so again for the sake of improvement"

CRICKETERS OF THE YEAR 1950 – Performances in the English season 1949

Name	Age*		Matches	Runs	Bat ave	Wickets	Bowl ave	Catches (/st)
TE Bailey	26	First-class	30	1380	35.38	130	24.20	14
		Tests	4	219	73.00	16	37.43	0
RO Jenkins	31	First-class	33	1183	28.16	183	21.19	27
JG Langridge	40	First-class	28	2914	60.70	2	14.00	32
RT Simpson	30	First-class	29	2525	63.12	16	31.93	11
		Tests	2	171	85.50	0		0
B Sutcliffe	26	First-class	29	2627	59.70	16	40.87	32
		Tests	4	423	60.42	1	95.00	4

as at 1/4/1950

1951

Five Cricketers of the Year

Godfrey Evans (Kent and England) ⋔
Sonny Ramadhin (West Indians) ●
Alf Valentine (West Indians) ●
Everton Weekes (West Indians) /
Frank Worrell (West Indians) /

- County champions – Lancashire and Surrey share title

- West Indies win their first series in England, 3-1

THIS IS THE YOUNGEST FIVE EVER CHOSEN – average age 24 at selection – and the youthful look was due to a new generation of West Indians shaking the game's old order with its innovation and brilliance. John Goddard's team not only trounced England 3–1 in the 1950 Tests but played breathtaking cricket, scoring runs fast and taking wickets by unorthodox means. The chosen four were largely uncoached.

Sonny Ramadhin and Alf Valentine, who had previously made only two first-class appearances apiece, claimed more than 250 wickets between them, and acquired a near-mystic reputation. The combined contribution of Everton Weekes and Frank Worrell exceeded 4,000 runs. Hubert Preston regretted not having room for Clyde Walcott [1958], who scored 1,775 runs. Five other players passed 1,000.

This first West Indies triumph on English soil inspired a generation of newly-arrived immigrants, who sang victory calypsos on the outfield after the win at Lord's, and eventually a string of Caribbean cricketers. Each of their next nine tours of England produced at least one Cricketer of the Year.

As it happened, the 1951 quartet forged close links with England. They played in the leagues, Worrell attended university in Manchester, and Ramadhin took up residence there.

Weekes and Worrell – both of whom were originally from Barbados, one short and strong, the other slim and lithe – were already established figures. Worrell had scored a triple-century for Barbados as a 19-year-old in a stand of 502 with Goddard, and had later shared in a world-record partnership of 574 with Walcott. He had also scored heavily against the English visitors of 1947-48. His maiden Test century came in the third match of that series, while Weekes's arrived in the fourth – what proved to be the first of five consecutive Test hundreds by him.

With only one century, Weekes was relatively subdued in the 1950 Tests, but unstoppable in other matches, recording one triple-century and four doubles by mid-July. Worrell was more influential in games that mattered: by scoring 261 in the Trent Bridge Test and 138 at The Oval, he helped West Indies total 500 and dictate proceedings.

Both men were knighted, Worrell having become one of the most significant of all

The strong West Indian touring team of 1950. Back row (l-r): Cecil Williams, Roy Marshall [1959], **Alf Valentine**, Lance Pierre, Clyde Walcott [1958], Hines Johnson, Allan Rae, Ken Trestrail, Bill Ferguson (baggage master). Seated: **Sonny Ramadhin**, Prior Jones, **Frank Worrell**, Rev. Palmer Barnes (assistant manager), John Goddard (captain), Gerry Gomez, Jeff Stollmeyer, Robert Christiani, **Everton Weekes**

cricketers – the first non-white captain of West Indies, a champion of positive, decent cricket, and a unifier of the Caribbean islands. He was appointed a senator in Jamaica, where he died of leukaemia aged 42. Weekes, who was forced to retire at 33 through injury, later had a long administrative career. A son, David Murray, played for West Indies but later fell on hard times.

Ramadhin, who was of part-Asian extraction and bowled in a cap with his sleeves buttoned down, was so small – fully grown he stood 5ft 4in – that he was overlooked for batting at his club in Trinidad. Instead he developed as a bowler who could turn the ball either way with a flick of fingers and wrist. One of the two games he played for Trinidad before the tour was watched by Goddard, who spotted his potential.

Few batsmen could pick Ramadhin in England; many ended up bowled or stumped.

Valentine held England's batsmen in an even firmer grip. He sent down 422.3 overs in four Tests: nearly half of them were maidens, and his 33 wickets set a record for a visiting player in England not broken until 1981 (by Terry Alderman in a six-Test Ashes series).

Like Ramadhin, Valentine came from a family with no cricketing links, but he made rapid strides at school in Spanish Town, Jamaica. At 17 he met Jack Mercer [1927], who encouraged him to spin the ball, but his lack of success before the England tour – two wickets in two games – made his selection an even bigger gamble than Ramadhin's. He only clinched a place in the First Test with 13 wickets against Lancashire in

Everton Weekes:
"Perhaps no batsman since Bradman has made such an impression on his first English tour as a ruthless compiler of big scores"

the final warm-up. Mid-tour it was discovered he needed glasses, which may explain his poor batting (though it never greatly improved).

Valentine also made an impact in his first series against Australia and India, but then lost his deadliness, the nadir coming in England in 1957 when he and Ramadhin were negated by pad-play. Ramadhin's decline was less steep, but he never touched the heights of 1950 again.

Godfrey Evans, who had come into the England side in 1946, was one of the most energetic and colourful of English cricketers. He was not infallible – he had been dropped in South Africa in 1948-49 and would be dropped again in 1951 – but as a wicketkeeper he was the best England had had up to this point, not the least of his contributions being to maintain the spirits of the side.

A good boxer in his youth before Kent asked him to choose sports, Evans first played for them as a batsman. In his fourth Test, at Adelaide, he scored 10 not out in 133 minutes to save the game, but could attack when necessary, and in an innings lasting only seven minutes longer in the First Test of 1950 scored 104. *Wisden* said that on his performances that

The 1950 spin twins **Alf Valentine** (left) and **Sonny Ramadhin** at Lord's with Brian Lara [1995]

season he must rank as the best keeper in the world. He remained an England regular until 1959, and his total of 219 Test dismissals was not bettered until another Kent keeper, Alan Knott [1970], went past it in 1976.

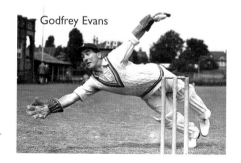

Godfrey Evans

CRICKETERS OF THE YEAR 1951 – Performances in the English season 1950

Name	Age*		Matches	Runs	Bat ave	Wickets	Bowl ave	Catches (/st)
TG Evans	30	First-class	21	1021	29.17			42/17
		Tests	3	224	37.33			3/6
S Ramadhin	21	First-class	21	36	5.14	135	14.88	3
		Tests	4	10	3.33	26	23.23	0
AL Valentine	20	First-class	21	49	3.06	123	17.94	7
		Tests	4	15	3.00	33	20.42	2
ED Weekes	26	First-class	23	2310	79.65	2	20.50	30
		Tests	4	338	56.33			11
FMM Worrell	26	First-class	22	1775	68.26	39	24.87	11
		Tests	4	539	89.83	6	30.33	4

as at 1/4/1951

Sonny Ramadhin:
"Batsmen [were] looking for mysterious deliveries which rarely came as they anticipated"

1952

Five Cricketers of the Year

Bob Appleyard (Yorkshire) ●

Tom Dollery (Warwickshire) /

Jim Laker (Surrey and England) ●

Peter May (Cambridge University, Surrey and England) /

Eric Rowan (South Africans) /

THESE FIVE ALMOST PICKED THEMSELVES FOR Norman Preston, the new editor. Bob Appleyard took 200 wickets in his first full season, and Peter May topped the batting averages in his second. Jim Laker bowled England to victory in the series decider with South Africa, while Eric Rowan was the leading batsman for the touring team. Tom Dollery became the first professional to captain his county to the title since Alfred Shaw in the 1880s.

May and Laker must rank among England's all-time greats – May would feature in any debate about the country's finest post-war batsmen, while Laker is a strong contender as its best off-spinner – but they were uneasy allies. Laker's bowling was a key factor in many of May's successes as Surrey and England captain, but they fell out after May rashly accused Laker of not trying during a county match in 1958. Laker's subsequent criticism of May in a book expedited the end of his Surrey career, while May, never easy with the public attention of leadership, soon quit at the age of 31 with a glittering record.

May's arrival was an early harbinger of England's dominance in the 1950s. On the evidence of his time at Charterhouse, plus a few games for Services teams and Cambridge University, he was picked for a Test trial in 1950 (failing twice against Laker). In 1951, he scored four centuries for Cambridge against counties and an unbeaten 119 for Gentlemen v Players, before celebrating news of his England call-up with a hundred on debut for Surrey. He then scored 138 on his first Test appearance at Headingley.

The next ten years brought May almost uninterrupted success: Surrey won seven straight titles (the last two under his captaincy), and England's next series loss did not come until 1958-59 – under May they won 20 out of 41 Tests between 1955 and 1961. In English conditions, he was without peer, averaging 57.30 in home Tests and smashing the threat of Sonny Ramadhin and Alf Valentine [both 1951] with an unbeaten 285 at Edgbaston in 1957.

Laker, who was raised in Yorkshire but settled in London after the war, had a bad time against the Australians in 1948 and, despite taking an astonishing eight for two in the 1950 Test Trial, was saddled with a reputation as a suspect international performer. Ten South African wickets at The Oval was his first major match-winning effort, but up until his miraculous year of 1956 he never played all five Tests of a series and was taken on tour only to the West Indies.

The Ashes of '56 changed perceptions of Laker forever: 46 wickets in the series, 19 in one match at Old Trafford (a feat unmatched in first-class cricket), and a second all-ten for Surrey against the touring team bore testimony both to his skill and to Australian mediocrity. He later became a long-standing and respected BBC TV commentator.

Like Laker, Rowan – a fearless opener who would bat without gloves or box – had his spats with authority. He had led South Africa's batting averages in England in 1935, but missed the 1947 trip because of personality clashes (though his younger brother Athol, a fine off-spinner, made the tour). When England toured South Africa in 1948-49 he saved the Second Test with an unbeaten 156 after being told he would be dropped for the next match. Promptly recalled, he scored 86 not out to save the Fourth Test.

Eric Rowan

Bob Appleyard

Tom Dollery

By 1951, Rowan was vice-captain. His 236 at Leeds was then a record score for South Africa, and on five other occasions he top-scored for his side in the Tests. But he did not play for his country again after this tour, something which may have been connected to an incident during an early match against Lancashire when he and John Waite were barracked for slow scoring and sat down on the pitch in protest; Rowan was later involved in a scuffle in the pavilion.

Appleyard – who suffered a number of family tragedies, including as a teenager discovering his father, stepmother and two sisters dead from a gas leak – was picked up from the leagues by Yorkshire at the age of 26. He was a versatile bowler of pace and off-spin who added leg- and off-cutters to his armoury.

After his astonishing season in 1951 he was diagnosed with tuberculosis, and did not play much until 1954, when a remarkable recovery saw him finish second in the national bowling averages and win a first Test cap. Tailoring his game to conditions, he topped the Test averages in Australia in 1954-55, but played only twice more for England. Injury forced his retirement in 1958.

Dollery had been a consistent run-scorer for Warwickshire since 1935, and was picked for the cancelled tour of India in 1939-40. He had appeared in four home Tests without success, but was a high-class county performer who in 1951 scored centuries against his county's nearest Championship rivals, Yorkshire and Lancashire. "In Dollery they [Warwickshire] possessed a man able to get the best out of his team both on and off the field," Preston wrote. "[He] showed that the paid player can become a captain in the real sense of the word."

Dollery, like May, came from Reading; Appleyard, like Laker, from Bradford. May married into the family of Arthur Gilligan [1924]; Dollery's grand-daughter married Jonathan Trott [2011].

A Surrey trio: **Peter May** (left) and **Jim Laker**, with Tony Lock [1954]

Jim Laker:
"When the pitch is helpful he bowls round the wicket to three or four men placed close to the batsman on the leg side and the ball whips viciously across in their direction"

Peter May:
"Success has not touched him. He is genuinely modest"

CRICKETERS OF THE YEAR 1952 – Performances in the English season 1951

Name	Age*		Matches	Runs	Bat ave	Wickets	Bowl ave	Catches (/st)
R Appleyard	27	First-class	31	104	5.77	200	14.14	11
HE Dollery	37	First-class	30	1549	38.72			26/1
JC Laker	30	First-class	28	624	19.50	149	17.99	22
		Tests	2	46	23.00	14	14.85	1
PBH May	22	First-class	26	2339	68.79	0		17
		Tests	2	171	57.00			1
EAB Rowan	42	First-class	26	1852	50.05	0		15
		Tests	5	515	57.22	0		3

as at 1/4/1952

1953

Five Cricketers of the Year

Harold Gimblett (Somerset) *

Tom Graveney (Gloucestershire and England) *

David Sheppard (Cambridge University, Sussex and England) *

Stuart Surridge (Surrey) ●

Fred Trueman (Yorkshire and England) ●

FOR THE FIRST TIME SINCE 1938, ALL THE FIVE were English. Tom Graveney, David Sheppard and the season's standout star Fred Trueman featured in the home Tests against India – who were spared a 4–0 drubbing only by rain – while Stuart Surridge led Surrey to a first outright Championship in 38 years. The selection of Harold Gimblett, one of 15 players to score 2,000 runs in 1952, was reward for long being among the most entertaining batsmen in county cricket.

Norman Preston wrote that the choice had not been easy: "A good case could have been made for nearly 20 players." Among those overlooked were five men who did the double – Brian Close [1964], Len Muncer, Ray Smith, George Tribe [1955] and Jack Walsh.

The chosen five were all attractive cricketers. Trueman was the most colourful, a solidly built fast bowler with a classic action who often sent batsmen on their way with an oath. Born into a mining community as the fourth of seven children, he saw cricket as a chance to escape poverty. He took 90 wickets at 20.57 in 1951, but the India Tests of 1952 were his breakthrough. He took three wickets in eight balls as India

crashed to 0 for 4 at Leeds, and eight for 31 as they capitulated for 58 at Old Trafford.

Trueman's immaturity led him into trouble on his first tour, to the West Indies in 1953-54, though some antics were wrongly ascribed to him, and he played only three Tests in the next three years. However, he later established himself as England's premier bowler, especially on home soil, and in 1964 became the first to reach 300 Test wickets. A subsequent media career did little to burnish a rightful legend.

Handling Trueman was one of the tests for Len Hutton [1938] as England's first professional captain. Those who thought it would be better if the team was still led by an amateur rallied around Sheppard. Coached at Hove by Patsy Hendren [1920], Sheppard captained Cambridge in 1952, was put in charge of Sussex for 1953 (when they finished second), and briefly stood in for the unwell Hutton as England captain in 1954. But Hutton remained in charge, and in 1954-55 retained the Ashes he had won in 1953.

Sheppard, who had toured Australia with little success in 1950-51, topped the averages in 1952, hitting 1,581 runs in 13 matches at Cambridge, 453 in six for Sussex, and 34 and 119

HEADLINE EVENTS FROM 1952

• County champions – Surrey

• England beat India 3-0, the sides having drawn 1-1 in India in 1951-52

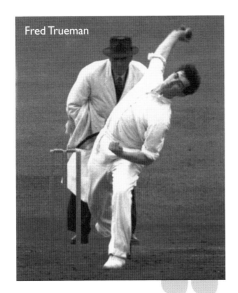

Fred Trueman

Fred Trueman:

"[He] gives promise of becoming a second Harold Larwood... some of the India batsmen visibly retreated before his onslaught"

Harold Gimblett

in two Tests for England. But as an evangelical Christian he was set on joining the church, and played only fleetingly after being ordained in 1955. He did tour Australia in 1962-63, scoring a match-winning century at Melbourne, but fielding errors prompted Trueman to accuse him of keeping his hands together only on Sundays. He later became Bishop of Woolwich, then Liverpool, and a Lord.

Graveney, born in Northumberland, educated at Bristol Grammar School and with a brother who joined the Gloucestershire staff before him, was a stylish cover-driver who drew comparisons with Wally Hammond [1928]. He was the leading batsman on the 1951-52 tour of India, scoring 175 in a Test at Bombay, and followed up in 1952 with 158 and 42 not out for MCC against the Indians and seventies in the First and Second Tests. Several years of underachievement followed, and before 1962 he had averaged 50 in only two Test series. He switched to Worcestershire in 1961 because of a captaincy dispute, and helped them win two titles. He was the first player to score 100 hundreds in the post-1945 era.

Graveney embarked on his most productive period for England after being recalled on his 39th birthday to face a powerful West Indies side in 1966; he scored 1,775 runs in his next

24 matches before being suspended for playing a benefit match on the rest day of a Test, an incident that ended his international career. He was MCC president in 2004-05, the first old-style professional appointed to the post.

By leading Surrey to titles in each of his five seasons in charge of Surrey, Surridge stands as the most successful captain in Championship history. With Peter May [1952] the team's only high-class batsman, Surridge focused on taking wickets and catches, and had the players to

Tom Graveney

CRICKETERS OF THE YEAR 1953 – Performances in the English season 1952

Name	Age*		Matches	Runs	Bat ave	Wickets	Bowl ave	Catches (/st)
H Gimblett	38	First-class	29	2134	39.51	0		24/1
TW Graveney	25	First-class	28	2066	48.04	10	24.90	13
		Tests	4	191	47.75			2
DS Sheppard	24	First-class	23	2262	64.62	0		21
		Tests	2	153	76.50			1
WS Surridge	35	First-class	32	541	17.45	78	25.21	58
FS Trueman	22	First-class	9	40	40.00	61	13.78	5
		Tests	4	17	17.00	29	13.31	1

as at 1/4/1953

Stuart Surridge (left) and Surrey's vice-captain Peter May [1952] with the county champions' pennant, which stayed at The Oval for seven years

David Sheppard

Stuart Surridge:
"[Surrey] amply justified Surridge's stated formula for successful captaincy: 'Attack all the time, whether batting, bowling or fielding'"

do it. During his reign, Surrey won 86 of 140 Championship matches, losing only 20, and in 1956 became the first county in 44 years to beat the Australians.

Surridge, who came from a family of bat-makers, was a terrific close catcher and a useful support bowler, who originally cemented a place as stand-in for Alec Bedser [1947]. In 267 matches he took 506 wickets and 375 catches (58 of them in 1952). An inspirational leader with a reckless bent, he paid little heed to the amateur–professional divide.

Gimblett, a big man from farming stock, was the finest batsman to have hailed from within Somerset to this point. He arrived sensationally in 1935 by scoring 123 in 80 minutes as a late call-up against Essex at Frome after going in at No. 8, and the following year played twice for England. But he was uneasy with the limelight, and had an ultra-attacking game perhaps not best suited to Test cricket (*Wisden* noted that he had hit 232 sixes in his career so far): he played only once more for England (in 1939). He did not enjoy his one tour, with a Commonwealth XI to India in 1950-51, and was most at home in the shires.

Gimblett had scored heavily since the war, and hit Somerset's first triple-century at Eastbourne in 1948, but 1952 – his benefit season – was his most prolific year, although he could not save the county from finishing bottom. Sadly, his positive play did not reflect his personality, and a few months after his selection by *Wisden* he suffered a breakdown and spent several months in a psychiatric institution. He died of an overdose in 1978.

1954

Five Cricketers of the Year

Neil Harvey (Australians) *

Tony Lock (Surrey and England) ●

Keith Miller (Australians) * ●

Johnny Wardle (Yorkshire and England) ●

Willie Watson (Yorkshire and England) *

HEADLINE EVENTS FROM 1953

- County champions – Surrey

- England beat Australia 1-0 to regain the Ashes after 19 years

AFTER A WAIT OF 19 YEARS, IN 1953 ENGLAND regained the Ashes in a fascinating and fluctuating series settled with an emotionally charged victory at The Oval. *Wisden*'s Five all featured in the drama, with the three England players the only significant contributors for the home side who had not been chosen before.

Keith Miller and Neil Harvey, two of the most exciting cricketers of the era, both had good tours for Australia, having come close to selection on their previous visit. By the end of the summer, the left-handed Harvey had scored 11 hundreds in 29 Tests with an average of 58.76, while Miller had joined Wilfred Rhodes [1899] in passing 2,000 runs and 100 wickets in Tests.

One innings was enough to secure Willie Watson's award. A Yorkshire player whose county career had begun before the war, he had appeared in six Tests with moderate success when he was recalled for the second game of the series at Lord's. England looked doomed early on the last day, but the left-handed Watson, first in partnership with Denis Compton [1939] and then in a stand lasting four and a quarter hours with Trevor Bailey [1950], guided England

towards safety. His innings of 109 spanned almost six hours.

Watson lost his place for the final Test, but was promoted to open on the winter tour of the Caribbean, and scored the second of his two Test hundreds in the first match in Jamaica. His self-belief was always fragile, though, and his form soon slipped again; by the summer of 1954 he was out of the side once more. He played only occasionally for England thereafter, and moved to Leicestershire as captain in 1958. He was also a notable wing-half who won four England caps in 1949-50 and went to the 1950 World Cup in Brazil.

Johnny Wardle and Tony Lock were both exceptional left-arm spinners of varied style and fiery temperament, competing – in the main – for the same England place. Both had made their first-class debuts in 1946, but Wardle rose faster; by 1953 he had taken 100 wickets in six seasons to Lock's three, though in 1953 Lock's average was far lower. Generally Wardle, who spun the ball more sharply, was viewed as the better asset overseas and Lock at home.

In 1953, with Lock unfit, Wardle started the series, but was replaced by Lock after the Third

Johnny Wardle

Johnny Wardle:

"Who could do anything except chuckle – at Lord's of all places – when Wardle was hit on the thigh by a Lindwall express and immediately began to rub his elbow?"

Test, even though Wardle took seven wickets in that game. Lock made little impact in the Fourth Test but, in tandem with Jim Laker [1952], set up the win at The Oval with five for 45 as Australia were dismissed for 162.

Wardle and Lock both toured the West Indies in 1953-54, where neither was a great success with the ball, though Wardle helped level the series with an innings of 66. Lock was called for throwing in the First Test, as he had been in a match for Surrey in 1952 (and would be again in 1959 and 1960). It was his faster ball that caused concern, and after studying film of his action Lock eventually modified his style.

Wardle, of mining stock, fell out with Yorkshire in 1958, and his public criticism of them led to his invitation to tour Australia in 1958-59 being withdrawn. He never played for England again – leaving him with a record of 102 Test wickets at the strikingly low average of 20.39 – and retreated to Minor Counties and league cricket.

Lock, by contrast, extended his first-class career into the 1970s. After retiring from Surrey in 1963, he proved an outstanding leader at Leicestershire, where he built on the work of Watson, and at Western Australia, whom he led

Neil Harvey

CRICKETERS OF THE YEAR 1954 – Performances in the English season 1953

Name	Age*		Matches	Runs	Bat ave	Wickets	Bowl ave	Catches (/st)
RN Harvey	25	First-class	25	2040	65.80	4	10.75	13
		Tests	5	346	34.60	0		0
GAR Lock	24	First-class	19	274	18.26	100	15.90	36
		Tests	2	21	7.00	8	20.62	3
KR Miller	34	First-class	24	1433	51.17	45	22.51	8
		Tests	5	223	24.77	10	30.30	2
JH Wardle	31	First-class	31	580	17.57	146	24.24	19
		Tests	3	57	28.50	13	26.46	0
W Watson	34	First-class	31	1769	45.35	0		22
		Tests	3	168	33.60			1

* as at 1/4/1954

to their first Sheffield Shield title. He played the last of his 49 Tests in 1967-68, and finished with 174 wickets for England. He was also one of the finest of all close catchers.

Miller can lay claim to being Australia's finest all-rounder, a hard-hitting batsman, acrobatic slip catcher and fast bowler who, in partnership with Ray Lindwall [1949], had already asserted Australian authority over England in three post-war Ashes series. His bowling lacked some of its old potency in 1953, but he got through an immense amount of work at Headingley, where he nearly helped Lindwall bowl Australia to victory. Two games earlier at Lord's his second-innings century created the opening for an Australian win that Watson blocked. He ended the tour with an innings of 262 not out in a day against Combined Services.

Miller's appeal went beyond mere runs and wickets. He played the game with energy and a sense of fun, and was all the more dangerous for not caring too much about the outcome. He had fought in the war as a fighter pilot, and was also a successful Australian Rules footballer and an avid racegoer. His rebellious streak contributed to his never being appointed captain of Australia.

Harvey was the fifth of six cricketing brothers, and good enough to play for Australia by the age of 19. A quick-footed and audacious strokemaker as well as a brilliant fielder (a skill developed by his baseball play), he became the youngest to score a century for Australia, in his second Test against India, and added another hundred in his first Ashes Test in England in 1948. With Don Bradman [1931] retired, Harvey cemented his position as Australia's leading batsman with four hundreds in a series in South Africa in 1949-50, a feat he repeated when South Africa paid a return visit to Australia in 1952-53.

Harvey scored ten centuries in first-class matches in 1953, but he struggled to deal with Alec Bedser [1947], and only one of these hundreds came in the Tests. He was set to see

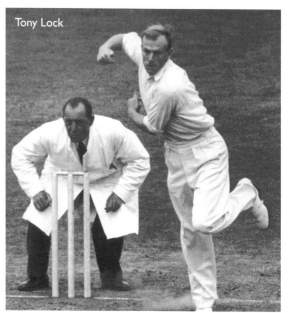
Tony Lock

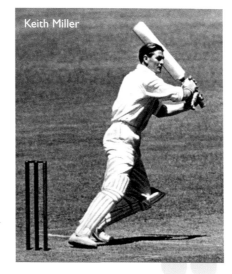
Keith Miller

Keith Miller:
"Even the Golden Age of cricket would have been enriched by a character so colourful as Keith Ross Miller... a man with the instinctive flair for turning a crowd's annoyance into instant delight"

Australia home at Leeds before England's time-wasting denied them.

On his next tour in 1956 Harvey endured a torrid time from Laker and Lock, and by his own high standards his career tailed off, perhaps in part through disenchantment at being passed over – like Miller – for the Australian captaincy. Harvey served as Australia's chairman of selectors from 1971 to 1979, and was later a trenchant critic of the modern game.

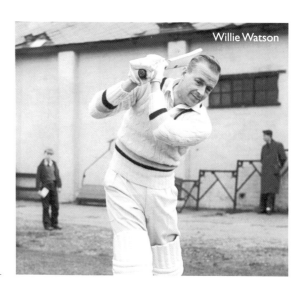
Willie Watson

1955

Five Cricketers of the Year

Bruce Dooland (Nottinghamshire) **/ •**
Fazal Mahmood (Pakistanis) **•**
Eric Hollies (Warwickshire) **•**
Brian Statham (Lancashire and England) **•**
George Tribe (Northamptonshire) **/ •**

FOR THE FIRST TIME SINCE 1933, THE FIVE contained no specialist batsman. Bruce Dooland and George Tribe – the first Cricketer of the Year from Northamptonshire for 21 years – were Australian all-rounders who had abandoned careers in their homeland to settle in England; both did the double. The other three were frontline bowlers. Brian Statham was one of the finest and most accurate fast bowlers England ever produced, while Fazal Mahmood, who was born in Lahore while it was still part of India, was the first Cricketer of the Year to represent Pakistan.

Pakistan, created as a nation on the Partition of India in 1947, had first played Tests in 1952-53, and in 1954 made their first full tour of England, under the captaincy of Abdul Hafeez Kardar. They performed creditably, losing only three of their 30 first-class fixtures, but England fielded an experimental team in the final Test at The Oval and Fazal, who narrowly missed selection for India's 1946 tour, bowled his side to an historic win to draw the series 1–1.

The son of a college professor and the first of a long line of strong Pakistan bowlers to hail from the Punjab, Fazal bowled a mixture of swing and cutters ideally suited to English conditions,

as his match figures of 60–27–99–12 at The Oval suggested, but he proved effective around the world, and his success against visiting sides had contributed to Pakistan gaining Test status.

Fazal was particularly adept at bowling on coir-matting pitches: in such conditions he delivered Pakistan their first wins over India (at Lucknow in 1952-53) and Australia (Karachi 1956-57). His match figures on those occasions were respectively 51.4–19–94–12 and 75–28–114–13. He later succeeded Kardar as captain.

Foreigners in county cricket remained a rarity, and this was the first time that two had been chosen in the same year. Both Tribe (who bowled orthodox and unorthodox left-arm spin) and Dooland (right-arm wrist-spin) had played state and briefly Test cricket in Australia in the 1940s before moving to England. Tribe joined Milnrow in the Lancashire League before being recruited by Northamptonshire in 1952; Dooland signed for East Lancashire in 1949 before being specially registered for Nottinghamshire, for whom he first played in 1953.

They had toured together with a Commonwealth XI in 1950-51, but struggled in the unofficial Tests against India.

HEADLINE EVENTS FROM 1954

- County champions – Surrey

- Pakistan win a Test match on their first tour of England to draw the series 1-1

- England draw 2-2 in the West Indies in 1953-54

Both were influential figures in county cricket, but overall Tribe made a bigger impact, performing the double seven times in eight years between 1952 and 1959. Dooland performed the feat in 1954 and 1957, but was more destructive with the ball, claiming 770 wickets in five seasons, including a Nottinghamshire record of 181 in 1954, when they finished fifth. He also developed a devastating flipper – or off-spinning top-spinner – that he passed on to Richie Benaud [1962].

Tribe helped Northamptonshire finish runners-up in 1957, their best for 45 years. Dooland, from Adelaide, also represented Australia at baseball, while Tribe, a Victorian, was a noted Australian Rules footballer.

Wisden praised Dooland for doing "much to restore right-arm leg-break and googly bowling to an important place in the strategy of the game", but Eric Hollies – a near-pick by *Wisden* in 1950 – was a bowler of similar type who had played for Warwickshire since 1932 with great success. Five inches shorter than Dooland, he made the ball spin and bounce less, but was very accurate and took county wickets by the bucketload.

He still holds two major Warwickshire records: most wickets in a season (180 in 1946, when he took all ten against Nottinghamshire without help from fielders), and most in a career

George Tribe

Fazal Mahmood

Fazal Mahmood:
"A special feature of Fazal's bowling is his astonishing stamina. For this he owes much to his father, who insisted on a rigid training schedule. From 1940 to 1947 Fazal went to bed no later than 10pm. He rose each morning at 4.30, and whatever the weather, walked five miles and ran five miles"

CRICKETERS OF THE YEAR 1955 – Performances in the English season 1954

Name	Age*		Matches	Runs	Bat ave	Wickets	Bowl ave	Catches (/st)
B Dooland	31	First-class	30	1012	28.11	196	15.48	21
Fazal Mahmood	28	First-class	16	286	20.42	77	17.53	4
		Tests	4	70	11.66	20	20.40	1
WE Hollies	42	First-class	29	130	6.50	122	19.58	9
JB Statham	24	First-class	22	231	10.50	92	14.13	16
		Tests	4	3	1.50	11	19.36	4
GE Tribe	34	First-class	33	1117	27.92	149	19.79	34

* as at 1/4/1955

He stayed on the fringe of the England side until the West Indies tour of 1953-54, when he topped the averages with 16 wickets at 28.75 and helped set up a win in Georgetown; he then played all four home Tests against Pakistan. *Wisden* said purists felt Statham's action lacked rhythm, but he was a natural bowler whose accuracy belied significant pace.

He was to be a mainstay of the England attack until 1963, and formed notable partnerships with Fred Trueman [1953] and, more fleetingly, Frank Tyson [1956]. Trueman had the better average and strike-rate, but Statham was more dependable overseas. He remains Lancashire's leading wicket-taker with 1,816 at just 15.12. Easygoing and popular, Statham was awarded the CBE. He endured hard times in later life before dying of leukaemia, aged 69.

Brian Statham: "He was a youngster who carried his flannels in a canvas bag and his boots in a brown-paper parcel"

Brian Statham (centre) leads England off after victory at Melbourne in January 1955. Captain Len Hutton [1938] (left) leads the applause as Statham walks in with Frank Tyson

Eric Hollies

Bruce Dooland

(2,201). His path to England selection was usually blocked by Doug Wright [1940], but he had a good record from 13 Tests, and famously ended the career of Don Bradman [1931] with a googly at The Oval in 1948. A hopeless batsman, Hollies made his career-best score in 1954 –47 against Sussex.

Statham had recently become an established member of the England side. Raised near Manchester, he was identified as a prospect after completing National Service in 1950. After attracting the attention of good judges in that year's Roses Match, he was summoned as a replacement by England the following winter, and made his Test debut in New Zealand aged 20.

1956 Five Cricketers of the Year

Colin Cowdrey (Kent and England) *
Doug Insole (Essex and England) *
Jackie McGlew (South Africans) *
Hugh Tayfield (South Africans) ●
Frank Tyson (Northamptonshire and England) ●

HEADLINE EVENTS FROM 1955

• County champions – Surrey

• England beat South Africa 3-2

• England retain the Ashes in Australia in 1954-55, winning 3-1

REGARDLESS OF HOW THEY HAD DONE DURING the 1955 season, Colin Cowdrey and Frank Tyson all but guaranteed their selections for what they achieved on England's victorious Ashes tour of Australia in 1954-55.

Cowdrey, who turned 22 on the tour, scored 319 runs in the Tests, including a defiant hundred at Melbourne, while Tyson destroyed Australia with blistering pace bowling, sweeping up 28 wickets in the series to general astonishment.

In fact, both returned to do well at home. Cowdrey's opportunities were limited by brief conscription to the RAF and a hand injury, and he appeared in only one Test, but still finished second in the national batting averages. Tyson produced another devastating spell to complete an innings win in the First Test against South Africa, and took 14 wickets at 18.42 in two Tests. He missed the others because of a foot problem that was to undermine his career.

There have been few English cricketing prodigies to match Cowdrey, who played for Tonbridge at 13 and for Kent at 17, and scored what proved to be the first of 107 first-class hundreds at 18. In 1953, while in his second year at Oxford, he scored 1,917 runs, and by dealing well with Ray Lindwall [1949] and Keith Miller [1954] paved the way for his selection for Australia, where he topped 1,000 runs in all matches.

Cowdrey was an automatic selection for England until 1971, and was recalled to bolster the team in Australia in 1974-75 when he was almost 42. He retired with more England caps and runs to his name than anyone to that point, but although he captained in 27 Tests he was considered too diffident and vacillating to be first-choice leader.

Born and raised in Lancashire, Tyson turned to Northamptonshire after his native county lost interest in signing him in 1950. While attending Durham University, he made his county debut against the Indians in 1952, by which point, *Wisden* said, his captain Freddie Brown [1933] reckoned he was already "the fastest bowler of all time". Against the 1953 Australians he took two wickets in his opening over. Coaching from Alf Gover [1937] helped refine his action and maximise his rhythm.

On debut against Pakistan in 1954, Tyson took four for 35, shortly after his surprise

Jackie McGlew in characteristic defensive mode against England

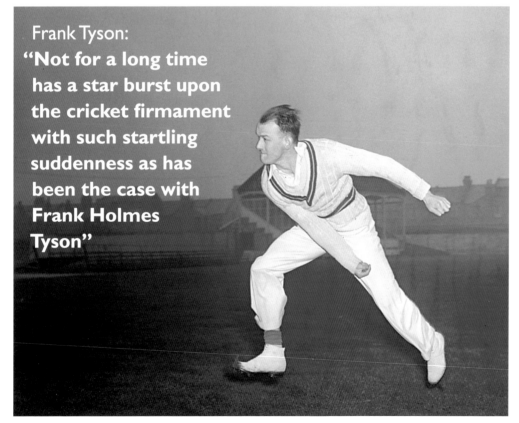

Frank Tyson:

"Not for a long time has a star burst upon the cricket firmament with such startling suddenness as has been the case with Frank Holmes Tyson"

selection for Australia. He returned one for 160 in the First Test, but on Gover's advice shortened his run-up, and in the next three matches, all won, picked up 25 wickets – creating a legend that lasts to this day.

But "Typhoon Tyson" soon blew out. Hampered by unsuitable pitches at Northampton, and a heel injury, he played only seven more Tests and retired at the age of 30.

Jackie McGlew belonged to a long line of adhesive South Africa openers. Despite collecting a pair at Lord's he scored 476 runs in the Tests and averaged almost twice as much as any team-mate. In the two matches his side won, which he captained in place of the injured Jack Cheetham, he scored 104 not out, 48, 23 and 133. He was also a brilliant cover fieldsman.

McGlew, who made his Test debut in England in 1951, was a key figure in a strong South African side during this period. At Wellington in 1952-53 he scored 255 not out, and at Durban in 1957-58 compiled what was then the slowest Test century on record, at 545 minutes.

Hugh Tayfield – who like McGlew came from Natal – was one of the finest off-spinners of all time, and the first South African to take 100 Test wickets. Utterly tireless, he bowled over the wicket and close to the stumps, and could keep even good players quiet.

His fingerprints were on most South Africa wins of this period: he took 13 wickets at Melbourne in 1952-53 when they beat Australia for the first time in 42 years, and nine at Headingley where they levelled the series with England. He first came to prominence when Australia were skittled for 75 on a "sticky dog" at Durban in 1949-50 (they still won).

Known as "Toey", from his habit of stubbing his boot into the ground before every ball, Tayfield came from an extended cricketing family: an uncle, Sidney Martin, played for Worcestershire in the 1930s, and two brothers and two cousins for Transvaal.

When Tayfield took 37 wickets in the 1956-57 series, Doug Insole topped England's averages with 312 runs at 39.00, scoring a fine unbeaten 110 in the only drawn game (the series ended 2–2). But that was to be the only full series the unorthodox but effective Insole ever played: he otherwise appeared in four one-off Tests in England, including at Leeds in 1955.

No one fared better than he did, though, in the 1955 season as a whole, when he scored more runs and centuries than anyone. For Essex he hit 129 against the South Africans, and home and away hundreds against Yorkshire. After leaving Cambridge in 1949, Insole was soon handed the Essex captaincy, a post he held until 1960. He was also a noted amateur footballer.

Insole and Cowdrey were both long-serving cricket administrators. Cowdrey was appointed a knight and life peer, and his son Chris was awarded the England captaincy in 1988 (though only for one match). Tyson emigrated to Australia, where he worked as schoolmaster and journalist. McGlew stood as a candidate for the pro-apartheid National Party. Tayfield was married and divorced five times (equalling the Test record held by Bill Edrich [1940]!).

Hugh Tayfield

Doug Insole

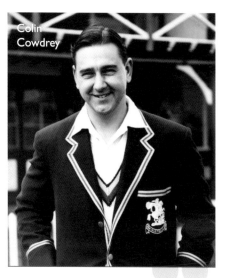

Colin Cowdrey

CRICKETERS OF THE YEAR 1956 – Performances in the English season 1955

Name	Age*		Matches	Runs	Bat ave	Wickets	Bowl ave	Catches (/st)
MC Cowdrey	23	First-class	14	1038	49.42	3	39.00	6
		Tests	1	51	25.50			0
DJ Insole	29	First-class	34	2427	42.57	24	32.12	30
		Tests	1	50	25.00			0
DJ McGlew	27	First-class	22	1871	58.46	0		4
		Tests	5	476	52.88			2
HJ Tayfield	27	First-class	23	392	15.07	143	15.75	21
		Tests	5	117	16.71	26	21.84	5
FH Tyson	25	First-class	20	257	12.23	75	19.26	9
		Tests	2	10	3.33	14	18.42	0

as at 1/4/1956

Colin Cowdrey:
"From the moment he was born at Bangalore on Christmas Eve, 1932, Michael Colin Cowdrey was destined for cricket. In naming him, his father gave him his initial start, MCC"

1957

Five Cricketers of the Year

Dennis Brookes (Northamptonshire) *
Jim Burke (Australians) *
Malcolm Hilton (Lancashire) •
Gil Langley (Australians) Ⅲ
Peter Richardson (Worcestershire and England) *

HEADLINE EVENTS FROM 1956

- County champions – Surrey

- England retain the Ashes, beating Australia 2-1, with Jim Laker taking a world record 19 wickets for 90 in the fourth Test at Old Trafford

ONLY THREE OF THE 20 PLAYERS WHO ASSISTED England in a famous Ashes victory in 1956 had not already been recognised by *Wisden*, and of these Peter Richardson alone was a regular in the side. In what was his debut series, Richardson opened in all five Tests, and scored more runs than anyone but Peter May [1952]. There was more scope to select Australians, and although they were a moderate side Jim Burke, their leading batsman, and wicketkeeper Gil Langley were both selected, even though Langley announced his retirement shortly after the tour.

Malcolm Hilton, aged 28, a slow left-armer at Lancashire, and Dennis Brookes, the Northamptonshire captain who was, at 41, the oldest specialist English batsmen chosen since 1906, made up a Five lacking a little star quality.

Richardson, of Hereford farming stock, was filling the boots of Len Hutton [1938], and did a capable job for several years. To add to the hundred he scored against Australia at Old Trafford, he took centuries off South Africa, West Indies (twice) and New Zealand, and although he lost his place after taking a year out to move from New Road, where he had played as an amateur while acting as captain and

joint-secretary, to join Kent as a professional, he subsequently won another nine caps.

A resourceful and enterprising left-hander, Richardson was the eldest of three brothers, one of whom, Dick (another left-handed bat), joined him in the England side for one match in 1957. Peter had topped 2,000 runs in 1953, but two years in the army interrupted his progress before his appointment as Worcestershire captain for 1956 gave him fresh momentum. A match-saving 130 not out in his first match against the Australians, followed by a gutsy unbeaten 36 against them for MCC, paved the way for his England call.

Brookes was also a stylish opening batsman who, *Wisden* argued, would probably have figured prominently in Test cricket had he played for his native Yorkshire. But his performances in league cricket around Kippax were first spotted by a Northamptonshire scout, and he was offered a trial in 1932. In fact his only Test came at No. 3 for an under-strength England side in the West Indies in 1947-48, when a broken finger severely cut short his tour.

Brookes, who scored an unbeaten 144 against the Australians in 1956, was already

Malcolm Hilton

Gil Langley

the highest run-scorer and century-maker in Northamptonshire's history (a record he still holds), but his qualities as a professional captain also contributed to his selection. In three seasons he had led the county to seventh, seventh and fourth; in 1957, his last year in charge, they finished second, equalling their best-ever finish.

Hilton took 1,006 first-class wickets, but he struggled to cope with his early success, and to an extent underachieved. Signed by Lancashire as a teenager, he caused a sensation in only his third first-class match by twice dismissing Don Bradman [1931].

He took 262 wickets in the 1950 and 1951 seasons combined, and made four Test appearances around this time – two in India in 1951-52, when he took nine wickets at Kanpur – but could not maintain this form, and sometimes did not even make his county XI. Tony Lock and Johnny Wardle [both 1954] became England's preferred slow left-armers.

Hilton finished third in the bowling averages in 1956, taking six for 10 for The Rest v Surrey and 14 for 88 against Somerset (for whom his younger brother Jim took eight for 69), but his form fell away in 1957, and by 1959 he was out of favour with Lancashire for good.

Dennis Brookes

A brilliant all-round fielder, he was a frequent 12th man for England.

Langley had been Australia's first-choice keeper since the retirement of Don Tallon [1949] in 1953, although he had played a full series against West Indies in 1951-52 when Tallon was unavailable (claiming 21 victims). He was unorthodox but effective, and widely praised for his anticipation. This skill may have been honed

Gil Langley:

"His waiting squat, with his right foot flat and left heel raised, is as informal as a Boy Scout grilling a chop at a campfire"

CRICKETERS OF THE YEAR 1957 – Performances in the English season 1956

Name	Age*		Matches	Runs	Bat ave	Wickets	Bowl ave	Catches (/st)
D Brookes	41	First-class	30	1916	42.57	0		6
JW Burke	26	First-class	21	1339	47.82	6	30.16	4
		Tests	5	271	30.11	0		0
MJ Hilton	28	First-class	34	459	14.34	158	13.96	28
GRA Langley	37	First-class	16	112	22.40	0		37/9
		Tests	3	21	10.50			18/1
PE Richardson	25	First-class	29	1718	39.95	1	30.00	8
		Tests	5	364	45.50			1

as at 1/4/1957

Peter Richardson on the attack against New Zealand, whose stand-in wicketkeeper is John Reid [1959]

encouraged him to put safety first, although an expanded repertoire of shots helped him earn selection for the 1956 tour of England, on which he was promoted to opener. By playing off the back foot, he survived more balls from Jim Laker [1952] than anyone bar Neil Harvey [1954].

Burke was retained as opener on tours of India and South Africa, scoring painstaking centuries at Bombay and Cape Town, but, after being criticised for slow scoring and a suspect bowling action, suddenly retired after the 1958-59 series with England.

Burke, who hid personal and financial difficulties, committed suicide in 1979. Langley was a prominent figure in South Australia politics for 20 years. Brookes became a Justice of the Peace.

Jim Burke

Peter Richardson:

"A curious feature of his eight Test innings against Australia was his dismissal each time by a catch to the wicketkeeper, but more than once he sacrificed his wicket in endeavouring to get runs quickly"

during a career as an outstanding Australian Rules footballer that ended around the time he was selected for his first tour, to South Africa in 1949-50.

Langley missed the Third and Fourth Tests in 1956 through injury, but still claimed 19 dismissals in the series, including what was then a record nine in Australia's victory at Lord's; he was reckoned to have missed only one chance. He played his last Test in India in November, and retired after scoring a hundred for South Australia v New South Wales a few weeks later.

Burke, whose parents emigrated to Sydney from Kent, had scored a century in his first Test, against England at Adelaide in 1950-51 at the age of 20, but struggled to hold down a regular place and was dropped several times. This only

1958

Five Cricketers of the Year

Peter Loader (Surrey and England) ●
Arthur McIntyre (Surrey) ⋒
Collie Smith (West Indians) ⫽
Micky Stewart (Surrey) ⫽
Clyde Walcott (West Indians) ⫽

HEADLINE EVENTS FROM 1957

• County champions – Surrey

• England beat West Indies 3-0

• England and South Africa draw 2-2 in South Africa in 1956-57

WICKETKEEPERS APART, MICKY STEWART BECAME the first Cricketer of the Year chosen in large part for his fielding. He was one of three players drawn from Surrey, who in 1957 won the sixth of seven straight Championships, and they were joined by Clyde Walcott and Collie Smith, two members of a West Indies side soundly beaten by England. Tragically, Smith was to be killed in a car accident in September 1959 aged 26. No other Cricketer of the Year has died so young.

Stewart had a fine season as an opener, and his highest score of 147 not out came against the West Indians, but nine batsmen not chosen by *Wisden* before bettered his aggregate. Norman Preston conceded: "The matter [choosing a Five] caused me considerable thought, so numerous were the candidates."

Stewart was one of several fielders who backed up Surrey's powerful bowling with brilliant reflex catching. It was a strategy devised by the now-retired Stuart Surridge [1953], who believed catches could be taken off defensive shots if fielders dared to stand close. Stewart, who was young and agile, and played professional football in the winter, was perfect for the job. Usually occupying short leg, he took 77 catches in the season (one short of the record) and seven in one innings at Northampton (still a joint record).

Stewart devoted his life to cricket. He was picked for eight Tests as an opener between 1962 and 1964, and captained Surrey for ten seasons, in 1971 leading them to their first Championship since their seven in a row. In retirement, he managed Surrey and England (the first man ever to hold that post), and made improving the fitness of England's players one of his priorities. His son, Alec, was a Cricketer of the Year in 1993.

As Surrey's regular wicketkeeper since 1947, Arthur McIntyre was one of the orchestrators of the high-pressure fielding tactics. Alec Bedser [1947] rated him as the equal of Godfrey Evans [1951] in standing up to him. But for Evans, McIntyre would have played more often for England. He won three Test caps, two when Evans was injured and one in Australia in 1950-51 as a batsman.

McIntyre, who was born and raised near The Oval, won his Second XI cap as leg-spin bowler and his First XI cap as batsman, only turning to keeping after the war (during which he was wounded in Italy). He was an aggressive batsman who topped 10,000 runs at a better average than Evans (22.83 to 21.22). He retired after the 1958 season to become Surrey's coach, a post he held until 1978.

Peter Loader was Bedser's new-ball partner at Surrey, and the fourth member of an all-conquering quartet with Jim Laker [1952] and Tony Lock [1954] that captured 448 wickets in the 1957 Championship. Loader had played his first full season in 1953, and been in the thick of Surrey's triumphs ever since.

His selection was also acknowledgment of his efforts for England: preferred to Trueman [1953] for South Africa in 1956-57, he played four Tests and bowled with great skill but no luck; the good fortune came when he was called up for the Fourth Test against West Indies at Headingley, and performed the first hat-trick for England at home since 1899. He took nine wickets in the game.

Loader was unfortunate to play only 13 Tests. He was tall, swung the ball late, and possessed imagination as well as skill. He took 1,326 wickets in a career that ended in 1963-64 with a match for Western Australia, where he settled.

Walcott, who narrowly missed selection following his match-winning century at Lord's in 1950, was overdue recognition. Hampered by a leg injury, he scored only 247 runs in the 1957 Tests, but his overall figures placed him fifth in the first-class averages.

Tall and powerful, Walcott had meted out brutal treatment to international bowlers for nearly ten years, especially in the Caribbean, where 11 of his 15 Test hundreds were scored. One of the Three Ws from Barbados, alongside Everton Weekes and Frank Worrell [both 1951], he established himself as a wicketkeeper–batsman, but gave up the gloves to the benefit of his batting. *Wisden* said he rivalled Len Hutton [1938] as the world's best batsman in the mid-1950s.

In 1954 Walcott had moved to Guyana to coach, and helped create a golden era of cricket there. He later became a noted administrator in the Caribbean and at the ICC, and was knighted in 1994.

Smith, a cheerful, carefree cricketer, was the star of the West Indies tour. Born and raised in a poor area of Kingston, Jamaica, his brilliance as a fielder saw him act as 12th man in Tests before playing at first-class level.

He announced himself with innings of 169 and 104 against the Australians in 1954-55 – the first for Jamaica, the second on Test debut – but was soon obliged to tighten up his game. He showed the benefit in England, where he scored 161 in the First Test and 168 in the Third, a

Clyde Walcott

The Surrey team after winning the sixth of their seven successive Championship titles in 1957. Back row (l-r): Bert Strudwick [1912] (scorer), David Sydenham, Mike Willett, Tony Lock [1954], Bernie Constable, Derek Pratt, Ken Barrington [1960], **Micky Stewart**, David Gibson, Tom Clark, **Peter Loader**, Dennis Cox, Andy Sandham [1923] (coach), Sandy Tait (masseur). Seated: David Fletcher, Jim Laker [1952], Lord Tedder (president), Peter May [1952] (captain), Alec Bedser [1947], Brian Castor (secretary), **Arthur McIntyre**, Eric Bedser

Collie Smith

performance that did much to save the game. He was also a capable off-spinner.

It was because of his success in 1957 that Smith returned to play for Burnley, and it was while travelling to a charity match with Garry Sobers [1964], who was at the wheel, that he was fatally injured. "In all my innings, I played with him inside me," Sobers said later.

CRICKETERS OF THE YEAR 1958 – Performances in the English season 1957

Name	Age*		Matches	Runs	Bat ave	Wickets	Bowl ave	Catches (/st)
PJ Loader	28	First-class	34	214	9.72	133	15.47	14
		Tests	2	1	0.50	10	10.00	1
AJW McIntyre	39	First-class	34	747	23.34			50/9
OG Smith	24	First-class	26	1483	41.19	34	27.05	13
		Tests	5	396	39.60	5	44.60	0
MJ Stewart	25	First-class	34	1801	36.75			77
CL Walcott	32	First-class	21	1414	45.61	0		28
		Tests	5	247	27.44	0		4

*as at 1/4/1958

1959

Five Cricketers of the Year

Les Jackson (Derbyshire) ●
Roy Marshall (Hampshire) /
Arthur Milton (Gloucestershire and England) /
John Reid (New Zealanders) /
Derek Shackleton (Hampshire) ●

THE NEW ZEALANDER JOHN REID ASIDE, FOUR of this group enjoyed outstanding county careers while playing extraordinarily little international cricket. Derek Shackleton took 2,857 first-class wickets and Les Jackson 1,733, while Roy Marshall scored 35,725 runs and Arthur Milton 32,150. Yet they mustered fewer than 20 Test caps between them.

Marshall played four Tests for West Indies as a youngster before effectively cutting himself off by building a life in England, but the three Englishmen perhaps suffered from belonging to counties that were fashionable neither with national selectors nor with *Wisden*. Jackson was Derbyshire's first Cricketer of the Year since 1937, and Shackleton – along with Marshall – Hampshire's first since 1933. Milton was only the second player from Gloucestershire since the war.

By contrast, Reid's presence was essential to a New Zealand Test side that had won only one Test in their history. That had come against West Indies at Auckland in March 1956, and Reid, who had then only just taken over the captaincy, played a starring role with a battling 84 in the first innings.

In a career spanning 16 years from the tours of England in 1949 and 1965, Reid appeared in 58 consecutive Tests, scoring 3,431 runs and taking 85 wickets with skilful fast-medium bowling. He remained captain until the end, and in 1961-62 led the side to two more wins in South Africa, where he had an immense tour.

In a team hopelessly out of their depth in a wet English summer in 1958, Reid struggled in the Tests, vainly attempting to hit his way out of trouble. His one highlight was an unbeaten 51 on the final afternoon that spared his side a 5–0 whitewash. He later lived for a time in South Africa, where he opposed the anti-apartheid sports boycott on the grounds that it was unworkable.

Shackleton and Marshall were key figures in Hampshire pushing Surrey close for the title in 1958 – and later helping to deliver it in 1961. It was a measure of the extent to which Marshall had adapted a distinctively Caribbean style of play to alien conditions that in such a difficult season he was one of only two batsmen to top 1,500 Championship runs.

Born and raised in Barbados as the son of a plantation owner, the bespectacled Marshall had

Derek
Shackleton

Derek Shackleton:
"Good-looking with neat dark wavy hair, he always looks clean-cut and immaculate. He takes little out of himself... and his high action and follow-through are models which could well be copied"

toured England in 1950 – when an innings of 135 at Southampton brought him to Hampshire's attention – and Australia in 1951-52. After two seasons of league cricket in Lancashire he began to qualify for Hampshire, and scored more than 2,000 runs in his first full season for them in 1955. In retirement he became involved in Somerset cricket.

Shackleton, born to a family of weavers in Todmorden, was recruited for Hampshire by Sam Staples [1929]. Despite being blind in one eye – a fact he kept secret until his career ended – he started as a useful batsman and top-scored on his England debut in 1950.

Shackleton was a precise and tireless medium-pacer who was armed with late swing and numerous variations. Utterly relentless, he regularly featured high on the seasonal lists of overs bowled and wickets taken; his record of 100 wickets in 20 successive seasons – from 1949 to 1968, a year in which he turned 44 – is unmatched. Nor has anyone taken more first-class wickets in post-war cricket.

Shackleton might have played more often for England, but he was initially deemed too similar to Alec Bedser [1947]. He was recalled in 1963 after a 12-year absence, and took 15 wickets in four Tests against West Indies.

Even in a bowler's summer, Jackson enjoyed amazing success in 1958, topping the national averages with 143 wickets at 10.99, the lowest average by a bowler taking 100 wickets since Tom Richardson [1897] in 1894. Normally a lively fast-medium bowler, Jackson operated at two-thirds capacity because of a persistent groin injury, but found he moved the ball more than normal. He effectively put paid to Hampshire's Championship ambitions by twice bowling Derbyshire to victory over them.

The youngest of 13 children in a mining family from Whitwell, Jackson made his county debut at 26, and two years later played one Test against New Zealand at Old Trafford in 1949.

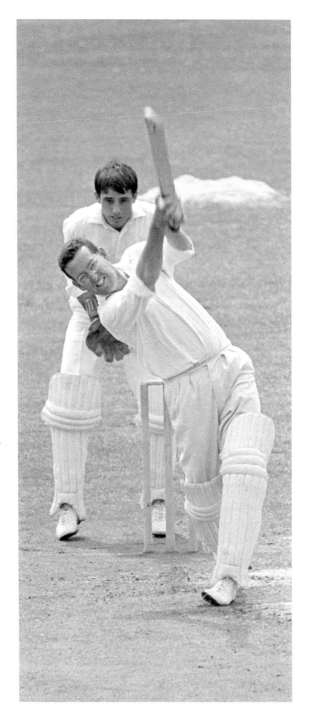

Roy Marshall hits out, watched by the Leicestershire wicketkeeper Roger Tolchard

But like Shackleton he found his path to the England side blocked by a golden generation of fast bowlers. He played one more Test against Australia in 1961 as a stand-in; aged 40, he contributed to a famous victory. He spent his winters working at the local colliery.

Milton's Test selection in 1958 made him what proved to be the last sportsman to represent England at cricket and football; he had won one international soccer cap in 1951-52. Having started with Gloucestershire in 1948, he moved up to open in 1954. A watchful batsman who liked to play late, he hit form at the right time in 1958, because England were looking for an opening partner for Peter Richardson [1957] and were happy to experiment against New Zealand.

Chosen for the Third Test at Headingley, Milton scored an unbeaten 104 in 102 overs before England declared at 267 for two in a rain-shortened match. An injury ruled him out of the Fourth Test, but he played the Fifth and went to Australia. Unfortunately, he did little in the two Tests he played there, and never established himself in the side. He was a brilliant close fielder who took more than 750 catches in his career. He later worked as a postman.

By an extraordinary coincidence, Milton and Jackson died on the same day in 2007 – April 25 – while Shackleton died five months later on September 28.

Arthur Milton

John Reid

John Reid:
"A powerful driver, sure hooker and adept with the cut, Reid does not like to waste time at the crease"

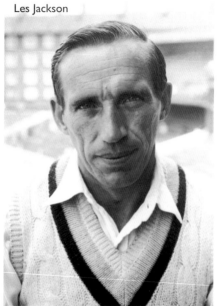
Les Jackson

CRICKETERS OF THE YEAR 1959 – Performances in the English season 1958

Name	Age*		Matches	Runs	Bat ave	Wickets	Bowl ave	Catches (/st)
HL Jackson	37	First-class	26	102	6.37	143	10.99	15
RE Marshall	28	First-class	33	2118	39.22	8	34.87	22
CA Milton	31	First-class	29	1431	31.80	1	64.00	34
		Tests	2	140	140.00	0		4
JR Reid	30	First-class	28	1429	39.69	39	22.74	32/1
		Tests	5	147	16.33	6	31.16	4/1
D Shackleton	34	First-class	29	347	12.85	165	15.44	11

as at 1/4/1959

1960

Five Cricketers of the Year

Ken Barrington (Surrey and England)
Donald Carr (Derbyshire)
Ray Illingworth (Yorkshire and England)
Geoff Pullar (Lancashire and England)
Mike Smith (Warwickshire and England)

ENGLAND'S SELECTORS EMBARKED ON A rebuilding programme following a surprising 4–0 defeat in Australia in 1958-59, and among the beneficiaries were Ken Barrington, Mike Smith, Geoff Pullar and Ray Illingworth, all of whom played against India in 1959 and toured the West Indies the following winter.

The summer of 1959 ranks among the great batting seasons, and Barrington, Smith and Pullar were among a record 23 batsmen who topped 2,000 runs; Smith in fact totalled 3,245, the most by any Cricketer of the Year in the season preceding his selection. Illingworth, an all-rounder, had the best batting season of a career spanning 33 years, with 1,726 runs.

Donald Carr, who scored 2,165 runs for Derbyshire, which remains the county record, made up an all-English quintet, something that did not happen again until 2005.

MJK Smith was easy to underestimate. He was tall and bespectacled, and scored runs mainly through the on side, but batted with enterprise, captained with purpose and was a predatory catcher. He gained a reputation as a shaky starter in Tests, but produced innings of real substance. Recalled for the last two Tests against India,

he scored 100 and 98; then in the Caribbean contributed a battling century in the decisive win and 96 to ensure a draw in the finale.

He broke batting records at Oxford with centuries against Cambridge in all three years; having switched from his native Leicestershire to Warwickshire, he made an immediate impact with the bat, and in 1959 lifted them from 16th to fourth. He fell out of favour with England in 1962, but returned as a popular leader for 25 Tests, winning in South Africa in 1964-65 and drawing in Australia in 1965-66. He represented England at rugby in 1956.

Illingworth became one of the finest of all captains – regaining the Ashes in 1970-71 after a 12-year hiatus, retaining them in 1972, and delivering Leicestershire (whom he joined after the 1968 season, having fallen out with Yorkshire) a first Championship in 1975. However, he had to wait until 1969 for his chance to lead England, though he had by then accumulated a vast knowledge central to his success.

In 1959 Illingworth was a key figure in Yorkshire finally taking the title from Surrey, and one of several contenders to fill the shoes of Jim Laker [1952] as England's first-choice off-spinner.

HEADLINE EVENTS FROM 1959

- County champions – Yorkshire

- England beat India 5-0

- Australia regain the Ashes, thrashing England 4-0 in Australia in 1958-59

He embarked on a run of 11 Tests, but it was years before he cemented a place.

Born to a joiner and undertaker in the cricketing nursery of Pudsey, Illingworth soon came to Yorkshire's attention, but it was on the advice of Bill Bowes [1932] – who wrote Illingworth's *Wisden* profile – that he turned from medium-pace to off-spin. He made rapid strides as a miserly bowler, less certain ones with the bat, before performing the double six times between 1957 and 1964.

Barrington was returning to the England side after a four-year gap, a wait that shaped his subsequent career as an obdurate batsman who sold his wicket so dearly that he was once dropped for slow scoring, but he averaged more in Tests (58.67) than anyone who has played 100 innings.

Having come into a Surrey side chasing titles, Barrington – who was born and raised in Reading – was expected to score quick runs, but on bowler-friendly pitches this was not always

Donald Carr

Ken Barrington

Geoff Pullar

Ken Barrington:
"Built on solid lines with a mop of dark hair, Barrington has always possessed a powerful square cut and brilliant cover-drives. Nowadays he is equipped with a very wide range of strokes"

easy. But he unleashed a wide range of shots in the better batting conditions of 1959, and earned *Wisden*'s praise as an entertainer. In six innings against India, he failed to pass 45 just once and finished the series as leading run-scorer. That was to be a familiar position.

Pullar started the season with seven straight fifties batting at No. 3, and later scored a hundred against the Indians for his county. He was brought in for the Third Test as an opener and was an immediate success, scoring 75 at Headingley and 131 at Old Trafford, the first Lancastrian to make a Test century on his home ground. He also took three hundreds off Yorkshire during the season, which he finished third in the averages.

A left-hander with a good technique and temperament, Pullar suited England's needs, and he was a regular selection for the next three years, during which he averaged 43.86. He was an international table-tennis triallist, and fond of fast cars (Barrington was also a car enthusiast). Like Malcolm Hilton [1957], Pullar was a product of the Werneth club.

Carr was a late example of the old-school amateur, but a classic one. One of three sporting sons of an army officer – whose posting in Germany led to Donald's birth in Wiesbaden – he was a gifted all-round sportsman who excelled at Repton before spending three years in the army en route to Oxford. Chosen for a sub-strength team to tour India in 1951-52, he played two Tests – the second as stand-in captain – and played his finest innings of 76 to save the first one at Delhi.

As the club's assistant secretary, Carr had since played regularly for Derbyshire, and led them since 1955. He was an intelligent captain, a capable batsman, good fielder and unorthodox slow-left arm spinner, but given his brilliant beginnings – he was chosen for a Victory Test aged 18 – he never quite fulfilled his promise. The only season in which he averaged more than 40 was in this summer of 1959.

Carr, like Smith, later became heavily involved in the game's administration. Smith

Ray Illingworth bats against Australia

was a long-serving chairman of Warwickshire, twice England tour manager and also an ICC match referee; Carr was an assistant secretary of MCC before becoming secretary of the TCCB. Barrington was an influential and valued assistant manager of several England tours before suffering a fatal heart attack on duty in the Caribbean in 1981. Illingworth was a powerful chairman of selectors and England manager in the 1990s. Pullar ran a fish and chip shop.

M. J. K. Smith

M. J. K. Smith:
"It is fair to say that no other county captain gave quite the same personal inspiration to his side"

CRICKETERS OF THE YEAR 1960 – Performances in the English season 1959

Name	Age*		Matches	Runs	Bat ave	Wickets	Bowl ave	Catches (/st)
KF Barrington	29	First-class	32	2499	54.32	20	34.55	45
		Tests	5	357	59.50	5	27.00	5
DB Carr	33	First-class	33	2292	44.07	21	43.61	35
R Illingworth	27	First-class	33	1726	46.64	110	21.46	30
		Tests	2	118	59.00	4	31.00	5
G Pullar	24	First-class	31	2647	55.14	1	28.00	18
		Tests	3	242	60.50			0
MJK Smith	26	First-class	36	3245	57.94	0		49
		Tests	2	207	69.00			1

* as at 1/4/1960

1961

Five Cricketers of the Year

Neil Adcock (South Africans) ●

Ted Dexter (Sussex and England) /

Roy McLean (South Africans) /

Raman Subba Row (Northamptonshire and England) /

Vic Wilson (Yorkshire) /

THE 1960 SEASON WAS DEPRESSING ON SEVERAL fronts. The weather was poor, attendances were in decline, and yet another touring team – this time South Africa – failed to give England a contest. Norman Preston decried the "plodders and prodders" happy to scrape 1,200 runs a year. The numbers of amateurs playing the game was dropping off; so, too, adventurous spirit.

Ted Dexter – along with Raman Subba Row the last amateur to be chosen as a Cricketer of the Year – proved a glorious exception. His enterprising batting, aggressive medium-fast bowling and leadership were central to Sussex's rise from 15th to fourth in the table. Although he had a quiet series against South Africa, he had scored 526 Test runs the previous winter in the Caribbean, where he proved his courage dealing with fast bowling.

Dexter's most eye-catching moment of the season – in which he was first to 1,000 runs – was throwing down the stumps from long-on from the last ball to deny the Players the run they needed to win at Lord's.

Born in Milan, and educated at Radley and Cambridge, Dexter might have pursued golf, but in his final year at university was chosen for

England, scored 52, and was soon on his way to Australia. He would remain the most electric batsman in England until his retirement in 1965, aged only 30, to pursue other interests, having already unsuccessfully stood as a parliamentary candidate against James Callaghan in the 1964 General Election (he returned briefly to cricket in 1968).

He was one of the first to master one-day cricket, leading Sussex to the Gillette Cup in its first two years in 1963 and 1964, and was a colourful chairman of selectors from 1989 to 1993.

Raman Subba Row lacked Dexter's captivating style, but was an effective and doughty left-handed batsman for Cambridge, Surrey, Northamptonshire and – briefly – England. He had made his Test debut alongside Dexter in 1958, scored a maiden century at Georgetown in 1959-60, and fell ten short of a hundred as opener against South Africa at Lord's in 1960. His finest achievement came in the months following his *Wisden* selection, with centuries against Australia at Edgbaston and The Oval in 1961, but soon afterwards the abolition of amateur status cost him his post as assistant

HEADLINE EVENTS FROM 1960

• County champions – Yorkshire

• England beat South Africa 3-0

• England beat West Indies 1-0 in the Caribbean in 1959-60

England's captain **Ted Dexter** with Frank Worrell [1951] of West Indies

Ted Dexter:

"No English cricketer bred since the war has so captured the imagination of those inside, outside and far from, the boundary ropes of our big cricket grounds"

Adcock, who came from English stock, had first played Tests in 1953-54, and caused England problems at home in 1956-57 when he and Peter Heine were a formidable pairing; in 1960, though, with Geoff Griffin no-balled for throwing at Lord's, he had to work largely alone. A pre-tour fitness regime paid dividends, and some rated him the fastest bowler in the game. The first South African fast bowler to top 100 wickets, he retired in 1963 and later worked as a radio commentator.

Roy McLean was an entertainer in the Dexter mould, only less reliable – as a Test average of 30.28 suggests. He was making his third and last Test tour of England in 1960; in 1955 he had struck a luminous if lucky 142 at Lord's, and a rapid fifty in a run-chase at Old Trafford. This time he returned to Manchester to score 109 in 160 minutes in a total of 229, but his most breathtaking display came in a festival match

secretary at Northamptonshire, forcing him into retirement aged 29.

Born in Streatham to an English mother and Indian father who worked as a barrister and privy councillor, and educated at Whitgift School, Subba Row had thought about giving up after a poor season with Surrey, but Northamptonshire invited him to join them in 1955 and he promptly set a county record with 260 not out against Lancashire, a mark he beat with 300 against Surrey in 1958, when he was captain. His tour of Australia in 1958-59 was spoiled by injury. He later served as an England tour manager, and a reforming chairman of TCCB.

Neil Adcock was South Africa's outstanding figure in a fateful summer. A tall, lean and hostile fast bowler, he returned exceptional figures in all matches, surprised himself by staying fit through a long tour, and consistently troubled the best players. In the Tests he dismissed Dexter four times and Colin Cowdrey [1956] five.

Roy McLean (left) with his South African team-mate Hugh Tayfield [1956]

Neil Adcock traps **Raman Subba Row** lbw during the 1960 Old Trafford Test. The non-striker is Ken Barrington [1960]

Vic Wilson

Raman Subba Row:

"Courage and team spirit are important factors in cricket, and Subba Row has these in abundance"

at Hastings, where he reached a century in 76 minutes despite spending half an hour over his first six runs. He was also a fine fielder.

McLean's approach went against the grain of South African cricket at the time, and was not always appreciated. He was criticised for impetuosity, and sometimes dropped by

exasperated selectors, but showed greater responsibility in 1960 and finished as the leading scorer in Tests and first-class matches. He returned to England in 1961 as captain of a development team that formed the core of the great South African side of the late 1960s. He quit in 1964-65, and later worked as an insurance salesman.

Social change in English cricket was further marked by Yorkshire winning their first official Championship under a professional captain. Discipline and unity had been under strain at the club, but Vic Wilson, a pleasant and unruffled character, restored order during three years in charge in which the county finished first, second and first. He only narrowly won the appointment; he had not averaged more than 30 since 1956, and what may have clinched it was an end-of-season century against the Rest of England in 1959.

Wilson, the son of a Malton farmer, was a gritty, determined left-hander who topped 20,000 runs for Yorkshire between 1946 and 1962, when he retired to take up full-time farming himself. He never played for England but, as a left-field pick for Australia in 1954-55, acted as 12th man in all five Tests; he was an exceptional close fielder.

CRICKETERS OF THE YEAR 1961 – Performances in the English season 1960

Name	Age*		Matches	Runs	Bat ave	Wickets	Bowl ave	Catches (/st)
NAT Adcock	30	First-class	20	71	4.73	108	14.02	7
		Tests	5	20	5.00	26	22.57	1
ER Dexter	25	First-class	30	2217	43.47	46	25.30	31
		Tests	5	241	26.77	5	31.40	0
RA McLean	30	First-class	26	1516	37.90	2	14.00	22
		Tests	5	269	33.62			7
R Subba Row	29	First-class	18	1503	55.66	2	41.50	9
		Tests	4	251	50.20			2
JV Wilson	40	First-class	37	1064	27.28	0		32

as at 1/4/1961

1962 Five Cricketers of the Year

Bill Alley (Somerset) / ●
Richie Benaud (Australians) / ●
Alan Davidson (Australians) / ●
Bill Lawry (Australians) /
Norman O'Neill (Australians) /

HEADLINE EVENTS FROM 1962

• County champions – Hampshire

• Australia retain the Ashes, winning the series 2-1

RICHIE BENAUD'S 1961 AUSTRALIANS WON THEIR first series in England for 13 years, and played an enterprising brand of cricket that earned widespread praise. *Wisden* acknowledged this welcome development by picking four of the tour party, while a fifth Australian playing county cricket, Bill Alley, made himself impossible to ignore by scoring 3,019 runs and taking 62 wickets in the season aged 42.

The Australian monopoly was bad news for two Englishmen. Colin Ingleby-Mackenzie, like Benaud a captain of positive intent, led Hampshire to their first title in 1961, while contributing 1,219 runs. David Allen, the Gloucestershire all-rounder, did the double and performed creditably in four of the five Ashes Tests. Neither was ever a Cricketer of the Year.

Benaud arrived for his third tour of England fresh from a starring role in an epic home series with West Indies which Australia won 2–1, with one match tied. He and Frank Worrell [1951] demonstrated that with the right attitude from the players Test cricket could still be attractive to watch.

Benaud, a fourth-generation Australian of Huguenot extraction whose brother also played for his country and whose father was a good grade cricketer, had been a Test player for ten years. By the 1957-58 tour of South Africa he was a world-class all-rounder – a hard-hitting batsman and skilled leg-spin and googly bowler.

In his first series in charge he regained the Ashes in 1958-59, but his finest hour now came at Old Trafford, where he bowled Australia to victory on the final afternoon to secure the Ashes. England had victory in sight until Benaud, who carried a shoulder injury for most of the tour, turned the game around, finishing with six for 70.

After retiring from Tests in 1964 with 2,201 runs and 248 wickets, Benaud used his experience as a newspaper reporter on the Sydney *Sun* to develop a distinguished media career, achieving iconic status as a TV commentator in Australia and England.

Benaud's journalistic experience prompted Norman Preston to ask him to write the profile of Alan Davidson, a naturally gifted left-handed cricketer whom Benaud had known since schooldays. Benaud hailed Davidson as "one of the greatest all-rounders in the history of the

Richie Benaud bowls against England in 1961, watched by Fred Trueman [1953]

against Surrey. This was his debut series, but he scored centuries in both Australia's wins – at Lord's, where he displayed immense tenacity on a difficult pitch, and Old Trafford. He was the third post-war Australian after Don Bradman [1931] and Neil Harvey [1954] to score 2,000 runs on an England tour.

Lawry, who developed a strong arm through playing baseball, remained a thorn in English sides throughout the 1960s before being removed as player and captain during the 1970-71 Ashes. He, like Benaud, became a long-serving commentator in Australia's Channel Nine box.

Norman O'Neill was Australia's most exciting batsman. That he was a product of the St George club in Sydney that produced Bradman was only one reason he aroused expectation: he was also blessed with the physique and array of back-foot shots to suggest he could be the country's next great batsman. Unfortunately his temperament was unequal to the task.

Inspired by Keith Miller [1954], O'Neill had already played some of the most dazzling innings of the post-war period. He had shone against England in 1958-59, on the subcontinent in 1959-60, and against West Indies in 1960-61, when he was the leading run-scorer of the series.

But he was an anxious beginner who never acquired the consistency his talent deserved. He scored 117 at The Oval in the final Test in 1961, but managed only one more century before the selectors decided that, at 28, he was no longer the answer to their prayers. His son Mark played state cricket for 12 years.

Alley, a noted middleweight boxer who won all his 28 bouts before a broken jaw at cricket ended his pugilism, had without coaching risen to play for NSW after the war before switching to the Lancashire leagues. He spent five seasons with Colne and four with Blackpool before joining Somerset in 1957 aged 38.

Alley was a steady performer, but his feats in 1961 were on another level altogether. He scored

game"; certainly there have been few finer left-arm fast bowlers.

Davidson had been consistently excellent for several years, contributing to games in ways that mattered. In the famous tied Test at Brisbane, he took 11 wickets and scored 44 and 80; at Old Trafford in the Test Benaud won with his bowling, Davidson gave his side a chance with an attacking 77 not out.

He was also a prehensile catcher, but it was his wicket-taking bursts that marked him out. No post-1918 bowler has taken 150 Test wickets at lower cost than Davidson's 186 at 20.53. He retired in 1963 to work in a bank, and later served as an administrator in cricket and horse racing.

Bill Lawry – the one Victorian among four New South Welshmen – was little known before the tour, selection for which he secured with a double-century against NSW. Tall at 6ft 2in, he was a left-hander with the reach to defend well, and a master of placement; although he was reckoned to have few attacking shots, he cemented his Test place with a powerful century

Richie Benaud:

"If one player, more than any other, has deserved well of cricket for lifting the game out of the doldrums, that man is Richard Benaud... He has succeeded in his aim to recreate interest in cricket"

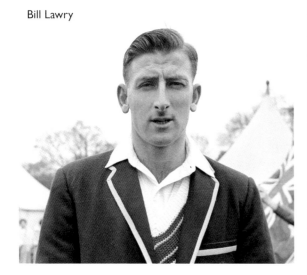
Bill Lawry

Norman O'Neill

Bill Alley bats for Somerset against Sussex, whose wicketkeeper is Mike Griffith

Bill Alley:

> "The presence in England of Richie Benaud and his gay Australian cavaliers seems to have been an inspiration to their fellow-countryman, who surprised not only himself but all followers of cricket by amassing an aggregate of 3,019 runs in the late summer of his career"

three unbeaten centuries against Surrey, and four innings against the Australians yielded 365 runs. He did his only double in 1962 and played for Somerset until his 50th year, before spending 16 years as an umpire, standing in ten Tests.

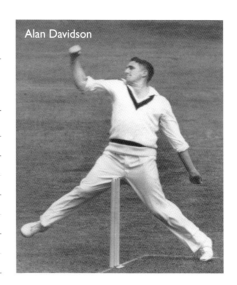
Alan Davidson

CRICKETERS OF THE YEAR 1962 – Performances in the English season 1961

Name	Age*		Matches	Runs	Bat ave	Wickets	Bowl ave	Catches (/st)
WE Alley	43	First-class	35	3019	56.96	62	25.33	29
R Benaud	31	First-class	22	627	25.08	61	23.54	18
		Tests	4	45	9.00	15	32.53	4
AK Davidson	32	First-class	20	607	30.35	68	22.30	15
		Tests	5	151	30.20	23	24.86	4
WM Lawry	25	First-class	23	2019	61.18	1	33.00	15
		Tests	5	420	52.50			2
NCL O'Neill	25	First-class	24	1981	60.03	6	44.83	20
		Tests	5	324	40.50	0		6

*as at 1/4/1962

1963

Five Cricketers of the Year

Don Kenyon (Worcestershire) *

Mushtaq Mohammad (Pakistanis) *

Peter Parfitt (Middlesex and England) *

Phil Sharpe (Yorkshire) *

Fred Titmus (Middlesex and England) * ●

HEADLINE EVENTS FROM 1962

- County champions – Yorkshire

- England beat Pakistan 4-0

- England lose 2-0 to India but beat Pakistan 1-0 during the winter of 1961-62

FOR THE 100TH EDITION OF THE ALMANACK, Mushtaq Mohammad became at 19 the youngest Cricketer of the Year chosen outside the schoolboy selections of 1918 and 1919 – a record he still holds – while two Middlesex players, Peter Parfitt and Fred Titmus, were picked for the first time since Stanley Scott and Drewy Stoddart in 1893.

Mushtaq's membership of a large cricketing family – originating in Gujarat, India, but relocated to Karachi upon Partition in 1947, when he was four years old – aided his swift rise. With two older brothers, Wazir and Hanif [1968], already Pakistan Test players, he gained a first-class debut aged 13 and at 15 toured England with the Pakistan Eaglets before becoming the youngest Test cricketer to that point when he made his debut against West Indies in 1958-59.

Mushtaq soon justified the faith. Initially chosen by Pakistan as a leg-spinner, he was already an accomplished batsman, and in his sixth match he scored a match-saving century at Delhi in 1960-61. A similar innings denied England at Trent Bridge in the only one of the five Tests in 1962 that Pakistan did not lose. He was capable of fluent strokemaking, as he showed in

the final match at The Oval, where he scored 43 and 72, and finished as the tour's leading batsman.

After two years qualifying, in 1966 Mushtaq, who stood only 5ft 7in, began a long career with Northamptonshire, whom he led to their first trophy in 1976, the Gillette Cup, while continuing a successful international career; by the time of his last Test in 1979, only Hanif had scored more runs for Pakistan. A fourth brother, Sadiq (two years younger than Mushtaq), also represented Pakistan.

Titmus too was a precocious all-rounder, first playing for Middlesex at 16 in 1949. Primarily a highly skilled off-spinner – England's best since Jim Laker [1952] – but also a resourceful and courageous batsman who in 53 Tests batted in every position from No. 2 to No. 10, Titmus performed his seventh double in eight seasons in 1962, and earned a long-awaited recall from England.

He had played two Tests without joy in 1955 (when he set a Middlesex record of 158 wickets in the season), but now became an England regular for the next four years. He enjoyed a fine tour of Australia in 1962-63, taking 21 wickets in the five Tests, did less well there three years later,

Fred Titmus (left) congratulates his Middlesex and England team-mate **Peter Parfitt** on the birth of his son

---

Fred Titmus:

"He knows how to bowl short of a length to discourage quick scoring, but he far prefers to pit his wits against opponents by keeping the ball up to them and introducing subtle changes of pace and flight for their discomfiture"

---

but toured Down Under again in 1974-75 aged 42. A swimming accident with a boat's propeller during the 1967-68 tour of West Indies cost him four toes and threatened to end his career, but he made a remarkable recovery. He played his last county match aged 49, and remains one of only five players to score 20,000 runs and take 2,500 wickets in first-class cricket. No one has taken more wickets for Middlesex.

Like Titmus, Parfitt secured for himself several years of Test cricket from 1962 onwards. Having scored a century on his fourth appearance, at Karachi in 1961-62, he followed up with hundreds in the First, Third and Fourth Tests of the home series against Pakistan. He scored two more centuries against them for Middlesex.

A stockily built left-hander, Parfitt had moved from his native Norfolk to Middlesex with the help of Bill Edrich [1940]. He was slow to trust his attacking instincts, but a

breakthrough came in 1961 when he topped 2,000 runs, leading to his selection for the winter tour of India and Pakistan.

Parfitt averaged 40.91 in a career spanning 37 Tests but, primarily a front-foot player, his record against the stronger nations was unimpressive, though he did begin the 1962-63 Ashes series with an innings of 80 at Brisbane. Later in that series he acted as an emergency wicketkeeper; he was an agile close fielder.

Wisden described Philip Sharpe as "probably the best slips fieldsman in the country". A low centre of gravity – he, like Mushtaq, stood only 5ft 7in – probably enhanced his technique. A tendency to get square-on in defence hampered his batting until 1961, up to when he averaged only 27.02, but Yorkshire kept faith partly because the bowlers liked him at slip. He was also a sunny personality.

Ironing out the technical kinks, he transformed himself in 1962, when he amassed 2,252 runs – only five batsmen made more – as well as taking 71 catches, a tally exceeded only twice in an English season. Yorkshire had the bowlers to create the chances, and he missed almost nothing.

The son of a mill executive and educated at Worksop College, Sharpe only narrowly missed selection for Australia, but played three Tests against West Indies in 1963. He coped well, scoring an unbeaten 85 at Edgbaston on debut and 63 and 83 at The Oval, but featured little for England until he played all six home Tests of 1969, when he took 13 catches – and a century off New Zealand at Trent Bridge.

Don Kenyon's selection was reward for his enterprising leadership of Worcestershire, who narrowly missed out on their first Championship title. He scored only two hundreds, but 16 half-centuries reflected his consistency and knack for shaping games.

The best was yet to come, though. In 1964 Kenyon did lead his county to their first title,

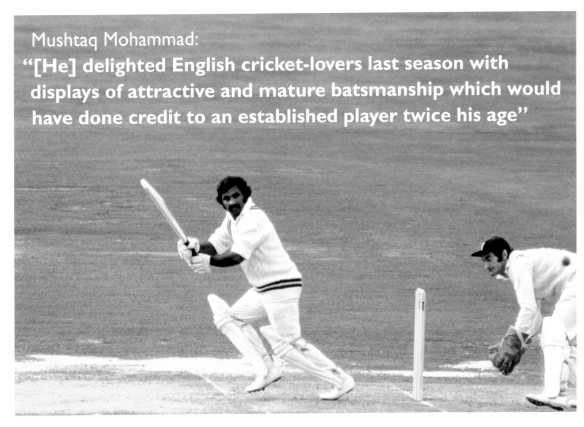

Mushtaq Mohammad:

"[He] delighted English cricket-lovers last season with displays of attractive and mature batsmanship which would have done credit to an established player twice his age"

Don Kenyon

and they were champions again the following year. When he retired in 1967 he stood as easily Worcestershire's most prolific run-scorer and century-maker (he remains their highest run-maker). This was a considerable effort given that war delayed his debut until 1946, when he was 22.

Kenyon, whose father had bowled fast for a local gasworks XI in Staffordshire, was a fine cover-driver who played eight Tests between 1951 and 1955, but with little success.

Kenyon, Sharpe and Titmus all served spells as England Test selectors, while Mushtaq had two stints as coach of Pakistan.

Phil Sharpe

CRICKETERS OF THE YEAR 1963 – Performances in the English season 1962

Name	Age*		Matches	Runs	Bat ave	Wickets	Bowl ave	Catches (/st)
D Kenyon	38	First-class	33	1941	35.29			19
Mushtaq Mohammad	19	First-class	26	1614	41.38	3	37.00	12
		Tests	5	401	44.55	0		1
PH Parfitt	26	First-class	31	2121	45.12	6	30.00	26
		Tests	5	340	113.33	0		5
PJ Sharpe	26	First-class	37	2252	40.94	0		71
FJ Titmus	30	First-class	31	1238	30.95	136	20.76	31
		Tests	2	13	13.00	3	24.66	2

*as at 1/4/1963

1964

Five Cricketers of the Year

Brian Close (Yorkshire and England) / ●
Charlie Griffith (West Indians) ●
Conrad Hunte (West Indians) /
Rohan Kanhai (West Indians) /
Garry Sobers (West Indians) / ●

HEADLINE EVENTS FROM 1963

- County champions – Yorkshire

- Sussex win the inaugural 65-over Knockout Competition

- West Indies beat England 3-1 to take the Wisden Trophy

- England draw 1-1 in Australia, who thus retain the Ashes

As in 1951, West Indies claimed four Cricketers of the Year – three from Barbados and, for the first time, one from British Guiana (now Guyana) in Rohan Kanhai. It was a fitting tribute to their exuberant cricket under Frank Worrell [1951], who led them to a 3–1 win over England in 1963 before retiring.

A silken athlete in everything he did, Garry Sobers was by now the world's leading all-rounder, a position he retained for the rest of the decade. Knighted in 1975, he has as good a claim as anyone to be the best all-rounder the game has seen.

A Test player at 17, Sobers announced himself to the world at 21 with a Test-record 365 not out in Jamaica in 1957-58 against a weak Pakistan attack; in the next match he scored 125 and 109 not out.

He was a star of the series in Australia in 1960-61, which led to him joining South Australia, for whom he topped 1,000 runs and 50 wickets in 1962-63 (a rare feat he repeated in 1963-64). On Australian pitches he bowled left-arm seam and swing, as he did in England, rather than the orthodox left-arm spin he began with. He could also bowl wrist-spin, and was a brilliant fielder in any position.

Sobers played more matches on the 1963 tour than anyone, and in almost every one contributed some outstanding performance. In the Tests, he took five for 60 at Edgbaston and scored a century at Leeds that laid the platform for a decisive victory.

There was seemingly nothing he could not do, but he proved a disappointing captain after Worrell. He returned to England in 1966 to enjoy his greatest series, and two years later joined Nottinghamshire, becoming the first man to hit six sixes in an over, and staying until 1974.

Like Sobers, Kanhai, Conrad Hunte and Charlie Griffith came from large, poor families – all were sons of plantation workers – but none had a tougher journey than Hunte. He was a Barbados player for seven years before playing for West Indies, and his invitation to join the 1957 tour of England went astray.

When he eventually made his debut in January 1958 against Pakistan, he made scores of 142, 260 and 114 in his first series, and would remain a top-order anchor for nine years. In 1963, he reined in his shotmaking to play two vital innings: 182 in the series opener at Old Trafford and 108 not out to take his side home in the finale at The Oval.

As Worrell's vice-captain, Hunte was upset to be passed over for the top job, but his attempted proselytising in the dressing-room hardly helped. A committed Christian, he was an advocate of the Moral Re-Armament movement, which promoted harmonious race relations and for whom he worked full-time after retiring in 1967. He was a key figure in the reconstruction of post-apartheid South African cricket.

Wisden described the 5ft 7in Kanhai as a "near batting genius". He had a wide array of shots, most audacious, many not seen before in England, and although he managed only one first-class century he was pivotal in the Tests. Batting at No. 3, he made important runs in all three wins – 90 at Old Trafford, 92 at Headingley, and a dazzling 77 in 70 minutes at The Oval.

Born a third-generation Indian at Port Mourant, Kanhai grew up playing the game without gloves or pads, which encouraged his attacking play. He kept wicket in three Tests in England in 1957 before cementing himself as a Test batsman with two double-centuries on the subcontinent in 1958-59.

He surprised team-mates by secretly marrying an English girl during the 1963 tour. He joined Warwickshire in 1968, helped them win the title in 1972, and stayed until 1977. He succeeded Sobers as West Indies captain and proved steelier, leading them to victory in England in 1973.

Griffith's new-ball partnership with Wes Hall was among the finest, fastest and most muscular of all time. Griffith easily outshone Hall in 1963 – his 32 wickets in the Test series was then a record for a fast bowler visiting England – but he never approached such heights again, and ended with 94 Test wickets to Hall's 192.

He had arrived uncertain of a Test place, but he cut an immediate swathe through county

Brian Close tosses up before the 1966 Oval Test with **Garry Sobers**

sides, taking 13 for 58 against Gloucestershire. He had previously appeared in one Test against England in 1959-60, but his career received a grave setback two years later when, while playing for Barbados, he fractured the skull of Nari Contractor, the Indian captain, and was also no-balled for throwing.

Questions over Griffith's action were to resurface after 1963, and he was again no-balled

> Brian Close:
> **"His field-placings were as intelligent and antagonistic as any seen in the county for 25 years, and if a fieldsman was required in a suicide position the captain himself was first for the job"**

> Garry Sobers:
> **"Sobers is essentially a cricketer for the big occasion. The tougher the struggle the more he enjoys it"**

Charlie Griffith

Rohan Kanhai

against Lancashire on the 1966 tour. He later served as West Indies' chairman of selectors.

Brian Close was chosen 14 years after performing the double during his first season at Yorkshire in 1949, when he also became, at 18, England's youngest-ever Test cricketer. He had been largely out of favour with England since; in a rare appearance in 1961, he was widely blamed for his part in the defeat by Australia at Old Trafford.

He was recognised now for leading Yorkshire to the title in his first season as captain and for his brave batting against Hall and Griffith, especially during an innings of 70 at Lord's.

By the end of the 1966 series, Close was captaining England in opposition to Sobers, breaking the grip the Oxbridge set had held on the job since the mid-1950s – but, after winning six out of seven Tests, some time-wasting tactics in a county match gave the Establishment an excuse to remove him.

Close fell out with Yorkshire in 1970 and moved to Somerset, where he laid the foundations of a trophy-winning side and mentored Viv Richards [1977], Ian Botham [1978], Brian Rose [1980] and Peter Roebuck [1988]. A close-in fielder of legendary

fearlessness, Close was a fanatical competitor with a considerable record, but ultimately achieved less than he should.

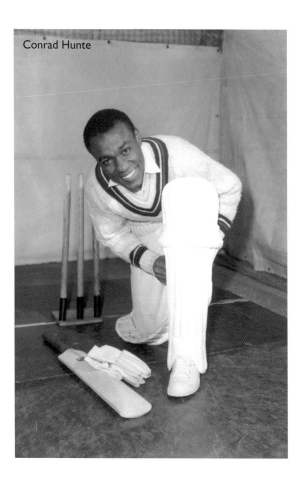

Conrad Hunte

CRICKETERS OF THE YEAR 1964 – Performances in the English season 1963

Name	Age*		Matches	Runs	Bat ave	Wickets	Bowl ave	Catches (/st)
DB Close	33	First-class	31	1529	32.53	43	27.34	27
		Tests	5	315	31.50	0		2
CC Griffith	25	First-class	20	164	10.25	119	12.83	7
		Tests	5	32	6.40	32	16.21	3
CC Hunte	31	First-class	21	1367	44.09	5	22.40	12
		Tests	5	471	58.87			4
RB Kanhai	28	First-class	21	1149	41.03			12
		Tests	5	497	55.22			5
GS Sobers	27	First-class	24	1333	47.60	82	22.48	29
		Tests	5	322	40.25	20	28.55	8

as at 1/4/1964

1965 Five Cricketers of the Year

Geoffrey Boycott (Yorkshire and England) *
Peter Burge (Australians) *
Jack Flavell (Worcestershire and England) ●
Graham McKenzie (Australians) ●
Bob Simpson (Australians) *

HEADLINE EVENTS FROM 1964

- County champions – Worcestershire

- Sussex retain the county one-day knockout competition, now sponsored Gillette Cup

- Australia beat England 1-0 to retain the Ashes

- England draw all five Tests in India in 1963-64

BOB SIMPSON LED AN EXPERIMENTAL AUSTRALIA side to a 1–0 win over England in 1964. Simpson's safety-first methods attracted criticism – he himself batted almost 13 hours for 311 in the Old Trafford Test – but his side possessed the best bowler in Graham McKenzie (the first Cricketer of the Year to be born in Western Australia), and Peter Burge played the decisive innings.

The arrival of Geoff Boycott, who scored a century in his first Test series, was a consolation for England. Every bit as tenacious an opener as Simpson, Boycott would be batsman of the series when England finally regained the Ashes in 1970-71, and when England next won a home series against Australia in 1977.

Simpson's triple-century ended a wait for a maiden Test hundred spanning 30 matches, a surprise for such a gifted batsman who had started for New South Wales at 16 and already scored seven first-class double-centuries, including a career-best 359.

Within months he had added twin centuries in a Test at Karachi and a double-century against West Indies in Barbados, where he and Bill Lawry [1962] posted a stand of 382. They formed one of the most successful of all opening Test partnerships, with an average (60.94) unsurpassed among leading post-1945 pairings.

Simpson, who had grown up in Sydney to Scottish parents, retired in 1967-68 at the age of 32, but ten years later answered an emergency call to captain Australia after mass defections to Kerry Packer's World Series Cricket. He was still good enough to score 539 runs in five Tests against India. He was also a useful leg-spin bowler and brilliant slip fieldsman.

Burge played 42 Tests, but was rarely guaranteed selection and at times came close to quitting. He saved his best performances for England, against whom he had scored a maiden Test century at The Oval in 1961 – when he finished second in the tour averages – and another hundred in the final game of the 1962-63 series to give Australia the draw they needed to retain the Ashes.

Burge arrived in England in 1964 troubled by a foot injury sustained during an innings of 283, then a record score for Queensland, and he was still without a century going into the Third Test at Headingley. When England took the second new ball Australia were 187 for seven, still 81 behind. But in trying to bounce him out, Fred Trueman [1953] fed Burge's great hook shot. Burge ended with 160 and Australia with 389. "He looks a fighter; he is a fighter," *Wisden* declared.

Burge's father Jack, a former grade cricketer, was involved in administration and managed some of his son's early Test tours before dying of a heart attack in 1957.

McKenzie followed his father and uncle in representing Western Australia at cricket and hockey. Taken as an untried youngster on the 1961 tour of England, he was called in for the Second Test and scored 34 runs and took five for 37. He was to spearhead Australia's attack for the next ten years.

McKenzie's abilities went beyond pace and strength: he could conjure wickets from unhelpful conditions. After taking 29 wickets in the 1964 series – equalling the Australian record in England held by Clarrie Grimmett [1931] – he picked up 21 in four Tests in Asia on the way home. On a typical Adelaide featherbed in 1965-66, he claimed six England wickets for 48.

McKenzie was at the time the youngest to take 100 and 200 Test wickets; he ended with 246 from 60 Tests. After turning full-time pro, he joined Leicestershire in 1969 and helped them win their first trophies, including a maiden Championship in 1975.

In Boycott, England found the opening batsman they had been looking for since the retirement of Len Hutton [1938] in 1955. A crease-occupier first and run-scorer second, he was a near-automatic selection until 1974, when he withdrew from Test cricket for three years through a probable combination of disappointed captaincy ambitions and stress.

A product of south Yorkshire's mining community, the bespectacled Boycott scored 1,628 runs in his first full season in 1963, and 2,110 in 1964, when he took two centuries off the Australians, one for county and the other for country in the final Test at The Oval.

Jack Flavell

Geoffrey Boycott

Geoffrey Boycott:
"He is ruthlessly dedicated to the job of scoring runs, analyses his own game, and takes the trouble to learn about the others"

Peter Burge

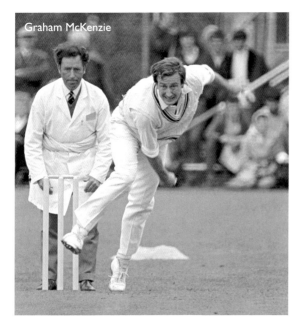
Graham McKenzie

player which led to ugly bouts of infighting.

Jack Flavell, whose new-ball partnership with Len Coldwell had for years been among the best in the country, helped Worcestershire to their first Championship title in 1964. His contribution of 101 wickets at 15.08 included a burst of 46 in five matches in August. No great batsman, he also hit the winning runs in a one-wicket win over Nottinghamshire.

Flavell had started in 1949 as a tearaway fast bowler, a year after escaping a lightning strike that killed two colleagues on a football field. He became more effective after sacrificing pace for control and topped the national averages in 1961, when he played two Tests. He played two more in 1964, but made little impact. He took 132 wickets when Worcestershire retained the title in 1965.

From 1967, he was rarely far from the top of the averages; in 1971 he became the first Englishman to average 100 in a season, and he repeated the feat in 1979. His technique was robust enough for him to score three Test centuries after his 40th birthday. He briefly stood as Test cricket's highest scorer, but as Yorkshire entered a long period of struggle a cult grew up around their best

Simpson coached Australia for ten years from 1986, laying the groundwork for much of their success in the modern era. Boycott became a trenchant and respected commentator. Burge worked as an administrator and match referee. McKenzie worked as a teacher and later in finance. Flavell ran a restaurant and guest house.

Bob Simpson

Bob Simpson:
"The flashing straight-drive and devastating square cut show him at his best and these strokes, as well as the on-drive perfectly taken off his toes, are examples of power and elegance which never fail to evoke admiration"

CRICKETERS OF THE YEAR 1965 – Performances in the English season 1964

Name	Age*		Matches	Runs	Bat ave	Wickets	Bowl ave	Catches (/st)
G Boycott	24	First-class	27	2110	52.75	0		6
		Tests	4	291	48.50	0		0
PJP Burge	32	First-class	23	1114	37.13	0		18/1
		List A	1	124	†			0
		Tests	5	322	46.00			3
JA Flavell	35	First-class	24	121	6.36	107	18.07	8
		Tests	2	17	5.66	2	68.00	0
GD McKenzie	23	First-class	22	290	16.11	88	22.45	15
		Tests	5	14	3.50	29	22.55	0
RB Simpson	29	First-class	22	1714	57.13	32	32.28	36
		Tests	5	458	76.33	1	159.00	10

† Not out, so no overage   * as at 1/4/1965

1966 Five Cricketers of the Year

Colin Bland (South Africans)
John Edrich (Surrey and England)
Dick Motz (New Zealanders)
Peter Pollock (South Africans)
Graeme Pollock (South Africans)

HEADLINE EVENTS FROM 1965

- County champions – Worcestershire

- Gillette Cup – Yorkshire

- England beat New Zealand 3-0 and lose to South Africa 1-0 in the first summer of double Test tours

- England beat South Africa 1-0 in 1964-65

GRAEME AND PETER POLLOCK PROVIDED THE first (and so far only) instance of brothers being chosen together as Cricketers of the Year. They were only young but had already made considerable marks, Graeme with bat and Peter with ball. In 1965 they combined to win South Africa a series confined to three matches because for the first time in the modern era England hosted twin Test tours.

John Edrich, who had an outstanding English season capped by an unbeaten 310 in the Headingley Test against New Zealand, provided another family "double", as he was the cousin of Bill Edrich [1940].

Graeme Pollock ranks among the all-time batting greats, a tall, imperious left-hander who inspired a wide following before the anti-apartheid sports boycott cut him adrift from international competition at the age of 26. A career average of 60.97 from 23 Tests places him second only to Don Bradman [1931].

Pollock was highly precocious. He made his first-class debut at 16, and his maiden Test series in Australia aged 19 saw his genius burst into full flower with innings of 122 at Sydney and 175 at Adelaide. Shortly before the England tour he

ended the 1964-65 series against England with 137 and 77 not out at Port Elizabeth, his home city, but it was his performance in Nottingham – 125 out of 160 while he was at the crease – that drove attendant reporters to hymns of praise. Rarely had an England attack been treated with such disdain.

Experience made little difference to his batting; he already knew what to do. For Peter, bowling was an art he had to learn. He was playing first-class cricket at 17 and Tests at 20. He took nine wickets on debut against New Zealand, and in 1963-64 claimed 40 wickets in eight Tests in Australia and New Zealand. But he did all that through pace and aggression; at home to England he found this was not always enough.

In England in 1965 he cut his run-up, reined himself in, and found he could do more with the ball; his rewards came at Trent Bridge, where he bowled as immaculately as England might have done had Graeme allowed. Peter took ten for 87 in the match. He would also have added handsomely to his 116 Test wickets but for the boycott.

The sons of a Scottish father who played provincial cricket, the two boys played fierce

Colin Bland

Colin Bland:
"Bland demonstrated that fielding can be both a delight and an exhilarating spectacle through scientific precision"

backyard games before attending Grey High School in Port Elizabeth, where they were coached by George Cox, once of Sussex. Both were later heavily involved in the game's administration, selection and coaching; Peter was an influential chairman of South Africa's selectors. Graeme had two sons who played first-class cricket, and Peter's son Shaun was a Cricketer of the Year in 2003.

Colin Bland scored 127 in the Oval Test, but was picked primarily for his work in the field; he was the first Cricketer of the Year whose photograph showed him fielding. Bland was a brilliant retriever and thrower from the boundary, but in England patrolled the covers or midwicket, from where he changed the course of the Lord's Test by running out Ken Barrington [1960] and Jim Parks [1968]. People came just to watch him in action, even at practice. He set standards matched by few, even in today's athletic game.

Bland, who was born in Rhodesia, was also an attacking batsman. He first played for South Africa in 1961-62, scored a century at Sydney two years later, and was a thorn in England's side in the 1964-65 series, when he saved the

Second Test with an unbeaten 144. A crash into a boundary fence ended his Test career in 1966-67; he played at provincial level for another seven years.

The left-handed Edrich had scored 120 against Australia the previous year, but started the 1965 season surplus to England's requirements. A run of five centuries, two nineties and a fifty earned him a recall when injury sidelined Geoff Boycott [1965]; his response was an unbeaten triple-century that contained 52 fours and five sixes.

A blow to the head from Peter Pollock ended his involvement in the South Africa series, but Edrich was unfazed, scored Test centuries at Melbourne and Sydney in 1965-66, and became England's bravest and most belligerent batsman of the next ten years. He spent more than 33 hours at the crease during the 1970-71 Ashes.

Edrich, the fifth member of his family to play first-class cricket, scored 1,799 runs in his first full season in 1959, and forged an effective opening partnership with Micky Stewart [1958]. He captained Surrey from 1973 to 1977, when he retired with 103 first-class centuries to his name. He was later an England selector and

CRICKETERS OF THE YEAR 1966 – Performances in the English season 1965

Name	Age*		Matches	Runs	Bat ave	Wickets	Bowl ave	Catches (/st)
KC Bland	27	First-class	17	969	40.37	1	18.00	6
		Tests	3	286	47.66			1
JH Edrich	28	First-class	28	2319	62.67	0		12
		List A	4	176	44.00			3
		Tests	2	317	317.00			1
RC Motz	26	First-class	14	355	19.72	54	22.98	0
		Tests	3	43	7.16	11	35.36	0
PM Pollock	24	First-class	12	182	22.75	50	17.02	5
		Tests	3	87	29.00	20	18.30	2
RG Pollock	22	First-class	14	1147	57.35	8	50.50	6
		Tests	3	291	48.50	2	13.50	1

* as at 1/4/1966

batting coach. In 2000 he was diagnosed with leukaemia, but confounded predictions about his prospects.

Dick Motz, a big-hearted fast bowler and big-hitting lower-order batsman, was the engine of a New Zealand attack put through an extraordinary journey in 1965. For almost six months they were on the road, in India (three Tests), Pakistan (one) and England (three) before returning home via Holland, Bermuda and Los Angeles. From the hot-house of Calcutta to the

Dick Motz

Brothers in arms: **Graeme** (left) and **Peter Pollock**

ice-box of Edgbaston he showed tremendous courage. In England, he was the team's leading bowler, and bludgeoned 95 off champions Worcestershire.

Motz played for Canterbury while still at school, and was in his early twenties when he took 81 wickets at 17.7 apiece on the 1961-62 tour of South Africa. In 1969 he became the first to take 100 Test wickets for New Zealand. He later worked as taxi driver and publican, and his weight rose to over 30 stone. He was married to Loretta Todd, herself a cricketer; their son was murdered in 1989.

John Edrich

1967 Five Cricketers of the Year

Bob Barber (Warwickshire and England)

Basil D'Oliveira (Worcestershire and England)

Colin Milburn (Northamptonshire and England)

John Murray (Middlesex and England)

Seymour Nurse (West Indians)

HEADLINE EVENTS FROM 1966

- County champions – Yorkshire

- Gillette Cup – Warwickshire

- West Indies beat England 3-1

- England draw 1-1 in Australia, who retain the Ashes

DESPITE ENGLAND ONLY DRAWING WITH Australia in 1965-66 and then losing heavily to West Indies at home in 1966, *Wisden* chose four of their players. Several West Indies stars had already been picked, though Wes Hall and Lance Gibbs [1972] were overlooked; instead, Seymour Nurse became the eighth Cricketer of the Year to come from Barbados in 16 years. "I looked at those whose performances in these times of so much mediocrity did most to draw the crowds," Norman Preston explained.

But these were five cricketers with chequered stories, for whom 1966 remained among their career high points.

Basil D'Oliveira, a Cape Coloured who had emigrated to England, became in 1968 the reluctant focal point of a political row with South Africa's apartheid regime, which refused to accept him in a visiting English team. The "D'Oliveira Affair" marked the start of South Africa's sporting isolation, and although D'Oliveira played for England until 1972 the episode deeply affected him.

D'Oliveira did brilliantly in the marginalised world of non-white cricket in South Africa, and moved to England aged 28 in search of broader

challenges (fearing he might be thought too old, he knocked at least three years off his real age). He played four seasons of league cricket at Middleton before joining Worcestershire.

He was first selected for England in 1966, and justified his all-rounder's role, scoring three fifties and bowling 160 overs in four Tests. Strong in every sense, he repeatedly proved himself a man for a crisis. He was an important component in the Ashes successes of 1970-71 and 1972, but his innings of 158 against Australia in 1968 is remembered most, as it led to his fateful selection for the South Africa tour.

In 2004, England and South Africa started competing in Tests for the Basil D'Oliveira Trophy. His son and grandson both played for Worcestershire.

Colin Milburn was one of the most exciting and popular cricketers in England in 1966, but three years later, aged just 28, his career was ruined by a car crash which deprived him of much of his sight.

Milburn tipped the scales at 18 stone, and played the shots of the huge and jovial man he was, bludgeoning boundaries with a joyous power that masked an orthodox technique. He was not confused or bothered by theory, and played the same for his country as he had when, as a 17-year-old, he clubbed a hundred for his native Durham, then a Minor County, off the 1959 Indians.

Having signed for Northamptonshire, he scored 100 and 88 against the 1963 West Indians, and clinched an England debut in 1966 with some explosive Championship innings. He was an immediate hit, scoring 94 on debut at Old Trafford and an unbeaten 126 at Lord's. Even so, he was dropped for the final Test because it was reckoned his weight immobilised him in the field. His response was to batter a double-century against Essex.

Milburn played only five more Tests, in the last of which he scored a spectacular 139 at Karachi shortly before his accident. During two seasons with Western Australia, he once reached a century in 77 minutes and another time scored 181 in a session. He died of a heart attack in 1990, aged 48.

Bob Barber and John Murray were heroes of England's consolation win in the final Test at The Oval in 1966. Barber had returned for the previous Test, and contributed to both games with runs and important wickets, but his relationship with the selectors was fraught and he played just once more for England.

Barber turned out as an amateur before 1962. He appeared for Lancashire while at Ruthin School, attended Cambridge and captained Lancashire for two seasons before his removal by a meddling committee. His first nine Test caps were chiefly as a leg-spinner, but a move to Warwickshire in 1963 saw him blossom into an attacking left-handed opener. He toured South Africa and Australia under his county captain MJK Smith [1960] with great success.

Barber's 185 off 255 balls on the opening day at Sydney in January 1966 rates as one of the great Test assaults. But he joined

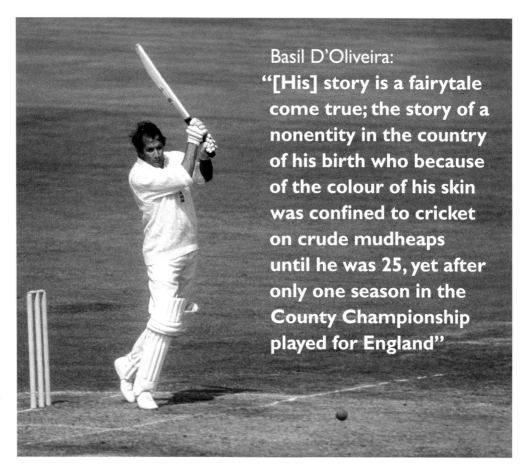

Basil D'Oliveira:

"[His] story is a fairytale come true; the story of a nonentity in the country of his birth who because of the colour of his skin was confined to cricket on crude mudheaps until he was 25, yet after only one season in the County Championship played for England"

Seymour Nurse

the family business and was available only for selected matches, a move that riled the hierarchy. He did, however, help Warwickshire win the 1966 Gillette Cup, top-scoring in the final. He retired in 1971 and moved to Switzerland.

Murray was an accomplished and dapper keeper, and a capable batsman who in 1957 did the double of 1,000 runs and 100 dismissals. But he was restricted to 21 Test caps by England's preference for Jim Parks [1968], who was foremost a batsman.

Replacing Parks for The Oval in 1966, he had the game of his life with the bat. When he went in his side were 166 for seven, but Murray, dealing bravely with the fast bowling, put on 217 with Tom Graveney [1953], and England won by an innings. However, he soon relinquished his place, after collecting a pair against Pakistan in 1967.

Murray claimed what was at the time a record 1,527 dismissals, but in a career spanning 23 years never won a county trophy. He later served as an England selector.

Nurse in 1965 converted a maiden Test century against Australia into a double, and was the second-highest run-scorer in the Tests in England the following year, behind Garry Sobers. He delighted spectators with his power and fluency. A keen footballer, he also attended the World Cup final at Wembley.

But Nurse's Test career was blighted by a lack of opportunities and poor handling: in the next series he was unwisely turned into a makeshift opener. He then hit 434 runs against England in 1967-68 but, a year later, was ready to retire, fearful in his mid-thirties that he would be axed. His farewell tour, to Australia and New Zealand, saw him make scores of 137, 168 and 258, but he stuck to his decision.

Nurse's first Test was against England in 1959-60 as a stand-in. Using a borrowed bat, he hit his first ball for four and scored 70.

The victorious England team which turned the tables on West Indies at The Oval in 1966. Back row (l-r): Geoff Boycott [1965], John Edrich [1966], **Basil D'Oliveira**, John Snow [1973], Dennis Amiss [1975], **Bob Barber**. Seated: Ray Illingworth [1960], Tom Graveney [1953], Brian Close (captain) [1964], **John Murray**, Ken Higgs [1968]

Colin Milburn

Colin Milburn:
"A pearl of great price in modern cricket. Few have been blessed with his genius for attack; fewer still with the nerve to go through with it come triumph or failure"

CRICKETERS OF THE YEAR 1967 – Performances in the English season 1966

Name	Age*		Matches	Runs	Bat ave	Wickets	Bowl ave	Catches (/st)
RW Barber	31	First-class	13	693	30.13	20	30.30	11
		List A	5	312	62.40	0		1
		Tests	2	97	32.33	6	30.33	2
BL D'Oliveira	35	First-class	28	1536	38.40	73	20.76	23
		Tests	4	256	42.66	8	41.12	2
C Milburn	25	First-class	23	1861	48.97			22
		Tests	4	316	52.66			2
JT Murray	32	First-class	19	784	37.33			31/7
		Tests	1	112	112.00			3
SM Nurse	33	First-class	19	1105	44.20	0		17
		List A	2	175	175.00	1	22.00	0
		Tests	5	501	62.62			5

as at 1/4/1967

1968

Five Cricketers of the Year

Asif Iqbal (Pakistanis) *

Hanif Mohammad (Pakistanis) *

Ken Higgs (Lancashire and England) ●

Jim Parks junior (Sussex) ⑩

Nawab of Pataudi junior (Indians) *

HEADLINE EVENTS FROM 1967

- County champions – Yorkshire

- Gillette Cup – Kent

- England beat India 3-0 and Pakistan 2-0

FOR THE FIRST TIME, WISDEN CHOSE THE SON OF a former Cricketer of the Year – and did so twice. The Nawab of Pataudi's father had been selected in 1932, Jim Parks's father in 1938. The two sons had been regular team-mates at Sussex, for whom Pataudi had played intermittently between 1957 and 1966.

Pataudi was a significant figure in India's history. He led them from 1962 to 1969, and began to rid them of their inferiority complex. As a prince he had the clout to demand the best players were chosen, and he handled the side with diplomacy and determination. Under him, India won nine times in 40 Tests, and in New Zealand in 1967-68 secured their first series win away from home.

It was amazing Pataudi achieved so much, because he lost the sight in his right eye in a car accident in 1961. The prognosis was poor, but within five months he made his Test debut (scoring a century in his third game), and after eight months was elevated to the captaincy (at 21, the youngest in Tests at that stage).

His batting was understandably erratic, but he played occasional magical innings, one of which came at Headingley in 1967, when he made the last of his six Test hundreds, an innings of 148 that could not avert defeat but saw India score a face-saving 510 in the follow-on.

Pataudi was brought up in a palace, was educated at Winchester and Oxford, and was an undisputed prodigy. After the princely titles were scrapped in 1971, he played on as Mansur Ali Khan Pataudi. He married a Bollywood star, and dabbled in politics, media work and cricket administration. In 2007, the Pataudi Trophy was inaugurated for Tests between England and India in England. He died, aged 70, a month after England won the 2011 series.

Hanif Mohammad, brother of Mushtaq [1963] and standing only 5ft 6in, was of more humble origin, but gave similar inspiration to Pakistan. He was his country's first cricketing star, and took the game to the people with two great feats – batting 16 hours 30 minutes for 337 to save a match in Barbados in 1957-58 (the longest innings in Tests), and a year later scoring 499 in a domestic game (the highest first-class innings for 35 years until Brian Lara's 501).

Hanif could attack, but his speciality in a weak side was using an impeccable defence to bat whole days (he once did so in Dhaka for

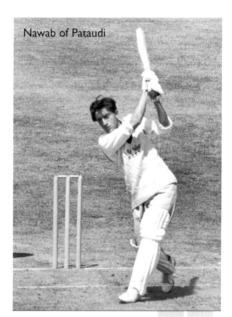

Nawab of Pataudi

Nawab of Pataudi:
"Adversity was no strange experience to the young captain. If he could lose an eye and play Test cricket six months later, he could measure up to most situations"

64 runs). In the First Test of 1967 at Lord's, he ensured Pakistan would not lose by staying nine hours for an unbeaten 187.

He had by then been Pakistan captain for three years during which he was at his peak as a player; when he was replaced as leader after the tour – he played only four more Tests – his average as captain stood at 58.73. Having started his Test career at 17, he had known some lean times, notably in England in 1962. His son Shoaib also played for Pakistan.

While a crisis prompted stonewalling from Hanif, it inspired Asif Iqbal to mount an emotional charger and gallop into the fray. An all-rounder of restless energy, he had set out as a lively fast-medium bowler but developed into a batsman of substance, ending his Test career with 11 hundreds.

In essence, *Wisden* chose him on the basis of just one innings, but what an innings it was. In the final Test at The Oval in 1967, Pakistan were facing a heavy defeat, and it was planned that if the game finished early a exhibition match would be staged. Asif was incensed at this, and during the next three hours was the driving force behind a partnership with Intikhab Alam worth 190 (a Test record for the ninth wicket at the time).

Jim Parks

CRICKETERS OF THE YEAR 1968 – Performances in the English season 1967

Name	Age*		Matches	Runs	Bat ave	Wickets	Bowl ave	Catches (/st)
Asif Iqbal	24	First-class	9	498	33.20	19	39.57	2
		Tests	3	267	53.40	11	25.27	1
Hanif Mohammad	33	First-class	14	855	45.00	5	29.40	11
		Tests	3	228	57.00	0		3
K Higgs	31	First-class	23	307	13.95	95	16.92	10
		Tests	4	22	7.33	18	18.83	0
JM Parks	36	First-class	29	1571	38.31	0		45/2
MAK Pataudi	27	First-class	16	777	35.31	0		9
		Tests	3	269	44.83	0		2

* as at 1/4/1968

Asif finished with 146 – *Wisden* called his innings "an amalgam of pure batting genius and joyous cheek" – and followed up with two wickets before England scrambled home.

Asif was signed by Kent for 1968, and over the next ten years helped them win ten trophies. After retiring he divided his time between England and the Middle East, where he ran cricket in Sharjah for many years.

Ken Higgs was a strong fast-medium bowler, and occasionally dangerous left-handed tail-end batsman, who had shouldered a big load in recent home Tests. He arrived at Lancashire in 1958 from Staffordshire, and learnt his trade sharing the new ball with Brian Statham [1955]. He was England's most incisive bowler against West Indies in 1966, and in the final Test scored a vital 63 in a tenth-wicket stand of 128 with John Snow [1973]. He had another excellent series against Pakistan in 1967. Overall, he took 71 wickets in 15 Tests; his average of 20.74 has been bettered by few for England.

It turned out that Higgs was less than halfway through his professional career. He quit Lancashire in 1969, but three years later Ray Illingworth [1960] recruited him to Leicestershire, where he stayed until his mid-forties, helping them win a Championship and four one-day trophies. He later coached Leicestershire and Nottinghamshire.

Parks had a fine season in 1967, which led to an England recall at the age of 36 for the winter tour of the West Indies (where he played the last of his 46 Tests). He had taken over the Sussex captaincy from Pataudi, and done a fine job: his side played enterprisingly, and he averaged more than he had in any domestic season for eight years.

Parks was already known as an attractive batsman, and had one England cap to his name when he took up keeping in 1958. He was an immediate success, and his 2,313 runs and 91 dismissals in 1959 paved the way for an

Asif Iqbal

emergency call-up in the West Indies, where his unbeaten century helped clinch the series.

Between 1963 and 1966 Parks was England's first-choice wicketkeeper, and although he committed occasional errors with the gloves he averaged more with the bat (32.34) than any England keeper before him except Les Ames [1929]. He later spent a few seasons with Somerset. His son, Bobby, had a long career as Hampshire's wicketkeeper.

Hanif Mohammad

Hanif Mohammad:
"The massive strength of Hanif is an unwavering, single-minded concern for the success of Pakistan cricket"

Ken Higgs

Part Four: 1969 to 1992

THE INTRODUCTION OF OVERSEAS PLAYERS INTO county cricket in 1968 transformed the face of the English game, and transformed the demographics of the Cricketers of the Year. For the next 20 years, before clubs cut back on numbers in the belief that foreign imports were hindering the development of home-grown talent, many of the world's leading stars congregated on a scale not seen in domestic tournaments until the Indian Premier League arrived in 2008. It was a "golden age".

In this period, overseas county players made up 31 of the 120 Cricketers of the Year, whereas previously in all years dating back to 1889 foreigners settled in England had collected the award just 13 times. West Indies provided the most overseas players with 12, followed by South Africa with eight, many South Africans being especially keen to play county cricket because the anti-apartheid boycott which ran in cricket from 1970 to 1992 prevented them taking part at international level. Four came from Pakistan, three from New Zealand, two from Australia (the twin brothers Steve and Mark Waugh), and one each from India and Zimbabwe.

The scope for bringing in top-quality players on immediate registrations brought about a dramatic shift in the balance of power, with counties which had previously won few trophies now able to challenge the bigger clubs for prizes – as well as for the attention of the *Wisden* editor. Essex, Glamorgan, Hampshire and Somerset provided only seven Cricketers of the Year between 1947 and 1968; this now rose to 31 from 1969 to 1992, of which 13 were from overseas. Whereas they had previously won only two titles between them (a Championship apiece for Glamorgan and Hampshire), these four counties raised their collective trophy haul to 24 – eight Championships and 16 one-day trophies, with Essex claiming a total of 11, Hampshire seven, Somerset five and Glamorgan one. Yorkshire, on the other hand, paid a heavy price for sticking with local players until 1992; having been routine Championship winners, they now failed to win the title once, while their number of *Wisden* representatives plummeted to two.

Taking the 31 overseas county players and 36 members of touring teams together, foreign Cricketers of the Year outnumbered English ones for the first time by 62 to 58. Three further players born and raised overseas were qualified as English by the time they were chosen by *Wisden*: Tony Greig (1975) and the brothers Chris (1984) and Robin Smith (1990). Allan Lamb (1982) and Graeme Hick (1987) were categorised as overseas players at the time of their *Wisden* selection, though they were in the process of qualifying for England.

The percentage of Cricketers of the Year who had appeared for England the previous home season fell to 25% from 37.3% in 1947–68, although because of South Africa's ostracism England did undertake fewer tours. Five of the seven selections from 1981 to 1987 contained no England Test players from the previous summer (Robin Jackman, chosen in 1981, played no Tests the previous year, although he did appear in one-day internationals).

The award's criteria came under some scrutiny during this period. Norman Preston, the editor from 1952 to 1980, subtly revised the parameters in 1977 by stating that a player need not "necessarily" be judged solely on his accomplishments during the previous English season. He did this to accommodate the long-serving wicketkeeper Bob Taylor, who passed 1,000 career dismissals in 1976. In his final year Preston appeared to use the same device to recognise Derek Randall, who did little in the 1979 season but had played an Ashes-winning innings in Australia a few months earlier.

John Woodcock, who succeeded Preston, was editor during six of the seven years in which few home players were chosen. As he pointed out in his Preface on more than one occasion, this was partly because several prominent England cricketers had been chosen already. In his Preface to the 1983 edition he went to some lengths to answer criticism that the previous year's Almanack, covering the famous 1981 Ashes series, had not contained any England players among the Five, noting that those such as Ian Botham and Mike Brearley had already been Cricketers of the Year. He wrote of the feature: "Never in any of its guises, has the same player been chosen twice." He returned to the issue in the 1985 edition to explain why many of the stars of the 1984 England–West Indies series had not been chosen.

Among notables from this period who missed out completely were Bishan Bedi, Abdul Qadir and Jeff Thomson, all of whom took more than 200 Test wickets, and Sarfraz Nawaz and Geoff Lawson, both of whom topped 150, with Lawson taking 63 of his in England. Gundappa Viswanath scored more than 6,000 Test runs, and John Wright more than 5,000, without being picked. Wasim Bari executed 228 dismissals for Pakistan. England's most-capped players not to be chosen were Phil Edmonds (51 Tests; the only England cricketer with 50 caps not to be picked), Graham Dilley 41, Geoff Miller 34, Chris Tavaré 31 and Paul Downton 30. Tony Lewis and Chris Cowdrey both captained England without being selected.

Sixteen English players were Cricketers of the Year in this period without ever playing what are now regarded as Tests, although one of them, Alan Jones, was given a cap against the Rest of the World in 1970 in a series later downgraded from Test status. Four of them came from Lancashire – Jack Bond, Peter Lee, Jack Simmons and David Hughes – which contrasts oddly with three notable players from the same county being overlooked: David Lloyd and Graeme Fowler, both of whom scored Test double-centuries, and Peter Lever, who played 17 Tests as a fast bowler. In explaining Simmons's selection in 1985, John Woodcock wrote that he represented the game's unsung heroes – "As others have before him, though not often." The next year Woodcock chose Phil Bainbridge, who never represented England, ahead of Edmonds.

The selection of Hughes, who captained Lancashire to second place in the Championship in 1987, by Graeme Wright represented one of the boldest of all picks. Hughes's credentials lay entirely in leadership: a first-class return of 503 runs and three wickets presented the weakest statistical case since Lord Hawke. At 40 Hughes was the third-oldest Cricketer of the Year from this period, behind Simmons (44) and Don Shepherd (42). The youngest were Craig McDermott, Graeme Hick and Waqar Younis, all aged 20.

The space devoted to the profiles of the Cricketers of the Year during this period peaked at 16 pages in 1973, before gradually contracting to eight by the time of John Woodcock's last year as editor in 1986. Graeme Wright, editor from 1987 to 1992, generally kept the entries to fewer than ten pages. The first colour photographs were used in the 1988 edition. After protective headgear came into vogue, inset photographs were sometimes used to show the faces of helmeted players.

This period also saw a rise in the number of former players – and former Cricketers of the Year – contributing profiles. Richie Benaud, who had written an appreciation of Alan Davidson in 1962, wrote the profiles of all four Australians chosen in 1973, as well as the two Australians selected in 1976. In 1974 Trevor Bailey became the third former Cricketer of the Year to turn contributor, after Benaud and Bill Bowes, with a portrait of his former Essex team-mate Keith Fletcher

David Green, chosen as a Cricketer of the Year in 1969 while playing for Gloucestershire, contributed in 1987 a piece on the West Indian

CRICKETERS OF THE YEAR 1969–92

(Teams they represented in the English season prior to selection)

Team	Years	Awards	Batsmen	Bowlers	Allrounders	WK
Essex	1972-91	9	4	3	1	1
Somerset	1971-90	8	6	1	1	0
Glamorgan	1969-91	7	5	2	0	0
Hampshire	1969-90	7	3	2	2	0
Kent	1969-86	7	3	2	1	1
Lancashire	1971-92	7	3	1	3	0
Warwickshire	1972-92	6	2	3	0	1
Middlesex	1977-91	6	4	1	1	0
Gloucestershire	1969-90	5	2	1	1	1
Worcestershire	1971-89	5	3	2	0	0
Nottinghamshire	1980-89	5	2	0	3	0
Surrey	1972-92	3	0	3	0	0
Sussex	1973-83	3	0	1	2	0
Northamptonshire	1976-83	3	2	0	1	0
Derbyshire	1977-89	3	1	1	0	1
Leicestershire	1979-88	3	2	1	0	0
Yorkshire	1969-79	2	0	1	0	1
Cambridge University	–	0	0	0	0	0
Oxford University	–	0	0	0	0	0
England	1969-92	30	16	9	3	2
Australians	1973-89	13	8	4	0	1
West Indians	1974-92	11	6	4	0	1
Indians	1972-91	6	3	1	2	0
Pakistanis	1971-88	3	2	0	1	0
New Zealanders	1974-86	2	1	0	1	0
Sri Lankans	1985	1	1	0	0	0
South Africans	–	0	0	0	0	0
TOTAL		**155***	**79**	**43**	**23**	**10**

*In total, there were 120 Cricketers of the Year between 1969 and 1992. However, the figure of 155 awards shown in the table reflects the fact that thirty-five players appeared for two teams during the season in question (30 for counties plus Tests for England, five for counties plus touring teams). Thirty-one overseas cricketers were chosen while playing for the following counties: Somerset 4, Essex 3, Glamorgan 3, Hampshire 3, Nottinghamshire 3, Warwickshire 3, Gloucestershire 2, Middlesex 2, Northamptonshire 2, Worcestershire 2, Kent 1, Lancashire 1, Surrey 1 and Sussex 1. Derbyshire and Leicestershire had no overseas players chosen; nor did Yorkshire, who only began selecting overseas players in 1992

fast bowler Courtney Walsh, who was an overseas player at the club at the time. In 1992, Jonathan Agnew and Peter Roebuck (both Cricketers of the Year in 1988) wrote respectively on Phillip DeFreitas, a former Leicestershire team-mate of Agnew's, and Waqar Younis, a dangerous fast bowler Roebuck was required to deal with as Somerset's opening batsman.

Robin Hobbs wrote an appreciation of Javed Miandad, a team-mate of his at Glamorgan in the previous summer of 1981, Hobbs's last in first-class cricket. Other former players who wrote profiles included Jack Bannister, Ian Brayshaw, Eric Hill and Peter Walker.

1969 Five Cricketers of the Year

Jimmy Binks (Yorkshire) 🎟
David Green (Gloucestershire) /
Barry Richards (Hampshire) /
Derek Underwood (Kent and England) ●
Ossie Wheatley (Glamorgan) ●

HEADLINE EVENTS FROM 1968

- County champions – Yorkshire

- Gillette Cup – Warwickshire

- England and Australia draw 1-1, with Australia retaining the Ashes

- England's proposed tour of South Africa in 1968-69 is cancelled as a result of the "D'Oliveira Affair"

- Overseas players admitted into county cricket

AUSTRALIA RETAINED THE ASHES BY DRAWING 1–1 in England in 1968, but for the first time since 1905 not one of their touring players was chosen (Wisden did not select a Five after the 1912 team visited). This was despite only two of their party having been chosen before: captain Bill Lawry [1962] and Graham McKenzie [1965]. It was a fair reflection of a disappointing side.

England were not much better represented, but then 11 of them had been chosen already. Their sole addition was Derek Underwood, the hero of a momentous series-levelling victory against the clock at The Oval. Either side of a lengthy rain-break, he took seven for 50, completing the job on a drying surface ideally suited to his brisk left-arm spin with a spell of four wickets in 27 balls.

That performance brought Underwood national celebrity aged only 23, but he had long been a formidable bowler for Kent. He first took 100 wickets in a season in 1963 aged 18 (a record). By 1970-71 he would reach 1,000 first-class wickets at the age of 25 (the third-youngest to do so) and 100 Test wickets in only his 23rd match.

Before the move to covered pitches in the 1980s, Underwood was known as "Deadly", for his ability to exploit pitches softened by rain. He was a key figure in Kent winning their first Championship for 57 years in 1970, later helping them to share the title in 1977 and win it outright the following year; they also lifted many one-day trophies in his time.

Later on, Underwood's mystique was eroded during spells with Kerry Packer's World Series Cricket and a rebel tour of South Africa, where he came up against Barry Richards.

If Underwood was as good a left-arm orthodox spinner as there was during the 1970s, Richards had a strong claim to the title of world's best batsman.

Another in a long line of great batsman from Natal, Richards was a beneficiary of the new rules allowing overseas cricketers into the county game; unlike some other arrivals, he came little known outside his native country. He had experience of English conditions through spells in Second XI cricket, but to score 2,395 runs, more than anyone else, in a wet summer was an amazing effort. According to Wisden, only

Jimmy Binks

Derek Underwood

Derek
Underwood:
**"Given the slightest
help from the pitch
he can be truly
devastating"**

Garry Sobers [1964] made a bigger impact. Richards's cover-drives evoked memories of Walter Hammond [1928].

Over the years that followed Richards would display his genius time and again, and launched his Test career in spectacular style at home to Australia in 1969-70. Only in one fatal sense was his timing awry. Thanks to apartheid, South African cricket was heading for the wilderness, and he never added to the four caps he won in that series.

Deprived of the biggest stage, he became disillusioned, though he still gave some astonishing performances for Hampshire, South Australia and Natal, and formed one of the most captivating opening partnerships county cricket has seen with Gordon Greenidge [1977].

At least Richards enjoyed one full Test series, which was more than could be said for Jimmy Binks, David Green or Ossie Wheatley. Binks played two Tests, Green and Wheatley none. All three were at this point nearing the ends of their careers.

Binks, a rarity among Yorkshire cricketers in that he came from Hull, might have played many more times for England had the competition for the wicketkeeping gloves not been so stiff from the likes of John Murray [1967] and Jim Parks [1968]. As it happened he did not keep particularly well in his Tests in India in 1963-64. Nor did he ever score a first-class century, though because of emergency he opened for England.

His selection by *Wisden* was recognition of a career spent in the relative shadows, though playing for Yorkshire was hardly that: the Championship title he won with them in 1968 was their seventh in nine seasons, and Binks was so integral to their plans that he played 412 consecutive Championship matches from his debut in 1955 until he retired in 1969.

Green was on his second county in 1968, having freshly arrived at Gloucestershire from Lancashire, where he had learned his cricket. Like Bob Barber [1967] he found a move from Old Trafford beneficial, scoring more runs in the 1968 season than anyone bar Richards. His success only fuelled the ire of Lancashire supporters who felt their county had erred again in letting a good player go.

Green was a gifted sportsman who played for Lancashire Second XI while still at Manchester Grammar School, and also represented Sale at rugby union before going to Oxford. An attractive and attacking batsman, he was

Barry Richards

remembered most for the curious feat of topping 2,000 runs in 1965 without making a century, but he deserved recognition as an early master of the one-day Gillette Cup format. Moving into business, he played little Championship cricket after the age of 30.

Wheatley, the first Glamorgan cricketer to be chosen by *Wisden* since 1931, was a fine outswing bowler with a strong action who took 1,099 first-class wickets at 20.85, a haul that narrowly failed to match his career runs. He started at Warwickshire in the same year he first played for Cambridge, but after four seasons switched to Glamorgan.

Wheatley had only planned to play occasionally in 1968, but enjoyed such success that he appeared in 16 Championship matches and took 82 wickets at only 12.95 to top the national averages. As captain from 1961 to 1966, he paved the way for Glamorgan to win their first Championship in 1969, a campaign in which he played only a minor part before retiring.

Wheatley was later an influential administrator, who vetoed the reappointment of Mike Gatting [1984] as England captain in 1989. Underwood's rebel days were forgiven when he was appointed MCC president in 2008. Richards, in television, and Green, as a respected newspaper reporter on county cricket, both had long careers in the media.

Barry Richards:

"It will be fascinating to see how far his talents will take him. Few, anywhere in the world, have his possibilities"

David Green

Ossie Wheatley

CRICKETERS OF THE YEAR 1969 – Performances in the English season 1968

Name	Age*		Matches	Runs	Bat ave	Wickets	Bowl ave	Catches (/st)
JG Binks	33	First-class	33	414	12.54			53/17
DM Green	29	First-class	30	2137	40.32	8	28.87	13
		List A	4	141	35.25	1	27.00	1
BA Richards	23	First-class	33	2395	47.90	12	22.00	37
DL Underwood	23	First-class	29	280	11.20	123	14.80	9
		Tests	4	69		20	15.10	2
OS Wheatley	33	First-class	16	55	6.11	82	12.95	5

as at 1/4/1969

1970

Five Cricketers of the Year

Basil Butcher (West Indians) *

Alan Knott (Kent and England) ▥

Majid Khan (Glamorgan) *

Mike Procter (Gloucestershire) * ●

Don Shepherd (Glamorgan) ●

HEADLINE EVENTS FROM 1969

• County champions –
  Glamorgan

• Gillette Cup – Yorkshire

• John Player League (40 overs)
  – Lancashire

• England beat both West Indies
  and New Zealand 2-0

• England draw all three Tests in
  Pakistan in 1968-69

BEFORE 1969, GLAMORGAN HAD WON JUST ONE Championship and seen only three of their players chosen as Cricketers of the Year. Now they surprised even themselves by carrying off the title as an unbeaten team, and were further rewarded by seeing their most dangerous batsman, Majid Khan, and hardest-working bowler, Don Shepherd, named among the Almanack's Five. However, their triumphant captain, Tony Lewis, was not selected – nor would he ever be, even though he later went on to captain England.

Majid belonged to one of cricket's greatest dynasties. His father played for India, and two cousins, Javed Burki and Imran Khan [1983], captained Pakistan, as Majid himself would do in one series against England in 1972-73. Schooled at Aitchison College, Lahore – and from 1970 to 1972 at Cambridge – he enjoyed a privileged existence, and his father encouraged him to enjoy his cricket. A free-spirited approach was central to his success.

First chosen for Pakistan at 18 in 1964, having scored 111 on his first-class debut at 15, Majid's route into county cricket in 1968 was sealed by a breathtaking display against his future county

at Swansea on Pakistan's 1967 tour. Majid failed in the Tests, but in 89 minutes he pulverised the Glamorgan bowling to the tune of 147 runs, more than half of which came in sixes.

Majid would play many such innings over the years, most notably a century before lunch on the first day of a Test against New Zealand at Karachi in 1976-77, a feat not accomplished since. He promised to return to the county after leaving Cambridge and duly did so, captaining them from 1973 to 1976 before quitting amid some acrimony.

Majid was one of several Glamorgan fielders who gave bowlers such as Shepherd outstanding support close to the wicket. Hailing from a hamlet on the Gower peninsula, Shepherd could hardly have had a more different upbringing from Majid, but he had adorned the game for more than 20 years as an intelligent and tireless bowler of immense accuracy who had switched from medium-pace to brisk off-cutters in 1956.

Fittingly, it was Shepherd who took the wickets in the final home game of the season that sealed the title for Glamorgan. In the same match he also claimed the 2,000th first-class wicket of his career, making him the first

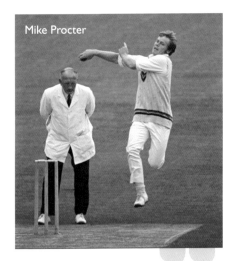
Mike Procter

Mike Procter:

"If the unique Garry Sobers is accepted as the best of the overseas imports in county cricket, there is a strong case for naming Procter as the next-best"

Alan Knott

non-English-born bowler to reach this mark. He retired in 1972, aged 45, having taken more wickets for Glamorgan than any other bowler, and more wickets than anyone never to have played Test cricket, both records that still stand.

Mike Procter's brilliant fast bowling was the chief reason why Gloucestershire pushed Glamorgan hardest in the Championship. A young South African all-rounder whose returns from his first season of county cricket in 1968 had been 1,167 runs and 69 wickets, Procter in 1969 made his main contributions with the ball – his 103 Championship wickets were more than anyone else managed in the competition – as his batting suffered what proved to be a temporary dip. Within months of being named by *Wisden*, Procter scored six successive centuries in domestic cricket in South Africa, equalling the world record.

Procter, who bowled with an ungainly open-chested action that relied on a long run-up and a powerful and fast delivery arm, made an impact with the ball in two series against Australia in 1966-67 and 1969-70 but, like his friend Barry Richards [1969], was soon lost

CRICKETERS OF THE YEAR 1970 – Performances in the English season 1969

Don Shepherd

Name	Age*		Matches	Runs	Bat ave	Wickets	Bowl ave	Catches (/st)
BF Butcher	36	First-class	15	984	61.50	6	17.16	2
		Tests	3	238	39.66	0		1
APE Knott	23	First-class	21	644	20.77	0		46/9
		List A	11	223	22.30			14/4
		Tests	6	193	21.44			19/3
Majid Khan	23	First-class	28	1547	39.66	15	19.86	19
		List A	18	413	25.81	12	12.50	4
MJ Procter	23	First-class	25	562	16.05	108	15.02	33
		List A	16	274	19.57	20	17.20	8
DJ Shepherd	42	First-class	27	91	11.37	81	22.59	10
		List A	14	24	6.00	18	16.72	6

* as at 1/4/1970

to Test cricket because of the anti-apartheid boycott. He remained an immense presence for Gloucestershire until 1981, and was central to them winning their first trophies, the Gillette Cup in 1973 and Benson and Hedges Cup in 1977.

Alan Knott was the fourth England wicketkeeper chosen by *Wisden* in as many years, and one of the best the country ever had. He was a natural gloveman, beautifully economical in his movements and armed with tremendous powers of concentration. He became Kent's regular keeper at the age of 18, and England's first choice behind the stumps after taking over from Jim Parks [1968] in the West Indies in 1967-68 when only 21.

When Knott did have a rare dip in form, his batting skills were guaranteed to save him his place; he played many crucial innings for England during a career spanning 95 Tests, scoring five hundreds and 30 fifties as well as claiming a then Test record of 269 dismissals. He manufactured all manner of strokes, but had a fundamentally sound technique. He would have played even more for England had he not joined World Series Cricket and a rebel tour of South Africa.

Basil Butcher's selection probably owed as much to what he had done on previous tours of England as anything he did in 1969. Like Rohan Kanhai [1964], the only previous Guyana-born cricketer to be chosen by *Wisden*, Butcher had grown up in the remote region around Port Mourant, Berbice, with an uncoached batting style, but that did not stop him playing some accomplished innings in difficult conditions.

He scored a great century at Lord's in 1963 on a day he had learned of his wife's miscarriage, and changed the course of the Trent Bridge Test of 1966 with an unbeaten double-century which involved a long partnership with Kanhai. His innings of 91 at Headingley in 1969, in what turned out to be his 44th and final Test, almost

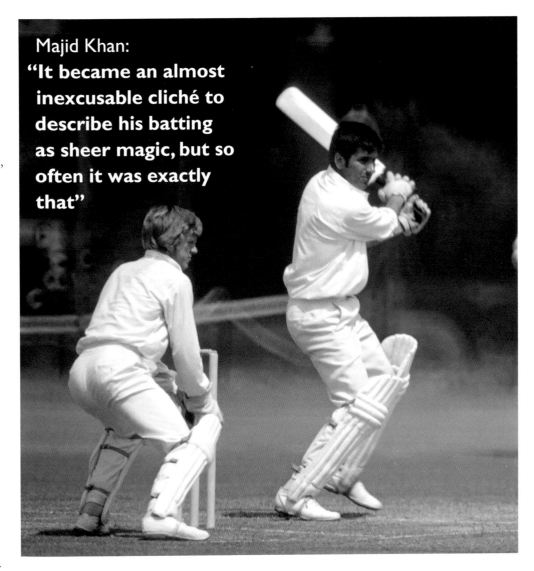

Majid Khan:
"It became an almost inexcusable cliché to describe his batting as sheer magic, but so often it was exactly that"

Majid Khan bats for Cambridge University against Sussex, whose wicketkeeper is Alan Mansell

won the game for West Indies, who lost by 30 chasing 303. He finished top of the batting averages on the tour, after which he announced his retirement at the age of 36.

Majid Khan became a principled cricket administrator in Pakistan, while Shepherd worked in coaching and local radio. Procter remained a prominent figure in South African cricket as coach, selector and administrator; he also acted as an ICC match referee. Knott worked occasionally as a wicketkeeping coach before settling in Cyprus.

Basil Butcher

1971

Five Cricketers of the Year

Jack Bond (Lancashire) *i*

Clive Lloyd (Lancashire) *i*

Brian Luckhurst (Kent) *i*

Glenn Turner (Worcestershire) *i*

Roy Virgin (Somerset) *i*

HEADLINE EVENTS FROM 1970

• County champions – Kent

• Gillette Cup – Lancashire

• John Player League – Lancashire

• England lose to a Rest of the World team 4-1, a series that replaces a cancelled tour by South Africa

LANCASHIRE'S GREAT SEASON IN 1970 WAS JUSTLY marked by *Wisden*'s selection of Jack Bond, their captain, and Clive Lloyd, the star player. Having won the inaugural John Player League in 1969, the county's first trophy since they shared the Championship in 1950, they now finished third in the Championship and won both John Player League and Gillette Cup. They lost only four matches all season, and two of those were rain-affected Sunday League games.

Bond's story was remarkable. Good enough to top 2,000 first-class runs in 1962, he never quite recovered his best form after suffering a broken arm the following year, and by 1967 he was spending more time out of the Lancashire first team than in it.

No one was more surprised than him when at the end of that year the county, needing a new captain, turned to him as a man who always fought, never complained and only wanted best for the club. He almost immediately changed the culture, demanding greater fitness and restoring pride and confidence.

His own contributions were useful rather than spectacular: he only ever scored one more first-class hundred (in 1972), but in 1970

averaged more than he had in any season since his big year in 1962.

Bond saw attractive cricket as a key to success, and in Lloyd he possessed one of the most glamorous county cricketers. Lloyd, bespectacled and 6ft 4in, struck the ball with awesome power, bowled useful medium-pace, and as a cover fielder was probably without peer. The big crowds that came to Old Trafford were as much his doing as anyone's.

Lloyd was picked up by Lancashire after spending the 1967 season in league cricket at Haslingden, improving his batting technique. He was already a Test cricketer by then, having toured India a few months earlier, and had since scored hundreds on his first appearances against England and Australia.

Two of his finest international innings came during the 1970 season for the Rest of the World against England in a five-match series that replaced a cancelled tour by South Africa. He scored a dashing 114 not out in seam-friendly conditions at Trent Bridge, and 101 at Edgbaston.

Lloyd, a cousin of Lance Gibbs [1972], took over the West Indies captaincy in 1974, and did a similar job to Bond in turning a team unaccustomed to winning into a unified and successful outfit (if one with a super-abundance of talent). Over the course of 11 years, Lloyd led West Indies in 74 Tests, winning 36 and losing only 12, and took them to two World Cup victories. When he retired from Tests in 1985, only four batsmen had scored more than his 7,515 runs.

Lloyd retained his ties with Lancashire, and captained them for four seasons in the 1980s while Bond was the manager. Bond retired as a player in 1974 after spending one season as player-coach at Notts. Lloyd later managed various West Indies sides, worked as an ICC match referee and chaired its cricket committee. His son Jason kept goal for Guyana's football team.

Brian Luckhurst was one of the stars of Kent's dramatic Championship win – they were bottom of the table on July 1 – and secured a place on the 1970-71 tour of Australia with runs as an opener against the Rest of the World. He played the decisive innings in England's victory at Trent Bridge, a painstaking 113 not out as they chased down 284 to win, and 92 in a tight match at Headingley lost by only two wickets.

When the 1971 *Wisden* went to press, the outcome of the Ashes in Australia was not known, but England led 1–0 and Luckhurst, who sustained two broken fingers on the tour, had scored the first of his two centuries in the series at Perth. He added two more Test hundreds at home in 1971, but after coming to international cricket relatively late at 31 his England career was over by 1975. He remained closely involved in the administration of Kent until his death in 2005.

Glenn Turner scored more runs (2,379) and centuries (ten, as well as being run out for 99 by Lloyd) than anyone else in the 1970 season, a striking effort for a young New Zealand batsman with a reputation for slow scoring (in 1969 he had carried his bat through 75.5 overs for 43 not out in the Lord's Test). But the requirement of scoring fast in one-day cricket was transforming his approach.

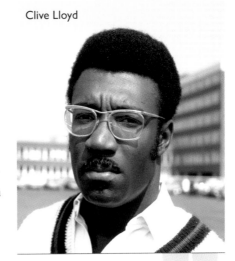

Clive Lloyd

Glenn Turner (right) goes out to bat for Worcestershire with Ron Headley

Clive Lloyd:

"He has set an example with the bat, the ball, and in the field, that has inspired every other member of the team"

Jack Bond

Such was his improvement that when he next toured England in 1973 he scored 1,000 runs before the end of May, and when in 1982 he became the first New Zealander to score 100 first-class centuries he got there by scoring 128 before lunch (and 311 in the day).

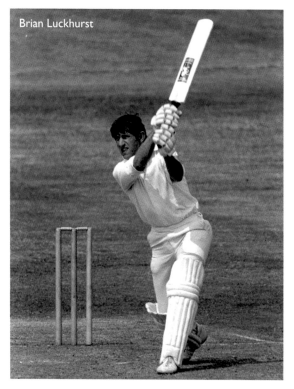

Brian Luckhurst

That innings came against Warwickshire, who in 1967 turned down the chance to sign him because they already had their quota of overseas players; Turner was snapped up by Worcestershire instead. Raised in Dunedin and coached by Bert Sutcliffe [1950], Turner worked in a bakery for 13 months to raise money to travel to Edgbaston for a trial.

Twin centuries from Turner at Christchurch in 1973-74 sealed New Zealand's first Test win over Australia. As a player his relationship with New Zealand cricket was often turbulent, but in retirement he was closely involved in its administration.

Roy Virgin's tallies for 1970 – 2,223 runs and seven hundreds – were the most by an English batsman, and a marked improvement on anything he had previously done in 14 seasons. After leaving Somerset for Northamptonshire he had another big year in 1974, in his second season at his new club, when his hauls of 1,936 runs and seven hundreds were the best by any player in the country. In both years he was spoken of as a possible England player, but the call never came. He later served as Northamptonshire's cricket committee chairman.

Roy Virgin

Roy Virgin:
"In general terms, he made 50% more runs than usual about 50% faster, with a most attractive method"

CRICKETERS OF THE YEAR 1971 – Performances in the English season 1970

Name	Age*		Matches	Runs	Bat ave	Wickets	Bowl ave	Catches (/st)
JD Bond	38	First-class	25	780	32.50			25
		List A	20	150	21.42			5
CH Lloyd	26	First-class	23	1603	47.14	28	29.21	12
		List A	18	678	52.15	16	25.93	9
BW Luckhurst	32	First-class	23	1633	48.02	0		26
		List A	13	664	55.33			6
GM Turner	23	First-class	25	2379	61.00	1	19.00	25
		List A	18	411	25.68	3	29.66	13
RT Virgin	31	First-class	24	2223	47.29			15
		List A	18	596	39.73	1	1.00	6

as at 1/4/1971

1972 Five Cricketers of the Year

Geoff Arnold (Surrey) ●
Bhagwat Chandrasekhar (Indians) ●
Lance Gibbs (Warwickshire) ●
Brian Taylor (Essex) Ⓜ
Zaheer Abbas (Pakistanis) Ⓘ

HEADLINE EVENTS FROM 1971

• County champions – Surrey

• Gillette Cup – Lancashire

• John Player League – Worcestershire

• India win their first series in England 1-0. England beat Pakistan 1-0

• England regain the Ashes, winning 2-0 in Australia in 1970-71

ON AUGUST 24, 1971, INDIA WON A TEST MATCH on English soil for the first time, and they had the bowling of Bhagwat Chandrasekhar to thank. Chandra had been recalled for the tour after being out of Test cricket for more than three years, in the belief that English batsmen were vulnerable to wrist-spin. The theory was right: he took six second-innings wickets for 38 in the final Test at The Oval, and India emerged victorious by four wickets.

Chandra was a childhood victim of polio, and his bowling arm was withered as a result. In fact, while this rendered him a hopeless batsman, it helped give his bowling whip: he mainly bowled fast top-spinners and googlies, supplemented by the occasional leg-break.

Though deadly on his day he could be erratic, and had previously been the match-winner in only one Test, against Australia at Bombay in 1964-65, but he had done well on the tour of England in 1967 even as a heavy workload was starting to take its toll on his slight frame.

Much success still lay ahead. When England toured India in 1972-73, Chandra's 35 wickets in the series – which still stands as an India record

– was decisive in the outcome. He retired with 242 Test wickets to his name.

Unlike Chandra, Zaheer Abbas arrived for the English summer of 1971 as an unknown outside his homeland. The young Pakistan batsman had one Test cap to his name, and made a minor tour of Ireland in 1969.

There was general amazement, therefore, when the bespectacled Zaheer – the eldest of seven brothers, who had developed his game through Karachi schools and club cricket and a devotion to practice – scored 110 on his first appearance against Worcestershire and a mammoth 274 in the First Test at Edgbaston. The England attack was missing only John Snow [1973] from those who had just helped win the Ashes in Australia. Apart from the sheer size of the innings, Zaheer's classical style drew widespread admiration.

His second-innings duck in the only Test to produce a positive result, at Headingley, perhaps cost Pakistan victory – England won by only 25 runs – but on the back of this tour Zaheer was recruited for Gloucestershire for the 1972 season.

He continued to play for the county until he retired from all cricket in 1985 with an imposing record as a free-flowing scorer against all but the

Zaheer Abbas

Zaheer Abbas:

"Few overseas players on their maiden tour of England have mastered conditions and bowlers alike with such complete efficiency"

Brian Taylor keeps wicket as Geoff Boycott [1965] hits out

very best attacks (he made few runs against the powerful West Indies pace battery). He hit 240 in the Third Test of the 1974 series in England – eight of his 12 Test centuries were scores above 150 – and in 1982-83 became the first Asian batsman to score 100 first-class centuries.

Geoff Arnold and Lance Gibbs were the leading bowlers for Surrey and Warwickshire respectively, the two counties who finished level on points at the top of the Championship table, Surrey being declared champions by virtue of more wins.

Arnold, whose stock ball was the outswinger although he could move the ball both ways,

Geoff Arnold

CRICKETERS OF THE YEAR 1972 – Performances in the English season 1971

Name	Age*		Matches	Runs	Bat ave	Wickets	Bowl ave	Catches (/st)
GG Arnold	27	First-class	21	92	5.41	83	17.12	8
		List A	14	54	13.50	18	22.72	2
BS Chandrasekhar	26	First-class	13	16	2.66	50	24.86	9
		Tests	3	4		13	29.15	3
LR Gibbs	37	First-class	26	116	9.66	131	18.89	24
		List A	8	17	4.25	19	14.36	6
B Taylor	39	First-class	27	751	19.25	0		54/15
		List A	19	436	24.22			18/2
Zaheer Abbas	24	First-class	19	1508	55.85	0		14
		Tests	3	386	96.50	0		3

* as at 1/4/1972

finished top of the national bowling averages, paving the way for his recall by England in 1972, which proved to be the start of a three-year run in the team. He took six for 45 in his first overseas Test at Delhi in 1972-73, but was most suited to conditions in England, where he was among the most dangerous new-ball bowlers.

Arnold first played for England in 1967, taking five for 58 against Pakistan in his second Test in helpful conditions on his home ground at The Oval. That year he took 109 wickets at 18.22, but missed most of the following summer through injury. He moved to Sussex in 1978, and spent five years there before returning to Surrey as a coach.

Gibbs was a hugely experienced cricketer in his late thirties, a long-fingered master in the subtle arts of off-spin bowling. He had entered first-class cricket in 1953-54, first appeared for West Indies in 1957-58, and had more than 200 Test wickets to his name (he would retire in 1975-76 with 309, a Test record until 1981-82).

Gibbs had done sterling work for Warwickshire since joining them in 1968, but nothing was as impressive as his efforts in 1971, when he promised the club he would not only take 100 wickets but get to the mark first. Shouldering an immense amount of work – he bowled 1,024.1 overs in the season – he was as good as his word.

Originally it was planned that 1971 would be his last season of county cricket, but Gibbs announced he would return for 1972, and in the event played a prominent part in Warwickshire clinching the title that had narrowly eluded them the previous year.

Gibbs, a cousin of Clive Lloyd [1971], emigrated to the United States after retiring as a player, but remained involved in West Indies cricket on an occasional basis.

Brian Taylor owed his *Wisden* selection to his leadership of an Essex side operating on a small staff and shoestring budget. A long-serving wicketkeeper-batsman who had made his debut

in 1949, Taylor forged a strong team spirit based on mutual support and energetic fielding, virtues that proved especially valuable in the John Player League.

Essex, having finished in the top four in the league's two previous seasons, ended as runners-up in 1971 with Taylor, known as "Tonker" for his aggressive batting, leading the way by opening the innings; against Derbyshire at Buxton he scored 100 off 84 balls.

Taylor had toured South Africa as understudy to Godfrey Evans [1951] in 1956-57, but a path to the England side never opened up. He retired in 1973 with 1,294 dismissals to his name; at the time, only three keepers could claim more.

Bhagwat Chandrasekhar

Lance Gibbs

Bhagwat Chandrasekhar: **"He must be unique in that he has turned his deformity, a withered arm, into an instrument of success"**

1973

Five Cricketers of the Year

Greg Chappell (Australians)
Dennis Lillee (Australians)
Bob Massie (Australians)
John Snow (Sussex and England)
Keith Stackpole (Australians)

HEADLINE EVENTS FROM 1972

- County champions – Warwickshire

- Gillette Cup – Lancashire

- John Player League – Kent

- Benson & Hedges Cup – Leicestershire

- England retain the Ashes by drawing 2-2 with Australia

AUSTRALIA FAILED TO REGAIN THE ASHES IN 1972, but four of their players were still chosen by *Wisden*, their first Cricketers of the Year for eight seasons. John Snow, England's spearhead, made up the Five (most of his team-mates had already been picked), though Tony Greig [1975] was surprisingly overlooked.

England retained the Ashes with a match to spare, but Australia were their equal and, as time would confirm, a team on the rise. None of their quartet had toured England before, but all had experience of the conditions, Greg Chappell having spent two seasons at Somerset, and Dennis Lillee and Keith Stackpole a season each in the Lancashire League, while Bob Massie had worked as pro in Kilmarnock.

In Chappell and Lillee Australia had two all-time greats in the making. Both had made their Test debuts during the home series against England in 1970-71, Chappell scoring 108 on his first appearance, at Perth, and Lillee taking eight wickets in the last two games as Australia fought a losing tide.

Chappell's quality had been immediately obvious, and he confirmed it with two more superb innings in England, the first at Lord's where he made a magnificent 131, the second at The Oval where he helped turn the final match Australia's way in a partnership of 201 with Ian Chappell [1976], his elder brother (a third brother, Trevor, also played Test cricket). These were the two games Australia won.

Chappell had both style and substance. He only turned 24 during the tour, but his batting technique was by now fully rounded – he had started out favouring the on side – and he was to prove himself among the most difficult batsmen in the game to bowl at. He scored 608 runs at home to England in 1974-75, and 702 at home to West Indies in 1975-76 in his first series after taking over the captaincy from brother Ian.

Chappell's availability was sometimes limited by business commitments, and he missed two years of Test cricket due to his involvement with World Series Cricket, but he still retired as Australia's leading Test run-scorer. He was also an immaculate slip fielder, and briefly held the world Test catching record for a non-keeper.

Lillee was the fast bowler Australia had been waiting for, someone of genuine pace who could back up their naturally aggressive style of play. With unruly flowing hair, extravagant

Greg Chappell

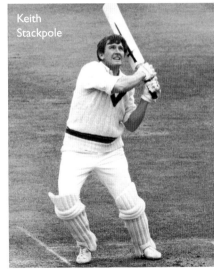
Keith Stackpole

John Snow

moustache and long run-up, he looked the part too, but he was acquiring the brain to go with the brawn of his tearaway youth. To destroy a World XI with figures of eight for 29 on his pace-friendly home ground at Perth in 1971-72, and take 31 wickets in five Tests in England in 1972 (then an Australian record in England) was to show two different sides of the same bowler.

Lillee started the tour suffering from back and hip problems, and feared he might not play the Tests. Early in 1973 he broke down with a stress fracture of the back, and spent more than a year in rehab, but when he returned he soon showed he had lost nothing. He retained a remarkable capacity to get through immense workloads and played for Australia until his 35th year, retiring with a then-record 355 Test wickets

to his name, 167 of them against England.

Massie's international career was as short as Lillee's was long, but an incredible performance in the Lord's Test, in which he took 16 wickets through extravagant swing bowling from round the wicket, guaranteed it will not be forgotten. No Test debutant had previously taken so many wickets.

Born and raised like Lillee in Perth, Massie had first played for Western Australia in 1965-66, but struggled to establish himself in a strong state side; he even failed a trial with Northamptonshire in 1970 following his spell in Scotland. He did just enough to be chosen for three of Australia's matches against a World XI in 1971-72, and secured his place to England by taking seven for 76 at Sydney.

John Snow:
"A haul of 55 wickets in two series against Australia is his passport to cricket immortality"

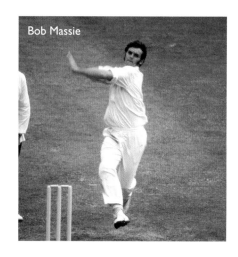
Bob Massie

Dennis Lillee

Dennis Lillee:

"This was the fast and furious Lillee, who… concentrated only on getting the ball from his end to the batsman's end in the shortest possible time"

He was left out of the First Test despite taking six for 31 at Worcester, and came nowhere near to bowling as well again as he did at Lord's. He took seven wickets in the rest of the series, but struggled to achieve any swing on a West Indies tour in 1973, and retired two years later.

Stackpole, whose father played for Victoria before him, was an aggressive opening batsman who scored more runs in the 1972 Tests than any batsman on either side, even if he rode his luck. He was also an able vice-captain to Ian Chappell, alongside whom he made his Test debut against England in 1965-66 as an all-rounder who batted at No. 8 and bowled leg-spin.

Despite a maiden Test hundred at No. 7 in South Africa, Stackpole missed the England tour in 1968, but within a few months had embarked on his career as opener. In that position he scored hundreds in India and West Indies, as well as 207 against England at Brisbane in 1970-71 and 114 at Trent Bridge during the 1972 series.

Snow, who played a big part in England winning the First Test at Old Trafford, might have been picked a year earlier following a great series in Australia in which he took 31 wickets, but he played only two home Tests in 1971 through injury and disciplinary action following a collision with Sunil Gavaskar [1980] at Lord's.

The son of a sporting vicar and the author of two books of poetry, Snow was a mercurial character who enjoyed several outstanding series for England, but he was mistrusted and only made two major tours. Few doubted he was the country's best fast bowler, accurate and hostile when everything clicked. He was still making an impact against Australia in 1975 and West Indies in 1976.

Like Chappell and Lillee, Snow joined World Series Cricket. He later worked as a travel agent. Lillee became a fast-bowling coach. Chappell coached India, ran academies in Australia, and worked as a selector.

CRICKETERS OF THE YEAR 1973 – Performances in the English season 1972

Name	Age*		Matches	Runs	Bat ave	Wickets	Bowl ave	Catches (/st)
GS Chappell	24	First-class	18	1260	70.00	19	25.68	26
		Tests	5	437	48.55	2	62.50	8
		ODI	3	101	33.66	2	37.00	0
DK Lillee	23	First-class	14	30	5.00	53	22.58	3
		Tests	5	10	3.33	31	17.67	0
		ODI	3	13	13.00	5	26.00	0
RAL Massie	25	First-class	12	45	5.00	50	17.02	0
		Tests	4	22	4.40	23	17.78	0
		ODI	3	16		3	43.00	1
JA Snow	31	First-class	14	171	10.68	50	22.12	6
		List A	18	101	12.62	29	13.55	0
		Tests	5	111	13.87	24	23.12	2
		ODI	3	5		4	24.25	0
KR Stackpole	32	First-class	21	1309	43.63	2	82.00	15
		Tests	5	485	53.88	0		4
		ODI	3	150	50.00	0		1

as at 1/4/1973

1974

Five Cricketers of the Year

Keith Boyce (Essex and West Indians)
Bevan Congdon (New Zealanders)
Keith Fletcher (Essex and England)
Roy Fredericks (Glamorgan and West Indians)
Peter Sainsbury (Hampshire)

HEADLINE EVENTS FROM 1973

- County champions – Hampshire

- Gillette Cup – Gloucestershire

- John Player League – Kent

- Benson & Hedges Cup – Kent

- England beat New Zealand 2-0 and lose to West Indies 2-0

- England lose to India 2-1 and draw 0-0 with Pakistan in 1972-73

THE ENGLAND TEAM ENDURED SOME DIFFICULT months during 1973, but out of adversity Keith Fletcher, five years a Test player but until now unsure of his place, emerged as a batsman of real substance.

In February he scored a century to secure a draw at Bombay. In June he batted six hours 20 minutes for 178 at Lord's to deny New Zealand a first Test win against England. In August, again at Lord's, he could not prevent a massacre at the hands of West Indies, but stood firm to top-score in both innings.

Circumstances hardly allowed him to show how fluently he could bat, but there was finally no doubting his character after 15 previous Tests without a hundred, or a score of more than 31 at home.

With his confidence bolstered, Fletcher enjoyed two more productive years with England, scoring another match-saving hundred in Barbados in 1974 and withstanding a battering from Australia's pace attack in 1974-75 to score 146 in a winning cause in the series finale. He lost his place soon after, but his skill at playing spin led to a recall for tours of India in 1976-77 and 1981-82, when he was appointed captain only to be peremptorily sacked after an attritional series was lost.

An acute reader of the game, Fletcher led Essex to their first trophies, including three Championships and five one-day prizes, before assisting them in various coaching capacities until 2001. He had a short and unsuccessful stint as England's team manager in the early 1990s.

Keith Boyce and Roy Fredericks were exuberant and important figures in West Indies' first series win since 1966-67 and England's heaviest home series defeat since 1966. Boyce was a joyous cricketer in the spirit of Learie Constantine [1940]. He bowled fast, batted without inhibition, and threw the ball further than most men ever have.

Recruited to Essex by Trevor Bailey [1950], who had played against him in a match in Barbados in 1965, Boyce spent two years qualifying for the county, during which he was nearly co-opted on to the 1966 West Indies tour. He quickly became one of the best all-rounders in English cricket, but rarely appeared for his native Barbados and had played only five Tests, all at home, before the 1973 tour.

His impact was immediate and decisive: in

the First Test at The Oval he took 11 for 147, then the best match figures for West Indies, as well as scoring 72; in the Third at Lord's he took another eight wickets as England sank to a huge innings defeat.

Boyce did not share with Fletcher the trophy-winning years at Essex; he retired in 1977 due to injury. By then, though, he had helped West Indies win the inaugural World Cup in 1975, when he scored a rapid 34 and took four wickets in the final against Australia. Retirement in Barbados was not kind to him: he liked to drink, his marriage broke up, and his house was destroyed in a hurricane. He died on his 53rd birthday in 1996.

Wisden described Fredericks, who stood only 5ft 4in, as the world's best left-handed opener. Like Fletcher, he took time to settle in Test cricket. He had scored 1,000 first-class runs on the England tour of 1969, but it was signing for Glamorgan in 1971 that led to a tightening of his technique as he found his ultra-attacking approach too hit-and-miss in English conditions.

By 1973, he could be seen in two styles: the steady accumulator who ground out 150 in eight and a half hours in the Edgbaston Test, or the dasher who won the second one-day international against England with a ruthless 105 off 111 balls.

Fredericks scored two more Test hundreds on his final tour of England in 1976, but his most famous innings came a few months earlier when he plundered 169 off 145 balls (including the first 100 off 71) against Australia's pacemen at Perth. The fifth cricketer from Guyana to be chosen by *Wisden* in 11 years, Fredericks later worked as minister for sport in the Guyanese government, but died of cancer in 2000, aged 57.

Bev Congdon so nearly led New Zealand

Roy Fredericks

Bevan Congdon

Bevan Congdon:
"His concentration became immense – the pitch his working world"

to glory in 1973. A Test cricketer since 1965 and on his third tour of England, he twice almost brought his country an elusive first victory over opponents of more than 40 years' standing. When New Zealand were left to score 479 to win the First Test at Trent Bridge, no one except their captain gave them a prayer. He scored 176 and they lost by only 38. At Lord's, his 175 left England facing a long fight for survival which, thanks to Fletcher, they managed.

Congdon, the youngest of six boys, grew up in Motueka in a remote region of South Island; he was coached by Les Townsend [1934], but getting noticed was not easy. He credited an improvement in his Test performances from 1972 to observing Glenn Turner [1971]. Although he never played in a winning side against England, he led New Zealand to their first Test victory over Australia in 1973-74.

Peter Sainsbury played a big part in Hampshire winning the Championship in 1973 without losing a game. A genuine all-rounder, he finished third in their batting averages and top of the bowling with his left-arm spin.

Sainsbury first played for Hampshire in 1954, took more than 100 wickets in his first full season the following year and was – uniquely – also a member of their first title-winning side in 1961. Losing and then rediscovering the art of flight in the late 1960s (he was not a big spinner of the ball), he revived his career and nearly achieved the double in 1971.

A brilliant short-leg fielder, he took more than 600 catches, and because of his fielding often acted as England's twelfth man. He retired in 1976 but remained closely involved with his county as a coach for many years. He was the first Cricketer of the Year to be born in Hampshire.

Keith Boyce:
"Graced with a lithe athletic frame, his every movement suggests physical power to spare"

Keith Boyce bowls, watched by Geoff Boycott [1965]

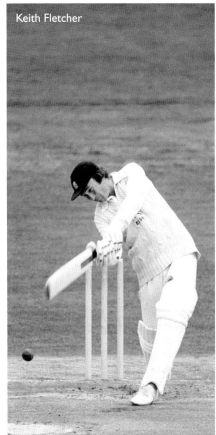

Keith Fletcher

CRICKETERS OF THE YEAR 1974 – Performances in the English season 1973

Name	Age*		Matches	Runs	Bat ave	Wickets	Bowl ave	Catches (/st)
KD Boyce	30	First-class	17	603	33.50	59	22.05	10
		List A	13	111	11.10	17	27.47	3
		Tests	3	129	25.80	19	15.47	0
BE Congdon	36	First-class	16	1081	60.05	20	30.50	7
		Tests	3	362	72.40	3	41.00	2
KWR Fletcher	29	First-class	19	1259	50.36			10
		List A	20	602	33.44			4
		Tests	6	575	63.88			2
		ODI	4	106	35.33			1
RC Fredericks	31	First-class	20	1506	43.02	1	165.00	10
		List A	14	357	25.50			4
		Tests	3	251	50.20	0		4
		ODI	2	109	54.50			0
PJ Sainsbury	39	First-class	22	758	34.45	53	17.83	10
		List A	20	173	15.72	18	35.77	12

* as at 1/4/1974

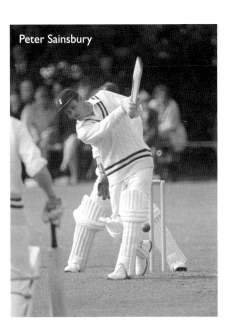

Peter Sainsbury

1975

Five Cricketers of the Year

Dennis Amiss (Warwickshire and England) /
Mike Denness (Kent and England) /
Norman Gifford (Worcestershire) ●
Tony Greig (Sussex and England) / ●
Andy Roberts (Hampshire) ●

HEADLINE EVENTS FROM 1974

- County champions – Worcestershire

- Gillette Cup – Kent

- John Player League – Leicestershire

- Benson & Hedges Cup – Surrey

- England beat India 3-0 and draw 0-0 with Pakistan

- England draw 1-1 with West Indies in the Caribbean in 1973-74

THIS WAS A POWERFUL GROUP. IT CONSISTED OF two England Test captains in Mike Denness and Tony Greig, who led a winning tour of India in 1976-77 and contributed to a reshaping of the game through his role in the creation of Kerry Packer's World Series Cricket; a batsman in Dennis Amiss who scored 102 first-class hundreds and pioneered the helmet; one of the great fast bowlers in Andy Roberts, who mentored a generation of West Indian speedsters; and a Championship-winning captain in Norman Gifford, who took more than 2,000 first-class wickets.

Denness had succeeded Ray Illingworth [1960] as England captain for the 1973-74 tour of West Indies, where thanks in part to Greig his team escaped with a 1–1 draw. At home in 1974, Denness, like most of the other batsmen including Greig, scored heavily against a weak India side, who were crushed 3–0, before England battled out three draws with Pakistan.

Denness went to Australia secure in his post, but by the time the 1975 *Wisden* was published he and his side had been so battered by Dennis Lillee [1973] and Jeff Thomson that he dropped himself for one Test. With Australia's attack weakened for the final match, Denness rallied to score 188 in an innings victory, but after a further defeat to Australia at home in 1975 he was sacked and replaced by Greig.

Denness was born in Scotland and educated at Ayrshire Academy, during which time he excelled at rugby union and represented Scotland at cricket. Spotted by George Duckworth [1929], he joined Kent in 1962, and as stand-in captain played a major role in Kent's 1970 Championship win. A fine, aggressive batsman against all but the best bowling, Denness led Kent to five one-day trophies as official captain between 1972 and 1976 before spending four seasons at Essex.

Greig also had Scottish roots. His father, a fighter pilot in the war, was from Edinburgh but emigrated to South Africa, where Tony and younger brother Ian, who also played for England, grew up around the Cape. Sussex coaches working there recommended him to Hove, and Greig was an immediate hit with bat and ball in 1967.

Greig, who stood 6ft 7in, was a charismatic figure whose relish for the big occasions made him the natural man to take over from Denness;

The England team for the first Test against Australia in 1975. Back row (l-r): Keith Fletcher [1974], Geoff Arnold [1972], **Tony Greig**, Chris Old [1979], Graham Gooch [1980], **Dennis Amiss**. Seated: Derek Underwood [1969], John Snow [1973], **Mike Denness** (captain), John Edrich [1966], Alan Knott [1970]

Tony Greig:

"His impact upon the English cricket scene matched his striking physical presence"

a rapier-like century at Brisbane had typified his unflinching response to Australia's short-pitched assaults, and he had two years' experience as Sussex captain behind him.

In his first match in charge he played an attacking innings of 96 at Lord's, but reached his height as strategist and motivator in India 18 months later as England pulled off a 3–1 series win against the odds.

Greig, who was also an exceptional fielder, deserved to rank among England's finest all-rounders, but before his untimely death in 2012 his record remained overshadowed by his controversial role in Packer's breakaway enterprise in 1977. As England captain at the time, Greig's sacking was inevitable, and by the age of 33 his playing career was effectively over.

Dennis Amiss, who was first tried by England in 1966, had a stupendous year in 1974; his aggregate of 1,379 Test runs remained an England record for a calendar year until beaten

by Michael Vaughan [2003]. His promotion to opener on the subcontinent in 1972-73 was the making of him: he did little in India, but returned from Pakistan with two hundreds and a 99 to his credit.

In 1974, he played a great match-saving innings of 262 not out in Jamaica, and scored two further centuries against West Indies before giving further evidence at home of his appetite for crease-occupation with scores of 188 against India and 183 against Pakistan.

He, like Denness, struggled badly in Australia, where his recent prolific form made him the target-in-chief; he too was dropped during the 1975 Ashes. Amiss was no quitter, though, and returned with a remodelled technique to compile a gutsy 203 against West Indies in 1976. He lost his Test place for good a year later, but scored 2,000 first-class runs in 1978 wearing protective headgear he had designed himself; he retired in 1987 with 102

Norman Gifford

Andy Roberts

first-class centuries and as Warwickshire's leading run-scorer.

Roberts, the son of a fisherman and one of a family of 14, was the most feared bowler in England in 1974. That he had seemingly come out of nowhere – islands such as Antigua were not known for producing cricketers, and he had played only once for Hampshire after a spell at the London indoor school run by Alf Gover [1937] – only added to the menace. He ran amok, taking 111 wickets in 19 Championship matches at an average of 13.45 and strike-rate of 35.6.

Roberts was armed with rare speed but also an instinctive grasp of how to vary his line of attack, the speed of his bouncers and use of the seam. By the time he toured England in 1976, he was in his pomp and ensured Greig's unfortunate boast that he could make West Indies "grovel" backfired.

Roberts took 202 wickets in 47 Tests, but his lasting gift to West Indies cricket was passing on his knowledge to the likes of Michael Holding [1977], Joel Garner [1980] and Malcolm Marshall [1983]. He also had a spell at Leicestershire.

Gifford's calm and experienced leadership helped deliver the Championship to New Road when the race with Hampshire appeared lost. By winning their last three games, Worcestershire nicked the title by two points.

Gifford, who was coached by Charles Hallows [1928], had been a member of the Worcestershire sides that won their first titles in 1964 and 1965. He had made his Test debut in 1964, but as a left-arm spinner faced stiff competition for a place from Derek Underwood [1969]; even so, in many of the 13 Tests Gifford played between 1971 and 1973 he was preferred to his rival. He went on to spend six years at Warwickshire, and was then coach at Sussex and, later, Durham.

In retirement, like Gifford, Amiss and Denness filled various coaching and administrative roles. Roberts was a coach and curator at Antigua's Recreation Ground, and Amiss was Warwickshire's chief executive. Greig settled in Australia and worked for Kerry Packer's Channel Nine as a colourful commentator until his death in December 2012. Denness died within four months, in April 2013.

Andy Roberts:
"He was the centre of discussion, especially among batsmen, either in retrospect or awesome anticipation"

CRICKETERS OF THE YEAR 1975 – Performances in the English season 1974

Name	Age*		Matches	Runs	Bat ave	Wickets	Bowl ave	Catches (lst)
DL Amiss	31	First-class	18	1510	53.92	1	17.00	6
		List A	14	559	39.92			3
		Tests	6	590	73.75			1
MH Denness	34	First-class	15	760	40.00			13
		List A	20	410	25.62			9
		Tests	6	380	54.28			6
N Gifford	35	First-class	22	270	12.85	69	19.31	16
		List A	22	165	11.78	33	22.90	7
AW Greig	28	First-class	18	669	24.77	55	30.49	24
		List A	17	453	32.35	23	24.26	6
		Tests	6	249	41.50	14	28.42	13
AME Roberts	24	First-class	21	67	6.70	119	13.62	2
		List A	21	54	18.00	35	11.34	4

* as at 1/4/1975

1976 Five Cricketers of the Year

Ian Chappell (Australians) *

Peter Lee (Lancashire) *

Rick McCosker (Australians) *

David Steele (Northamptonshire and England) *

Bob Woolmer (Kent and England) *

HEADLINE EVENTS FROM 1975

- County champions – Leicestershire

- Gillette Cup – Lancashire

- John Player League – Hampshire

- Benson & Hedges Cup – Leicestershire

- Australia beat England 1-0

- West Indies win the inaugural World Cup

- England are beaten 4-1 in Australia in 1974-75

IN THE SUMMER OF 1975 ENGLAND GOT LITTLE joy out of Ian Chappell's Australians, who knocked them out of the inaugural World Cup at the semi-final stage and beat them 1–0 in a four-Test series, but they regained a fair bit of pride through the defiance of two newcomers, David Steele and Bob Woolmer.

After the First Test was lost by an innings, Steele answered England's call for batsmen armed with the technique and temperament to stand firm against fast bowling. Grey-haired and bespectacled, England cap on head and sweatband on right forearm, he could hardly have looked less suited to holding the fort at No. 3, but he coped so coolly that he achieved national celebrity as "the bank clerk who went to war".

His selection was inspired. In six innings he was never out for less than 39, and at home to West Indies in 1976 he scored a phlegmatic hundred in the first match of the series. Unfortunately for him, England's next assignment was to India and Steele was not rated a good player of spin, so he was left at home, and being by then 35 years old he was not recalled.

Steele, whose younger brother John had a long career at Leicestershire, did not join Northamptonshire from his native Staffordshire until he was 21, and then took seven seasons to average 30 with the bat. This rose to 52.19 in 1972, and when England did not call on him then he thought his chance of Test cricket had gone. In 1979 he moved to Derbyshire, initially as captain, but after three years returned to Northampton.

Though a capable left-arm spinner, Steele was primarily a batsman, but Woolmer was originally picked by England as an all-rounder who swung the ball at medium-pace. In his first Test, he came on as first change and batted at No. 8, but his resourceful batting soon led to promotion.

Woolmer missed the Third Test at Leeds but returned for the Fourth at The Oval, where he went in at No. 5 and in the follow-on scored 149 in eight hours 20 minutes. This included what was then the slowest century scored for England against Australia at six hours 34 minutes, and helped secure an unlikely draw.

Woolmer made himself into a successful cricketer through close study and hard work. He spent several winters coaching and playing in South Africa, and the demands of one-day

Ian Chappell bats at Lord's with **Bob Woolmer** at short leg; the wicketkeeper is Alan Knott [1970]

At the end of the 1975 series in England, Chappell surprisingly announced that at the age of 31 he was standing down as captain, though continuing as a player. It was a surprise because he had just scored 192 at The Oval, and overall as captain averaged 50 with the bat. He was a more rugged, less graceful, batsman than his brother Greg Chappell [1973], but a more purposeful leader.

Chappell created a team that took its catches (he was a fine slip catcher) and knew how to win. He also fought the players' corner on remuneration, and was instrumental in the setting up of World Series Cricket, which transformed pay levels. He remained outspoken in his later work as a TV commentator.

Rick McCosker, who topped Australia's batting averages in the Tests in England, made a remarkable rise. Born at Inverell, more than 400 miles from Sydney, he genuinely was a bank clerk, and did not make his state debut until two weeks short of his 27th birthday. A year later the national selectors gambled on him as opener midway through the 1974-75 Ashes; he confirmed a reputation for neatness and courage by scoring 80 in his first innings.

He opened in England and thrived in generally favourable batting conditions, scoring an unbeaten 95 at Headingley before the pitch was sabotaged and the match abandoned, followed by 127 at The Oval, where he shared a big stand with his captain.

McCosker returned to England in 1977 and scored a hundred at Trent Bridge, but his most famous innings came a few months before that in the Centenary Test at Melbourne when he batted with a broken jaw wired up and heavily bandaged. He contributed 25 brave runs to a partnership with Dennis Lillee [1973] of 54 – in a game Australia won by 45.

Peter Lee was a former Northamptonshire team-mate of Steele's who moved to Lancashire in 1972 after struggling to establish himself with

cricket, at which Kent were highly successful, raised his game. He had been chosen for three one-day internationals against Australia in 1972 and done well.

Woolmer had risen to No. 3 by the time he scored two hundreds in the 1977 Ashes, but he signed for World Series Cricket and played only four more Tests. His analytical mind later served him well as a successful and innovative coach, notably with Warwickshire and South Africa. He died while working with Pakistan at the 2007 World Cup.

Like Steele and Woolmer, Ian Chappell was another who relished life at first wicket down, as fine a player of the hook stroke as there has been, but it was as a captain that he had his most profound impact. He did as much as anyone to turn around Australia's fortunes in the early 1970s. The uncompromising brand of cricket his team played did not gain universal approval, but there was no doubting the success of the method. Of the seven full series he led, Australia won five and drew two.

> Ian Chappell:
> **"Although his candid speech and honesty can be refreshing, the same attributes also have landed him in trouble with administrators on several occasions"**

David Steele

serious shoulder injury in 1978, and he was released by Lancashire in 1982, after which he retreated to Minor Counties cricket for Durham.

Brian Davison, Leicestershire's leading batsman in a Championship year and scorer of 189 against the Australians, was unlucky to miss out.

Peter Lee

David Steele:

"Test cricket has not enjoyed such a romantic story for decades. In the space of three matches... Steele emerged as the much-needed national hero"

his native county, where he was coached by Jack Mercer [1927]. He was a big-hearted medium-fast bowler whose tirelessness and persistence were much needed on the batsmen's pitches of 1975, when he was the only English bowler to claim more than 100 first-class wickets, as he had been in 1973. He also took three for 38 in Lancashire's Gillette Cup final victory over Middlesex.

Lee's career went into decline following a

Rick McCosker batting. The wicketkeeper is **Alan Knott** [1970]

CRICKETERS OF THE YEAR 1976 – Performances in the English season 1975

Name	Age*		Matches	Runs	Bat ave	Wickets	Bowl ave	Catches (/st)
IM Chappell	32	First-class	11	1022	53.78	6	30.50	4
		Tests	4	429	71.50	1	82.00	2
PG Lee	30	First-class	21	77	15.40	112	18.45	5
		List A	25	2	2.00	30	22.23	6
RB McCosker	29	First-class	11	1078	59.88			3
		Tests	4	414	82.80			1
DS Steele	34	First-class	21	1756	48.77	11	13.45	26
		List A	20	536	29.77	0		5
		Tests	3	365	60.83	2	10.50	4
RA Woolmer	27	First-class	17	1193	42.60	30	30.70	12
		List A	15	149	24.83	17	22.58	7
		Tests	2	218	54.50	2	36.00	1

as at 1/4/1976

1977

Five Cricketers of the Year

Mike Brearley (Middlesex and England) /
Gordon Greenidge (West Indians) /
Michael Holding (West Indians) ●
Viv Richards (West Indians) /
Bob Taylor (Derbyshire) ⋔

HEADLINE EVENTS FROM 1976

• County champions – Middlesex

• Gillette Cup – Northamptonshire

• John Player League – Kent

• Benson & Hedges Cup – Kent

• West Indies beat England 3-0

EACH OF THESE FIVE WAS A LEADER IN HIS field. Viv Richards ranks among the greatest batsmen of all time, Gordon Greenidge among the most effective openers. Michael Holding deserves prominent mention among the most captivating and deadly of fast bowlers, while as a wicketkeeper Bob Taylor had few peers. As a thinker and strategist, Mike Brearley acquired a unique status among captains.

Norman Preston, *Wisden*'s editor, said that four of the five picked themselves, while Taylor was chosen as a wicketkeeper "who excels in ability and consistency coupled with artistry". Taylor's selection was essentially down to long service: he claimed his 1,000th dismissal in 1976.

The selection of three West Indians was a fair reflection of their team's dominance during the long hot summer of 1976. Had Clive Lloyd [1971], Roy Fredericks [1974] and Andy Roberts [1975] not already been chosen, the touring team could have made a clean sweep.

Richards pulverised England's bowling in Tests and one-day internationals, and despite missing a Test through illness set a West Indies record of 829 runs in a series that included scores of 232 at Trent Bridge and 291 at The Oval. Earlier in the year he scored four hundreds in six Tests – one in Australia and three at home to India – and finished the calendar year of 1976 with a then-record 1,710 Test runs.

The tour of Australia was the making of him. West Indies may have been crushed, but Richards's belief soared. He already possessed the gifts; now he had the motivation to make his team the best in the world. His mission was to neutralise the most dangerous fast bowlers, pointedly doing so without recourse to the helmets that would soon be in vogue. On his day he was unstoppable.

Richards came to England with fellow Antiguan Roberts in 1973, and honed his technique at Somerset, for whom he played regularly until 1986. He was chaired from the field after his fifth and final tour in 1991, when he retired unbeaten in 12 series as captain.

Richards, who spent his best years at No. 3, conceded he owed much to the openers who drew the bowlers' sting. Greenidge was invariably one, in company first with Fredericks, later with Desmond Haynes [1991]. Greenidge's ability to deal with the new ball owed much to his formative years being spent in England: though born and raised in Barbados, he moved to England at 14, and three years later joined Hampshire, where he would open with Barry Richards [1969].

Greenidge could cut and hook with tremendous power, but his improvement in 1976 – when he scored more runs and centuries than anyone on the tour – was in part down to knowing when to attack and when not, an adjustment made necessary by his horrible failure in Australia the previous winter.

Six of his 19 Test hundreds were scored in England – one of two double-hundreds on the 1984 tour made light work of a run-chase at Lord's – and 92 first-class centuries put him second only to Richards's 114 among West Indians.

Holding was perhaps the most natural fast bowler of his generation. Never mind his bowling: his long run-up, graceful and rhythmic, was spellbinding enough. Unfortunately for the batsmen, it did not stop there. He could swing the ball, move it off the pitch and propel it at speeds to rival Jeff Thomson.

This encouraged him to give his all even in the most unpromising conditions, as happened when he blasted out 14 England batsmen (nine bowled, three lbw) at The Oval in 1976, still the best match figures for West Indies. Earlier in the series, he relished his speed as he and Roberts [1974] worked over the ageing Brian Close [1964] and John Edrich [1966].

The Oval was Holding's first big performance, though he had recently taken six for 65 in a Test in Trinidad which India had still won. He had been promising but expensive in Australia, before which he had taken only 16 wickets in three seasons with Jamaica.

Holding, who battled injuries later in his career, formed great new-ball partnerships with Roberts and then Malcolm Marshall [1983] before dropping down to first change. He retired

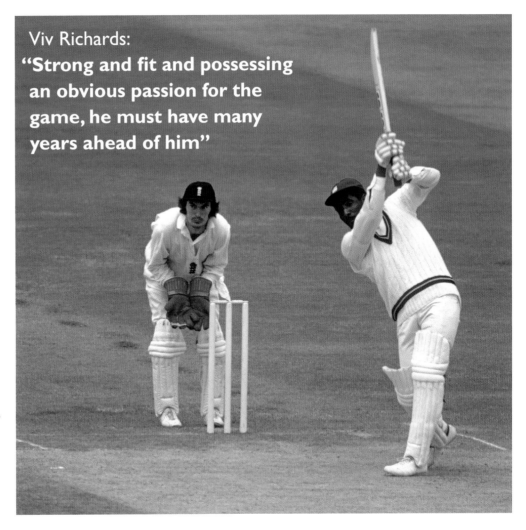

Viv Richards:
"Strong and fit and possessing an obvious passion for the game, he must have many years ahead of him"

Viv Richards, watched by Alan Knott [1970]

Mike Brearley

in 1987 with 249 Test wickets, a close second to Joel Garner [1980] as the most successful West Indies fast bowler to that point.

Mike Brearley's solid showing against Holding and Roberts for MCC earned him his first Test cap at the age of 34, and although he lasted only two matches he played three composed innings and was taken on the winter tour of India and Australia as vice-captain to Tony Greig [1975].

Brearley had shone at Cambridge as batsman and occasional wicketkeeper, before his development was arrested by a teaching career that took him to Newcastle and California.

Michael Holding

Gordon Greenidge

Turning full-time to cricket from 1971, when he became Middlesex captain, he developed into one of the best county openers in the country. Middlesex's results also picked up: they reached both cup finals in 1975, and in 1976 won their first outright Championship since 1947.

Greig's defection to Kerry Packer meant the England captaincy passing to Brearley in 1977. This was lucky, as was the weakness of England's opponents, but Brearley's gift for leadership was beyond dispute.

Under him, England won three Ashes series – on the third occasion in 1981 after he was recalled mid-series and masterminded a famous comeback – but as a batsman he never cracked Test cricket, failing to score a hundred in 39 appearances.

Taylor's modest talent with the bat – he scored one century in a career spanning more than 600 games – was the chief reason why he was unable to displace Alan Knott [1970] as England's No. 1 keeper. But Knott's departure to Kerry Packer in 1977 created an opening, and Taylor eventually played 57 Tests, the last of them at the age of 43. He only enhanced his reputation for unfussy but near-immaculate glovework.

He retired with a world-record 1,646 dismissals to his name. He later worked for a cricket-equipment manufacturer. Richards briefly coached the West Indies team before moving into media work. Holding became a respected TV commentator, and Brearley became a psychoanalyst.

Bob Taylor

Bob Taylor:

"It is a measure of his consistency that Taylor could be regarded as a cricketer of any year, not merely the last one"

CRICKETERS OF THE YEAR 1977 – Performances in the English season 1976

Name	Age*		Matches	Runs	Bat ave	Wickets	Bowl ave	Catches (/st)
JM Brearley	34	First-class	25	1695	40.35	0		15
		List A	16	423	28.20			6
		Tests	2	70	17.50			1
CG Greenidge	25	First-class	20	1952	55.77			28
		Tests	5	592	65.77			7
MA Holding	23	First-class	12	152	12.66	55	14.38	5
		Tests	4	41	8.20	28	12.71	0
IVA Richards	25	First-class	16	1724	71.83	1	56.00	17/1
		Tests	4	829	118.42	1	56.00	2
		ODI	3	216	108.00	1	4.00	1
RW Taylor	35	First-class	21	641	20.03			47/10
		List A	23	220	18.33			24/7

* as at 1/4/1977

1978 Five Cricketers of the Year

Ian Botham (Somerset and England)

Mike Hendrick (Derbyshire and England)

Alan Jones (Glamorgan)

Ken McEwan (Essex)

Bob Willis (Warwickshire and England)

HEADLINE EVENTS FROM 1977

- County champions – Middlesex and Kent (shared)

- Gillette Cup – Middlesex

- John Player League – Leicestershire

- Benson & Hedges Cup – Gloucestershire

- England beat Australia 3-0 to regain the Ashes

- Australia beat England by 45 runs in the Centenary Test in 1976-77

In Bob Willis, Mike Hendrick and Ian Botham, *Wisden* chose the most influential members of England's pace attack in the Ashes triumph of 1977. Between them the trio took 51 wickets, even though Hendrick and Botham did not join Willis until the third match and Botham was ruled out of the final game with a fractured foot.

At Trent Bridge, where Botham coolly collected a five-for on his first day of Test cricket at the age of 21, they claimed 15 wickets; at Headingley, where the series was won, they took 16. Australia were missing key personnel but were totally outplayed.

In the case of Botham and Willis this proved the start of a wonderful relationship: in all they would play 60 Tests together in which they took 476 wickets between them, Botham in his early days swinging the ball prodigiously while Willis, tall and angular, was constantly lifting it nastily towards rib-cages and throats.

Hendrick, prone to injury and less proficient in the knack of taking wickets, appeared less often – the three of them played 15 times together overall – but when Botham reached his 100th Test wicket in 1979 (in what was then a record

two years and five days after his debut) he said that the bowler he most enjoyed working with was Hendrick because of his relentless accuracy.

Not only were their bowling styles complementary: Hendrick and Botham were among the finest close catchers of their generation and held on to many of the edges that came their way. Botham set England records for most Test wickets (383) and catches (120), of which the former still stands with Willis (325) his nearest rival.

Willis took longer to reach the heights than Botham, who was seven years younger. Willis was tried early by England and discarded; switched from Surrey to Warwickshire; and went through serious knee surgery before finally embarking on a long run in the Test side from 1976. He was a key player in England's series win in India in 1976-77, a tour for which Botham was overlooked even though he had made his first one-day appearances at home in 1976.

Although he spent some early years at Leicestershire, Hendrick took his place in a distinguished line of Derbyshire fast-medium seam bowlers armed with well-grooved actions and powerful physiques, though it was not until

1977 that he translated the excellence he displayed at county level to the international arena.

Botham, whose solid build and Herculean stamina enabled him to play almost injury-free until 1984, was more than just a bowler, though. To the surprise of those who had seen his early efforts on the Lord's groundstaff or at Somerset and thought him merely a courageous lower-order hitter, he developed into a batsman of real substance whose appetite for big hitting was backed by a sound technique.

In the winter of 1977-78 and summer of 1978, Botham hit three Test hundreds at No. 7, but was good enough by 1982 to score a double-century against India from No. 5. In all he hit 14 Test hundreds, and even though his game declined as his fitness deteriorated he finished with a record that statistically puts him head and shoulders above all England's other all-rounders.

One area in which neither Botham nor Willis excelled was captaincy, either with their counties or country, though Botham was stand-in leader when Somerset lifted the last of the five one-day trophies they won between 1979 and 1983, their first-ever prizes. In between their respective brief stints as England captain, Botham and Willis starred in the 1981 Ashes series, particularly in the legendary Headingley Test. Botham later moved to Worcestershire and Durham. Hendrick ended his career at Nottinghamshire.

Willis retired in 1984, in part because his knee problems resurfaced, but his total of 90 Test caps has been bettered by few genuine fast bowlers.

Alan Jones led Glamorgan to the Gillette Cup final in 1977, a notable effort given the turbulence the previous year surrounding the departure of Majid Khan [1970]. Jones, in his 40th year, was one of the most competent opening batsmen in English cricket during the 1970s, and was unlucky not to win an official Test cap.

In fact Jones, a left-hander, had played what was at the time regarded as an official Test, for England v Rest of the World at Lord's in 1970 – he was presented with a cap and blazer – but in 1980 this series was downgraded in the record books. He came close to selection for the Ashes

Bob Willis:
"Determination is one virtue Willis does not lack"

Ian Botham:
"A straightforward, pleasant character, who knows where he is aiming and who, in the best old-fashioned sense, has a good conceit of himself"

CRICKETERS OF THE YEAR 1978 – Performances in the English season 1977

Name	Age*		Matches	Runs	Bat ave	Wickets	Bowl ave	Catches (/st)
IT Botham	22	First-class	17	738	30.75	88	22.53	15
		List A	17	423	28.20	20	25.80	10
		Tests	2	25	12.50	10	20.20	1
M Hendrick	29	First-class	21	66	6.60	67	15.94	17
		List A	16	40	13.33	19	20.73	4
		Tests	3	20	6.66	14	20.71	5
A Jones	39	First-class	21	1272	37.41	0		6
		List A	23	619	26.91			4
KS McEwan	25	First-class	23	1702	51.57	0		14
		List A	21	646	35.88			9
RGD Willis	28	First-class	16	124	12.40	58	20.39	5
		List A	18	70	8.75	23	24.00	2
		Tests	5	49	24.50	27	19.77	2
		ODI	3	7	7.00	5	15.80	0

as at 1/4/1978

Ken McEwan

Alan Jones bats; in the background is
Allan Lamb [1981]

England's team for the 1978-79 Australian
tour, just before departure. Back row
(l-r): John Lever [1979], Geoff Miller,
John Emburey [1984], Graham Gooch
[1980]. Second row: **Ian Botham**, **Mike
Hendrick**, Phil Edmonds, Chris Old [1979].
Third row: Geoff Boycott [1965],
Mike Brearley [1977] (captain), **Bob Willis**,
Bob Taylor [1977]. Front: David Gower
[1979], Clive Radley [1979], Roger Tolchard,
Derek Randall [1980]

tour in 1970-71, but missed out and was not
considered again.

He remains the batsman to have scored
most first-class runs (36,049) without ever
playing a Test. The eighth of nine boys to a
South Wales miner, he played alongside his
only younger brother Eifion for Glamorgan for
more than 20 years.

Ken McEwan was similarly unfortunate when
it came to missing out on Test cricket. By the
age of 20, when McEwan first played for Eastern
Province and was recommended to Sussex by
Tony Greig [1975], who coached him at school,
South Africa's sporting isolation was entrenched
and his prospects of playing international cricket
all but non-existent.

Sussex turned him down because they had
filled their quota of overseas players, but Essex

invited him for a trial and signed him for 1974.
He topped 1,000 runs and continued to improve
year by year, totalling 1,821 runs in 1976 and
1,702 in 1977, when he scored more first-class
hundreds (eight) than anyone else. Including a
score of 104 in the Sunday League, he struck five
centuries in 11 days between June 26 and July 6.

McEwan, who had a gift for timing and
attacking strokeplay, was a key component in
Essex's domination of county cricket between
1979 and his retirement in 1985, during which
time they won three Championships and five
one-day trophies.

Botham, who was knighted for his services
to cricket and charity work in 2007, became
a prominent TV commentator, often working
alongside Willis. Hendrick and Jones went
into coaching.

1979

Five Cricketers of the Year

David Gower (Leicestershire and England) /
John Lever (Essex and England) ●
Chris Old (Yorkshire and England) ●
Clive Radley (Middlesex and England) /
John Shepherd (Kent) / ●

HEADLINE EVENTS FROM 1978

- County champions – Kent

- Gillette Cup – Sussex

- John Player League – Hampshire

- Benson & Hedges Cup – Kent

- England beat Pakistan 2-0 and New Zealand 3-0

- England draw 0-0 in Pakistan and 1-1 in New Zealand in 1977-78

ENGLAND COPED BETTER THAN SOME FOLLOWING the defections to Kerry Packer's World Series Cricket. Among those they brought into a reshaped batting line-up in 1978 were Clive Radley and David Gower, one a veteran of 33 years, the other a promising stripling of 21. Both were instant hits, though only one built on this early success.

Gower, the first Cricketer of the Year from Leicestershire since 1933, was a golden-haired left-hander who struck the ball with an easy elegance that sent onlookers into raptures and historians in search of English batsmen who had similar time to spare.

He was never much inspired by county cricket – the first time he averaged 35 in a Championship season was in 1981 – but liked the big stage. Chosen for the First Test of the 1978 season against Pakistan after hitting an unbeaten 114 in a one-day international at The Oval, he pulled his first ball in Test cricket for four, and in eight Test innings that summer reached at least 39 in seven of them.

He scored 111 in the First Test against New Zealand, and during the winter tour struck 102 at Perth, the first of nine hundreds he took off Australia. An unbeaten double-century at home to India followed in 1979. The last batsman to score a hundred for England at so young an age was Denis Compton [1939].

Gower was occasionally dropped by England, but not for long, at least not until cultural differences with the captaincy of Graham Gooch [1980] left him marginalised in his later years. Even so, and despite the suspicion that he might have scored more had he cared about statistics, he retired in 1993 as England's leading Test run-scorer with 8,231.

Radley, in fact, needed more than Packer's intervention to get into the England side. Only when Mike Brearley [1977] suffered a broken arm did he receive a summons to leave Sydney, where he was coaching, and join England's touring team in the winter of 1977-78.

Brought in to strengthen the batting after England were routed for 64 at Wellington, Radley dropped anchor for almost 11 hours in his second match at Auckland for 158, and followed this with another, brisker hundred against Pakistan at Edgbaston, where he partnered Gower in his first Test innings. When they put

Clive Radley

John Shepherd

John Lever

on 114 in the final Test against New Zealand, Radley matched Gower's strokeplay.

Radley, who helped Middlesex to four outright Championships as well as one shared title, had grown up playing cricket in Norfolk before migrating to Middlesex, where he rose to vice-captain under Mike Brearley. Hit on the head by Rodney Hogg in the opening first-class match, Radley spent the 1978-79 tour of Australia on the margins and slipped out of the England reckoning.

Two more members of that Ashes tour party were among *Wisden*'s Five, although neither played much part, Chris Old appearing only in the First Test and John Lever in the Second as they found themselves squeezed out by the triumvirate of Botham, Hendrick and Willis [all 1978].

Old, a tall fast-medium bowler from Middlesbrough armed with outswingers and break-backs, whose brother Alan played rugby union for England, first appeared for England in India in 1972-73. He took six wickets in his first game and claimed his 100th Test scalp in 1977, but was plagued by fitness issues; he had played only two full series before facing Pakistan in 1978. In the First Test at Edgbaston, he produced an amazing burst of four wickets in five balls, the fifth delivery being a no-ball.

Old's aspirations as a Test all-rounder remained unfulfilled. He once hit a Championship century in just 37 minutes, but was uncomfortable against short-pitched bowling. He did, however, play a key role in England's fightback at Headingley in 1981, staying with Botham while 67 runs were added.

Lever was among the finest swing bowlers in the country, and the best left-arm fast-medium bowler England had had since Bill Voce [1933]. He too started his Test career in India, in his case in 1976-77, and with spectacular results, taking ten for 70 at Delhi (as well as scoring 53) to get England off to a winning start. He finished the series with 26 wickets.

John Lever:
"No cricketer places more emphasis on physical fitness – and it has paid off"

David Gower

David Gower: "The mantle of cricket's 'golden boy' slips easily over Gower's lithe shoulders"

Chris Old

Lever was unlucky not to play any of the home Tests in 1978, but Botham had the role of swinger-in-chief covered; by the end of that summer they had played only one Test together. Lever instead focused on spearheading Essex's drive for a first Championship title, a role enhanced after the retirement of Keith Boyce [1974]. He performed magnificently, taking 97 wickets in 19 Championship matches.

Both Old and Lever joined a rebel tour of South Africa in 1981-82, but Lever's superb fitness meant he was still wanted by England after his ban was served: he played one Test at Headingley in 1986 and took six wickets.

John Shepherd, a long-serving all-rounder from Barbados, was chosen by *Wisden* for his part in helping Kent win the Championship and Benson and Hedges Cup in 1978, his benefit season. He had played for the county since 1966 after being spotted at the same time as his childhood friend Boyce; while Boyce went to Essex, Shepherd headed for Kent.

He made his Test debut for West Indies in England in 1969, and would have played many more Tests had he not joined a multinational tour of South Africa in 1973, leading to his excommunication from West Indian cricket. He returned to South Africa and became the first black cricketer to play in the Currie Cup.

Wisden may have thought it was paying a late tribute to Shepherd; in fact he played county cricket until 1987 when he was 43, in his later years with Gloucestershire, and finished with 13,359 runs and 1,157 wickets in the first-class game.

Shepherd later worked as a development officer in the Americas. Lever became a master at Bancroft's School. Radley worked as head coach at MCC, Gower became a well-known presenter of cricket on Sky Television. Old ran a fish-and-chip shop in Cornwall.

CRICKETERS OF THE YEAR 1979 – Performances in the English season 1978

Name	Age*		Matches	Runs	Bat ave	Wickets	Bowl ave	Catches (/st)
DI Gower	22	First-class	21	1098	37.86	0		6
		List A	19	685	42.81			10
		Tests	6	438	54.75			0
		ODI	4	201	67.00			3
JK Lever	30	First-class	22	85	10.62	106	15.18	9
		List A	22	27	9.00	35	20.11	2
CM Old	30	First-class	14	236	23.60	64	17.31	5
		List A	17	171	17.10	29	14.75	5
		Tests	4	21	7.00	14	17.64	1
		ODI	2	31		4	8.00	1
CT Radley	34	First-class	18	923	36.92	0		17
		List A	19	661	44.06	0		2
		Tests	6	308	38.50			4
		ODI	4	250	83.33			0
JN Shepherd	35	First-class	20	785	35.68	44	35.75	12
		List A	21	380	27.14	34	13.91	10

*as at 1/4/1979

1980

Five Cricketers of the Year

Joel Garner (Somerset and West Indians) ●
Sunil Gavaskar (Indians) /
Graham Gooch (Essex and England) /
Derek Randall (Nottinghamshire and England) /
Brian Rose (Somerset) /

HEADLINE EVENTS FROM 1979

- County champions – Essex

- Gillette Cup – Somerset

- John Player League – Somerset

- Benson & Hedges Cup – Essex

- England beat India 1-0

- West Indies win the World Cup

- England beat Australia 5-1 in 1978-79 to retain the Ashes

THE 1979 SEASON WAS HISTORIC FOR TWO counties previously in no need of trophy cabinets: Essex won the Championship and Benson and Hedges Cup, while Somerset lifted the Gillette Cup and John Player League. *Wisden* marked the occasion by naming among its Five Graham Gooch, who scored 120 for Essex in their Lord's final, and Brian Rose and Joel Garner, respectively captain and principal strike bowler at Somerset. Garner also helped West Indies win the World Cup in England in June.

Sunil Gavaskar was the first touring cricketer picked in three years. Given his record over the previous ten years and his success in keeping a strong England pace attack at bay in their own conditions, his selection must have been automatic.

The innings he played at The Oval typified him. Set 438 to win, India were given little chance, but Gavaskar played in masterly fashion, starting in defence but moving smoothly onto the attack as the target approached: he had more shots in his locker than he often showed. When he fell for 221, the chase faltered and the game was drawn, but his audacity almost paid off. On the back of his

success, Gavaskar was signed by Somerset for 1980 as stand-in for Garner.

Gavaskar can lay strong claim to be the finest opening batsman of modern times. No one has scored more Test runs as an opener, his versatility was demonstrated by him averaging more outside the subcontinent than on it, and at 5ft 5in he was almost impossible to bounce out.

Gavaskar was raised in Bombay (now Mumbai) in a cricketing environment – an uncle, Madhav Mantri, kept wicket for India – and after six first-class matches he was chosen for his first tour: in four Tests he scored 774 runs, including 124 and 220 in the same game in Trinidad despite suffering toothache. He scored one of his best hundreds at Old Trafford on India's 1974 tour.

Gooch batted at No. 3 or 4 in the Tests against India in 1979 before taking up the role of opener during England's tour of Australia the following winter, having not even made the side for the first match.

Unlike the safety-first Gavaskar, Gooch knew well how to play one-dayers, and his tremendous success in limited-overs games in 1979 proved a stepping stone to finally conquering Test cricket

Derek Randall doffs his cap to bowler Dennis Lillee [1973] during the Centenary Test at Melbourne

Derek Randall:

"In his never-dull career he has fallen at a few fences, but much of his appeal is that he picks himself up with a smile"

in failure, the Sydney innings overturned a deficit of 142 and turned the game – and series – England's way; it probably did more than anything to secure his *Wisden* selection. Randall's performances in the home season of 1979 were moderate, at least until a spectacular double of 209 and 146 against Middlesex in his final match.

Randall was a fidget whose restless energy came out in his shuffles around the crease and acrobatic patrolling of the cover and midwicket regions, from which he executed many unlikely run-outs and catches.

Garner stood a towering 6ft 8in, and for a fast bowler of deceptive speed this created almost impossibly difficult trajectories to score off. Two performances in 1979 stood out: in the World Cup final he took five England wickets for 38, and in the Gillette Cup final against Northamptonshire six for 29; of his 11 wickets in these games, seven were bowled, one lbw and one hit-wicket. His economy rate in limited-overs cricket was 2.7 runs per over, in first-class matches 1.9.

Another in the long line of Test fast bowlers from Barbados, Garner was given his chance as stand-in against Pakistan in 1976-77 and claimed 25 wickets in five games; around the same time he came to Somerset's attention while playing for Littleborough in the Lancashire League.

Garner did sterling work for his captains, Clive Lloyd [1971] especially using him as stock bowler while attacking from the other end, yet he finished with more Test wickets (259) at a lower cost (20.97 each) than most contemporaries. By the time he was controversially sacked by Somerset in 1986 his fitness was fading fast.

After several years of near-misses under Brian Close [1964], Somerset finally laid hands on trophies under Rose, who took over the reins late in 1977 just as he was leaving for his first full England tour. That trip was not a great personal

in 1980, when he struck a glorious maiden hundred against West Indies five years after collecting a pair on debut.

Gooch was a wonderful striker of the ball; his problem was reining in his shots like Gavaskar. The penny dropped after he moved up to opening the innings for Essex in 1978, and grasped the need to get fitter.

He became a formidable run-scorer at county and international level, though not reaching his peak until his late thirties. He stands tenth among first-class run-scorers and top of England's list in Tests. He also scored more runs in first-class and List A one-day matches combined (67,057) than anyone in history.

Derek Randall opened in the First Test against India in 1979, not something he was ever particularly suited to, but being shunted around the order was to be his fate. He scored seven hundreds for England in five different positions, although his two most famous innings came at No. 3 on earlier tours of Australia – an iridescent 174 at Melbourne in the Centenary Test of 1976-77, and a painstaking 150 in searing Sydney heat in January 1979.

Although the Melbourne effort ended

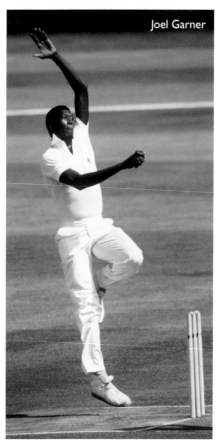

Joel Garner

Graham Gooch

success, but at Somerset he came to the captaincy at just the right time.

In 1978 the county narrowly missed out on winning the same two competitions they would claim 12 months later, but Rose remained positive going into the 1979 season, though he erred when he declared a one-day innings closed after six balls of a Benson and Hedges Cup group match to ensure his side's qualification on run-rate. Somerset were expelled from the competition, and Rose took the flak.

Rose, whose development was slowed by teacher training, was a fluent opening batsman who briefly regained his England place in 1980, but health issues undermined his game, and by 1983 he was a marginal presence in the Somerset side.

He was later a shrewd manager at Taunton. Garner rose to president of the Barbados Cricket Association. Gooch became batting coach to Essex and England. Randall coached at Bedford School. Gavaskar worked for the Indian board and in television.

Sunil Gavaskar

Graham Gooch:
"[He] has the passion and promise to suggest we shall hear a lot more of his name in the years ahead"

Brian Rose

CRICKETERS OF THE YEAR 1980 – Performances in the English season 1979

Name	Age*		Matches	Runs	Bat ave	Wickets	Bowl ave	Catches (/st)
J Garner	27	First-class	14	106	17.66	55	13.83	4
		List A	24	136	15.11	47	12.23	2
		ODI	4	10	10.00	8	21.50	1
SM Gavaskar	30	First-class	13	1062	55.89	0		15
		Tests	4	542	77.42			3
GA Gooch	26	First-class	17	838	36.43	4	50.25	28
		List A	24	1137	54.14	2	60.00	9
		Tests	4	207	41.40	1	49.00	6
		ODI	5	210	52.50	0		0
DW Randall	29	First-class	14	1138	47.41			12
		List A	18	371	28.53			5
		Tests	3	83	27.66			4
BC Rose	29	First-class	21	1317	41.15	0		11
		List A	23	701	41.23			6

as at 1/4/1980

1981

Five Cricketers of the Year

Kim Hughes (Australians) /
Robin Jackman (Surrey and England) •
Allan Lamb (Northamptonshire) /
Clive Rice (Nottinghamshire) / •
Vintcent van der Bijl (Middlesex) •

HEADLINE EVENTS FROM 1980

- County champions – Middlesex

- Gillette Cup – Middlesex

- John Player League – Warwickshire

- Benson & Hedges Cup – Northamptonshire

- West Indies beat England 1-0

- England and Australia draw the Centenary Test at Lord's

- England lose 3-0 in Australia in 1979-80

FOR HIS FIRST SET OF CRICKETERS OF THE YEAR, John Woodcock chose three overseas players, the first time so many had appeared in one go. All three came from South Africa, and he said he could easily have picked a fourth – probably Kepler Wessels at Sussex or Peter Kirsten of Derbyshire. The Five were made up by Kim Hughes, who batted brilliantly for Australia in the Centenary Test at Lord's, and Robin Jackman, the one English representative.

As Jackman was born in India, for the first time since 1962 none of the five was English by birth. Nor was anyone picked from the powerful West Indies touring team.

Vintcent van der Bijl was an automatic pick. Middlesex won two trophies and competed strongly for two more, and he was central figure on all fronts. Standing 6ft 7½in, he posed many of the same problems to batsmen as Joel Garner [1980], and their answers were generally as ineffective. He was particularly effective in the Championship, in which he took all his 85 first-class wickets at 14.72 each. With Wayne Daniel, he formed the most daunting new-ball partnership in the county game.

Van der Bijl, the third generation of his family to play first-class cricket, had been little known outside South Africa because of the boycott. He was a prolific wicket-taker for Natal, but had never been on a major tour, though he was selected for South Africa's cancelled Test tour of Australia in 1971-72.

A switch from teaching to business opened up the possibility of time off to play a season in England. It proved a one-off, and he retired from playing in 1983. In 2008 he was appointed the ICC's umpires' and referees' manager.

If there was a new-ball attack to rival Middlesex's it was Clive Rice and Richard Hadlee [1982] at Nottinghamshire, although injuries curtailed Hadlee's availability in 1980. Rice was a genuine all-rounder who finished with more than 25,000 runs and 900 wickets at first-class level, but his vibrant leadership was held in special regard.

He had no sooner been appointed captain at Nottinghamshire in 1978 than he was sacked for signing for World Series Cricket. When he was restored midway through 1979 the decision caused friction, but had little impact on Rice's game. In 1980, he topped the county's batting averages and led the team to third in the Championship. Better was to come: in 1981 they took the title, and repeated the feat in Rice's final season in 1987.

Hostile with the new ball and aggressive with the bat, Rice was an uncompromising cricketer who could have carved a significant Test record had he been granted the chance. Like van der Bijl, he was chosen for the cancelled tour of Australia in 1971-72; however, he played long enough to captain South Africa in their historic comeback series of one-day internationals in India in 1991-92.

Being several years younger, Allan Lamb had time to spend four years qualifying for England. He moved from Cape Town in 1977, aged 22, with a view to gaining a county contract and possibly qualifying for the country where his parents were born. He played Second XI cricket for Derbyshire and Northamptonshire, but failed to land a contract with either; then, a few months later, Northants came knocking.

Lamb soon adjusted to English conditions. In his second season in 1979 he scored 1,747 first-class runs, and in 1980 went better with 1,797 and first place in the batting averages. He also played the deciding innings of 72 in the Benson

Vince van der Bijl (left) with the Middlesex captain Mike Brearley [1977]

and Hedges Cup final to give the county only their second major trophy.

Lamb qualified in 1982 and, with England having lost several players to a rebel tour, was immediately chosen. He scored a hundred in his third Test and remained a regular for the

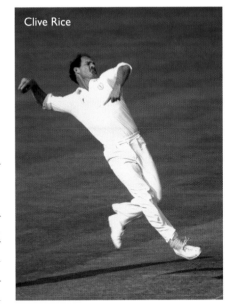

Clive Rice

Vintcent van der Bijl:
"Few cricketers have made a bigger impact in a single season of English county cricket"

CRICKETERS OF THE YEAR 1981 – Performances in the English season 1980

Name	Age*		Matches	Runs	Bat ave	Wickets	Bowl ave	Catches (/st)
KJ Hughes	27	Tests	1	201	100.50			0
		ODI	2	171	171.00			1
RD Jackman	35	First-class	23	363	22.68	121	15.40	14
		List A	23	230	19.16	36	17.69	4
AJ Lamb	26	First-class	23	1797	66.55	1	27.00	11
		List A	23	467	24.57	0		6
CEB Rice	31	First-class	23	1448	53.62	39	22.02	16
		List A	23	693	40.76	21	24.19	13
VAP van der Bijl	33	First-class	20	331	25.46	85	14.72	5
		List A	26	286	22.00	25	25.08	6

as at 1/4/1981

next ten years, thanks in part to his courage against fast bowling (he scored six hundreds against West Indies). A highly attacking style contributed to a relatively low average of 36.09.

Jackman, the son of a British army colonel in India who brought him to England as an infant, was one of the most reliable and hard-working seam bowlers on the county circuit. His game went up a level with the arrival of Sylvester Clarke to share the new ball at Surrey, and he took 93 wickets in 1979 and 121 in 1980, when he led the wicket-taking list by a distance.

That he was not chosen by England for any of the six home Tests – he appeared in a one-day international against Australia at The Oval – was a matter of general surprise. It seemed that, being in his mid-thirties, he was too old.

In fact, Jackman was called up as a replacement for the winter tour of the West Indies, where he played two Tests (he would appear in two more at home in 1982) but found himself at the centre of a political row over his contacts with South Africa, where he spent his

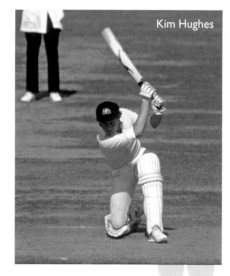

Kim Hughes

Allan Lamb

Robin Jackman

Kim Hughes:
"The marvellous appeal of Hughes's batting lies in the repertoire of his strokes and his unashamed enthusiasm in playing them"

winters. The Test in Guyana was cancelled. Jackman later settled in South Africa, where he became a noted TV commentator.

Hughes's cavalier strokeplay was the one memorable feature of a Centenary Test spoiled by rain. He skipped up and down the Lord's pitch like an Olympic fencer, enjoying himself as much as spectators during twin innings of 117 and 84. In the two preceding one-days he took England's bowling for 73 and 98.

Hughes had always been in a hurry. Impatient to play for Western Australia, he scored a quickfire 119 when he finally got the chance aged 21. In his fourth Test, he played a different game, grafting eight hours for a hundred against England at Brisbane in 1978-79. Because of the Packer split, he was fast-tracked into captaincy.

In the summer of 1981, Hughes was on his way back to England to lead a full Ashes tour. Australia were 1–0 up after two; then came the heroics of Ian Botham [1978], and Hughes's fortunes nosedived. He later quit the captaincy in tears, headed to South Africa on a rebel tour, and spent a long time awaiting Australia's forgiveness.

1982 Five Cricketers of the Year

Terry Alderman (Australians) ●
Allan Border (Australians) ⫽
Richard Hadlee (Nottinghamshire) ⫽ ●
Javed Miandad (Glamorgan) ⫽
Rod Marsh (Australians) ⋔

HEADLINE EVENTS FROM 1981

- County champions – Nottinghamshire

- NatWest Trophy – Derbyshire

- John Player League – Essex

- Benson & Hedges Cup – Somerset

- Ian Botham inspires England to regain the Ashes 3-1

- England lose 1-0 in West Indies in 1980-81

EVEN THOUGH ENGLAND ACHIEVED A FAMOUS Ashes victory in 1981, for only the third time there were no English players among *Wisden*'s Five – most of the main performers had already been picked – but this was nevertheless a star-studded quintet.

Indeed, there would be a time when the principal individual Test career records rested in the hands of three of them: Allan Border (most runs and catches by an outfielder), Richard Hadlee (most wickets) and Rod Marsh (most dismissals by a wicketkeeper).

Border emerged as an indisputably world-class player on Australia's tour – and arguably the best left-handed batsman in the world – as he led resistance to England's often rampant bowlers.

He made the highest score of a low-scoring First Test which Australia won, but it was his obduracy and bravery during the last two matches that won greatest acclaim: two unbeaten hundreds followed by a score of 84 spanned 15 hours, a task made no easier by a broken finger on his left hand. His century at Old Trafford was slower than any previously for Australia.

Raised in Sydney as one of four boys, Border spent two summers in England playing club

and league games before moving swiftly through state cricket to Australia's Test team, which needed fresh recruits during the Packer split. Two unbeaten innings in a losing cause in his second Test showed his worth.

Border remained Australia's best batsman even after taking over the captaincy in 1984-85. Difficult times followed, but he painstakingly built a team to beat the world. He counted wins at a World Cup and in three Ashes series among his many triumphs.

Terry Alderman had an extraordinary season, taking 42 wickets in the six Tests, a record for Australia in an Ashes series. He had not played Test cricket before, but his game was perfectly suited to English conditions, although it required refinement in the early days of the tour when Dennis Lillee [1973], his Western Australia team-mate, advised him to bowl faster than at home and aim to hit the seam rather than swing the ball. It worked like a dream, in part because some of the pitches played into his hands.

Alderman's career was not straightforward. He had lengthy lay-offs from Test cricket after badly injuring a shoulder tackling an on-field intruder during a match at Perth

Javed Miandad:
"He is a natural sportsman of rare talent. His relaxed but commanding attitude is immediately convincing"

special understanding with Lillee, as they also played together for Western Australia. He scored three Test hundreds; no previous Australian wicketkeeper had scored one.

Marsh retired after the 1983-84 season, disappointed in his ambition to captain Australia; he might well have provided more stability than was provided by the chopping and changing between Greg Chappell [1973] and Kim Hughes [1981]. He later worked as a respected head coach at academies in Australia, England and Dubai. His son Dan captained Tasmania to their first state title.

Hadlee, a fast bowling all-rounder, was along with Clive Rice [1981] the architect of Nottinghamshire's first Championship title since 1929. From a shorter run than he used for New Zealand, Hadlee's pace was lively enough to leave batsmen little time to adjust to his subtle movement off an unerringly accurate line. He got through a lot of work and finished with 105 wickets, the most in the country.

He also brought 745 runs to the Championship cause as a dangerous left-handed hitter at No. 7 whose batting had improved with the advent of helmets. In 1984, he became the first to perform the double in an English season for 17 years.

Hadlee, whose father captained New Zealand while two brothers also represented the country, was originally signed by Nottinghamshire in 1978 to replace Rice, only for Rice to stay. He had by 1981 bowled New Zealand to some rare Test wins over the stronger sides, but such results were soon to become more common as, with Hadlee's help, New Zealand entered the best period in their history. He was knighted for services to cricket in 1990, during his final tour of England.

Javed Miandad, a Pakistani batsman in his early twenties but already hugely experienced, scored 2,083 runs and eight hundreds in first-class cricket in 1981. He had joined Glamorgan

and for joining a rebel tour, and he was never the force elsewhere that he was in England. He had three good seasons with Kent and Gloucestershire before returning for the 1989 Ashes and having another bonanza with 41 wickets in six Tests.

Marsh did not have a particularly notable series – his side waited in vain for one of his muscular efforts with the bat before it was too late – and his *Wisden* selection owed much to his overtaking Alan Knott [1970] as the leading Test wicketkeeper in terms of dismissals, a record he held until 1998-99.

Marsh began as a batsman, scoring a hundred on first-class debut in 1968-69 at No. 5, and took time to master the art of keeping. But he gained a reputation as an athletic taker of the fastest bowling, especially Lillee [1973] and Jeff Thomson in their pomp. Marsh developed a

Terry Alderman

the previous year after spending four part-seasons at Sussex, who had other overseas signings they preferred.

Miandad provided the most striking exception yet to the rule that the very best Pakistan players enjoyed privileged upbringings; he was one of seven children from a modest family in Karachi which turned all three sons into cricketers. His batting was unorthodox and audacious, and he was incredibly fast on his feet whether batting or fielding close to the wicket.

The most remarkable of several astonishing innings he played was a double-century at Colchester that almost took his side home after Essex had set Glamorgan 325 on a dusty, difficult pitch. Miandad was already Pakistan captain by this point, but perhaps because of his origins he was mistrusted and soon replaced. He could also irritate opponents, and in November 1981 was involved in an ugly spat with Lillee [1973] during a Test in Perth.

He retired in 1996 as Pakistan's leading run-scorer in Tests, but was especially suited to one-day cricket and played in the first six World Cups. He later had several stints as national coach.

Allan Border

Allan Border:
"The beady, pale-blue eyes above the stubbly chin watched the English bowlers with an unrelenting concentration"

Richard Hadlee (left) and Clive Rice [1981] celebrate after Nottinghamshire win the County Championship in 1981

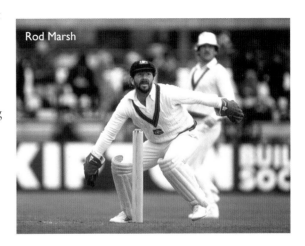

Rod Marsh

CRICKETERS OF THE YEAR 1982 – Performances in the English season 1981

Name	Age*		Matches	Runs	Bat ave	Wickets	Bowl ave	Catches (/st)
TM Alderman	25	First-class	12	34	6.80	51	20.86	11
		Tests	6	22	5.50	42	21.26	8
AR Border	26	First-class	13	807	50.43	2	32.50	16
		Tests	6	533	59.22			12
		ODI	3	95	47.50			1
RJ Hadlee	30	First-class	21	745	32.39	105	14.89	14
		List A	19	377	37.70	23	19.52	10
Javed Miandad	24	First-class	22	2083	69.43	3	36.00	11
		List A	21	746	46.62	1	17.00	9
RW Marsh	34	First-class	10	368	24.53	1	0.00	26/2
		Tests	6	216	19.63			23

* as at 1/4/1982

1983

Five Cricketers of the Year

Imran Khan (Sussex and Pakistanis) ⚫ ●
Trevor Jesty (Hampshire) ⚫ ●
Alvin Kallicharran (Warwickshire) ⚫
Kapil Dev (Indians and Northamptonshire) ⚫ ●
Malcolm Marshall (Hampshire) ●

HEADLINE EVENTS FROM 1982

- County champions – Middlesex

- NatWest Trophy – Surrey

- John Player League – Sussex

- Benson & Hedges Cup – Somerset

- England beat India 1-0 and Pakistan 2-1

- England lose 1-0 in India in 1981-82

THIS SELECTION CONTAINED SOME ILLUSTRIOUS figures. Kapil Dev took 434 Test wickets, Malcolm Marshall 376 and Imran Khan 362. Kapil Dev captained India to the World Cup in 1983, a few weeks after his *Wisden* selection was unveiled, and Pakistan became world champions under Imran in 1992. Alvin Kallicharran was briefly captain of West Indies, for whom he scored more than 4,000 Test runs. Only Trevor Jesty failed to hit the big time, his international career confined to ten one-day games during the winter of 1982-83.

Marshall was relatively small at 5ft 11in, but emerged as the equal of any fast bowler in the world in 1982, a worthy rival for the older, more experienced Imran. He could bowl as swiftly as anyone, and in his third full season of county cricket knew how to take wickets by pitching the ball up and moving it late. His haul of 134 first-class wickets was the most by anyone in an English season since 1967, and helped promote him from the margins of the West Indies side.

Marshall got through more than 800 first-class overs for Hampshire. He had a beautifully fluid action and loved bowling, especially when a game was in the balance. He bowled out Surrey when they needed 104 to win, and Somerset for 74 when their target was only 85.

Marshall, who grew up in Barbados with Garry Sobers [1964] as a hero, aspired to an all-rounder status he never quite achieved. His bowling always came first. After finally being given the new ball for West Indies in early 1983 he only got better, and came to be regarded as the best of all the great Caribbean fast bowlers.

He played for Hampshire until 1993, and later did sterling work playing and coaching in Natal before his premature death from cancer in 1999, aged only 41.

Jesty deputised as Hampshire captain in the early weeks of the season, but his heaviest run-scoring came later, all six of his Championship centuries dating from late July onwards – a run of form that played its part in his call-up as a replacement on the winter tour to Australia and New Zealand. Before that late burst he took hundreds off the Indian and Pakistani touring teams.

Jesty was a capable all-rounder who twice reached 50 first-class wickets in a summer with his medium-pace bowling. He turned 34 during the 1982 season, which proved his best with the bat by a distance (he did not average more than 45 in any other season), but played on until his early forties, spending three years at Surrey and four at Lancashire. He then became a long-serving county umpire.

Imran's cricket took a huge step forward in 1982 with his elevation to the Pakistan captaincy at the expense of Javed Miandad [1982]. Imran's background was in keeping with the traditions of the job – Aitchison College Lahore and Oxford University – and he filled the role with assurance.

Alvin Kallicharran

His all-round return of 212 runs and 21 wickets in three Tests in England outshone Ian Botham [1982], and with better umpiring luck Pakistan might have won the series. Although Imran was a very capable middle-order batsman, bowling was his strongest suit. His pace was quick, he had a good bouncer and yorker, and he had learned how to bowl outswingers during World Series Cricket.

Since 1980 he had shared the new ball at Sussex with Garth le Roux, narrowly missing out on the Championship in 1981. Before Pakistan's tour, they helped the county win four early-season Championship matches.

Imran remained Pakistan's first-choice leader until the World Cup triumph of 1992, supervising their first series win in England in 1987. He later raised funds to build a cancer hospital in memory of his mother, married into the Goldsmith family, and founded a political party called Movement for Justice.

Kapil Dev also gave Botham a run for his money during 1982. This was less to do to with his potent fast-medium bowling than his explosive batting, which secured him the player of the series award, even though England won 1–0.

Despite previously doing little with the bat in Tests outside India, Kapil scored runs in all four innings, and in the last three appeared on course for one of the fastest Test centuries. In the second innings at Lord's, with his side in trouble, he struck 89 off 55 balls. After the tour he rejoined Northamptonshire – for whom he had briefly appeared in 1981 – and contributed two quickfire hundreds.

Kapil Dev's family came originally from Pakistan, so had they not moved to Chandigarh, where his father was a successful building contractor, he might have shared the new ball with Imran. Physically hardy, he bowled tirelessly in India's cause and in 1980 reached the Test double just 16 months after making his debut.

Kapil took over the India captaincy early in 1983, and within six months had led his country

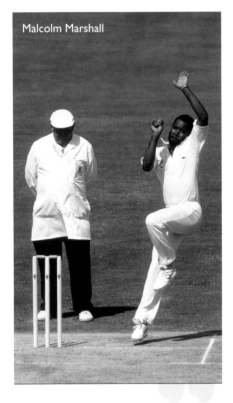

Malcolm Marshall

Malcolm Marshall: "[He] earned admiration for his ability, his work-rate and his cheerful Barbadian humour"

Kapil Dev (left) and Imran Khan at a reunion of World Cup-winning captains in 2011

left-hander, was the only man to pass 2,000 runs in 1982, and matched Jesty's eight hundreds, three of them doubles. His unbeaten 230 against Lancashire at Southport involved a fourth-wicket stand of 470 with Geoff Humpage [1985].

Perhaps his best innings was his 131 at Southampton, when he countered Marshall's pace with unrivalled expertise. He also scored a brilliant match-winning century in the NatWest Trophy against a Somerset attack containing Joel Garner [1980]. However, his runs could not prevent Warwickshire finishing bottom of the Championship.

By this stage, Kallicharran had finished a Test career spanning 66 Tests for West Indies. Dropped during the 1980-81 season, he signed to play in South Africa in 1981-82, a move that led to a ban from the West Indian board. He continued to play in England and South Africa until 1990, when the ban was lifted.

One of 11 children to a rice and coconut farmer, Kallicharran started at the Port Mourant club that produced Rohan Kanhai [1964] and Basil Butcher [1970], and at 16 he was the youngest to represent Guyana.

Imran Khan:

"Responsibility turned a fine cavalier into a great cricketer"

to a surprise victory in the World Cup final over West Indies. Though his bowling declined, by playing on until 1993-94 he took the Test wicket-taking record off Richard Hadlee [1982].

Alvin Kallicharran, a small, accomplished

CRICKETERS OF THE YEAR 1983 – Performances in the English season 1982

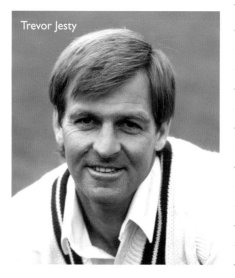

Trevor Jesty

Name	Age*		Matches	Runs	Bat ave	Wickets	Bowl ave	Catches (/st)
Imran Khan	30	First-class	16	588	45.23	64	16.85	2
		List A	13	197	19.70	20	16.80	0
		Tests	3	212	53.00	21	18.57	0
TE Jesty	34	First-class	22	1645	58.75	35	21.42	13
		List A	22	598	29.90	28	23.25	6
Al Kallicharran	34	First-class	23	2120	66.25	14	41.28	8
		List A	24	512	25.60	10	64.40	6
Kapil Dev	24	First-class	14	770	42.77	29	41.86	13
		Tests	3	292	73.00	10	43.90	0
		ODI	2	107	53.50	0		0
MD Marshall	24	First-class	22	633	22.60	134	15.73	4
		List A	22	258	17.20	26	24.84	6

* as at 1/4/1983

1984 Five Cricketers of the Year

Mohinder Amarnath (Indians) 🏏 ●
Jeremy Coney (New Zealanders) 🏏 ●
John Emburey (Middlesex) 🏏 ●
Mike Gatting (Middlesex and England) 🏏
Chris Smith (Hampshire and England) 🏏

HEADLINE EVENTS FROM 1983

• County champions – Essex

• NatWest Trophy – Somerset

• John Player League – Yorkshire

• Benson & Hedges Cup – Middlesex

• England beat New Zealand 3-1

• India win the World Cup

• England lose 2-1 in Australia in 1982-83

MOHINDER AMARNATH WAS THE FIRST FOR 65 years to be chosen as a Cricketer of the Year without playing a first-class match in the previous English season. His credentials were excellent, but his selection rested on his match-winning exploits as an all-rounder at the World Cup in England in June 1983: he was Man of the Match in the semi-final and final victories over England and West Indies.

Wisden's profile also gave prominent mention to Amarnath's brave batting earlier in the year against Pakistan and West Indies, when he daringly took on some of the world's best fast bowlers so successfully that he garnered 1,182 runs in 11 Tests.

Amarnath had lived and died by such belligerent methods many times before. His father Lala Amarnath, the scorer of India's first Test century, encouraged his sons to play the hook – brother Surinder also played for India – but a fractured skull courtesy of Richard Hadlee [1982] at Trent Bridge in 1979 had set him back. A few months later he made a one-off attempt at batting in a topee, and the 1982-83 Tests were his next attempt at a return.

Amarnath's scores in the final stages of the World Cup were only 46 and 26, but they were significant in the context of the two low-scoring games, as was his gentle medium-pace swing bowling off an ambling run-up: his combined figures in semi-final and final were 19–1–39–5. West Indies soon exacted revenge in the Test arena, dismissing him for five ducks in his next six innings.

Only John Emburey made an unarguable case for selection, according to John Woodcock in his Preface. Emburey was an interesting choice insofar as he was serving a three-year England ban after joining a rebel tour of South Africa, but given a free run with Middlesex for the whole summer he had an outstanding all-round season with 782 runs and 103 wickets. Emburey's career spanned 25 seasons from 1973 to 1997, but this was his best.

He rarely ripped through a side with his off-spin, but was consistently effective through bowling a tight wicket-to-wicket line and getting the ball to drift across the right-hander. He had also become more assertive as a batsman since the ban started in 1982, when he also topped 750 first-class runs; for much of the 1983 season he batted at No. 6.

Jeremy Coney

Jeremy Coney:
"He regards international cricket as an experience unparalleled in joy and excitement"

Emburey joined Middlesex in 1971 after failing to find an opening at Surrey, and learned much from Fred Titmus [1963], even though Titmus's presence made him wait a long time before securing a regular place in the team. Emburey returned to Test cricket after his ban to help England win Ashes series in 1985 and 1986-87. He joined a second rebel tour of South Africa in 1989, but again regained his England place after the ban ended.

The one blot on Middlesex's season was that the Championship, in which they held a handsome lead at one point, slipped away to Essex. Even so the summer was a very good one for Mike Gatting, who at the start had taken over the captaincy from Mike Brearley [1977]. Under pressure to maintain the record of his predecessor, Gatting got off to the best possible start by delivering the Benson and Hedges Cup in a tight final demanding a cool nerve, Middlesex winning by four runs.

Gatting had a tremendous season with the bat too, averaging more than 60 and being the highest qualified Englishman in the batting averages. He forced his way back into the England side for the last two of the four Tests against New Zealand, scoring 81 in his first innings.

Up to this point his Test career, spanning 22 matches, had been a disappointment, glimpses of classy strokeplay mixed in with self-inflicted downfalls. Gatting went on the winter tour but was dropped once more

Chris Smith

CRICKETERS OF THE YEAR 1984 – Performances in the English season 1983

Name	Age*		Matches	Runs	Bat ave	Wickets	Bowl ave	Catches (/st)
M Amarnath	33	ODI	8	237	29.62	8	22.25	0
JV Coney	31	First-class	9	437	31.21	14	24.21	14
		Tests	4	238	34.00	5	23.00	7
		ODI	6	197	49.25	9	20.33	1
JE Emburey	31	First-class	25	782	27.92	103	17.88	23
		List A	22	253	25.30	23	20.78	4
MW Gatting	26	First-class	18	1494	64.95	5	46.00	19
		List A	27	651	31.00	13	18.76	9
		Tests	2	121	30.25	0		4
CL Smith	25	First-class	23	1923	53.41	17	32.17	19
		List A	19	703	43.93			1
		Tests	2	78	19.50	2	15.50	2

as at 1/4/1984

before finally breaking through on the tour of India in 1984-85.

Some glory years followed, including captaining England to victory in the 1986-87 Ashes in Australia, but so too did further disappointments. After retiring he was briefly an England selector, and then an ECB administrator.

Chris Smith, the Durban-born son of an English father and Scottish mother, scored more than 2,600 runs in all competitions in 1983, making him the most prolific batsman in the country. He had a textbook technique, concentration by the bucketload and character enough not to be fazed by leading a chase in pursuit of 407 to beat the eventual champions Essex. Smith's share was 163.

When Graeme Fowler was ruled unfit for the Third Test, Smith was the natural replacement. Crushingly, he was out first ball to Hadlee, but responded with a gutsy 43 in the second innings and played five of the six Tests on the winter tour of 1983-84.

His season was all the more impressive because he had spent the previous two summers confined largely to Second XI cricket while he qualified by residence for England. After three seasons with Natal, he had joined Hampshire in 1980 as stand-in for Gordon Greenidge [1977], but lost his place when Greenidge returned.

Smith's younger brother Robin, who played alongside him at Hampshire between 1985 and 1991, was a Cricketer of the Year in 1990. Chris later emigrated to Western Australia, where he took up an administrative post at the WACA ground.

Jeremy Coney proved an inspired selection. In terms of statistics his 1983 tour with New Zealand was unexceptional, but he showed great character on several occasions. He saw his side home in a difficult run-chase in a group match against England at the World

The strong Middlesex side of the early 1980s. Back row (l-r): Simon Hughes, Wilf Slack, Andrew Miller, Norman Cowans, Wayne Daniel, John Carr, Paul Downton, Roland Butcher. Seated: Phil Edmonds, **John Emburey**, **Mike Gatting** (captain), Clive Radley [1979], Graham Barlow

Mohinder Amarnath

Mohinder Amarnath:
"The half-year or so of personal success... [is] as triumphant as any cricketer can have known"

Cup, and in the Test at Headingley which New Zealand won he took four wickets with his medium-pace.

Even so, by the end of the tour he had – like Gatting – appeared in more than 20 Tests without making a hundred, despite having almost always batted in the top six. That finally changed in January 1984 when he struck an unbeaten 174 in the First Test of a series in which New Zealand finally beat England for the first time.

Coney had always been courageous, often jumping in the air to defend bouncers, and this gutsiness was in evidence in the Caribbean in 1984-85 when his arm was fractured by Joel Garner [1980]. Appointed New Zealand captain soon after, he oversaw historic series wins away to both Australia and England. He later developed a career in theatre-lighting design in London while also being a much-respected TV pundit.

1985

Five Cricketers of the Year

Martin Crowe (Somerset) *
Larry Gomes (West Indians) *
Geoff Humpage (Warwickshire) ⋔
Jack Simmons (Lancashire) * ●
Sidath Wettimuny (Sri Lankans) *

HEADLINE EVENTS FROM 1984

- County champions – Essex

- NatWest Trophy – Middlesex

- John Player League – Essex

- Benson & Hedges Cup – Lancashire

- England lose to West Indies 5-0

- Sri Lanka draw their first Test in England at Lord's

- England lose to both New Zealand and Pakistan 1-0 in 1983-84

WITH MANY OF THE KEY WEST INDIANS WHO took part in a 5–0 trouncing of England in 1984 already chosen, there was an opportunity to recognise Sidath Wettimuny as the first Cricketer from Sri Lanka, and two English county players who never appeared in Tests, Geoff Humpage and Jack Simmons. John Woodcock, the editor, wrote that Simmons – the oldest Cricketer of the Year for 52 years – represented the game's unsung heroes.

Larry Gomes was the sole West Indian representative, and only the fourth *Wisden* Cricketer of the Year born in Trinidad. The Five was completed by Martin Crowe, a highly talented young New Zealand batsman whose prodigious season would have made him a deserving choice any time.

Wettimuny was the star of Sri Lanka's inaugural Test in England, which followed the West Indies series. The England players might have fancied boosting their averages, but Wettimuny was determined to show that his country's cricket had substance as well as style (they had lost eight of their previous 13 Tests).

Sri Lanka kept their opponents in the field until the third morning when Wettimuny,

battling cramp, fell for 190 after more than ten and a half hours at the crease, the longest innings in a Test at Lord's and an eloquent statement that Sri Lanka did indeed belong at the top table.

Wettimuny was one of three sons to an engineer who studied the writings of C. B. Fry [1895] and built an indoor school. All three boys, who attended Ananda College, the leading Buddhist school in Colombo, went on to open the batting for Sri Lanka. Sidath had performed well on a tour of England in 1981, and scored his country's first Test hundred in Pakistan in 1981-82.

His form fell away after his Lord's marathon, and he subsequently averaged less than 20 in Tests before retiring in 1987.

Gomes arrived for England tour unsure of his future, having recently lost his No. 3 spot to Richie Richardson [1992], who was eight years his junior. But Gomes used his time out of the West Indies side to make technical adjustments, and won back his place after outperforming Richardson in the warm-ups.

He scored 143 at Edgbaston, an unbeaten 92 in a run-chase at Lord's, and 104 at Headingley, where only one other top-six batsman got beyond 50. An ultra-cautious leg-side game, which often led to him being underestimated, had paid rich dividends. He followed the England tour with two Test hundreds in Australia, but after that his form went into steady decline.

Gomes's previous experience of English conditions must have helped: he spent four seasons with Middlesex in the early 1970s, and toured with West Indies in 1976. He might have joined the 1980 tour as replacement but, disaffected by his treatment, he turned down the offer. When Gomes was 16 a mentor gave him a set of goals, one of which was to be a *Wisden* Cricketer of the Year.

Crowe joined Somerset as a youthful stand-in for Viv Richards [1977] and Joel Garner [1980], who were touring with West Indies, and got off to a terrible start, suffering a string of low scores in May before his character and superb technique came to the rescue. He scored four centuries in successive Championship games, culminating in a courageous display against Andy Roberts [1975] in which he scored 190 to win the game. He ended the season with more than 2,600 runs and 70 wickets in all matches.

Martin Crowe

Martin Crowe:
"In terms of cricket, the esteem of colleagues and public respect, he managed to fill, with poise and dignity, the enormous gap left in Somerset's ranks by the absence of Vivian Richards"

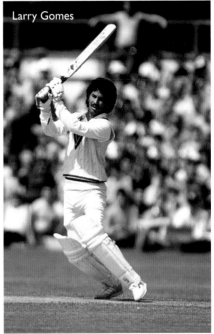

Larry Gomes

CRICKETERS OF THE YEAR 1985 – Performances in the English season 1984

Name	Age*		Matches	Runs	Bat ave	Wickets	Bowl ave	Catches (/st)
MD Crowe	22	First-class	25	1870	53.42	44	30.75	28
		List A	23	750	34.09	26	25.34	5
HA Gomes	31	First-class	12	841	70.08	2	40.50	2
		List A	4	162	54.00	2	29.50	1
		Tests	5	400	80.00			1
GW Humpage	30	First-class	26	1891	48.48	2	28.50	55/11
		List A	26	777	38.85			33/5
J Simmons	44	First-class	21	748	25.79	63	26.09	15
		List A	26	202	20.20	31	23.38	5
S Wettimuny	28	First-class	7	505	50.50	1	7.00	2
		Tests	1	203	101.50			0

* as at 1/4/1985

Crowe's father had played first-class cricket, and his brother Jeff regularly played alongside him in Tests. More gifted than his brother, Martin was playing for New Zealand by the age of 19, shortly after completing a season on the Lord's groundstaff.

The 1984 season accelerated his development. He had at that stage scored one Test hundred; he would finish in 1996 with 17, still a New Zealand record, as is his highest score of 299.

Crowe's season at Taunton had far-reaching consequences, because such was his beneficial effect on other players that Somerset controversially sacked Richards and Garner in order that he could return in 1987. A cousin of Russell Crowe, the Hollywood actor, Crowe married a former Miss Universe.

In terms of runs scored, Humpage enjoyed one of the best seasons by any wicketkeeper-batsman, his 1,891 first-class runs in 1984 being bettered only by Les Ames [1929] and Jim

Sidath Wettimuny

Parks [1968] among those who kept regularly. Humpage, who usually batted at No. 5, had topped 1,300 first-class runs in five seasons and would do so three times more.

Thickly set and heavily bearded, Humpage was a manufactured wicketkeeper, having come to the role only shortly before starting his county career in 1974, but he was considered good enough to be given three one-day caps against Australia in 1981. Sadly, he was put low in the order, where his batting ability was wasted.

Not selected for the winter tour of 1981-82, he joined a rebel tour of South Africa; his three-year ban ended with the 1984 season. Humpage hoped to win back an England place, but lost out to Paul Downton, Bruce French and Jack Richards.

Simmons, aged 43, used all his guile to assist in Lancashire's Benson and Hedges Cup victory, stifling Warwickshire's batsmen in the final with 11 overs costing just 18 runs. In three knockout matches his combined analysis was 33–9–66–3.

As an off-spinning all-rounder, Simmons had long been suited to one-day cricket – he had played a central part in Lancashire's revival in the early 1970s – but he remained effective at the longer game and in 1984 enjoyed his best first-class season in 16 years with 748 runs and 63 wickets. He had never made so many runs, and had only once taken more Championship wickets.

Simmons was playing first-team cricket at Enfield aged 14, but at 19 turned down a county contract to continue his apprenticeship as a draughtsman while playing as a pro in the leagues. Only when he was 27 did he accept Lancashire's renewed offer. He spent seven seasons skippering Tasmania, but was never official Lancashire captain. He retired in 1989 aged 48. He was later Lancashire chairman and the ECB's cricket chairman.

Vic Marks, with 1,262 runs and 86 wickets, was unlucky to be overlooked.

Geoff Humpage

Jack Simmons

Jack Simmons:
"Lancashire can seldom have had a more popular player"

1986

Five Cricketers of the Year

Phil Bainbridge (Gloucestershire) *

Richard Ellison (Kent and England) ●

Craig McDermott (Australians) ●

Neal Radford (Worcestershire) ●

Tim Robinson (Nottinghamshire and England) *

HEADLINE EVENTS FROM 1985

- County champions – Middlesex

- NatWest Trophy – Middlesex

- John Player League – Essex

- Benson & Hedges Cup – Lancashire

- England beat Australia 3-1 to regain the Ashes

- England win 2-1 in India in 1984-85

THREE OF THESE FIVE STARRED IN THE 1985 Ashes series, won by England 3–1. Tim Robinson opened the batting for England in all six Tests, scoring two big hundreds in games they won. Richard Ellison was brought in to bolster their bowling with the series standing at 1–1 after four matches, and swung the ball to devastating effect, claiming ten wickets at Edgbaston and seven at The Oval.

Craig McDermott, a strongly built fast bowler from Queensland who turned 20 shortly before the tour, laboured tirelessly in Australia's cause and finished with 30 wickets in the series.

The surprise was that *Wisden* did not pick Phil Edmonds, Middlesex's left-arm spinner who took 15 wickets in the Ashes having played an important role in England's series win in India in 1984-85. Edmonds was also Middlesex's leading spinner as they won the Championship.

Robinson enjoyed a tremendous first 12 months in Test cricket. Surprisingly chosen ahead of Chris Broad, his Nottinghamshire opening partner, for the tour of India – Robinson scored 2,000 runs in 1984 and was rated the better player of spin – he responded with 444 runs, including a maiden Test hundred spanning almost nine hours at Delhi.

He followed that with 490 runs in the Ashes, playing match-shaping innings of 175 in the First Test at Headingley and 148 in the Fifth at Edgbaston, while maintaining his county form, scoring six hundreds and playing a big part in Nottinghamshire reaching the NatWest Trophy final, which they lost to Essex by one run despite Robinson scoring 80.

Unfortunately, by the time the 1986 *Wisden* appeared, Robinson had endured a nightmare in the Caribbean – 72 runs in eight Test innings – and was dropped after the first home Test of 1986. He was never secure at Test level again, and joined a rebel tour of South Africa in 1989-90.

Robinson first played for Nottinghamshire as an undergraduate, and captained them for seven years from 1988, leading them to two trophies. He retired in 1999 and later took up umpiring.

Ellison had made his England debut in 1984, and bowled well in India without luck. He learned to bowl outswing at Tonbridge School under Alan Dixon, a former Kent player, and this weapon helped him top 50 first-class wickets in 1983 and 1984; in 1985 he went better with 65 wickets at just 17.20 apiece, putting him top of the national averages.

This was a particularly good return considering a sprained ankle kept him out of the first three Championship matches, but he worked hard at his fitness and was reckoned to have gained a yard of pace when he regained his England place in mid-August.

Like Robinson, Ellison's fortunes soon declined. After a bright start his tour of the West Indies faded, and he also lost his place after the First Test of the 1986 season, in his case never to return. He came home from a season in Tasmania in 1986-87 with a stress fracture of the back and was out for a year; when the offer of a rebel tour in 1989-90 came along he too signed up. He left Kent after his benefit season in 1993 and became coach at Millfield School.

McDermott was also an outswing bowler (though of livelier pace) who would also be plagued by injuries, though one of richer achievement. He suffered from bowling too much too soon, before his body could cope. He was brought into the Australian side, aged

Neil Radford

Neil Radford:

"Radford was undoubtedly county cricket's success story of 1985"

Craig McDermott:
"He looked set for a long and distinguished Test career"

CRICKETERS OF THE YEAR 1986 – Performances in the English season 1985

Name	Age*		Matches	Runs	Bat ave	Wickets	Bowl ave	Catches (/st)
P Bainbridge	27	First-class	24	1644	56.68	19	30.00	10
		List A	22	288	18.00	19	28.57	6
RM Ellison	26	First-class	18	539	26.95	65	17.20	4
		List A	18	171	17.10	23	23.08	1
		Tests	2	3	3.00	17	10.88	1
CJ McDermott	20	First-class	16	183	16.63	51	31.54	2
		List A	4	0		8	21.87	1
		Tests	6	103	12.87	30	30.03	2
NV Radford	28	First-class	24	306	17.00	101	24.68	4
		List A	23	158	19.75	28	25.75	7
RT Robinson	27	First-class	18	1619	59.96	0		13
		List A	21	970	51.05			6
		Tests	6	490	61.25			5

as at 1/4/1986

19, a few months before the England tour and remained raw. His inexperience showed at times, but then so did his promise. When Australia won at Lord's, he took six for 70.

McDermott claimed 291 wickets from 71 Tests, but after 1985 never took another one in England, missing the 1989 tour and withdrawing in 1993 with a twisted bowel. Only from 1990-91 did he assume the position of attack leader that had been predicted for him for so long: he took 18 England wickets in two Tests that winter, and four years later captured 32 in what proved to be his last Ashes series.

After retiring as a player in his early thirties, he set up a real-estate business that failed, leaving him bankrupt. He later went into coaching and was Australia's fast-bowling coach in 2011-12.

Neal Radford was the only bowler to take 100 first-class wickets in 1985, a remarkable feat for a bowler in his first season at Worcestershire who had done little of note in five years at Lancashire.

Born in Northern Rhodesia (now Zambia) and a successful fast-medium bowler for Transvaal, Radford had completed his qualification for England when Lancashire released him, which made him a more attractive signing for a new county, and Worcestershire saw him fitting in to a team eager to go places. Duly inspired, he got through a lot of work and consistently moved the ball off the seam in a fashion he never managed at Old Trafford.

His golden form earned him a place on standby for the West Indies tour, and in 1986 he played two home Tests. After again finishing as leading wicket-taker in the country in 1987, with 109 victims, he played another Test at Auckland, but he did little in any of his England appearances. He retired after his benefit season at New Road in 1995.

Phil Bainbridge was Gloucestershire's most consistent batsman in a year in which they rose from bottom of the Championship in 1984 to third. He raised his average from 32.37 to 56.68

while wearing a special splint to protect a wrist broken while playing football, batting at No. 4 and acting as vice-captain. At various points in the season he sustained a broken finger, fractured a cheekbone and was concussed. He was also a useful medium-pace support bowler.

Bainbridge's fine season made him a contender for the winter tours, but this was as close as he came to representative honours, his batting average dropping to 27.30 in 1986. He left Bristol in 1990 to be among the first recruits to the newly elevated Durham, and captained them in 1994.

Richard Ellison bowls Allan Border [1982] as England close in on victory at Edgbaston in 1985

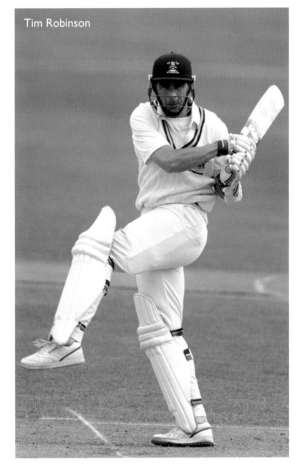

Tim Robinson

Phil Bainbridge

1987

Five Cricketers of the Year

John Childs (Essex) ●
Graeme Hick (Worcestershire) /
Dilip Vengsarkar (Indians) /
Courtney Walsh (Gloucestershire) ●
James Whitaker (Leicestershire) /

- County champions – Essex

- NatWest Trophy – Sussex

- John Player League – Hampshire

- Benson & Hedges Cup – Middlesex

- England are beaten 2-0 by India and 1-0 by New Zealand

- England lose 5-0 in West Indies in 1985-86

WHILE ENGLAND WERE LOSING HOME SERIES TO India and New Zealand for the first time in 1986, Graeme Hick, a young batsman at Worcestershire, was forging a career that would soon see him cast as their potential saviour. Hick was born and raised in Zimbabwe, and played county cricket as an overseas player, but with Zimbabwe not yet holding Test status he was invited to qualify for New Zealand and England. He chose England.

Hick's output belied his years. He turned 20 in May 1986, but such was his strength that he had no difficulty surviving a long season. He scored a century in the final Championship match just as he had in the first, and accumulated 2,004 runs in first-class matches and another 889 in one-dayers. He was the youngest to score 2,000 runs in a season, beating a record held by Len Hutton [1937], and the youngest Cricketer of the Year since Mushtaq Mohammad [1963].

The son of a tobacco farmer, Hick was a fine all-round sportsman who shone in schools matches in Harare and was still at school when he was chosen for Zimbabwe's 1983 World Cup squad. He was sent to Worcestershire on a scholarship in 1984, and in his first full season the following year topped 1,000 runs.

Hick continued breaking records in county cricket, but when he qualified for England in 1991 life became tougher. With his reputation preceding him, he was ruthlessly targeted by opposition pace attacks. He played 65 Tests, but his final average of 31.32 was a grave disappointment, and something only partially compensated for by a county career laden with runs.

Hick's best innings of the season came against Gloucestershire, in which he survived a bruising from their West Indian spearhead Courtney Walsh to score 134.

Walsh was the bowler of the season. He carried the Gloucestershire attack without complaint and did most to ensure they finished second in the Championship, equalling their highest finish. In the eight matches they won without contrivance, Walsh took 70 wickets, including 23 in two games against Hampshire, 11 against Surrey and 10 against Somerset.

Walsh started at the Melbourne club in Kingston, Jamaica, for which Michael Holding [1977] also played. He toured England in 1984 without appearing in the Tests, but his efforts for

Gloucestershire – he claimed 85 wickets in his first season with them in 1985 – helped propel him towards a regular place in the West Indies side from late 1986.

When Walsh finally got to take the new ball on a regular basis from 1993-94, his record only improved further, and thanks to his amazing strength and stamina he extended his career until 2001, when he retired aged 38 with a then-record 519 Test wickets.

The qualities that brought him international success were those applied on Gloucestershire's behalf in the early days. He generated steep bounce from his 6ft 5½in frame, angling the ball into the right-hander but making it move away off the seam. He learned from Holding and Andy Roberts [1975] that out-thinking a batsman was as important as raw pace.

Dilip Vengsarkar, a tall batsman who played the ball late, top-scored in all four innings of the two Tests won by India against England, including two high-quality centuries. The first came at Lord's, where he completed a third hundred in three Test appearances, a unique feat for a visiting batsman there, and the second on a poor batting pitch at Headingley. In both cases everyone else struggled, and by the time Vengsarkar reached his century he had No. 11 for company.

Like Hick, Vengsarkar was a batting prodigy. He was first chosen by India at the age of 19 in his first season of first-class cricket; he was originally tried as an opener but the move did not work, and it was to be almost three years before he established himself at No. 3. The tour of England in 1986 saw him embark on the best period in his career, 16 Tests yielding eight hundreds, only for him to not make another in four years before he retired in 1992. He later ran an academy in Mumbai.

John Childs accomplished a remarkable transformation in 1986, taking 85 wickets at

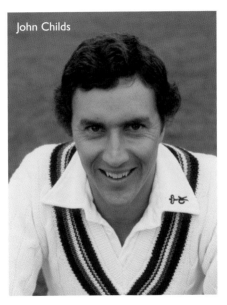
John Childs

15.03 to help Essex win the Championship, 12 months after fearing he would never play again. Childs, a freelance sign-writer in the winter, left Gloucestershire in 1984 after ten mixed seasons but made no impact as a left-arm spinner in his first year at Chelmsford, his five wickets costing 105.60 apiece.

Essex, though, kept faith in him and with advice from Fred Titmus [1963] and Don Wilson he adopted a longer, faster approach to the wicket. It brought rich dividends and took Childs close to selection for the Ashes tour of 1986-87. He finally won two England caps in 1988 aged 36, and was picked for a tour of India in 1988-89 that was cancelled. He played in two

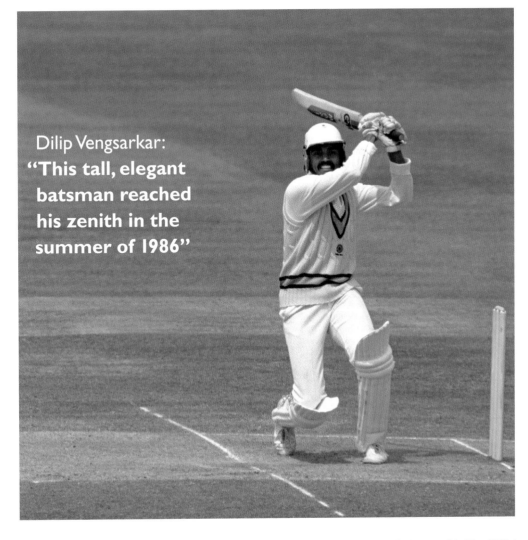
Dilip Vengsarkar: "This tall, elegant batsman reached his zenith in the summer of 1986"

Courtney Walsh

more Championship-winning sides, and retired in 1996 with more than 1,000 first-class wickets to his name. He later worked as director of Essex's academy.

James Whitaker confirmed himself as among the most aggressive and exciting young batsmen in the country, scoring 1,526 first-class runs despite missing almost five weeks after both hands were fractured in the same game by Malcolm Marshall [1983]. In his comeback match he scored 100 and 82 against Yorkshire, both unbeaten.

His average of 66.34 was the best by an England-qualified player, and secured him a place for Australia, where he played one Test as stand-in for the injured Ian Botham [1978]. Against the odds, he never played for England again. Only in his mid-thirties, when he captained Leicestershire to two Championships, did he regularly average over 40.

Whitaker, who was educated at Uppingham, spent winters working in the family chocolate-manufacturing business. He retired from playing to take up a managerial position at Leicestershire, and later worked as an England selector.

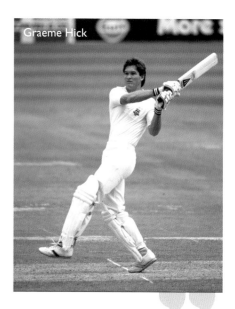
Graeme Hick

Graeme Hick:
"It is hard to think that there have been many better players at his age"

James Whitaker

CRICKETERS OF THE YEAR 1987 – Performances in the English season 1986

Name	Age*		Matches	Runs	Bat ave	Wickets	Bowl ave	Catches (/st)
JH Childs	35	First-class	22	214	13.37	89	16.28	4
GA Hick	20	First-class	24	2004	64.64	3	36.33	29
		List A	26	889	40.40	6	23.66	9
DB Vengsarkar	30	First-class	8	536	67.00			3
		Tests	3	360	90.00			1
CA Walsh	24	First-class	23	221	12.27	118	18.17	7
		List A	18	73	9.12	22	28.77	1
JJ Whitaker	24	First-class	22	1526	66.34	1	47.00	18
		List A	16	231	16.50	0		2

* as at 1/4/1987

1988

Five Cricketers of the Year

Jonathan Agnew (Leicestershire) ●
Neil Foster (Essex and England) ●
David Hughes (Lancashire) / ●
Peter Roebuck (Somerset) /
Salim Malik (Pakistanis) /

HEADLINE EVENTS FROM 1987

- County champions – Nottinghamshire

- NatWest Trophy – Nottinghamshire

- Refuge Assurance League – Worcestershire

- Benson & Hedges Cup – Yorkshire

- England lose 1-0 to Pakistan

- England retain the Ashes, winning 2-1 in Australia in 1986-87

- Australia win the World Cup in 1987-88

TWO COUNTY CAPTAINS WHO NEVER PLAYED FOR England were chosen for their parts in hoisting their clubs out of difficult times in 1987. Neither David Hughes nor Peter Roebuck lifted a trophy, but Hughes led Lancashire to the runners-up spot in the Championship and within four points of a first outright title in 53 years, while Roebuck oversaw an improvement in Somerset's performances that was not fully reflected in results.

For Hughes, selection as Cricketer of the Year was the second surprise in 12 months. In 1986, aged 39, having spent the summer unwanted by the first team and leading the seconds to their title, he was stunned to be invited to take charge of the First XI in 1987. Shelving thoughts of retirement, he turned his attention to restoring pride at a club that had spent 11 seasons in the bottom six of the Championship.

Hughes's contributions with the bat were disappointing and his slow left-arm spin bowling was virtually non-existent, but his captaincy was inspirational and commanding – as it remained until he stepped down, a year after taking Lancashire to a unique double in the Lord's cup finals in 1990, to move into a managerial role.

Hughes was the son of a cricket pro in the Bolton League. His best years as a player came under Jack Bond [1971], during which he was the twilight hero in a famous Gillette Cup semi-final win over Gloucestershire and forged a potent spin partnership with Jack Simmons [1985]. By the 1980s, his bowling faded away as his batting blossomed, but then he discovered a third string to his bow.

Roebuck took over the Somerset captaincy in 1986, but things did not improve straight away; in fact, they got worse as, partly with his encouragement, the club dismissed Viv Richards [1977] and Joel Garner [1980]. Ian Botham [1978], who was already minded to leave the club, departed in sympathy for the West Indians.

Much acrimony followed, but eventually with the air cleared a young team played with renewed purpose, as did the bespectacled Roebuck, who had a fine season in 1987, finishing eighth in the national averages and scoring some of his best and grittiest hundreds: one with a broken finger at Headingley and others against Hampshire's Malcolm Marshall [1983] and Sylvester Clarke of Surrey.

Roebuck, who played for Somerset Second XI at 13 before developing his game at Millfield and Cambridge (where he took a First in Law), was a contender to open the batting for England, but it never happened. He quit the Somerset captaincy after 1988, and retired from the professional game in 1991 to pursue a career as a cricket writer and broadcaster, while leading Devon to four successive Minor Counties titles.

He rarely returned to England after receiving a suspended sentence in 2001, having admitted three charges of common assault on young men. He was found dead outside a Cape Town hotel in 2011; police said he had jumped from a sixth-floor window after officers arrived to question him about an alleged sexual assault on a Zimbabwean man.

Neil Foster had been an England cricketer for five years, but the 1987 series against Pakistan was the first in which he was involved throughout. A tall, lean, seam and swing bowler, Foster's promise was evident from early days – he made his Essex debut at 18 – but he battled severe back and knee injuries and took time to settle to international cricket.

His finest hour came at Madras (now Chennai) in 1984-85 when he bowled England to victory with 11 wickets, but 1987 had several highlights, even if he could not prevent Pakistan winning their first Test series in England. Foster took eight wickets in the Headingley Test and six more at Edgbaston, and claimed 86 first-class wickets overall to follow his haul of 105 in 1986. He also bowled well at the business end of the World Cup on the subcontinent late in the year.

But the good days proved short-lived, and by 1989 Foster had signed for a rebel tour of South Africa. A Test record of 88 wickets in 29 matches was disappointing, but he did help Essex win five Championship titles.

Jonathan Agnew was a fast bowler built along similar lines to Foster, whose presence was possibly the chief obstacle to Agnew breaking

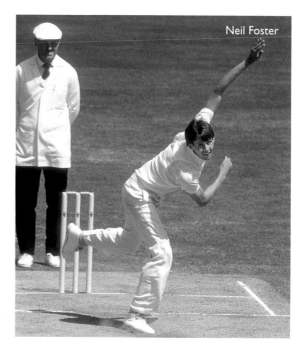

Neil Foster

into the England side in 1987 despite taking 194 first-class wickets over the course of that season and the previous one. Nor did he get picked for the winter tours.

The official reason was doubts over his fitness, although Agnew, operating off a shorter

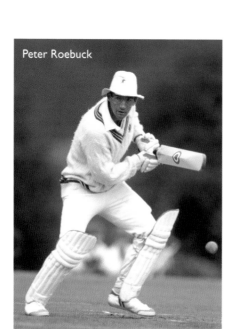

Peter Roebuck

Peter Roebuck:
"He seems to thrive on contest, competition and conflict"

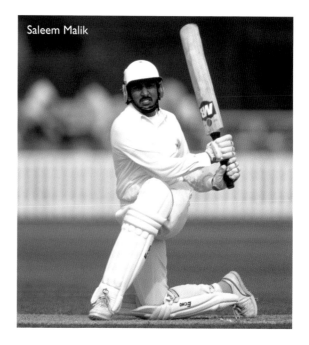

Saleem Malik

run than in his early days while still swinging the ball, got through more Championship overs in the season than any other fast bowler.

Agnew made his county debut at 18 while at Uppingham School, and joined Leicestershire after a spell with Surrey Second XI. He played three Tests in 1984 and 1985 with little success. Close to giving up the game in 1986, he started developing a second career in radio, and a year after retiring as a player in 1990 embarked on a distinguished career as BBC Radio's cricket correspondent.

Salim Malik played the decisive innings of the only match of the 1987 Test series to produce a positive result. On an uneven pitch at Headingley, Malik demonstrated the purity of his technique with a patient 99 occupying five and a half hours. He blamed nerves on his dismissal, as he had not made a hundred for 18 Tests; he ended the drought in the final Test at The Oval, where he contributed 118 to a stand of 234 with Javed Miandad [1982].

Malik grew up in Lahore, the son of a linen exporter, and rose fast through the ranks. At the age of 18, he toured Australia and scored

a hundred on debut against Sri Lanka; at 19, he toured England, and at 21 had scored five centuries in his 21 Tests.

He scored further Test hundreds on the 1992 and 1996 tours of England, and spent two seasons with Essex, but during a year as Pakistan captain in 1994-95 allegations surfaced of match-fixing, and he was subsequently banned for life following an inquiry by Justice Malik Qayyum in 2000.

David Hughes (left) after captaining Lancashire to victory in the NatWest Trophy, with Man of the Match Phillip DeFreitas [1992]

David Hughes:
"Hughes's contribution as a batsman was disappointing, as a bowler non-existent"

CRICKETERS OF THE YEAR 1988 – Performances in the English season 1987

Name	Age*		Matches	Runs	Bat ave	Wickets	Bowl ave	Catches (/st)
JP Agnew	27	First-class	25	387	16.82	101	24.26	1
		List A	20	65	16.25	24	27.83	2
NA Foster	25	First-class	21	419	19.95	86	22.00	6
		List A	17	265	44.16	31	17.12	5
		Tests	5	93	15.50	15	22.60	1
		ODI	3	19	19.00	7	12.85	0
DP Hughes	40	First-class	25	503	17.34	3	33.00	20
		List A	19	240	17.14	8	23.25	10
PM Roebuck	32	First-class	16	1199	49.95	0		15
		List A	16	648	46.28			5
Salim Malik	24	First-class	17	901	50.05	2	35.50	8
		Tests	5	248	49.60			4

* as at 1/4/1988

Jonathan Agnew bowls, watched by umpire Jack Bond [1970]

1989

Five Cricketers of the Year

Kim Barnett (Derbyshire and England) **/**
Jeff Dujon (West Indians) **M**
Phil Neale (Worcestershire) **/**
Franklyn Stephenson (Nottinghamshire) **/** **●**
Steve Waugh (Somerset) **/**

HEADLINE EVENTS FROM 1988

- County champions – Worcestershire

- NatWest Trophy – Middlesex

- Refuge Assurance League – Worcestershire

- Benson & Hedges Cup – Hampshire

- West Indies beat England 4-0

- England beat Sri Lanka 1-0

- England lose 1-0 in Pakistan and draw 0-0 in New Zealand in 1987-88. England and Australia draw the Bicentenary Test in Sydney

FRANKLYN STEPHENSON, AN ALL-ROUNDER FROM Barbados, enjoyed in 1988 one of the finest county seasons by anyone in the fully professional era. Signed by Nottinghamshire as replacement for Clive Rice [1981] and Richard Hadlee [1982], he not only matched Hadlee's 1984 feat of the double but reached the mark in two fewer games.

Stephenson attacked with bat and ball. He missed two matches after breaking his nose hooking at a ball in May, but was unrepentant. As a tall fast bowler who angled the ball into right-handers and seamed it away, he compelled batsmen to play. He also had perhaps the best slower ball in the game, using it to dupe around a quarter of his 125 first-class victims.

He completed the double in spectacular style. Needing 210 runs from the last fixture against Yorkshire for his 1,000, he made light of the task: quite apart from bowling 71 overs and taking 11 wickets, he bludgeoned 111 in the first innings and 117 in the second. Remarkably Nottinghamshire still lost, though they finished fifth in the table.

Stephenson was one of the most travelled cricketers of his era. Initially he worked as a waiter, and his early games were for hotel teams before he progressed to the northern leagues in England. A rebel tour of South Africa in 1981-82 cut him off from Caribbean cricket, but he was rarely without year-round employment. He stayed at Trent Bridge until 1991, then spent four years with Sussex. Most of his employers got value for money. After retiring from cricket he became a golf professional in Barbados.

As Stephenson was banned from playing internationally, West Indies had lacked a batting and bowling all-rounder since the departure of Garry Sobers [1964]. Fortunately they were able to balance their side in the 1980s thanks to Jeff Dujon, who was a slim, elegant batsman as well as capable keeper to their pace-centric attacks.

Dujon's batting record was easily the best of any Test keeper during this decade. His five hundreds were scored in varied conditions, and although his best score in England in 1988 was 67, he made four fifties and shared in the biggest stand of the innings on five of the seven occasions he batted. When Gordon Greenidge [1977] missed the Fourth Test at Leeds through injury, Dujon opened in his place.

Phil Neale

Waugh had helped Australia win the World Cup a few months before this, when his cool medium-pace death bowling was vital to the outcome, but he had yet to fulfil his potential as a batsman in Test cricket, to which he gained early exposure because Australian cricket was at a low ebb.

This would soon change. Waugh returned to England with Australia in 1989 and scored his maiden Test hundred in the first match; many more centuries followed over the next 15 years, and Waugh's love of a scrap meant that his hundreds usually came as guarantees of victory. Inheriting the captaincy in 1999, he built on the work of Allan Border [1982] and Mark Taylor [1990] in ensuring Australia remained the team to beat.

Waugh was raised as one of four boys to sporting parents in suburban Sydney; his twin brother Mark was a Cricketer of the Year in 1991.

Phil Neale led Worcestershire to Championship and Sunday League titles in 1988. It was an exhausting season, as the county also reached the quarter-finals of the Benson and Hedges Cup and the NatWest Trophy final, where despite Neale's 64 they paid the price for losing an important toss. It was also his benefit season.

Early in the year he discovered he son was ill with leukaemia, and shortly before the NatWest final he himself was admitted to hospital for viral tests; a week later he scored a crucial century in the Championship that took him to 1,000 for the season. Neale was used to multi-tasking. He pursued sport while taking a degree in Russian Studies, and for ten years played cricket for Worcestershire and football for Lincoln City (initially under Graham Taylor, the future England manager). Two of his best seasons as a batsman came towards the end of this period, when he began captaining the county. Worcestershire retained the Championship under him in 1989.

Franklyn Stephenson

Franklyn Stephenson:
"His timekeeping was a constant source of irritation"

Steve Waugh

Dujon came from a cricketing family – his father also represented Jamaica – but what seemed an inevitable rise to the top was delayed by the island keeping him waiting six years to take over the gloves. The West Indies job was then his after David Murray joined the South African rebels. Dujon retired from Tests after the 1991 tour of England, and his 270 dismissals still stands as a West Indies record.

Steve Waugh was, like Stephenson, another newish face to county cricket in 1988. He had played three matches for Somerset the previous year as fill-in for Martin Crowe [1985]; now he was summoned back from a spell with Smethwick in the Birmingham and District League when Crowe broke down with a back problem.

Hot-footing it to Southampton, Waugh arrived in time to bat at No. 7 and retrieve a mini-crisis with an unbeaten 115, which he completed on his 23rd birthday. In 14 Championship appearances he scored six hundreds and finished second in the national averages.

Jeff Dujon

for England. His call-up came for the end-of-season Test against Sri Lanka, in which he scored 66. He would have played in the previous match against West Indies but for a hand injury. It was deserved recognition of a fine season in which only two batsmen scored more runs at a better average. He was also Man of the Match in the only one-day international he ever played.

However, his England career stalled in 1989, and three weeks after he was dropped it emerged he had signed for a South African rebel tour.

Barnett joined Derbyshire as a leg-spinning all-rounder in 1979, but promotion to the captaincy four years later accelerated his development, as did winters in South Africa. Despite a fidgety way at the crease, he thrived as attacking opener and led Derbyshire to the 1993 Benson & Hedges Cup.

Leaving Derbyshire in 1998 as their highest-ever run-scorer, he joined Gloucestershire and shared in their glory year in one-day cricket. But his marriage broke up and, after retiring in 2003, he fell out of work. In March 2013 he was fined £380 for harassing his former wife.

He later forged a long career as operations manager of the England national team, starting in 1999 and spanning many triumphs.

Kim Barnett became the first Derbyshire batsman since Donald Carr [1960] to be picked

Kim Barnett

Kim Barnett:

"Captaincy turned Barnett into an opening batsman because he felt... he should go over the top first"

CRICKETERS OF THE YEAR 1989 – Performances in the English season 1988

Name	Age*		Matches	Runs	Bat ave	Wickets	Bowl ave	Catches (/st)
KJ Barnett	28	First-class	19	1623	57.96	14	29.57	17
		List A	24	1014	50.70	0		6
		Tests	1	66	33.00			1
		ODI	1	84	84.00			0
PJL Dujon	32	First-class	12	601	50.08			31
		Tests	5	305	50.83			20
		ODI	3	69	34.50			4/1
PA Neale	34	First-class	21	1036	39.84	0		8
		List A	25	740	43.52			10
FD Stephenson	29	First-class	22	1018	29.08	125	18.31	10
		List A	20	168	14.00	31	19.51	4
SR Waugh	23	First-class	15	1314	73.00	3	20.00	20
		List A	16	716	59.66	8	34.12	6

as at 1/4/1989

1990

Five Cricketers of the Year

Jimmy Cook (Somerset) *

Dean Jones (Australians) *

Jack Russell (Gloucestershire and England) ▥

Robin Smith (Hampshire and England) *

Mark Taylor (Australians) *

HEADLINE EVENTS FROM 1989

- County champions – Worcestershire

- NatWest Trophy – Warwickshire

- Refuge Assurance League – Lancashire

- Benson & Hedges Cup – Nottinghamshire

- Australia beat England 4-0

AUSTRALIA TROUNCED ENGLAND 4–0 IN 1989 in one of the most lopsided Ashes series in memory, and it was a surprise that Graeme Wright, the editor, contented himself with picking only two of their players. Aside from Mark Taylor and Dean Jones, who were named among the Five, David Boon scored 442 runs in the Tests and Geoff Lawson took 29 wickets.

Taylor, who was introduced into the Australia side earlier in the year, was the missing link in the batting plans of team coach Bob Simpson [1965], who wanted one opener to be left-handed. Taylor teamed up with Geoff Marsh while Boon dropped to No. 3. Jones, who had been inconsistent against the new ball, moved down into the middle order to play a more aggressive role.

Taylor was temperamentally suited to drawing the bowlers' sting. He did this to perfection on a tricky first day of the series at Headingley, batting until stumps for 96; he reached his maiden Test hundred next morning and Australia totalled 601. Thanks in large part to him they topped 400 in the first innings of all six Tests, and in nine straight games during the year.

Taylor's aggregate of 839 runs, spanning 38 hours, was the third-highest in any Ashes series, and he became the first to score 1,000 Test runs in the calendar year of his debut. He also batted through the first day of the Trent Bridge Test, in which he and Marsh posted a stand of 329.

Taylor, who grew up in rural New South Wales, had tasted English conditions with a season in the Bolton League in 1988. In 1994 he embarked on five years as Australia's captain, and his enterprise won many admirers as well as buying him time when he went through troughs in form. He was a superb slip fielder, and briefly held the Test catching record for non-keepers.

Jones was an ideal man to run floundering opponents ragged, but his Test hundreds at Edgbaston and The Oval began with Australia in moderate positions. At other less pressured times, he played selflessly and scored more runs in the series than anyone but Taylor. He also made the season's highest score of 248 against Warwickshire.

Jones was a gifted player who set new standards in one-day batting with his inventive movement around the crease and fast running between the wickets, but in Tests he played some great innings without being a great player. He established himself with a heroic double-century in a tied Test in Madras (now Chennai) in 1986-87, and sealed his place on the England tour with another double against West Indies. But he was inconsistent, and Australia jettisoned him when he was only 31.

One of three cricketing brothers, Jones could be abrasive to deal with. He had turbulent spells as captain of Victoria and Derbyshire, and was later an outspoken media pundit.

Like Jones, Robin Smith – the younger brother of Chris [1984] – might have achieved more at Test level. His performances in the 1989 Tests suggested a maturity of mind that previously had not always been in evidence since he arrived at Hampshire from Natal at the age

Jack Russell

Jimmy Cook:
"The batting exploits of Jimmy Cook in his first season of county cricket were truly astonishing"

of 17. Strongly built, he had broken many sports records at school.

Even though he made three early Championship hundreds in 1989, Smith only started the Ashes series after injury ruled out Mike Gatting [1984], but he scored runs in every game he played and, unfazed by the sledging of Merv Hughes [1994], was leader of England's resistance as well as their run chart. He scored 143 out of a total of 260 at Old Trafford, and 101 out of 255 at Trent Bridge.

Two more big home summers followed, but he coped with spin less well than pace and by the age of 32 Smith was finished with international cricket, although he continued to play for Hampshire until 2003.

Jack Russell did every bit as much as Smith to boost bedraggled English morale, although he cut a very different figure. He was of slight build, wore a floppy white hat, and came from Stroud. He might have played for England earlier, but there were fears that his batting was not up to it. He scotched that theory by scoring 94 on debut against Sri Lanka in 1988 and by batting for more than 16 hours in the Ashes, while still maintaining high standards behind the stumps.

Australia suspected he was fragile against pace, until he stood firm for an unbeaten 64 at Lord's and answered their sledging in kind; an innings of 128 not out at Old Trafford was a poignant act of defiance on the day the Ashes were lost and news of defections to South Africa emerged.

Later in the year, Russell looked the best keeper in the world at the Nehru Cup one-day tournament, but England still spent the next nine years vacillating over whether he or Alec Stewart [1993] was the best bet as keeper. After they came down on Stewart's side for good, Russell focused on helping Gloucestershire win six one-trophies in five years. He also developed a career as an artist.

Robin Smith

Robin Smith:

"The way he faced up to the intimidation offered by Merv Hughes made for colourful cricket"

Mark Taylor

Jimmy Cook enjoyed a spectacular first season in county cricket, being the leading batsman in terms of first-class runs, centuries and average, and in all matches totalling 3,143 runs with 11 hundreds. He turned 36 during the season but did not miss a match, though after July he reached 50 only once.

The highlight was carrying his bat through both innings at Trent Bridge for 120 (out of 186) and 131 (out of 218), an eloquent tribute to an unruffled, uncomplicated method that had served him well for Transvaal since 1972-73.

Cook played two more seasons at Somerset and, remarkably, improved on his output both times; in all, he scored 7,604 runs and 28 hundreds for them in 71 first-class matches. He played three Tests after South Africa's return to the international arena in 1991-92. He later filled various coaching roles and was an early mentor to Graeme Smith [2004]. His son Stephen was also a successful batsman.

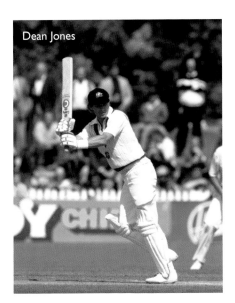
Dean Jones

CRICKETERS OF THE YEAR 1990 – Performances in the English season 1989

Name	Age*		Matches	Runs	Bat ave	Wickets	Bowl ave	Catches (/st)
SJ Cook	36	First-class	23	2241	60.56			13
		List A	24	902	39.21			10
DM Jones	29	First-class	14	1510	88.82	0		8
		List A	5	168	42.00	1	0.00	2
		Tests	6	566	70.75			4
RC Russell	26	First-class	19	586	26.63			51/7
		List A	17	191	27.28			21/2
		Tests	6	314	39.25			14/4
RA Smith	26	First-class	18	1577	58.40	0		11
		List A	19	817	58.35			9
		Tests	5	553	61.44			1
MA Taylor	25	First-class	17	1669	57.55			23
		Tests	6	839	83.90			5

as at 1/4/1990

1991

Five Cricketers of the Year

Michael Atherton (Lancashire and England) *

Mohammad Azharuddin (Indians) *

Alan Butcher (Glamorgan) *

Desmond Haynes (Middlesex) *

Mark Waugh (Essex) *

HEADLINE EVENTS FROM 1990

- County champions – Middlesex

- NatWest Trophy – Lancashire

- Refuge Assurance League – Derbyshire

- Benson & Hedges Cup – Lancashire

- England beat both New Zealand and India 1-0

- England lose 2-1 in West Indies in 1989-90

RUNS WERE NEVER MORE PLENTIFUL THAN IN the hot summer of 1990, and unsurprisingly *Wisden*'s editor Graeme Wright made up his Five for 1991 entirely of batsmen who had shone the previous summer. In first-class and one-day matches combined, Desmond Haynes scored 3,699 runs, Michael Atherton 2,996, Alan Butcher 2,821 and Mark Waugh 2,761. Mohammad Azharuddin, who toured with India, played relatively few matches but produced two spell-binding centuries in the Tests.

Even in such a run-gorged season, Haynes's commitment to Middlesex's cause was remarkable. Six days after completing back-to-back hundreds in a tight Test series with England in the Caribbean, he made an unbeaten 107 in a Sunday League match, and before the end of April had muscled 358 runs from five innings in three different competitions. He simply never let up, even scoring twin hundreds in a relatively unimportant match against the New Zealanders.

His contributions went beyond brisk, attractive runs. He had joined Middlesex in 1989 following the untimely death of Wilf Slack, and was determined to be the perfect antidote: cheerful, helpful, professional. But in 1990 he

wanted to do better still – and did. So too, did Middlesex, who won the Championship again.

Haynes was already famous as one half of Test cricket's most successful opening partnership with fellow Barbadian Gordon Greenidge [1977], in which Haynes tended to rein himself in. When he occasionally stood in as West Indies captain he was no less pragmatic, once using delaying tactics to save a Test in Trinidad. His careers with Middlesex and West Indies ended in 1994, after which he held various administrative posts.

Ten years younger than Haynes, Mark Waugh stood to benefit more from county cricket – which he entered in 1988, a year after his twin brother Steve [1989]. While playing in the Bolton League Mark was approached by Allan Border [1982] about taking over his place in the Essex side; eager to develop as Steve had done, he accepted.

In 1989 he topped 1,500 runs, but it was 1990 that really boosted his confidence, as he scored four hundreds against county attacks containing some of the best West Indies and Pakistan fast bowlers. He showed himself undemonstrative, organised and stylish – and ready for the next step up.

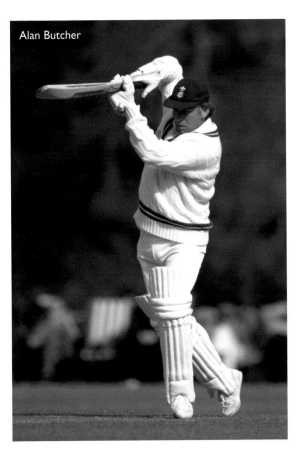

Alan Butcher

earlier in the year, was by this time back playing at his best after struggling to live up to the expectations generated by three hundreds in his first three Tests against England in 1984-85. In fact, his instinctive style of play was best suited to true pitches, and over a career spanning 15 years and 99 Tests he never fully mastered dealing with livelier pitches or short-pitched bowling.

Azharuddin captained India for much of the 1990s, but his career ended abruptly in 2000 amid allegations of match-fixing. In 2009 he moved into politics.

Atherton was brought into the England side in 1989 following defections to a rebel tour; he played two Tests at No. 3 and was then left out of the winter tour of the West Indies.

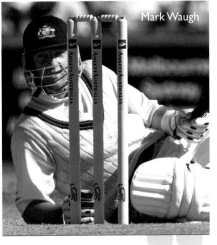

Mark Waugh

Mohammad Azharuddin

In January 1991 he was chosen for his first Test, and scored 138 against England. He was to be a near-fixture in the Australian team for the next 11 years, and finished with more than 8,000 runs in both Tests and one-day internationals. He was also among the finest of slip fielders, as was Mohammad Azharuddin.

Waugh could be a lovely player to watch but Azharuddin, who wielded some of the lightest bats around, was an artist of an altogether superior strain. His counter-attacking 121 at Lord's in 1990 stood out even in a Test match stuffed with runs, as he uncannily flicked straight balls through square leg and midwicket with a roll of the wrists. He followed it with an innings of 179 at Old Trafford that was scarcely less good.

Azharuddin, a Muslim from Hyderabad who had been promoted to the Indian captaincy

Mark Waugh:
"He can have 30 on the board without the bowlers realising he has his pads strapped on"

Michael Atherton

Michael Atherton:
"It was not just his class which shone through; it was the temperament"

He therefore had something to prove when the 1990 season began, and used his bat to make his feelings plain, scoring 856 runs in all competitions by the end of May. He got back his England place, this time as an opener, and in 11 Test innings scored two hundreds and six fifties. He also took 45 first-class wickets, though his career as a leg-break bowler did not last.

This was Atherton's first full season of county cricket after three summers split between Cambridge University and Lancashire, in the first of which he passed 1,000 runs.

Neither his quality nor temperament was ever in serious doubt. He captained Manchester Grammar School at 15, Cambridge at 20 and a Combined Universities team to victories over two counties in one-day matches at 21. He would lead England in more Tests (54) than anyone. He was unlucky, though, to be an opener in an era of great fast bowlers and to play when neither England, nor their selection policy, was strong. He was later a distinguished Sky TV commentator and *Times* correspondent.

For fifth spot, Alan Butcher beat off competition from Ashley Metcalfe, Chris Broad and his Glamorgan opening partner Hugh Morris, all of whom, like him, topped 2,000 first-class runs in 1990.

Butcher, who was in his 19th season of county cricket, was the first English-born batsman to 1,000 runs, as he had been in 1989, and his positive, thoughtful captaincy contributed to Glamorgan finishing eighth, their highest Championship position for 20 years.

One of Butcher's chief strengths was in dealing with fast bowling: he was of short build, spent five years in Australia in his youth, and developed his game at The Oval, where he played for Surrey until 1986. It was the reason why he won his one Test cap in 1979, and why he and fellow left-hander Morris were viewed as the best opening pair in county cricket.

His finest innings of the season came in a NatWest Trophy quarter-final against Middlesex, even though his unbeaten 104 could not prevent defeat. He retired in 1992 and moved into coaching roles with Surrey and Zimbabwe. Two brothers, two sons and a daughter also played to county standard; son Mark played 71 Tests.

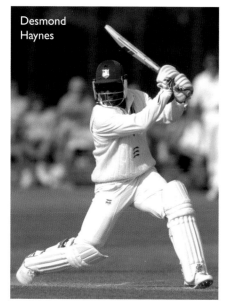

Desmond Haynes

CRICKETERS OF THE YEAR 1991 – Performances in the English season 1990

Name	Age*		Matches	Runs	Bat ave	Wickets	Bowl ave	Catches (/st)
MA Atherton	23	First-class	20	1924	71.25	45	31.06	24
		List A	25	1072	51.04	12	25.08	13
		Tests	6	735	66.81	1	178.00	6
M Azharuddin	28	First-class	9	770	77.00			3
		Tests	3	426	85.20			1
		ODI	2	118	*			2
AR Butcher	37	First-class	23	2116	58.77	1	153.00	8
		List A	24	705	35.25	1	20.00	10
DL Haynes	35	First-class	23	2346	69.00	2	56.50	14
		List A	27	1353	61.50	6	66.16	12
ME Waugh	25	First-class	22	2072	76.74	12	64.25	18
		List A	23	689	34.45	10	38.10	6

as at 1/4/1991

1992

Five Cricketers of the Year

Curtly Ambrose (West Indians) ●
Phillip DeFreitas (Lancashire and England) ●
Allan Donald (Warwickshire) ●
Richie Richardson (West Indians) /
Waqar Younis (Surrey) ●

HEADLINE EVENTS FROM 1991

- County champions – Essex

- NatWest Trophy – Hampshire

- Refuge Assurance League – Nottinghamshire

- Benson & Hedges Cup – Worcestershire

- England and West Indies draw 2-2

- England beat Sri Lanka 1-0

- England lose 3-0 in Australia in 1990-91

AFTER CHOOSING FIVE BATSMEN IN 1991, GRAEME Wright opted for four specialist fast bowlers in 1992, the first time so many of this type had been chosen in the same year.

The background of none of the five was traditional: Curtly Ambrose, Richie Richardson and Phillip DeFreitas all hailed from small islands in the eastern Caribbean; Allan Donald was the first Cricketer of the Year born in South Africa's Free State; while Waqar Younis grew up in a remote part of the Punjab and the United Arab Emirates.

DeFreitas spent his first ten years in Dominica before moving to London, where he shone at cricket and football. Opting for cricket, he joined the MCC Young Cricketers and was recommended to Leicestershire, for whom he took 94 wickets in his first full season. That won him a place on the 1986-87 tour of Australia where he performed capably in Tests and one-day internationals.

This steep rise created expectations that were not met until 1991 when, having just finished another tour of Australia strongly, he concentrated on bowling accurately and seaming the ball both ways. The results were

dramatic: with 22 wickets at 20.77 apiece in five Tests against West Indies (figures that rivalled Ambrose's) and a career-best seven for 70 against Sri Lanka, he was England's spearhead. He also scored a maiden Test fifty and fielded superbly as England, given little chance, held West Indies 2–2.

It proved a fleeting high point. DeFreitas returned to being inconsistent in Tests; in one-dayers, where the need for economy was imperative, he bowled much better. While England's faith in him wavered, he kept jumping counties, getting through three before returning to Leicestershire, where he retired aged 40.

Ambrose, who stood 6ft 7in, was of similar build to Joel Garner [1980] and posed similar problems. He was uncannily accurate for his pace, and filled many batsmen with dread. In 1991 he did more than anyone to ruin the debut series of Graeme Hick [1988].

Ambrose had also been responsible for turning around the series with England in the Caribbean in 1989-90, his final-day figures of eight for 45 snatching a late series-levelling victory in Barbados, before West Indies went on to win the deciding game in Antigua easily.

There were many such irresistible spells.

Ambrose's height had encouraged thoughts of basketball, but after taking up cricket seriously at 17 he progressed fast. Andy Roberts [1975] dispensed wise counsel, and Viv Richards [1977] facilitated three seasons of league cricket in England ahead of his first major tour there in 1988, when he took 22 wickets in the series.

There were misguided concerns that Ambrose was disposed neither mentally nor physically to the long haul, in fact. He relished lengthy series – averaging 23 wickets in his seven against England and 21 in six against Australia – and retired aged 36 with 405 Test wickets to his name. He also spent several seasons at Northamptonshire.

Richardson was the leading run-scorer in the 1991 Tests, which was a personal triumph given his record in English conditions. In 1984, he was not chosen for any of the Tests, and in 1988 did little in three games before injury. Several seasons in English and Welsh leagues had hardly helped. But in 1991 he worked out a method, resisting the urge to push at the ball, and staying patient. Grafting hundreds in the Fourth and Fifth Tests were his reward.

On the harder wickets of West Indies and Australia, where his previous 12 Test hundreds were scored, Richardson was a strokeplayer of the highest quality, a fine hooker and square-driver. Like Viv Richards, he eschewed the helmet.

After the 1991 tour, Richardson was appointed Richards's successor as West Indies captain. It was a sad reign – his batting suffered as a once-great team entered decline – but he was always dignified. He retired following the 1996 World Cup, suffering from fatigue.

He became the first prominent signing for English all-star club team Lashings, played bass guitar alongside Ambrose in a reggae band called Big Bad Dread and The Baldhead, and in 2011 was appointed West Indies manager.

Even though this was a pace-dominated era, Waqar Younis was greeted as something out of the ordinary after he took 45 wickets in six Tests against New Zealand and West Indies in 1990-91, then mowed down 113 victims in 17 Championship matches for Surrey in 1991. Delivering the ball with a low arm, after a galloping run-up, he tended to pitch it full and swing it late. Stumps were shattered, toes crushed, well-set batsmen

Waqar Younis:
"A bowler who could become... the greatest of them all"

CRICKETERS OF THE YEAR 1992 – Performances in the English season 1991

Name	Age*		Matches	Runs	Bat ave	Wickets	Bowl ave	Catches (/st)
CEL Ambrose	28	First-class	10	53	7.57	51	17.03	1
		Tests	5	37	5.28	28	20.00	0
PAJ DeFreitas	26	First-class	18	499	20.79	73	24.38	2
		List A	23	161	16.10	29	26.34	11
		Tests	6	135	16.87	30	19.06	1
AA Donald	25	First-class	21	96	8.00	83	19.68	10
		List A	18	18	6.00	25	26.80	4
RB Richardson	30	First-class	15	1403	66.80	0		14
		Tests	5	495	55.00			4
Waqar Younis	20	First-class	18	177	14.75	113	14.65	4
		List A	21	48	6.00	39	17.87	3

as at 1/4/1992

Allan Donald

Richie Richardson

Curtly Ambrose

Phillip DeFreitas

Curtly Ambrose:
"Ambrose has the ability to exert a debilitating psychological influence which so often precipitates a cluster of wickets"

rendered helpless. His strength and stamina were exceptional.

Such was Waqar's success at swinging an old ball against the shine – reverse-swing – that suspicions were aroused of ball-tampering. These allegations resurfaced when Pakistan beat England 2–1 in Tests in 1992.

Waqar needed luck to get started. Spotted while playing in a televised domestic match in 1988 by the then Pakistan captain Imran Khan [1983], he was introduced into the national side in 1989-90 and recommended to Surrey in 1990. Waqar helped Glamorgan win the Championship in 1997, and retired in 2003 with more than 350 wickets in both Tests and one-day internationals at strike-rates bettered by few.

Donald finished second to Waqar in the 1991 averages, and nearly took Warwickshire to the Championship title. He put in heroic efforts, notably a spell of 20 overs with a back injury to set up a win over Northamptonshire.

Donald bowled a full length from a classical action that created movement off the seam or shaped the ball away. After starting his provincial career with Free State in 1985-86 he joined Warwickshire in 1987, and created headlines with his pace two years later when he took 86 first-class wickets and helped them win the NatWest Trophy.

Donald remained close to Warwickshire throughout his career, and assisted their title win in 1995, but in late 1991 his focus shifted to South Africa's readmission to international cricket. He spearheaded their attack for the next ten years.

His finest series came in England in 1998, when he took 33 wickets in a losing cause. He finished, in 2002, with 330 Test wickets at a strike-rate of 47.0 that was only slightly inferior to Waqar's (43.4) and better than Ambrose's (54.5). He later worked as a fast-bowling coach and media pundit.

Part Five: 1993 to 2013

THIS PERIOD CEMENTED THE MULTINATIONAL flavour of the Cricketers of the Year award, with the number of English players – men and women, as England's Claire Taylor in 2009 became the first female cricketer chosen – again outnumbered by the foreign contingent, this time by 54 to 50.

While there was a shift in the totals of overseas and touring players – overseas cricketers at counties fell from 31 to 15, while those with touring teams rose from 36 to 43 (four appeared for both counties and touring teams in the same year) – this mainly reflected an expanding international schedule and a corresponding decline in the quality of overseas players available to counties.

Further evidence of the spread in the game's global reach could be seen in the first cricketers chosen while representing Zimbabwe (in 2002) and Bangladesh (in 2011).

Indeed, the desire to recognise the world's best talent led to a temporary relaxing of the rules of selection. In 1997, Sanath Jayasuriya was picked without having played in England the previous year, the first time this had happened since Dick Pilling in 1891. The Sri Lankan batsman had starred as an explosive pinch-hitter at the 50-overs World Cup in Asia in 1996, and Matthew Engel, whose arrival as editor in 1993 marks the start of this period, justified Jayasuriya's selection on the grounds that his innovative play had had a significant influence on the English season that followed.

In 2000, Engel went further and based the award on a player's impact on cricket worldwide rather than on the preceding English season, a policy that was followed when Graeme Wright was editor in 2001-02 and Tim de Lisle in 2003. During this time three more foreign cricketers were picked who had not appeared the previous English season: Andy Flower and V. V. S. Laxman in 2002, and Matthew Hayden in 2003. However in 2004, when Engel began a second spell as editor (he oversaw 12 editions of the Almanack in total), the decision was reversed and a separate award introduced for the Leading Cricketer in the World. An introductory paragraph to the Cricketers of the Year thereafter explained the criteria for selection.

In his first issue as editor, Engel ran a list of those active players (37 at the time) who had already been Cricketers of the Year and were therefore ineligible for consideration. It is the only time this has been done. The percentage of Cricketers of the Year who appeared for England during the home season prior to their selection rose from 25% in 1969–92 to 34, not far short of the level in 1947–68 of 37%. However, there were two distinct phases: between 1993 and 2002, when the England team generally struggled, they managed only 11 selections, while from 2003 to 2013, when results were much improved, 24 players were chosen. There were no England players – indeed no *English* players – chosen in 1997, 2000 and 2002, but in 2005 all five Cricketers of the Year appeared for England the previous summer, only the third time a frontline team (ie Test or county side) from the previous English season had achieved such a clean sweep, following in the footsteps of an earlier crop of England players in 1938 (no more than four of whom appeared together at any one time during the 1937 Tests) and the famous Australians who swept the board in 1949.

Almost half the 35 England cricketers were specialist bowlers, who outnumbered England batsmen for the first time since 1889–1917. Possibly the switch to a County Championship made up exclusively of four-day matches in 1993 gave bowlers greater scope to develop their skills. Overall during this period bowlers achieved a healthy representation, despite bat apparently dominating ball.

With international stars in the ascendant, the number of English cricketers chosen solely for their efforts in the county game fell markedly to just 14, whereas there had been 28 English players who played only for counties in 1969–92. Of these, eight were members of Championship-winning sides, six of them captains. Nigel Briers (1993) and Alan Richardson (2012) were the only Cricketers of the Year from this period never to play international cricket.

The rise of one-day cricket in its various guises was reflected not only in Jayasuriya's selection but in the inclusion of Aravinda de Silva, a star in one-day games for Kent in 1995, and Lance Klusener and Tom Moody in the year following the 1999 World Cup. Ian Austin was picked in 1999 for helping Lancashire win the NatWest Trophy and Sunday League, and Mark Alleyne after leading Gloucestershire to a one-day treble in 2000. Australian all-rounder Ian Harvey, another stalwart of many Gloucestershire one-day triumphs, was chosen in 2004.

Durham, who only entered the County Championship in 1992, finished as the joint-best-represented county with seven – all selected between 2005 and 2010 – although four were overseas players. Warwickshire also provided seven Cricketers of the Year, of whom two were imports. The seven best-represented counties were those from all the major Test-match grounds.

Inevitably, with the net spread so wide, some outstanding players missed out. These included Inzamam-ul-Haq, who scored more than 20,000 international runs, Sourav Ganguly and Virender Sehwag, Stephen Fleming, who captained New Zealand and briefly Nottinghamshire with distinction, and Mark Butcher, the son of a Cricketer of the Year and the maker of a match-winning century in a home Ashes Test. Michael Bevan was one of the leading one-day batsmen of the era, and Mike Hussey was also a great servant of the Australian team as well as being, like Bevan, a heavy scorer in county cricket. Chris Gayle scored Test triple-centuries as well as being an early champion in Twenty20. Chaminda Vaas, Daniel Vettori and Harbhajan Singh all took over 350 Test wickets, as did Makhaya Ntini, who took ten of them in one match at Lord's.

Engel's second spell as editor also saw changes in presentation. He moved away from the standard action photographs of the Five in favour of more varied images. Chris Adams, captain of champions Sussex, was pictured in front of celebrating supporters at Hove. In 1995 five headshots were used, and in 2006 some of the Five were pictured in civvies. When Scyld Berry took over as editor he restored the use of action images during his four years, the only exception being Chris Read holding the Championship trophy in 2010.

Berry introduced two striking "firsts" by picking the first woman cricketer, England's Claire Taylor in 2009, and two years later selecting only four Cricketers of the Year after one of his original five – widely assumed to be Pakistan fast bowler Mohammad Aamer, though never actually specified – faced serious allegations of corruption. Tim de Lisle's one year as editor in 2003 was notable for his devoting 20 pages to the Five, twice the usual space.

CRICKETERS OF THE YEAR 1993–2013

(Teams they represented in the English season prior to selection)

Team	Years	Awards	Batsmen	Bowlers	Allrounders	WK
Warwickshire	1995-2011	7	3	2	2	0
Durham	2005-10	7	4	3	0	0
Surrey	1993-2007	6	2	2	1	1
Yorkshire	1993-2012	6	3	2	1	0
Middlesex	1996-2011	4	3	1	0	0
Lancashire	1999-2012	4	0	4	0	0
Nottinghamshire	2008-11	4	0	2	1	1
Sussex	1993-2010	3	1	1	0	1
Glamorgan	1994-2006	3	1	2	0	0
Worcestershire	1995-2012	3	0	1	1	1
Essex	1998-2012	3	3	0	0	0
Somerset	2001-13	3	2	1	0	0
Leicestershire	1993-97	2	2	0	0	0
Derbyshire	1995-96	2	0	2	0	0
Kent	1996-2005	2	2	0	0	0
Northamptonshire	1996-2007	2	0	2	0	0
Gloucestershire	2001-04	2	0	0	2	0
Hampshire	2006	1	1	0	0	0
England	1993-2012	35	12	17	3	3
Australians[†]	1994-2010	14	6	5	1	2
South Africans	1995-2013	10	6	1	2	1
Pakistanis	1993-2007	5	2	3	0	0
Sri Lankans[†]	1997-2012	5	4	1	0	0
Indians[†]	1997-2008	4	3	1	0	0
West Indians	2008-13	2	2	0	0	0
New Zealanders	2000	1	0	0	1	0
Zimbabwe[†]	2002	1	0	0	0	1
Bangladeshis	2011	1	1	0	0	0
England Women	2009	1	1	0	0	0
TOTAL		**143***	**64**	**53**	**15**	**11**

*In total, there were 104 Cricketers of the Year between 1993 and 2013. However, the figure of 143 awards shown in the table reflects the fact that thirty-nine players appeared for two teams during the season in question (35 for counties plus Tests for England, four for counties plus touring teams). Fifteen overseas cricketers were chosen while playing for the following counties: Durham 4, Warwickshire 2, Essex 1, Gloucestershire 1, Kent 1, Leicestershire 1, Middlesex 1, Northamptonshire 1, Surrey 1, Worcestershire 1 and Yorkshire 1

†Sanath Jayasuriya (Sri Lanka, 1997), Andy Flower (Zimbabwe, 2002), V. V. S. Laxman (India, 2002) and Matthew Hayden (Australia, 2003) were chosen for their general impact on the game and did not play in the previous English season

The number of former or current players contributing profiles rose to a new high; they made up 13 of the 65 authors used during this period. Jonathan Agnew, Michael Atherton and Angus Fraser were all former Cricketers of the Year themselves. Other former players included Paul Allott, Ian Bishop, Simon Hughes, Steve James, Vic Marks, Derek Pringle, Mike Selvey and Alec Swann (who profiled his brother Graeme). Mark Nicholas and Robin Martin-Jenkins wrote profiles while still active county players. Christopher Martin-Jenkins, Robin's father and a distinguished commentator, wrote his first profile on Jacques Kallis for the 2013 edition, but died before it appeared.

Tanya Aldred in 2001 was the first woman to write a profile, and Emma John became the second in 2007. Tanya Aldred wrote four profiles in all, the last in 2012, when her husband Andy Wilson also contributed one.

1993 Five Cricketers of the Year

Nigel Briers (Leicestershire)
Martyn Moxon (Yorkshire)
Ian Salisbury (Sussex and England)
Alec Stewart (Surrey and England)
Wasim Akram (Pakistanis)

HEADLINE EVENTS FROM 1992

- County champions – Essex

- NatWest Trophy – Northamptonshire

- Sunday League – Middlesex

- Benson & Hedges Cup – Hampshire

- England are beaten 2-1 by Pakistan

- Pakistan win the World Cup in 1991-92

- England beat New Zealand 2-0 in 1991-92

IN HIS FIRST YEAR AS EDITOR, MATTHEW ENGEL made two orthodox picks in Wasim Akram and Alec Stewart, for their performances in Test cricket, and three left-field choices in Nigel Briers and Martyn Moxon, respectively captains of Leicestershire and Yorkshire, and Ian Salisbury, that rarest of breeds, a young English wrist-spinner.

Wasim and Waqar Younis [1992] were described as the most successful cricketers in the world, whose variety and aggression made them as potent a new-ball partnership as the game had seen. Wasim, the taller of the two, bowled fast left-arm swing, and together they were the difference as Pakistan won their series in England 2–1, Wasim taking 21 wickets in four Tests to Waqar's 22 in five.

The means by which they prodigiously swung the old ball came under suspicion – the umpires changed a ball during a one-day international at Lord's, and England players grumbled about illegal tampering – but in later years, as they continued under greater scrutiny to manipulate the ball with dexterity, "reverse swing" became accepted as fair innovation.

Wasim attended a fee-paying school in Lahore, where he rose fast as an all-rounder. After chancing to bowl in the nets at Javed Miandad [1982], he was fast-tracked into international cricket, and claimed ten wickets in his second Test aged 18. He signed a six-year deal with Lancashire in 1988 and was an instant hit.

Wasim did not entirely fulfil his promise as a batsman, but as a bowler remained durable and potent until his retirement in 2003 as the leading left-armer in history with 414 wickets in Tests and 502 in one-dayers. When Pakistan won the World Cup in 1992, prior to their tour of England, Wasim was Man of the Match in the final. His reputation was stained by the Qayyum Report into match-fixing in Pakistan cricket, which in 2000 barred him from holding the national captaincy.

Stewart proved himself an indispensable member of England's side in 1992. During the Pakistan series he played as specialist opener in three matches and wicketkeeper in two, in one of which he also opened. Against a formidable bowling attack he made most runs at the best average, scoring 190 at Edgbaston and carrying his bat at Lord's.

Stewart, the son of Micky [1958], who was manager during his son's early seasons with

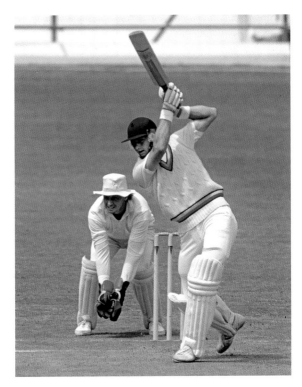

Martyn Moxon bats for England against New Zealand, whose wicketkeeper is Ian Smith

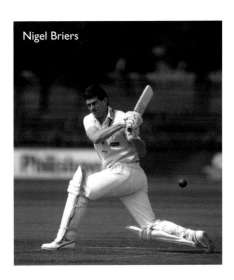

Nigel Briers

Wasim Akram

first game, and he contributed a half-century in his second appearance. Subsequently dropped, he responded with 23 wickets in his last two Championship matches of the season.

Salisbury developed his game for a village side in Northamptonshire, and arrived at Sussex, where he was coached by Norman Gifford [1975], via the Lord's groundstaff. He made his county debut in 1989, and after two seasons was taken on his first England A tour.

Though it had started promisingly, his Test career was to prove a grave disappointment, 15 appearances bringing only 20 wickets at an average of 76.95, but Salisbury long remained a potent force at county level. After leaving Sussex, he helped Surrey win three Championships, and after a short stint at Warwickshire rejoined Surrey in a coaching capacity in 2009.

Engel said Moxon was chosen for his batting – "and for displaying qualities of leadership that enabled Yorkshire to raise their ancient bar on outsiders [playing for the county] with a minimum of fuss".

Yorkshire finished 16th out of 18 in the 1992 Championship, having previously ended 14th and 10th under him as captain, but the club had turned a corner. Moxon took them to eighth in his last season as leader in 1995 and, immediately moving into management after retiring in 1997, he paved the way for the club's first title for 33 years in 2001. He spent six seasons coaching Durham, who also won the Championship soon after he returned to Yorkshire.

Moxon was also a nearly man as player, a technically accomplished opening batsman who learnt at the knee of Geoff Boycott [1964]. He first played for Yorkshire as Boycott's stand-in in 1981, and scored two hundreds in his first three Championship matches – but was afforded only ten Tests in five spells between 1986 and 1989. He would have played for England in 1984 but was thwarted by injury; his top score was 99, and on another occasion rain stymied him on 81

Surrey and England, had been slow to make an impact with either, but the long apprenticeship, and winters of grade cricket in Perth, produced a hardened competitor. Two winning performances against West Indies and Sri Lanka in 1991 earned him his first extended run in the England side.

Stewart was rarely out of England's thoughts again until he was chaired from his home field at The Oval in 2003 after his 133rd and last Test appearance (he remains England's most-capped player). He could have been remembered as one of England's finest openers, but to accommodate the team's need for a wicketkeeper-batsman he played mostly in the middle order. He was later mentor to Matt Prior [2010].

Salisbury had a stunning season in 1992, claiming 87 first-class wickets and becoming the first specialist leg-spin bowler to appear for England in 21 years. His maiden Test victim was Javed Miandad, one of five wickets in his

Wasim Akram:
**"He stands…
as perhaps the
fastest and most
destructive left-arm
bowler the world
has seen"**

Alec Stewart

Alec Stewart:

"Brisk and polished, he became the very model of a modern professional"

Ian Salisbury

not out. Even in 1992, he came close to a recall.

Briers was chosen for the character he showed in reviving a Leicestershire side that had suffered a string of departures and poor results. A trained schoolteacher, he imposed a discipline that brought surprising results: in late July Leicestershire were vying for the Championship (though they fell away to finish eighth) and in September they reached their first final of the NatWest Trophy (formerly Gillette Cup), losing to Northamptonshire. He finished 74th in the first-class batting averages, but in all cricket topped 2,100 runs as an opener.

Briers first played for Leicestershire at 16, and was a regular from 1975, when they won their first Championship. A badly broken arm in 1986 nearly forced his retirement, but the captaincy, which came to him in 1990, proved the making of him. He stepped down in 1995 and was unable to play on because of a knee injury, but his wish to leave behind a good side was granted. Leicestershire won the title again in 1996 and 1998. He later became director of sport at Marlborough College.

CRICKETERS OF THE YEAR 1993 – Performances in the English season 1992

Name	Age*		Matches	Runs	Bat ave	Wickets	Bowl ave	Catches (/st)
NE Briers	38	First-class	24	1372	38.11			12
		List A	26	799	31.96			11
MD Moxon	32	First-class	19	1385	53.26	0		9
		List A	16	372	23.25	4	22.00	7
IDK Salisbury	23	First-class	20	279	14.68	87	28.96	15
		List A	20	77	15.40	24	28.50	11
		Tests	2	66	22.00	5	61.20	0
AJ Stewart	29	First-class	19	1234	42.55	0		22
		List A	25	995	47.38			31/4
		Tests	5	397	56.71			5
		ODI	5	238	47.60			5/2
Wasim Akram	26	First-class	14	299	19.93	82	16.21	5
		List A	5	78	19.50	6	35.66	2
		Tests	4	118	19.66	21	22.00	0

* as at 1/4/1993

1994

Five Cricketers of the Year

David Boon (Australians) *

Ian Healy (Australians) Ⅲ

Merv Hughes (Australians) ●

Shane Warne (Australians) ●

Steve Watkin (Glamorgan and England) ●

HEADLINE EVENTS FROM 1993

- County champions – Middlesex

- NatWest Trophy – Warwickshire

- Axa Equity & Law League – Glamorgan

- Benson & Hedges Cup – Derbyshire

- Australia beat England 4-1

- England lose 3-0 to India and 1-0 to Sri Lanka in 1992-93

AUSTRALIA PROVIDED THE FIRST INSTANCE SINCE 1973 of a touring team providing four Cricketers of the Year. They were among nine players who appeared in all six Tests for a side that won the Ashes 4–1. David Boon scored 555 runs, Ian Healy executed 26 dismissals, while Shane Warne and Merv Hughes both topped 30 wickets. It was a rout.

Boon was Australia's leading batsman, and one of the most dependable No. 3s they ever had. Short in build, luxuriant of moustache, and a run-maker of grit rather than glamour, he was the archetypal Aussie battler and a popular figure, not least with beer producers, who used him to promote their products.

After a poor tour in 1985 and a solid one in 1989, Boon's third visit was a triumph. He struck hundreds in the Second, Third and Fourth Tests, and finished as his side's leading scorer. It was the best series away from home he ever had. His method was simple: concentrate fiercely and wait to put the bad balls away. He was also a fine short leg.

Boon, whose mother represented Australia at hockey and whose father was a respected sports administrator who died three months before the tour, made his debut for Tasmania aged 17 only a year after they entered the Sheffield Shield. He was indebted to Jack Simmons [1985], his first state captain, and named his son after him.

After retiring from international cricket, Boon was an inspirational captain of Durham from 1997 to 1999. He later worked as an Australian selector and ICC match referee.

Warne was not so much a surprise packet as an explosive device which sent tremors through the cricket world. He arrived in England with 11 Test caps, and a couple of decent performances, behind him – but nothing was preparation for his first ball in an Ashes Test. Suggesting one thing as it swerved towards leg, only to do another by fizzing off the pitch to clip the top of off stump, it summed up his genius.

Mike Gatting [1984], the recipient, was dumbstruck – something that became commonplace among England's middle order, several of whom were dropped during the series. Warne bowled 439.5 overs, took 34 wickets (then a record for a visiting spinner in England, though he himself bettered it in 2005), and conceded fewer than two runs per over, thus confounding the idea that wrist-spinners must be expensive.

Warne's bleached blond hair, ear-stud and junk-food diet led many to underestimate him, but a few had seen at close quarters what he could do and pushed his case. He was a leg-spinner without a great googly, but he hardly needed it as he spun the ball hugely, had a terrific flipper, and made the ball swerve through the air. He was also nerveless and, when it came to reading an opponent, very clever.

Australia built their attack around him until 1999, when injuries and scandals started to take a toll – but eager for redemption he kept coming back. When he finally retired in 2007 he was the leading Test wicket-taker in history. He later developed a career as a TV pundit and a competitive poker player, and became engaged to Liz Hurley, the actress and model.

Without Hughes to spearhead the pace attack, even Warne might have struggled. A burly 6ft 4in Victorian who had long tried to play the part of tearaway quick without convincing many, Hughes metamorphosed from support act to leading man when Craig McDermott [1986] was forced out of the tour because of illness.

Hughes led the attack manfully, delivering 296.2 overs and taking crucial wickets on a regular basis. He still approached the crease with mincing steps and a stuttering run, still uttered oaths from beneath a moustache even more extravagant than Boon's, but showed that, while the body might have been errant to the task, the mind was not.

Like Warne, Hughes grew up in the suburbs of Melbourne harbouring a love for cricket and Aussie Rules, only his suburb was less fashionable. He first played for Australia in 1985-86, and became a Test regular three years later. He took 19 Test wickets in England in 1989, and in the fourth match of the 1993 series claimed his 200th Test scalp.

Hughes played only two more Tests before his knees finally packed up. Like Boon he served as a national selector and appeared in commercials – in his case for pizzas and dieting.

David Boon

David Boon:
"His performances… elevated him to the stature of a diminutive but formidable national treasure"

Merv Hughes

An extraordinary bowler such as Warne also needed a great collaborator behind the stumps, and he found one in Healy, who brought a rare dedication and analysis to his work. Australia had been looking for a reliable keeper since Rod Marsh [1982], and in Healy, a surprise pick in 1988-89 after only six first-class appearances, they discovered one.

Healy grew up in Biloela, 600 miles north of Brisbane, where he excelled at several sports and learnt to be self-reliant and competitive. He turned himself into a resourceful batsman, as England discovered at Old Trafford when he recorded a maiden first-class century – the first of his four Test hundreds.

Healy's combativeness may have been one reason why he, like Marsh, never rose to the Australian captaincy. He claimed 27 dismissals on the 1997 tour, which remains the record for a series in England, and retired two years later with 395 to his name in all, then a Test record.

Healy later worked as a TV commentator for Channel Nine. His niece Alyssa Healy kept wicket for the Australian women's team.

Steve Watkin was a key figure in England's consolation victory at The Oval, where his second-innings burst of three wickets set up a first win over Australia in 19 matches. He also led the attack at Glamorgan, who achieved their highest Championship finish (third) in 23 years, and finished as the top first-class wicket-taker in the country.

Watkin, who learned the game in Maesteg, was a wholehearted trier with a superb action and physique that made him ideally suited to English conditions as he seamed the ball from a high release point. He sent down more first-class overs in 1993 than any other fast bowler.

Watkin's first Test appearance, at Headingley in 1991, saw him contribute to England's first home win over West Indies for 22 years, but he was dropped after one more game. He toured the West Indies in 1993-94 without featuring in the Tests, and never represented England again. With Waqar Younis [1992] as new-ball partner, he helped Glamorgan win the title in 1997. He later ran the Welsh Cricket Academy.

Shane Warne:
"Gatting remained rooted at the crease for several seconds – in disbelief rather than dissent – before trudging off to the pavilion like a man betrayed"

A winning double act: **Shane Warne** (left) and **Ian Healy**

Steve Watkin

CRICKETERS OF THE YEAR 1994 – Performances in the English season 1993

Name	Age*		Matches	Runs	Bat ave	Wickets	Bowl ave	Catches (/st)
DC Boon	33	First-class	14	1437	75.63			10
		Tests	6	555	69.37			5
IA Healy	29	First-class	16	499	38.38			42/11
		Tests	6	296	59.20			21/5
MG Hughes	32	First-class	14	299	33.22	48	29.58	3
		Tests	6	76	15.20	31	27.25	0
SK Warne	24	First-class	16	246	22.36	75	22.64	8
		Tests	6	113	37.66	34	25.79	4
SL Watkin	29	First-class	19	204	12.75	92	22.80	7
		List A	21	7	1.75	31	22.74	4
		Tests	1	17	8.50	6	25.33	1

*as at 1/4/1994

1995

Five Cricketers of the Year

Brian Lara (Warwickshire) *

Devon Malcolm (Derbyshire and England) ●

Tim Munton (Warwickshire) ●

Steven Rhodes (Worcestershire and England) ⋔

Kepler Wessels (South Africans) *

HEADLINE EVENTS FROM 1994

- County champions – Warwickshire

- NatWest Trophy – Worcestershire

- Axa Equity & Law League – Warwickshire

- Benson & Hedges Cup – Warwickshire

- England beat New Zealand 1-0 and draw 1-1 with South Africa

- England lose 3-1 in West Indies in 1993-94

BRIAN LARA'S EXTRAORDINARY FEATS IN 1994 made him an automatic pick. Shortly after breaking the world Test record with 375 against England in Antigua, this compact left-hander with an extravagant backlift joined Warwickshire, and reeled off six centuries in seven innings, culminating in a first-class record of 501 not out against Durham.

This amazing run inspired his new team-mates at Edgbaston to rare heights: they won the Championship, Benson and Hedges Cup and Sunday League, as well as finishing runners-up in the NatWest Trophy. Tim Munton led their bowling unfailingly, and ended with 109 wickets in all competitions.

Lara's achievements were a matter of great pride in his native Trinidad, which had not previously produced a batting superstar, but no surprise to those who had known him since early days. The tenth of 11 children, he repaid his family's support with many astonishing performances for school and youth teams. In his second first-class match he scored 92 against Joel Garner [1980] and Malcolm Marshall [1983].

He had to wait for a run in the West Indies side, but showed he was ready to lead the batting with a magnificent 277 at Sydney in 1992-93.

Anything seemed possible after 1994, and in many respects he did not disappoint. He produced plenty more spellbinding performances – setting another new mark in Tests with 400 not out in 2003-04 and retiring in 2007 as the leading Test run-scorer – but with West Indian cricket in inexorable decline he allowed a cult of personality to build around him.

No such thing could have happened with Munton, a selfless, genial and hard-working cricketer who blossomed under the responsibility of leadership when Dermot Reeve [1996] was injured for half the 1994 campaign. Reeve insisted the Championship pennant be presented to Munton.

Aware that Allan Donald [1992] would be unavailable – his absence with the touring South Africans created the opening for Lara – Munton, who stood 6ft 6in, trained for the strike bowler's role rather than that of support act, and his haul of 81 first-class wickets was his best.

Munton first played for Leicestershire's seconds while at school, but there was no opening in their first team, and after three seasons he signed for Warwickshire. In 1989-90 he learnt to swing the ball, and in 1992 played two Tests without making much of a mark. He perhaps lacked the pace to make a big impact at international level.

Munton missed much of the 1995 season recovering from a back operation, and suffered various injury problems before retiring in 2001 after two seasons with Derbyshire.

Kepler Wessels, who led South Africa to victory in their first Test in England since the end of their sporting isolation, scoring a century

Devon Malcolm

himself in the process, was in his own way almost as remarkable a cricketer as Lara. He was not pretty to watch, and rarely smiled, but overcame numerous hurdles to forge a successful international career which ended when he stepped down as captain in November 1994.

Wessels did much to restore South African cricket to a position of respect. He never flinched from a physical challenge, and by scoring 18 with a smashed finger at Sydney in early 1994 in a Test won by five runs set an unarguable example.

Wessels, who excelled at many sports as a youngster including boxing, was the first Afrikaner cricketer to make an impact, and it took time for him to be accepted. He took himself off to Sussex at 18 and played five seasons, scoring heavily in the last two. At 21, he emigrated to Brisbane, and did so well that he played 24 Tests for Australia before being unfairly blamed for recruiting rebels.

He received mixed support on first returning to his native country, but led South Africa to the semi-finals of the 1992 World Cup. After retiring in 2000, he coached with

Kepler Wessels

Kepler Wessels:
"He led them in from the cold, a modest man with a private face and a lion's heart"

CRICKETERS OF THE YEAR 1995 – Performances in the English season 1994

Name	Age*		Matches	Runs	Bat ave	Wickets	Bowl ave	Catches (Ist)
BC Lara	25	First-class	15	2066	89.82	0		11
		List A	22	634	28.81			9
DE Malcolm	32	First-class	18	89	6.84	69	29.20	2
		List A	15	2	1.00	19	29.73	1
		Tests	2	4	4.00	12	18.50	1
TA Munton	29	First-class	18	106	10.60	81	21.58	4
		List A	25	16		28	26.10	5
SJ Rhodes	30	First-class	18	896	56.00			59/8
		List A	22	231	25.66			33/6
		Tests	6	222	55.50			26/2
KC Wessels	37	First-class	12	679	42.43	0		17
		Tests	3	238	39.66			3

as at 1/4/1995

Steven Rhodes

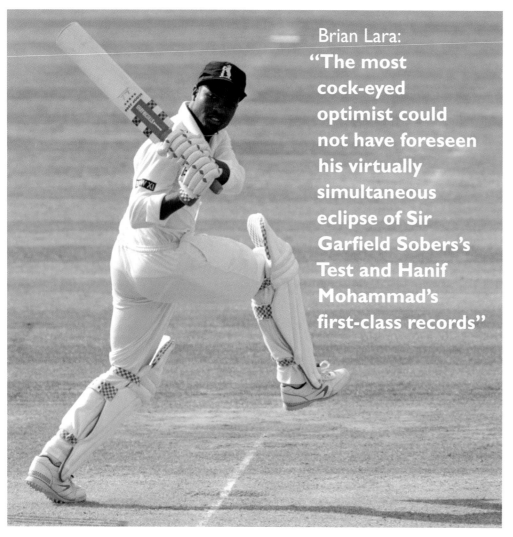

Brian Lara:
"The most cock-eyed optimist could not have foreseen his virtually simultaneous eclipse of Sir Garfield Sobers's Test and Hanif Mohammad's first-class records"

once more and in the second innings swept them aside with figures of nine for 57, then the sixth-best return in Test history.

Malcolm was born in Jamaica, and moved to Sheffield at 16 to join his father, who worked there to support the family. He caused havoc in club cricket, but Yorkshire still only picked people born inside the county borders then, so in 1984 he joined Derbyshire, where Michael Holding [1977] acted as guide. He played his first Test in 1989 and a few months later on his native island starred in England's first Test win over West Indies for 16 years.

Malcolm's fitness and love for the game kept him playing – via three counties – until he was 40 and past 1,000 first-class wickets.

Steve Rhodes, who caught three of Malcolm's nine wickets at The Oval, had an outstanding first season as England wicketkeeper, finishing with 26 catches, two stumpings and a batting average of 55.50. He scored 49 on debut, and batted two hours to save the Lord's Test against New Zealand. Michael Atherton [1991], his captain, saluted him as his player of the year, not only for his practical contributions but his unquenchable spirit.

Like Malcolm, Rhodes (whose father kept wicket for Nottinghamshire in the 1960s) was raised in Yorkshire before moving elsewhere to further his career. He left for Worcestershire in 1984, and shared in the club's most successful period in the late 1980s while earning various representative honours. Worcestershire were the side who denied Warwickshire a clean sweep of domestic trophies in 1994.

At 29 Rhodes might have embarked on a long run in the England side, but he failed badly with the bat on the winter tour of Australia and, shortly after the 1995 *Wisden* appeared, lost his place to Alec Stewart [1993], never to get it back. He remained until 2004 an excellent performer for Worcestershire, whom he later coached.

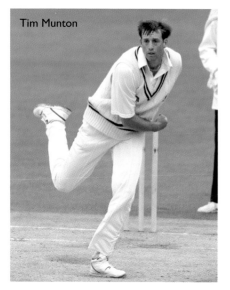

Tim Munton

mixed success at Northamptonshire, for whom his son Riki played.

Even Wessels could not keep Devon Malcolm at bay in the Oval Test. Malcolm was an unlikely hero: he was hopelessly short-sighted, one of the worst No. 11s in the game, and as a fast bowler could be wildly inaccurate. But he had the strength and athleticism to bowl lightning fast and straight, and on this occasion did just that.

Malcolm had been given numerous chances, and it looked like he might never feature again. But the Third and final Test against South Africa was a must-win game, so he was summoned

1996

Five Cricketers of the Year

Dominic Cork (Derbyshire and England) ●
Aravinda de Silva (Kent) /
Angus Fraser (Middlesex and England) ●
Anil Kumble (Northamptonshire) ●
Dermot Reeve (Warwickshire) / ●

HEADLINE EVENTS FROM 1995

- County champions – Warwickshire

- NatWest Trophy – Warwickshire

- Axa Equity & Law League – Kent

- Benson & Hedges Cup – Lancashire

- England and West Indies draw 2-2

- England lose 3-1 to Australia in 1994-95

HAVING LOST 3–1 IN THE CARIBBEAN the previous year – an eighth loss in nine series for the *Wisden* Trophy – England halted the West Indies juggernaut in 1995 with a 2–2 draw. Two players were key – Dominic Cork, an outswing bowler playing his first series, and Angus Fraser, an accurate seamer who had been around the side for six years. Several West Indians had already been chosen, though Ian Bishop, the leading wicket-taker in the series, was overlooked.

Cork's entrance was explosive. His seven for 43 to bowl England to victory at Lord's were the best innings figures by an Englishman on debut. Two months later he seized the first hat-trick by an England bowler in a Test since 1957, in a game in which he also scored an unbeaten half-century. His celebrity was such that he was asked to hand over a cheque for £21 million to the winner of the National Lottery.

Cork, the youngest of three brothers whose father was a decent league fast bowler, played his early cricket for Staffordshire. His talent for swinging the ball and lung-bursting appeals owed something to Ian Botham [1978], his hero, though he credited Kim Barnett [1989] as his mentor. He had been on several England A tours, but clinched Test selection with nine for 43 for Derbyshire against Northamptonshire.

Sadly, he could not meet expectations. In 15 months he had taken 67 Test wickets but his seam-and-swing bowling was really only effective in English conditions. His batting flattered to deceive, though he famously hit the winning runs when West Indies next visited Lord's in 2000.

After an acrimonious split with Derbyshire, he enjoyed some success with Lancashire and Hampshire, whom he led to the Twenty20 title in 2010 at the age of 38.

Fraser was another very English type of bowler, but his virtues translated better overseas. Almost half his 177 Test wickets came abroad, including 54 in the Caribbean where, with his 6ft 5in height, he capitalised on uneven bounce. He and Cork also teamed up at home to South Africa in 1998, when Fraser took 18 wickets in the victories at Nottingham and Leeds.

Fraser lumbered to the crease and delivered the ball without a big leap or long stride, but a strong, high arm action was so well grooved that the ball stuck faithfully to an off-stump line. If conditions were helpful, he was dangerous; if they weren't, he still gave his captain control.

He was central to many of England's finest wins of the period – Jamaica 1990, The Oval 1993, Barbados 1994, Trinidad 1998 – but he was treated cruelly by injuries and, sometimes, the selectors. He was inexplicably left out of the 1994-95 Ashes tour and the First Test in 1995 against West Indies; when he returned, his first-innings five for 66 played its part in another significant victory.

Fraser, who developed his game at Stanmore alongside his brother Alastair, who played occasionally for Middlesex, retired in 2002 to become cricket correspondent of *The Independent* before rejoining Middlesex in a coaching capacity.

Aravinda de Silva's selection was inspired, because around the time the 1996 Almanack appeared he was winning the World Cup final for Sri Lanka with an unbeaten century against Australia.

He was chosen for his one-day batting for Kent, specifically a brilliant 112 off 95 balls (in a losing cause) in the Benson & Hedges Cup final against Lancashire. He also played a big part in Kent winning the Sunday League, but his 1,781 first-class runs were unable to prevent them finishing bottom of the Championship.

As their World Cup triumph showed, Sri Lankan cricket was on the rise, and de Silva used his Man of the Match performance at Lord's to air grievances about Sri Lanka not being given enough Tests in England. When next they visited in 1998, de Silva followed words with action, scoring 152 as Sri Lanka won what remained a one-off Test.

Standing less than 5ft 4in, de Silva was a master on Asian pitches, which yielded 16 of his 20 Test centuries. But, as he showed with Kent, he had the technique to thrive anywhere. He was an avid collector of sports cars.

Anil Kumble and Dermot Reeve were chosen principally for their parts in a tight Championship race between Reeve's Warwickshire, who took the

Angus Fraser

> Angus Fraser:
> **"It is all rather inelegant and unathletic: a man trampling through a nettle-bed pursued by a swarm of bees"**

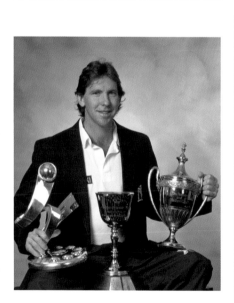
Captain **Dermot Reeve** with the three trophies Warwickshire won in 1994

title, and Northamptonshire, for whom Kumble captured 105 wickets. The counties also contested the NatWest Trophy final, won by Warwickshire as well.

Kumble was a tall, strong Indian who bowled fast, bouncing leg-breaks that did not need to turn much to be troublesome, though on crumbling surfaces in India they were particularly effective. Northamptonshire prepared pitches to suit him, and he took 64 of his wickets at home.

His unusual style was simply too much for many county batsmen, and he became the first spinner to take 100 wickets in an English season since Derek Underwood [1969] in 1983. Not one of his victims was stumped; 20 were leg-before and 21 bowled. He conceded only 2.3 runs per over.

Kumble, who like Bhagwat Chandrasekhar [1972], another fast leg-break bowler, came from Bangalore, worked hard at all aspects of his game. Having made his Test debut in England in 1990 he took his 100th Test wicket in his 21st match in October 1995, but this was barely the start. When he retired in 2008 he had taken 619 wickets in 132 Tests, an Indian record, including all ten in an

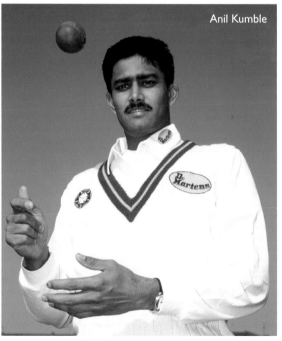
Anil Kumble

innings against Pakistan at Delhi in 1999. He also scored a century at The Oval in 2007.

Reeve was an unorthodox cricketer, and easy to underestimate. He was not an outstanding batsman, swing bowler or fielder, yet was inventive enough to make each part count along with his restless leadership. He was sharp, disciplined and competitive, and knew how to motivate his team while irritating the opposition. There was simply no arguing with the facts: Warwickshire had won six trophies in three seasons under him.

The Man of the Match award he took in the NatWest Trophy final was his third on such an occasion, an unprecedented feat. Born and raised in Hong Kong to English parents, he represented the territory at the 1982 ICC Trophy, and gained entry into the English game via the MCC groundstaff. He left Sussex for Warwickshire in 1987 in search of a club whose ambitions matched his own.

Reeve played three Tests in 1991-92, but was more in demand as a one-day cricketer. He joined Somerset as player-coach in 1997, and retired the following year. A career as TV pundit was derailed after he confessed to cocaine addiction.

Dominic Cork (left) celebrates a wicket for England with Michael Atherton [1991]

Aravinda de Silva

Aravinda de Silva:
"The ball was feathered, not bludgeoned, persuaded, not carved"

CRICKETERS OF THE YEAR 1996 – Performances in the English season 1995

Name	Age*		Matches	Runs	Bat ave	Wickets	Bowl ave	Catches (/st)
DG Cork	24	First-class	18	589	21.81	90	20.00	8
		List A	23	305	19.06	29	27.03	6
		Tests	5	197	28.14	26	25.42	1
PA de Silva	30	First-class	16	1781	59.36	5	128.20	3
		List A	24	722	36.10	15	34.33	7
ARC Fraser	30	First-class	17	95	7.30	56	29.14	2
		List A	23	48	12.00	38	15.92	4
		Tests	5	22	5.50	16	35.18	1
A Kumble	25	First-class	17	321	20.06	105	20.40	11
		List A	19	24	4.00	30	22.83	5
DA Reeve	32	First-class	16	652	36.22	38	17.39	17
		List A	24	347	26.69	33	19.51	9

*as at 1/4/1996

1997

Five Cricketers of the Year

Sanath Jayasuriya (Sri Lanka) *I*
Mushtaq Ahmed (Pakistanis) ●
Saeed Anwar (Pakistanis) *I*
Phil Simmons (Leicestershire) *I* ●
Sachin Tendulkar (Indians) *I*

HEADLINE EVENTS FROM 1996

- County champions – Leicestershire

- NatWest Trophy – Lancashire

- Axa Equity & Law League – Surrey

- Benson & Hedges Cup – Lancashire

- England beat India 1-0 and lose to Pakistan 2-0

- Sri Lanka win the World Cup in 1995-96

- England lose 1-0 in South Africa in 1995-96

FOR THE FIRST TIME SINCE 1982, THERE WERE NO English-qualified players among the Five. The inclusion of four Asians reflected the way the game's axis had shifted towards the subcontinent. That three of them were openers who gave their sides explosive starts in one-day cricket was a sign of what that shift meant in practical terms.

Other batsmen were looking to take advantage of flat pitches and fielding restrictions in the first 15 overs, but at the 1996 World Cup Sanath Jayasuriya did it most destructively. Also an effective left-arm spinner, he ended as player of the tournament, and editor Matthew Engel felt compelled to name him among his Five even though he did not take part in the 1996 English season, which started exactly a month after the final.

At this point, Jayasuriya had scored only three hundreds in one-day internationals, but by the time he retired in 2011 he had 28 to his name, all from the top of the order. By April 2013, he was one of only four players to have scored 20 ODI hundreds while opening, the others being Sachin Tendulkar (45), Chris Gayle and Saeed Anwar (both 20).

To widespread astonishment at the World Cup, Jayasuriya repeatedly took three steps down the pitch and carved the ball over cover. His 82 off 44 balls that despatched England at the quarter-final stage was just one example of his audacity. "Pinch hitting" was truly born.

Most Sri Lankan cricketers emerged from Colombo colleges. Jayasuriya came from Matara, a southern fishing village, with no obvious links to the sport, and emerged while civil unrest on the island left cricket struggling for cohesion. He recorded a maiden Test fifty at Lord's in 1991, but his five-day career was initially modest.

Shortly after the World Cup, he scored – against Pakistan in Singapore – a century off 48 balls and a fifty off 17, both then ODI records. No surprise there. What was a surprise was an innings of 340 in a Test against India in August 1997, and a blistering double-century against England in 1998. He had blossomed into a serious player.

Tendulkar might have been picked by *Wisden* after his first tour of England in 1990 when, at just 17, he scored a maiden century to save the Old Trafford Test and began to fulfil the rich predictions made for the young prodigy from Bombay.

Having spent a season with Yorkshire in 1992 as their first-ever overseas player, he returned to England in 1996 a seasoned campaigner and master craftsman. In the interim he had scored two stunning centuries on a tour of Australia, and another one in South Africa. Now he added two more polished jewels to his crown: 122 out of 219 at Edgbaston and 177 at Trent Bridge. He was 23 years of age and possessed the technique, confidence and vision of a batting genius.

Tendulkar was more of a focused technician than Jayasuriya but, since promotion to open India's one-day batting in 1994, he too had become adept at kick-starting an innings. It was a role that helped make him the most prolific run-scorer in ODI history (a record he also claimed, more predictably, in Tests) as well as the first batsman to score 100 international centuries.

Tendulkar was appointed India's captain shortly after the England tour, but it was a short-lived reign. He was happiest in the ranks, churning out runs to the delight of the millions of Indians who worshipped him as a god, a task he fulfilled with modesty.

Anwar, like Jayasuriya a left-hander, first made his name as a one-day player, but it was clear during Pakistan's 1996 tour of England that he was actually a batsman of real substance.

His innings of 176 in the Oval Test was perhaps the most beautiful of the summer, and an impressive response to England's tactics, which had worked in the previous Test at Leeds, of attacking him outside off stump. He square-drove the bowlers to distraction. He also made 74 and 88 in the Lord's Test, as well as scoring heavily in the one-day internationals and other matches on the tour.

Anwar remained a Test regular until 2001, when he withdrew from the game following the death of his daughter, but it was his 50-over batting for which he was best remembered. A month after the 1997 Almanack appeared he set a new mark for one-day internationals with

Sanath Jayasuriya

Sanath Jayasuriya:
"His World Cup exploits promised that the course of the game would change forever"

Phil Simmons

194 against India, a score not bettered until Tendulkar passed it with 200 in 2010.

Mushtaq Ahmed was a more conventional leg-spinner than Shane Warne [1994] or Anil Kumble [1996], trying to wear down batsmen with indecipherable googlies. He spun Pakistan to two victories over England on the final afternoon – with spells of five for 11 at Lord's and six for 67 (in 30 overs unchanged) at The Oval. A few months earlier he had taken 18 wickets in two Tests in Australia, followed by ten in Christchurch.

He had modelled himself on Abdul Qadir, and made his Test debut as Qadir's replacement in Australia in 1989-90. He played a starring role in Pakistan's 1992 World Cup win, before honing his game with three seasons at Somerset, during which he took 217 wickets. Only after consulting Warne did he show more patience. He had always been tireless.

Mushtaq Ahmed

Sachin Tendulkar

Saeed Anwar

captaining Pakistan, but in 2008 joined England as spin-bowling coach.

Phil Simmons was the cornerstone of Leicestershire's 1996 Championship triumph. He had played for them before, but this was his first full season; he had built his upper-body strength and was armed to bludgeon the ball and propel it at serious speed. The results were exceptional: in all competitions he amassed more than 2,100 runs, 70 wickets and 45 catches, mainly at slip.

At the business end of the campaign he contributed a burst of six for 14 at Durham and an innings of 142 against Middlesex.

Simmons was raised in Arima, Trinidad, near the home of Larry Gomes [1985], and was coached by Rohan Kanhai [1964]. His first England tour in 1988 nearly ended in tragedy; he was hit on the head by David Lawrence, his heart stopped, and he needed emergency brain surgery. His second in 1991 was a grave disappointment. Unable to cement a Test place, he turned to county cricket as an alternative career.

After missing the 1997 season he returned to Grace Road in 1998, but made less impact. He later coached Zimbabwe and Ireland, and his nephew Lendl Simmons also played for West Indies.

Mushtaq played the last of 52 Tests in 2003, the same year he helped Sussex to their first Championship title with 103 wickets; when they won again in 2006 and 2007 he took 100 and 90. He was barred by the Qayyum Report from

CRICKETERS OF THE YEAR 1997 – Performances in the English season 1996

Name	Age*		Matches	Runs	Bat ave	Wickets	Bowl ave	Catches (/st)
ST Jayasuriya	27	Did not play in England in 1996						
Mushtaq Ahmed	26	First-class	7	118	14.75	41	21.00	4
		Tests	3	44	11.00	17	26.29	3
Saeed Anwar	28	First-class	10	1224	68.00			6
		Tests	3	362	60.33			2
		ODI	3	151	50.33			0
PV Simmons	33	First-class	17	1244	56.54	56	18.23	35
		List A	20	939	49.42	17	35.11	10
SR Tendulkar	23	First-class	7	707	64.27	1	109.00	5
		Tests	3	428	85.60	0		2

* as at 1/4/1997

Saeed Anwar:
"His wrists hovered, hawk-like, over the advancing ball, extending further and further as if they were elastic"

1998

Five Cricketers of the Year

Matthew Elliott (Australians)
Stuart Law (Essex)
Glenn McGrath (Australians)
Matthew Maynard (Glamorgan)
Graham Thorpe (Surrey and England)

HEADLINE EVENTS FROM 1997

- County champions – Glamorgan

- NatWest Trophy – Essex

- Axa Life League – Warwickshire

- Benson & Hedges Cup – Surrey

- England lose 3-2 to Australia

- England draw 0-0 in Zimbabwe and win 2-0 in New Zealand in 1996-97

AUSTRALIA'S DOMINANCE OVER ENGLAND continued in 1997, the 3–2 scoreline doing scant justice to their superiority. They had the best fast bowler in Glenn McGrath, while Matthew Elliott was easily the leading run-scorer. They did not even have room in the side for Stuart Law, who instead spent the summer scoring more than 2,500 runs for Essex.

McGrath was a bush cricketer of the type Australians like to celebrate. He came from Dubbo, a wheat and sheep farming centre 200 miles north-west of Sydney, and did not move to the city, where he initially lived in a caravan, to pursue his sport until he was 19.

It turned out he was built for the job: the mechanics of bowling fast and straight took little out of his body, and in a career spanning 14 years McGrath was rarely injured and barely changed. He stuck the ball in the same place and asked the same questions: the result was 563 Test wickets, more than any fast bowler in history, at an average of just 21.64, plus 381 more in one-day internationals. Along with Ricky Ponting [2006] he played in four consecutive World Cup finals, winning three of them.

The wickets came in clutches after the 1994-95 Ashes, and before arriving in England in 1997 he had taken 26 in five Tests against West Indies. He misjudged the conditions at Edgbaston, but bounced back with eight for 38 as England were skittled for 77 at Lord's. He was integral to Australia's wins in the Third and Fifth Tests, and took seven for 76 in a losing cause at The Oval.

McGrath was a more dignified figure than his habitual sledging of opponents suggested. He married an English girl, Jane Steele, in 1999 and, after she died of cancer in 2008, shortly after he retired, he devoted much time to the Jane McGrath Foundation.

Elliott, a tall left-handed opener from Victoria, corresponded to another popular Australian type, the fierce battler who shrugged off problems for the greater good. He broke into the side the previous home season only to be injured in his second match in a mid-pitch collision with his batting partner. Sidelined for several weeks, he returned in South Africa and made runs in belligerent fashion.

Before leaving for England he suffered knee trouble, and played through the Ashes unsure if his body would withstand the demand. He scored

Stuart Law

Glenn McGrath

Stuart Law:

"An unashamed sledger, he was as energetic and rasping with his tongue as he was with his strokes"

In fact Elliott's temperament was less solid than it looked, and within months he lost his place after struggling against South Africa. Two subsequent recalls were short-lived, the second coming in 2004 during a flying visit home from England for the birth of his son. Elliott assisted Glamorgan for four seasons, but was most successful at Yorkshire in 2002, when his unbeaten 128 won the C&G Trophy final against Somerset.

Elliott may have been someone Law had most in mind when he reacted to his omission from Australia's tour party by saying he had consistently outplayed the Australian batsmen and England bowlers who would feature in the Ashes.

His response confirmed an estrangement from the Australian selectors, who picked him for the one-day side until early 1999 but never asked him to add to the one Test cap he earned as stand-in against Sri Lanka in 1995-96 (when he scored 54 not out).

Law was a plain speaker, uncompromising competitor, and entertaining batsman in all formats. The son of a Brisbane grade cricketer, he struck 179 in his second match for

112 at Lord's and 199 at Leeds, an innings that effectively resolved the series; that he survived let-offs both times only accentuated the resolve.

CRICKETERS OF THE YEAR 1998 – Performances in the English season 1997

Name	Age*		Matches	Runs	Bat ave	Wickets	Bowl ave	Catches (/st)
MTG Elliott	26	First-class	12	1091	57.42	0		7
		Tests	6	556	55.60			4
SG Law	29	First-class	17	1482	57.00	5	71.20	19
		List A	25	1088	45.33	13	41.23	14
GD McGrath	28	First-class	11	25	6.25	49	20.65	4
		Tests	6	25	12.50	36	19.47	2
MP Maynard	32	First-class	18	1170	65.00	0		21
		List A	20	691	40.64	0		14
GP Thorpe	28	First-class	14	1160	61.05	0		17
		List A	19	679	45.26			15
		Tests	6	453	50.33			8
		ODI	3	127	127.00			3

* as at 1/4/1998

Queensland, a state he led to their first Sheffield Shield titles in 1994-95 and 1996-97.

Unwanted by his country, he rejoined Essex for a second season, and churned out runs with pointed insistence. The highlight was an unbeaten 80 to win the NatWest Trophy final. He spent six seasons at Essex followed by seven at Lancashire, and served both richly. He scored exactly 100 hundreds in all competitive cricket. Ironically Australia later employed him as a coach.

Graham Thorpe was easily England's best batsman in the Ashes. He scored most runs, and averaged 50.33 when no other player topped 40. His left-handedness and quick feet helped him deal with Shane Warne [1994] as well as anyone had.

Having found centuries hard to come by since making an unbeaten 114 on debut during Australia's previous tour, he reeled off three in four matches, two in New Zealand followed by 138 in the First Test against Australia, when a stand of 288 with Nasser Hussain [2003] set up a big England win.

Thorpe, whose performances in the Surrey Championship earned him an invitation to The Oval at 16, was the most accomplished English batsman of his generation. He was fast-tracked into the A team at 20, and once he'd got into the full England side was rarely left out again.

Back problems restricted his appearances in 1998-99, and the collapse of his marriage – triggered by newspaper allegations stemming from the New Zealand tour of 1997 – led him to drop out of the England side for a year, but he made a glorious return in 2003. After retiring in 2005 he became a highly regarded batting coach, joining England's one-day side in 2013.

Matthew Maynard led Glamorgan to their third Championship title in 1997. It was an unlikely story, because his career had been a tale of talent wasted, but captaincy brought out his best. With the title on the line he played two major innings: an unbeaten 75 against Essex and a breathtaking 142 at Somerset.

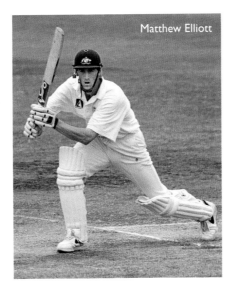
Matthew Elliott

Matthew Maynard

Matthew Maynard:
"No one in the modern game... has converted so much talent into so few England caps"

Maynard grew up on Anglesey, where his father ran a pub. It was remote cricket territory, and he tried his luck at Kent before getting a chance with Glamorgan. Given a late-season debut in 1985, he blazed one of the more remarkable maiden hundreds, 102 in 87 minutes against Yorkshire, going to his hundred with three sixes. Maintaining form, he was given a Test debut in 1988 at 22, failed twice and was dropped.

With England seemingly uninterested, and a young family to consider, he joined a rebel tour in 1989-90 and was banned until 1993. England gave him three more Tests, but he failed to take advantage.

Five years as Glamorgan captain from 1996 was only the start of an unexpected career in management; he later worked as England's assistant coach and Glamorgan's head coach. His son Tom played for Glamorgan and Surrey before his tragic death in an accident on a railway line in 2012.

Graham Thorpe

1999

Five Cricketers of the Year

Ian Austin (Lancashire and England) ●
Darren Gough (Yorkshire and England) ●
Muttiah Muralitharan (Sri Lankans) ●
Arjuna Ranatunga (Sri Lankans) /
Jonty Rhodes (South Africans) /

HEADLINE EVENTS FROM 1998

- County champions – Leicestershire

- NatWest Trophy – Lancashire

- Axa League – Lancashire

- Benson & Hedges Cup – Essex

- England beat South Africa 2-1

- Sri Lanka win their first Test in England in a one-off match at the Oval

- England lose 3-1 in West Indies in 1997-98

THE FIRST TEST WIN ON ENGLISH SOIL OF EVERY visiting team bar Australia, who pre-dated the award, had been marked by at least one player being named among *Wisden*'s Five, and following their sensational trouncing of England at The Oval in 1998 Sri Lanka were accorded two.

Arjuna Ranatunga, the captain, was chosen as much for his leadership, in its broadest sense, as his batting. He had guided a team finding their way in the cricketing world to somewhere near the top. They won the World Cup in 1996, and six other one-day tournaments in three years, and were now winning as many Tests as they were losing.

Ranatunga was raised and educated in Colombo, but showed faith in those like Sanath Jayasuriya [1997] and Muttiah Muralitharan who came from elsewhere. He scored 51 at The Oval, and made a fifty in the triangular one-day series with England and South Africa which Sri Lanka also won, but that wasn't why he was picked.

Ranatunga, three of whose brothers also played internationally, had appeared in all but five of his country's 87 Tests since their first in 1981-82, and had captained most of their matches since 1989. He instilled the belief that

they could beat anyone. That he was tubby and often walked his singles only reinforced his defiance of the established order. It was no surprise that after retiring in 2000 he went into cricket administration and politics.

Murali, one of four sons of a biscuit-maker from Kandy, was Ranatunga's main weapon. Ranatunga raised eyebrows by putting England in on a good pitch, but he needed Murali to rest between bowling them out twice. Murali duly took seven wickets in the first innings and – after Sri Lanka amassed 591 – nine in the second.

A key ingredient in Murali's success was that he rarely tired. He bowled 113.5 overs at The Oval, but routinely got through 60 or 70 overs per match in a career spanning 18 years, 133 Tests and a record 800 wickets.

His methods were unusual and controversial, and the England camp's mutterings about the legitimacy of his action were not the first. He was no-balled for throwing by a local umpire in Australia in 1995-96, and when he returned there in 1998-99 he was no-balled again, prompting Ranatunga to lead his team from the field.

Murali, shaken by all questioning of his integrity, was subjected to many tests to demonstrate that his bowling arm naturally had a kink in it; his wrist was also unusually flexible. At this point he was essentially an off-spinner, but in 2003 developed a "doosra" that made him even harder to keep out, let alone score off. He became a much-prized asset in the Twenty20 game.

The exoticism of Sri Lanka's cricket left their English opponents looking colourless, with the glorious exception of the effervescent Darren Gough. The son of a Barnsley pest-control officer, Gough burst on to the Test scene in 1994 with an eye-catching all-round performance against New Zealand (65 runs, four wickets) that he trumped the following winter at Sydney (51 runs, six wickets), but the intervening period had been one of disappointments and injury frustrations.

He broke a finger and was slow to get into the South Africa series in 1998, but played a full part in England's unexpected fightback at Trent Bridge and Headingley, where with the match on the line he took six for 42. In Australia in 1998-99 he was at the heart of England's

Darren Gough

Darren Gough:

"He was young, good-looking, an authentic Yorkshireman with that air of sleeves-up defiance which the nation adores"

Jonty Rhodes

CRICKETERS OF THE YEAR 1999 – Performances in the English season 1998

Name	Age*		Matches	Runs	Bat ave	Wickets	Bowl ave	Catches (/st)
ID Austin	32	First-class	13	304	23.38	36	27.16	7
		List A	28	134	11.16	39	18.87	3
		ODI	3	29	14.50	3	42.00	0
D Gough	28	First-class	11	269	19.21	42	25.40	1
		List A	19	112	11.20	42	16.45	4
		Tests	5	62	8.85	19	25.78	0
		ODI	6	18	6.00	13	21.07	0
M Muralitharan	26	Tests	1	30	30.00	16	13.75	1
		ODI	3	22	11.00	6	19.66	1
A Ranatunga	35	Tests	1	51	51.00			0
		ODI	3	92	30.66			1
JN Rhodes	29	First-class	11	562	43.23			4
		Tests	5	367	52.42			1
		ODI	5	155	38.75			5

as at 1/4/1999

Muttiah Muralitharan

Arjuna Ranatunga

Ian Austin

dramatic victory at Melbourne, and followed up with a hat-trick at Sydney.

Gough was short for a fast bowler, but bulldog strong and quick, and in the later years of his England career was a highly skilled operator, never more so than during back-to-back series wins in Pakistan and Sri Lanka in 2000-01. He was the first England bowler to top 200 wickets in both Tests and one-day internationals. He gained wider celebrity by winning *Strictly Come Dancing* in 2005.

Jonty Rhodes almost stole victory from under Gough's nose at Headingley, where his pugnacious 85, begun amid the ruins of 12 for four chasing 219, was typical of his fighting spirit. That innings capped an outstanding series which re-established him as a Test player; it was Rhodes's century that laid the platform for South Africa's win at Lord's.

Rhodes's credentials as a Test batsman were often questioned, but no one doubted his worth

**Ian Austin:
"His success confounded a few people. Cricketers are not supposed to look like Ian Austin any more"**

in one-day cricket. He scored fast and was, quite simply, the best outfielder in the world. A highlight of the summer was a leaping catch at short cover to dismiss Robert Croft. He was Man of the Series in the Texaco Trophy.

Rhodes, who came from a sporting, god-fearing family from Pietermaritzburg, was taught the value of fielding by his father, and he attracted global attention for a diving run-out of Inzamam-ul-Haq at the 1992 World Cup. His speed also helped to earn him South African caps at hockey.

He retired from Tests in 2001 to prolong his one-day career, but a farewell at the 2003 World Cup was spoiled by a broken hand. He later worked as a fielding coach.

Ian Austin bowled a great spell to win the NatWest Trophy final for Lancashire, seaming and swinging his way to figures of 10–5–14–3 to trigger a Derbyshire collapse from 70 for no wicket to 108 all out. The next day Lancashire clinched the Sunday League. By taking the NatWest match award Austin completed a rare double, having also won it in one of Lancashire's three Benson & Hedges Cup victories during his time.

In his Editor's Notes, Matthew Engel justified Austin's selection: "Nowadays it is a rarity for someone to come along and establish a special rapport with his home crowd. Ian Austin is an exception… There ought to be dozens like him, but there aren't. That is why he is a Cricketer of the Year."

Austin, from Haslingden, was popular not least because he looked as though he had just stepped off the village green. His waistline may have been old-fashioned – like Ranatunga's – but his bowling possessed all the modern tricks, and Wasim Akram [1993] described him as the best death bowler he'd seen. A big-hitting left-hander, he once took a hundred off Yorkshire in 61 balls.

Austin played nine one-day internationals in 1998 and 1999, but was unable to replicate his county form. He finished with Lancashire in 2002 before returning to the leagues.

2000 Five Cricketers of the Year

Chris Cairns (New Zealanders) / ●
Rahul Dravid (Indians) /
Lance Klusener (South Africans) / ●
Tom Moody (Worcestershire and Australians) / ●
Saqlain Mushtaq (Surrey and Pakistanis) ●

HEADLINE EVENTS FROM 1999

- County champions – Surrey

- NatWest Trophy – Gloucestershire

- CGU National League – Lancashire

- Benson & Hedges Cup – Gloucestershire

- Australia win the World Cup

- England lose 2-1 to New Zealand

- England lose 3-1 in Australia in 1998-99

For the first time, the award took account of a player's impact on cricket worldwide rather than purely on the preceding English season. In fact, because the World Cup was staged in England in 1999, the chosen Five – for the only time representing five different nationalities – had all appeared during the English season. The England team performed so poorly at the World Cup and in four Tests against New Zealand that few of them merited consideration.

Even though India failed to go far in the tournament, Rahul Dravid finished as the World Cup's leading run-scorer, cementing a reputation as someone who knew how to score on alien pitches. Earlier in the year, he had made 190 and 103 not out in a Test at Hamilton, and his maiden Test century had come at Johannesburg in 1996-97.

Dravid was sufficiently undemonstrative in personality and batting style to be easily underestimated, but it was becoming clear that he was a very special talent. He had played his first Tests for India in England in 1996 when, batting at No. 7, he crafted innings of 95 at Lord's on debut and 84 at Trent Bridge. He had since moved up to No. 3, a position with which he became synonymous: when he retired in 2012, he had scored more than 10,000 Test runs from there.

Dravid, who graduated from Bangalore University while developing his batting with Karnataka, signed for Kent in 2000, when he gave a masterclass at Portsmouth in how to deal with Shane Warne [1994]. A year, later at Kolkata, he played one of his most famous innings against Warne to help win a Test after India followed on.

Tom Moody was central to Australia winning the 1999 World Cup. As an all-rounder, he gave the side a balance it badly needed and his presence was appreciated in several tight finishes. He scored only 117 runs, but made them fast, and took seven wickets. It was an implausible story: he was 33 years old, had suffered injuries and was only belatedly added to the squad.

Moody had also been a young member of Australia's 1987 World Cup-winning squad. Soon after that he was given a run in the Test side, and fared reasonably well until he came unstuck in the role of opener. He then concentrated on careers with Western Australia and Worcestershire, both of whom he captained and helped to trophies.

Tom Moody:

"He is one of the courtly Australians with beautiful manners: not merely a practitioner of the game but an ambassador for it"

Tom Moody (right) with Shane Warne [1994]

Chris Cairns

Moody stood 6ft 6in, struck the ball cleanly and bowled useful medium-pace swing, but was above all a natural leader. He did not play much beyond the 1999 season before becoming a successful coach at state and county level, later guiding Sri Lanka to the World Cup final in 2007.

The man who came closest to denying Australia the World Cup was South Africa's all-rounder Lance Klusener. He took 17 wickets in the tournament, but it was his left-handed hitting that created a sensation. Batting late in the innings, he cleared his front leg and swung the ball through the leg side time after time.

He won three matches with innings struck at better than a run a ball, and an unbeaten 31 off 16 deliveries failed by only one to win a semi-final with Australia, Klusener's last shot creating a mix-up with Allan Donald [1992], who was

run out. The match was tied, and Australia went through, having finished higher in an earlier group stage.

Such precise hitting under pressure has rarely been bettered: overall in the tournament, Klusener scored 281 runs off 230 balls, and was out only twice.

Klusener, raised on his family's sugar-cane farm near Durban, had the build of a man who spent three years in the army. He was mentored at Natal by Malcolm Marshall [1983], and a rich Test career beckoned when, in his first five matches, he completed a century off 102 balls and took an eight-for, but he struggled for consistency. He scored 174 against England in December 1999, but was effectively cut adrift from Tests after 2001. He later had spells at three counties.

Chris Cairns enjoyed a more substantial career as Test all-rounder; indeed in 1999 he was arguably the world's best. He began the year by taking a Test century off India at Hamilton, and returned to the ground in December to score 72 and take seven for 27 against West Indies (and 10 for 100 in the match).

At the World Cup, he scored 60 in a victory over Australia, but his best efforts came in the Tests in England. Cairns was to the fore in the wins at Lord's and The Oval, taking wickets and turning the Oval match with an explosive 80 from 94 balls after New Zealand had collapsed to 39 for six.

Life was rarely so uncomplicated. He was the son of Lance Cairns, another New Zealand all-rounder and a folk hero of the early '80s. However, Chris's careers with New Zealand and Nottinghamshire were frequently interrupted by injury. In 1993, his sister Louise was killed in a train crash. He retired from Tests as the sixth player to pass 3,000 runs and 200 wickets. In 2012 he won a libel suit against former IPL chairman Lalit Modi over allegations relating to his stint in the Indian Cricket League.

Saqlain Mushtaq was a genuine innovator,

the pioneer of the off-spinner's "doosra". He developed the skill while playing street cricket with his brothers in Lahore with a taped tennis ball. After playing organised cricket at college he rose fast, and by the age of 18 was taking wickets for Pakistan. A highly aggressive bowler for a spinner, he proved consistently successful and became the fastest to reach 100 wickets in one-day internationals.

He enjoyed diverse triumphs in 1999. He took two match ten-fors in Pakistan's first Test meetings with India for ten years, winning a nailbiter at Chennai by snapping up three of the last four wickets when India had been within 17 of victory. He helped Pakistan to reach the World Cup final – though defeat reduced him to tears – and Surrey to win their first Championship since 1971. In seven Championship matches, Saqlain took 58 wickets at just 11.37 apiece.

Before the summer was out, though, his knees were playing up, a problem that eventually cut short his international career before he was 30, though he played in two more Surrey Championship-winning sides.

Saqlain Mushtaq

Rahul Dravid

Rahul Dravid:
"[He] has the time… to graduate into the very highest company, and to do it with an understated, old-fashioned grace"

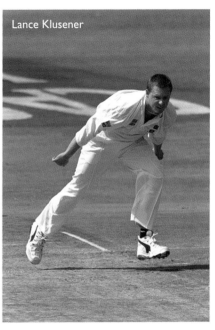

Lance Klusener

CRICKETERS OF THE YEAR 2000 – Performances in the English season 1999

Name	Age*		Matches	Runs	Bat ave	Wickets	Bowl ave	Catches (/st)
CL Cairns	29	Tests	4	183	30.50	19	21.26	0
		ODI	9	182	36.40	12	27.75	2
RS Dravid	27	ODI	8	461	65.85			2
L Klusener	28	ODI	8	281	140.50	12	27.41	0
TM Moody	34	First-class	5	286	35.75	6	44.50	5
		List A	14	317	45.28	11	34.27	2
		ODI	7	117	117.00	7	31.42	2
Saqlain Mushtaq	23	First-class	7	46	15.33	58	11.37	1
		List A	18	53	10.60	37	15.81	4
		ODI	10	40	13.33	17	22.29	3

*as at 1/4/2000

2001

Five Cricketers of the Year

Mark Alleyne (Gloucestershire) / ●
Martin Bicknell (Surrey) ●
Andrew Caddick (Somerset and England) ●
Justin Langer (Middlesex) /
Darren Lehmann (Yorkshire) /

HEADLINE EVENTS FROM 2000

- County champions – Surrey

- NatWest Trophy – Gloucestershire

- Norwich Union National League – Gloucestershire

- Benson & Hedges Cup – Gloucestershire

- England beat Zimbabwe 1-0 and West Indies 3-1 to regain the Wisden Trophy for the first time since 1973

- England lose 2-1 in South Africa in 1999-2000

COUNTY CRICKETERS WERE UNUSUALLY WELL represented. Mark Alleyne led Gloucestershire to an unprecedented clean sweep of the three one-day prizes. Martin Bicknell assisted in Surrey's defence of their Championship title. Justin Langer and Darren Lehmann, two Australian batsmen of contrasting character, were influential figures at their respective clubs.

The exception was Andrew Caddick, whose selection was due to a terrific return to the England side after a wilderness period in which his ability and semi-detached demeanour (he was actually just shy) were questioned.

Caddick had come back with 20 wickets against New Zealand in 1999. He had then bowled with devastating effect in South Africa and at home to West Indies, whose two most serious collapses were triggered by Caddick at his hottest: he took five for 16 at Lord's and five for 14 at Headingley, four of them in one extraordinary over. He had never been this reliable during earlier spells in the team.

There was no doubting his natural gifts: he was tall, generated good bounce, and when the wickets started to come he could be relentless.

Having grown up in New Zealand (to English parents) he was sometimes likened to Richard Hadlee [1982] – a stretch version of the limousine of fast bowlers. Caddick moved to England because he felt under-valued, and joining Somerset certainly did him good. One injury-affected season apart, he had averaged 75 wickets every year since. When he took 105 in 1998, though, it failed to convince the sceptics and he was omitted from an Ashes tour.

Caddick played his last Test in 2003 – delivering victory with ten wickets at Sydney – but carried on at Somerset until his 41st year. Of his 1,180 first-class wickets, 234 came in Tests.

Gloucestershire's many one-day triumphs – they had also won both knockout cups in 1999 – were a tribute to their spirit under Alleyne. While Jack Russell [1990] intimidated from behind the stumps, Alleyne brought calmness, tolerance and paternalism – and made the one-per-cents count.

He was not an insignificant player. He scored 112 off 91 balls in the Benson & Hedges Cup final in 1999. He bowled canny seamers, and seemed elasticated in the field. He had scored his first county hundred at 18, and between 1993 and 1999 topped 6,000 runs and 200 wickets in

Darren Lehmann (left) with his Australian team-mate **Justin Langer**

Mark Alleyne

the Championship. He won ten one-day caps in 1999 and 2000.

But leadership transformed him when he took over as Gloucestershire captain from Courtney Walsh [1987], becoming the first Briton of Afro-Caribbean stock regularly to lead a first-class county. Born in England, Alleyne was raised until 15 in Barbados before returning to London and entering the Haringey Cricket College. After retiring in 2005, he became head coach at MCC.

Martin Bicknell might have enjoyed a similar England career to Caddick, but was out of favour for much longer. He too topped 1,000 first-class wickets, a classic English bowler who swung the ball away and nipped it back, but perhaps rose too fast for his own good.

He played for Surrey at 17 and was taken as a reserve on the 1990-91 Ashes tour at 21. When he played two Tests at 23 and did little he was jettisoned, but between regular injuries maintained exemplary standards for his county, routinely exceeding 50 wickets. Some thought him short on speed, but he kept getting people out.

In 2000 he had a terrific season, taking 60 Championship wickets – 16 of them against Leicestershire at Guildford – as well as weighing in with 500 runs.

Bicknell, whose brother Darren also had a long county career as a batsman, must rate among the best bowlers never given a regular run by England – and when, in 2003, he was recalled after a ten-year break, and bowled his country to victory on his home ground at The Oval, it seemed to confirm the error of the selectors' ways. He retired to take up a post at Charterhouse school.

Lehmann, an attacking left-hander of the highest class, had enjoyed a phenomenal 12 months: he scored 1,142 runs in ten matches for South Australia, then topped the chart in England in 2000 with 1,477 to carry Yorkshire to third in the Championship, equalling their highest finish since 1975. A Championship hundred off 89 balls against Kent was the season's fastest.

Lehmann was another Australian who could have played many more Tests than he did. Like Bicknell, his precocity did him few favours. He made his state debut at 17, and became the youngest Australian to score 1,000 runs in a season, but by 2000 had appeared in only five Tests and, at 30, must have feared his chance had gone.

In fact, he was recalled in 2002 and played regularly for two years, during which he scored five Test hundreds, while continuing to be an important member of Australia's one-day side.

Lehmann possibly gained most satisfaction from helping Yorkshire, in 2001, win their first Championship for 33 years. He played for them until 2006, when he signed off with 339 against Durham. He had married the sister of team-mate Craig White at Christmas 1999.

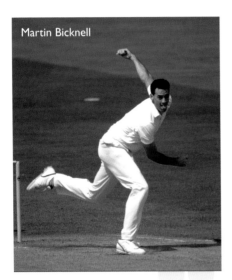

Martin Bicknell

Martin Bicknell:

"A classic English new-ball bowler: all short run, high arms and high knees, a natural outswinger with the knack of cutting the ball back into the right-hander"

Justin Langer, also a left-hander, whose uncle Robbie played in World Series Cricket, was 27 before he nailed down a place in the Australian side in 1998-99. He too had had a big 12 months, scoring more than 1,800 first-class runs during the winter in Australia, New Zealand and Zimbabwe, when four of his eight hundreds came in Tests.

He then rejoined Middlesex for a third season, in which his aggregate of 1,472 fell just short of Lehmann's. Middlesex, though, finished only one place off bottom of the second division.

Only on the Ashes tour of 2001 did Langer move up from No. 3 to form with Matthew Hayden [2003] a famously imposing alliance that lasted until Langer's Test retirement in 2006-07. Their complementary styles served both well: Langer was shorter and, brought up on pitches in Perth, stronger square of the wicket.

Langer bowed out with four seasons at Somerset alongside Caddick, the last three as captain, scoring a county-record 342 against Surrey in 2007. His 86 first-class hundreds put him second among Australians, behind Bradman [1931] and just ahead of Lehmann's 82. Both Langer and Lehmann went into coaching.

Andy Caddick dismisses Damien Martyn [2002]

CRICKETERS OF THE YEAR 2001 – Performances in the English season 2000

Name	Age*		Matches	Runs	Bat ave	Wickets	Bowl ave	Catches (/st)
MW Alleyne	32	First-class	16	410	17.08	25	27.36	14
		List A	26	400	23.52	23	33.08	16/1
MP Bicknell	32	First-class	15	500	31.25	60	17.53	5
		List A	17	62	15.50	23	16.21	4
AR Caddick	32	First-class	10	141	10.84	55	15.41	3
		List A	16	26	3.25	11	31.45	2
		Tests	7	89	8.90	30	18.46	2
		ODI	6	3	1.00	6	21.33	1
JL Langer	30	First-class	16	1472	61.33	1	35.00	25
		List A	19	566	33.29			14
DS Lehmann	31	First-class	16	1477	67.13	8	38.75	8
		List A	24	757	39.84	9	23.77	6

* as at 1/4/2001

2002 Five Cricketers of the Year

Andy Flower (Zimbabwe) 🅜
Adam Gilchrist (Australians) 🅜
Jason Gillespie (Australians) ●
V. V. S. Laxman (India) ⫽
Damien Martyn (Australians) ⫽

HEADLINE EVENTS FROM 2001

- County champions – Yorkshire

- C&G Trophy – Somerset

- Norwich Union League – Kent

- Benson & Hedges Cup – Surrey

- England draw 1-1 with Pakistan and lose 4-1 to Australia

- England win 1-0 in Pakistan and 2-1 in Sri Lanka in 2000-01

FOR THE SIXTH AND LAST TIME, BUT FOR THE third time in six years, no English-qualified players featured among the Five.

Andy Flower and Adam Gilchrist, possibly the two finest batting wicketkeepers in Test history, were both riding high, although at different stages of their careers. A year after this, at the 2003 World Cup, Flower – already well into his thirties – made a black-armband protest against what he called the "death of democracy" in Zimbabwe, and his international playing days were over. Gilchrist, having come to Test cricket late, still had six big years ahead of him.

Unlike his fellow left-hander Gilchrist, who toured with another irresistible Australian side, Flower did not appear in the 2001 English season. He was, though, in the form of his life. In late 2000, he gave an amazing demonstration of batting against spin – and his command of the conventional and reverse sweeps – by scoring 540 runs in two Tests in India. His unbeaten 232 at Nagpur remains a record for a wicketkeeper-batsman.

In September 2001 he became the first keeper to score a century in each innings of a Test, against South Africa at Harare –

occupying the crease for almost 15 hours for 142 and 199 not out – and in early 2002 displaced Alan Knott [1970] as the leading Test run-scorer among wicketkeepers. He briefly topped the Test batting rankings.

Flower and elder brother Grant were instrumental in Zimbabwe achieving Test status in 1991-92 and, before injury in 2001, Andy had appeared in every international they had played since their inaugural Test. He captained the side before politics intervened and he returned to the ranks following an England tour in 2000.

Forced to leave Zimbabwe in 2003, Flower settled in England – he was married to an English girl – and after playing for Essex took up a coaching post with England, becoming team director in 2009. Bringing to the role the professionalism that had marked his play, he guided England to many triumphs.

Gilchrist outdid many of Flower's batting feats, including most Test runs and centuries by a keeper. Playing in a stronger side gave him licence to attack even when Australia got into trouble.

He was the first to hit 100 Test sixes, and his strike-rate of 81.95 was bettered only by

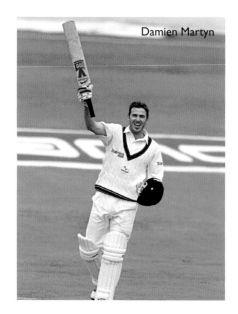

Damien Martyn

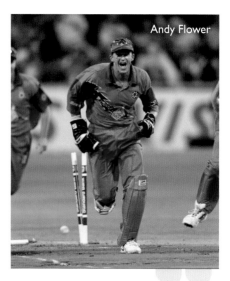

Andy Flower

Andy Flower:

"He may not be the prettiest batsman to watch... but he is considered by some to be the finest exponent of the reverse sweep"

Virender Sehwag, whose best years came later. Sehwag and others followed where Gilchrist first trod: his double-century at Johannesburg in February 2002 was briefly the fastest on record; a century at Perth in 2006-07 remains the speediest in Ashes Tests. Though he gripped the bat high on the handle, his technique was fundamentally sound.

Gilchrist moved from New South Wales to Western Australia to pursue his ambitions. He became Australia's one-day keeper in 1996-97, but did not depose Ian Healy [1994] in Tests until late 1999. He promptly won a match at Hobart against Pakistan from a near-hopeless position.

A rapier-like century in the opening Test of the 2001 Ashes set Australia on a dominant course, though the series provided a rare blemish on Gilchrist's CV when, as stand-in captain, he lost control as England chased down 315 at Headingley. After retiring from Tests in 2007-08, he became an early star of the IPL, and remained a big drawcard in Twenty20 leagues in 2013.

Damien Martyn, like Gilchrist, developed his cricket at Western Australia, his family having been driven out of Darwin by Cyclone Tracy, in which they lost everything.

VVS Laxman (left) with Rahul Dravid [2000] during their epic stand against Australia at Kolkata in 2001

He rose fast, captaining the 1991 Young Australia side in England, and returning with the senior team two years later. He played his first Test at 21, but success had come too easily; squandering his early chances, he was cast into the wilderness. He nearly gave up the game, only to return against New Zealand in 1999-2000, and this time he made it count.

Martyn arrived in England still a relative unknown, but that changed when a maiden Test hundred at Edgbaston was followed by a serene 118 off 135 balls at Headingley, his seemingly

CRICKETERS OF THE YEAR 2002 – Performances in the English season 2001

Name	Age*		Matches	Runs	Bat ave	Wickets	Bowl ave	Catches (/st)
A Flower	33	Did not play in England in 2001						
AC Gilchrist	30	First-class	8	663	82.87			28/4
		Tests	5	340	68.00			24/2
		ODI	6	248	49.60			7/5
JN Gillespie	26	Tests	5	41	13.66	19	34.31	2
		ODI	3	9	9.00	4	25.75	1
VVS Laxman	27	Did not play in England in 2001						
DR Martyn	30	First-class	9	942	104.66	2	26.50	3
		Tests	5	382	76.40			0
		ODI	5	99	49.50	1	66.00	0

as at 1/4/2002

effortless back-foot drives wowing onlookers. He added three hundreds against South Africa in 2001-02 and four more in vital situations on the subcontinent in 2004.

He endured a rare poor series in England in 2005 and, never comfortable with the limelight, suddenly quit as an international player after two quiet matches in the 2006-07 Ashes.

No one did more to ensure Australia retained the Ashes in double-quick time than Jason Gillespie. In the three straight wins that clinched the series, he took 17 wickets and broke the hand of England's captain Nasser Hussain [2003].

Gillespie was a formidable new-ball partner for Glenn McGrath [1998]. Operating off a shorter run-up than in the past, he bowled with pace and accuracy, and held such an immaculate

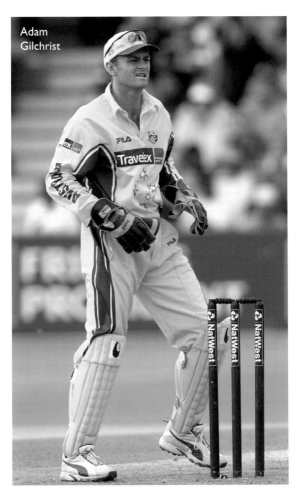

Adam Gilchrist

seam position that the ball was guaranteed to wobble dangerously.

He had won Australia a Test on the 1997 tour with figures of seven for 37 at Headingley, but his career had since been hampered by injuries severe even for a bowler of his type. However, he had delivered some outstanding spells during a recent epic series in India.

Gillespie had a colourful background: his ancestry was part-Aborigine, he named a daughter Sapphire, and he wore a ponytail in his early days. When his form tailed off in England in 2005 he became a figure of fun for English crowds, but he had the last laugh early the following year when he scored 201 not out as a nightwatchman at Chittagong in what proved to be his last Test. He later had spells with Yorkshire and Glamorgan, before taking over as Yorkshire's head coach.

Laxman also did not play in England in 2001, but his inclusion was recognition of one of the greatest of all Test innings in March, when he and Rahul Dravid [2000] batted all day at Kolkata to turn the tables on Australia, who lost after enforcing the follow-on. Laxman scored 281 and drove Shane Warne [1994] to distraction with his attacking strokeplay on a wearing pitch.

Laxman, who grew up among a Hyderabad family of doctors and was inspired by the artistry of Mohammad Azharuddin [1991], was not so much a great batsman as a batsman who played great innings. Many of these came against Australia, off whom he scored ten hundreds, six in Tests and four in one-day internationals, a format in which otherwise he did not particularly excel.

On his day there was no stopping him. His fine hands also made him one of the best slip catchers. England were the only major Test team against whom he failed to make a hundred, though English audiences glimpsed his brilliance during brief appearances for Lancashire from 2007 to 2009.

Jason Gillespie

Jason Gillespie:
"He combined high pace with such incisive accuracy and pronounced seam movement that there were times when he was unplayable"

2003 Five Cricketers of the Year

Matthew Hayden (Australia) /
Adam Hollioake (Surrey) / •
Nasser Hussain (Essex and England) /
Shaun Pollock (Warwickshire) / •
Michael Vaughan (Yorkshire and England) /

HEADLINE EVENTS FROM 2002

- County champions – Surrey

- C&G Trophy – Yorkshire

- Norwich Union League – Glamorgan

- Benson & Hedges Cup – Warwickshire

- England beat Sri Lanka 2-0 and draw 1-1 with India

- England lose 1-0 in India and draw 1-1 in New Zealand in 2001-02

NASSER HUSSAIN'S SELECTION WAS BELATED recognition of his service to English cricket since taking over the national captaincy in 1999 with the team's fortunes at a low ebb. His resignation as one-day leader after the 2003 World Cup was known before the Almanack's publication, but not who would replace him. In fact, by July Michael Vaughan had taken charge of all captaincy affairs.

Hussain was passionate about raising standards. He refused to accept mediocrity, and harangued his players into seriously competing with all but Australia; even they were beaten in the final Test of the 2002-03 series, a result that paved the way for the Ashes to be reclaimed under Vaughan in 2005, for the first time since 1986-87.

Hussain also advanced the moral argument for England not playing in Zimbabwe at the World Cup, an act that cost them their place in the next round. He was perhaps too intense to inspire mass affection, but he gave his all.

Born in Chennai to an Indian father and English mother, Hussain moved as a youngster to Essex, where his father ran an indoor school at Ilford. He started as a leg-spinner but lost the knack, and became a manufactured but effective batsman. He first played for England at 21 against West Indies in 1989-90, but had to wait until 1996 for a decent run. He scored 207 against Australia in 1997.

He was an unlikely choice as captain, but forged a special relationship with Duncan Fletcher, the coach, and benefited from England's best players being put on central contracts from 2000. Hussain was prone to injury and bouts of poor form, but led the side to four straight series wins. He retired as a player after hitting a match-winning Test century at Lord's in 2004, and moved into commentary with Sky TV, becoming their sharpest observer.

Vaughan was a more classical batsman and more rational strategist, though he had better players at his command. He enjoyed a golden year in 2002, finally turning promise into substance. Promoted to open, he scored 1,481 runs in 12 Tests and in the first week of 2003 added a third century in an Ashes series that brought him 633 runs. Statistically it remains the finest year an England Test batsman has had.

At his best Vaughan struck the ball imperiously, but during a long reign as captain – he led in 51 Tests, 26 of which were won – these days became rarer, though a sublime innings of 166 at Old Trafford played its part in the 2005 Ashes victory. A knee operation in the autumn of 2002 was an ominous sign of things to come: his knee gave way in late 2005, and he was out for more than a year.

Vaughan, a great-great-nephew of Ernest Tyldesley [1920], moved from Manchester to Sheffield when he was nine, and joined Yorkshire just as their bar against outsiders was lifting. He resigned as England captain in 2008 and retired the following year, before moving into media work.

Shaun Pollock, like Hussain, paid for World Cup failure. South Africa were hosts and favourites, but performed erratically and went out after Pollock misread the Duckworth/Lewis charts and thought they had beaten Sri Lanka when in fact the scores were tied. A dignified if conservative captain since the departure in disgrace of Hansie Cronje in 2000, he was sacked soon after.

Pollock was one of the finest bowling all-rounders. Batting low in the order, he averaged 32.31 in Tests, but this aspect of his game was overshadowed by his talent as a relentlessly accurate seam bowler in partnership with Allan Donald [1992]. He was another Natal protégé of Malcolm Marshall [1983].

By January 2003, Pollock had taken 278 Test wickets at the low average of 20.71, but he was losing his nip, and this rose to 23.11 by 2008 when he retired with a South African-record 421 wickets. He bowled well enough, though, in the Tests in England in 2003.

The son of Peter Pollock and nephew of Graeme [both 1966], Shaun was most effective in 2002 as a one-day player for Warwickshire, who first recruited him as a young international in 1996, when he marked his debut with four wickets in four balls.

Hollioake's third Championship title in four seasons as Surrey captain was emotionally charged. In March 2002, his younger brother

Adam Hollioake (left) and his brother Ben receive their England caps on the same day, from Michael Atherton

Shaun Pollock

Ben, himself a member of the team, was killed in a car crash in Australia, and Adam did not rejoin the side until mid-June. But when he did, Ben's death liberated his play: captaincy had eroded his form, but he now enjoyed hitting the ball again, with spectacular results. He averaged almost 70 in the Championship, and struck 117 off 59 balls in a cup quarter-final.

Hollioake was born in Melbourne, moving to England at 12. He developed into a serious batting all-rounder, and in 1997 was given one-day and Test opportunities by England (as was Ben). These proved short-lived, but his leadership had made its mark at Surrey and he briefly acted as stand-in captain of England's 50-overs team, guiding them to a rare if inconsequential trophy in Sharjah in 1997-98. He also led Surrey to five one-day trophies, the last in 2003.

Hollioake retired after 2004, but briefly reappeared for Essex's Twenty20 side in 2007. Re-settling in Australia, he was declared bankrupt in 2011 after a property company he ran collapsed. He took up professional boxing and cage-fighting in 2012, aged 40.

Matthew Hayden was another chosen for his global impact – and what an impact it had been in the two years since the dam burst in India in early 2001, when he plundered 549 runs in three Tests. A big man, broad and powerful, he made the most of his reach to sweep spinners or, as in Australia where he scored most of his runs, to batter fast bowlers off the front foot. It was intimidatory batting, and it worked. As a pair of contrasting left-handed openers, he and Justin Langer [2001] were a nightmare to bowl at.

Starting with the India series, Hayden plundered 2,560 runs in 25 Tests, and the flow continued unabated through 2003, when he took brief possession of the world Test record with 380 against Zimbabwe at Perth. He also became a major force in one-day cricket. These were his peak years. His output dipped slightly thereafter, though not hugely. He had two relatively quiet series in England in 2001 and 2005, having also toured in 1993 without appearing in the Tests.

Hayden, who grew up in rural Queensland and loved surfing, fishing and triathlons, was in his late twenties before becoming a Test regular, but he had always scored heavily, for his state and during spells with Hampshire and Northamptonshire.

Nasser Hussain (right) with **Michael Vaughan**

Matthew Hayden

CRICKETERS OF THE YEAR 2003 – Performances in the English season 2002

Name	Age*		Matches	Runs	Bat ave	Wickets	Bowl ave	Catches (/st)
ML Hayden	31	Did not play in England in 2002						
AJ Hollioake	31	First-class	9	738	67.09	5	35.60	10
		List A	15	351	35.10	30	14.86	9
N Hussain	35	List A	15	690	57.50			6
		Tests	7	478	47.80			6
		ODI	7	244	40.66			3
SM Pollock	29	First-class	10	425	25.00	28	26.17	13
		List A	20	550	36.66	37	14.29	5
MP Vaughan	28	First-class	9	976	75.07	4	46.25	5
		Tests	7	900	90.00	4	41.00	5

* as at 1/4/2003

2004 Five Cricketers of the Year

Chris Adams (Sussex) /
Andrew Flintoff (Lancashire and England) / ●
Ian Harvey (Gloucestershire) / ●
Gary Kirsten (South Africans) /
Graeme Smith (South Africans) /

HEADLINE EVENTS FROM 2003

• County champions – Sussex

• C&G Trophy – Gloucestershire

• National League – Surrey

• Twenty20 Cup – Surrey

• England beat Zimbabwe 2-0 and draw 2-2 with South Africa

• England lose 4-1 in Australia in 2002-03

• Australia win the World Cup

BETWEEN THEM, GARY KIRSTEN AND GRAEME Smith spanned almost South Africa's entire Test experiences of the post-apartheid era.

Kirsten regularly opened the batting from 1993 to 2002, when he moved into the middle order to accommodate Smith, the rising star. Within a year, Smith was in possession of the captaincy, a post he still held ten years later. They rank among South Africa's finest openers, no-frills left-handers set on laying the ground for match-winning totals. Much of their team's success depended on them.

Kirsten, one of four cricketing brothers and half-brothers, who for eight years lived at Newlands where his father worked as groundsman, was an anonymous-looking batsman who ground out more than 7,000 runs in 101 Tests thanks in part to Duncan Fletcher, then coach at Western Province, convincing him of his mental toughness.

He had an especially good record against England, scoring 72 and 44 when South Africa won at Lord's in 1994, and double-centuries at Old Trafford in 1998 and Durban in 1999-2000 (batting 14½ hours to save the game), but his contributions in 2003 were perhaps most satisfying. He scored hundreds in both matches

South Africa won, his gutsy effort at Headingley where the ball seamed and swung being a classic of its type.

He wanted to retire after the tour, but agreed to delay until March 2004. He later turned himself into an excellent coach, guiding India to the top of the Test rankings and to victory in the 2011 World Cup, before rejoining South Africa where he worked closely with Smith. Within a year he had helped them become the No. 1 Test side in turn.

In giving the captaincy to Smith when only three months past his 22nd birthday, South Africa were aiming for a fresh start, and got it. He was unfazed by the challenge, even though his country's cricket politics were complex. He was intent on leading by example, and did so once the Tests in England got under way, scoring 277 and 85 at Edgbaston and 259 at Lord's, breaking Don Bradman's 1930 record for a visiting Test batsman there.

England managed to stifle his strong leg-side game in later matches and draw the series 2–2, but it was only a temporary stay. Smith's method was ungainly but effective, and he wasn't prone to prolonged self-doubt. He returned to England to achieve series victories in 2008 and 2012, playing a great innings of 154 to chase down the runs at Edgbaston on the first tour and lay the platform for a massive win with 131 at The Oval (in his 100th Test) on the second. He was also an outstanding slip fielder.

The rise of Andrew Flintoff, an amiable Lancastrian, as an international class all-rounder was the most exciting thing to happen to English cricket in 2003. It had been a long time coming. The period since he first appeared for England in 1998 had been littered with injuries, grumbles about excess weight – even when fit he was a giant man – and variable form.

Finally, things had come together. He was the most economical bowler at the 2003 World Cup, and battered South Africa's Test attack on both sides of London: to the tune of 142 at Lord's, where his bat split amid the assault, and 95 at The Oval. During the winter of 2003-04 he added a more sober century in match-saving mode in Antigua, and a first five-for at Bridgetown.

For the next two years he airily lived up to the label of England's best fast-bowling all-rounder since Ian Botham [1978], climaxing in a career-defining 2005 Ashes series, before his body creaked under the load. When he took on the captaincy as stand-in for Michael Vaughan [2003], the mind struggled to cope too. Fitness was fleeting thereafter, and so were the match-shaping performances. The England team stopped relying on him long before his last international at the age of 31.

He subsequently embarked on various media ventures while retaining few direct links with cricket. He won his only fight as a professional boxer in 2012.

Chris Adams led Sussex, one of the oldest clubs, to their first Championship title in 2003, special reward for a painful career journey. He had parted acrimoniously from Derbyshire in 1997 to further his ambitions with Sussex, but

Ian Harvey

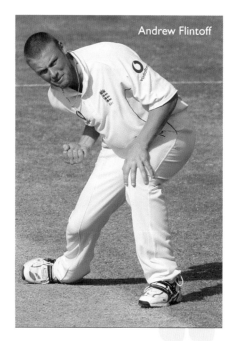

Andrew Flintoff

Andrew Flintoff:

"[An] amiable giant who carved into the bowling, a farmhand delighting in the coconut shy"

Chris Adams celebrates Sussex's first County Championship title

when he finally played for England in South Africa in 1999-2000 it was a disaster.

He might have given up disenchanted. Instead he threw himself into making Sussex a force, the captaincy having been part of the bait when he joined them. He was a hard-hitting batsman and equally aggressive captain, and in three years took the team from bottom of the second division to top of the first. Personally, 2003 was difficult. It was his benefit year, and by mid-season he was struggling for form. But he turned things round and played some vital innings during the title run-in.

Adams, who developed his batting and fine fielding in Derbyshire club cricket and at Repton School, led Sussex to two further Championships, as well as two one-day trophies, before retiring to join Surrey as team director in 2009.

Ian Harvey was a stocky one-day specialist and early star of Twenty20, which launched in

England in 2003. He scored the first Twenty20 hundred, against Warwickshire in 50 balls, and was the first to make three centuries, but his main strength was as a bag-of-tricks medium-pace death bowler. He could also throw with either arm.

In the 2000 Benson & Hedges Cup final against Glamorgan, he captured five for 34, and in early 2003, when he played six matches during Australia's victorious World Cup campaign (though not the final), he took four wickets in the opening encounter with Pakistan. Although he took the match award in the 2003 C&G Trophy final against Worcestershire partly for scoring 61, he had earlier returned figures of two for 37 off ten overs. This was the sixth one-day trophy he had helped Gloucestershire win in five seasons.

In 2004, with his international career coming to a close, Harvey joined Yorkshire for two seasons before returning to Gloucestershire for one. He then played for three more counties – Derbyshire, Hampshire and Northamptonshire – in as many seasons, latterly as a Twenty20 specialist.

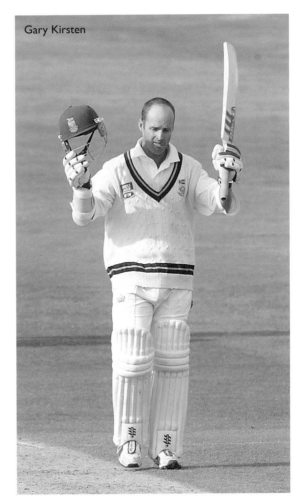

Gary Kirsten

Graeme Smith

Graeme Smith:
"He imposed his will upon England emphatically ... Never had the tone for a series been set so devastatingly"

CRICKETERS OF THE YEAR 2004 – Performances in the English season 2003

Name	Age*		Matches	Runs	Bat ave	Wickets	Bowl ave	Catches (/st)
CJ Adams	33	First-class	16	966	35.77	0		18
		List A	15	601	66.77			8
A Flintoff	26	First-class	10	942	72.46	15	48.46	7
		List A	17	430	35.83	25	18.56	13
		Tests	5	423	52.87	10	59.20	0
		ODI	10	279	39.85	15	18.13	5
IJ Harvey	31	First-class	6	404	44.88	27	23.14	4
		List A	9	337	37.44	24	15.45	1
G Kirsten	36	First-class	7	713	71.30			5
		Tests	4	462	66.00			4
GC Smith	23	Tests	5	714	79.33			3
		ODI	7	223	31.85			3

as at 1/4/2004

2005 Five Cricketers of the Year

Ashley Giles (Warwickshire and England) ●
Steve Harmison (Durham and England) ●
Robert Key (Kent and England) /
Andrew Strauss (Middlesex and England) /
Marcus Trescothick (Somerset and England) /

HEADLINE EVENTS FROM 2004

- County champions – Warwickshire

- C&G Trophy – Gloucestershire

- Totesport League – Glamorgan

- Twenty20 Cup – Leicestershire

- England win all seven home Tests, beating New Zealand 3-0 and West Indies 4-0

- England beat West Indies 3-0 in the West Indies in 2003-04

FOR THE FIRST TIME SINCE 1938 ALL FIVE Cricketers of the Year had appeared for England the previous summer, reflecting the team's achievement in winning all seven home Tests in 2004 and 11 out of 13 in the year as a whole. It was also the first time since 1960 that there had been no foreigners.

Andrew Strauss was newest to the England team. Drafted in for the first Test of the summer to replace the injured Michael Vaughan [2003], he scored 112 and 83 against New Zealand at Lord's, and never looked back. He added another century against West Indies and three more in South Africa, and his three-figure scores at Old Trafford and The Oval were highly influential in the outcome of the 2005 Ashes.

Strauss had a big-match temperament, and although he briefly lost his place in 2007-08 was soon back. He was obvious captaincy material, but waited until 2009 to get the job full-time. He inherited a difficult situation but quickly turned things round, and inspired home and away Ashes series wins not only as leader but with the bat (scoring hundreds at Lord's and Brisbane) and as a slip catcher.

By the time he took England to No. 1 in the Test rankings in August 2011 the strain was telling, and after losing to South Africa in 2012 he stepped down from all forms of the game.

Strauss was born in Johannesburg to South African parents before moving to England when he was eight. He played cricket at Radley and Durham University, but took four years at Middlesex to make a mark and was 27 when he played his first Test.

Marcus Trescothick formed an effective all-left-handed opening partnership with Strauss from 2004 to 2006, before Trescothick dropped out of international cricket suffering from depression. He had missed few matches for England in Tests or one-dayers since his debut in 2000, during which time his duties as batsman, slip catcher and first lieutenant were all-consuming. He played on for Somerset, as captain from 2010, but refused to countenance an England comeback.

He struggled in the West Indies early in 2004, but returned strongly with a match-shaping 132 against New Zealand at Leeds and twin hundreds against West Indies at Edgbaston. During the following winter he played one of his

Marcus Trescothick (left) with
Robert Key

Marcus Trescothick:
**"With puppy fat
and slogger's
muscles, [he] hit
his first hundred
aged II"**

Born into a cricket-loving family, Trescothick was a heavy scorer from his early years with Keynsham in Somerset. He played for the county at 17, but was still a mercurial talent when Duncan Fletcher picked him for England on the back of a free-wheeling hundred against Glamorgan in 1999.

Steve Harmison was arguably the world's best fast bowler in 2004, his 67 wickets in Tests and 26 in one-day internationals bearing testimony to his consistent menace. He was tall and with an open-chested action angled the ball into right-handers; few relished the challenge.

This was his peak. The previous winter he left a tour of Bangladesh early and was told to get fit, which he did training with Newcastle United's footballers. When he next played he demolished West Indies with seven for 12 in Jamaica, and for months barely bowled a bad spell. He fired the first shot in the 2005 Ashes with five wickets at Lord's, and took the wicket that clinched a two-run win at Edgbaston.

But his fitness was fading, and a woeful opening wide at Brisbane in 2006 symbolised his unpreparedness. He spearheaded Durham's title wins of 2008 and 2009 – he was the first

finest innings, a rapid 180 at Johannesburg that opened the door to victory.

He relied more on eye than footwork, but his penchant for hitting the ball made him one of England's best one-day batsmen. He capped the 2004 season with 104 in the Champions Trophy final defeat to West Indies.

CRICKETERS OF THE YEAR 2005 – Performances in the English season 2004

Name	Age*		Matches	Runs	Bat ave	Wickets	Bowl ave	Catches (/st)
AF Giles	32	Tests	7	219	31.28	31	26.16	3
		ODI	9	93	23.25	9	23.77	5
SJ Harmison	26	Tests	7	80	20.00	38	25.42	2
		ODI	12	21	10.50	22	19.90	2
RWT Key	25	First-class	16	1896	79.00			8
		Tests	4	378	63.00			3
AJ Strauss	28	List A	18	668	51.38			2
		Tests	7	590	45.38			11
		ODI	12	403	44.77			2
ME Trescothick	29	Tests	7	641	53.41	0		6
		ODI	12	403	33.58	2	22.50	9

* as at 1/4/2005

Durham player picked by *Wisden* – and his last act for England was to help regain the Ashes in 2009, but his career was tinged with disappointment.

Harmison left school at 15 and worked as a labourer before Durham spotted him playing for Northumberland. David Boon [1994] was an early mentor. Harmison's younger brother Ben played for Durham and Kent.

Ashley Giles had played his first Test in 1998, and been derided as a left-arm spinner of marginal worth in English conditions, but in 2004 he confounded the sceptics by twice bowling England to victory over West Indies with fourth-innings five-fors. At Lord's he bowled Brian Lara [1995] with a ball that turned extravagantly: as a supposedly defensive bowler who rarely moved it off the straight, Giles was not expected to do that.

Giles, whose lack of fluidity betrayed an early career as a medium-pacer, specialised in bit parts, whether doughty runs at No. 8, sound fielding, or occasional wickets, and the England dressing-room valued them all. In the 2005 Ashes, he took important wickets at Edgbaston and hit the winning runs in a nailbiter at Trent Bridge. He was Vaughan's soulmate and took newcomers under his wing; he was the ultimate team man.

Late in 2005, however, he broke down with hip trouble during a tour of Pakistan, and although he recovered to be controversially selected ahead of Monty Panesar [2007] in Australia at the start of the 2006-07 Ashes series, it was a short-lived return. Forced into retirement, he moved seamlessly into management – as Warwickshire's director of cricket, as England selector, and from 2012-13 as coach of England's limited-overs sides.

Robert Key, a solidly built, rosy-cheeked biffer in the mould of Trescothick, might have gained more opportunities but for Trescothick and Strauss. In 2004 he broke back into the England team at No. 3 through sheer weight of runs at

Steve Harmison

Steve Harmison:

"He was at last hiding his disappointment that he was not Alan Shearer. England could hardly hide their glee"

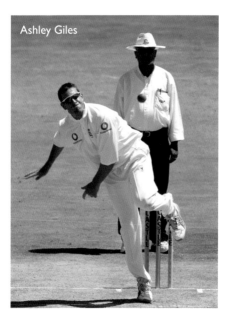

Ashley Giles

the top of Kent's order – he reached 1,000 for the season by June 2 – and on his return punished a wayward West Indies attack for 221 at Lord's. Two matches later a measured 93 not out took the team home at Old Trafford. Even so, he did not start in South Africa, and some mixed performances permanently cost him his place.

Key came to notice with England's Under-19 World Cup-winning squad of 1998, and was among the first intake at the national academy. Eight Tests in 2002 and 2003 revealed glimpses of promise, but only one half-century.

He took the Kent captaincy in 2006 to enhance his England chances, but his form suffered. He was perhaps not best suited to the shorter formats, but Kent lifted the Twenty20 Cup in 2007 and were runners-up in two domestic finals in 2008, prompting England to recall him for the World Twenty20 in 2009. He quit the Kent captaincy in 2012.

Andrew Strauss

2006 Five Cricketers of the Year

Matthew Hoggard (Yorkshire and England) ●
Simon Jones (Glamorgan and England) ●
Brett Lee (Australians) ●
Kevin Pietersen (Hampshire and England) /
Ricky Ponting (Australians) /

HEADLINE EVENTS FROM 2005

- County champions –
  Nottinghamshire

- C&G Trophy – Hampshire

- Totesport League – Essex

- Twenty20 Cup – Somerset

- England regain the Ashes
  for the first time since 1989,
  beating Australia 2-1

- England beat Bangladesh 2-0

- England win 2-1 in South Africa
  in 2004-05

THE 2005 ASHES PRODUCED ONE OF THE greatest Test series, and with it many heroes. Six of the England side, and seven of the Australians, had already been picked by *Wisden,* but the chosen five were major players in the drama.

Kevin Pietersen was the first to convince England's batsmen that Shane Warne [1994] and Glenn McGrath [1998] could be conquered. He treated them with near-contempt in the First Test, and then with the fate of the Ashes in the balance on the final afternoon at The Oval launched a fearless attack on Brett Lee and Shaun Tait that took the game out of Australia's reach long before he was out for 158.

Pietersen was not unhappy to be famous. Born in Pietermaritzburg, to a South African father and English mother, he left for England at 19 frustrated at his progress, and beat a path to the top by scoring heavily for Nottinghamshire. When he felt they had no more to offer he joined Hampshire. He qualified for England in October 2004 and took the one-day team by storm, sealing his Test place with a match-winning 91 against Australia at Bristol.

His wristy style was original but risky: being tall, he had the reach to dominate

bowling, and applied cool logic to the manufacture of strokes such as the switch-hit. His average was not exceptional, but he played innings that were. In 2008 England made him captain, then got cold feet when he challenged Peter Moores, the head coach. His desire to spend more time at the IPL caused further conflict with the management in 2012.

Simon Jones also brought a magical element to England's game. A strapping and feisty fast bowler, his command of reverse swing peaked when he returned six for 53 at Old Trafford and five for 44 at Trent Bridge to secure his side the advantage. The ball that extracted off stump as Michael Clarke [2010] shouldered arms summed up his skill. He also lent Andrew Flintoff [2004] vital support in a last-wicket stand of 51 at Edgbaston.

Jones, whose father Jeff also bowled fast for England, had struggled to reach this point. Glamorgan had picked him for his pace, but he had no-ball problems and tinkered with his run-up. He learned about reverse swing at the national academy, but neither county nor country, who first called on him in 2002, always trusted him. He lost more than a year to a ruptured cruciate ligament. But in South Africa in 2004-05 his accuracy grew.

Sadly, his best years were behind him. An ankle injury brought an early end to his involvement in the 2005 Ashes, and a comeback in India in 2006 stalled. A painful battle for fitness ensued. A move to Worcestershire took him close to an England recall in 2008 before injury struck again, and he eked out his career playing one-dayers for Hampshire before rejoining Glamorgan.

Matthew Hoggard was England's leading conventional swing bowler. If the ball didn't move he could be a liability – and went long periods without being called on – but if it did he was dangerous. He served England well by three times accounting cheaply for Matthew Hayden [2003]. At Trent Bridge he took five wickets and scored eight not out in a tight finish.

Hoggard emerged from a crop of fast bowlers at Yorkshire, making his debut for England in 2000. But he served a long apprenticeship before cementing a place in 2004 in the West Indies, where he took a hat-trick at Bridgetown. This was the start of 40 consecutive Tests. He won match and series against South Africa with 12 wickets at Johannesburg in January 2005.

Brett Lee (left) celebrates another wicket with **Ricky Ponting**

Brett Lee:
"[He] had a remarkable Ashes… and made an impact that transcended figures"

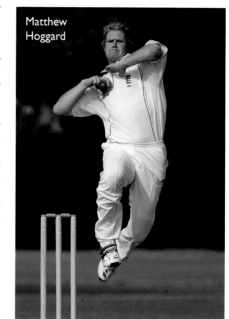

Matthew Hoggard

CRICKETERS OF THE YEAR 2006 – Performances in the English season 2005

Name	Age*		Matches	Runs	Bat ave	Wickets	Bowl ave	Catches (/st)
MJ Hoggard	29	First-class	13	161	12.38	50	27.72	4
		Tests	7	45	6.42	30	21.80	2
SP Jones	27	Tests	6	66	33.00	23	21.13	1
		ODI	6	1	1.00	4	49.75	0
B Lee	29	Tests	5	158	26.33	20	41.10	2
		ODI	8	39	39.00	14	22.07	0
KP Pietersen	25	First-class	11	897	44.85	0		4
		List A	19	518	39.84	1	1.00	8
		Tests	5	473	52.55			0
		ODI	10	228	45.60			8
RT Ponting	31	Tests	5	359	39.88	1	9.00	4
		ODI	10	303	33.66			4

as at 1/4/2006

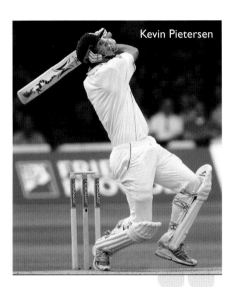

Kevin Pietersen

Kevin Pietersen: **"Now we stand back to find out whether he will be remembered as the cricketer who ate himself or a legend of the willow"**

Creditably, he finished with more Test wickets, at a lower average, away than at home.

Having lost some nip, he was dropped in favour of James Anderson [2009] in New Zealand in 2008, and never played for England again. He joined Leicestershire in 2010, captaining them for three years.

Ricky Ponting had a bad series as captain of Australia. Having been in charge for a year, he lost the Ashes at the first attempt. He mistakenly asked England to bat at Edgbaston, and lost his temper when run out by a substitute, Gary Pratt, at Trent Bridge. But he played one of the great defensive innings – worth 156 – to save the Old Trafford Test. Without him Australia might have disintegrated.

Ponting, whose tendency to play across his front pad sometimes made him appear vulnerable, was the most complete Australian batsman since Don Bradman [1931]. Raised in Tasmania, he played his first Test at 20, and in 1997 scored a flawless hundred on his first tour of England at 22. He ironed out a wild streak, and in 2001 moved up to No. 3 to shape matches on a regular basis. He was also the world's best all-round fielder.

His response to the 2005 defeat was immense. In the next 12 matches, he led Australia to 11 wins and a draw, and scored eight hundreds, before in 2006-07 spearheading a 5–0 demolition of England and another Australian World Cup triumph (he appeared in three World Cup-winning sides, taking the Man of the Match award in the 2003 final).

But both he and the team subsequently declined together, suffering back-to-back Ashes defeats that triggered Ponting's resignation as captain. He retired as a Test player in 2012, after 168 matches and 13,378 runs, second only to Sachin Tendulkar [1997] in both categories.

Brett Lee's 20 wickets in the series cost 41.10 apiece, but his efforts were heroic. With McGrath and Jason Gillespie [1998] either absent or diminished, he carried Australia's pace attack as they pushed for victory at Edgbaston and The Oval. That they failed was scarcely his fault. He had Pietersen dropped on 15 at The Oval.

Flintoff's consolatory pat on the back after Lee's unbeaten 43 went unrewarded at Edgbaston provided one of the images of the summer.

Lee, whose brother Shane played ODIs, had had a chequered career. When he was young Dennis Lillee [1973] helped remodel his action. His long run-up and leaping action were sights to behold, and Lee enjoyed his speed as much as everyone else bar the batsmen. Steve Waugh [1989] was an unalloyed fan, and oversaw Lee's sensational arrival in Test cricket in 1999-2000, but he had yet to play a Test under Ponting before this tour.

Lee was central to much of Australia's success over the next two years, including the 2006-07 rout of England. Injury scuppered his hopes of playing in the 2009 Ashes, but he continued to be effective in one-day internationals until his retirement in 2012.

Simon Jones

2007 Five Cricketers of the Year

Paul Collingwood (Durham and England) /
Mahela Jayawardene (Sri Lankans) /
Mohammad Yousuf (Pakistanis) /
Monty Panesar (Northamptonshire and England) ●
Mark Ramprakash (Surrey) /

HEADLINE EVENTS FROM 2006

- County champions – Sussex

- C&G Trophy – Sussex

- NatWest Pro40 – Essex

- Twenty20 Cup – Leicestershire

- England draw 1-1 with Sri Lanka and beat Pakistan 3-0

- England lose 2-0 to Pakistan and draw 1-1 with India in 2005-06

MAHELA JAYAWARDENE, MOHAMMAD YOUSUF and Mark Ramprakash were accomplished batting technicians. Jayawardene and Yousuf were masters in Asian conditions and on the way to amassing immense Test records. Ramprakash's international days had been a disappointment, and were behind him. He compensated by continuing to score hugely in county cricket even in his late thirties.

Jayawardene came to England in 2006 under pressure. He was a recent appointment as Sri Lanka's captain, and in poor form for a player of his class. He gave the perfect riposte, leading a young side with verve while scoring elegantly crafted runs when they mattered most.

He led an amazing escape at Lord's, his six-hour 119 paving the way for his team to bat 14 hours in the follow-on. Sri Lanka lost the Second Test but won the Third, and then he went on the attack in the one-day series, plundering 328 runs at a strike-rate of 101.86. Sri Lanka won it 5–0.

Jayawardene developed his game at Nalanda College, Colombo, made his Test debut at 20, and scored his first hundred at 21. He was slow to churn out regular hundreds, but then got a taste

for really big scores: a few weeks after the England tour, in August 2006, he took 374 off South Africa on a bland pitch in Colombo, the fourth-highest innings in Tests. By 2013, he was averaging 61.12 in home Tests and 37.36 elsewhere.

Captaincy proved no hardship, the years from 2006 to 2009, when he stepped down, being his most productive. He returned for a one-year spell in 2012-13.

Programmed to play the ball at the last instant, Yousuf was as lovely to watch as Jayawardene. He batted No. 4 during Pakistan's tour of England and retrieved tricky situations, with grit never outshining glamour. His efforts counted for little in terms of the overall outcome, but he entertained royally with 202 at Lord's, 192 at Leeds and 128 at The Oval.

In his next series, at home to West Indies, he operated even more ruthlessly, racking up 665 runs in three matches to end 2006 with a calendar-year record of 1,788 runs. He would never have won a prize for fielding, though.

Born Yousuf Youhana, a Christian, into poverty in Lahore, he for years had to put cricket second to earning a wage. His father worked at the railway station, and he was briefly employed as a tailor. He played a season in the Bradford League, but his background hampered his progress in Lahore cricket. His first Test came in 1998 and he, like Jayawardene, took time to fulfil his talent. The regular big scores came with a conversion of religion, and name, in 2005.

The runs that came so effortlessly in 2006 soon dried to a trickle, and he lost his place for good after the 2010 tour of England amid recriminations about losses in Australia under his captaincy and spot-fixes involving team-mates.

Ramprakash had an astonishing season with Surrey in 2006, reaching 2,000 runs in 20 innings, and making scores of 150 in five successive matches, both records, as was his average of 103.54, the best-ever by an Englishman. The only quibble was that his runs came in the Championship's second division. In the autumn he followed Darren Gough [1999] by winning *Strictly Come Dancing*.

Monty Panesar

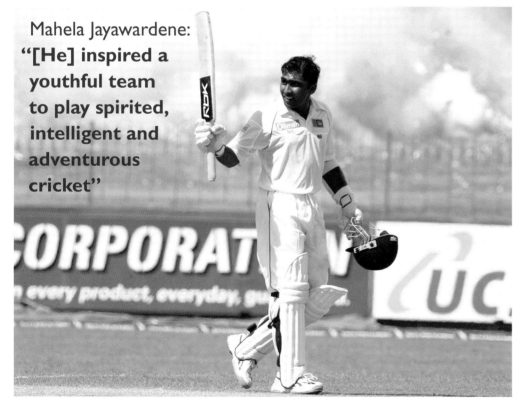

Mahela Jayawardene: "[He] inspired a youthful team to play spirited, intelligent and adventurous cricket"

Mahela Jayawardene after his 374 against South Africa in 2006

Ramprakash's England career had produced very different numbers: an average of 27.32 from 52 Tests, with just two hundreds. The defence was that he was messed around by vacillating selectors; the prosecution that the big stage made him too taut to do well, something that seemed unlikely when he took the match award in the NatWest Trophy final as a teenager.

Ramprakash, whose mother was Irish and father Guyanese, expressed himself more freely when he left Middlesex in 2001. With his England days behind him, his season's average rose above 60 and then beyond 70. In 2007 his average again exceeded 100, and in 2009, when he turned 40, it touched 90. He retired in 2012 with 114 first-class hundreds to his name, and became a batting coach.

If Ramprakash was an underachiever, the opposite was possibly true of Paul Collingwood, who had less talent but no end of guts. It looked as though one-day internationals might be his pinnacle – he batted, bowled canny medium-pace and was a brilliant fielder – but his versatility made him a good reserve player on Test tours, and eventually his chances came.

In 2005-06, scores of 96 and 80 at Lahore and an unbeaten 134 at Nagpur earned him an extended run which went surprisingly well. He made 186 against Pakistan at Lord's in 2006, and at Adelaide the following winter recorded a double-century that would have been sweeter had England not lost.

Collingwood, raised near Durham, was best on low, slow wickets, but less good when the ball bounced high on off stump. He experienced bouts of poor form, but was adept at ending them before the selectors' axe fell. His all-round status helped prolong his Test life until he retired on the day the 2010-11 Ashes series was won. He captained England to the World Twenty20 title in 2010, their first global one-day trophy.

Monty Panesar, the son of Punjabi immigrants and the first Sikh to play Test

Mohammad Yousuf

Paul Collingwood

Mohammad Yousuf:
"A Ferrari when he is batting and a truck when he isn't"

Mark Ramprakash

cricket for anyone but India, was propelled into the England team in India in early 2006 by an injury to Ashley Giles [2005], the senior left-arm spinner. Panesar had yet to play a full county season, though he had spent time at the national academy and could already bowl well for hours.

He proved a natural. His first wicket was Sachin Tendulkar [1997], and in the course of the summer's Tests he confirmed a knack for getting good players out, including Yousuf three times. But when Giles was fleetingly fit again Panesar was dropped, only to return unfazed, claiming eight wickets at Perth.

Confusion sometimes arose about how many variations he should attempt and what fields he should set, but he still raced to 100 wickets two years after his debut.

When the more multi-faceted Graeme Swann [2010] arrived on the scene, Panesar – who was a hopeless batsman and fielder – was once again soon surplus to requirements, and this time his confidence did ebb. A change from Northamptonshire to Sussex did him good, and in 2012, when England required two spinners in Asian conditions, he returned to snaffle 33 wickets in six Tests.

CRICKETERS OF THE YEAR 2007 – Performances in the English season 2006

Name	Age*		Matches	Runs	Bat ave	Wickets	Bowl ave	Catches (/st)
PD Collingwood	30	Tests	7	460	41.81	1	134.00	10
		ODI	9	231	28.87	6	31.33	6
DPMD Jayawardene	29	Tests	3	230	38.33			7
		ODI	5	328	109.33			3
Mohammad Yousuf	32	Tests	4	631	90.14			1
		ODI	6	232	77.33			1
MS Panesar	24	First-class	17	136	10.46	71	28.57	3
		Tests	7	39	13.00	27	26.85	1
MR Ramprakash	37	First-class	15	2278	103.54			13
		List A	11	403	50.37			3

as at 1/4/2007

2008 Five Cricketers of the Year

Ian Bell (Warwickshire and England) *

Shivnarine Chanderpaul (West Indians and Durham) *

Ottis Gibson (Durham) ●

Zaheer Khan (Indians) ●

Ryan Sidebottom (Nottinghamshire and England) ●

ZAHEER KHAN AND RYAN SIDEBOTTOM WERE both left-arm fast-medium bowlers who had big summers in 2007. Zaheer was the difference between the sides as India ended England's six-year unbeaten run at home. By spring 2008, Sidebottom was named England's player of the year, and in 13 months captured 70 Test wickets.

India surprised England by using two left-armers coming at them from round the wicket, R. P. Singh lending Zaheer good support, and the English batsmen admitted they couldn't read which way Zaheer would swing the ball. His nine wickets decided the Test at Trent Bridge, where he generated lavish conventional swing – although he was capable of reverse swing too.

Zaheer had come from a town in Maharashtra without a turf pitch, and played for the unfashionable state of Baroda. He first appeared for India in 2000, but came and went for several years, not helping himself by neglecting gym work.

The turning point was a season at Worcestershire in 2006, when he had time to experiment, develop rhythm, and master the tricks of his trade. He took 78 wickets, and returned home equipped to bowl in all conditions.

A capable batsman who once scored 75 in a Test from No. 11, Zaheer starred in India's 2011 World Cup triumph with 21 wickets at 18.76, but his fitness declined rapidly after that and he was axed during the home defeat by England in 2012-13.

Sidebottom, who had played one Test in 2001, owed his recall aged 29 to injuries and to the replacement of Duncan Fletcher (who was not a fan) by Peter Moores as England's head coach. He took eight wickets against West Indies on his comeback at Headingley, a former home ground, and gave the attack much-needed control all summer. Not only his straggly hair was unruly; he could berate errant fieldsmen and showed he was no respecter of reputations in his duel with Sachin Tendulkar [1997] at Trent Bridge.

Sidebottom went on to an outstanding winter. He was player of the series in the one-dayers in Sri Lanka and Tests in New Zealand, where he took ten wickets at Hamilton, including a hat-trick, and eight at Napier. He maintained his form in the home Tests against New Zealand in 2008, but carrying the attack then began to take its toll on his form and fitness. He remained integral to England's

Ian Bell

Ryan Sidebottom

Shivnarine Chanderpaul

Shivnarine
Chanderpaul:
**"After more than
13 years on the
international
treadmill his love
for batting remains
undiminished"**

one-day plans, and helped win the World Twenty20 in 2010.

Sidebottom, whose father Arnie played one Test in 1985, revitalised himself by moving in 2004 from Yorkshire to Nottinghamshire, where he was given the new ball. Having won one Championship with Yorkshire, he added two more at Trent Bridge. Rejoining Yorkshire in 2011, he had his best-ever Championship season.

Ian Bell showed signs in 2007 of fulfilling an immense talent. Armed with a pure technique, he had been touted as a future "great" since starting his first-class career at 17 and reaching the fringe of the England team at 19. When he debuted two years later he scored 70, and in his third match struck 162 against Bangladesh.

He was briefly dropped in 2006, but had he converted his 97 against West Indies at Old

Trafford in 2007 into a hundred it would have been his fifth century in seven Tests at No. 6. Later, against India, he struck a pair of cultured sixties at The Oval, and took the player of the series award in the ODIs.

But there were twists to come. A fragility in high-pressure situations led to his being dropped again in the Caribbean in 2009. He toughened up, and two big years followed. He did well on tour in South Africa and Australia, and during 2011 averaged 118.75 in Tests; he was finally saving matches and winning them. In 2012, he was restored to England's one-day team as opener, and flourished. He was a brilliant short-leg fielder.

Shivnarine Chanderpaul, a diminutive left-hander from Guyana with a freakishly open stance, was one of the best of all defensive batsmen. In England he batted 24 hours in three Tests (he missed Headingley with a knee injury), including 18 hours unbeaten. When Monty Panesar [2007] bowled him at Chester-le-Street he was the first spinner to do so in a Test for 13 years.

Chanderpaul passed fifty in all five Test innings against England in 2007 – a sequence he later extended to a record-equalling seven – and twice finished with unbeaten hundreds; his 116 in testing conditions at Old Trafford, which he described as his best innings, took his side within striking distance of a target of 455.

After the tour he joined Durham and helped them secure their first prize, the Friends Provident Trophy, with 78 off 79 balls in the final – as if to remind everyone that he could score fast if he wanted to. He was a good one-day player, and in 2003 took a 69-ball Test hundred off Australia.

The first Indo-Caribbean to play 100 Tests for West Indies, Chanderpaul made his debut as a teenager in 1993 and was immediately difficult to shift, although it took him many attempts to turn a fifty into a hundred. His son Tagenarine played for Guyana as a batsman in 2013, aged 16.

Ottis Gibson, Man of the Match for Durham in that FP Trophy final, was a Bajan whose West

Indies career had been unjustly brief. He settled in England, where he worked as an ECB coach before cutbacks pushed him back into county cricket with Leicestershire in 2004 (he had a spell with Glamorgan in the mid-1990s).

Initially he was a tearaway, but coaching taught him more about the subtleties of his craft, and during two seasons at Grace Road and two more at Durham he became a highly skilled and effective operator. He reached a peak in 2007 at the age of 38 when he took 80 first-class wickets, including all ten for 47 against Hampshire, as Durham finished Championship runners-up.

In the FP Trophy, Gibson shared a match-winning stand in the semi-final and took three wickets, including two with the first two balls of the innings, in the final, which was also against Hampshire. The previous year, a career-best 155 had ensured Durham's first division survival.

At the end of the season he was appointed England's bowling coach, effectively ending his playing career. In 2010 he became West Indies head coach, and two years later took them to the World Twenty20 title. His cousin Deandra Dottin played for West Indies Women.

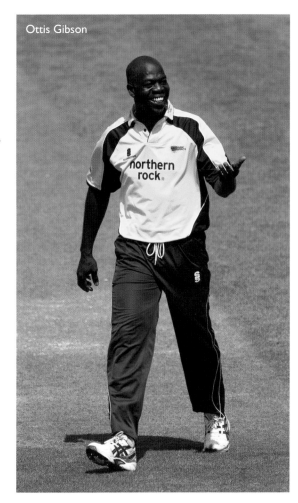

Ottis Gibson

Zaheer Khan

Zaheer Khan: **"England = India minus Zaheer: this is the equation that summed up the Test series of 2007"**

CRICKETERS OF THE YEAR 2008 – Performances in the English season 2007

Name	Age*		Matches	Runs	Bat ave	Wickets	Bowl ave	Catches (/st)
IR Bell	25	Tests	7	417	37.90			5
		ODI	10	507	56.33			6
S Chanderpaul	33	First-class	7	670	74.44	0		4
		List A	11	465	116.25			0
		Tests	3	446	148.66	0		0
		ODI	5	202	202.00			0
OD Gibson	39	First-class	15	578	27.52	80	20.75	6
		List A	18	120	24.00	34	20.02	4
Zaheer Khan	29	Tests	3	28	9.33	18	20.33	1
		ODI	9	62	12.40	7	53.42	0
RJ Sidebottom	30	First-class	13	169	15.36	39	29.89	3
		Tests	6	107	26.75	24	25.75	2

as at 1/4/2008

2009 Five Cricketers of the Year

James Anderson (Lancashire and England) ●

Dale Benkenstein (Durham) /

Mark Boucher (South Africans) ⫛

Neil McKenzie (Durham and South Africans) /

Claire Taylor (England Women) /

HEADLINE EVENTS FROM 2008

- County champions – Durham

- Friends Provident Trophy – Essex

- NatWest Pro40 – Sussex

- Twenty20 Cup – Middlesex

- England beat New Zealand 2-0 and lose 2-1 to South Africa

- England lose 1-0 to Sri Lanka and beat New Zealand 2-1 in 2007-08

CLAIRE TAYLOR BECAME THE FIRST WOMAN TO BE named a Cricketer of the Year. According to Scyld Berry, the editor, her selection was made partly in general recognition of the advances made in the women's game in England.

During the winter of 2007-08, the England Women's team had retained the Ashes in Australia, before returning home and going unbeaten through the season. Taylor had seen her team through to victory in the Bowral Test, in which she scored 79 and 64 not out.

"*Wisden* has never set any parameters such as limiting the Five Cricketers to men, and there is no element of political correctness, or publicity-seeking about her selection," Berry wrote in his Notes. "The best cricketers in the country should be recognised, irrespective of gender."

Taylor, who was born in Amersham to sporting parents, did not take up cricket until the age of 13, but not long after leaving Oxford, where she studied maths, she had established herself as an England regular.

Taylor brought a rare level of dedication and professionalism to her game, and briefly gave up work to concentrate on cricket (most women players were amateurs at this time). In 2006 she

scored an unbeaten 156 not out against India, the highest score in any one-day international at Lord's, and by 2008 topped the world one-day batting rankings.

Better was yet to come. In 2009 Taylor helped England win both the World Cup, in which she was leading run-scorer, and World Twenty20, for which she was player of the tournament. She retired in 2011 having played more than 250 times for England.

For James Anderson, 2008 was a seminal year. A talented young bowler and natural athlete, he burst on to the scene in 2002-03 as a replacement in England's one-day team in Australia, after making only 11 Championship appearances for Lancashire. His ability to swing the ball at pace was demonstrated in a match-winning performance against Pakistan at the World Cup.

Years of frustration followed as he struggled to master control in the Test arena on the few occasions when he was chosen to play. He also lost a year to injury following a misguided attempt to remodel his action.

Heading into the 2007-08 tour of New Zealand he was at a low ebb, but mid-series the selectors made a bold move to include him and

James Anderson: **"The Burnley Express had been late out of the sidings"**

Another wicket for **James Anderson**, congratulated by Ian Bell [2008]

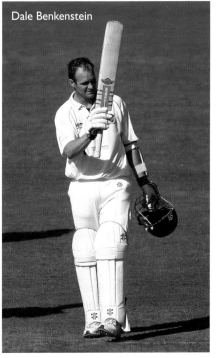

Dale Benkenstein

Stuart Broad [2010] ahead of Matthew Hoggard [2006] and Steve Harmison [2005].

Anderson relished his new role as attack leader, and at home in 2008 took the first seven New Zealand wickets at Trent Bridge, where he demonstrated his mastery of late swing. He could be deadly in classic English conditions, but it took longer for him to learn how to bowl elsewhere.

Armed with intelligence and a burning desire to improve, he ultimately proved a champion on every continent, taking 24 wickets in Australia in 2010-11 and 15 in India in 2012-13, by which time he had dismissed Sachin Tendulkar [1997] more times than anyone in Tests. He also overtook Ian Botham [1978] as England's leading wicket-taker across all formats.

Despite Anderson's efforts South Africa won their Test series in England in 2008, with Mark

CRICKETERS OF THE YEAR 2009 – Performances in the English season 2008

Name	Age*		Matches	Runs	Bat ave	Wickets	Bowl ave	Catches (/st)
JM Anderson	26	First-class	10	92	13.14	49	21.04	9
		Tests	7	91	18.20	34	25.76	6
		ODI	11	13	6.50	6	53.16	4
DM Benkenstein	34	First-class	15	817	43.00	1	60.00	5
		List A	16	399	30.69	7	38.28	8
MV Boucher	32	Tests	4	138	27.60			18
		ODI	5	55	18.33			3
ND McKenzie	33	First-class	10	546	32.11	0		10
		Tests	4	339	48.42			2
SC Taylor	33	Women's ODI	11	292	73.00			4

as at 1/4/2009

Mark Boucher (left) and **Neil McKenzie**

Boucher and Neil McKenzie, both valued senior members of the team, playing important parts. Boucher was a stabilising force during a difficult chase at Edgbaston, scoring an unbeaten 45 in partnership with Graeme Smith [2004]. Boucher scored few Test hundreds in a long career, but played many smaller innings of great influence, such as this.

Early on, Boucher's batting kept him in the side when his glovework was a little scruffy. He was actually dropped in 2004-05, but his dedication saw him regain his place for the remainder of his career. He retired as the record-holder for most dismissals in Tests (555) and all internationals (999).

Key to his longevity was staying fit, although ironically his career ended during the early days of his fourth tour of England in 2012 when he was hit in the eye by a bail while keeping at Taunton. There were brief fears, happily unfounded, that he might lose his sight.

Since his recent recall to the Test side, McKenzie had forged a formidable opening partnership with Smith; shortly before coming to England they had shared a world-record

Claire Taylor

Claire Taylor:

"In the men's college team she learned to play off the back foot, whereas women's cricket is more of a front-foot game"

stand of 415 in Bangladesh. They both scored hundreds in the follow-on to save the Lord's Test, McKenzie's obdurate 138 lasting more than nine hours. He faced more deliveries in the series than any other player.

McKenzie, whose father played for Transvaal, had led a South African under-19 team to England in 1995, and spent four years in the Test team as a capable but inconsistent batsman from 2000 to 2004. During his early days his preparation involved many superstitious rituals, such as taping a bat to the dressing-room ceiling.

Within months of his selection by *Wisden*, McKenzie lost his Test place again, this time for good, but he was resourceful enough to reinvent himself for the Twenty20 age, helping Hampshire to two domestic titles.

McKenzie prepared for the 2008 England tour with an early-season stint at Durham, where he played under fellow South African Dale Benkenstein, who went on to lead them to their first Championship title.

Benkenstein was not only the county's best batsman, but managed to get the best out of a talented squad. In search of trophies, Durham had begun to import outside help on short-term contracts, but Benkenstein was totally committed to the cause. Joining Durham in 2005 after a spell in league cricket in Cumbria, he was quickly named as captain and in 2007 led them to the FP Trophy.

Born in Rhodesia, he had moved with his family to Natal when he was six; there he learnt the game in the back yard with two older brothers who also played first-class cricket, as did their father.

Benkenstein showed an early aptitude for captaincy, and took over from Malcolm Marshall [1983] at Natal in 1996. Touted as a potential Test leader, he in fact played only 22 one-day internationals, the last in 2002. He surprisingly resigned the Durham captaincy after the 2008 season, but carried on playing in the ranks.

2010

Five Cricketers of the Year

Stuart Broad (Nottinghamshire and England) ◗ ●
Michael Clarke (Australians) ◗
Graham Onions (Durham and England) ●
Matt Prior (Sussex and England) ⬛
Graeme Swann (Nottinghamshire and England) ●

HEADLINE EVENTS FROM 2009

- County champions – Durham

- Friends Provident Trophy – Hampshire

- NatWest Pro40 – Sussex

- Twenty20 Cup – Sussex

- England beat West Indies 2-0 and Australia 2-1 to regain the Ashes

- Pakistan win the World Twenty20

- England lose 1-0 to both India and West Indies in 2008-09

WISDEN MARKED ENGLAND'S ACHIEVEMENT IN regaining the Ashes in 2009 by picking four of the victorious side – three bowlers in Stuart Broad, Graham Onions and Graeme Swann, plus wicketkeeper-batsman Matt Prior – none of whom was even in the team at the start of 2008. Australia's best batsman Michael Clarke completed the Five.

Broad, whose father Chris played 25 Tests as a batsman, had long been earmarked as a future star. He too started out as a batsman, but eventually his 6ft 6in height gave him natural advantages as a bowler. He began in England's one-day teams (being hit for six sixes in an over by Yuvraj Singh in the World Twenty20 in 2007) and had only been a Test regular since 2008.

Broad started the Ashes quietly, but as would often happen produced his best under pressure, taking six wickets and sharing a whirlwind stand of 108 with Swann in the fourth match at Headingley that shifted momentum even in defeat. In the decider at The Oval, he produced the spell that settled the outcome. Often criticised for not pitching the ball up, he did so devastatingly, capturing five wickets in 47 balls.

Broad's form remained mercurial, and he

was briefly dropped from the Test side in 2012. Although he scored 169 in a world-record eighth-wicket partnership of 332 with Jonathan Trott [2011] at Lord's in 2010, his batting did not develop as much as expected, but he was capable of match-shaping spells with the ball. He became the third England Test player to top 1,500 runs and 150 wickets after Ian Botham [1978] and Andrew Flintoff [2004].

He was appointed England's Twenty20 captain in 2011. His sister Gemma worked as an England team analyst.

Overall, Swann's Ashes series was nothing remarkable, but he starred in England's two wins, taking four second-innings wickets in both. This confirmed his talent for performing under pressure – his wisecracking nature showed a love of the limelight – and completed a remarkable comeback.

Swann, whose brother Alec also played county cricket, had first toured with England in 1999-2000, aged 20, but was plainly not ready. After years of hard graft, during which he switched from Northamptonshire to Nottinghamshire, he returned to the England squad and finally played his first Test in

Matt Prior:

"Like a good football referee, his best work went unnoticed"

Graeme Swann:

"His eagerness to be involved in everything... is Swann's dominant characteristic"

Matthew Prior (left) with **Graeme Swann**

December 2008, taking two wickets in his first over at Chennai.

Over the next few months he displaced Monty Panesar [2007] as England's first-choice spinner. His timing was perfect: left-handed batsmen (the off-spinner's preferred prey) were playing international cricket in greater numbers than ever, and the Decision Review System, which assisted spin bowlers in getting verdicts, was starting to be introduced. Four years after his debut, he overtook Jim Laker [1952] as England's most successful Test off-spinner.

The stylish, quick-footed Clarke played Swann as well as anyone. He scored a wonderful century at Lord's in a losing cause, made an unbeaten hundred to draw the Test at Edgbaston, and fell seven short of a third century at Headingley. However, he failed twice at The Oval.

Clarke had long seemed destined for great things. He learnt a lot at the cricket centre run by his father Les, and by 18 was captaining Australia under-19s and signing his first New South Wales contract.

In his first Test, at Bangalore in 2004, he made a seemingly effortless 151, and a month

CRICKETERS OF THE YEAR 2010 – Performances in the English season 2009

Name	Age*		Matches	Runs	Bat ave	Wickets	Bowl ave	Catches (/st)
SCJ Broad	23	Tests	7	300	33.33	26	28.73	I
		ODI	5	32	10.66	8	32.62	0
MJ Clarke	28	Tests	5	448	64.00	I	75.00	8
		ODI	7	269	44.83	0		2
G Onions	27	First-class	14	52	6.50	69	19.95	5
		Tests	5	19	6.33	20	25.15	0
MJ Prior	28	First-class	13	788	41.47			30/1
		Tests	7	366	36.60			14/1
		ODI	10	239	23.90			7/1
GP Swann	31	Tests	7	312	44.57	21	32.66	4
		ODI	8	38	7.60	12	21.33	3

* as at 1/4/2010

later added 141 in his first home Test. But the golden-boy image took a number of hits. He was dropped after the 2005 England tour, and in 2010 and 2011 averaged less than 40. He had issues with the short ball, and with a dodgy back.

His ascension to the Test captaincy in 2011 was greeted with some scepticism, as he wasn't that popular within the team, but the job transformed him. During 2012 he four times topped 200 in Tests, a unique feat: this included a sublime 329 not out against India in his home city of Sydney, and two double-centuries against South Africa's vaunted pace attack; so much for the supposed flaws in his game.

Like Swann, Prior returned to the England set-up in India in 2008-09. During his first run in the side he had scored a hundred on debut against West Indies at Lord's in 2007, but his keeping proved fallible and he lost his place. He returned a better player and contributed some vital, selfless innings in the Ashes, finishing as England's fastest scorer.

Over the next two years, Prior was the focal point of an athletic, vibrant England fielding unit. He also played many fine innings tailored to the needs of the side. By March 2013 he had scored seven Test hundreds, but despite several spells in the team had failed to establish himself in England's 50-over or Twenty20 sides.

Prior was born in Johannesburg to a South African mother and English father. The family moved to England when he was 11, and he won a sports scholarship to Brighton College. He initially faced competition from Tim Ambrose for the gloves at Sussex and with England, but from 2009 made the Test position his own, keeping in 50 consecutive matches.

Onions was not even in the Durham team at the end of 2008, but in 2009 he stayed free from injury and picked up 20 Test wickets in the summer as well as helping Durham retain the Championship. He took five for 38 on debut against West Indies at Lord's and four for 58

against Australia at Edgbaston, where he began the second day by taking two wickets with the first two balls.

Onions had a penchant for gaining assistance off the pitch through long, accurate spells, and either side of his Test debut took 45 wickets in five Championship games.

He was left out of the Ashes decider at The Oval, but regained his place in South Africa, where he attained unlikely celebrity as a No. 11 batsman, twice batting out the final six balls for draws, at Centurion and Cape Town. He again didn't finish the series due to concerns about his stamina.

Onions underwent major back surgery in 2011, but fought his way back into various England squads. On being released from the party for the Lord's Test against South Africa in 2012, he drove up to Trent Bridge and took nine for 67 for Durham, also running out the tenth man.

Stuart Broad

Graham Onions

Michael Clarke

2011

Four Cricketers of the Year

Eoin Morgan (Middlesex and England) *

Chris Read (Nottinghamshire) ♛

Tamim Iqbal (Bangladeshis) *

Jonathan Trott (Warwickshire and England) *

HEADLINE EVENTS FROM 2010

- County champions – Nottinghamshire

- Clydesdale Bank 40 – Warwickshire

- Twenty20 Cup – Hampshire

- England beat Bangladesh 2-0 and Pakistan 3-1

- England win the World Twenty20

- England draw 1-1 with South Africa and beat Bangladesh 2-0 in 2009-10

SCYLD BERRY AGAIN BROKE WITH TRADITION, BY naming only four Cricketers of the Year. He had originally chosen five but, as he explained in his Preface, "serious allegations of corruption were then made against one of them, and subsequent events rendered his selection in my opinion unsustainable".

Although *Wisden* did not identify the player in question, because at the time he along with two Pakistan team-mates faced criminal charges brought by the Crown Prosecution Service, it was widely assumed that he was Mohammad Aamer.

Aamer played six Tests in England in the summer of 2010 – two against Australia in a series that would have been played in Pakistan had security allowed, and four against England. In them he captured the striking haul of 30 wickets. For one who was only 18 years old, he showed remarkable skill in swinging the ball at pace, while remaining so accurate. He also demonstrated impressive tactical nous.

A few months after *Wisden* 2011 appeared, the three Pakistanis were jailed for their involvement in the bowling of three prearranged no-balls during the Lord's Test against England. They had already received playing bans from the ICC.

Tamim Iqbal became the first Bangladeshi cricketer to be chosen by *Wisden*. Bangladesh made their second Test tour of England in 2010, and thanks to Tamim they put up a much better fight than in 2005. He scored two brilliant centuries, one at Lord's off 94 balls, the other off exactly 100 at Old Trafford.

Driven by the desire to become the first Bangladeshi to get his name on the Lord's honours board, Tamim was mortified to be run out for 55 in the first innings, and vowed not to leave without making a hundred. Not only did he have his wish in the second innings, he got there by hitting Tim Bresnan [2012] for 4, 4, 2 and 4 from successive balls, before gesturing to the visitors' dressing-room to have his team-mates write his name on the board. He later said that the hundred in Manchester on a bouncier, more alien surface, gave him greater satisfaction.

Tamim, who was only 21, was born within a stone's throw of the Test ground in Chittagong, and grew up in a family obsessed by cricket. An uncle, Akram Khan, had captained Bangladesh to success in the 1997 ICC Trophy which led to their Test status; an elder brother, Nafis Iqbal, also opened the batting for Bangladesh. His father, a football coach by trade, coached Tamim

Tamim Iqbal

A youthful involvement in hurling had helped him develop a range of wristy sweeps and reverse sweeps while playing Twenty20 cricket for Middlesex. Like Kevin Pietersen [2006], Morgan had an ability to hit the ball in unusual areas, which made him an invaluable asset to an England batting line-up often too conventional for its own good. *Wisden* actually described Morgan as the most versatile limited-overs batsman in world cricket. He was certainly an important factor in England winning the World Twenty20 in May 2010, their first global trophy.

However, Morgan's idiosyncratic technique served him less well in the Test arena, and by early 2012 he had lost his place in the side and been forced to refine his methods. He remained a brilliant match-winner in the shorter formats.

Jonathan Trott might have been picked after his Ashes-winning performance at The Oval in 2009, but could be ignored no longer after consistent run-making in 2010. He played two massive innings at Lord's – 226 against Bangladesh and 184 against Pakistan, in the first and last Tests of England's summer.

Trott was an old-fashioned style of cricketer who loved to bat time, setting himself to survive the day as a matter of course. His painstaking marking of his guard exasperated many onlookers and opponents, but for him it was an essential ritual before each ball. Trott batted a total of 33 hours in the six home Tests, and in the winter in Australia notched up another 20 hours in the process of scoring 445 runs.

Trott was born in Cape Town into a sporting family, both his parents being talented hockey players. His brother-in-law, Kenny Jackson, played for Western Province and was a mentor. Trott worked his way through the South African youth system, but shortly after representing their under-19s opted to follow his English-born father to the UK. He quickly won a contract with Warwickshire after scoring 245 in a trial match.

Trott married Abi Dollery, Warwickshire's

Chris Read

tirelessly before his death in 2000.

Equally important to his development was watching Sanath Jayasuriya [1997] at the 1996 World Cup. Unfortunately, Bangladesh's struggles led to their international fixture list being trimmed, and Tamim's form suffered.

Like Tamim, Eoin Morgan broke new ground. Born on a council estate in north Dublin, he was the first Irishman to be chosen by *Wisden,* although after appearing in 23 one-day internationals for his country of birth he switched allegiance to England in 2009 because of the greater opportunities it afforded. He made his maiden Test century in his third match, against Pakistan at Trent Bridge, but *Wisden* was mainly recognising his brilliant and innovative batting in limited-overs cricket.

Jonathan Trott

press officer and the grand-daughter of Tom Dollery [1951], while his own father was reputedly a descendant of Harry [1894] and Albert Trott [1899].

Chris Read led Nottinghamshire to the Championship in 2010. In a thrilling finale, Read was the driving force behind an aggressive bid to win the title on the last day of the season. Read gambled that neither Yorkshire nor Somerset would win elsewhere, and that his side could get home on bonus points alone in their match at Old Trafford. Nottinghamshire, 89 for two overnight, duly raced to 400 and took three quick Lancashire wickets to seal the title.

Read was a precocious talent. He had played for his native Devon, and Gloucestershire, and toured with England A by the time he moved at the age of 20 to Nottinghamshire in 1998. Fifteen Test caps followed between 1999 and 2007, but while he was widely regarded as the best gloveman in the country, he failed to cement a Test place or ever win a central contract. He later said he never felt "comfortable" as an England player.

Although perhaps never good enough as a batsman for England, or vocal enough for them behind the stumps, he was a substantial county cricketer.

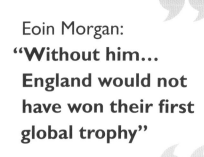

Eoin Morgan

Eoin Morgan:

"Without him... England would not have won their first global trophy"

CRICKETERS OF THE YEAR 2011 – Performances in the English season 2010

Name	Age*		Matches	Runs	Bat ave	Wickets	Bowl ave	Catches (Ist)
EJG Morgan	24	Tests	6	256	32.00			4
		ODI	14	512	46.54			7
CMW Read	32	First-class	17	945	45.00			60/4
		List A	12	263	43.83			8/3
Tamim Iqbal	22	Tests	2	268	67.00			0
		ODI	6	143	23.83			2
IJL Trott	29	First-class	12	1084	57.05	5	18.80	14
		List A	19	940	55.29	0		7
		Tests	6	669	83.62	I	23.00	4
		ODI	7	335	47.85	0		I

as at 1/4/2011

2012 Five Cricketers of the Year

Alastair Cook (Essex and England)

Tim Bresnan (Yorkshire and England)

Kumar Sangakkara (Sri Lankans)

Glen Chapple (Lancashire)

Alan Richardson (Worcestershire)

HEADLINE EVENTS FROM 2011

- County champions – Lancashire

- Clydesdale Bank 40 – Surrey

- Twenty20 Cup – Leicestershire

- England beat Sri Lanka 1-0 and India 4-0

- England retain the Ashes in 2010-11, beating Australia 3-1

- India win the World Cup

ENGLAND WENT TOP OF THE WORLD TEST rankings for the first time in 2011, when they won five out of seven home Tests, and two of the key players in this rise were Alastair Cook and Tim Bresnan. In the innings victory over India at Edgbaston in which England sealed the No. 1 spot, Cook scored 294, having the previous winter amassed a record 766 runs in an historic Ashes series win.

It was a surprise that Cook had not been chosen before by *Wisden,* as he had been a consistent scorer in Tests since his debut in 2006. In fact, in the 2011 *Wisden*, Scyld Berry, the editor, said that he had been tempted to change the parameters so Cook could be picked on the back of his performances in Australia, but he hoped that continued good form would soon see Cook picked – as indeed happened.

Bresnan, by contrast, had first played Test cricket in 2009 and rarely been an automatic choice. However he hadn't let England down when he had played, and one of his best games came against India at Trent Bridge, where he scored 90 and took five for 48 in the second innings. After the India series, he was averaging 45.42 with bat and 23.60 with ball. He became

something of a lucky mascot for England: they won the first 13 Tests in which he appeared.

The backgrounds of Cook and Bresnan could not have been much different. Cook was educated at St Paul's choir school and Bedford, while Bresnan went to a state school in Pontefract, and played his early cricket for Townville Miners Welfare Club.

Cook was identified from an early age as a cricketer of rare talent and application, and received early guidance from Keith Fletcher [1974] and Graham Gooch [1980]. Drafted into the England team in emergency in India early in 2006 at the age of 21, he scored a hundred on debut and became an automatic selection thereafter.

Less obviously suited to one-day cricket, he nevertheless made a big impact when he was appointed England's 50-overs captain in 2011, broadening his range of strokes and being named Man of the Series in his first outing against Sri Lanka.

He took over the reins of the Test side in 2012-13, and led England to their first series win in India since 1984-85, scoring hundreds in each of the first three matches of the series (to add to the two in two he had made as stand-in captain

Alastair Cook (left) places the field with Tim Bresnan

Tim Bresnan:
"He still has the air of a man with an emergency cheese sandwich in his back pocket"

in Bangladesh in 2010). That gave him 23 Test hundreds, an England record.

Bresnan, in fact, first played for England a year earlier than Cook, at 20, though only in the one-day team; for a while he found it difficult to be regarded as anything more than a useful support player.

He moved to centre stage during the Ashes in 2010-11, when he was brought into the side for the Fourth Test in place of Steven Finn, and on his first day of action played a starring role in Australia's Boxing Day rout for 98 at the MCG. Bresnan took four for 50, and finished the series at the top of the averages with 11 wickets at 19.54.

Gradually his talents had emerged: tireless, good at reverse and conventional swing, both at a deceptive pace; a useful No. 8 batsman and good team man. A persistent elbow problem requiring two operations saw a tailing-off of his form in 2012.

Kumar Sangakkara was one of the most complete batsmen to come out of Asia. He scored prolifically on the subcontinent, but had the technique to replicate his success abroad. On his third tour of England in 2011 he filled one of the few gaps in his CV by recording a

gritty first Test century there, scoring 119 to save the game at the Rose Bowl. During 2011 as a whole he scored 1,000 runs in both Tests and one-day internationals for an unprecedented third time.

In his early years, Sangakkara successfully combined wicketkeeping and batting, but when he concentrated his energies on the pivotal No. 3 position in Tests, he took his batting up to another level, raising his average by more than 25 points.

Like Cook, Sangakkara had a privileged upbringing, studied music at school, and batted left-handed; unlike Cook, he also studied law. He masked a teak-hard toughness with an impressive elegance. He led Sri Lanka from 2009 until 2011, when he resigned after their defeat by India in the World Cup final. Free to speak, he issued withering criticism of Sri Lanka's political Establishment when he delivered the Cowdrey Lecture at Lord's.

Glen Chapple and Alan Richardson were both long-serving bowlers who earned their recognition outside the international arena. Chapple, who toured several times with England A in the mid-1990s, never played a Test, though he was once named in a squad in 2003. His only

In 2011 **Glen Chapple** captained Lancashire to their first outright County Championship title since 1934

Kumar Sangakkara

Championship in 2011, their first outright title since 1934.

Like Chapple, Richardson was a classical English bowler: accurate and looking to take wickets through seam or swing. It is arguable whether a more itinerant cricketer has been chosen by *Wisden* than Richardson, who had already played for Derbyshire, Staffordshire, Warwickshire and Middlesex before signing for Worcestershire in 2009.

He did what he described as "some shocking jobs" to subsidise his cricket, including landscape gardening, nights in warehouses and putting studs into golf shoes. He was part of Warwickshire's unbeaten 2004 Championship campaign, but described it as the "lowest point" of his career as he took just six wickets in seven matches. He did, though, tour with England Lions in 2007-08.

After a slow start at New Road, he took 55 wickets in 2010 and 73 in 2011. Not only was he the leading wicket-taker in the first division, but he bowled more overs than any other fast bowler, and played a big part in Worcestershire escaping relegation.

Although Chapple and Richardson both did well again with the ball, neither could prevent their counties dropping into the second division in 2012.

Kumar Sangakkara:

"[He has] an impulsive nature and a principled belief in right and wrong"

one-day cap came in a game against Ireland in 2006 that typified his misfortune, as he broke down after four overs.

Chapple's years of toil were finally rewarded after he was handed the Lancashire captaincy for 2009. In both 2010 and 2011 he took more than 50 first-class wickets at less than 20 apiece, the best returns of his career, but his crowning achievement came when he led Lancashire to the

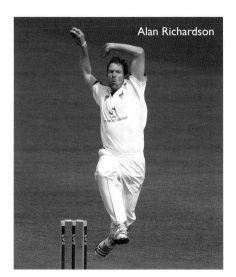

Alan Richardson

CRICKETERS OF THE YEAR 2012 – Performances in the English season 2011

Name	Age*		Matches	Runs	Bat ave	Wickets	Bowl ave	Catches (/st)
TT Bresnan	27	Tests	3	154	77.00	16	16.31	0
		ODI	10	112	18.66	14	33.85	5
G Chapple	38	First-class	13	380	18.09	57	19.75	2
AN Cook	27	First-class	14	1372	57.16			12
		Tests	7	738	73.80			7
		ODI	10	467	58.37			4
A Richardson	36	First-class	16	151	10.06	73	24.42	5
KC Sangakkara	34	Tests	3	184	30.66			0
		ODI	5	221	44.20			3/4

* as at 1/4/2012

2013

Five Cricketers of the Year

Hashim Amla (South Africans) *

Nick Compton (Somerset) *

Jacques Kallis (South Africans) * ●

Marlon Samuels (West Indians) *

Dale Steyn (South Africans) ●

HEADLINE EVENTS FROM 2012

- County champions – Warwickshire

- Clydesdale Bank 40 – Hampshire

- Twenty20 Cup – Hampshire

- England beat West Indies 2-0 and lose 2-0 to South Africa

- West Indies win the World Twenty20

- England lose 3-0 to Pakistan and draw 1-1 with Sri Lanka in 2011-12

THE SELECTION OF THREE SOUTH AFRICAN players maintained the country's record of producing a Cricketer of the Year on all but one of their tours of England since 1904 (the one time they did not, following the 1912 tour, *Wisden* did not actually choose a Five).

However, the selection of Hashim Amla, a Durban-born Muslim whose family originated in India, broke new ground. He was the first from the country's non-white community to be a Cricketer of the Year while playing for South Africa. Two Cape Coloureds, Charles Llewellyn [1911] and Basil D'Oliveira [1967], were chosen while playing for English sides. Amla modestly declined to see himself as a role model.

He had a sublime tour. He batted 13 hours for South Africa's first triple-century at The Oval, setting them on course for a crushing win while confirming a reputation for zen-like patience, superb positioning around the crease and precision strokeplay. He also scored the only hundred of the game at Lord's in which South Africa clinched the series and the No. 1 position in the rankings. Carrying his form into the shorter formats, he finished with 900 runs and eight top-scores in 11 international innings.

When South Africa then won in Australia, Amla was again to the fore, with hundreds at Brisbane and Perth. The team travelled a lot in 2012, and Amla's haul of 1,712 international runs overseas was a record for one year.

Amla, whose elder brother Ahmed played provincial cricket, was earmarked for great things from schooldays. He captained South Africa under-19s, and the Dolphins (formerly Natal) at the age of 21, shortly before making his Test debut. He had to work on ironing out some flaws, but by 2010 the dam burst; that year he plundered 1,000 runs in both Tests and one-dayers at averages in excess of 75.

Jacques Kallis, who had previously had three relatively quiet tours of England, was the game's most formidable all-rounder since Ian Botham [1978], if often more impressive to watch than exciting. His performance in the Oval Test was typical. He captured two important wickets in the first innings with his muscular medium-pace bowling, kept Amla company for seven hours while contributing 182 towards a stand of 377 between two of batting's coolest technicians, and held two catches at slip, where he generally missed little.

The engine room of the South African side that became the top-ranked Test team in 2012: **Hashim Amla**, **Dale Steyn**, Graeme Smith [2004] and **Jacques Kallis**

That hundred was his 43rd in Tests, second only to Sachin Tendulkar [1997]. He was less prominent in the other Tests, partly because he suffered two contentious decisions and was hampered at Leeds by back spasms. His fitness had become a constant concern, and he missed the one-day series.

A protégé of Duncan Fletcher's at Western Province, Kallis was first picked by South Africa at 20, and sealed his place two years later by saving a Test in Australia, shortly after spending a season at Middlesex. He was not always a fast scorer, but he upped his game after being dropped from South Africa's 2007 World Twenty20 squad. He was competitive but always chivalrous.

South Africa's attack had been spearheaded since the retirement of Shaun Pollock [2003] in 2008 by Dale Steyn, who for much of that time

Hashim Amla:
"Whereas others see fielders, Amla sees gaps"

had been ranked the world's No. 1 bowler. Short and wiry, Steyn was a relative pygmy in a world of fast-bowling giants but, swinging the ball from a fullish off-stump line, he was consistently the fastest and the best, and rarely injured.

Unusually, he did not take the new ball in England for tactical reasons, but he was responsible for stirring South Africa into action at The Oval, bounding in on the second morning to peg back England's total. He added a five-for in the second innings and finished with 15 wickets in the three-Test series, including Jonathan Trott [2011] four times and Alastair Cook [2012] thrice.

Steyn grew up in the remote town of Phalaborwa, near the Kruger national park, but still gained a debut with Northerns aged 20. His early Tests were unremarkable, and he failed at Essex in 2005, but soon after that his fist-pumping celebrations were becoming more common. In January 2013 he reached 300 Test wickets in 61 matches; only Dennis Lillee [1973] and Muttiah Muralitharan [1999] have done so in fewer matches.

Nick Compton, whose father played for Natal and whose grandfather was Denis Compton [1938], used his immense concentration and exemplary technique to score prolifically at Somerset in 2012. He topped the national averages by 26 points and was the leading run-scorer despite missing three matches with back trouble. But for rain he would probably have scored 1,000 runs before the end of May; as it was, he got there on June 1, the earliest date for 24 years.

Such form left him strongly placed for Test selection, as at the end of the season England were looking for an opener to replace the retired Andrew Strauss [2005], and Compton duly formed a productive alliance with Cook [2011] during the winter, first in India and then New Zealand, where he scored two hundreds.

Compton was, like Amla, born in Durban in 1983, and played under him at Durban High

Marlon Samuels leads the celebrations after West Indies win the World Twenty20 in 2012

Marlon Samuels, a Jamaican, arrived in England in 2013 with a Test batting average below 30 and a chequered past. Some thought him wayward; he thought he was waywardly handled. Whatever, he had not given up, even when he was accused by Indian police in 2007 of giving team information to a known bookmaker, and banned by the ICC for two years. He maintained his innocence and went into training for his return.

In 2013, he negotiated to miss some West Indies matches to play in part of the IPL, but not to miss the England tour; that was a challenge he wanted. Nor did he take a backward step, hitting 86 at Lord's, 117 and 76 not out at Trent Bridge, and 76 at Edgbaston, and engaging verbally with the England players as well.

In October 2012, Samuels played perhaps the finest innings seen in a 20-overs match when he turned around the World Twenty20 final against Sri Lanka with a breathtaking 78 off 56 balls, pulverising Lasith Malinga in the process. The following month he took 260 off Bangladesh in a Test.

He was a useful off-spinner, but twice barred because of a suspect action. One of six siblings, elder brother Robert, also played for West Indies.

Marlon Samuels:
"[He] made the stump mike essential listening with his ice-cool rejoinders"

School before being spotted on a schools tour and offered a sports scholarship to Harrow. He first played for Middlesex at 18, but both his opportunities and fortunes fluctuated wildly. A big season in 2006 won him a place on an England A tour, but in 2010 he left for Somerset, where his game moved onto a consistent upward trajectory.

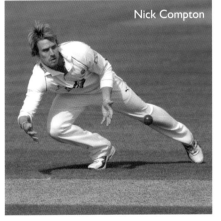

Nick Compton

CRICKETERS OF THE YEAR 2013 – Performances in the English season 2012

Name	Age*		Matches	Runs	Bat ave	Wickets	Bowl ave	Catches (/st)
HM Amla	30	Tests	3	482	120.50			2
		ODI	5	335	111.66			2
NRD Compton	29	First-class	14	1494	99.60			9
		List A	6	237	47.40			1
JH Kallis	37	Tests	3	262	65.50	4	45.00	6
MN Samuels	32	Tests	3	386	96.50	5	30.00	0
		ODI	2	43	21.50	2	27.00	0
DW Steyn	29	Tests	3	38	9.50	15	29.20	1
		ODI	3	4	4.00	5	20.60	0

* as at 1/4/2013

Cricketers of the Century

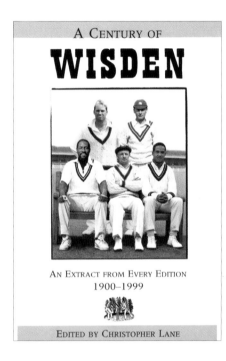

The Five Cricketers of the Century in a mock team picture on the cover of a book which accompanvied the Millennium Edition. From left: (back row) **Warne**, **Hobbs**, (front row) **Richards**, **Bradman**, **Sobers**

IN 2000, WISDEN NAMED ITS FIVE CRICKETERS of the Century. To arrive at a "Five", Matthew Engel, the editor, drew on the votes of an electorate of 100 cricketers, journalists, historians and observers spanning all nine (at that time) Test-playing countries. Voters were asked to consider the contributions of cricketers in the broadest sense – taking account of such things as leadership qualities and impact on the public – and to discount W. G. Grace on the basis that he was primarily a 19th Century cricketer.

The chosen Five were:

Don Bradman	(Australia, 100 votes)
Garry Sobers	(West Indies, 90 votes)
Jack Hobbs	(England, 30 votes)
Shane Warne	(Australia, 27 votes)
Viv Richards	(West Indies, 25 votes)

Others who received more than one vote were:

19 votes:	Dennis Lillee, Sir Frank Worrell
18 votes:	Wally Hammond
14 votes:	Denis Compton
13 votes:	Sir Richard Hadlee, Imran Khan
12 votes:	Sunil Gavaskar
11 votes:	Sydney Barnes, Sir Len Hutton
10 votes:	Bill O'Reilly
9 votes:	Sir Ian Botham
6 votes:	Harold Larwood, Ray Lindwall, Sachin Tendulkar
5 votes:	Richie Benaud, George Headley, Kapil Dev
4 votes:	Graeme Pollock, Wilfred Rhodes, Victor Trumper
3 votes:	Godfrey Evans, Malcolm Marshall, Wasim Akram
2 votes:	Sir Alec Bedser, Clarrie Grimmett, Fred Trueman, Frank Woolley

Matthew Engel said that the electorate was "weighted to reflect each country's role in international cricket over the century, judged – very roughly – on the number of Tests played. So there were 28 English voters, 20 from Australia and so on down the line to just one from Zimbabwe… They were a mixture of cricketers, journalists (indeed many count as both), historians or even just expert observers of the game like Sir Carlisle Burton of Barbados. More than half had played Test cricket; all of them had watched copious amounts of it." He added that a major problem was "that no one watched all the cricket of the century. Some, however, came close, led by E. W. Swanton, whose first-hand knowledge of all cricket since the First World War was unsurpassable."

In *Wisden*'s 100th edition in 1963, Neville Cardus, the eminent cricket writer, was invited to select "Six Giants of the *Wisden* Century". He chose players who had "enriched the game by expanding in a fresh way some already established method… masters of the old and initiators of the new". His six were: Sydney Barnes (England), Don Bradman (Australia), W. G. Grace (England), Jack Hobbs (England), Tom Richardson (England) and Victor Trumper (Australia).

Schools Cricketer of the Year

Jos Buttler

In 2008, under Scyld Berry's editorship, *Wisden* introduced a Schools Cricketer of the Year award. It was the first time the Almanack had annually recognised school cricketers, although the Five Cricketers of the Year in 1918 and 1919 were drawn from public-schools cricket when the county and international games were suspended due to war. The first three winners of the award had all played for England by 2011.

2007	Jonny Bairstow (St Peter's School, York)
2008	James Taylor (Shrewsbury School)
2009	Jos Buttler (King's College, Taunton)
2010	Will Vanderspar (Eton College)
2011	Daniel Bell-Drummond (Millfield School)
2012	Thomas Abell (Taunton School)

Daniel Bell-Drummond

Will Vanderspar

Thomas Abell

James Taylor and **Jonny Bairstow**

The Leading Cricketer in the World

In 2004, Wisden introduced a new award, the Leading Cricketer in the World, based on worldwide performances during the previous calendar year. Like the Five Cricketers of the Year, the choice was that of the editor, in consultation with the game's most experienced writers and commentators, but unlike selection for the Five this global award could be won more than once.

Virender Sehwag, whose explosive batting for India set new standards for opening an innings in Test cricket, became the first man to receive the award twice, and by 2013 was the only Leading Cricketer in the World not to have been chosen as a Cricketer of the Year. Ricky Ponting (Leading Cricketer for 2003, Cricketer of the Year 2006) and Jacques Kallis (Leading Cricketer for 2007, Cricketer of the Year 2013) were both chosen for the global award before they were selected among a Five. Kumar Sangakkara was, in the 2012 *Wisden*, chosen for both.

In 2007, *Wisden* produced a retrospective list of Leading Cricketers in the World for each year – minus war years when play was suspended – dating back to 1900. Selection was supervised by *Wisden* editor Matthew Engel in consultation with a panel of experts, and used the same criteria as the award introduced in 2004. Like Sehwag, three players on the retrospective list – Aubrey Faulkner (1910), Herbie Collins (1920) and Jeff Thomson (1974) – were never chosen as Cricketers of the Year.

Virender Sehwag

Jeff Thomson

2003	Ricky Ponting (Australia; selected by Wisden in 2004)
2004	Shane Warne (Australia)
2005	Andrew Flintoff (England)
2006	Muttiah Muralitharan (Sri Lanka)
2007	Jacques Kallis (South Africa)
2008	Virender Sehwag (India)
2009	Virender Sehwag (India)
2010	Sachin Tendulkar (India)
2011	Kumar Sangakkara (Sri Lanka)
2012	Michael Clarke (Australia)

Aubrey Faulkner

Herbie Collins

The most frequent winners of the Leading Cricketer award (including retrospective winners) are: Don Bradman 10, Garry Sobers 8, Jack Hobbs, Viv Richards and Shane Warne 3.

1900	K. S. Ranjitsinhji (England)
1901	C. B. Fry (England)
1902	Victor Trumper (Australia)
1903	C. B. Fry (England)
1904	Bernard Bosanquet (England)
1905	Stanley Jackson (England)
1906	George Hirst (England)
1907	Ernie Vogler (South Africa)
1908	Monty Noble (Australia)
1909	Wilfred Rhodes (England)
1910	Aubrey Faulkner (South Africa)
1911	Victor Trumper (Australia)
1912	Sydney Barnes (England)
1913	Sydney Barnes (England)
1914	Jack Hobbs (England)
1919	Jack Gregory (Australia)
1920	Herbie Collins (Australia)
1921	Charles Macartney (Australia)
1922	Jack Hobbs (England)
1923	Patsy Hendren (England)
1924	Maurice Tate (England)
1925	Jack Hobbs (England)
1926	Charles Macartney (Australia)
1927	Bill Ponsford (Australia)
1928	Tich Freeman (England)
1929	Walter Hammond (England)
1930	Don Bradman (Australia)
1931	Don Bradman (Australia)
1932	Don Bradman (Australia)
1933	Harold Larwood (England)
1934	Don Bradman (Australia)
1935	Stan McCabe (Australia)
1936	Don Bradman (Australia)
1937	Don Bradman (Australia)
1938	Don Bradman (Australia)
1939	Don Bradman (Australia)
1946	Don Bradman (Australia)
1947	Denis Compton (England)
1948	Don Bradman (Australia)
1949	Len Hutton (England)
1950	Frank Worrell (West Indies)
1951	Keith Miller (Australia)
1952	Len Hutton (England)
1953	Alec Bedser (England)
1954	Clyde Walcott (West Indies)
1955	Frank Tyson (England)
1956	Jim Laker (England)
1957	Peter May (England)
1958	Garry Sobers (West Indies)
1959	Richie Benaud (Australia)
1960	Garry Sobers (West Indies)
1961	Alan Davidson (Australia)
1962	Garry Sobers (West Indies)
1963	Fred Trueman (England)
1964	Garry Sobers (West Indies)
1965	Garry Sobers (West Indies)
1966	Garry Sobers (West Indies)
1967	Graeme Pollock (South Africa)
1968	Garry Sobers (West Indies)
1969	Graeme Pollock (South Africa)
1970	Garry Sobers (West Indies)
1971	Mike Procter (South Africa)
1972	Dennis Lillee (Australia)
1973	Barry Richards (South Africa)
1974	Jeff Thomson (Australia)
1975	Clive Lloyd (West Indies)
1976	Viv Richards (West Indies)
1977	Dennis Lillee (Australia)
1978	Viv Richards (West Indies)
1979	Garry Chappell (Australia)
1980	Viv Richards (West Indies)
1981	Ian Botham (England)
1982	Imran Khan (Pakistan)
1983	Kapil Dev (India)
1984	Joel Garner (West Indies)
1985	Richard Hadlee (New Zealand)
1986	Malcolm Marshall (West Indies)
1987	Martin Crowe (New Zealand)
1988	Malcolm Marshall (West Indies)
1989	Allan Border (Australia)
1990	Graham Gooch (England)
1991	Curtly Ambrose (West Indies)
1992	Wasim Akram (Pakistan)
1993	Shane Warne (Australia)
1994	Brian Lara (West Indies)
1995	Brian Lara (West Indies)
1996	Sanath Jayasuriya (Sri Lanka)
1997	Shane Warne (Australia)
1998	Sachin Tendulkar (India)
1999	Steve Waugh (Australia)
2000	Muttiah Muralitharan (Sri Lanka)
2001	Glenn McGrath (Australia)
2002	Matthew Hayden (Australia)

Facts and Figures

CRICKETERS OF THE YEAR 1889-2013

Team	Years	Awards	Batsmen	Bowlers	Allrounders	WK
Surrey	1889–2007	49	22	18	5	4
Yorkshire	1889–2012	43	20	13	8	2
Lancashire	1889–2012	34	14	15	3	2*
Nottinghamshire	1890–2011	29	13	8	6	2
Middlesex	1892–2011	28	15	6	6	1
Kent	1892–2005	26	11	8	4	3
Essex	1898–2012	24	11	6	6	1
Warwickshire	1897–2011	23	9	7	5	2
Sussex	1895–2010	21	9	4	6	2
Somerset	1893–2013	19	12	3	4	0
Gloucestershire	1896–2004	17	8	3	5	1
Worcestershire	1900–2012	16	8	4	3	1
Hampshire	1900–2006	15	8	3	4	0
Northamptonshire	1905–2007	14	6	3	5	0
Derbyshire	1899–1996	13	5	5	1	2
Glamorgan	1927–2006	12	7	5	0	0
Leicestershire	1904–1997	8	5	1	2	0
Durham	2005–2010	7	4	3	0	0
Staffordshire	1910	1	0	1	0	0
Cambridge University	1889–1953	10	6	1	2	1
Oxford University	1893–1948	7	6	1	0	0
Public Schools	1918–1919	10	2	6	1	1
England	1889–2012	152	70	52	19	11
Australians†	1889–2010	70	34	19	9	8
South Africans	1905–2013	28	17	6	2	3
West Indians	1934–2013	26	16	7	2	1
Indians†	1933–2008	14	8	2	4	0
Pakistanis	1955–2007	12	6	4	2	0
New Zealanders	1928–2000	8	3	1	4	0
Sri Lankans†	1985–2012	6	5	1	0	0
Zimbabwe†	2002	1	0	0	0	1
Bangladeshis	2011	1	1	0	0	0
England Women	2009	1	1	0	0	0

Teams shown are those the players represented in the English season prior to selection

In total, there have been 570 Cricketers of the Year up to 2013. However, the total number of awards listed in this table is more than 570 because several played for country and county; some played for country, county and university in the same season (see individual sections for full details)

* Dick Pilling (Lancashire) did not appear in the previous season because of illness

† Sanath Jayasuriya (Sri Lanka, 1997), Andy Flower (Zimbabwe, 2002), V. V. S. Laxman (India, 2002) and Matthew Hayden (Australia, 2003) were chosen for their general impact on the game and did not play in the previous English season.

YOUNGEST CRICKETERS OF THE YEAR

Age at April 1 in the year of Wisden selection

16	Harry Calder (1918)
17	Clement Gibson (1918), Greville Stevens (1918)
18	John Firth (1918), Gerard Rotherham (1918), Norman Partridge (1919), Percy Adams (1919), Percy Chapman (1919), Adrian Gore (1919), Lionel Hedges (1919)
19	Mushtaq Mohammad (1963)
20	Jack Crawford (1907), Donald Knight (1915), Denis Compton (1939), Alf Valentine (1951), Craig McDermott (1986), Graeme Hick (1987), Waqar Younis (1992)

OLDEST CRICKETERS OF THE YEAR

Age at April 1 in the year of Wisden selection

48	Lord Hawke (1909)
47	WG Grace (1896)
45	Ewart Astill (1933)
44	Levi Wright (1906), Jack Simmons (1985)
43	Bill Alley (1962)
42	Alex Kennedy (1933), Eric Rowan (1952), Eric Hollies (1955), Don Shepherd (1970)

CHAMPIONSHIP WINNING CAPTAINS

1909	Lord Hawke (Yorkshire, champions in 1908)
1912	Frank Foster (Warwickshire, 1911)
1940	Brian Sellers (Yorkshire, 1939)
1952	Tom Dollery (Warwickshire, 1951)
1953	Stuart Surridge (Surrey, 1952)
1961	Vic Wilson (Yorkshire, 1960)
1964	Brian Close (Yorkshire, 1963)
1975	Norman Gifford (Worcestershire, 1974)
1977	Mike Brearley (Middlesex, 1976)
1989	Phil Neale (Worcestershire, 1988; the county also won the Refuge Assurance League)
1996	Dermot Reeve (Warwickshire, 1995; the county also won the NatWest Trophy)
1998	Matthew Maynard (Glamorgan, 1997)
2003	Adam Hollioake (Surrey, 2002)
2004	Chris Adams (Sussex, 2003)
2009	Dale Benkenstein (Durham, 2008)
2011	Chris Read (Nottinghamshire, 2010)
2012	Glen Chapple (Lancashire, 2011)

Mark Alleyne (2001) led Gloucestershire to a treble of one-day trophies in 2000. Jack Bond (1971) and Brian Rose (1980) respectively led Lancashire and Somerset to two one-day trophies in 1970 and 1979

FAMILY RELATIONS

Brothers

Harry Trott (1894) and Albert Trott (1899)

RE "Tip" Foster (1901) and Henry Foster (1911)

John Gunn (1904) and George Gunn (1914). They were nephews of William Gunn (1890)

Johnny Tyldesley (1901) and Ernest Tyldesley (1920)

James Langridge (1933) and John Langridge (1950)

Graeme Pollock and Peter Pollock (both 1966). Shaun Pollock, son of Peter and nephew of Graeme, was picked in 2003

Mushtaq Mohammad (1963) and Hanif Mohammad (1968)

Greg Chappell (1973) and Ian Chappell (1976)

Chris Smith (1984) and Robin Smith (1990)

Steve Waugh (1989) and Mark Waugh (1991). They are the only twins

Fathers and sons

Jim Parks, sen. (1938) and Jim Parks, jun. (1968)

Nawab of Pataudi, sen. (1932) and Nawab of Pataudi, jun. (1968)

Micky Stewart (1958) and Alec Stewart (1993)

Peter Pollock (1966) and Shaun Pollock (2003)

Grandfather and grandson

Denis Compton (1939) and Nick Compton (2013)

Cousins

Jack Hearne (1892) and Alec Hearne (1894). JW Hearne, a distant relation, was picked in 1911

Syd Gregory (1897) and Jack Gregory (1922)

Tich Freeman and AC "Jack" Russell (both 1923)

Bill Edrich (1940) and John Edrich (1966)

Clive Lloyd (1971) and Lance Gibbs (1972)

Majid Khan (1969) and Imran Khan (1983)

Uncles and nephews

William Gunn (1890); John Gunn (1904) and George Gunn (1914)

Ranjitsinhji (1897) and Duleepsinhji (1930)

James Hallows (1905) and Charles Hallows (1928)

Graeme Pollock (1966) and Shaun Pollock (2003)

Majid Khan (1969) and Imran Khan (1983)

Jonathan Trott (2011) is reputedly related to the Australian Trott brothers (see above); he also married a grand-daughter of Tom Dollery (1952). Michael Vaughan (2003) was the great-great-nephew of Ernest Tyldesley (1920)

WOODEN SPOONISTS

Cricketers of the Year who represented a county finishing bottom of the championship the previous season

1897	KS Ranjitsinhji (Sussex, who finished 14th out of 14 in 1896)
1904	Albert Knight (Leicestershire, joint bottom out of 15 in 1903)
1953	Harold Gimblett (Somerset, 17th out of 17 in 1952)
1983	Alvin Kallicharran (Warwickshire, 17th out of 17 in 1982)
1996	Aravinda de Silva (Kent, 18th out of 18 in 1995)

Steve Harmison was a Cricketer of the Year in 2005, after his club Durham finished bottom of the Championship second division in 2004, but he only appeared for them in one-day matches

CRICKETERS OF THE YEAR AFTER DEBUT SEASON

The following were chosen after the English seasons in which they made their first-class debuts

Wilfred Rhodes (1899)
Douglas Carr (1910)
Lionel Tennyson (1914)
Herbert Sutcliffe (1920)

CRICKETERS OF THE YEAR WHO DID NOT PLAY AGAIN

No first-class appearance after April 1 of the year of Wisden selection

Dick Pilling (1891)	He died on March 28, 1891
Harry Calder (1918)	He never played first-class cricket
Bill Ponsford (1935)	
Jock Cameron (1936)	He died on November 2, 1935
Gil Langley (1957)	
Gary Kirsten (2004)	
Ottis Gibson (2008)	

ALL 570 CRICKETERS OF THE YEAR, BY CATEGORY

All-rounder:	92 (16.1%)
Batsman:	283 (49.6%)
Bowler:	158 (27.7%)
Wicketkeeper:	37 (6.5%)

MOST PLAYERS FROM ONE TEAM IN THE SAME YEAR

Appearing for teams in the English season prior to selection

5	England 1938, 2005; Australians 1949
4	Yorkshire 1901; England 1930, 1947, 1960, 1967, 1979, 2010; West Indians 1951, 1964; Australians 1962, 1973, 1994

In 1912 and 1929, Wisden's Five were all drawn from the England teams chosen to tour Australia in 1911-12 and 1928-29 respectively

FULL ENGLAND XIs OF CRICKETERS OF THE YEAR

All 11 players who were Cricketers of the Year by April 1 of the year in question

Three Tests v Australia 1902 – Edgbaston, Lord's and The Oval
One Test v South Africa 1907 – The Oval
One Test v Australia 1909 – Edgbaston
One Test v Australia 1924-25 – Sydney (First Test)
Two Tests v Australia 1930 – Trent Bridge and Headingley
Two Tests v Australia 1958-59 – Melbourne (Second Test) and Adelaide

The most Cricketers of the Year for any other Test XI is nine for Australia v Sri Lanka, Darwin, 2004

NON-TEST PLAYERS

Of the 570 Cricketers of the Year, 68 never played in men's Test matches

Other Internationals:

Alan Jones	(1978 he played what was regarded at the time as an official Test in 1970 but the status of the game was later downgraded)

One-day internationals:

Mark Alleyne	(2001; England)
Ian Austin	(1999; England)
Dale Benkenstein	(2009; South Africa)
Glen Chapple	(2012; England)
Ian Harvey	(2004; Australia)
Geoff Humpage	(1985; England)
Trevor Jesty	(1983; England)
Clive Rice	(1981; South Africa)

Women's Test and one-day internationals:

Claire Taylor	(2009; England)

Other English Players:

Hubert Ashton (1922)	Phil Bainbridge (1986)	Hugh Bartlett (1939)
Jack Bond (1971)	Nigel Briers (1993)	Jack Bryan (1922)
Frederick Bull (1898)	Cuthbert Burnup (1903)	Arthur Day (1910)
Henry Foster (1911)	David Green (1969)	Louis Hall (1890)
Albert Hallam (1908)	John Hallows (1905)	Alfred Hartley (1911)
Robert Henderson (1890)	Herbie Hewett (1893)	David Hughes (1988)
James Iremonger (1903)	John Langridge (1950)	Peter Lee (1976)
Bev Lyon (1931)	Jack Mercer (1927)	Phil Neale (1989)
Jack Newstead (1909)	Percy Perrin (1905)	Alan Richardson (2012)
Peter Roebuck (1988)	Peter Sainsbury (1974)	Stanley Scott (1893)
Brian Sellers (1940)	Don Shepherd (1970)	Jack Simmons (1985)
"Razor" Smith (1911)	Stuart Surridge (1953)	Brian Taylor (1972)
Tom Taylor (1901)	John Tunnicliffe (1901)	Roy Virgin (1971)
Tom Wass (1908)	Ossie Wheatley (1969)	Vic Wilson (1961)
Levi Wright (1906).		

Other Foreign Players:

Bill Alley (1962)	Ken McEwan (1978)	Alan Marshal (1909)
Frank Tarrant (1908)	Sydney Smith (1915)	Franklyn Stephenson (1989)
Vintcent van der Bijl (1981).		

Public Schools Cricketers:

Percy Adams (1919)	Harry Calder (1918)	John Firth (1918)
Clem Gibson (1918)	Adrian Gore (1919)	Lionel Hedges (1919)
Norman Partridge (1919)	Gerard Rotherham (1918).	

SHORTEST-LIVED CRICKETERS OF THE YEAR

Collie Smith (1958)	26
Major Booth (1914)	29
Ken Farnes (1939)	30
Jock Cameron (1936)	30
Alan Marshal (1909)	32
Lionel Hedges (1919)	32
John Ferris (1889)	33
Kenneth Hutchings (1907)	34
Jack Brown (1895)	35
Frederick Bull (1898)	35
Dick Pilling (1891)	35

LONGEST-LIVED CRICKETERS OF THE YEAR

Wilfred Rhodes (1899)	95
Bill Brown (1939)	95
Sydney Barnes (1910)	94
Harry Calder (1918)	94
Jack Mercer (1927)	94
Bob Wyatt (1930)	93
Alf Gover (1937)	93
Reg Simpson (1950)	93 (as at May 1, 2013)
Percy Fender (1915)	92
Don Bradman (1931)	92

CRICKETERS OF THE YEAR WHO WROTE PROFILES

Eight Cricketers of the Year later contributed profiles of subsequent Cricketers of the Year

Bill Bowes (1932)	wrote nine profiles of Yorkshire cricketers between 1952 and 1969
Richie Benaud (1962)	wrote seven profiles of Australian cricketers from 1962 to 1976
Trevor Bailey (1950)	wrote a profile of Keith Fletcher in 1974
David Green (1969)	wrote a profile of Courtney Walsh in 1987
Jonathan Agnew (1988)	wrote three profiles between 1992 and 1997
Peter Roebuck (1988)	wrote a profile of Waqar Younis in 1992
Michael Atherton (1991)	wrote a profile of Graeme Smith in 2004
Angus Fraser (1996)	wrote a profile of Eoin Morgan in 2011

TOP NON-WISDEN CRICKETERS OF THE YEAR

Those who were never selected, and their places on the all-time lists.

All-time first-class runs	LG Berry & KG Suttle: *both* 30,225 (61st)
All-time first-class wickets	RTD Perks: 2,233 (20th)
	EG Dennett: 2,147 (23rd)
	JA Newman: 2,032 (31st)
	A Shaw: 2,027 (32nd)
All-time first-class dismissals	FH Huish: 1,310 (6th)
	D Hunter: 1,253 (9th)
	HR Butt: 1,228 (10th)
All-time Test dismissals	Wasim Bari: 228 (8th)
All-time Test runs	Inzamam-ul-Haq: 8,830 (14th)
	V Sehwag: 8,586 (18th)
	SC Ganguly: 7,212 (36th)
	SP Fleming: 7,172 (37th)
All-time England Test runs	MA Butcher: 4,288
All-time Australia Test runs	MEK Hussey: 6,235
All-time South Africa Test runs	HH Gibbs: 6,167
All-time West Indies Test runs	CH Gayle: 6,603
All-time Sri Lanka Test runs	MS Atapattu: 5,502
All-time Test wickets	Harbhajan Singh: 413 (10th)
	M Ntini: 390 (12th)
	DL Vettori: 360 (17th)
	WPUJC Vaas: 355 (18th)
	BS Bedi: 266 (29th)
All-time England Test wickets	GR Dilley: 138
All-time Australia Test wickets	SCG MacGill: 208
All-time West Indies Test wickets	WW Hall: 192
All-time Pakistan Test wickets	Danish Kaneria: 261
All-time ODI runs	Inzamam-ul-Haq: 11,739 (4th)
All-time ODI wickets	WPUJC Vaas: 400 (4th)
All-time List A runs	MG Bevan: 15,103 (13th)
All-time List A wickets	WPUJC Vaas: 506 (17th)

Index

Name	birth date	death date	year of selection	birthplace	page
Abel, R	30.11.1857	10.12.1936	1890	Rotherhithe, Surrey	8
Adams, CJ	6.5.1970		2004	Whitwell, Derbyshire	337
Adams, PW	5.9.1900	28.9.1962	1919	St Pancras, London	91
Adcock, NAT	8.3.1931		1961	Sea Point, Cape Town, South Africa	200
Agnew, JP	4.4.1960		1988	Macclesfield, Cheshire	285
Alderman, TM	12.6.1956		1982	Subiaco, Perth, Western Australia	267
Alley, WE	3.2.1919	26.11.2004	1962	Hornsby, Sydney, Australia	203
Alleyne, MW	23.5.1968		2001	Tottenham, Middlesex	328
Amarnath, M	24.9.1950		1984	Patiala, Punjab, India	273
Ambrose, CEL	21.9.1963		1992	Swetes Village, Antigua	297
Ames, LEG	3.12.1905	27.2.1990	1929	Elham, Kent	117
Amiss, DL	7.4.1943		1975	Harborne, Birmingham, Warwickshire	246
Amla, HM	31.3.1983		2013	Durban, Natal, South Africa	364
Anderson, JM	30.7.1982		2009	Burnley, Lancashire	352
Appleyard, R	27.6.1924		1952	Wibsey, Bradford, Yorkshire	173
Armstrong, WW	22.5.1879	13.7.1947	1903	Kyneton, Victoria, Australia	46
Arnold, GG	3.9.1944		1972	Earlsfield, Surrey	237
Ashton, H	13.2.1898	17.6.1979	1922	Calcutta (now Kolkata), Bengal, India	98
Asif Iqbal	6.6.1943		1968	Hyderabad, Andhra Pradesh, India	221
Astill, WE	1.3.1888	10.2.1948	1933	Ratby, Leicestershire	129
Atherton, MA	23.3.1968		1991	Failsworth, Manchester, Lancashire	294
Attewell, W	12.6.1861	11.6.1927	1892	Keyworth, Nottinghamshire	14
Austin, ID	30.5.1966		1999	Haslingden, Lancashire	322
Azharuddin, M	8.2.1963		1991	Hyderabad, Andhra Pradesh, India	294
Bailey, TE	3.12.1923	10.2.2011	1950	Westcliff-on-Sea, Essex	167
Bainbridge, P	16.4.1958		1986	Sneyd Green, Stoke-on-Trent, Staffordshire	279
Bakewell, AH	2.11.1908	23.1.1983	1934	Walsall, Staffordshire	132
Barber, RW	26.9.1935		1967	Withington, Manchester, Lancashire	218
Bardsley, W	7.12.1882	20.1.1954	1910	Warren, New South Wales, Australia	67
Barnes, SF	19.4.1873	26.12.1967	1910	Smethwick, Staffordshire	67
Barnes, W	27.5.1852	24.3.1899	1890	Sutton-in-Ashfield, Nottinghamshire	8
Barnett, CJ	3.7.1910	28.5.1993	1937	Fairview, Cheltenham, Gloucestershire	141
Barnett, KJ	17.7.1960		1989	Stoke-on-Trent, Staffordshire	288
Barrington, KF	24.11.1930	14.3.1981	1960	Reading, Berkshire	197
Bartlett, HT	7.10.1914	26.6.1988	1939	Balaghat, India	147
Bedser, AV	4.7.1918	4.4.2010	1947	Reading, Berkshire	158
Bell, IR	11.4.1982		2008	Walsgrave, Coventry, Warwickshire	349
Benaud, R	6.10.1930		1962	Penrith, New South Wales, Australia	203

Name	birth date	death date	year of selection	birthplace	page
Benkenstein, DM	9.6.1974		2009	Salisbury (now Harare), Rhodesia (now Zimbabwe)	352
Bicknell, MP	14.1.1969		2001	Guildford, Surrey	328
Binks, JG	5.10.1935		1969	Hull, Yorkshire	228
Blackham, JM	11.5.1854	28.12.1932	1891	North Fitzroy, Melbourne, Australia	11
Bland, KC	5.4.1938		1966	Bulawayo, Rhodesia (now Zimbabwe)	215
Blunt, RC	3.11.1900	22.6.1966	1928	Durham	114
Blythe, C	30.5.1879	8.11.1917	1904	Deptford, Kent	49
Bond, JD	6.5.1932		1971	Kearsley, Bolton, Lancashire	234
Boon, DC	29.12.1960		1994	Launceston, Tasmania, Australia	307
Booth, MW	10.12.1886	1.7.1916	1914	Lowtown, Pudsey, Yorkshire	77
Border, AR	27.7.1955		1982	Cremorne, Sydney, Australia	267
Bosanquet, BJT	13.10.1877	12.10.1936	1905	Bulls Cross, Enfield, Middlesex	52
Botham, IT	24.11.1955		1978	Oldfield, Heswall, Cheshire	255
Boucher, MV	3.12.1976		2009	East London, South Africa	352
Bowes, WE	25.7.1908	4.9.1987	1932	Elland, Yorkshire	126
Bowley, EH	6.6.1890	9.7.1974	1930	Leatherhead, Surrey	120
Boyce, KD	11.10.1943	11.10.1996	1974	Castle, St Peter, Barbados	243
Boycott, G	21.10.1940		1965	Fitzwilliam, Yorkshire	212
Bradman, DG	27.8.1908	25.2.2001	1931	Cootamundra, New South Wales, Australia	123
Braund, LC	18.10.1875	23.12.1955	1902	Clewer, Berkshire	43
Brearley, JM	28.4.1942		1977	Harrow, Middlesex	252
Brearley, W	11.3.1876	30.1.1937	1909	Bolton, Lancashire	64
Bresnan, TT	28.2.1985		2012	Pontefract, Yorkshire	361
Briers, NE	15.1.1955		1993	Southfields, Leicester	304
Briggs, J	3.10.1862	11.1.1902	1889	Sutton-in-Ashfield, Nottinghamshire	5
Broad, SCJ	24.6.1986		2010	Nottingham	355
Brockwell, W	21.1.1865	30.6.1935	1895	Kingston-upon-Thames, Surrey	23
Brookes, D	29.10.1915	9.3.2006	1957	Kippax, Leeds, Yorkshire	188
Brown, FR	16.12.1910	24.7.1991	1933	Lima, Peru	129
Brown, JT	20.8.1869	4.11.1904	1895	Great Driffield, Yorkshire	23
Brown, WA	31.7.1912	16.3.2008	1939	Toowoomba, Queensland, Australia	147
Bryan, JL	26.5.1896	23.4.1985	1922	Beckenham, Kent	98
Bull, FG	2.4.1875	16.9.1910	1898	Hackney, London	31
Burge, PJP	17.5.1932	5.10.2001	1965	Kangaroo Point, Brisbane, Australia	212
Burke, JW	12.6.1930	2.2.1979	1957	Mosman, Sydney, Australia	188
Burnup, CJ	21.11.1875	5.4.1960	1903	Blackheath, Kent	46
Butcher, AR	7.1.1954		1991	Croydon, Surrey	294
Butcher, BF	3.9.1933		1970	Port Mourant, Berbice, British Guiana (now Guyana)	231
Caddick, AR	21.11.1968		2001	Christchurch, Canterbury, New Zealand	328
Cairns, CL	13.6.1970		2000	Picton, Marlborough, New Zealand	325
Calder, HL	24.1.1901	15.9.1995	1918	Cape Town, South Africa	88
Cameron, HB	5.7.1905	2.11.1935	1936	Port Elizabeth, South Africa	138
Carr, AW	21.5.1893	7.2.1963	1923	Mickleham, Surrey	101
Carr, DB	28.12.1926		1960	Wiesbaden, Germany	197
Carr, DW	17.3.1872	23.3.1950	1910	Cranbrook, Kent	67
Catterall, RH	10.7.1900	3.1.1961	1925	Port Elizabeth, South Africa	107

Name	birth date	death date	year of selection	birthplace	page
Chanderpaul, S	16.8.1974		2008	Unity Village, East Coast, Demerara, Guyana	349
Chandrasekhar, BS	17.5.1945		1972	Mysore, India	237
Chapman, APF	3.9.1900	16.9.1961	1919	The Mount, Reading, Berkshire	91
Chappell, GS	7.8.1948		1973	Unley, Adelaide, South Australia	240
Chappell, IM	26.9.1943		1976	Unley, Adelaide, South Australia	245
Chapple, G	23.1.1974		2012	Skipton, Yorkshire	361
Childs, JH	15.8.1951		1987	Lipson, Plymouth, Devon	282
Clarke, MJ	2.4.1981		2010	Liverpool, New South Wales, Australia	355
Close, DB	24.2.1931		1964	Rawdon, Leeds, Yorkshire	209
Collingwood, PD	26.5.1976		2007	Shotley Bridge, Co Durham	346
Compton, DCS	23.5.1918	23.4.1997	1939	Hendon, Middlesex	147
Compton, NRD	26.6.1983		2013	Durban, Natal, South Africa	364
Coney, JV	21.6.1952		1984	Wellington, New Zealand	273
Congdon, BE	11.2.1938		1974	Motueka, Tasman, New Zealand	243
Constantine, LN	21.9.1901	1.7.1971	1940	Petit Valley, Diego Martin. Trinidad	150
Cook, AN	25.12.1984		2012	Gloucester	361
Cook, SJ	31.7.1953		1990	Johannesburg, Transvaal, South Africa	291
Copson, WH	27.4.1908	13.9.1971	1937	Stonebroom, Derbyshire	141
Cork, DG	7.8.1971		1996	Newcastle-under-Lyme, Staffordshire	313
Cowdrey, MC	24.12.1932	4.12.2000	1956	Bangalore, India	185
Crawford, JN	1.12.1886	2.5.1963	1907	Cane Hill, Surrey	58
Crowe, MD	22.9.1962		1985	Henderson, Auckland, New Zealand	276
Cuttell, WR	13.9.1863	9.12.1929	1898	Sheffield, Yorkshire	31
Darling, J	21.11.1870	2.1.1946	1900	Glen Osmond, Adelaide, South Australia	37
Davidson, AK	14.6.1929		1962	Lisarow, Gosford, New South Wales, Australia	203
Day, AP	10.4.1885	22.1.1969	1910	Blackheath, Kent	67
de Silva, PA	17.10.1965		1996	Colombo, Ceylon (now Sri Lanka)	313
DeFreitas, PAJ	18.2.1966		1992	Scotts Head, Dominica	297
Dempster, CS	15.11.1903	14.2.1974	1932	Wellington, New Zealand	126
Denness, MH	1.12.1940	19.4.2013	1975	Bellshill, Lanarkshire, Scotland	246
Denton, D	4.7.1874	16.2.1950	1906	Thornes, Wakefield, Yorkshire	55
Dexter, ER	15.5.1935		1961	Milan, Italy	200
D'Oliveira, BL	4.10.1931	18.11.2011	1967	Signal Hill, Cape Town, South Africa	218
Dollery, HE	14.10.1914	20.1.1987	1952	Reading West, Berkshire	173
Donald, AA	20.10.1966		1992	Bloemfontein, Orange Free State, South Africa	297
Donnelly, MP	17.10.1917	22.10.1999	1948	Ngaruawahia, Waikato, New Zealand	161
Dooland, B	1.11.1923	8.9.1980	1955	Cowandilla, Adelaide, South Australia	182
Douglas, JWHT	3.9.1882	19.12.1930	1915	Clapton, London	80
Dravid, R	11.1.1973		2000	Indore, Madhya Pradesh, India	325
Druce, NF	1.1.1875	27.10.1954	1898	Denmark Hill, London	31
Ducat, A	16.2.1886	23.7.1942	1920	Brixton, London	94
Duckworth, G	9.5.1901	5.1.1966	1929	Warrington, Lancashire	117
Dujon, PJL	28.5.1956		1989	Kingston, Jamaica	288
Duleepsinhji, KS	13.6.1905	5.12.1959	1930	Sarodar, Kathiawar, India	120
Edrich, JH	21.6.1937		1966	Blofield, Norfolk	215
Edrich, WJ	26.3.1916	24.4.1986	1940	Lingwood, Norfolk	150

Name	birth date	death date	year of selection	birthplace	page
Elliott, MTG	28.9.1971		1998	Chelsea, Victoria, Australia	319
Ellison, RM	21.9.1959		1986	Willesborough, Ashford, Kent	279
Emburey, JE	20.8.1952		1984	Peckham, London	273
Evans, TG	18.8.1920	3.5.1999	1951	Finchley, Middlesex	170
Farnes, K	8.7.1911	20.10.1941	1939	Leytonstone, Essex	147
Fazal Mahmood	18.2.1927	30.5.2005	1955	Lahore, India (now in Pakistan)	182
Fender, PGH	22.8.1892	15.6.1985	1915	Balham, London	80
Ferris, JJ	21.5.1867	17.11.1900	1889	Sydney, Australia	5
Fielder, A	19.7.1877	30.8.1949	1907	Plaxtol, Tonbridge, Kent	58
Firth, JDE	21.2.1900	21.9.1957	1918	The Park, Nottingham	88
Fishlock, LB	2.1.1907	25.6.1986	1947	Battersea, London	158
Flavell, JA	15.5.1929	25.2.2004	1965	Wall Heath, Staffordshire	212
Fletcher, KWR	20.5.1944		1974	Worcester	243
Flintoff, A	6.12.1977		2004	Preston, Lancashire	337
Flower, A	28.4.1968		2002	Cape Town, South Africa	331
Foster, FR	31.1.1889	3.5.1958	1912	Deritend, Birmingham, Warwickshire	73
Foster, HK	30.10.1873	23.6.1950	1911	Malvern, Worcestershire	70
Foster, NA	6.5.1962		1988	Colchester, Essex	285
Foster, RE	16.4.1878	13.5.1914	1901	Malvern, Worcestershire	40
Fraser, ARC	8.8.1965		1996	Billinge, Lancashire	313
Fredericks, RC	11.11.1942	5.9.2000	1974	Blairmont, East Bank, Berbice, British Guiana (now Guyana)	243
Freeman, AP	17.5.1888	28.1.1965	1923	Ladywell, Lewisham, London	101
Fry, CB	25.4.1872	7.9.1956	1895	West Croydon, Surrey	23
Garner, J	16.12.1952		1980	Enterprise, Christ Church, Barbados	261
Gatting, MW	6.6.1957		1984	Kingsbury, Middlesex	273
Gavaskar, SM	10.7.1949		1980	Bombay (now Mumbai), India	261
Geary, G	9.7.1893	6.3.1981	1927	Barwell, Leicestershire	111
Gibbs, LR	29.9.1934		1972	Queenstown, Georgetown, British Guiana (now Guyana)	237
Gibson, CH	23.8.1900	31.12.1976	1918	Entre Rios, Argentina	88
Gibson, OD	16.3.1969		2008	Sion Hill, St Peter, Barbados	349
Giffen, G	27.3.1859	29.11.1927	1894	Norwood, Adelaide, South Australia	20
Gifford, N	30.3.1940		1975	Ulverston, Lancashire	246
Gilchrist, AC	14.11.1971		2002	Bellingen, New South Wales, Australia	331
Giles, AF	19.3.1973		2005	Chertsey, Surrey	340
Gillespie, JN	19.4.1975		2002	Darlinghurst, Sydney, Australia	331
Gilligan, AER	23.12.1894	5.9.1976	1924	Denmark Hill, London	104
Gimblett, H	19.10.1914	30.3.1978	1953	Bicknoller, Somerset	176
Goddard, TWJ	1.10.1900	22.5.1966	1938	Gloucester	144
Gomes, HA	13.7.1953		1985	Arima, Trinidad	276
Gooch, GA	23.7.1953		1980	Whipps Cross, Leytonstone, Essex	261
Gore, AC	14.5.1900	7.6.1990	1919	Ayr, Scotland	91
Gough, D	18.9.1970		1999	Monk Bretton, Barnsley, Yorkshire	322
Gover, AR	29.2.1908	7.10.2001	1937	Woodcote, Epsom, Surrey	141
Gower, DI	1.4.1957		1979	Tunbridge Wells, Kent	258
Grace, WG	18.7.1848	23.10.1915	1896	Downend, Bristol	26
Graveney, TW	16.6.1927		1953	Riding Mill, Northumberland	176

Name	birth date	death date	year of selection	birthplace	page
Green, DM	10.11.1939		1969	Llanengan, Caernarvon	228
Greenidge, CG	1.5.1951		1977	Black Bess, St Peter, Barbados	252
Gregory, JM	14.8.1895	7.8.1973	1922	North Sydney, Australia	98
Gregory, SE	14.4.1870	31.7.1929	1897	Moore Park, Randwick, Sydney, Australia	28
Greig, AW	6.10.1946	29.12.2012	1975	Queenstown, South Africa	246
Griffith, CC	14.12.1938		1964	Pie Corner, St Lucy, Barbados	209
Grimmett, CV	25.12.1891	2.5.1980	1931	Caversham, Dunedin, New Zealand	123
Gunn, G	13.6.1879	29.6.1958	1914	Hucknall Torkard, Nottinghamshire	77
Gunn, JR	19.7.1876	21.8.1963	1904	Hucknall Torkard, Nottinghamshire	49
Gunn, W	4.12.1858	29.1.1921	1890	St Anne's, Nottingham	8
Hadlee, RJ	3.7.1951		1982	St Albans, Christchurch, New Zealand	267
Haigh, S	19.3.1871	27.2.1921	1901	Berry Brow, Huddersfield, Yorkshire	40
Hall, L	1.11.1852	19.11.1915	1890	Batley, Yorkshire	8
Hallam, AW	12.11.1869	24.7.1940	1908	East Leake, Nottinghamshire	61
Halliwell, EA	7.9.1864	2.10.1919	1905	Drayton Green, Ealing, Middlesex	52
Hallows, C	4.4.1895	10.11.1972	1928	Little Lever, Lancashire	114
Hallows, J	14.11.1873	20.5.1910	1905	Little Lever, Lancashire	52
Hammond, WR	19.6.1903	1.7.1965	1928	Buckland, Dover, Kent	114
Hanif Mohammad	21.12.1934		1968	Junagadh, Gujarat, India	221
Hardinge, HTW	25.2.1886	8.5.1965	1915	Greenwich, London	80
Hardstaff, J	3.7.1911	1.1.1990	1938	East Kirkby, Kirkby-in-Ashfield, Nottinghamshire	144
Harmison, SJ	23.10.1978		2005	Ashington, Northumberland	340
Hartley, A	11.4.1879	9.10.1918	1911	New Orleans, USA	70
Harvey, IJ	10.4.1972		2004	Wonthaggi, Victoria, Australia	337
Harvey, RN	8.10.1928		1954	Fitzroy, Melbourne, Australia	179
Hassett, AL	28.8.1913	16.6.1993	1949	Geelong, Victoria, Australia	164
Hawke, Lord	16.8.1860	10.10.1938	1909	Willingham Rectory, Gainsborough, Lincolnshire	64
Hayden, ML	29.10.1971		2003	Kingaroy, Queensland, Australia	334
Hayes, EG	6.11.1876	2.12.1953	1907	Peckham, London	58
Haynes, DL	15.2.1956		1991	Holders Hill, St James, Barbados	294
Hayward, TW	29.3.1871	19.7.1939	1895	Cambridge	23
Headley, GA	30.5.1909	30.11.1983	1934	Colon, Panama	132
Healy, IA	30.4.1964		1994	Spring Hill, Brisbane, Australia	307
Hearne, A	22.7.1863	16.5.1952	1894	Ealing, Middlesex	20
Hearne, JT	3.5.1867	17.4.1944	1892	Chalfont St Giles, Buckinghamshire	14
Hearne, JW	11.2.1891	14.9.1965	1912	Hillingdon, Middlesex	73
Hedges, LP	13.7.1900	12.1.1933	1919	Streatham, London	91
Henderson, R	30.3.1865	28.1.1931	1890	Newport, Monmouthshire	8
Hendren, EH	5.2.1889	4.10.1962	1920	Turnham Green, Middlesex	94
Hendrick, M	22.10.1948		1978	Darley Dale, Derbyshire	255
Hewett, HT	25.5.1864	4.3.1921	1893	Norton Manor, Norton Fitzwarren, Somerset	17
Hick, GA	23.5.1966		1987	Salisbury (now Harare), Rhodesia (now Zimbabwe)	282
Higgs, K	14.1.1937		1968	Kidsgrove, Staffordshire	221
Hill, C	18.3.1877	5.9.1945	1900	Hindmarsh, Adelaide, South Australia	37
Hilton, MJ	2.8.1928	8.7.1990	1957	Chadderton, Lancashire	188
Hirst, GH	7.9.1871	10.5.1954	1901	Kirkheaton, Yorkshire	40

Name	birth date	death date	year of selection	birthplace	page
Hitch, JW	7.5.1886	7.7.1965	1914	Radcliffe, Lancashire	77
Hobbs, JB	16.12.1882	21.12.1963	1909	Cambridge	64
Hoggard, MJ	31.12.1976		2006	Leeds, Yorkshire	343
Holding, MA	16.2.1954		1977	Half Way Tree, Kingston	252
Hollies, WE	5.6.1912	16.4.1981	1955	Old Hill, Staffordshire	182
Hollioake, AJ	5.9.1971		2003	Melbourne, Australia	334
Holmes, ERT	21.8.1905	16.8.1960	1936	Calcutta (now Kolkata), India	138
Holmes, P	25.11.1886	3.9.1971	1920	Oakes, Huddersfield, Yorkshire	94
Hughes, DP	13.5.1947		1988	Newton-le-Willows, Lancashire	285
Hughes, KJ	26.1.1954		1981	Margaret River, Western Australia	264
Hughes, MG	23.11.1961		1994	Euroa, Victoria, Australia	307
Humpage, GW	24.4.1954		1985	Sparkbrook, Birmingham, Warwickshire	276
Hunte, CC	9.5.1932	3.12.1999	1964	Shorey's Village, St Andrew, Barbados	209
Hussain, N	28.3.1968		2003	Madras (now Chennai), India	334
Hutchings, KL	7.12.1882	3.9.1916	1907	Southborough, Kent	58
Hutton, L	23.6.1916	6.9.1990	1938	Fulneck, Pudsey, Yorkshire	144
Illingworth, R	8.6.1932		1960	Pudsey, Yorkshire	197
Imran Khan	25.11.1952		1983	Lahore, Pakistan	270
Insole, DJ	18.4.1926		1956	Clapton, London	185
Iremonger, J	5.3.1876	25.3.1956	1903	Norton, Yorkshire	46
Jackman, RD	13.8.1945		1981	Simla, India	264
Jackson, FS	21.11.1870	9.3.1947	1894	Allerton Hall, Chapel Allerton, Leeds, Yorkshire	20
Jackson, HL	5.4.1921	25.4.2007	1959	Whitwell, Derbyshire	194
Jardine, DR	23.10.1900	18.6.1958	1928	Malabar Hill, Bombay (now Mumbai), India	114
Javed Miandad	12.6.1957		1982	Karachi, Pakistan	267
Jayasuriya, ST	30.6.1969		1997	Matara, Ceylon (now Sri Lanka)	316
Jayawardene, DPMD	27.5.1977		2007	Colombo, Sri Lanka	346
Jenkins, RO	24.11.1918	22.7.1995	1950	Rainbow Hill, Worcester	167
Jessop, GL	19.5.1874	11.5.1955	1898	Cheltenham, Gloucestershire	31
Jesty, TE	2.6.1948		1983	Gosport, Hampshire	270
Johnston, WA	26.2.1922	25.5.2007	1949	Beeac, Victoria, Australia	164
Jones, A	4.11.1938		1978	Velindre, Glamorgan	255
Jones, AO	16.8.1872	21.12.1914	1900	Shelton, Nottinghamshire	37
Jones, DM	24.3.1961		1990	Coburg, Melbourne, Australia	291
Jones, SP	25.12.1978		2006	Morriston, Swansea, Glamorgan	343
Jupp, VWC	27.3.1891	9.7.1960	1928	Burgess Hill, Sussex	114
Kallicharran, AI	21.3.1949		1983	Paidama, Berbice, British Guiana (now Guyana)	270
Kallis JH	16.10.1975		2013	Pinelands, Cape Town, South Africa	364
Kanhai, RB	26.12.1935		1964	Port Mourant, Berbice, British Guiana (now Guyana)	209
Kapil Dev	6.1.1959		1983	Chandigarh, India	270
Keeton, WW	30.4.1905	10.10.1980	1940	Shirebrook, Derbyshire	150
Kelly, JJ	10.5.1867	14.8.1938	1903	Sandridge (now Port Melbourne), Victoria, Australia	46
Kennedy, AS	24.1.1891	15.11.1959	1933	Edinburgh, Midlothian	129
Kenyon, D	15.5.1924	12.11.1996	1963	Wordsley, Staffordshire	206
Key, RWT	12.5.1979		2005	East Dulwich, London	340
Kilner, R	17.10.1890	5.4.1928	1924	Low Valley, Wombwell, Yorkshire	104

Name	birth date	death date	year of selection	birthplace	page
Kinneir, S	13.5.1871	16.10.1928	1912	Pickwick, Corsham, Wiltshire	73
Kirsten, G	23.11.1967		2004	Cape Town, South Afrioca	337
Klusener, L	4.9.1971		2000	Durban, Natal, South Africa	325
Knight, AE	8.10.1872	25.4.1946	1904	Leicester	49
Knight, DJ	12.5.1894	5.1.1960	1915	Sutton, Surrey	80
Knott, APE	9.4.1946		1970	Belvedere, Kent	231
Knox, NA	10.10.1884	3.3.1935	1907	Clapham, London	58
Kumble, A	17.10.1970		1996	Bangalore, India	313
Laker, JC	9.2.1922	23.4.1986	1952	Frizinghall, Bradford, Yorkshire	173
Lamb, AJ	20.6.1954		1981	Langebaanweg, South Africa	264
Langer, JL	21.11.1970		2001	Perth, Western Australia	328
Langley, GRA	14.9.1919	14.5.2001	1957	North Adelaide, South Australia	188
Langridge, J	10.7.1906	10.9.1966	1932	Chailey, Sussex	126
Langridge, JG	10.2.1910	27.6.1999	1950	Chailey, Sussex	167
Lara, BC	2.5.1969		1995	Cantaro, Santa Cruz, Trinidad	310
Larwood, H	14.11.1904	22.7.1995	1927	Nuncargate, Nottinghamshire	111
Law, SG	18.10.1968		1998	Herston, Brisbane, Australia	319
Lawry, WM	11.2.1937		1962	Thornbury, Melbourne, Australia	203
Laxman, VVS	1.11.1974		2002	Hyderabad, Andhra Pradesh, India	331
Lee, B	8.11.1976		2006	Wollongong, New South Wales, Australia	343
Lee, PG	27.8.1945		1976	Arthingworth, Northamptonshire	249
Lees, WS	25.12.1875	10.9.1924	1906	Sowerby Bridge, Yorkshire	55
Lehmann, DS	5.2.1970		2001	Gawler, South Australia	328
Lever, JK	24.2.1949		1979	Stepney, London	258
Leyland, M	20.7.1900	1.1.1967	1929	New Park, Harrogate, Yorkshire	117
Lillee, DK	18.7.1949		1973	Subiaco, Perth, Western Australia	240
Lilley, AFA	28.11.1866	17.11.1929	1897	Holloway Head, Birmingham, Warwickshire	28
Lindwall, RR	3.10.1921	23.6.1996	1949	Mascot, Sydney, Australia	164
Llewellyn, CB	26.9.1876	7.6.1964	1911	Pietermaritzburg, Natal, South Africa	70
Lloyd, CH	31.8.1944		1971	Queenstown, Georgetown, British Guiana (now Guyana)	234
Loader, PJ	25.10.1929	15.3.2011	1958	Wallington, Surrey	191
Lock, GAR	5.7.1929	30.3.1995	1954	Limpsfield, Surrey	179
Lockwood, WH	25.3.1868	26.4.1932	1899	Old Radford, Nottinghamshire	34
Lohmann, GA	2.6.1865	1.12.1901	1889	Kensington, London	5
Luckhurst, BW	5.2.1939	1.3.2005	1971	Sittingbourne, Kent	234
Lyon, BH	19.1.1902	22.6.1970	1931	Caterham, Surrey	123
Macartney, CG	27.6.1886	9.9.1958	1922	West Maitland, New South Wales, Australia	98
Macaulay, GG	7.12.1897	13.12.1940	1924	Thirsk, Yorkshire	104
MacBryan, JCW	22.7.1892	14.7.1983	1925	Box, Wiltshire	107
McCabe, SJ	16.7.1910	25.8.1968	1935	Grenfell, New South Wales, Australia	135
McCosker, RB	11.12.1946		1976	Inverell, New South Wales, Australia	249
McDermott, CJ	14.4.1965		1986	Raceview, Ipswich, Queensland, Australia	279
McDonald, EA	6.1.1891	22.7.1937	1922	Launceston, Tasmania, Australia	98
McEwan, KS	16.7.1952		1978	Bedford, South Africa	255
McGahey, CP	12.2.1871	10.1.1935	1902	Stepney, London	43
McGlew, DJ	11.3.1929	9.6.1998	1956	Pietermaritzburg, Natal, South Africa	185

Name	birth date	death date	year of selection	birthplace	page
McGrath, GD	9.2.1970		1998	Dubbo, New South Wales, Australia	319
MacGregor, G	31.8.1869	20.8.1919	1891	Merchiston, Edinburgh, Scotland	11
McIntyre, AJW	14.5.1918	26.12.2009	1958	Kennington, London	191
McKenzie, GD	24.6.1941		1965	Cottesloe, Perth, Western Australia	212
McKenzie, ND	24.11.1975		2009	Johannesburg, Transvaal, South Africa	352
MacLaren, AC	1.12.1871	17.11.1944	1895	Whalley Range, Manchester, Lancashire	23
McLean, RA	9.7.1930	26.8.2007	1961	Pietermaritzburg, Natal, South Africa	200
Majid Khan	28.9.1946		1970	Ludhiana, Punjab, India	231
Malcolm, DE	22.2.1963		1995	Kingston, Jamaica	310
Mankad, MH	12.4.1917	21.8.1978	1947	Jamnagar, Gujarat, India	158
Marsh, RW	4.11.1947		1982	Armadale, Perth, Western Australia	267
Marshal, A	12.6.1883	23.7.1915	1909	Warwick, Queensland, Australia	64
Marshall, MD	18.4.1958	4.11.1999	1983	Bridgetown, St Michael, Barbados	270
Marshall, RE	25.4.1930	27.10.1992	1959	Farmers Plantation, St Thomas, Barbados	194
Martin, F	12.10.1861	13.12.1921	1892	Dartford, Kent	14
Martyn, DR	21.10.1971		2002	Darwin, Northern Territory, Australia	331
Mason, JR	26.3.1874	15.10.1958	1898	Blackheath, Kent	31
Massie, RAL	14.4.1947		1973	Subiaco, Perth, Western Australia	240
May, PBH	31.12.1929	27.12.1994	1952	The Mount, Reading, Berkshire	173
Maynard, MP	21.3.1966		1998	Oldham, Lancashire	319
Mead, CP	9.3.1887	26.3.1958	1912	Battersea, London	73
Mead, W	1.4.1868	18.3.1954	1904	Clapton, London	49
Melville, A	19.5.1910	18.4.1983	1948	Carnarvon, Cape Province, South Africa	161
Mercer, J	22.4.1893	31.8.1987	1927	Southwick, Sussex	111
Merchant, VM	12.10.1911	27.10.1987	1937	Bombay (now Mumbai), India	141
Milburn, C	23.10.1941	28.2.1990	1967	Burnopfield, Co Durham	218
Miller, KR	28.11.1919	11.10.2004	1954	Sunshine, Melbourne, Australia	179
Milton, CA	10.3.1928	25.4.2007	1959	Bedminster, Somerset	194
Mitchell, B	8.1.1909	1.7.1995	1936	Ferreira Deep Gold Mine, Johannesburg, South Africa	138
Mitchell, F	13.8.1872	11.10.1935	1902	Market Weighton, Yorkshire	43
Mohammad Yousuf	27.8.1974		2007	Lahore, Pakistan	346
Mold, AW	27.5.1863	29.4.1921	1892	Middleton Cheney, Northamptonshire	14
Moody, TM	2.10.1965		2000	Adelaide, South Australia	325
Morgan, EJG	10.9.1986		2011	Dublin, Ireland	358
Morris, AR	19.1.1922		1949	Bondi, Sydney, Australia	164
Motz, RC	12.1.1940	29.4.2007	1966	Christchurch, Canterbury, New Zealand	215
Moxon, MD	4.5.1960		1993	Stairfoot, Barnsley, Yorkshire	304
Munton, TA	30.7.1965		1995	Melton Mowbray, Leicestershire	310
Muralitharan, M	17.4.1972		1999	Kandy, Ceylon (now Sri Lanka)	322
Murray, JT	1.4.1935		1967	North Kensington, London	218
Mushtaq Ahmed	28.6.1970		1997	Sahiwal, Pakistan	316
Mushtaq Mohammad	22.11.1943		1963	Junagadh, Gujarat, India	206
Nayudu, CK	31.10.1895	14.11.1967	1933	Nagpur, Maharashtra, India	129
Neale, PA	5.6.1954		1989	Scunthorpe, Lincolnshire	288
Newstead, JT	8.9.1877	25.3.1952	1909	Marton-in-Cleveland, Yorkshire	64
Nichols, MS	6.10.1900	26.1.1961	1934	Stondon Massey, Essex	132

Name	birth date	death date	year of selection	birthplace	page
Noble, MA	28.1.1873	22.6.1940	1900	Chinatown, Sydney, Australia	37
Nourse, AD	12.11.1910	14.8.1981	1948	Durban, Natal, South Africa	161
Nurse, SM	10.11.1933		1967	Jack-My-Nanny Gap, Black Rock, St Michael, Barbados	218
Old, CM	22.12.1948		1979	Middlesbrough, Yorkshire	258
Oldfield, WAS	9.9.1894	10.8.1976	1927	Alexandria, Sydney, Australia	111
O'Neill, NCL	19.2.1937	3.3.2008	1962	Carlton, Sydney, Australia	203
Onions, G	9.9.1982		2010	Gateshead, Co Durham	355
O'Reilly, WJ	20.12.1905	6.10.1992	1935	White Cliffs, New South Wales, Australia	135
Owen-Smith, HGO	18.2.1909	28.2.1990	1930	Rondebosch, Cape Town, South Africa	120
Paine, GAE	11.6.1908	30.3.1978	1935	Paddington, London	135
Palairet, LCH	27.5.1870	27.3.1933	1893	Broughton East, Grange-over-Sands, Lancashire	17
Panesar, MS	25.4.1982		2007	Luton, Bedfordshire	346
Parfitt, PH	8.12.1936		1963	Billingford, Fakenham, Norfolk	206
Parker, CWL	14.10.1882	11.7.1959	1923	Prestbury, Gloucestershire	101
Parkin, CH	18.2.1886	15.6.1943	1924	Eaglescliffe, Co Durham	104
Parks, JH	12.5.1903	21.11.1980	1938	Haywards Heath, Sussex	144
Parks, JM	21.10.1931		1968	Haywards Heath, Sussex	221
Partridge, NE	10.8.1900	10.3.1982	1919	Great Barr, Staffordshire	91
Pataudi, Nawab of, jun.	5.1.1941	22.9.2011	1968	Bhopal, India	126
Pataudi, Nawab of, sen.	16.3.1910	5.1.1952	1932	Pataudi, India	221
Paynter, E	5.11.1901	5.2.1979	1938	Oswaldtwistle, Lancashire	144
Peebles, IAR	20.1.1908	27.2.1980	1931	Aberdeen, Scotland	123
Peel, R	12.2.1857	12.8.1941	1889	Churwell, Leeds, Yorkshire	5
Perrin, PA	26.5.1876	20.11.1945	1905	Abney Park, Stoke Newington, London	52
Pietersen, KP	27.6.1980		2006	Pietermaritzburg, Natal, South Africa	343
Pilling, R	11.8.1855	28.3.1891	1891	Old Warden, Bedfordshire	11
Pollock, PM	30.6.1941		1966	Pietermaritzburg, Natal, South Africa	215
Pollock, RG	27.2.1944		1966	Durban, Natal, South Africa	215
Pollock, SM	16.7.1973		2003	Port Elizabeth, South Africa	334
Ponsford, WH	19.10.1900	6.4.1991	1935	North Fitzroy, Melbourne, Australia	135
Ponting, RT	19.12.1974		2006	Launceston, Tasmania, Australia	343
Poore, RM	20.3.1866	14.7.1938	1900	Carysfort House, Dublin, Ireland	37
Prior, MJ	26.2.1982		2010	Johannesburg, Transvaal, South Africa	355
Procter, MJ	15.9.1946		1970	Durban, Natal, South Africa	231
Pullar, G	1.8.1935		1960	Swinton, Lancashire	197
Quaife, WG	17.3.1872	13.10.1951	1902	Newhaven, Sussex	43
Radford, NV	7.6.1957		1986	Luanshya, Northern Rhodesia (now Zambia)	279
Radley, CT	13.5.1944		1979	Hertford	258
Ramadhin, S	1.5.1929		1951	St Charles Village, Trinidad	170
Ramprakash, MR	5.9.1969		2007	Bushey, Hertfordshire	346
Ranatunga, A	1.12.1963		1999	Colombo, Ceylon (now Sri Lanka)	322
Randall, DW	24.2.1951		1980	Retford, Nottinghamshire	261
Ranjitsinhji, KS	10.9.1872	2.4.1933	1897	Sarodar, Kathiawar, India	28
Ransford, VS	20.3.1885	19.3.1958	1910	South Yarra, Melbourne, Australia	67
Read, CMW	10.8.1978		2011	Paignton, Devon	358
Read, JM	9.2.1859	17.2.1929	1890	Thames Ditton, Surrey	8

Name	birth date	death date	year of selection	birthplace	page
Read, WW	23.11.1855	6.1.1907	1893	Reigate, Surrey	17
Reeve, DA	2.4.1963		1996	Kowloon, Hong Kong	313
Reid, JR	3.6.1928		1959	Auckland, New Zealand	194
Relf, AE	26.6.1874	26.3.1937	1914	Burwash, Sussex	77
Rhodes, JN	27.7.1969		1999	Pietermaritzburg, Natal, South Africa	322
Rhodes, SJ	17.6.1964		1995	Dirk Hill, Bradford, Yorkshire	310
Rhodes, W	29.10.1877	8.7.1973	1899	North Moor, Kirkheaton, Yorkshire	34
Rice, CEB	23.7.1949		1981	Johannesburg, Transvaal, South Africa	264
Richards, BA	21.7.1945		1969	Morningside, Durban, South Africa	228
Richards, IVA	7.3.1952		1977	St John's, Antigua	252
Richardson, A	6.5.1975		2012	Newcastle-under-Lyme, Staffordshire	361
Richardson, PE	4.7.1931		1957	Hereford	188
Richardson, RB	12.1.1962		1992	Five Islands Village, Antigua	297
Richardson, T	11.8.1870	2.7.1912	1897	Byfleet, Surrey	28
Roberts, AME	29.1.1951		1975	Urlings Village, Antigua	246
Robertson, JD	22.2.1917	12.10.1996	1948	Chiswick, Middlesex	161
Robins, RWV	3.6.1906	12.12.1968	1930	Stafford	120
Robinson, RT	21.11.1958		1986	Skegby, Sutton-in-Ashfield, Nottinghamshire	279
Roebuck, PM	6.3.1956	12.11.2011	1988	Oxford	285
Rose, BC	4.6.1950		1980	Dartford, Kent	261
Rotherham, GA	28.5.1899	31.1.1985	1918	Allesley, Coventry, Warwickshire	88
Rowan, EAB	20.7.1909	30.4.1993	1952	Johannesburg, Transvaal, South Africa	173
Russell, CAG	7.10.1887	23.3.1961	1923	Leyton, Essex	101
Russell, RC	15.8.1963		1990	Stroud, Gloucestershire	291
Saeed Anwar	6.9.1968		1997	Karachi, Pakistan	316
Sainsbury, PJ	13.6.1934		1974	Chandlers Ford, Hampshire	243
Salim Malik	16.4.1963		1988	Lahore, Pakistan	285
Salisbury, IDK	21.1.1970		1993	Northampton	304
Samuels, MN	5.1.1981		2013	Kingston, Jamaica	364
Sandham, A	6.7.1890	20.4.1982	1923	Streatham, London	101
Sangakkara, KC	27.10.1977		2012	Matale, Sri Lanka	361
Saqlain Mushtaq	29.12.1976		2000	Lahore, Pakistan	325
Schwarz, RO	4.5.1875	18.11.1918	1908	Lee, London	61
Scott, SW	24.3.1854	8.12.1933	1893	Bombay (now Mumbai), India	17
Sellers, AB	5.3.1907	20.2.1981	1940	Keighley, Yorkshire	150
Shackleton, D	12.8.1924	28.9.2007	1959	Todmorden, Yorkshire	194
Sharpe, JW	9.12.1866	19.6.1936	1892	Ruddington, Nottinghamshire	14
Sharpe, PJ	27.12.1936		1963	Shipley, Yorkshire	206
Shepherd, DJ	12.8.1927		1970	Port Eynon, Glamorgan	231
Shepherd, JN	9.11.1943		1979	Belleplaine, St Andrew, Barbados	258
Sheppard, DS	6.3.1929	5.3.2005	1953	Reigate, Surrey	176
Sherwin, M	26.2.1851	3.7.1910	1891	Greasley, Nottinghamshire	11
Shrewsbury, A	11.4.1856	19.5.1903	1890	New Lenton, Nottinghamshire	8
Sidebottom, RJ	15.1.1978		2008	Huddersfield, Yorkshire	349
Simmons, J	28.3.1941		1985	Clayton-le-Moors, Lancashire	276
Simmons, PV	18.4.1963		1997	Arima, Trinidad	316

Name	birth date	death date	year of selection	birthplace	page
Simpson, RB	3.2.1936		1965	Marrickville, Sydney, Australia	212
Simpson, RT	27.2.1920		1950	Sherwood Rise, Nottingham	167
Smith, CIJ	25.8.1906	8.2.1979	1935	Corsham, Wiltshire	135
Smith, CL	15.10.1958		1984	Durban, Natal, South Africa	273
Smith, D	24.1.1907	12.9.1979	1936	Somercotes, Derbyshire	138
Smith, GC	1.2.1981		2004	Johannesburg, Transvaal, South Africa	337
Smith, MJK	30.6.1933		1960	Westcotes, Leicester	197
Smith, OG	5.5.1933	9.9.1959	1958	Boys Town, Kingston, Jamaica	191
Smith, RA	13.9.1963		1990	Durban, Natal, South Africa	291
Smith, SG	15.1.1881	25.10.1963	1915	San Fernando, Trinidad	80
Smith, TPB	30.10.1908	4.8.1967	1947	Ipswich, Suffolk	158
Smith, WC	4.10.1877	15.7.1946	1911	Oxford	70
Snow, JA	13.10.1941		1973	Peopleton, Worcestershire	240
Sobers, GS	28.7.1936		1964	Chelsea Road, Bay Land, St Michael, Barbados	209
Spooner, RH	21.10.1880	2.10.1961	1905	Litherland, Lancashire	52
Stackpole, KR	10.7.1940		1973	Collingwood, Melbourne, Australia	240
Staples, SJ	18.9.1892	4.6.1950	1929	Newstead Colliery, Nottinghamshire	117
Statham, JB	17.6.1930	10.6.2000	1955	Gorton, Manchester, Lancashire	182
Steele, DS	29.9.1941		1976	Bradeley, Staffordshire	249
Stephenson, FD	8.4.1959		1989	Halls, Holders, St James, Barbados	288
Stevens, GTS	7.1.1901	19.9.1970	1918	Hampstead, London	88
Stewart, AJ	8.4.1963		1993	Merton, Surrey	304
Stewart, MJ	16.9.1932		1958	Herne Hill, London	191
Steyn, DW	27.6.1983		2013	Phalaborwa, Northern Province, South Africa	364
Stoddart, AE	11.3.1863	4.4.1915	1893	Westoe, South Shields, Co Durham	17
Storer, W	25.1.1867	28.2.1912	1899	Butterley, Derbyshire	34
Strauss, AJ	2.3.1977		2005	Johannesburg, Transvaal, South Africa	340
Strudwick, H	28.1.1880	14.2.1970	1912	Mitcham, Surrey	73
Subba Row, R	29.1.1932		1961	Streatham, London	200
Sugg, FH	11.1.1862	29.5.1933	1890	Ilkeston, Derbyshire	8
Surridge, WS	3.9.1917	13.4.1992	1953	Herne Hill, London	176
Sutcliffe, B	17.11.1923	20.4.2001	1950	Ponsonby, Auckland, New Zealand	167
Sutcliffe, H	24.11.1894	22.1.1978	1920	Summerbridge, Harrogate, Yorkshire	94
Swann, GP	24.3.1979		2010	Northampton	355
Tallon, D	17.2.1916	7.9.1984	1949	Bundaberg, Queensland, Australia	164
Tamim Iqbal	20.3.1989		2011	Chittagong, Bangladesh	358
Tarrant, FA	11.12.1880	29.1.1951	1908	Fitzroy, Melbourne, Australia	61
Tate, MW	30.5.1895	18.5.1956	1924	Preston, Brighton, Sussex	104
Tayfield, HJ	30.1.1929	24.2.1994	1956	Durban, Natal, South Africa	185
Taylor, B	19.6.1932		1972	West Ham, Essex	237
Taylor, HW	5.5.1889	8.2.1973	1925	Durban, Natal, South Africa	107
Taylor, MA	27.10.1964		1990	Leeton, New South Wales, Australia	291
Taylor, RW	17.7.1941		1977	Stoke-on-Trent, Staffordshire	252
Taylor, SC	25.9.1975		2009	Amersham, Buckinghamshire	352
Taylor, TL	25.5.1878	16.3.1960	1901	Headingley, Leeds, Yorkshire	40
Tendulkar, SR	24.4.1973		1997	Bombay (now Mumbai), India	316

Name	birth date	death date	year of selection	birthplace	page
Tennyson, Lord	7.11.1889	6.6.1951	1914	Westminster, London	77
Thompson, GJ	27.10.1877	3.3.1943	1906	Cogenhoe, Northampton	55
Thorpe, GP	1.8.1969		1998	Farnham, Surrey	319
Titmus, FJ	24.11.1932	23.3.2011	1963	Kentish Town, Middlesex	206
Townsend, CL	7.11.1876	17.10.1958	1899	Clifton, Bristol	34
Townsend, LF	8.6.1903	17.2.1993	1934	Long Eaton, Derbyshire	132
Trescothick, ME	25.12.1975		2005	Keynsham, Somerset	340
Tribe, GE	4.10.1920	5.4.2009	1955	Yarraville, Melbourne, Australia	182
Trott, AE	6.2.1873	30.7.1914	1899	Abbotsford, Melbourne, Australia	34
Trott, GHS	5.8.1866	10.11.1917	1894	Collingwood, Melbourne, Australia	20
Trott, IJL	22.4.1981		2011	Cape Town, South Africa	358
Trueman, FS	6.2.1931	1.7.2006	1953	Stainton, Yorkshire	176
Trumble, H	12.5.1867	14.8.1938	1897	Abbotsford, Melbourne, Australia	28
Trumper, VT	2.11.1877	28.6.1915	1903	Darlinghurst, Sydney, Australia	46
Tunnicliffe, J	26.8.1866	11.7.1948	1901	Low Town, Pudsey, Yorkshire	40
Turnbull, MJL	16.3.1906	5.8.1944	1931	Cardiff, Glamorgan	123
Turner, CTB	16.11.1862	1.1.1944	1889	Bathurst, New South Wales, Australia	5
Turner, GM	26.5.1947		1971	Dunedin, Otago, New Zealand	234
Tyldesley, GE	5.2.1889	5.5.1962	1920	Roe Green, Worsley, Lancashire	94
Tyldesley, JT	22.11.1873	27.11.1930	1902	Roe Green, Worsley, Lancashire	43
Tyldesley, RK	11.3.1897	17.9.1943	1925	Westhoughton, Lancashire	107
Tyson, FH	6.6.1930		1956	Farnworth, Lancashire	185
Underwood, DL	8.6.1945		1969	Bromley, Kent	228
Valentine, AL	28.4.1930	11.5.2004	1951	Kingston, Jamaica	170
van der Bijl, VAP	19.3.1948		1981	Rondebosch, Cape Town, South Africa	264
Vaughan, MP	29.10.1974		2003	Manchester, Lancashire	334
Vengsarkar, DB	6.4.1956		1987	Rajapur, Maharashtra, India	282
Verity, H	18.5.1905	31.7.1943	1932	Headingley, Leeds, Yorkshire	126
Vine, J	15.5.1875	25.4.1946	1906	Willingdon, Sussex	55
Virgin, RT	26.8.1939		1971	Taunton, Somerset	234
Voce, W	8.8.1909	6.6.1984	1933	Annesley Woodhouse, Nottinghamshire	129
Vogler, AEE	28.11.1876	9.8.1946	1908	Swartwater, Queenstown, South Africa	61
Wainwright, E	8.4.1865	28.10.1919	1894	Tinsley, Sheffield, Yorkshire	20
Walcott, CL	17.1.1926	26.8.2006	1958	New Orleans, St Michael, Barbados	191
Walsh, CA	30.10.1962		1987	Kingston, Jamaica	282
Walters, CF	28.8.1905	23.12.1992	1934	Bedlinog, Glamorgan	132
Waqar Younis	16.11.1971		1992	Vehari, Pakistan	297
Ward, A	21.11.1865	6.1.1939	1890	Waterloo, Leeds, Yorkshire	8
Wardle, JH	8.1.1923	23.7.1985	1954	Ardsley, Yorkshire	179
Warne, SK	13.9.1969		1994	Ferntree Gully, Victoria, Australia	307
Warner, PF	2.10.1873	30.1.1963	1904	The Hall, Port-of-Spain, Trinidad	49
Washbrook, C	6.12.1914	27.4.1999	1947	Barrow, Clitheroe, Lancashire	158
Wasim Akram	3.6.1966		1993	Lahore, Pakistan	304
Wass, TG	26.12.1873	27.10.1953	1908	Sutton-in-Ashfield, Nottinghamshire	61
Watkin, SL	15.9.1964		1994	Duffryn Rhondda, Maesteg, Glamorgan	307
Watson, W	7.3.1920	23.4.2004	1954	Bolton-on-Dearne, Yorkshire	179

Name	birth date	death date	year of selection	birthplace	page
Waugh, ME	2.6.1965		1991	Canterbury, Sydney, Australia	294
Waugh, SR	2.6.1965		1989	Canterbury, Sydney, Australia	288
Weekes, ED	26.2.1925		1951	Pickwick Gap, Westbury, St Michael, Barbados	170
Wellard, AW	8.4.1902	31.12.1980	1936	Southfleet, Kent	138
Wessels, KC	14.9.1957		1995	Bloemfontein, Orange Free State, South Africa	310
Wettimuny, S	12.8.1956		1985	Colombo, Ceylon (now Sri Lanka)	276
Wheatley, OS	28.5.1935		1969	Low Fell, Gateshead, Co Durham	228
Whitaker, JJ	5.5.1962		1987	Skipton, Yorkshire	282
White, JC	19.2.1891	2.5.1961	1929	Holford, Somerset	117
Whysall, WW	31.10.1887	11.11.1930	1925	Woodborough, Nottinghamshire	107
Willis, RGD	30.5.1949		1978	Sunderland, Co Durham	255
Wilson, JV	17.1.1921	5.6.2008	1961	Scampston, Malton, Yorkshire	200
Wood, A	25.8.1898	1.4.1973	1939	Fagley, Bradford, Yorkshire	147
Wood, H	14.12.1853	30.4.1919	1891	Dartford, Kent	11
Woodfull, WM	22.8.1897	11.8.1965	1927	Maldon, Victoria, Australia	111
Woods, SMJ	13.4.1867	30.4.1931	1889	Ashfield, Sydney, Australia	5
Woolley, FE	27.5.1887	18.10.1978	1911	Tonbridge, Kent	70
Woolmer, RA	14.5.1948	18.3.2007	1976	Kanpur, India	249
Worrell, FMM	1.8.1924	13.3.1967	1951	Bank Hall, St Michael, Barbados	170
Worthington, TS	21.8.1905	31.8.1973	1937	Bolsover, Derbyshire	141
Wright, DVP	21.8.1914	13.11.1998	1940	Sidcup, Kent	55
Wright, LG	15.1.1862	11.1.1953	1906	Oxford	150
Wyatt, RES	2.5.1901	20.4.1995	1930	Milford Heath House, Surrey	120
Yardley, NWD	19.3.1915	3.10.1989	1948	Gawber, Barnsley, Yorkshire	161
Zaheer Abbas	24.7.1947		1972	Sialkot, India (now in Pakistan)	237
Zaheer Khan	7.10.1978		2008	Shrirampur, Maharashtra, India	349

Acknowledgements

GREAT CREDIT IS DUE TO THE EFFORT AND inspiration of Christopher Lane, who has given so many years in the service of *Wisden* and whose concept this book was; to Philip Bailey, who provided swathes of relevant and fascinating statistics; to Harriet Monkhouse and Steven Lynch, two of the sharpest brains and pairs of eyes ever to work on *Wisden*'s behalf; to Freddie Wilde, whose assistance was great and who is handily placed to help *Wisden* with its bicentenary; to former editors Matthew Engel, Graeme Wright and Scyld Berry; to Marcus Duck for all his work on the book's elegant and reader-friendly design; to Charlotte Atyeo at Bloomsbury; to Peter Bathurst; and to Nick Humphrey, who proved such a diligent and enthusiastic editor.

All photographs courtesy of Getty Images apart from the following: Harry Wood (p12); Harry Trott (p21); Frank Druce (p33); Ernest Halliwell (p53); Alfred Hartley (p71); Charles Llewellyn (p72); William Smith (p72); Major Booth (p79); Sydney Smith (p81); G. T. S. Stevens (p90); Hubert Ashton (p100); Jack Bryan (p100); Jack Russell (p102); George Macaulay (p106); Dodger Whysall (p109); Jack Mercer (p113); Walter Robins (p121); Tuppy Owen-Smith (p122); Bev Lyon (p125); Alex Kennedy (p130); C. K. Nayudu (p131); Cyril Walters (p134); Jim Smith (p137); Denis Smith (p140); Stan Worthington (p142); Bill Copson (p142); Tom Goddard (p145); Roly Jenkins (p168); Tom Dollery (p174); Bruce Dooland (p184); Malcolm Hilton (p189); Aubrey Faulkner (371); Herbie Collins (371) all courtesy of The Roger Mann Collection. Jack Mercer (p113) courtesy of Glamorgan Cricket Archives. Will Vanderspar (p369) courtesy of Eton College. Thomas Abell (p369) courtesy of Scott Nelmes, Imagination Photography.

murder of a Soho prostitute. He was committed to a mental hospital, and died in 1958.

Kinneir did not play first-class cricket until he was 27, and had failed to average 30 in the previous four years: the 1911 season was easily his best. He clinched his tour place with five centuries in 33 days, including 158 for Players v Gentlemen. *Wisden* questioned whether he was not too old for England, and was proved right; he did little in Australia, playing only one Test, and had a poor season in England in 1912. He missed most of the 1913 season after contracting syphilis. He was killed in a motorbike crash aged 57.

Like Kinneir a left-hander, Mead had one of the most effective if workmanlike methods in the game, which sustained him through a first-class career spanning 28 seasons, in 27 of which he topped 1,000 runs. To this point his form for Hampshire – whom he joined after Surrey released him – had been sound rather than spectacular. In 1911 he totalled 2,562 runs with nine centuries, but so many of his runs came in the second half of the season that he nearly missed selection for Australia. Mead averaged 21 in four Tests, and was overlooked at home in 1912; indeed he played only two of his 17 Tests in England, despite scoring 182 in one of them.

"Young Jack" Hearne, a distant relation of J. T. [1892] and Alec Hearne [1894], was at 21 the youngest professional batsman chosen so far by *Wisden*. He had joined the Lord's groundstaff at 15, and by 1910 was winning Championship matches with bat and ball, being rated one of the best googly bowlers in the country. Even though he toured the West Indies with MCC in 1910-11, and performed the double in 1911, Middlesex needed persuading that he was old enough to tour Australia. His career suffered badly from the interruption of the 1914–18 war, and although he was one of only five all-rounders with 35,000 runs and 1,750 wickets in first-class cricket, he never quite fulfilled his potential for England.

Strudwick's qualities as wicketkeeper had been evident since he executed a record 91 dismissals in his first full season in 1903, as a result of which he went to Australia as understudy to Dick Lilley [1897]. *Wisden* rated his footwork peerless: "Strudwick had from the first a touch of genius," it said, while proposing that Surrey fine him for his habit of leaving his post to chase the ball to the boundary. However, his batting was not strong – he never scored a century in 675 first-class matches – and he was rarely assured of an England place. Having averaged more than 20 for the first time in 1911, he kept in the First Test in Australia, but then lost his place to Tiger Smith, who kept better to Foster. Five other keepers were tried during Strudwick's 28-match Test career, but he remained the favourite. He held the record for most first-class dismissals until 1975.

CRICKETERS OF THE YEAR 1912 – Performances in the English season 1911

Name	Age*		Matches	Runs	Bat ave	Wickets	Bowl ave	Catches (/st)
FR Foster	23	First-class	23	1614	42.47	141	20.31	12
JW Hearne	21	First-class	27	1627	42.81	102	22.00	12
S Kinneir	40	First-class	20	1629	49.36			7
CP Mead	25	First-class	29	2562	54.51	21	33.95	25
H Strudwick	32	First-class	35	629	21.68	0		66/14

* as at 1/4/1912

1913

No award

Sydney Pardon opted to forego Five Cricketers of the Year and instead celebrate the Almanack's 50th edition by commemorating the life of its founder John Wisden (who had died in 1884), an act that suggests a certain confidence about *Wisden*'s standing in the world. Pardon invited five people – three knights, a canon and a reverend – who had played with or against Wisden, or been coached by him, to contribute their recollections. Their words were accompanied by a reproduction of a coloured plate originally published by John Corbet Anderson of Wisden in his playing days.

The 1912 season, although blighted by bad weather, saw England, Australia and South Africa compete in a Triangular Tournament of nine Tests won by England. Several players eligible to be a Cricketer of the Year performed well. They included two South Africans – Sid Pegler, a bowler of fast-medium leg-cutters who took 189 wickets during the season, and Aubrey Faulkner, who did the double and was described in the Editor's Notes as his team's "one great batsman". For Australia, Charles Kelleway scored 360 runs in six Tests, including a century and five for 33 against South Africa at Old Trafford, where Jimmy Matthews took two hat-tricks for Australia. Harry Dean, a left-armer from Lancashire, took 162 wickets at 13.67 apiece. Tiger Smith, preferred to Strudwick as England's keeper, had a strong all-round season. None of these six players was ever chosen as a Cricketer of the Year.

HEADLINE EVENTS FROM 1912

- County champions – Yorkshire

- A triangular Test tournament is staged in England and won by the hosts, who beat Australia 1-0 and South Africa 3-0

- England win back the Ashes under J. W. H. T. Douglas in Australia in 1911-12, taking the series 4-1